HEAVEN

AND

HELL

Paul Caponigro

The New Century Edition
of the Works of Emanuel Swedenborg

Jonathan S. Rose

Series Editor

Stuart Shotwell

Managing Editor

Heaven

and Its Wonders

AND

Hell

Drawn from Things Heard & Seen

EMANUEL SWEDENBORG

Translated from the Latin by George F. Dole
With an Introduction by Bernhard Lang
And Notes by George F. Dole, Robert H. Kirven,
and Jonathan S. Rose

SWEDENBORG FOUNDATION
West Chester, Pennsylvania

Printed in the United States of America

ISBN (library) 0-87785-475-0
ISBN (paperback) 0-87785-476-9

Library of Congress Cataloging-in-Publication Data

Swedenborg, Emanuel, 1688–1722.
    [De coelo et ejus mirabilibus. English]
    Heaven and its wonders and hell : drawn from things heard and seen/Emanuel Swedenborg ; translated from the Latin by George F. Dole ; with an introduction by Bernhard Lang ; and notes by George F. Dole, Robert H. Kirven, and Jonathan S. Rose.
        p. cm.— (The new century edition of the works of Emanuel Swedenborg)
    Includes bibliographical references (p.) and indexes.
    ISBN 0-87785-475-0 (lib.bdg. : alk.paper)
    1. Heaven—Christianity. 2. Hell—Christianity. 3. Future life—Christianity—Early works to 1800. I. Dole, George F. II. Lang, Bernhard, 1946– III. Kirven, Robert H. IV. Rose, Jonathan S. V. Title.

BX8712.H513 2000
236'.24—dc21

                                                                                    00-037533

Cover designed by Caroline Kline
Text designed by Joanna V. Hill
Ornaments from the first Latin edition, 1758
Diagrams set in electronic form by Caroline Kline
Indexes by Bruce Tracy
Typeset by Nesbitt Graphics

For information contact:
        Swedenborg Foundation
        320 North Church Street
        West Chester PA 19380 USA

Contents

Part I. Heaven and Hell

Part II. The World of Spirits and Our State After Death

Part III. Hell

Notes and Indexes

Translator's Preface

HEAVEN and Hell is one of five works that Emanuel Swedenborg published in 1758.[1] These works differ markedly from *Secrets of Heaven*, Swedenborg's first theological work, which he had published between 1749 and 1756. The latter set out to demonstrate that there was spiritual meaning within the literal meaning of Scripture, of "the Word," by beginning at Genesis 1:1 and proceeding verse by verse with an exposition of this meaning. It is compendious to say the least, filling a dozen or more volumes in English translation.

There are clear indications that when he began the massive *Secrets of Heaven,* he expected to carry it to completion by proceeding consecutively through from Genesis to the Book of Revelation.[2] This would have complied quite literally with his divine commission as he first heard it, "to open to people the spiritual sense of Scripture."[3] However, he stopped at the end of Exodus (volume 8 in the first Latin edition, 1756), and presumably began work on the material that would be published in 1758.

---

1. The other four are *New Jerusalem, Last Judgment, White Horse,* and *Other Planets.* (See the list of short titles in this volume for details about the full Latin and English titles of these and other works by Swedenborg. For information about standards for referring to Swedenborg's works, see note 5 below.) Any discussion of the works of 1758 should note that it is difficult to determine in what order they were written or published. *Other Planets* may well have been the first, since it does not refer to any of the other works, but is referred to in *Heaven and Hell* (§§321, 417, and 419) and *Last Judgment* (§10). However, the lack of references may be due simply to the fact that the text was to all intents and purposes copied from *Secrets of Heaven. Heaven and Hell* (§1) and *White Horse* (§9) refer to each other, as do *Heaven and Hell* (§78) and *New Jerusalem* (§3). Furthermore, while *Heaven and Hell* refers to *Last Judgment* twice, once in the future tense (§§508, 559), this latter work is cited by section number in *New Jerusalem* (§1). It is striking also that in the chapter on Sacred Scripture in *New Jerusalem,* there is no reference to *White Horse,* which is devoted to that subject. Apparently, Swedenborg worked on at least the latter four (all but *Other Planets*) simultaneously, and may have sent them to the printer together. When he lists his own works, he gives the order as *Heaven and Hell, New Jerusalem, Last Judgment, White Horse,* and *Other Planets.* (See Acton 1952, 2:745, and the last page of Swedenborg's edition of *Marriage Love.*)

2. See Wunsch 1929, 22 note 13. See also the printer's advertisement describing the project as "an explanation of the whole Bible" (Hindmarsh 1861, 3).

3. This quotation is translated from the only primary account of the circumstances of this commission, found in a memoir by one of Swedenborg's friends, Carl Robsahm, which is based on a conversation late in Swedenborg's life. See Hjern 1989, 29–65. For secondary accounts, see Acton 1927, 40–47, and Sigstedt 1981, 197–199.

We have no record of his reasons for the change of course, but it is a striking one.[4] It involves both a shift in genre from exegesis to topical theology and a shift in form from the multivolume to the book and even the booklet. *Secrets of Heaven* belongs on the theologian's bookshelf. *Heaven and Hell* might feel at home in the airport book rack.

This is consistent with his statement of the purpose of the present work. In his prefatory remarks, he deplored the prevalence of biblical literalism, which in his view could lead only to increasing skepticism. He continued:

> To prevent this negative attitude—especially prevalent among people who have acquired a great deal of worldly wisdom—from infecting and corrupting people of simple heart and simple faith, I have been allowed to be with angels and to talk with them person to person. I have also been allowed to see what is in heaven and in hell, which has been going on for thirteen years. Now I am being allowed therefore to describe what I have heard and seen, in the hopes of shedding light where there is ignorance and dispelling skepticism. (*Heaven and Hell* 1)[5]

This suggests that he had a particular readership in mind. While it was surely unrealistic to expect "people of simple heart and simple faith" to read Latin, the book would be quite accessible to the parish clergy closest to such people. It would be accessible also to "amateur intellectuals," often in positions of responsibility, who delighted in keeping up with new discoveries. Further, its ideas were vivid and concrete, easy to remember and to communicate, and its Latin simple and accessible. It may be no accident that *Heaven and Hell* has been far and away the most popular of Swedenborg's works.

---

4. Swedenborg may have felt a change in course was necessary because of the poor public response to *Secrets of Heaven*. In §4422 of his diary (published posthumously under the title *Spiritual Diary* or, more accurately, *Spiritual Experiences* [= Swedenborg 1983–1997]), he reports being informed that only four copies of one of his works have been sold in the past two months. He does not name the work in question. Though the diary entry itself is undated, the nearest dated entry, §4388, was written September 14, 1749, which suggests a time frame of late 1749 for the surrounding entries. Accepting this time frame, we can deduce that §4422 refers to the first volume of *Secrets of Heaven*, which was at that time being offered at his bookseller's. Judging from the diary entry, Swedenborg seems at that time to have been content to follow angelic advice to leave the apparent difficulty with distribution to the Lord's providence. Nevertheless, seven years later he shifts to shorter works. Another possible reason for the shift from major exegesis to the shorter topical works is Swedenborg's reaction to the Last Judgment, which he reports as an event he witnessed in the spiritual world in 1757. However, this connection remains speculative, as we have no evidence to support it. (For a discussion of the Last Judgment in Swedenborg's theology, see the introduction to this volume.)

5. As is common in Swedenborgian studies, text citations refer not to page numbers but to Swedenborg's section numbers, which are uniform in all editions.

If *Heaven and Hell* is written for a broader readership than *Secrets of Heaven,* there is nevertheless a strong continuity in content. With the exception of *Last Judgment,* all of the 1758 works draw heavily on *Secrets of Heaven* and refer the reader directly to it. The most direct dependence is found in *Other Planets,* which is taken from material in *Secrets of Heaven* with only very slight editing. *New Jerusalem* consists of very short chapters, each presenting a basic theological concept and each save the last followed by a kind of appendix comprising extensive references to *Secrets of Heaven. White Horse,* as its full title indicates,[6] is material extracted from *Secrets of Heaven* on the nature of the Word.

Heaven and Hell's relationship to *Secrets of Heaven* is less direct. In *Secrets of Heaven,* the general subject of what awaits us after death is dealt with in the first series of interchapter articles,[7] but much less extensively than in *Heaven and Hell.* In his table of the repeated passages that appear in Swedenborg's works, John Faulkner Potts identifies just thirty-four of *Heaven and Hell*'s 603 sections as cited from *Secrets of Heaven* (Potts 1888–1902, 6:859–864).[8] Further, the sequence of presentation is very different. The earlier presentation begins with an account of his own experience of what it is like to die, proceeds with generalizations about awakening in the other world, and then has substantial material about hell before dealing with the general structure and some of the characteristics of heaven. *Heaven and Hell* begins by asserting the centrality of the Lord and deals with heaven, the world of spirits (as the intermediate realm we enter immediately after death), and hell, in that order.

Swedenborg was clearly concerned to convey the connection between *Heaven and Hell* and *Secrets of Heaven.* He referred to the contents of *Heaven and Hell* as "secrets of heaven" in §1. He began the later work by citing Matthew 24:29–31, part of a description of the "last days," stating that it is misleading to understand it literally and sketching a spiritual interpretation. He then presented his claim to have been granted open communication with angels in order to counter this literalism and closed his preface with the brief but immense assertion that the revelation he had been granted was what was meant (in Matthew, presumably) by the Lord's

---

6. *The White Horse in Revelation Chapter 19, and the Word and Its Spiritual or Inner Sense (from* Secrets of Heaven).

7. The interchapter material consists of digressions from the main exegesis offered in each chapter. These digressions are often serial, or continued from one chapter to the next; if excerpted and combined, they form continuous accounts of several topics. Swedenborg himself excerpted one series to form *Other Planets.*

8. These passages are identified in the table of parallel passages.

coming. The details of his exegesis of the Matthew passage are carefully annotated with references to *Secrets of Heaven,* and through the rest of the book there are relatively few pages that do not have such footnotes.[9]

To *Heaven and Hell* 78–86, which form a chapter on the Lord and his Divine Human, Swedenborg appended an extensive set of references to passages in *Secrets of Heaven* that treat that subject; to *Heaven and Hell* 346–356, which is a chapter on wise and simple people in heaven, he added a similar set of references to *Secrets of Heaven* on the subject of "knowledge"; and after §§597–603, a chapter on the topic of freedom, he added a series of references to the earlier work's discussion of human freedom, the Lord's inflow into us, and spirits as means of communication with us. The obvious conclusion is that Swedenborg intended *Heaven and Hell* at least in part as a vehicle for information already published in *Secrets of Heaven.* As well as demonstrating a striking concern for consistency, the cross-references clearly indicate a hope that it would attract the reader to that larger work.

It is worth noting that Potts (1888–1902, 6:863–864) identified only five passages in *Heaven and Hell* as duplicated from Swedenborg's *Spiritual Experiences,* the running record of paranormal experiences that he kept for some twenty years (1746–1765). The most probable reason is that this diary records specific incidents, while *Heaven and Hell* usually generalizes from this experience and takes the form of a spiritual guidebook rather than a traveler's narrative. (We should not in any case expect formal references to the unpublished diary in Swedenborg's published writing.) In later works, notably *Marriage Love* and *True Christianity,* he would insert *memorabilia,* or accounts of memorable occurrences, many of which can be traced back to the diary.

It may not be amiss to alert the reader to the presence in *Heaven and Hell* of a pervasive ethical concern. Swedenborg had had a productive career as an engineer and civil servant, which he left only when his theological enterprise was well under way. Throughout his life, he remained an active and respected member of the *Riddarhus,* the Swedish House of Nobles; and one of the last things to issue from his pen was an extensive and thoughtful memorandum on Sweden's finances. For him personally, that is, experiences of the spiritual world were not an avenue of escape from earthly responsibilities. There is a recurrent emphasis in *Heaven*

---

9. His task of making these cross-references was made easier by an index to *Secrets of Heaven* that he had compiled himself. (There are extant a first and a second draft of this index in his own hand; see Swedenborg 1890.) Cross-references in *Secrets of Heaven* itself indicate that Swedenborg began his index as soon as the work reached a size that made such a resource necessary for consistent cross-referencing, about the middle of Genesis chapter 8; and he evidently updated it faithfully thereafter.

and Hell on a generous, honest, and useful life here and now as the only viable foundation for heavenly life hereafter.

Regarding the publication of *Heaven and Hell,* James Hyde provides the following information (1906, 221). The first edition of one thousand copies was printed by John Lewis, 1 Paternoster Row, in London, the proof sheets being read by John Marchant. There are two tables of typographical errata and a table of contents in autograph manuscripts in the Royal Library in Stockholm. As of the time Hyde wrote, a copy with notes by John Clowes was in the library of D. B. Bragg;[10] another with annotations by Samuel Taylor Coleridge was in the library of Lord Coleridge.

The first English translation of the work, by William Cookworthy and Thomas Hartley, was published in 1778. That of the redoubtable John Clowes appeared in 1817 and served as a guide to Samuel Noble for his 1839 version, which became the standard in England until 1899, when J. R. Rendell's translation was published. In the United States, Benjamin Barrett's translation was published in 1867, and served (with various revisions) until that of John Ager (1900). In England, Doris Harley's revision of the Ager translation succeeded the Rendell version in 1958. My own 1976 translation was intended for the paperback market and omitted the references to *Secrets of Heaven.*[11] The present translation is a fresh effort and not a revision: I regard myself as responsible for the previous version, but not responsible to it. The work has also been translated into Arabic, Bulgarian, Chinese, Czech, Danish, Dutch, Finnish, French, German, Hindi, Hungarian, Icelandic, Italian, Japanese, Korean, Latvian, Norwegian, Polish, Portuguese, Russian, Spanish, Swedish, Tamil, Ukranian, Welsh, and Zulu.

The Latin style of the book is remarkable for its simplicity—not really colloquial, but perhaps not far from that of courteous conversation. While there are touches of poetic imagery and phrasing from time to time, there is nothing that could be called sentimental and certainly nothing sensationalist. Swedenborg's primary concerns were evidently for clarity and accessibility. It is the effort of the present edition to represent

---

10. Clowes (1743–1831), an Anglican clergyman, accepted Swedenborg's doctrines in 1773 with such enthusiasm that, without leaving the established church, he devoted the remainder of his life to translating Swedenborg's theological works, and to teaching and preaching their contents. The major works he translated were *True Christianity, Secrets of Heaven, New Jerusalem, Life, Other Planets, Marriage Love,* and *Heaven and Hell;* but he translated or revised many others as well. For more on Clowes, see Clowes 1874 and Tafel 1890, 1166–1170.

11. For bibliographic data on the translations cited, see the list following this preface. Collections of translations are housed in the Swedenborg Library, 2875 College Drive, Bryn Athyn, Pa., 19009, U.S.A; and at the Swedenborg Society, 20/21 Bloomsbury Way, London, WC1A 2TH, U.K.

these qualities as faithfully as possible, qualities that the members of the editorial committee feel have too often been slighted in favor of a rather Latinate literalism. If at times the language of the present version seems stilted or obscure, the fault is with the translator, not with Swedenborg. Simplicity is not always easily come by.

In the sixth and final volume of his *Swedenborg Concordance,* published in 1902, Potts advised readers to mark in their own copies the "repeated passages" that he had identified, "until such time as an annotated edition of the Writings is made, which will of course contain them" (Potts 1888, 6:859).[12] Almost a century later, his expectation of such an annotated edition begins to be fulfilled. The New Century Edition owes its inception to the vision and energy of David Eller. This volume, as the first of the series to be published, although not first in Swedenborg's bibliography, has benefited from critique not only by my designated consultants, Sylvia Shaw, Stuart Shotwell, and Michelle Thorne, but also by fellow translators Lisa Hyatt Cooper and Jonathan Rose. Every page bears invisible evidence of their care, and their gentle spirit has been a constant source of support and delight. I am grateful also to Carolyn Andrews, Robin Cooper, Matthew L. Genzlinger, and Oula Synnestvedt for the painstaking labor of verifying references. Others who have helped to check and supply facts for this volume are Andrew Dole, John L. Hitchcock, Norman Ryder, Erik E. Sandström, and William Ross Woofenden.

My deep gratitude is due as well to the board of directors of the Swedenborg Foundation. This project dwarfs any single previous Foundation undertaking, and the courage and conviction of the directors deserve the highest commendation. On behalf of the entire editorial committee, I would express the hope that this initial result justifies their trust.

These words are being written not far from the home of Zina Hyde, who in the nineteenth century gave generously of his time and resources toward the publication of Latin editions of Swedenborg's theological works. Those volumes are now paying the price of their acid-bleached elegance; they stand as a reminder that we are limited by our times, and can do no more than our best. May this edition be good enough for now, and lead in time to something better.

GEORGE F. DOLE
Bath, Maine
February, 2000

---

12. I am grateful to William Ross Woofenden for calling my attention to the statement by Potts.

Works Cited
in the Translator's Preface

Acton, Alfred. 1927. *Introduction to the Word Explained*. Bryn Athyn, Pa.: Academy of the New Church.

———. 1955. *The Letters and Memorials of Emanuel Swedenborg*. Vol. 2. Bryn Athyn, Pa.: Swedenborg Scientific Association.

Clowes, John. 1874. *The Memoirs of John Clowes*. Edited by Theodore Compton. London: Longmans, Green & Co.

Hindmarsh, Robert. 1861. *The Rise and Progress of the New Jerusalem Church*. Edited by Edward Madeley. London: Hodson & Son.

Hjern, Olle. 1989. *Carl Robsahm: Anteckningar om Swedenborg*. Stockholm: ABA Cad/Copy & Tryck.

Hyde, James. 1906. *A Bibliography of the Works of Emanuel Swedenborg, Original and Translated*. London: Swedenborg Society.

Potts, John Faulkner. 1888–1902. *The Swedenborg Concordance*. 6 vols. London: Swedenborg Society.

Sigstedt, Cyriel Odhner. 1981. *The Swedenborg Epic: The Life and Works of Emanuel Swedenborg*. New York: Bookman Associates, 1952. Reprint, London: Swedenborg Society.

Swedenborg, Emanuel. 1890. *Index Verborum, Nominum, et Rerum in Arcanis Coelestibus*. Edited by Rudolph L. Tafel. London: Swedenborg Society. Translation available in: Emanuel Swedenborg. 1909. *Index of Words, Names, and Subjects in the Heavenly Arcana, from the Latin of Emanuel Swedenborg, to Which Is Added an Index to the Scripture Passages*. Translated and edited by J. Hyde. London: Swedenborg Society.

———. 1983–1997. *Experientiae Spirituales*. 6 vols. Edited by J. Durban Odhner. Bryn Athyn, Pa.: Academy of the New Church.

Tafel, Rudolph Leonard. 1890. *Documents concerning the Life and Character of Emanuel Swedenborg*. Vols. 2–3. London. Swedenborg Society.

Wunsch, William F. 1929. *The World Within the Bible*. New York: New Church Press.

Selected List of Editions
of *Heaven and Hell*

1. Latin Editions

Swedenborg, Emanuel. 1758. *De Coelo et Ejus Mirabilibus, et de Inferno, ex Auditis et Visis.* London.

————. [1758] 1862. *De Coelo et Ejus Mirabilibus, et de Inferno, ex Auditis et Visis.* Edited by Johann Friedrich Immanuel Tafel. Tübingen: Verlags-Expedition.

————. [1758] 1890. *De Coelo et Ejus Mirabilibus, et de Inferno, ex Auditis et Visis.* Edited by Samuel H. Worcester. New York: American Swedenborg Printing and Publishing Society.

2. English Translations

Swedenborg, Emanuel. [1758] 1778. *A Treatise Concerning Heaven and Hell.* Translated by William Cookworthy and Thomas Hartley. London: James Phillips.

————. [1758] 1817. *A Treatise Concerning Heaven and Its Wonders, and Also Concerning Hell: Being a Relation of Things Heard and Seen.* Translated by John Clowes. London: Society for Printing and Publishing the Writings of Emanuel Swedenborg.

————. [1758] 1839. *Heaven and Its Wonders Described; With an Account of Hell: From Actual Information and Observation.* Translated by Samuel Noble. London: J. S. Hodson.

————. [1758] 1867. *Heaven and Its Wonders, and Hell: From Things Heard and Seen.* Translated by Benjamin Barrett. Philadelphia: J. B. Lippincott.

————. [1758] 1899. *Heaven and Its Wonders, and Hell: From Things Heard and Seen.* Translated by J. R. Rendell. London: Swedenborg Society.

————. [1758] 1900. *Heaven and Its Wonders, and Hell: From Things Heard and Seen.* Translated by John C. Ager. New York: American Swedenborg Printing and Publishing Society.

————. [1758] 1958. *Heaven and Its Wonders and Hell, From Things Heard and Seen.* Translated by John C. Ager, revised and edited by Doris Harley. London: Swedenborg Society.

————. [1758] 1976. *Heaven and Hell.* Translated by George F. Dole. New York: Swedenborg Foundation.

On Heaven and Hell

A Historical Introduction to Swedenborg's Most Popular Book

BERNHARD LANG

Outline

Among all visionaries, Herr Swedenborg is probably the one who has written most explicitly. He discusses, quotes sources, adduces arguments and causes, etc. The whole edifice has a kind of coherence and with all its peculiarity is erected with studied thought. The book, moreover, has so many new and unexpected turns that it may be read through without boredom.

—CARL GUSTAF TESSIN,
Diary, entry of July 4, 1760
(Sigstedt 1981, 274–275)

But I again repeat my conviction, that Swedenborg's *Meaning* is the truth—and the duty of his followers is, to secure this meaning to the Readers of his works by collecting from his numerous Volumes those passages, in which this meaning is conveyed in terms so plain as not to be misconceived: an introduction of 50 pages would suffice for this purpose.

—SAMUEL TAYLOR COLERIDGE,
marginal note on Swedenborg, *Heaven and Hell*
(Coleridge 2000, 410)

E MANUEL Swedenborg (1688–1772) was a man of two careers: one in science and one in theology. The first career ended in 1747 when he retired from his position on the Royal Board of Mines in his home country, Sweden. With inherited resources augmented by a small salary, the fifty-nine-year-old scholar went abroad, spending much time in London and Amsterdam, cities he knew from earlier visits. London was the city where in April 1745 he had had a vision of "the Lord God, the Creator of the world and the Redeemer," who permitted him to see "the worlds of spirits, heaven, and hell" (Tafel 1875, 36).[1] From that time on he devoted all of his time and energy to the writing of theological books. The main fruit of his initial endeavors came to completion in 1756 with the publication of the eighth and final tome of *Arcana Coelestia, Quae in Scriptura Sacra, seu Verbo Domini Sunt, Detecta: . . . Una cum Mirabilibus Quae Visa Sunt in Mundo Spirituum, et in Coelo Angelorum* (A Disclosure of Secrets of Heaven Contained in Sacred Scripture, or the Word of the Lord, . . . Together with Amazing Things Seen in the World of Spirits

---

1. An analysis of this vision and a discussion of the authenticity of the relevant report can be found in Benz 1949, 278–288.

and in the Heaven of Angels).[2] At the express will of the writer, the volumes appeared without indication of authorship. Completed in his sixty-eighth year, they constitute Swedenborg's foundational theological work.

The learned author could now have retired for good, for on all accounts, he had achieved very much. Moreover, after all these years of writing, he must have been exhausted, or so one would think. In fact, this was not the case. Swedenborg must have felt that a work of eight huge quarto tomes of biblical exegesis, theological reflection, and reports on the author's visions would not find many readers, at least not immediately. So he prepared a number of smaller, less forbidding books, some of which were closely based on *Secrets of Heaven*. Five of these appeared in 1758, shortly after the author's seventieth birthday.[3] All of these books were in Latin, printed in London by John Lewis, who had a bookshop in Paternoster Row (Acton 1955, 523). They appeared anonymously and drew heavily on *Secrets of Heaven*, to which they seem meant to draw attention. These new, smaller books were based mainly on certain sections of *Secrets of Heaven* in which particular theological subjects are systematically developed—sections that stand out in contrast to the primary focus of the book, which is a running spiritual commentary on Genesis and Exodus.

One of these smaller books of 1758 was titled *De Coelo et Ejus Mirabilibus, et de Inferno, ex Auditis et Visis* (Heaven and Its Wonders and Hell: Drawn from Things Heard and Seen).[4] Apparently one thousand copies were printed (Acton 1955, 524). Designed as a kind of introduction to some of the ideas of *Secrets of Heaven,* it was short, concise, and well organized; the pedagogical aim is visible throughout in the uncomplicated Latin style, the frequent announcements of what will be discussed next, and the summaries that punctuate the book. Swedenborg himself has annotated the book with references to *Secrets of Heaven* and has appended to

---

2. Throughout the present edition, the short title *Secrets of Heaven* is used in place of the Latin title.

3. Swedenborg was not the only author of an abridgment of his *Secrets of Heaven* in his own time. In southern Germany, Friedrich Christoph Oetinger (1702–1782), a Lutheran minister, deplored the inaccessibility of the huge Latin quarto tomes and in 1765 published a hundred-page summary (Oetinger [1765] 1855, 15–116).

4. Throughout the present edition, the short title *Heaven and Hell* is used in place of the Latin title. As is common in Swedenborgian studies, text citations refer not to page numbers but to Swedenborg's section numbers, which are uniform in all editions. In this introduction, section numbers where no work is specified should be understood to refer to *Heaven and Hell.* Thus "§90" means "*Heaven and Hell,* §90."

individual chapters summaries of certain subjects dealt with in that work (for example, after §86), so that the reader is constantly reminded of the larger work. As an introductory text based on a more comprehensive theological work, *Heaven and Hell* forms part of a larger corpus of texts. Occasionally Swedenborg also refers to other writings such as *De Nova Hierosolyma et Ejus Doctrina Coelesti* (The New Jerusalem and Its Heavenly Teaching: see *Heaven and Hell* 78) and *De Ultimo Judicio, et de Babylonia Destructa* (The Last Judgment and Babylon Destroyed; see *Heaven and Hell* 559), both belonging to the same series of books printed in 1758.[5] Although meant as an accessible introduction for "church people these days" and specifically for "people of simple heart and simple faith" (§1), *Heaven and Hell* is not a work complete in itself, and any thorough study must take account of this fact. What Swedenborg really means, one might say, can be found out only by way of a thorough study of the entire corpus, not by a consideration of just one isolated, small part of it. A recognition of the importance of the context of *Heaven and Hell* led English romantic author Samuel Taylor Coleridge (1772–1834) to scribble in the margin of his Latin copy the comment cited in the epigraph above. In what follows, however, the incompleteness and openness of *Heaven and Hell* is not emphasized, for doing so would present an inconvenience, especially for first-time readers. Instead, *Heaven and Hell* is examined as a representative fragment that echoes and conveys the spirit and meaning of Swedenborg's theological *oeuvre*. It is viewed here as if it were a complete work, the contents of which can be summarized and understood as a coherent presentation of the author's teaching.

I. *Heaven and Hell*'s Map of the Universe

The best way to summarize the contents of *Heaven and Hell* is to reconstruct its teaching in the form of a maplike representation of the universe (see figure 1). The material world *(mundus)* in which we live is only a small part within the whole. Surrounded by vast spiritual worlds, it is comparable to a small principality surrounded by vast empires. The first of these empires is the *mundus spirituum* (§421), the world of the spirits of the dead. Immediately after death, people find themselves in this region.

---

5. In the present edition, these works are referred to by the short titles *New Jerusalem* and *Last Judgment* respectively, not by their Latin titles.

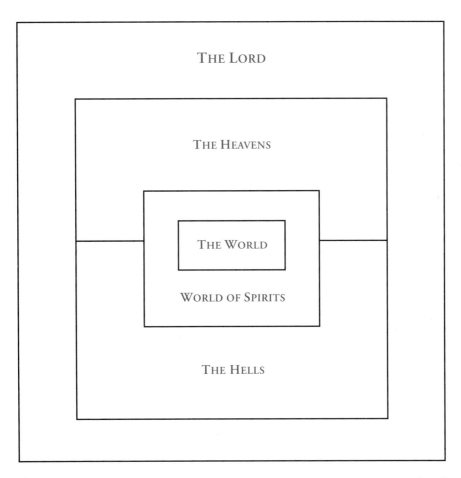

Figure 1. Swedenborg's map of the universe (first version). In *Heaven and Hell,* Swedenborg describes the various realms that make up the universe; this description could be schematized in various ways. The schema suggested here sets our world at the center of the realms; it should be contrasted with figure 2.

After some time, they either sink down into the infernal regions (*inferna,* the hells) or they rise up to heaven. Heaven has a complex structure that echoes the human form. On the grandest level it is differentiated into two kingdoms, the heavenly and the spiritual. Upon closer inspection it divides into three heavens: the first or outermost heaven, the second or middle heaven, and the third or inmost heaven. Each heaven contains innumerable communities, and each community, many angels. The structure of hell is similar to that of heaven, although upside down in relation to it. Each community of hell is balanced by a community of heaven devoted to an opposite form of love. The entire structure is encompassed and animated by the Lord *(Dominus)*.

In *Heaven and Hell,* Swedenborg describes his map of the universe starting from the top level, so that after commenting on God, he deals with heaven, then the realm of the spirits, and eventually hell, the lowest level. Our world, that is, the central area, is not dealt with in a separate section, but mentioned whenever necessary. The following description departs from Swedenborg's approach by starting with the map's central realm—our world—and then moves toward the realms that encompass our world: the world of spirits, heaven, hell, and eventually the Lord as the ultimate reality. But as soon as the map is understood, one can open Swedenborg's book anywhere and start reading wherever one pleases.

a. The World

The world *(mundus),* located at the center of the structure, is the material world in which we live. This world is composed of numerous earths scattered through the universe, of which our globe is merely one of many (§417). All the earths are peopled with human beings. For practical purposes, however, it suffices to equate the world with our earth. On the earth, we find the church, defined as "the Lord's heaven on earth" (§57). In the world, the Christian church is responsible for teaching people the proper worldview—that is, all about the various spiritual worlds surrounding and encompassing the *mundus.* However, the traditional churches have generally failed. Although *Heaven and Hell* does not have a separate section dealing with the world, Swedenborg nevertheless refers to it quite frequently, for whatever he explains is for the knowledge and the benefit of those living in this realm. Structurally, a most important feature of the world is its location between heaven and hell. Both of these realms try to influence the world and impinge upon individual lives; as a result, the two forces neutralize each other, so that humans are free—neither forced to submit to evil nor forced to yield to good (§§597–602). They can freely decide between good and evil. In the diagram, care has been taken to include a feature emphasized by Swedenborg: the influence of heaven and hell on our world is not immediate, but exercised through spirits active in the world of spirits (§600).

In a world of free decision, it is important to be guided morally. Swedenborg has much to say and to recommend about right and wrong living in the world and offers his advice. Central themes relate to work, marriage, and churchgoing. An active, productive life of service to society counts as the ideal. Swedenborg warns of idleness and asceticism. Idleness never makes one happy (§403), and withdrawal from active life, as takes place in monastic communities, tends to inflate people with a sense of their own worth and thus leads away from the divine forces with which one must associate to be happy both here and hereafter (§535). As for marriage, *Heaven and Hell* warns against any domineering attitude in the conjugal relationship, for "any love of control of one over the other utterly destroys marriage love" (§380). The book also warns against marriage between partners of divergent religions, for true marital love does not develop between them (§378). Even an interpretation of marital intimacy is offered: "Marital pleasure, which is a purer and more delicate pleasure of touch, surpasses all others because of its service, the procreation of the human race and thus of the angelic heaven" (§402). Concerning religion, Swedenborg pronounces a verdict on those who think constant churchgoing and praying are the right path (§535). He knew the limits and spiritual dangers of what outwardly appears to be a holy and devout life. In sum, the seer's ethical message is one of optimism: "It is not so hard to lead a heaven-bound life as people think it is" (title of §§528–535).

While still living in the material world, Swedenborg was granted glimpses of the vast realms that transcend and encompass the earthly realm. Whereas in the Middle Ages Dante could present his worldview in the form of a coherent narrative, Swedenborg prefers a more systematic, philosophical description. At many points, however, his description includes autobiographical narrative statements: as a visionary, Swedenborg conversed with the residents of the other regions. There is nothing strange about this communication, Swedenborg assures us, for all the beings he encounters are people who once lived a normal human life in this world.

b. The World of Spirits

The world of spirits *(mundus spirituum)* is the realm immediately encasing our material world. Swedenborg's observations about this realm can be found under the heading "The World of Spirits and Our State after Death" (§§421–535). As this heading indicates, death shifts people's primary consciousness from the material world into the world of spirits. During their stay in this intermediary world, people go through various stages:

1. The first stage can be described as a stage of introduction. Having arrived in this world, people seem to be still the same. They meet the same way as in their earthly lives—"we . . . can talk to anyone when we want to, to friends and acquaintances from our physical life, especially husbands and wives, and also brothers and sisters. I have seen a father talking with his six sons and recognizing them. I have seen many other people with their relatives and friends," reports the visionary (§427).

2. The second stage is a stage of transformation. People meet angels—former material human beings, delegated from heaven to offer instruction about the Lord, heavenly existence, and the values of goodness and truth (§548). Exposed to angelic instruction, people increasingly focus on their basic spiritual attitude so that their positive or negative character asserts itself. People sort out their true thoughts, feelings, and attitudes and so reveal their true nature. Some good people's personalities are found to include certain crude and false elements of thought and orientation. After a purgatory-like period of suffering, they can be reckoned among the good (§513). Eventually, people change. They shed the form of the physical body that they had from their parents, so that their own, individual, previously concealed inner form becomes visible, a form shaped by their true nature, character, and orientation. People of good character now have lovely faces, while people of evil orientation have ugly ones (§457).

3. Having reached their definitive form at the end of the second stage, the good and the wicked part company to lead their own lives. The wicked ones can leave the world of spirits immediately, sinking headlong down into hell. The good ones, by contrast, go through one more stage of angelic instruction that prepares them for heavenly existence (§512).

Although some people stay very long in the world of spirits—up to thirty years—most of the newcomers soon find their way either up to heaven or down into hell (§426). Which way one goes depends on the inner orientation that one has acquired during one's life in the flesh and that has asserted itself in response to angelic instruction. Evil people choose hell; good people, heaven.

c. Heaven

Heaven and Hell devotes most space to describing heaven and heavenly existence (§§20–420). Although much of the text relies on abstract psychological and philosophical notions and may seem impenetrable to some first-time readers, many have been attracted to and charmed by the seer's lively descriptions of the world of the angels. The angels, according to Swedenborg, are none other than the blessed ones—the people who, after having lived their lives in the world *(mundus)* and after having spent some time in the world of spirits *(mundus spirituum),* have found their permanent abode in one of the heavenly kingdoms. Speaking of all humans, Swedenborg says, "We have been created to enter heaven and become angels" *(homo creatus est ut in coelum veniat, & fiat Angelus,* §57).

Whereas many people think of angels as "minds without form," as "something airy with something alive within it," Swedenborg insists on their truly human form (§74). "They have faces, eyes, ears, chests, arms, hands, and feet. They see each other, hear each other, and talk to each other. In short, they lack nothing that belongs to humans except that they are not clothed with a material body" (§75). Like his father, the Lutheran bishop Jesper Swedberg (1653–1735), Swedenborg insists that the inhabitants of heaven are not deprived of the most elementary means of communication, language.[6] "Angels talk with each other just the way we do in this world. They talk about various things—domestic matters, community concerns, issues of moral life, and issues of spiritual life," the seer explains (§234). He adds that "angelic language, like human language, is differentiated into words. It is similarly uttered audibly and heard audibly" (§235). While his father had speculated that the Swedes would speak Swedish in heaven, but would understand other languages without difficulty, Swedenborg advances the more philosophical view that "all people in heaven have the same language," no matter where they come from (§236).

In heaven, like-natured and like-minded angels recognize each other easily, and so they come together to form communities *(societates)*. Swedenborg's description sounds very much like a description of cities, towns, and villages on earth: The larger forms of these communities consist of tens of thousands of individuals, the smaller of some thousands, and the smallest of hundreds. Some people live alone (§50). The seer repeatedly insists on the fact that the communities are not formed by a law imposed from outside; rather, each heavenly community is constituted from the inner being of every member. In Swedenborg's words: "Heaven is not outside angels but within them" (§53). The members of the heavenly communities live in houses; these are "just like the houses on earth that we call homes, but more beautiful. They have chambers, suites, and bedrooms in abundance, and courtyards with gardens, flower beds, and lawns around them" (§184). The houses form cities with streets and lanes and public squares "just like the ones we see in cities on our earth" (§184).

As former men and women, the angels are male and female (§366). As a consequence, they form couples. Mate is drawn toward mate when their minds can be united into one. They love each other at first sight and enter into marriage. With many people gathered around them, they also hold a feast in celebration of their union (§383). The Lord blesses their mutual love and makes them happy. Heavenly couples differ from their earthly counterparts only in that they have no children (§382b).

---

6. For Jesper Swedberg's interest in the language of the saints, see Lamm 1922, 5.

Does heavenly bliss consist of a life of leisure? No, answers the seer, for idleness never leads to happiness (§403). Far from being idle, heavenly life is an active life. Ecclesiastical, civic, and domestic affairs all keep the angels busy, not only within their own society (§388), but also outside. As a rule, heavenly societies are assigned specific duties. The inhabitants of some work as guardian angels in the world; their task is leading people away from evil feelings and thoughts and helping them to control their deeds (§391). Others work among the spirits that have newly arrived in the world of spirits. Again others raise the children who have died in infancy. Swedenborg assures the parents of these infants that "all children, whether born within or outside the church, are adopted by the Lord and become angels" (§416).

d. Hell

The infernal regions *(inferna),* with their division into an upper level called the region of spirits *(regnum spirituum)* and a lower level called the region of demons *(regnum geniorum,* see §596), are dealt with at length, though not nearly as extensively as the heavenly realms (§§536–588). The spirits *(spiritûs)* and demons *(genii)* are none other than former human beings. According to Swedenborg, there are no devils and demons made by God in a separate act of creation; this common belief, Swedenborg says, is quite unjustified. Both the spirits and the demons have lived on earth, have died, and have spent some time in the world of spirits. Why are they in hell, a place of "rank, foul stenches" (§429)? Swedenborg asserts that the reason sinners enter hell is not that the Lord is angry with them (§545). They dwell there because during their earthly existence they preferred evil over good and so associated themselves more and more with the infernal realms. As a result, they ended up as spirits in the region of evil spirits or, worse, in the region of demons.

What happens to the evil spirits and the demons in hell? No judgment based on records of past crimes and offenses is passed by a court,[7] and there is no prison per se, no fire, no devil with a fork. Instead, the evil ones suffer from their own spiritual state (§547). We must beware, however, of misunderstanding Swedenborg: He does not psychologize the tortures of hell by speaking of it in terms of inner unhappiness;[8] instead, he

---

7. It should be observed that §462b:7 comes uncharacteristically close to a suggestion of "court proceedings."

8. Inner agony *(dolor),* according to Swedenborg, is never a permanent state of unhappiness, but only a temporary state or feeling (see §400:3–4).

consistently refers to the tortures of hell as harm inflicted from the outside. "The hellish mob craves and loves nothing more than inflicting
harm, especially punishing and torturing" (§550). The Gospels describe
hell as a place of utter darkness, of "weeping and gnashing of teeth"
(Matthew 8:12), and the passage easily lends itself to a psychological interpretation. Swedenborg specifically comments on the biblical text, but
takes it to refer to "clashes and battles" between the citizens of hell (§575).
Unlike Swedenborg, his contemporary Jean-Jacques Rousseau (1712–1778)
comes close to defining hell in psychological terms. According to book 4
of *Émile,* human hearts are "eaten away by envy, avarice, and ambition,"
so that hell is "in the hearts of the wicked" (Rousseau [1762] 1991, 284).
Both Rousseau and Swedenborg consider wicked hearts and evil acts as a
unity, and both of them know that evil originates in the human heart.
Yet, despite this similarity, Rousseau emphasizes the human heart, and
Swedenborg accentuates the acts. Rousseau's hell can be described as an
insane asylum, whereas Swedenborg's inferno is a society in which the
wicked reign. In hell, freed from social constraints, the wicked heart at-
tempts to express itself freely in ever new evil acts.

What about punishment? In hell, punishment does exist, but it is
never based on records of sins committed during the earthly life. Instead,
punishment is incurred exclusively for deeds done in hell (§509). It is effected by other demons, who never abstain from frustrating and tormenting their like when permitted.

The state in which the wicked find themselves depends on their individual urges and inner qualities (§508), all of which reflect love of self
and love of the world in various degrees (§554). To the good, they appear
as "monsters" (§80) of "misshapen, black, and grotesque" form (§99),
wearing "nothing but rags, dirty and foul" (§182). "Some of their faces
are black, some like little torches, some pimply, with huge ulcerated
sores" (§553). But, Swedenborg asks, are they ultimately lost to heaven?
Yes! Definitely, it is in this world, the world of time and space, that we
can and must choose. Once the evil character of someone has asserted itself, there will be no more change, and so there will be no escape from
hell, in all eternity. "A great deal of experience has convinced me that after death we remain the same forever" (§480). Consequently, "the people
in the hells cannot be saved" (§595). Yet Swedenborg gives those in hell a
little hope: Sometimes the Lord sends angels to people in hell to prevent
them from tormenting each other excessively (§391).

Swedenborg briefly describes the woeful condition and activities of
the infernal spirits. Living in crude huts, the hellish spirits engage in "constant quarrels, hostility, beating, and violence. The streets and alleys are

full of thieves and robbers. In some hells there are nothing but brothels, foul to look at and full of all kinds of filth and excrement" (§586). The seer hints in one section (§600) that they try to influence people living in the earthly realm. The most evil of spirits, the demons *(genii),* "take particular delight in making themselves unnoticeable and floating around others like ghosts, doing their harm covertly, spraying it around like the venom of snakes" (§578). Swedenborg indicates that the spirits also make assaults on heaven (§595), but to no avail; for when the heavens defend themselves against hell, the angels by a mere effort of the will disperse evil spirits and cast them back into hell (§229). The result of this constant conflict and antagonism is a dynamic drama. Supervised and regulated by the Lord, who always supports the heavenly forces, the play of antagonistic powers results in a great cosmic equilibrium (§§592, 593). Far from being in a sterile state of homeostasis, the universe teems with life.

The dynamic character of Swedenborg's universe emerges even more clearly when it is compared with traditional scholastic notions of the afterlife. According to much of Christian tradition, human life will eventually come to a halt in heaven and hell. Having reached its goal, it ceases to exist. In heaven, the blessed would be rewarded, essentially by the beatific vision of God. In hell, the damned would be punished by eternal suffering. *Heaven and Hell* would have none of this. Heaven, a dynamic reality, means harmonious life under divine inflowing, whereas hell means disharmonious life apart from the Lord. For the author of *Heaven and Hell,* human life will continue forever—both in this world and in the spiritual universes that surround it.

e. The Lord

All of this life comes from the Lord *(Dominus),* who encompasses and sustains the entire cosmic structure. Everything that exists and lives owes its being to the Lord, and indeed draws its power of being at any moment from the Lord (§9). Cut off from its source of being, everything would immediately vanish into nothingness. In the world *(mundus),* not all people turn to the Lord as their source of being, but in the spiritual world, all the angels do. To the angels of the heavenly kingdom, he is visible as a sun high above the heavens (§118)—"reddish and gleaming, so brilliant as to be beyond description" (§159).

The solar metaphor for the Lord is used in a way that gives Swedenborg's theocentric universe a heliocentric structure: "Since the Lord is the sun of heaven . . . the Lord is the common center *[Dominus est Centrum commune]"* (§124). Elsewhere Swedenborg uses more traditional, vertical expressions according to which God is above everything else and the various heavens are called lower and higher ones (§22). However, a close reading reveals that Swedenborg often switches his language from vertical to centric metaphors. Thus the higher angels and heavens are also called "more inward" ones, that is, those that are closer to the divine center (§§22, 29, 31). "All perfection increases as we move inward and decreases as we move outward, because more inward things are closer to the Lord and intrinsically purer, while more outward things are more remote from the Lord and intrinsically cruder" (§34). Figure 2 is an attempt to show Swedenborg's centric language and offer an alternative to the previous map of the universe (figure 1).

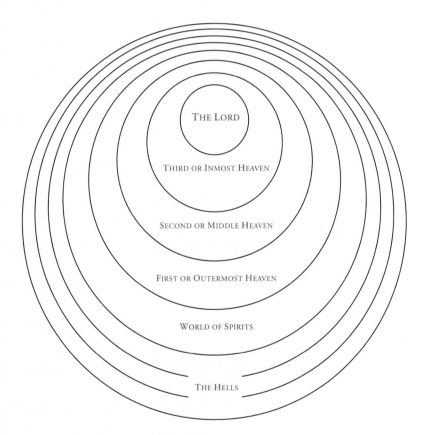

THE LORD

THIRD OR INMOST HEAVEN

SECOND OR MIDDLE HEAVEN

FIRST OR OUTERMOST HEAVEN

WORLD OF SPIRITS

THE HELLS

Figure 2. Swedenborg's map of the universe (second version). Whereas the schema offered in figure 1 places God at the periphery, making him encompass the universe, an alternative representation is implied in Swedenborg's text. The seer can also speak of the various levels of heaven as being closer to or farther from the divine center. This schema places the Lord at the center and relegates all else to the periphery.

Swedenborg takes care to correct common misunderstandings of the notion of God. Theologians have often misrepresented the nature of the Lord by believing in three divine beings (§2) or denying the divinity of the Lord while recognizing only the Father (§3). There is only one God, one Lord, who manifested himself on earth as Jesus, and who manifests himself in heaven as the sun or the moon (§§117–18). He may also manifest himself in angelic—that is, human—form (§§55, 121). The Lord's self-manifestation and visibility are facts much emphasized by Swedenborg; only misguided philosophers think of God as invisible and consequently as incomprehensible (§§82, 86). Those who describe God as the invisible soul of the universe, a being beyond the grasp of human cognition (§3), are clearly mistaken. Read as a critique of this naturalistic philosophy, Swedenborg's *Heaven and Hell* emerges as a celebration of the knowledge of divine realities. The seer was given that knowledge in two mutually supportive ways—by way of mystical communication with angels and by being enabled to understand the inner meaning of the biblical writings. "It has been granted to me to be with angels and to talk to them person to person," he explains. "Now I am being allowed therefore to describe what I have heard and seen, in the hopes of shedding light where there is ignorance and dispelling skepticism" (§1).

II. Elements of Interpretation

The words just cited are a solid starting point for an examination of the context of Swedenborg's times: "It has been granted to me to be with angels and to talk to them person to person. I have also been enabled to see what is in heaven and in hell, which has been going on for thirteen years" (§1). Since these words were written they have electrified many who have read or heard about them. During the last years of his life, Emanuel Swedenborg became a kind of celebrity, and people sought him out in his homes in Stockholm and London, or wherever they could find him. And he did not mind being approached. One of these visitors, the German poet Gottlieb Friedrich Klopstock (1724–1803), wanted to be put in touch with his departed friends—which, however, Swedenborg refused to do (Tafel 1890, 697). Klopstock and many others considered him a spirit-seer, and people wanted to hear him talk about angels or dead relatives, out of pure curiosity. They relied on hearsay and perhaps on a very superficial reading of books like *Heaven and Hell,* which seemed to them a conglomerate of disparate hallucinations. While it is true that Swedenborg did claim to be in contact with the other world, many contemporaries misunderstood or simply overlooked the fact that he wanted to lay the foundation of a new theology. They also were not aware of his sober, perfectly reasonable language and style of thought. Therefore the foregoing summary has sought to stress the systematic, coherent character of the teaching of *Heaven and Hell*.

In what follows Swedenborg's teaching is examined from a different angle—from a historical one. Historical understanding of a text that is as remote from our time and as complex as *Heaven and Hell* demands inquiry into the various layers of its cultural, philosophical, and religious background. The metaphor of layers immediately makes sense when the reader considers the fact that *Swedenborg's philosophy belongs to the eclectic tradition.* Today, eclecticism has a bad name, for it is given to systems of thought that arbitrarily combine elements from a variety of sources without adequate structure for the combination. In the seventeenth and eighteenth centuries, by contrast, many philosophers and scientists celebrated eclecticism as the only adequate procedure. Truth, they claimed, cannot be attained by committing oneself wholeheartedly to a traditional school such as the one founded by Plato (427–347 B.C.E.), Aristotle (384–322 B.C.E.), or the Stoics; it can only be found by experience and by carefully scrutinizing and possibly refining received ideas and notions found in the huge repertoire of already accumulated insight. Tradition, in the form of received ideas, and innovation, in the form of new insights gained through experiment and careful observation, interacted in the seventeenth and eighteenth centuries to produce new knowledge. Eclectic minds were open to all sorts of ideas, combined them into ever new configurations, developed them in ever new ways, and rarely sought to trace—or to reveal—their ultimate sources.

In science, the golden age of eclecticism was around 1700, when in Germany Johann Christoph Sturm (1635–1704) ranked as its leading representative (Albrecht 1994, 307–357). As a scholar of "natural philosophy" (as it was then called), Sturm wrote about mathematics and physics, introduced experimental physics in the courses he taught in Altdorf (the university of Nuremberg, Bavaria), interacted with specialists like the English chemist Robert Boyle (1627–1691), and caught the attention of the German philosopher Gottfried Wilhelm Leibniz (1646–1716). Sturm explained his approach in a treatise titled *De Philosophia Sectaria et Electiva* (On Sectarian and Eclectic Philosophy, 1679) and called his later collection of papers *Philosophia Eclectica* (Eclectic Philosophy; 1686, 1698). In order to make up one's mind about natural phenomena, Sturm insisted, it is not enough to study the ancient books; one has to research "the book of nature" as well. Sturm practiced a three-step method: first, one has to describe the phenomena as accurately as possible; then inventory the explanatory theories proposed by ancient and modern authorities; and finally, extract the proper explanation from the available literature. In science, eclecticism was both "modern" and "elitist" (Albrecht 1994, 330). When Swedenborg studied mathematics and physics in the early eighteenth century, the foremost scientists shared Sturm's basic philosophy, and the Swede made it his own. The spirit of eclecticism extended far beyond natural philosophy and came to include all of philosophy. All true philosophy, Denis Diderot (1713–1784) asserted in the *Encyclopédie*, is eclectic in nature. "La philosophie eclectique" existed in antiquity, but then "remained forgotten until the end of the sixteenth century," when it was reborn under Giordano Bruno (1548–1600), Francis Bacon (1561–1626), René Descartes (1596–1650), Thomas Hobbes (1588–1679), Gottfried Wilhelm Leibniz, Nicolas de Malebranche (1638–1715), and a long list of Diderot's heroes (Diderot [1755] 1876, 345). Among the eclectic philosophers, some would not have considered including Christian ideas in their system; others, however, were open to traditional Christian claims, accepted the notion of divine revelation, and rejected the purely mechanistic description of nature (Gaier 1984, 90–91; Dreitzel 1991, 332–333).

As befits a man of this philosophical persuasion, Swedenborg's learning was vast and eclectic, his thought stemming from a variety of sources. In retrospect, Ralph Waldo Emerson (1803–1882)—a man well acquainted with the merits of eclecticism—could write: "Swedenborg was born into an atmosphere of great ideas. It is hard to say what was his own" (Emerson [1849] 1903, 103). If Swedenborg's thought were to be compared to a house, it would be one in which building materials from different sources were combined to form a new, solid unity. But what were these building materials and where did they come from? The following is an attempt to define some of the intellectual materials out of which Swedenborg constructed his system and to trace their historical origins. Archaic, Neoplatonic, Renaissance, baroque, and romantic elements can be discerned. The first subject will be the archaic character of his worldview.

a. An Archaic Worldview

Ancient peoples found themselves in a world marked by two opposite, conflicting experiences (Cohn 1993, 3–76). There was stability and order, manifesting itself in the perennial cycle of day and night, birth and death. "As long as the earth endures, seedtime and harvest, cold and heat, summer and winter, day and night, shall not cease" (Genesis 8:22). That order extended from nature to society and was also seen as valid for the realm of the spirits and deities. Divinely appointed and unchanging, this order was essentially timeless. Yet it was never wholly tranquil and stable, for there was the second, equally impressive experience—that of instability, of conflict and chaos. Drought could upset the seasons, infertility threaten the continuity of the generations, disease and war give rulership to death rather than to life and prosperity. For all their disruptive power, however, the forces of chaos could never completely triumph over the divinely appointed order of creation. While the world is always liable to disturbance and full of conflict, the gods, it seemed, hold the world in timeless equilibrium between cosmos and chaos, with the balance usually tipped somewhat in the direction of cosmic order. The overall impression the world made on archaic humankind was one of visible and ultimately reliable stability, tempered by a strong sense of insecurity.

The world of the archaic peoples did not stop at the limits of everyday awareness; it extended well beyond those confines. Some form of heaven and hell—the abode of the favored and the less than favored of the dead—belonged to this worldview. The blissful realm is repeatedly described in the Rig-Veda, the ancient Sanskrit hymns composed around 1200 B.C.E. in India (Cohn 1993, 76). In these hymns, heaven appears as full of light, harmony, and joy. Its denizens are nourished on milk and honey. They make love—all the more deliciously because they have been freed from every bodily defect. The sound of sweet singing and of the flute is readily available. A typical hell was that of the ancient Mesopotamians: a netherworld peopled by demons who sometimes swarm out into the world of the living and even make assaults on the world of the gods. The same nether world also housed the spirits of dead human beings, or at least most of them. Pictured as a realm of darkness and ruled by an unfriendly goddess, hell was a gloomy, unpleasant place.

In his dialogue *Phaedo,* the Greek philosopher Plato discusses the fate of souls after death, assigning them places according to sinfulness or saintliness in life:

> When she [the soul] arrives at the place where the other souls are gathered, if she be impure and have done impure deeds, whether foul murders or other crimes which are the brothers of these, and the works of brothers in crime—from that soul every one flees and turns away; no one will be her companion, no one her guide, but alone she wanders in extremity of evil until certain times are fulfilled, and when they are fulfilled, she is borne irresistibly to her own fitting habitation. . . . Those who appear to be incurable by reason of the greatness of their crimes—who have

committed many and terrible deeds of sacrilege, murders foul and violent, or the like—such are hurled into Tartarus which is their suitable
destiny, and they never come out. . . . Those who have been pre-eminent
for holiness of life are released from this earthly prison [that is, the body],
and go to their pure home which is above, and dwell in the purer earth;
and of these, such as have duly purified themselves with philosophy live
henceforth altogether without the body, in mansions fairer still, which
may not be described, and of which the time would fail me to tell. (Plato
1952, *Phaedo* 108 B–C; 113 E; 114 B–C)

Plato seems to have added certain ideas of his own—calling the body the
soul's prison and seeing philosophy as the most powerful means of achiev-
ing a higher postmortem status; yet, when designating a particular destination for each type of soul, his basic view agrees with archaic notions.

The Iranian prophet Zoroaster, who lived sometime around 1200
B.C.E., revised the archaic worldview by intensifying its dramatic dimension.[9] The conflict between the forces of order and the powers of chaos
was not simply everlasting; instead, the conflict would some day escalate
to a final clash of arms and armies. This war of apocalyptic dimensions
would bring victory to the creator god and final defeat, if not annihila-
tion, to his opponents. As a result, human history would come to a final
halt. A new world without conflict would be established. Zoroaster's
worldview influenced ancient Jewish beliefs and through them Christian
eschatological doctrines. The war scenario was supplemented by a judgment scenario, so that the dramatic end and consummation of human
history came to be seen as consisting of two final acts—Satan's defeat and
the Last Judgment.

In *Heaven and Hell,* Swedenborg boldly brushes the Zoroastrian-
Christian doctrine aside in order to revert to the archaic worldview. For
him, history will continue forever as a place of conflict between good and
evil, truth and falsehood, order and disorder. He offers a radical new interpretation of traditional Christian teachings on the Last Judgment, arguing that the relevant biblical texts have been misunderstood (§§1, 307,
312). He claims to have been granted the discovery of the real meaning
concealed in the Bible. From *Heaven and Hell* alone, although it is not
discussed, one can infer that for Swedenborg the Last Judgment has already taken place as an event not on earth, but in the spiritual world. In

---

9. Boyce (1975, 190) dates Zoroaster between 1400 and 1000 B.C.E.

Last Judgment 45 he describes it as an event he had himself witnessed in 1757. *Heaven and Hell* includes a brief description:

> I have seen mountains that were the abode of evil people leveled and overturned, sometimes shaken from end to end as happens in our earthquakes. I have seen cliffs split down the middle right to the bottom and the evil people on them swallowed up. I have also seen angels scatter some hundreds of thousands of evil spirits and cast them into hell. (§229)

Although this report is accompanied by a reference to *Last Judgment*, which describes the actual event in detail, uninformed readers will hardly suspect that the author here speaks about the Last Judgment as a past event, an episode contemporaneous with human history rather than the culmination and end of this history. Swedenborg chose to devote a separate book—*Last Judgment*—to this important subject.

According to one Christian creed, Christ "will come again in glory to judge the living and the dead, and his kingdom will have no end."[10] This article of faith is generally understood in apocalyptic terms as a reference to a great cosmic drama that marks the end of human history. In modern theology, belief in the "end of the world" has become quite controversial, and many theologians are looking for a meaning beyond the mere words. For them, eschatological scenarios described in the New Testament and summarized in the creed are not meant as predictions of and information about future events. Instead, they must have some symbolic meaning, to be recovered by special strategies of interpretation.

Three of these strategies have become quite common among theologians. One school sees the New Testament apocalyptic drama as a secondary, post-Jesuanic level of early Christian tradition. On this premise Jesus' ministry can be understood within the archaic worldview. Seen from this perspective, his healings appear as temporary victories in the battle against the forces of evil, aiming at the establishment of God's royal rule among people. Even though Jesus may have hoped to cure Jewish society as a whole, he never went beyond hoping for the immediate though temporary triumph over the forces of evil. Jesus' reestablishment of divine rulership is small-scale and realistic and forms an episode of the struggle between order and chaos. There is no need to make it a minor prelude to an apocalyptic event of universal dimensions. The historical

---

10. From the Constantinopolitan Creed of 381 C.E. See Leith 1973, 33.

Jesus, as some modern historians see him, never gave his message a utopian and apocalyptic frame (Lang 1997, 94–96).

A second strategy of revising traditional Christian eschatological beliefs can be seen in the work of the twentieth-century Catholic theologian Gerhard Lohfink. According to him there will be only an individual judgment after the death of each person; as a cosmic drama, the Last Judgment will never take place, and it may be understood as expressing the fact that from God's timeless perspective, all individual judgments happen at the same time (Lohfink 1975, 70–81).

The third relevant strategy, represented by the twentieth-century Lutheran theologian Rudolf Bultmann, holds that the mythological eschatology must have an existential message. Rather than being a literal announcement of the Last Judgment, it serves as an urgent summons to confront God here and now and find our authentic inner being. When people discover God as the ultimate reality, then everything else—the material world and its history—vanishes. This is how Bultmann explains the real, inner meaning of the biblical message of the "end of the world":

> Eschatological preaching views the present time in the light of the future, and it says that this present world of nature and history, the world in which we live our lives and make our plans, is not the only world; that this world is temporal and transitory, yes, ultimately empty and unreal in the face of eternity. (Bultmann 1958, 23)

Like Swedenborg, much of modern theology eliminates apocalyptic scenarios. Swedenborg's Last Judgment is unique, however, inasmuch as he describes it as a single significant event that has already taken place.

b. Neoplatonic Features

One of the very first things we are told in *Heaven and Hell* is that "the Divine is one" (*quod Divinum unum sit*, §2). This One *(unum)* is the "First" *(Primum),* and whatever exists both in this world and in the other realms of the universe owes its existence to it. We must not think of existing beings—both material and immaterial, animate and inanimate, animal and human—as standing in themselves. Rather, their being has to be constantly replenished from the First, the source of all being. Everything depends on the First for strength and vitality. "If anything were not kept in constant connection with the First, through intermediate means, it would instantly collapse and disintegrate" (§9). Nothing stands in itself as a complete and independent substance; everything derives its power of being from a transcendent, otherworldly source—from the One, or the First.

These statements form the elementary ontological lesson not only of Swedenborg, but of a long and venerable philosophical tradition begun in ancient Greece by Plato in the fourth century B.C.E., and renewed as well as developed by Plotinus (205–270) in the third century C.E.[11]

Platonic philosophy teaches three main doctrines. First, that there are two worlds—a material one and a spiritual, transcendent one, with the spiritual world being the purer and more powerful realm. Second, that both worlds are ultimately derived from a common source of being and power that transcends everything spiritual and material. This source can be spoken of as the Good, the One, the First, or the Deity. Third, the human being belongs essentially to the spiritual or divine world and therefore transcends death; the general way of referring to this doctrine is to say that the individual human soul is immortal.

Stated in these very general terms, much if not all of Christian theology parallels Platonic or Neoplatonic thought. However, Swedenborg sometimes uses the very terminology employed by the school of Plato—for example, when calling God "the First." According to a most important doctrine of Plato, everything that exists gets its being from an ultimately transcendent source, and it must stay in contact with that source in order not to fall into nothingness. God, or the Good, in Plato as in Swedenborg symbolized by the sun, brings entities "into existence and gives them growth and nourishment"; they "derive from the Good . . . their very being and reality" (Plato 1952, *Republic* 6:509 B). Swedenborg also uses specifically Neoplatonic ideas and teachings. The statement already quoted above is a perfect example: "If anything were not kept in constant connection with the First, through intermediate means *[in nexu continue tenetur per intermedia cum Primo]*, it would instantly collapse and disintegrate" (§9). The First, in Platonic thought, is transcendent and very remote from most spiritual and material realities, so that there must be an *intermedium,* or intermediary, that connects it with its ultimate source of being. "Anything existing after the First must necessarily arise from that First, whether immediately or as tracing back to it through intervenients," states Plotinus (1952, 5:4, 1). Platonists have spent much time trying to define this *intermedium;* Plotinus, for instance, developed the theory of a cosmic soul that binds all things together, connecting them with the One or the First. In Swedenborg, we find angels in the *intermedium* function:

---

11. For an introductory summary of the philosophy of Plotinus and the impact it made in Western intellectual life, see Harris 1976.

"We cannot move a step without the inflow *(influxus)* of heaven," he observes. He adds that "angels have been allowed to activate my walking, my actions, my tongue, and my conversation as they wished, by flowing into my intention and thinking" (§228). In one passage, Plotinus too refers to divine guidance by way of inflow: "Once the soul receives an outflow [emanation] coming to her from the Good, she is excited and seized with Bacchic madness, and filled with stinging desires: thus love is born. . . . Once, however, a warmth from the Good has reached her, she is strengthened and awakened" (1952, 6:7, 22). The "outflow" (from the Divine) and "inflow" (into the soul) that in Plotinus excites the soul to love is in Swedenborg generalized to all movements of human will and human thought. All forms of love—marriage love *(amor conjugialis)* as well as simpler forms of mutual love *(amor mutuus)*—all derive also from heavenly inflow ("Marriage love comes down from the Lord through heaven"; *Amor conjugialis a Domino per Coelum descendat,* §385).

Plotinus and Swedenborg share a conspicuous feature of their writing and their way of arguing: the alternation of conceptual discussion with the vivid description of spiritual experiences. When writing in abstract ways about good and truth and their emanation from the Lord and their inflow into human beings, they rarely fail to conclude the discussion by illustrating the argument from "things heard and seen" in the spiritual world. The two philosophers agree in their endeavor to exhaust the resources of language and communication to make their point. Hence Plotinus's

> tendency to conclude passages of arid dialectical discussion with one of his vivid descriptions of contemplation or of mystical experience, and his stress that only in the light of such experiences can all difficulties be resolved. Also relevant in this context is Plotinus' use of imagery, especially of the so-called "dynamic images," in which processes drawn from the material world are used to illustrate the activity of the spiritual order. (Wallis 1972, 41)

The following parables, illustrating divine presence in the world, can give an idea of Plotinus's charming use of parable and imagery:

> The Soul [of the cosmos] watches the ceaselessly changing universe and follows all the fate of all its works: This is its life, and it knows no respite from its care, but is ever laboring to bring about perfection, planning to lead all to an unending state of excellence—like a farmer, first sowing and planting and then constantly setting to rights where rainstorms and long frosts and high gales have played havoc. (Plotinus 1952, 2:3, 16)

Imagine that a stately and varied mansion has been built. It has never been abandoned by its architect, who, yet, is not tied down to it. He has judged it worthy in all its length and breadth of all the care that can serve to its being—as far as it can share in being—or to its beauty, but a care without burden to its director, who never descends, but presides over it from above: This gives the degree in which the cosmos is ensouled, not by a soul belonging to it, but by one present to it; it is mastered not master; not possessor but possessed. The soul bears it up, and it lies within, no fragment of it unsharing. (Plotinus 1952, 4:3, 9)

The cosmic soul, for Plotinus, is an emanation from the One that, through presence in everything, connects everything with the One as its ultimate, divine source of being. One final example, the symbolic use of the human body, can serve to illustrate how Plotinian language can be very close to that of Swedenborg. The author of *Heaven and Hell* often uses the human body as an illuminating analogy in his arguments. Thus he asserts that the universe as a whole is in human form and that the highest or third heaven corresponds to the head of the Universal Human (§65). In the school of Plato we find similar ideas. Consider the following passage from Plotinus:

In every living being the upper parts—head, face—are the most beautiful, the mid and lower members inferior. In the Universe the middle and lower members are human beings; above them, the Heavens and the gods that dwell there. These gods with the entire circling expanse of the heavens constitute the greater part of the cosmos. (Plotinus 1952, 3:2,8)

If we substitute the angels for Plotinus's gods, then we have a statement that comes close to what Swedenborg might have written. Thus many of Swedenborg's ideas echo both the thought and the language of Europe's oldest and most venerable philosophy. This being said, one major difference between *Heaven and Hell* and the Neoplatonic view of God must be pointed out. In classical Neoplatonism the First or One stays remote from creation and is difficult to reach even by philosophical meditation. Swedenborg's Christian Neoplatonism insists that the One is the Lord, that is, Jesus Christ who manifested himself within the realm of the created world and therefore can be thought about, believed in, and loved. (Interestingly, Swedenborg does not offer a critique of Neoplatonism. His critique of those who speak about a deity that is somehow identical with nature but cannot be grasped by human thought or love, found in §3, seems to be directed against Neostoic philosophy.)

Not only the *Enneads* of Plotinus but also other Neoplatonic works can be compared fruitfully with *Heaven and Hell*. Here the most prominent source is the *Corpus Hermeticum,* a series of religious and philosophical treatises dating from the second and third centuries. According to one of the books included in this corpus and reminiscent of Swedenborg (Hermes Trismegistus, libellus 16), two powers compete for dominion over each human soul. One of these powers is represented by the host of demons, evil spirits that

> mould our souls into another shape, and pull them away to themselves, being seated in our nerves [or sinews] and marrow and veins and arteries, and penetrating even to our inmost organs. . . . These demons then make their way through the body, and enter into the two irrational parts of the soul; and each demon perverts the soul in a different way, according to his special mode of action. (Scott 1924, 271)

There is a third, rational part of the soul, however, and this part remains unassailed by demonic assaults:

> But the rational part of the human soul remains free from the dominion of the demons, and fit to receive God into itself. If then the rational part of the human soul is illumined by a ray of light from God, for that human being the working of the demons is brought to naught, for no demon and no god has power against a single ray of light of God. But such humans are few indeed. (Scott 1924, 271)

True to its Neoplatonic elitism, the *Corpus Hermeticum* argues that only a few people have been touched by the divine light.

Neoplatonic philosophy intrigued and inspired Christian thinkers in antiquity, including Origen (about 185 to about 254), Augustine (354–430), and Pseudo-Dionysius (who flourished around 500). The Italian philosopher Marsilio Ficino (1433–1499), enamored by the thought of Plotinus, translated that author's Greek works into Latin, making them accessible to European readers. Ficino also produced a Latin version of the *Corpus Hermeticum,* then thought to belong to the world's most ancient literature—a literature predating the biblical books written by Moses. In the seventeenth century the so-called Cambridge Platonists, a school represented by Henry More (1614–1687) and Ralph Cudworth (1617–1688), reinvigorated Platonic thought, defending it against those scientists who adopted a mechanistic worldview. Among earlier researchers, Martin Lamm emphasized Swedenborg's closeness to if not indebtedness to Neoplatonic philosophy (Lamm 1922). The author of

Heaven and Hell mentions Plotinus by name only once, in a quotation from Augustine (Swedenborg 1931, 138), but he seems to have known Plotinus' works in Ficino's translation. The Diocesan Library of Linköping in Sweden owns a Latin copy of Plotinus's works (published in Basel 1580) which Swedenborg had signed with his name in 1705 (Lamm 1922, 62). So at one point of his long intellectual career he must have become acquainted with Neoplatonic thought and it may have inspired him to think along similar lines. Among Swedenborg's known philosophical authorities, Leibniz is perhaps closest to Neoplatonism (Nemitz 1991 and 1994); see for instance his assertion that "the creature depends continually upon divine operation, and that it depends upon that no less after the time of its beginning than when it first begins. This dependence implies that it would not continue to exist if God did not continue to act" (Leibniz [1710] 1952, 355 = §385). On this important point, Plotinus, Leibniz, and Swedenborg all agree.

During the seventeenth and eighteenth centuries, European intellectuals strove to develop what we now call science but which was then called natural philosophy. Certain baroque authors—mainly those we now call Enlightenment scientists—rejected the notion of an animated nature, based their ideas exclusively on verifiable experience, and adopted a mechanistic worldview (Bonk 1999). By contrast others, such as George Berkeley (1685–1753), stayed closer to Neoplatonic traditions, upon which they drew, and made them key elements of their "philosophia eclectica" (Sladek 1984, 145). Although always religious, Swedenborg had adopted a mechanistic worldview in his early, philosophical works. Ultimately he found it wanting and came to prefer a more Neoplatonic perspective.

c. Renaissance Ideas and Ideals

Both Plotinus and Emanuel Swedenborg remained unmarried, did not care much about eating,[12] and spent all their life in intellectual pursuits. They also shared basic philosophical ideas about the divine. However, not all of Swedenborg's teachings echo Neoplatonic ideas. In certain respects, the author of *Heaven and Hell* was quite different from Plotinus. Their attitude toward wealth and worldly occupations differed considerably.

---

12. Porphyry [301] 1991, *Life of Plotinus* §8: "Even his sleep was kept light by abstemiousness that often prevented him taking as much as a piece of bread." In the years after his Christ-vision, Swedenborg apparently did not eat much (Tafel 1890, 537, 544; Cuno 1947, 11), often living on a simple diet of almonds and raisins (Tafel 1890, 540).

The ancient philosopher praised one of his friends, the Roman senator Rogatianus, holding him up as a model to those aiming at a philosophical life. Rogatianus, according to Porphyry's *Life of Plotinus,* had "advanced to such detachment from political ambitions that he gave up all his property, dismissed all his slaves, renounced every dignity. . . . He even abandoned his own house, spending his time here and there at his friends' and acquaintances', sleeping and eating with them and taking, at that, only one meal every other day" (Porphyry [301] 1991, §7). Plotinus recommended a life of poverty and world-renouncement, preferring contemplation and meditation to active life in the world. In its Augustinian form, Neoplatonic philosophy suited Christian ascetics and world-renouncers and could be invoked by medieval monks. Swedenborg would have none of this. Only ignorant people prefer an existence characterized by "spurning worldly interests, especially concerns for money and prestige, going around in constant meditation about God, salvation, and eternal life, devoting their lives to prayer, and reading the Word [that is, the Bible] and religious literature." No, says Swedenborg, "if we would accept heaven's life, we need by all means to live in the world and to participate in its duties and affairs" (§528). Ultimately based on selfishness and a high degree of self-love—as opposed to selflessness and usefulness to the community—mortification makes life mournful and gloomy; it prepares us for hell rather than for sainthood in heaven (§§528, 535).

What Swedenborg says of the life of worldly duties also applies to wealth: it does not stand in the way of spiritual authenticity.

> It is all right to acquire wealth and accumulate any amount of assets, as long as it is not done by fraud or evil devices. It is all right to eat and drink with elegance, as long as we do not invest our lives in such things. It is all right to be housed as graciously as befits one's station, to chat with others like ourselves, to go to games, to consult about worldly affairs. . . . There is no need to give to the poor except as the spirit moves us. (§358)

In other words, Swedenborg tells no one to sell his or her property and lead a different life. He would not have approved of Plotinus's friend Rogatianus. To him, Rogatianus must have appeared a strange man. He would have told him that what ultimately counts is not the outward behavior but the inner state, for "our quality is actually that of our affection and thought, or our love and faith" (*homo enim talis est qualis ejus affectio & cogitatio,* §358).

In his negative attitude toward world-renouncement and in his appreciation of wealth, the author of *Heaven and Hell* departs from the Neoplatonic and medieval Catholic traditions. His values are those of the Renaissance. While the medieval attitude continued to be visible in the eighteenth century, the Renaissance with its new cultural, intellectual, political, and religious style had penetrated all of Europe, including Sweden and England. Scholars and merchants, poets and prelates considered life "in the world" to be at least as pure and valuable as that of the monk's retreat. Rather than renouncing the world, they said, we should shape and enjoy it. Renaissance theology insisted that as noble beings we are invited to enjoy rather than renounce the world. The first chapter of the book of Genesis sanctioned the ideal of an active life, detailing how creative humankind reflects the image of God the Creator. By loving, enjoying, and participating in God's world, Christians display their love of God (Trinkaus 1970). In the early sixteenth century, Rodrigo Borgia (1431–1503; alias Pope Alexander VI), Erasmus of Rotterdam (1466?–1536), Machiavelli (1469–1527), and Michelangelo (1475–1564) symbolized the Renaissance interest in art and architecture, books and building, wealth, the opposite sex, and worldly power. In the eighteenth century, the very same interests still fascinated the intellectual and cultural elite, and Swedenborg's dictum "apart from an active life, a life has no happiness" (*absque vita activa, nulla vitae felicitas,* §403) can easily pass for a Renaissance maxim. There would have been no Gottfried Wilhelm Leibniz and Immanuel Kant (1724–1804) in Germany, no Voltaire (1694–1778) in France, no Isaac Newton (1642–1727) in England, no Emanuel Swedenborg in Sweden if the Renaissance had not prepared their way.

Lorenzo Valla (1405–1457), one of the most important Renaissance authors, broke with many medieval Catholic ideas. In *The Profession of the Religious* he denied that institutionalized monastic virtue had superior validity and asserted that spontaneous good actions were higher (Trinkaus 1948, 151). Swedenborg's critical attitude toward monasticism and his preference for giving to the poor "as the spirit moves us" (§358) speak the same language and reflect the same Renaissance atmosphere of thought.

As has been demonstrated, the Renaissance appreciation of wealth and worldliness rests on a firm theological basis: the insight into the goodness of creation. It also rests on a philosophical foundation—on the idea of human freedom and self-determination. Unlike animals, human beings can determine their fate free from the constraints of inborn dispositions. A few lines from Giovanni Pico della Mirandola's famous *Oratio de Hominis Dignitate* (Oration on Human Dignity, 1486) can serve as a condensed statement of the atmosphere in which Swedenborg thought. Pico puts the following words in the mouth of God as he speaks to Adam in Paradise:

> Neither a fixed abode nor a form that is yours alone nor any function peculiar to yourself have we given you, Adam, to the end that according to your longing and according to your judgment you may have and possess what abode, what form, and what functions you yourself shall desire. The nature of all other beings is limited and constrained within the bounds of laws prescribed by us. You, constrained by no limits, in accordance with your own free will, in whose hand we have placed you, shall ordain for yourself the limits of your nature. We have set you at the world's center that you may from thence more easily observe whatever is in the world. We have made you neither of heaven nor of earth, neither mortal nor immortal, so that with freedom of choice and with honor, as though the maker and moulder of yourself, you may fashion yourself in whatever shape you shall prefer. You shall have the power to degenerate into the lower forms of life, which are brutish. You shall have the power, out of your soul's judgment, to be reborn into the higher forms, which are divine. (Pico della Mirandola 1948, §3)[13]

Freedom, for Renaissance philosophers and for Swedenborg, has to do with the human faculty of will or volition. In this context, as in many others, the author of *Heaven and Hell* focuses on the distinction between volition and intellect as our basic mental capacities (§§423–425, 500). The vocabulary he uses can be presented as follows:

essential mental capacities:	will/volition/intention *(voluntas)*	intellect/understanding *(intellectus, cogitatio)*
mental states:	love *(amor)*	wisdom *(sapientia)*
extra-mental realities:	good *(bonum)* or evil *(malum)*	truth *(verum)* or falsehood *(falsum)*

If the human being is to be free, he or she must have a free will. Before Pico, Augustine had asserted this fact in *De Libero Arbitrio* (On Free Will, dating from 388–395); after him, the prince of humanists, Erasmus

---

13. I have adapted the translation of Elizabeth L. Forbes.

of Rotterdam, had done the same in a work of the same title—*De Libero Arbitrio* (On Free Will, 1524). Here we have to remember that in the Renaissance, philosophical discussion supported the idea that the action-oriented human will, rather than the contemplation-oriented intellect, was the noblest human faculty (Trinkaus 1970, 73). While medieval scholastics invoked the authority of Aristotle to defend their contemplative ideals, Renaissance writers preferred Cicero (106–43 B.C.E.), the active statesman and orator, the man of the will. This Renaissance tradition reached Swedenborg through authors such as Malebranche (died 1715), Leibniz (died 1715), and Christian Wolff (died 1754).[14] According to Swedenborg, the human faculty of volition *(voluntas)* also ranks above the intellect or cognitive ability. Priority is given to the human will and, consequently, to everything that is in the center of the diagram—volition, love, good. "Our volition," he states, "is the substance of our life . . . while our cognitive ability is the consequent manifestation of life" (§26, note i). In the spiritual world, the highest realm of heaven—the one called the heavenly kingdom—is defined as "the volitional side of heaven" (§95). In more philosophical terms, "thought is nothing but the form of our intention" (*cogitatio non aliud est quam voluntatis forma,* §500). In the order of the faculties of the human mind, then, volition holds the highest rank. For the author of *Heaven and Hell* it follows that "nothing is ever free unless it comes from our volition" (§598:2).

But how is it that the human person can be free? Swedenborg describes the atmosphere in which humans live as one in which good and evil influences blend: "By means of the spirits from hell we encounter our evil, and by means of the angels from heaven we encounter the good we have from the Lord. As a result, we are in a spiritual equilibrium—that is, in freedom" (§599). It is in freedom that humans can decide whether to associate with heaven or hell and thus fix their ultimate destiny. As the only free beings in the universe, men and women stand at the center of the cosmos. It is up to them whether they open themselves to the inflowing of good and truth from the Lord, or close themselves to such inflowing. Thus both heaven and hell are peopled with free beings. The Renaissance idea of human freedom has never been asserted more consistently.

All human beings enjoy this freedom, not just Christians. Therefore all human beings can live a moral life in which they attach themselves to the

---

14. See Swedenborg 1931, 54–59 for Swedenborg's excerpts on the notion of the will. Nemitz 1991 and 1994 comments on the influence of Leibniz and Wolff on Swedenborg.

good and to the Lord. And therefore all can attain heavenly existence. While traditional Christian theology was prepared to relegate pagans to hell (as did Dante in his *Inferno*), Swedenborg recognizes their capacity to enter heaven (§§318–328). In so doing he has famous Renaissance human- ists on his side: Erasmus of Rotterdam and the Swiss reformer Ulrich Zwingli (1484–1531). For Erasmus, one does not have to be a Christian to become a saint; and Christians may even rely on pagan intercession in heaven; so why not pray, *"Sancte Socrates, ora pro nobis*—Saint Socrates, pray for us"? (Erasmus [1552] 1997, 194). Unlike the other, less liberal re- formers, Zwingli also admitted pagans to heaven. Hoping to lure the French king François I (1494–1547) to the Protestant cause, Zwingli promised him eternal felicity in the company of his own pious ancestors as well as biblical figures. With a splendid humanist flourish he added that characters like Hercules, Socrates, the Catos, and the Scipios would also await the king in heaven (Zwingli [1531] 1953, 275–276; see Stephens 1995). Together with Jesus, Socrates formed the moral paradigm of the Renais- sance, and so it would not have made sense to exclude him from heaven. If all are free to lead a truly moral and spiritual life, then heaven is open to all.

The enjoyment of wealth and the universal ability of free self-deter- mination form part of what Renaissance philosophers have termed the dignity of the human being. But although wealth and freedom are impor- tant aspects of this dignity, they are in some way secondary. Swedenborg dug deeper, insisting that there must be more to human dignity. He ar- gued that in the human being there is an inner point of contact with the Deity that is the foundation of one's dignity. From his hesitant language we can see that Swedenborg found it difficult to express himself on this point; yet his meaning is clear enough. Within every human being there is "a central and highest something *[intimum & supremum quoddam]*, where the Lord's divine life flows in first and most intimately." It is this "central or highest level that makes us human and distinguishes us from the lower animals, since they do not have it. This is why we, unlike ani- mals, can be raised up by the Lord toward himself. . . . It is also why we live forever" (§39). The divine indwelling in the human person is beyond human perception or, in other words, it belongs to the basic ontological structure. It is this "central and highest something" that make us the cen- tral and highest something within the universe. It makes us the only in- telligent and responsive partners of the Lord himself.

The Lord's partners, according to some Renaissance thinkers, do not have to originate on the planet Earth. In the fifteenth century the cardinal Nicholas of Cusa (1401–1464) in *Of Learned Ignorance* (1440) held the idea of a plurality of worlds and the existence of life on the moon and sun. The most interesting Renaissance statement comes from the Franciscan theologian Guillaume de Vaurouillon (1392–1463), who taught in Paris. While he did not believe in the existence of worlds other than our own, he argued that it would not be difficult for God to create them. "Infinite worlds, more perfect than this one, lie hid in the mind of God. . . . It is possible that the species of each of these worlds is distinguished from those of our world" (quoted by O'Meara 1999, 15). Vaurouillon did not imagine knowledge of those worlds, far and separate, coming to earth except through angelic communication or some other special divine means. Soon the idea was to receive support from both traditional and scientific cosmology. In 1473 the recently discovered book *De Rerum Natura* (On the Nature of Things), written in the first century B.C.E. by the Epicurean philosopher Lucretius (about 96 to about 55 B.C.E.), became available in print; this book's pluralist teaching made European intellectuals acquainted with the idea. In the sixteenth century, scientific support came from Nicolaus Copernicus (1473–1543), whose heliocentric redescription of the universe made the earth a planet among other, possibly inhabited planets. By the eighteenth century, the idea of an inhabited universe had become commonplace and was shared by most philosophers and scientists (Crowe 1997, 152), including Swedenborg (see *Heaven and Hell* 417, and his work *Other Planets* throughout). When Pope Benedict XIV (1675–1758) lifted the ban on works expounding heliocentrism in 1757 (Randles 1999, 217), the story of the medieval cosmos ended, and a new story could begin—the story of an infinite universe with a plurality of worlds.

d. The Other Life in Baroque Thought

Biographies of Emanuel Swedenborg regularly include a plate showing one of the few portraits that exist of him: a man with erect and vigorous physique, big smiling eyes, wearing a white, curly, powdered wig, a dress-coat of black velvet, and a white shirt with frilled sleeves: a man easily recognized as a modestly attired aristocrat of the baroque age. The portrait reminds us of the fact that the author of *Heaven and Hell,* while thoroughly familiar with the traditions of the past, was also a man of his own century and his own culture. Known as the age of the baroque, the seventeenth and eighteenth centuries boasted a rich artistic, literary, religious, and political culture, of which the terms Enlightenment (that is, baroque rationalism) and "classical music" can capture no more than small fragments. One particular feature of the baroque mind that no one can miss is its almost excessive attention to and interest in detail, whether in map making, travel reports, painting, historiography, biography, diary writing, novels, theology, or any of the subjects of its fascination. Authors, artists, and scientists strove to satisfy the hunger for well-chronicled, detailed, precise knowledge, both of the visible world of the present and the invisible realms of the past; both of faraway places and the transcendent world.

While relevant examples of excessive attention to elaboration and detail in travel reports, diaries, and novels can be relegated to the notes, this mode of presentation in cartography, art, historiography, and theology deserves at least a brief commentary here.[15]

In 1492 Christopher Columbus discovered the continent that came to be known as America. During the following two centuries, explorers traveled throughout the world, often in the service of European royalty. Their aim was to win new islands, new wealth, and indeed new treasures for their masters and for themselves. Typically, the reports of these expeditions were considered secrets of the state and therefore remained unpublished. Since the way to the "treasure islands" was to remain secret, cartographers received little information that they could use in improving their maps (Schéuerbrandt 1993, 38). This attitude of secrecy changed around 1700, when a new era of exploration began. Eighteenth-century explorers such as the Dane Vitus Bering (1681–1741), the German Carsten Niebuhr (1733–1815), and the English Captain James Cook (1778–1779) sought knowledge, not treasures, and therefore took great care to have their discoveries chronicled in the form of detailed reports and ever more precise maps. They linked their maps to astronomically determined coordinates that had been established by French cartographers in the late seventeenth century (Musall 1993, 66–67). Around 1700, Europeans knew about 60.6 percent of the surface of the earth; by 1800, they knew 82.6 percent (Scheuerbrandt 1993, 41). By the end of the eighteenth century, cartographers could produce fairly reliable maps of most parts of the world, and these maps look very much like those we use today.

Baroque artists, as exemplified by the Dutch painters, left us a full, realistic, and almost photographic record of their world. Painters were

---

15. Mention may be made of Georg Forster (1754–1794), who chronicled one of Captain Cook's sea expeditions (*A Voyage round the World,* 1777) and Carsten Niebuhr (1733–1815), who explored and described Arabia and the adjacent countries (*Beschreibung von Arabien,* 1772). Typical baroque diaries include those of the Englishmen Samuel Pepys (1633–1703) and James Boswell (1740–1795). Here also belong Swedenborg's short journal of dreams and his long diary of spiritual experiences. The English novel is essentially an eighteenth-century product; unsurpassed in detail is *Tristram Shandy* (1760–1767), by Laurence Sterne (1713–1768), in which the author reaches the third volume before he gets around to having his hero born.

expected to show scenes of the past—historic battles, personalities, and encounters of great men—with the same realistic touch in the hopes of evoking patriotic or religious feelings. In the eighteenth century, history-painting could be considered the highest, most noble kind of art. "He that Paints a History well," Jonathan Richardson (1665–1745) wrote in 1725, "must be able to write it; he must be thoroughly inform'd of all things relating to it, and conceive it clearly, and nobly in his mind, or he can never express it upon the Canvas: He must have a solid Judgment, with a lively Imagination, and know what Figures, and what Incidents ought to be brought in, and what every one should Say, and Think. A painter therefore of this Class must possess all the good Qualities requisite to an Historian" (Richardson [1725] 1996, 215). The appreciation of history-painting reflects the wish of the baroque age to visualize everything as concretely and with as much detail as possible.

The eighteenth century saw the first development of modern historiography—Voltaire composed his *Essai sur les moeurs et l'esprit des nations,* David Hume (1711–1776) his *History of England,* and Edward Gibbon (1737–1794) the famous *History of the Decline and Fall of the Roman Empire,* works that still rank among the classics of historical narrative. A greater wealth of petty detail could of course be included in biographies (not to mention private, then unpublished diaries), of which *The Life of Samuel Johnson,* by James Boswell (1740–1795) remains the foremost example. People read these works with admiration and looked at the historian's craft with awe. Historians were expected to recreate the past in vivid detail, make us almost present at the great moments, and grant us glimpses of domestic and everyday life. But historiography did not aim at the mere accumulation of events, names, and descriptions. It aimed at giving a coherent picture and explaining the course of history: Why did the Roman empire decline (Gibbon)? What motivated the English monarchs to act as they did? What are the limits of institutional power (Hume)? How is history shaped by religion, economy, trade, and various customs and worldviews (Voltaire)? Far from identifying history with the mere listing of dynasties and chronicling of battles, historians considered their task as eminently philosophical and moral. Swedenborg was not a historian; but was he not of a kindred spirit as he strove to describe the other world as vividly as possible, while at the same time explaining the innermost dispositions of people, and God's dealing with them? When an early German defender of Swedenborg strove to characterize the seer, he compared him to a historian: "Whenever he [Swedenborg] refers to the revelatory states that he claims to have had, he appears as someone who, with the spirit of

a historiographer, observes with clear perception and narrates very truthfully and precisely."[16]

As an integral part of culture in the seventeenth and eighteenth centuries, religion shares the general craving for detail, specificity, and precision. Catholic moral casuistry described and defined sinful acts and their
circumstances in hairsplitting detail. Vying with each other in elaborate
moral descriptions and "pictures of manners," preachers of all churches inflicted long sermons on their congregations, often on both Sunday morning and Sunday afternoon (to the well-known displeasure of Swedenborg).
Baroque religiosity can be measured by the intensity of its will to imagine
scenes of the Bible, of the lives of the saints, and of the heavenly world.
Theologians, visionaries, and poets all strove to include as much detail in
their writing about the other world as history-painters used in their effort
to put it on canvas. In the seventeenth century, the classical book on heaven
came from the Puritan divine Richard Baxter (1615–1691). Titled *The Saints'
Everlasting Rest* (1649), it strove to depict with as many details as possible a
God-centered heaven—a heaven of saints praising the Lord for ever and
ever. While this theocentric perspective continued throughout the eighteenth century, it gradually gave way to a different, more human-centered
view (McDannell and Lang 1988, 177–180, 224–227). A first move in this
direction was the assumption, so ably argued by the Jesuit Athanasius
Kircher (1602–1680), that the eternal abode of the blessed must be a truly
human *environment,* one in which the physical senses function, colors can
be seen, sounds can be heard, and so on (Randles 1999, 165). Increasingly,
authors also insisted on the truly human character of the other *life,* imagined and described touching scenes of meeting again, and spoke of heaven
as home.

The general willingness to speculate about the details of eternal life
can be illustrated from a quite unexpected source—James Boswell's *Life
of Samuel Johnson* (1791). Dr. Johnson (1709–1784), the famous English
lexicographer, was immortalized in James Boswell's charming biography,
which ranks among the foremost works of English literature. Keen to
note everything Johnson said, he recorded a dialogue the two had one
evening in 1772. This is how Boswell described the conversation:

---

16. *Prüfungsversuch* 1786, xliv; my translation. The German reads: "Wenn er von seinen (von ihm
behaupteten) Offenbarungszuständen etwas erzählet, so findet man an ihm den Geist eines mit
gutem Bewußtsein beobachtenden, sehr treu und genau erzählenden Geschichtschreibers." The
anonymous author knew *Heaven and Hell,* of which he quotes §358 to assert the sober, practical
character of Swedenborg's ethics and to defend the seer against the reproach of sectarian enthusiasm (*Prüfungsversuch* 1786, xl–xli).

I [Boswell] again visited him [Dr. Johnson] at night. Finding him in a very good humour, I ventured to lead him to the subject of our situation in a future state, having much curiosity to know his notions on that point. Johnson: "Why, Sir, the happiness of an unembodied spirit will consist in the consciousness of the favour of God, in the contemplation of truth, and in the possession of felicitating ideas." Boswell: "But, Sir, is there any harm in our forming to ourselves conjectures as to the particulars of our happiness, though the scripture has said but very little on the subject? 'We know not what we shall be.'" Johnson: "Sir, there is no harm." (Boswell [1791] 1952, 192)

The conversation then goes into these various "particulars" of eternal happiness—meeting friends, listening to music, and having a body, for "there are some philosophers and divines who have maintained that we shall not be spiritualized to such a degree, but that something of matter, very much refined, will remain" (Boswell [1791] 1952, 193). Both Johnson and Boswell were normal Englishmen of their age, interested in everything, but not overly concerned about religion. In listening to them, we can get a glimpse of the baroque spirit: It was considered normal—"not doing any harm"—to offer speculations about heavenly life. The dialogue between the two supports the view recently suggested by Philip Almond in his study *Heaven and Hell in Enlightenment England:* In the seventeenth and eighteenth centuries, the influence of Platonic philosophers such as Henry More was pervasive and provided the background to the Boswell-Johnson dialogue. Moreover, the idea that at death the soul exchanges its terrestrial vehicle for one of air or a more refined one of ether was common to all Platonists of the period, including More in England (Almond 1994, 29–33) and Leibniz in Germany (Swedenborg 1931, 281).[17]

According to the modern Platonic school, the other world was not only coextensive with the physical universe; located within the universe, it shared the same spatiotemporal realm. The theory of the vehicle of the soul kept spirits, demons, and angels within the physical realm and thus susceptible to scientific investigation or, at least, reasonable speculation. Almond (1994, 36–37) describes the Platonist's map as consisting of the following two levels:

---

17. That angels, spirits, and human souls all have some kind of body was believed by many philosophers and theologians in early modern Europe. In his *Colloquium Heptaplomeres de Abditis Sublimium Arcanis* (1593), the French political writer and jurist Jean Bodin (1530–1596) summarizes the argument as follows: "If an angel has no body, as Aristotle and most theologians think, its substance would be everywhere, and it would have a being of infinite extension. Moreover, it would follow that Intelligences and Evil Spirits could do the same as God, and so everything would be confused. . . . We have, then, a clear demonstration . . . that angels, evil spirits, and souls have bodies and limits, and that their natures are subject to change" (Maxwell-Stuart 1999, 177–178).

1. The uppermost level was the ethereal heavenly kingdom where dwelt God, the angels, the saints, and the souls of the blessed.

2. Below the heavenly kingdom was an aerial kingdom, peopled by some of the souls. Unable to penetrate into the higher levels of the aerial kingdom, the wicked souls and the evil spirits had to stay close to earth. Some of the evil spirits lived in the cavities within the earth.

If the Platonists' views are compared with those of the other authors listed in appendix 1, several observations can be made. First, Swedenborg's *Heaven and Hell* finds an (as it were) natural place among the baroque authors. He shares their interest in life after death and their effort to give precise descriptions of the other life. Details of his description find parallels—the motif of meeting again with friends and relatives, intimations of sexual pleasures, and the placing of dead children in heaven rather than in hell. Second, among the works considered, *Heaven and Hell*—and its parent work, *Secrets of Heaven*—offers by far the most detailed description. No one prefigures Swedenborg's report of the spiritual kingdom as an upper-class world of aristocrats, complete with fine clothing, castles, and formal parks. No one has the idea that there could be an even higher heaven, the heavenly kingdom, in which the angels live in primitive, noble-savage circumstances, are naked, and have simple, wooden churches (§§179 and 223).[18] Third, Swedenborg departs from the Platonic paradigm established by Henry More and others in that he modifies the notions of time and space in heaven and hell (§§162–169, 191–199). Unlike the advocates of the new Platonic paradigm, Swedenborg does not include heaven and hell within the material universe as we know it, but rather asserts the existence of a spiritual universe connected to the physical by correspondences. Fourth, Swedenborg is the only author who claimed to have been in contact with the other world. In doing so, he was unique in his day. Some considered him insane, and Immanuel Kant's *Träume eines Geistersehers* (Dreams of a Spirit-Seer, [1766] 1969), with its apparently scathing critique of the Swedish visionary's work, demonstrates how foreign the visionary mode was to the Enlightenment temper. For the baroque age, speculation about the other world was possible, as even Kant conceded; yet it had to be done within the limits of reason, Kant argued, for there cannot be any real experience of

---

18. In his vision of the angels living in the heavenly kingdom, Swedenborg echoes ideas of the "noble savage" in a state of piety and morality uncorrupted by urban civilization. Perhaps this underlies his statement that "of non-Christians, the Africans are especially valued" (§326). For Swedenborg's view of Africa, see Odhner 1978. Swedenborg's description of the heavenly kingdom also parallels classical descriptions of the "Golden Age" (§115), on which see Frazier 1998.

the beyond. As a visionary, Swedenborg announces another intellectual movement: that of romanticism.

e. The Dawn of the Romantic Age

In 1772, a twenty-three-year-old youth reviewed several volumes of *Aussichten in die Ewigkeit* (Prospects of Eternity) by Johann Kaspar Lavater (1741–1801) in a learned journal printed in Frankfurt, Germany. Although the reviewer found some interesting passages in the letters that make up this treatise on the afterlife, his overall reaction was reserved: "In letter 17, the one on the social joys of heaven, there is a lot of warmth as well as goodness of the heart, but not enough to fill our soul with heaven."[19] He felt that the Swiss author had dealt with an interesting subject in a cold, bloodless, pedantic manner, full of reason but lacking the fire of feeling and the contagious power of enthusiasm. The review ends on a lyrical note. The author should seek the inspiration of

> that divinely chosen seer of our age, who was impregnated by the joys of heaven, to whom the spirits spoke through all senses and the entire body, in whose bosom the angels lived: the glory of this man should radiate on him, and, if possible, make him aglow, so that he can feel the bliss and appreciate the stammering voice of the prophets whose spirit is filled with unspeakable words.[20]

The young reviewer was Goethe (1749–1832), and the man he recommended, though did not name, was none other than Swedenborg (Peebles 1933, 148).[21]

---

19. Goethe [1772] 1987, 384.

20. Goethe [1772] 1987, 385.

21. That in the years 1772 and 1773 Goethe was quite willing to acknowledge the authority of a divinely inspired genius is evident not only from the Lavater review quoted above, but also from his essay "Zwo wichtige, bisher unerörterte biblische Fragen" ("Two Important, Heretofore Neglected Biblical Problems," 1773). This text ends with a rhetorical exhortation, addressed to those whom God has given experience of the divine reality: "When the eternal Spirit casts a glance of his wisdom, throws a spark of his love onto his elect one, then he must make himself known and stammer what he feels. He shall make himself known! and we will honor him! Blessed are you, wherever you come from! You, who enlighten the heathens! You, who excite the nations!" (Goethe [1773] 1987, 443; my translation here). The elect one is Swedenborg, and the reference to "wisdom and love" has a strong Swedenborgian ring (see, for example, §158—love and wisdom are from the Lord). Goethe presumably knew Oetinger's book on Swedenborg. In the papers of Goethe's friend Katharina von Klettenberg (1723–1774) a few pages of excerpts from Oetinger's book were found (Weis 1882, Fuchs 1900); these excerpts represent Oetinger's German translation of *Secrets of Heaven* 449–553, a text largely repeated in *Heaven and Hell* 395–414. Thus a case can be made for Goethe's indirect knowledge of at least one section of *Heaven and Hell.*

In Europe, from the middle of the eighteenth century, three intellectual and cultural movements vied with each other: the older baroque temper, represented by the pious and learned Lavater; the Enlightenment, which, in the person of Kant, was critical of traditional religion, hostile to mystical claims, and insisted on the limits of philosophical and theological speculation; and romanticism, which, firmly standing within the Christian tradition, expressed an interest in mysticism, dreams, and visionary experience, and often gave expression to its sentiments in poetry and novels. The spirit of the young Goethe was tinged with romantic sentiment, and Swedenborg united the baroque and the romantic temper within one single soul.[22]

Unlike their baroque predecessors, romantic minds were not satisfied with pious speculations about the hereafter. They wished to look beyond the everyday world in which people live their everyday lives, and actually experience higher worlds. According to the romantic tradition, only a thin veil divides our world from the divine realm, and dreams, mystical experiences, visions, clairvoyance, even telepathy and somnambulism were thought to give access to it. Both the uneducated and the educated believed in the existence of spirits, their activity in and influence on the material realm, and in the ability of gifted individuals to communicate with them (Sawicki 1999). Some dabbled in the occult arts and formed circles that eagerly sought information about the state of deceased persons through spiritistic messages (Sigstedt 1981, 343). In Germany, two women visionaries came to unexpected fame through romantic interest in their visions: the Catholic nun Anna Katharina Emmerich (1774–1824) and the Protestant lay woman Friedericke Hauffe (1801–1829). While Sister Anna's visions were transcribed and published by the poet Clemens Brentano (1778–1842) to become classics of Catholic devotional literature, Hauffe was immortalized as "the seeress of Prevorst" by her doctor, the Swabian writer Justinus Kerner (1786–1862).

An analysis that includes Swedenborg in the romantic movement should at the same time emphasize his independence from it. Rather than being dependent on that movement, he must be considered its forerunner and source of inspiration. Throughout the romantic movement, especially in Germany, Swedenborg's influence can be felt.[23] The ease with which romantic writers in England, Germany, and France could

---

22. See Lamm 1918, who writes about a romantic current within the eighteenth-century Enlightenment, mentioning Swedenborg as one of its major representatives.

23. See below, at the end of this introduction.

appreciate Swedenborgian ideas demonstrates the inherent romanticism of the author of *Heaven and Hell.*

Heaven and Hell frequently invokes visionary experience, often to illustrate abstract notions with more vivid descriptions, so that the romantic spirit supplements and sometimes prevails over baroque rationality. Swedenborg's teaching on heavenly "appearances" gives his otherworld a particularly visionary, romantic quality. The outward appearance of every angel expresses her or his inner being; thus inner goodness appears as shining beauty (§459), and an evil character manifests itself as visible ugliness. That the inner state creates the outer appearance is also true of the clothes the angels wear in the spiritual kingdom: the more elegant, shining, or festive the clothing, the more intelligence is present in that person. "The most intelligent wear clothes that gleam as though aflame, some radiant as though alight. The less intelligent wear pure white and soft white clothes that do not shine" (§178). The same inner-directedness is true of the environment in which the angels live, for "in the heavens, everything comes into being from the Lord in response to the deeper nature of the angels" (§173). To angels focused on intelligence "there appear gardens and parks full of all kinds of trees and flowers"; in these trees "there are fruits in keeping with the quality of the love these intelligent angels are absorbed in" (§176). One may compare this psychological world to one projected by a magic lantern: the lantern and its repertoire of images correspond to the angelic soul and its states, the projecting light corresponds to divine inflow, and the projected images to the angel's environment. All inner states not only manifest themselves in the outside world, but actually create that world. In Swedenborg's words: "It can never be said that heaven is outside anyone. It is within; because every angel accepts the heaven that is outside in keeping with the heaven that is within" (§54).

Partly due to divine inflowing, partly due to the angels' own mood, the nature of the angels is in constant change, so that they are never exactly the same (§155). And the same is again true of their surroundings. The houses in which the angels live "change slightly in response to the changes of state of their deeper natures" (§190). "As the states of the inner levels of angels' love and wisdom change, so too do the states of the various things that surround them and are visible to their eyes; for the things that surround angels are given their appearance according to the things that are within them" (§156). In other words: heavenly reality, though originating with the Lord, is constantly shaped and reshaped by the angels. As a result, the individual angels always find themselves in an environment congenial to their mental state, as if that environment were a projection or emanation of that state.

In heaven, one might say, all people have heaven within themselves, and this is why Swedenborg can call each individual a complete heaven: "Heaven is not outside angels but within them. Their deeper levels, the levels of their minds, are arranged in the form of heaven and therefore are arranged to accept all the elements of heaven that are outside them. . . . As a result, an angel is also a heaven" (§53).

The visionary's romantic notion of an ideal world in which everything emerges from the inner being of eternally young, beautiful men and women (§414) has inspired one of his most reserved biographers to acknowledge the master's achievement. Martin Lamm writes, "Thanks to his unique ability of giving symbolic meaning to a spiritual world fashioned out of earthly notions, [Swedenborg] could give it the same fantastic, dreamlike quality which it must have had in his own original visions" (Lamm 1922, 367).[24]

In addition to the visionary mode of experience and description, one more feature foreshadows—and eventually deeply impresses—the romantic age: the theme of heavenly love between men and women. The classical canon of Christian thought does not allow for the subject to be dealt with, for in heaven, according to standard Christian doctrine, all bliss derives from the soul's enjoyment of God alone. In baroque theology, the French Jesuit Pierre Nicole (1625–1695) summed this teaching up by saying that in heaven, the blessed will have no desire for anything else besides God. Their souls' "capacity to love, desire, and enjoy will be so exhausted that it will be impossible for them to love and desire anything besides God" (Nicole [1715–1732] 1971, 375). For Nicole, the communion of the blessed with each other is so unimportant that he speaks of heavenly existence as *solitude eternelle avec Dieu seul:* "The human being is created to live in an eternal solitude with God alone" (Nicole [1715–1732] 1971, 506).[25] During the age of the baroque, as has been shown, the classical teaching as expressed by Nicole was gradually modified, and the idea of love, even erotic love, between the blessed could be imagined. But while the subject itself occasionally surfaces in earlier writing, it never became so developed as in Swedenborg's work.

At first sight, what *Heaven and Hell* says about men and women sounds quite conventional: "As to innate nature, men do act on the basis of reason *[ex ratione],* while women act on the basis of their feelings *[ex*

---

24. My translation into English from the German.

25. This passage from Nicole and the preceding are my translation.

affectione]. As to form, the man has a rougher and less attractive face, a deeper voice, and a stronger body, while the woman has a softer and more attractive face, a gentler voice, and a softer body" (§368). A closer reading reveals that Swedenborg is more nuanced than this quotation seems to suggest. Feelings, for him, are related to volition, which as has been shown is valued more highly than the faculty of thinking and reasoning; thus *Heaven and Hell* comes close to admitting the superiority of women. But it is not the celebration of female superiority that interests Swedenborg. He celebrates the heavenly marital union as a merging of the two sexes, and the union is so complete that the two appear as one angel rather than two different beings (§367). Their sharing of reasoning *(ratio)* and feeling *(affectio)* is complete. "I have been told by angels," exclaims the seer, "that the more two spouses are engaged in this kind of union, the more they are caught up in marriage love and, at the same time, in intelligence, wisdom, and happiness" (§370). This is the stuff of which the romantic vision of love is made. Without Swedenborg, Novalis (1772–1801) would never have described heavenly bliss in terms of "sweet talk of whispered wishes: this is all we hear, and we gaze into blessed eyes forever, and taste nothing but mouth and kiss" (Novalis 1978, 401).[26] Swedenborg gave romanticism one of its most daring fantasies.

III. Some Early Readers of *Heaven and Hell*

From our attempt to offer elements of interpretation, *Heaven and Hell* emerges as a work echoing a variety of cultural and intellectual currents. Building on archaic views of the permanent conflict between good and evil; adopting Neoplatonic notions of the Deity; drawing on the Renaissance appreciation of the human will and a life in which wealth can be enjoyed legitimately; describing heaven and hell in the detailed manner of baroque spiritual writers and surpassing them; and, finally, developing bold ideas about marital love in heaven and trying to be true to the visionary experiences of his own romantic spirit, Emanuel Swedenborg created a work of imposing complexity. Despite the avowed aim of serving as a compendium of and introduction to the many-volumed *Secrets of Heaven* for "people of simple heart and simple faith" (§1), *Heaven and Hell* waits

---

26. My translation, from "Song of the Dead." This poem by Novalis was written in 1800 but published only posthumously.

for intelligent, educated readers. What follows is a sketch of the reactions of the first generation of such readers. Luckily, some of these people confided their thoughts to private diaries or expressed them freely in published reviews and anecdotes. While the relevant sources are scarce, they nevertheless permit a classification into four types: the reader of the gentle class, the translator, the theologian, and the founder of a new church.

a. Readers of the Gentle Class in Sweden, Amsterdam, and London

Two Swedes and one German, all personally known to Swedenborg, come within our first category—the educated reader of the gentle class. Writing private notes or memoirs between 1759 and 1770, Count Gustaf Bonde, Carl Gustaf Tessin, and Johann Christian Cuno have left us the earliest readers' responses to the original Latin edition of *Heaven and Hell.* To these three gentle readers a fourth can be added—the anonymous reviewer of *A Treatise concerning Heaven and Hell* in *The Gentleman's Magazine* of 1778.

After having published *Heaven and Hell* as well as four other books in London in 1758, Swedenborg returned to Sweden, carrying with him, it seems, only very few copies of his new publications (Tafel 1890, 397; Acton 1955, 529). One copy came into Sweden through unknown channels and was sold to Count Gustaf Bonde (1682–1764), then chancellor of the University of Uppsala, an old acquaintance of Swedenborg. Bonde or his bookseller must have been the first in Sweden to guess or find out that Swedenborg was the author of the anonymously printed work.

In a personal, unpublished note of uncertain date—1759 or 1760—Count Bonde lists several objections that he had when reading.[27] Swedenborg's teaching that "our nature after death depends on the kind of life we led in the world" (heading of §§470–484) seemed to contradict "our principle articles of faith and the hope of everlasting life for a poor sinner." Lutherans believe in the essential sinfulness of every human being, so that, were Swedenborg right, all of them would end in hell. According to Bonde, Swedenborg fails to consider Christ's merit and God's merciful intervention on behalf of the sinner. It is not the life we lead on earth, Bonde contends, but God's mercy that determines life everlasting; therefore there is the hope of everlasting life even for a poor sinner. Other Swedenborgian views were equally problematic: How could the serpent have

---

27. The short document is in the State Archives of Stockholm; a transcript can be found in the Academy Collection of Swedenborg Documents, vol. 6, no. 809 (Swedenborg Library, Bryn Athyn, Pennsylvania). The Academy Collection dates the document to 1760, whereas Sigstedt (1981, 270) proposes January 5, 1759.

tempted Eve in Paradise, if there were no angels and devils before human beings existed in Paradise? The count fears that if, instead of basing one's faith on the plain letter of Scripture, one has to look into it for an "internal sense," then anyone could make up a special religion to suit oneself, by searching out whatever meaning one pleases. What struck Count Bonde were Swedenborg's critique of the Lutheran doctrine of "salvation by faith through divine mercy" (see §§521 and 522) and his redefinition of angels, which amounted to a dismissal of traditional beliefs in angels as a separate, nonhuman species within God's creation (§311). Interestingly, Bonde does not seem to have been surprised by the author's claim of contact with angels. Bonde's Lutheran beliefs were tolerant of angelic revelations, but intolerant of everything that contradicted their doctrine of divine mercy.

Another very early recorded reader is Carl Gustaf Tessin (1695–1770), an architect and former president of the House of Nobles of Sweden. His surviving diary includes several notes on Swedenborg. The first records Tessin's visit with Swedenborg in Stockholm:

> Merely out of curiosity, to make the acquaintance of a singular man, I went to see Assessor Swedenborg on the afternoon of March 5, 1760. He lives far up on Hornsgatan in a neat little wooden house on a large plot of ground with a garden belonging to him. I found there an old man about seventy-three years of age with a countenance perfectly like that of the late Bishop Swedberg, but not so tall. He had feeble eyes, a large mouth, and a pale complexion, but he was cheerful, friendly, and talkative. It seemed that I was welcome, and as I had not intended to make many preludes, I began at once by speaking about the work on *Heaven and Hell.* (Tessin, as quoted in Sigstedt 1981, 273; see Tafel 1890, 398–399)

Tessin apparently had heard about this book, but he had not seen a copy. Swedenborg had to tell him that at the moment no copies were available in Sweden:

> He [Swedenborg] said that besides his own copy he had only two others, which he had intended, at the next Riksdag [meeting of parliament], to hand over to two bishops; but as he had heard that one copy of it had come into the country without his knowledge, having been sold to His Excellency Count Bonde, he had reconsidered the matter and given one of his copies to Senator Count Höpken and the other one to Councillor Oelreich, the censor of books. He expects fifty more copies from England next spring and then he will send one to me. (Tessin, as quoted in Sigstedt 1981, 273; see Tafel 1890, 399)

These fifty copies must have arrived promptly, for by July he had his own copy of *Heaven and Hell*. In a diary entry of July 4, 1760, Tessin comments on the book:

> Among all visionaries, Herr Swedenborg is probably the one who has written most explicitly. He discusses, quotes sources, adduces arguments and causes, etc. The whole edifice has a kind of coherence and with all its peculiarity is erected with studied thought. The book, moreover, has so many new and unexpected turns that it may be read through without boredom. What he says in [§]191 . . . concerning space in heaven is a well-reasoned dream. Throughout the entire work one recognizes Bishop Swedberg's son, who is dreaming with far greater profundity than the father. . . . All this may be read with the same credence one gives to Mohammed's Alkoran. (Tessin, as quoted in Sigstedt 1981, 274–275)[28]

Tessin read *Heaven and Hell* with much interest, recognized its coherence, appreciated its novelty and even profundity, but eventually decided to place it with the Qur'an—a book of other people's revelation, a book not accepted and acceptable as *our* normative source of religion. The reference to the Qur'an was to become standard in anti-Swedenborg polemics; it will also appear in the discussion below of the reactions of Johann Christian Cuno and John Wesley, but Tessin's note of 1760 seems to be the first attestation.[29]

Johann Christian Cuno (1708–1796)—the third and final reader to be mentioned in this section—was a well-educated German merchant and author living in Amsterdam. In the mid-nineteenth century, the librarian of the Royal Library in Brussels was alerted to the existence of a German autograph manuscript of four thousand folio pages—the autobiography of Cuno. August Scheler, the librarian, read the manuscript and decided to publish the section dealing with Swedenborg. (Cuno 1947 is an English translation.)

Cuno happened to meet Swedenborg in an Amsterdam bookstore on November 4, 1768, and the two men took a liking to each other. At the

---

28. The transcript in Tessin 1760 indicates that all three passages cited here were written on March 5, 1760. Sigstedt, however, cites the date of this particular diary entry as July 4, 1760; and it should be noted that she copied all of these entries from the original diaries of Tessin in his family library at Åkerö Castle in Södermanland in 1915. See Sigstedt 1981, notes 443 and 447.

29. The implication of the comparison to the Qur'an is that of a heavenly Paradise that is too sensuous. Eighteenth-century writers often refer to the Qur'an or "Mahometans" when rejecting sensuous notions of heaven; for an example, see *The Gentleman's Magazine* 1739, 9:5b, quoted in Appendix I.

time Swedenborg was living in Amsterdam to supervise the printing of some of his books, and it was in this city that Cuno became one of his friends and avid readers. Between 1768 and 1770, he saw Swedenborg frequently, and he often had an occasion to ask questions about his religious views and his publications. Cuno owned some of Swedenborg's books; others—including *Heaven and Hell*—he borrowed from the author (Cuno 1947, 17). He read *Heaven and Hell* in 1769, "eleven years" after its publication (Cuno 1947, 52), took many notes, jotted down comments, and included all of them in his autobiography. A pious man, a regular churchgoer, and himself an author of religious books, Cuno was fully conversant with theology and immediately realized that *Heaven and Hell* departed from biblical teaching as generally understood (Cuno 1947, 43–68). He noted that in Swedenborg's theology all the angels and evil spirits have formerly been humans on earth; there are marriages in heaven; resurrection actually means introduction into the world of spirits. He also suspected the author of falling into the trap of Manicheism, a heresy that posits the eternal coexistence of two conflicting principles, one good and one evil—the one realized in heaven, the other in hell. Cuno considered Swedenborg's visionary claims the most irritating feature of his friend's theology. Was it likely that a gentleman of the eighteenth century was superior to St. Paul, who had been unable to tell of his heavenly visions? Swedenborg himself had written about enthusiasts who, with their minds focused exclusively on matters of religion, delved into the world of spirits and were deceived by lying spirits (§249). Was it possible that Swedenborg, despite his claims to the contrary, belonged to these enthusiasts (Cuno 1947, 114)?

Nevertheless, Cuno admits of finding "here and there . . . a grain of gold" (Cuno 1947, 97), and he enjoyed what Swedenborg wrote about the admission of wise and virtuous pagans like Cicero into heaven (Cuno 1947, 52). All things considered, doubts remain:

> I myself [Cuno] cannot in the least defend the upright Swedenborg. But if, eleven years ago, when this work of his whereof I am speaking, namely *Heaven and Hell,* was published, a well-grounded theologian had left what is good therein in its place, and soberly refuted what was erroneous and contradictory, then the good man, if not diverted from his imaginations, would nevertheless have been constrained to be more careful in the future, and not to flood the world with his multifarious writings. (Cuno 1947, 52)

If the statements of Bonde, Tessin, and Cuno were representative of the early readers of *Heaven and Hell,* then one would have to say that the response was largely critical and only marginally appreciative. There were other readers, however, and some of them responded in a friendly way, if not with enthusiasm. When the first English translation of *Heaven and Hell* became available in 1778, a then fashionable monthly publication, *The Gentleman's Magazine* of London, honored it with a review of a little more than two columns in small print. The anonymous reviewer offered extensive excerpts from the translator's preface to introduce Swedenborg (spelled "Swedenberg" in the review), the scientist and visionary.[30] A tantalizingly brief comment on *A Treatise concerning Heaven and Hell* forms the conclusion:

> We shall only observe, upon the whole, that whatever judgment the public may entertain of the visionary part of this work, the doctrinal part is unexceptionable; and as the former has met with a very able advocate in the preface-writer, the latter will need no justification. (*Gentleman's Magazine* 1778, 326b)

No contemporary reader will have missed the friendly tone of the review, and so it may be concluded that in 1778, when the first public statement on Swedenborg's book appeared, the educated readers of England took the work seriously. Regrettably, no information about the reviewer can be found in the surviving files of the publisher (Kuist 1982). By contrast, the name of the "very able advocate" who wrote the preface of *A Treatise concerning Heaven and Hell* has been determined: Thomas Hartley. He belongs to those early readers of *Heaven and Hell* whose enthusiasm led them to produce vernacular versions of the Latin book.

b. Early Translators

Swedenborg's book had the chance to capture the attention not only of people of the gentle class with a passing interest in the subject, but also of pious people who sought to promote it in vernacular translations. Soon *Heaven and Hell* became *Vom Himmel und von den wunderbaren Dingen desselben* (1775, German), *A Treatise concerning Heaven and Hell* (1778), and *Les Merveilles du Ciel et de l'Enfer* (1782, French).

The first to translate *Heaven and Hell* was a German. Although *Vom Himmel und von den wunderbaren Dingen desselben* does not mention the

---

30. The April 1772 number of *The Gentleman's Magazine* (42:198b) included the following obituary note: "Hon. and learned Emanuel Swedenburgh [*sic*], famous for his mathematical works, and for his visionary [works]."

translator's name, a contemporary German biographical dictionary attributes it to Johann Christoph Lenz (1748–1791) who is identified as the clerk and master accountant of the University of Leipzig (Hamberger and Meusel 1797). Lenz must have had a sizeable collection of books he classified as "alchemistic and theosophical works" (Breymeyer 1984, 227). Most likely, he found Swedenborg's books more interesting than others and therefore chose two of them for translation: *Soul-Body Interaction,* which appeared as *Von der Vereinigung der Seele und des Leibes* (1772), and *Heaven and Hell,* issued as *Vom Himmel* (1775).

Hartley and Cookworthy, the two English translators, had known and admired Swedenborg personally, and their work made an enormous impact on many readers. Thomas Hartley (1709–1784) was an Anglican cleric. As an absentee rector of Winwick, Northhamptonshire, he paid a curate to do the regular parish work. Liberated from that duty, Hartley led the life of an intellectual and a writer interested in mysticism. He was acquainted with Selina, Countess of Huntingdon (1707–1791), the famous patroness of English baroque spirituality, as well as with William Law (1686–1761) and George Whitefield (1714–1770) (Beilby 1931). William Cookworthy (1705–1780), otherwise a busy chemist, porcelain manufacturer, and entrepreneur, found time to serve the Quaker community of Plymouth as an elder (Selleck 1978). During the 1760s, the two came to be interested in Swedenborg's work, eventually met each other, developed a friendship, and also visited the master in London. Their story is one of devotion to the work of Swedenborg. After Swedenborg's death, the two men collaborated on the translation of *Heaven and Hell.* Although Rev. Hartley was then a frail old man of over seventy, he reworked Cookworthy's draft. By 1778 Cookworthy had it published at his own expense, paying 100 pounds sterling to the printer (Tafel 1890, 539).

Hartley wrote a long introduction to *A Treatise concerning Heaven and Hell* in which he defended Swedenborg's claim to have knowledge of the spiritual world from experience.[31] He knew that his times were not favorable to such claims, for "the belief of all extraordinary or supernatural dispensations is at a very low ebb with us" (Hartley 1778, vi).

---

31. The introduction to *A Treatise concerning Heaven and Hell* is anonymous, but scholars generally admit Hartley's authorship. *The Gentleman's Magazine* 1791, 61:619b–620a, prints a letter by "Candidus." Candidus recommends to a correspondent who inquired after the true character of Swedenborg to read the preface of *A Treatise concerning Heaven and Hell,* stating that it was "written by the Rev. T. Hartley, a worthy and pious clergyman of the Church of England" (620a).

Contemporaries of Hartley would—and in one case known to him, actually did—obtain for persons who conversed with angels a "statute of lunacy" and order them to the madhouse (Hartley 1778, xviii). This attitude not only rests on "an undue exaltation of man's natural rational faculties and powers, as the sufficient test of revealed Truth," but also on the belief that miracles ceased sometime during the early church (Hartley 1778, vi). This, however, cannot be true, for it does not seem to be rational to dismiss all of the many reports on visions known from all periods of church history as inventions and forgeries (Hartley 1778, xiii). Thus Hartley felt that he could appeal to popular belief as if to common knowledge when defending the reality of otherworldly contacts:

> And who will say, that the natural eye of man is incapable . . . to discern the subtle vehicles of certain spirits, whether consisting of air or ether; certain it is, that either by condensation, or some other way, they can make themselves visible, and converse with us, as man with man, and so innumerable are the instances hereof, as also of their discoveries, warnings, predictions, &c. that I may venture to affirm, with an appeal to the publick for the truth of it, that there are few ancient families in any county of Great Britain, that are not possessed of records or traditions of the same in their own houses, however the prevailing Sadducism of these times may have sunk the credit of them, as well as in great measure cut off communications of this kind. (Hartley 1778, xxii–xxiii)

For many contemporaries of Hartley, this was a fragile argument. In Britain, the "Cock Lane" case of 1762 had left its mark on people's memory (Uglow 1997, 625–655). In January 1762, Fanny Lynes, who had recently died of smallpox, allegedly made herself known in the house of Richard Parsons in Cock Lane, London. Through peculiar knockings heard in the room of Parsons's eleven-year-old daughter, she was thought to indicate that she had been murdered. All of London discussed the case, and the investigating committee included celebrities like Dr. Samuel Johnson. Soon the "Cock Lane ghost" was exposed as a hoax. Though the fraud was still remembered in 1778, belief in ghosts was too firmly established in British popular lore to have been eradicated by one such exposure. The anonymous reviewer of *A Treatise concerning Heaven and Hell* quotes Hartley's appeal to British ghost-seeing without indicating any reservations against it (*Gentleman's Magazine* 1778, 326a).

Hartley ends his long preface with the explanation of two of Swedenborg's teachings: the doctrine of "correspondences" and the doctrine of the intermediate state in which the departed find themselves between death and relegation to either heaven or hell. By way of conclusion, here are Hartley's recommendations about reading *A Treatise concerning Heaven and Hell.* One can understand Swedenborg as "the enlightened Seer, and the extraordinary messenger of important news from the other world"; failing this, one may consider him as a "Christian divine and sage interpreter of the Scriptures." Failing this again, one may "read him as the judicious moralist, and acute metaphysician; or read him as the profound philosopher; or if he cannot please in any of these characters, read him at least as the ingenious author of a divine romance" (Hartley 1778, xxxviii).

Cookworthy and Hartley's translation of *Heaven and Hell* made a great impact on at least some contemporaries—both positively and negatively. There were two important readers of this translation. Both Robert Hindmarsh and John Wesley read *A Treatise concerning Heaven and Hell* early in 1782, and, as will become clear, came to vastly different conclusions. But before their views are discussed, another early translator should be mentioned: Abbé Pernety.

The life of Antoine Joseph Pernety (1716–1796), the French translator of *Heaven and Hell,* is marked by the unrest of a man who moved from a Benedictine monastery to the court of a prince; at the same time, the devout Catholic became a writer on esoteric themes (Williams-Hogan 1998, 235–239). In the same year in which Swedenborg had *Heaven and Hell* printed, Pernety published his *Fables égyptiennes et grecques dévoilées et réduites au même principe* (Fables of the Egyptians and Greeks Revealed and Epitomized According to a Common Principle, Paris, 1758). Pernety came to Prussia during the reign of Frederick the Great and served in the position of a librarian between 1767 and 1783. It was as a librarian that he came across Swedenborg's work; in 1779 he read *Marriage Love.* In his correspondence with Carl Fredrick Nordenskjöld, a Swede, he reports how he became convinced of the value and spiritual truth of Swedenborg's work. Pernety had gathered around himself a group of people interested in the esoteric arts with whom he practiced a kind of oracle. His Neoplatonic worldview did not permit him to communicate directly with the One, the Supreme Deity; but one of the emanations of the One, called "la Sainte Parole" (the Holy Word), could be contacted in an oracular procedure. The answer la Sainte Parole gave to his question about Swedenborg was entirely favorable: Swedenborg had spoken truthfully ("il a dit vrai").[32] As a result, Pernety produced a somewhat free French

---

32. Pernety is quoted in Williams-Hogan 1998, 236. For a transcript of the original letter of October 20, 1781, in which the quotation appears, see Pernety 1781. For more on Pernety, see Tafel 1875, 637.

version of *Heaven and Hell,* and the two volumes of *Les Merveilles du Ciel et de l'Enfer* were printed in Berlin in 1782.

Pernety's translation includes a long preface titled "Observations ou Notes sur Swédenborg" ("Notes and Observations on Swedenborg") in which Pernety comments on Swedenborg's life and work. Some of the anecdotes about the author of *Heaven and Hell* must have come to Pernety from his Swedish correspondents, the Nordenskjöld brothers, Carl Fredrick and August. One of the anecdotes relates how Swedenborg was asked whether his views were compatible with those of the German mystic Jacob Boehme (1575–1624). "He was a good man, answered Swedenborg; it is a pity that some errors crept into his writings, especially with regard to the Trinity." Similarly, Swedenborg was asked whether there was any truth in Hermetic philosophy: "Yes, he replied, I consider it to be true, and one of the greatest wonders of God; but I advise no one to work in this subject" (Pernety 1782, 78; Tafel 1875, 62). While there is no way of authenticating these anecdotes, they do reflect the interest of both August Nordenskjöld and Pernety in esoteric traditions.[33]

In obedience to "la Sainte Parole," Pernety eventually left Berlin and traveled south in order to establish the kingdom of the New Jerusalem. The nucleus of that kingdom was to be an esoteric society that he founded in the city of Avignon in Provence.

Little is known about the early reception of *Les Merveilles du Ciel et de l'Enfer,* but one anecdote deserves telling. The French writer Honoré de Balzac (1799–1850) knew the book, and when in 1832 he wrote his novel *Louis Lambert*—the story of a young genius—he put Pernety's translation in the hands of his protagonist. At age fourteen, Louis, a tanner's son, was found by Madame de Staël as he read "une traduction du *Ciel et de l'Enfer*"—a translation of *Heaven and Hell* (Balzac [1832] 1980, 595). The year is 1811, and Balzac adds that at this time only a handful of French intellectuals had heard of Swedenborg. In the story, Madame de Staël takes pity on the poor boy and pays for his schooling in a nearby convent. Balzac gives us the full reading list of his genius: when de Staël found him, he had already complemented his Bible studies by reading the great mystics—Saint Teresa of Avila, Madame Guyon, and *Les Merveilles du Ciel et de l'Enfer* (Balzac [1832] 1980, 594). This is how Balzac imagines a mystical life should get started. And in fact, some

---

33. Swedenborg may have echoed Augustine, who in the *City of God* (8, 23) suggests that Hermes "makes many statements agreeable to the truth concerning the one true God, maker of the world."

of the philosophical thoughts with which Balzac ends his novel betray Swedenborg's influence (Wilkinson 1996, 156–171).

c. A Theological Reader: John Wesley

Awesome supernatural visions of God and angels, communion with spirits, sensing angelic presence and help—all of this was reported in John Wesley's entourage (Ayling 1979, 300–303). Wesley (1703–1791) was fond of angels and believed that they sent messages into our consciousness, sometimes when we sleep, but sometimes also when we are awake (Wesley [1782] 1856, 77). The founder of the Methodist movement avidly believed in signs and wonders. It does not come as a surprise that Wesley, when he heard of Swedenborg, was intrigued by his otherworldly experience. Although both Wesley and Swedenborg lived in England, had heard of each other, and took an interest in each other's work, they never met. Shortly before his death in 1772, Swedenborg had sent him a copy of his last theological work, *True Christianity* (Wesley [1782] 1856, 403).

Wesley's experience of reading Swedenborg's work can be followed in his private diary from February 28, 1770, where he reports that he "sat down to read and seriously consider some of the writings of Baron Swedenborg" (Wesley n.d., 5:354). Although Wesley does not state which works he looked at, it may well be that *Heaven and Hell* was among them. In his diary entry of December 8, 1771, he comes back to the subject: "I read a little more of that strange book, Baron Swedenborg's *Theologia Coelestis*" (Wesley n.d., 5:440). The Latin title that he gives (which means *The Theology of Heaven)* seems to be a somewhat inaccurate version of the Latin title of *Heaven and Hell,* although it could also refer to *Secrets of Heaven.* Then Wesley seems to have abandoned the reading for many years. He resumed it only after having received some English versions of Swedenborg's books. His collection now included *A Treatise concerning Heaven and Hell,* the English translation of *Heaven and Hell* published in 1778. His diary entry of April 22, 1779, is longer and more detailed than the earlier ones, and refers to *A Treatise concerning Heaven and Hell* as "Baron Swedenborg's *Account of Heaven and Hell*" (Wesley n.d., 6:230)—in his diary, Wesley cared little about noting the exact titles of books that he read.

Between 1770 and early 1779, Wesley always found something positive in Swedenborg's works, even though he had his doubts and applied to him what Milton wrote of Satan: "His mind has not yet lost all its original brightness, but appears majestic, though in ruin" (Wesley n.d.,

5:440).[34] Despite this caution, his overall comments could be quite positive. In a letter addressed to his friend Miss Elizabeth Ritchie are found the following words: "I have abundant proof that Baron Swedenborg's fever,[35] which he had thirty years before he died, much affected his understanding. Yet his tract is 'majestic, though in ruins.' He has strong and beautiful thoughts, and may be read with profit by a serious and cautious reader" (Wesley [1782] 1856, 58). Wesley does not specify which "tract" he meant, but the reference may be to the recently published *Treatise concerning Heaven and Hell*. While Wesley's letter dated February 12, 1779, cautiously recommends Swedenborg, his diary entry of April 22, 1779, comes close to a total condemnation: "Of this work [that is, *A Treatise concerning Heaven and Hell*] in particular I must observe that the doctrine contained therein is not only quite unproved, quite precarious from beginning to end, as depending entirely on the assertion of a single brain-sick man; but that, in many instances, it is contrary to Scripture, to reason, and to itself" (Wesley n.d., 6:231).

It was not before early 1782 that John Wesley took the time to consider all the Swedenborg books that had accumulated in his study: volume 1 of *True Christianity* (published as *The True Christian Religion* in the first English edition of 1781), *A Treatise concerning Heaven and Hell* (the English edition of 1778), and *Marriage Love* (in the Latin edition of 1768). The Latin title of the latter, *Delitiae Sapientiae de Amore Conjugiali* (Wisdom's Delight in Marriage Love), he refers to as *De Nuptiis Coelestibus* (On the Marriages of Heaven) with characteristic disregard for exact citation. His "Thoughts on the Writings of Baron Swedenborg," completed May 9, 1782, and printed in 1783 in the *Arminian Magazine,* represent his only public statement on the subject. Here Wesley reviews Swedenborg's life, offers a selection of excerpts from Swedenborg's books, and ends with a detailed, nine-page review of *A Treatise concerning Heaven and Hell.* Compared with the diary entries, the tone has not changed. Again, Swedenborg is accused of insanity and his theology considered unacceptable. From Wesley's review, the following list of the most serious errors he sees in Swedenborg can be abstracted:

---

34. See *Paradise Lost* 2:305.

35. Wesley repeatedly refers to this "fever" (Wesley n.d. 5, 440; Wesley n.d. 6, 230; Wesley [1782] 1856, 402). Apparently answering Wesley, Hartley (1778, xxxii) dismisses the "fever" incident as constituting any evidence of Swedenborg's insanity. Recent scholarship considers Wesley's source apocryphal and doubtful; see Rogal 1988, 297–298.

1. Swedenborg does not believe in the divine Trinity, but only in one God.

2. He rejects the common belief that God created angels as such. "This grand position, which runs through all his Works, that all angels and devils were once men, without which his whole hypothesis falls to the ground, is palpably contrary to scripture" (Wesley [1782] 1856, 416).

3. He believes in a kind of purgation of certain souls after death, thereby coming close to affirming Catholic beliefs. "How exceeding small is the difference between the Romish and the Mystic purgatory!" (Wesley [1782] 1856, 415)

4. He believes in marriages in heaven. Wesley asks, "How is this consistent with our Lord's words, 'In the resurrection they neither marry, nor are given in marriage, but are as the angels of god in heaven'?" (Wesley [1782] 1856, 416, quoting Matthew 22:30).

5. He describes caverns in rocks, subterraneous mines, ruined houses, and rude cottages in hell. "But how does this agree with what we read in the Scripture concerning hell-fire?" (Wesley [1782] 1856, 418) According to Revelation 20:15, "whosoever is not found written in the book of life, will be cast into the lake of fire" (Wesley [1782] 1856, 422).

6. He describes, especially in *True Christianity*, a relatively decent life in hell: a life in which people work, rest, and even entertain themselves with the opposite sex.[36] Here he refers to Swedenborg as "a filthy dreamer . . . , who takes care to provide harlots, instead of fire and brimstone, for the devils and damned spirits in hell" (Wesley [1782] 1856, 422). "So the Christian Koran exceeds even the Mahometan! Mahomet allowed such to be in paradise; but he never thought of placing them in hell" (Wesley [1782] 1856, 421). "O how much more comfortable is the condition of these spirits in hell, than that of the galley-slaves at Marseilles, or the Indians in the mines of Potosi!" (Wesley [1782] 1856, 420). Wesley considers Swedenborg's description of hell "the most dangerous part of all his writings," for it "tends to familiarize it to unholy men, to remove all their terror, and to make them consider it, not as a place of torment, but a very tolerable habitation" (Wesley [1782] 1856, 417).

---

36. In hell, each man "is also informed that every one is at liberty to walk, to converse, and afterwards to sleep, when he hath done his Work; He is then led into an inner Part of the Cavern, where there are Harlots, and he is permitted to take one to himself, and to call her his Wife, but he is forbid on pain of Punishment, to connect himself with more than one" (*True Christianity,* in the translation read by Wesley; that is, Swedenborg 1781, §281).

Apart from what he sees as flagrant errors, Wesley is dissatisfied with the style of the *Treatise concerning Heaven and Hell,* for it lacks dignity. Of Swedenborg's description of heaven, Wesley writes:

> It would be tedious to point out the particular oddities and absurdities.
> . . . It may suffice to remark in general, that it contains nothing sub-
> lime, nothing worthy of the dignity of the subject. Most of the images
> are low, and mean, and earthly, not raising, but sinking, the mind of
> the reader; representing the very angels of God in such a light, as might
> move us, not to worship, but despise them. And there is a grossness
> and coarseness in the whole description of the invisible world, which I
> am afraid will exceedingly tend to confirm rational infidels in a total
> disbelief of it. (Wesley [1782] 1856, 417)

Elsewhere he exclaims: "How egregiously trifling is this account! So puerile, so far beneath the importance of the subject, that one who did not know the character of the writer [that is, Swedenborg], might natu-rally imagine he was turning it into burlesque" (Wesley [1782] 1856, 419).

John Wesley, at an age at which he was tending to look back to his own achievements, felt unable to adopt any of Swedenborg's views. Wesley's own theology of heaven and hell was quite conventional. Long ago, he had included an abridgment of Richard Baxter's *Saints' Everlasting Rest* in his fifty-volume set titled *A Christian Library* (1749–1755). In Baxter's heaven, the saints rested and praised God, rather than engaging in the more earthly employments described by Swedenborg. Apparently, the only result of Wesley's renewed consideration of Swedenborg's work was that he took up the subject of angels and hell in several sermons, in which he repeated fairly conventional views.[37] In Methodist circles, Swedenborg was to be *persona non grata.* "O my brethren," Wesley addressed the Methodist read-ers of the *Arminian Magazine,* "let none of you recommend such a writer any more!" (Wesley [1782] 1856, 422)

d. Founder of a New Church: Robert Hindmarsh

Wesley, a man in his old age, could not easily be impressed and shaken out of his long-standing, largely traditional theological views. Robert Hindmarsh presents a completely different—in many ways an opposite—story. At the impressionable age of twenty-two, Robert Hindmarsh

---

37. Three sermons dating from 1782/1783 are entitled "Of Good Angels," "Of Evil Angels," and "Of Hell" (Wesley 1986, 3–44).

(1759–1835), a printer, became acquainted with George Keen, a Quaker interested in Swedenborg. Keen loaned two books by Swedenborg to Hindmarsh on January 2, 1782, a day Hindmarsh remembered well: it was the very day that he met his future wife, Sarah Paramor (1761?–1833). The two works were *A Treatise concerning Heaven and Hell,* and *On the Commerce between the Soul and the Body.*[38] (Both books had been translated by Hartley.) Hindmarsh immediately read the two volumes and instantly became convinced of their "heavenly origin" (Hindmarsh 1861, 11); soon he was a convinced follower of Swedenborg. By 1784, he had founded an association "instituted for the purpose of promoting the heavenly doctrines of the New Jerusalem, by translating, printing, and publishing the theological writings of the honourable Emanuel Swedenborg" (Hindmarsh 1861, 23). With its seat in London, this "Theosophical Society" soon boasted close to one hundred individuals (all of them male), of whom one, John Flaxman (1755–1826), was to become a famous sculptor (Hindmarsh 1861, 23). In 1784, Hindmarsh also had the second edition of *A Treatise concerning Heaven and Hell* printed.

While the Theosophical Society was to dissolve within less than a decade, Hindmarsh did not give up the idea of organizing a group of people interested in Swedenborg's work. With Robert Hindmarsh as its leader, a separatist group originating within the Theosophical Society established itself as a church and asked Robert Hindmarsh's father, the Methodist minister James Hindmarsh (1731?–1812), to lead its first service of worship, on January 27, 1788. Today, the Swedenborgian "Church of the New Jerusalem" traces its origin back to this event. Without Robert Hindmarsh's enthusiasm for *A Treatise concerning Heaven and Hell,* this event would never have occurred.

The early readers of *A Treatise concerning Heaven and Hell* foreshadowed and even shaped the way later generations would respond to the book. Today it is clear that by 1782, the early readers had already formulated the three main responses of the nineteenth and twentieth centuries. Many would follow John Wesley's sharp critique and dismiss *A Treatise concerning Heaven and Hell* as pure fantasy, delusion, heresy, or, worse, as inspired by "the spirit of darkness" (Wesley [1782] 1856, 422). At times, Wesley comes close to satirizing Swedenborg's views, but for him and his audience, the subject was too serious to be amenable to satirical comment. This changed in the twentieth century, when Mark Twain (1835–1910)

---

38. In the present edition this work is referred to as *Soul-Body Interaction.*

published "Captain Stormfield's Visit to Heaven" ([1907] 1995). A second group would see *A Treatise concerning Heaven and Hell* the way his French translator, Antoine Joseph Pernety, understood the book: as an introduction to a new, esoteric worldview that permitted the reception of inspiration from spirits or angels. An impressive number of romantic poets and artists appreciated Swedenborg's book or were in some way or other influenced by it; these include William Blake (1757–1827) and Samuel Taylor Coleridge in England, Friedrich Wilhelm Schelling (1775–1854) in Germany, and Honoré de Balzac in France.[39] A third group, represented by Robert Hindmarsh, would either make *A Treatise concerning Heaven and Hell* part of the sacred writings recognized by a new Christian church and accepted as a strong revelatory and theological statement of life after death, or consider it the beginning of a new religious philosophy. This group, generally referred to now as the Swedenborgians, can be credited with translating *Heaven and Hell* into many modern languages. One Swedenborgian, Johann Friedrich Immanuel Tafel (1796–1863), head librarian of the University of Tübingen in Germany, also published a new edition of the original Latin text (1862). Due to the effort of its translators, Emanuel Swedenborg's *Heaven and Hell* ranks as one of the few eighteenth-century religious books still in print and still attracting considerable attention in comparison to many other writings dating from the same period. Thanks to them *Heaven and Hell* can still be discovered as a work that has, as Tessin said, "so many new and unexpected turns that it may be read through without boredom."

---

39. Secondary sources on Swedenborg's influence on romanticism include: Peebles 1933 (Goethe), Benz 1941 (Schelling), Schuchard 1949 (Goethe), Roos 1952 (Novalis and others), Heinrichs 1979 (Schelling, Goethe), Gaier 1984 and 1988 (Goethe), Paley 1985 (Blake), Bellin and Ruhl 1985 (Blake), Sjödén 1985 (Balzac and others), Bellin 1988 (Blake), Wilkinson 1996 (Balzac and others), Horn 1997 (Schelling), Ford 1998, 95–96, 147–151 (Coleridge). Coleridge annotated a copy of Swedenborg's *Heaven and Hell*; the notes, kept in the British Library, are printed in Coleridge 2000, 403–425; they seem to date from 1819/1820. Two embodiments of the French romantic temper, otherworld-utopias and spiritualism, also seem to include a Swedenborgian element (Kselman 1993, 143–162). America's most important romantic movement, transcendentalism, was also deeply influenced by Swedenborg (Taylor 1988).

The author acknowledges the kind help received from Jane Williams-Hogan, who has been a mentor on Swedenborg for many years. Valuable assistance also came from Reinhard Breymayer, Nancy Dawson, Heather Jackson, Carroll Odhner, Jonathan S. Rose, Stuart Shotwell, and Eberhard Zwink.

Appendix 1

*Some Baroque Ideas on Life after Death,
and on Heaven and Hell*

IN our generation, life after death and the nature of heaven and hell no longer form a subject that readily arises in conversation. In the seventeenth and eighteenth centuries people had a different attitude. Most took an interest in the matter, and not a few philosophers and theologians offered their thoughts on heaven and hell in print. Most often they discussed "the problem of immortality," but occasionally heaven and hell figured in the debate. In Britain from around 1650 onwards, and at least for one century, "almost every aspect of the afterlife gave rise to speculation or debate among scholars" (Houlbrooke 1998, 50). Not only in Britain, of course. One author has counted the books on immortality that were published in Germany between 1751 and 1758—the years immediately before *Heaven and Hell*—and noted fifty-four separate works (Unger 1929–1930, 433). In other European countries, one would no doubt find similar figures: baroque and enlightenment philosophers and theologians can be credited with the first real exploitation of the theme. The following brief list of relevant authors and viewpoints provides the context in which Swedenborg developed his thought and published *Heaven and Hell,* and suggests the works to which some of Swedenborg's early readers may have compared *Heaven and Hell* and its vernacular translations.

1. *The Immortality of the Soul* (1659). The Cambridge philosopher Henry More, well known as a follower of Plato, offered much more than the title of his book seems to indicate. Like other Platonists of his time, he tried to avoid a strict separation between the spiritual and the material worlds, making the spiritual world a part of the universe as we know it. For the seventeenth-century Platonists, explains the historian Philip Almond, "no great gulf was fixed between the living and the dead" (Almond 1994, 36). Both the living and the dead belonged to the same spatiotemporal realm, with angels, the blessed, and God placed in the higher regions, and the wicked souls and Satan in the air around the earth and in the cavities within the

earth (Almond 1994, 36–37). At times, the souls of the blessed "sing and play and dance together, reaping the lawful pleasures of the very animal life, in a far higher degree than we are capable of in this world" (More 1659, 420). According to More, the souls retain certain feminine and masculine features (McDannell and Lang 1988, 212; Almond 1994, 31). More's work was remembered for quite some time: Dr. Johnson mentioned it in a conversation he had with James Boswell in 1772 (Boswell [1791] 1952, 192–193).

2. *Two Treatises . . . of the Immortality of Reasonable Soules* (1644). Sir Kenelm Digby, a Catholic philosopher and scientist (Almond 1994, 70–71), denied the existence of divine judgment. He argued that "if a man die in disorderly affection to anything as to his chief good, he eternally remains, by the necessity of his own nature, in the same affection; and there is no imparity that, to eternal sin, there should be imposed eternal punishment" (Digby 1644, 445). Later Swedenborg would describe everlasting existence in hell in the same way.

3. *Von den vier letzten Dingen: nämlich von dem Tod, Gericht, Hölle und Himmelreich* (On the Four Last Things: Death, Judgment, Hell, and the Kingdom of Heaven, German, 1680). Written by the Capuchin friar Martin of Cochem, this work introduced baroque Catholics to a very sensuous otherworld. He refers to "a real river, real trees, real fruit, and real flowers that please our vision, taste, smell, and touch in unsurpassable ways" (Martin 1753, 170).[40]

4. *The Pilgrim's Progress* (1678–1684). In the second part of his Puritan bestseller, John Bunyan included a discussion of the joy Christian must feel when he is joined by his wife Christiana and their sons in the celestial city (Bunyan [1678–1684] 1965, 351).

5. *Systema Theologicum* (Theological System, 1686). In this manuscript the famous philosopher and mathematician Gottfried Wilhelm Leibniz argued that the spiritual state in which someone dies actually determines his or her fate in the spiritual world. "Whenever a soul leaves the body in the state of mortal sin, that is, being ill-affected toward God, it falls as it were automatically into the abyss of hell, just like a heavy thing that is broken off and not held back by some external agent. Estranged from God, it imposes damnation

---

40. This passage from Martin is my translation.

upon itself" (Leibniz 1966, 193). Human souls "obviously continue to follow the path which they have begun and stay in the spiritual state in which they died" (Leibniz 1966, 9).[41] While this document was not published before the nineteenth century, it nevertheless demonstrates that one of Swedenborg's teachings (*Heaven and Hell* 363, 477) was within the range of view of baroque thinkers.

6. *A Vindication of the Immortality of the Soul and a Future State* (1703). William Assheton, rector of Beckenham in Kent, sought to refute the idea that people who had died found that heavenly life consisted in "bare speculation, gazing upon each other, and admiring each other's perfections." In heaven, people will lead an active life. God's Kingdom will have "laws and statutes and governors and subjects, and those of different ranks, orders, and degrees" (Assheton 1703, 57–60).

7. *The Spectator,* no. 111, July 7, 1711. This issue of London's famous *Spectator,* one of the "moral dailies" in which Enlightenment authors sought to disseminate their views among the educated, is dedicated to "the Immortality of the Soul." The essayist Joseph Addison rejected the changeless character of sainthood, arguing that there must be movement and progress in the hereafter. God presents us with only the "rudiments of existence here, and afterwards [we will] be transplanted into a more friendly climate, where [we] may spread and flourish to all eternity" (Addison [1711] 1965, 458). Addison does not describe heaven. In a later issue of the *Spectator,* John Hughes refers to Cicero's dialogue *On Old Age,* in which Cato looks forward to meeting his friends and ancestors in the other world (Hughes [1712] 1965, 418–420). Swedenborg may have read the *Spectator* during one of his early stays in Britain (see editor's note on *Spiritual Experiences* 5565 in Swedenborg 1889).

8. *Death and Heaven; or the Last Enemy Conquered, and Separate Spirits Made Perfect* (1722). Isaac Watts, author of hymns ("O God, Our Help in Ages Past") and minister of an independent church in London, describes a heaven full of movement and life. The blessed will serve God "perhaps as priests in his temple, and as kings, or viceroys, in his wide dominions" (Watts [1722] 1812, 398–399). His examples of heavenly employments include the reporting of the

---

41. This passage from Leibniz and the preceding are my translation.

"faithful execution of some divine commission" and ruling "over inferior ranks of happy spirits" or over "whole provinces of intelligent beings in lower regions" (Watts [1722] 1812, 402–403). Although this is not mentioned in *Death and Heaven,* Watts also questioned traditional notions of the Trinity. *Death and Heaven* had been through four editions by 1737, and sixteen by 1818: This makes it the book on this topic most likely to have been already known to English readers of Swedenborg.

9. *Festum Magnum* (The Great Feast-Day, 1724, Swedish). Jesper Swedberg, Lutheran bishop of Skara in central Sweden and father of Emanuel Swedenborg, was a prolific author. Some of his devotional books, all written in Swedish, include references to heaven and heavenly life. In *Festum Magnum* he writes about the interest the blessed have in the life of their earthly relatives. In another book, *Sanctificatio Sabbati* (Observing the Sabbath, 1734, Swedish), he offers his views of how the blessed in heaven talk to each other: although everyone uses her or his native language, everyone understands the others. Although the bishop does not seem to have offered any sustained descriptions of the other life, his writings betray interest in the subject and the ease with which the subject could surface in baroque preaching (Lamm 1922, 5–6).

10. *The Gentleman's Magazine,* 1739. This famous monthly publication not only chronicled and commented on current events, but also included a correspondence section in which readers, often under pen names, expressed themselves freely on the subject of their choice. In the January number a "Theophilus" complains of authors who, following John Milton's *Paradise Lost,* are "corrupting our Notions of Spiritual Things, and sensualizing our Ideas of Heaven to a Degree that may have ill Effects on Religion in general: It is letting Fancy obtrude its wild Luxuriance into the Place of Truth and Reason, and making room for the grossest and most absurd kind of Enthusiasm, and if one is to interpret his [that is, Milton's] other Descriptions of Heaven by this Hint, it is every whit as sensual as the Mahometan's" (*Gentleman's Magazine,* 1739, 5b). In the April number of the same year, "Cleomenes" asks readers to discuss the afterlife of infants who die at an early age, suggesting that their souls are either annihilated after death, or that they transmigrate into other bodies again (*Gentleman's Magazine,* 1739, 177–179). Beginning with the January number of the *Gentleman's Magazine,* 1740, the editor included many responses to "Cleomenes" (*Gentleman's Magazine,*

1740, 3–4, 52–54, 167–168, 245–246, 341–342, 441–443; see Houl-brooke 1998, 52–53). "G. F.," the first contributor to the debate, in-sisted that any answer to the issue should be based on "Reason guided by Revelation" (*Gentleman's Magazine,* 1740, 4b).

11. *Émile ou de l'Education* (Emile, or on Education, 1762). Jean-Jacques Rousseau's famous treatise on education does not comment specifically on eschatological subjects, but rejects traditional notions about hell. According to these notions, unbaptized children who died in early infancy would spend eternal life suffering in hell. In *Émile,* book 4, Rousseau discusses and rejects this opinion: "We hold that no child who dies before the age of reason will be deprived of eternal happiness" (Rousseau [1762] 1991, 258). Swedenborg says the same thing (§410). See also the debate in *Gentleman's Magazine* 1739/40, referred to above.

12. *Aussichten in die Ewigkeit* (Prospects of Eternity, 1768–1778). The author of this work, Johann Caspar Lavater, was Reformed minister in Zurich, Switzerland, and ranked as a celebrity known to Moses Mendelssohn and Goethe. In eternal life, he claimed, "we will have bodies, live in corporeal worlds, will have to deal with material, sensual objects, and form one or more societies" (Lavater 1773, 93).[42] By the time of his writing, Lavater may have known the work of Swedenborg.[43] In 1772, Goethe reviewed the *Aussichten* in *Frankfurter Gelehrte Anzeigen* (Goethe [1772] 1987).

13. *Life of Samuel Johnson* (1791). As already mentioned, James Boswell recorded a conversation he had with Dr. Johnson on eternal life. After death, says Johnson, many friendships will no longer exist, for "we form many friendships by mistake, imagining people to be different from what they really are. After death, we shall see every one in a true light" (Boswell [1791] 1952, 193). This is something Swedenborg, too, could have said: the idea was not foreign at the time. John says of the Lord, "We shall see him as he is" (1 John 3:2), and the notion is readily applicable to others as well.

---

42. My translation.

43. For Lavater's knowledge of Swedenborg's work, see Acton 1955, vol. 2, 641–643, and Benz 1938. Benz speculates that Lavater was largely inspired by Swedenborg, whom he in vain tried to contact in order to have Swedenborg's opinion of his books. He also asked for information about a dead friend (Benz 1938, 155–156). Lavater seems to have avoided acknowledging his indebtedness to Swedenborg because of Immanuel Kant's critique in *Dreams of a Spirit Seer* (Kant [1766] 1969).

Appendix 2

Chronological Table

1688	January 29	Emanuel Swedberg born in Stockholm, Sweden
1719	May 26	The children of Bishop Jesper Swedberg ennobled and their name changed to Swedenborg
1745	April	Swedenborg receives a divine calling in London
1747	July 17	Swedenborg retires from Royal Board of Mines in Sweden
1749	Summer	First volume of *Secrets of Heaven* (Swedenborg's main theological work) published anonymously in London
1756	June	Final volume of *Secrets of Heaven* published
1758		Anonymous publication of *Heaven and Hell* in London
1759	January 5	First reaction to *Heaven and Hell* in short, un-published notes by Count Gustaf Bonde, Sweden
1760	March 5	Carl Gustaf Tessin visits Swedenborg in Stockholm, talks with him about *Heaven and Hell*
1769		Johann Christian Cuno's notes on *Heaven and Hell*
1770	February 28	John Wesley's first diary entry on Swedenborg, with possible reference to *Heaven and Hell*
1772	March 29	Swedenborg dies in London
		Goethe, in review of Lavater's *Aussichten in die Ewigkeit,* recommends Swedenborg's work

1775		*Vom Himmel und von den wunderbaren Dingen desselben* (German translation of *Heaven and Hell*) published in Leipzig, Germany
1778		*A Treatise concerning Heaven and Hell* (translation of *Heaven and Hell*) published in London
	July	*A Treatise concerning Heaven and Hell* favorably reviewed in *The Gentleman's Magazine*, London
1779	February 12	John Wesley recommends Swedenborg's work to Elizabeth Ritchie
1782		*Les Merveilles du Ciel et de l'Enfer* (French translation of *Heaven and Hell*) published in Berlin, Germany
	January 2	Robert Hindmarsh borrows *A Treatise concerning Heaven and Hell* from a friend
1783		John Wesley's article "Thoughts on the Writings of Baron Swedenborg" (written May 9, 1782) published in the *Arminian Magazine*
1784		Theosophical Society founded by Robert Hindmarsh in London
		Robert Hindmarsh publishes second printing of *A Treatise concerning Heaven and Hell*

Works Cited
in the Introduction

1. Sources

a. Ancient Sources

Hermes Trismegistus. *See* Scott, Walter.

Plato. 1952. *The Dialogues.* Translated by Benjamin Jowett. Chicago: Encyclopaedia Britannica.

Plotinus. 1952. *The Six Enneads.* Translated by Stephen MacKenna and B. S. Page. Chicago: Encyclopaedia Britannica.

Porphyry. [301] 1991. "On the Life of Plotinus." In Plotinus, *The Enneads,* translated by Stephen MacKenna and abridged by John Dillon. London: Penguin Books.

Scott, Walter, ed. and trans. 1924. *Hermetica: The Ancient Greek and Latin Writings Which Contain Religious or Philosophic Teachings Ascribed to Hermes Trismegistus.* Vol. 1. Oxford: Clarendon Press.

b. Renaissance and Early Modern Sources

Acton, Alfred. 1955. *The Letters and Memorials of Emanuel Swedenborg.* Vol. 2. Bryn Athyn, Pa.: Swedenborg Scientific Association.

Addison, Joseph. [1711] 1965. Essay no. 111 [July 7]. *The Spectator.* Vol. 1. Edited by Donald F. Bond. Oxford: Clarendon Press.

Assheton, William. 1703. *A Vindication of the Immortality of the Soul and a Future State.* London.

Balzac, Honoré de. [1832] 1980. *Louis Lambert.* In vol. 11 of *La Comédie humaine.* Edited by Pierre-Georges Castex. Paris: Gallimard.

Bonde, Count Gustaf. 1759/1760. Academy Collection of Swedenborg Documents. Vol. 6, no. 809. Swedenborg Library, Academy of the New Church. Bryn Athyn, Pa.

Boswell, James. [1791] 1952. *Life of Samuel Johnson.* Chicago: Encyclopaedia Britannica.

Bunyan, John [1678–1684] 1965. *The Pilgrim's Progress.* Edited by Roger Sharrock. Harmondsworth: Penguin.

Cuno, Johann Christian. 1947. *J. C. Cuno's Memoirs on Swedenborg.* Translated by Claire E. Berninger. Bryn Athyn, Pa.: The Academy Book Room.

Diderot, Denis. [1755] 1876. Entry for "Eclectisme" in *Encyclopédie.* In vol. 14 of *Ouevres complètes de Diderot.* Edited by J. Assézat. Paris: Garnier Frères.

Digby, Kenelm. 1644. *Two Treatises . . . of the Immortality of Reasonable Soules.* Paris: Blaizot.

Erasmus of Rotterdam. [1522] 1997. "The Godly Feast" *[Convivium Religiosum].* In vol. 39 of *Collected Works of Erasmus.* Translated by Craig R. Thompson. Toronto: University of Toronto Press.

Gentleman's Magazine. 1739. [Discussion of issues of the afterlife.] London: Edward Cave. Vol. 9.

———. 1740. [Continuation of discussion of issues of the afterlife.] London: Edward Cave. Vol. 10.

———. 1772. [Obituary note on Swedenborg.] London: D. Henry. Vol. 42, 198b.

———. 1778. [Anonymous review of Swedenborg, *A Treatise concerning Heaven and Hell.*] London: D. Henry. Vol. 48, 325a–326b.

———. 1791. [Letter by "Candidus."] London: John Nichols. Vol. 61, 619b–620a.

Goethe, Johann Wolfgang. [1772] 1987. Review of *Aussichten in die Ewigkeit in Briefen an J. G. Zimmermann,* by Johann Caspar Lavater. In Johann Wolfgang Goethe, *Sämtliche Werke, Münchener Ausgabe.* Vol. 1:2. Edited by Karl Richter. Munich: Carl Hanser Verlag.

———. [1773] 1987. "Zwo wichtige bisher unerörterte biblische Fragen." In Johann Wolfgang Goethe, *Sämtliche Werke, Münchener Ausgabe.* Vol. 1:2. Edited by Karl Richter. Munich: Carl Hanser Verlag.

Hamberger, Georg Christoph, and Johann Georg Meusel. 1797. Entry on "Lenz, Johann Christoph" in *Das gelehrte Teutschland; oder Lexikon der jetzt lebenden teutschen Schriftsteller.* 5th ed. Vol. 4. Lemgo: Meyersche Buchhandlung.

Hartley, Thomas. 1778. Preface to *A Treatise concerning Heaven and Hell,* by Emanuel Swedenborg. London: James Phillips.

Hindmarsh, Robert. 1861. *Rise and Progress of the New Jerusalem Church.* Edited by Edward Madeley. London: Hodson & Son.

Hughes, John. [1712] 1965. Essay no. 537 [November 15]. *The Spectator.* Vol. 4. Edited by Donald F. Bond. Oxford: Clarendon Press.

Kant, Immanuel. [1766] 1969. *Dreams of a Spirit Seer.* Translated by John Manolesco. New York: Vantage Press.

Lavater, Johann Caspar. 1773. *Aussichten in die Ewigkeit in Briefen an J. G. Zimmermann.* 2d ed. Vol. 3. Hamburg: Buchhändlergesellschaft.

Leibniz, Gottfried Wilhelm. [1710] 1952. *Theodicy.* Translated by Austin Farrar. New Haven: Yale University Press.

———. [1686] 1966. *Theologisches System.* Edited and translated by Carl Haas. Hildesheim: Olms.

Martin von Cochem. 1753. "Von den vier letzten Dingen: nämlich von dem Tod, Gericht, Hölle und Himmelreich," appendix in *Das große Leben Christi.* Mariazell: Holtzmayr.

Maxwell-Stuart, P. G., ed. and trans. 1999. *The Occult in Early Modern Europe: A Documentary History.* New York: St. Martin's Press.

More, Henry. 1659. *The Immortality of the Soul.* London: Morden.

Nicole, Pierre. [1715–1732] 1971. *Essais de Morale.* Vol. 1. Geneva: Slatkine.

Novalis. 1978. "Song of the Dead," in *Tagebücher und Briefe*. Vol. 1. Edited by Richard Samuel. Munich: Carl Hanser Verlag.

Oetinger, Friedrich Christoph. [1765] 1855. *Swedenborgs und anderer irdische und himmlische Philosophie*. Part 1. Edited by Karl C. E. Ehmann. Reutlingen: Rupp & Baur.

Pernety, Antoine Joseph. 1781. Academy Collection of Swedenborg Documents. Vol. 10, no. 1663.18. Swedenborg Library, Academy of the New Church. Bryn Athyn, Pa.

———. 1782. "Observations ou notes sur Swédenborg," in *Les Merveilles du Ciel et de l'Enfer*, by Emanuel Swedenborg, translated by Antoine Joseph Pernety. Vol. 1. Berlin: G. J. Decker.

Pico della Mirandola, Giovanni. 1948. "On the Dignity of Man," translated by Elizabeth L. Forbes. In *The Renaissance Philosophy of Man*. Edited by Ernst Cassirer, Paul Oskar Kristeller, and John H. Randall. Chicago: The University of Chicago Press.

"Prüfungsversuch, ob es wol ausgemacht sei, daß Swedenborg zu den Schwärmern gehöre." 1786. In *Revision der bisherigen Theologie* [German translation of *Survey*], by Emanuel Swedenborg. Breslau: Gottlieb Löwe.

Richardson, Jonathan. [1725] 1996. "An Essay on the Theory of Painting" in *Historienmalerei*. Edited by Thomas W. Gathgens and Uwe Fleckner. Berlin: Reimer.

Rousseau, Jean-Jacques. [1762] 1991. *Emile, or On Education*. Translated by Allan Bloom. London: Penguin Books.

Spectator. See Addison, Joseph, and Hughes, John.

Swedenborg, Emanuel. [1758] 1775. *Vom Himmel und von den wunderbaren Dingen desselben*. [Translated by Johann Christoph Lenz?] Leipzig: Gleditsch.

———. 1781. *True Christian Religion*. Vol. 1. Translated by John Clowes. London: R. Hawes.

———. [1758] 1782. *Les Merveilles du Ciel et de L'Enfer*. Translated by Antoine Joseph Pernety. Berlin: G. J. Decker.

———. 1931. *A Philosopher's Note Book*. Translated by Alfred Acton. Philadelphia: Swedenborg Scientific Association.

———. 1889. *The Spiritual Diary of Emanuel Swedenborg*. Vol. 4. Translated by G. Bush. Revised and edited by J. Buss. London: James Speirs.

Tafel, Rudolph Leonard. 1875. *Documents concerning the Life and Character of Emanuel Swedenborg*. Vol. 1. London: Swedenborg Society.

———. 1890. *Documents concerning the Life and Character of Emanuel Swedenborg*. Vol. 2–3. London. Swedenborg Society.

Tessin, Carl Gustaf. 1760. Academy Collection of Swedenborg Documents. Vol. 6, no. 793.12. Swedenborg Library, Academy of the New Church. Bryn Athyn, Pa.

Twain, Mark. [1907] 1995. "Captain Stormfield's Visit to Heaven." In *The Bible according to Mark Twain*. Edited by Howard G. Baetzhold and Joseph B. McCullough. Athens, Ga.: The University of Georgia Press.

Watts, Isaac. [1722] 1812. "The Happiness of Separate Spirits." In *Works*. London: Longman, Hurst, Rees, Orme, and Brown. Vol. 2. [This is discourse 2 of "Death and Heaven; or the Last Enemy Conquered, and Separate Spirits Made Perfect; With an Account of the Rich Variety of their Employments and Pleasures."]

Wesley, John. [1782] 1856. "Thoughts on the Writings of Baron Swedenborg." In *The Works of the Rev. John Wesley.* Vol. 13. Edited by Thomas Jackson. London: John Mason.

———. 1931. *The Letters of John Wesley.* Vol. 6. Edited by John Telford. London: The Epworth Press.

———. 1986. *The Works of John Wesley.* Edited by Albert C. Outler. Vol. 3. Nashville: Abingdon Press.

———. n.d. [1909–1916] *The Journal of the Rev. John Wesley.* Vols. 5 and 6. Edited by Nehemiah Curnock. London: Charles H. Kelly.

Zwingli, Ulrich. [1531] 1953. "Exposition of the Faith." In *Zwingli and Bullinger.* Edited by Geoffrey W. Bromiley. London: SCM Press.

2. Secondary Literature

a. Cultural History and Theology

Albrecht, Michael. 1994. *Eklektik: Eine Begriffsgeschichte mit Hinweisen auf die Philosophie- und Wissenschaftsgeschichte.* Stuttgart: Frommann-Holzboog.

Almond, Philip C. 1994. *Heaven and Hell in Enlightenment England.* Cambridge: Cambridge University Press.

Ayling, Stanley. 1979. *John Wesley.* London: Collins.

Beilby, A. E. 1931. *Rev. Thomas Hartley, A.M.* London: New Church Press.

Benz, Ernst. 1938. "Swedenborg und Lavater." *Zeitschrift für Kirchengeschichte.* 57:153–216.

———. 1949. "Nachwort," in *Ausgewählte religiöse Schriften,* by Emanuel Swedenborg, edited by Martin Lamm. Marburg: Simons-Verlag.

Bonk, Sigmund. 1999. *Abschied von der Anima mundi: Die britische Philosophie im Vorfeld der industriellen Revolution.* Freiburg: Verlag Karl Alber.

Boyce, Mary. 1975. *History of Zoroastrianism.* 3 vols. Leiden: Brill.

Breymeyer, Reinhard. 1984. "Ein radikaler Pietist im Umkreis des jungen Goethe." In *Pietismus und Neuzeit,* vol. 9. Edited by Martin Brecht and others. Göttingen: Vandenhoeck & Ruprecht.

Bultmann, Rudolf. 1958. *Jesus Christ and Mythology.* New York: Charles Scribner's Sons.

Cohn, Norman. 1993. *Cosmos, Chaos, and the World To Come: The Ancient Roots of Apocalyptic Faith.* New Haven: Yale University Press.

Crowe, Michael J. 1997. "A History of the Extraterrestrial Life Debate." *Zygon* 32:147–162.

Dreitzel, Horst. 1991. "Zur Entwicklung und Eigenart der eklektischen Philosophie." *Zeitschrift für historische Forschung* 18:281–343.

Frazier, Scott I. 1998. "Echoes from the Past: A Look at Classical Influences within Swedenborg's 'Golden Age.'" *Scripta: Bryn Athyn College Review* 1:27–44.

Harris, R. Baine. 1976. "A Brief Description of Neoplatonism." In *The Significance of Neoplatonism.* Edited by R. Baine Harris. Albany, N.Y.: State University of New York Press.

Houlbrooke, Ralph. 1998. *Death, Religion and the Family in England, 1480–1750.* Oxford: Clarendon Press.

Kuist, James M. 1982. *The Nichols File of* The Gentleman's Magazine: *Attributions of Authorship and Other Documentation in Editorial Papers at the Folger Library.* Madison, Wis.: University of Wisconsin Press.

Lamm, Martin. 1918. *Upplysningstidens romantik: Den mystik sentimentala strömingen i svensk litteratur.* Stockholm.

———. 1922. *Swedenborg: Eine Studie über seine Entwicklung zum Mystiker und Geisterseher.* Translated by Ilse Meyer-Lüne. Leipzig: Felix Meiner.

Lang, Bernhard. 1997. *Sacred Games: A History of Christian Worship.* New Haven: Yale University Press.

Leith, John H., ed. 1973. *Creeds of the Churches.* Rev. ed. Richmond: John Knox Press.

Lohfink, Gerhard. 1975. "Zur Möglichkeit christlicher Naherwartung." In Gisbert Greshake and Gerhard Lohfink, *Naherwartung—Auferstehung—Unsterblichkeit.* Freiburg: Herder.

McDannell, Colleen and Bernhard Lang. 1988. *Heaven: A History.* New Haven: Yale University Press.

Musall, Heinz. 1993. "Weltkarten vom Ende des 17. bis zur Mitte des 19. Jahrhunderts." In *Imago mundi moderna: Weltkarten des Zweiten Entdeckungszeitalters.* Edited by Gerhard Römer. Karlsruhe: Badische Landesbibliothek.

Nemitz, Kurt P. 1991. "Leibniz and Swedenborg." *The New Philosophy* 94:445–488.

———. 1994. "The German Philosophers Leibniz and Wolff in Swedenborg's Philosophic Development." *The New Philosophy* 97:411–425.

Odhner, J. Durban. 1978. "Reflections on Africa." *The New Philosophy* 81:255–270.

O'Meara, Thomas F. 1999. "Christian Theology and Extraterrestrial Intelligent Life." *Theological Studies* 60:1–30.

Randles, W.G.L. 1999. *The Unmaking of the Medieval Christian Cosmos, 1500–1760.* Aldershot: Ashgate.

Rogal, Samuel J. 1988. "Swedenborg and the Wesleyans: Opposition or Outgrowth?" In *Swedenborg and His Influence.* Edited by Erland J. Brock. Bryn Athyn, Pa.: The Academy of the New Church.

Sawicki, Diethard. 1999. "Die Gespenster und ihr Ancien régime: Geisterglauben als Nachtseite der Spätaufklärung." In *Aufklärung und Esoterik.* Edited by Monika Neugebauer-Wölk. Hamburg: Meiner.

Scheuerbrandt, Arnold. 1993. "Die Entdeckungs- und Forschungsreisen bis zum Beginn des 19. Jahrhunderts." In *Imago mundi moderna: Weltkarten des Zweiten Entdeckungszeitalters.* Edited by Gerhard Römer. Karlsruhe: Badische Landesbibliothek.

Selleck, A. Douglas. 1978. *Cookworthy and His Circle.* Plymouth: Baron Jay.

Sigstedt, Cyriel Odhner. 1981. *The Swedenborg Epic: The Life and Works of Emanuel Swedenborg.* New York: Bookman Associates, 1952. Reprint, London: Swedenborg Society.

Sladek, Mirko. 1984. *Fragmente der hermetischen Philosophie in der Naturphilosophie der Neuzeit.* Frankfurt: Verlag Peter Lang.

Stephens, W. Peter. 1995. "Zwingli and the Salvation of the Gentiles." In *The Bible, the Reformation and the Church.* Edited by W. P. Stephens. Sheffield: Sheffield Academic Press.

Trinkaus, Charles. 1948. Introduction [to Lorenzo Valla]. In *The Renaissance Philosophy of Man*. Edited by Ernst Cassirer, Paul Oskar Kristeller, and John H. Randall. Chicago: The University of Chicago Press.

———. 1970. *In Our Image and Likeness: Humanity and Divinity in Italian Humanist Thought*. Chicago: The University of Chicago Press.

Uglow, Jenny. 1997. *Hogarth: A Life and a World*. London: Faber and Faber.

Unger, Rudolf. 1929–1930. "Der Unsterblichkeitsgedanke im 18. Jahrhundert und bei unseren Klassikern." *Zeitschrift für systematische Theologie* 7:431–460.

Wallis, R.T. 1972. *Neoplatonism*. London: Gerald Duckworth.

Williams-Hogan, Jane. 1985. *A New Church in a Disenchanted World: A Study of the Formation and Development of the General Conference of the New Church in Great Britain*. Diss. University of Pennsylvania, Philadelphia. Ann Arbor: University Microfilms.

———. 1998. "Emanuel Swedenborg and Western Esotericism." In *Western Esotericism and the Science of Religion*. Edited by Antoine Faivre and Wouter J. Hanegraaff. Leuven: Peeters.

b. Swedenborg's Influence on the Romantic Movement

Bellin, Harvey F. 1988. "Opposition Is True Friendship: Swedenborg's Influences on William Blake." In *Emanuel Swedenborg: A Continuing Vision*. Edited by Robin Larsen. New York: Swedenborg Foundation.

Bellin, Harvey F., and Darrell Ruhl, eds. 1985. *Blake and Swedenborg: Opposition Is True Friendship*. New York: Swedenborg Foundation.

Benz, Ernst. 1941. "Swedenborg als geistiger Wegbahner des deutschen Idealismus und der deutschen Romantik." *Deutsche Vierteljahresschrift für Literaturwissenschaft und Geistesgeschichte* 19:1–32.

Coleridge, Samuel Taylor. 2000. *The Collected Works of Samuel Taylor Coleridge*. Vol. 12:5: *Marginalia*. Edited by H. J. Jackson and George Whalley. Princeton: Princeton University Press.

Emerson, Ralph Waldo. [1849] 1903. *Representative Men: Seven Lectures*. Boston: Houghton, Mifflin and Company.

Ford, Jennifer. 1998. *Coleridge on Dreaming: Romanticism, Dreams and the Medical Imagination*. Cambridge: Cambridge University Press.

Fuchs, G. F. 1900. "Zu dem Aufsatz: Von dem Himmel und der himmlischen Freude." *Goethe-Jahrbuch* 21:281–282.

Gaier, Ulrich. 1984. "Nachwirkungen Oetingers in Goethes *Faust*." In *Pietismus und Neuzeit. Ein Jahrbuch zur Geschichte des neueren Protestantismus*. Vol. 10. Göttingen: Vandenhoeck & Ruprecht.

———. 1988. "Könnt' in Magie von meinem Pfad entfernen—Swedenborg im Magischen Diskurs von Goethes *Faust*." In *Emanuel Swedenborg 1688–1772. Naturforscher und Kundiger der Überwelt*. Edited by Horst Bergmann and Eberhard Zwink. Stuttgart: Württembergische Landesbibliothek.

Gladish, Robert W. 1973. "Swedenborg among the Nineteenth-Century Literati." *The New Philosophy* 76:498–510.

Heinrichs, Michael. 1979. *Emanuel Swedenborg in Deutschland: Eine kritische Darstellung der Rezeption des schwedischen Visionärs im 18. und 19. Jahrhundert.* Frankfurt: Verlag Peter D. Lang.

Horn, Friedemann. 1997. *Schelling and Swedenborg.* Translated by George F. Dole. West Chester, Pa.: Swedenborg Foundation.

Kselman, Thomas A. 1993. *Death and the Afterlife in Modern France.* Princeton: Princeton University Press.

Paley, Morton D. 1985. "A New Heaven Is Begun: Blake and Swedenborgianism." In *Blake and Swedenborg: Opposition Is True Friendship.* Edited by Harvey F. Bellin and Darrell Ruhl. New York: Swedenborg Foundation.

Peebles, Waldo C. 1933. "Swedenborg's Influence upon Goethe." *The Germanic Review* 8:147–156.

Roos, Jacques. 1952. *Aspects littéraires du mysticisme philosophique et l'influence de Boehme et de Swedenborg.* Strasbourg: P.-H. Heitz.

Schuchard, Gottlieb C. L. 1949. "The Last Scene in Goethe's Faust." *Publications of the Modern Language Association* 64:417–444.

Sjödén, Karl-Eric. 1985. *Swedenborg en France.* Stockholm: Almqvist & Wiksell International.

Taylor, Eugene. 1988. "Emerson: The Swedenborgian and Transcendentalist Connection." In *Emanuel Swedenborg: A Continuing Vision.* Edited by Robin Larsen. New York: Swedenborg Foundation.

Weis, L. 1882. "Goethe und Swedenborg." *Goethe-Jahrbuch* 3:349–351.

Wilkinson, Lynn R. 1996. *The Dream of an Absolute Language: Emanuel Swedenborg and French Literary Culture.* Albany, N.Y.: State University of New York Press.

Short Titles and Other Conventions
Used in This Work

SWEDENBORG'S footnotes, referenced by superscript letters appearing in the main text, comprise references to his previously published *Secrets of Heaven* (1749–1756). These references sometimes have obvious errors. Where a plausible correction has been found, it has been inserted in square brackets. These corrections have, furthermore, been italicized as an indication that they are intended to replace the preceding entry, not augment it. In the two instances where no alternative has been found, the reading of the first edition is followed by a question mark in italicized square brackets: *[?]*; in another two instances, certain references that seem to have been intended by Swedenborg but were inadvertently omitted by him have been inserted in roman brackets. For the background of these references, see the translator's preface. It should be observed that Swedenborg used the lettering series *a–z, aa–zz,* and *aaa–zzz* before starting over at *a,* whereas in this edition the lettering starts over after each chapter heading. A few comments by the translator have been included in brackets within Swedenborg's footnotes.

The system used in Swedenborg's footnotes to indicate corrections and additions has also been applied to citations of the Bible and of Swedenborg's works that appear in the main text of the translation: that is, italicized brackets indicate a correction and roman brackets indicate an addition. Words not appearing in the original but necessary for the understanding of the text also appear in roman brackets; this device has been used sparingly, however, even at the risk of some inconsistency in its application.

The comments of the translator, indicated by the notation [GFD]; the annotator, indicated by [RHK]; and the series editor, indicated by [JSR], are printed as endnotes; these notes are referenced by superscript numbers appearing in the main text. Translations in the endnotes are those of the indicated writer.

Swedenborg did not number the chapters of *Heaven and Hell.* His decision not to do so seems to have been deliberate, and in accord with it chapter numbers are not included in the text. However, because some studies of this work make reference to chapter numbers, the table of contents provides them.

As is common in Swedenborgian studies, text citations of Swedenborg's works refer not to page numbers but to Swedenborg's section numbers, which are uniform in all editions. Thus "*Secrets of Heaven* 29" refers to section 29 (§29) of *Secrets of Heaven*. A reference such as 29:2 indicates subsection 2 of section 29, marked by [2] in the section itself.

References to Swedenborg's works in this volume accord with the short titles listed below, except where he gives his own version of a title in the text of the translation, or where other translations are cited by the annotators. In this list, the short title is followed by the traditional translation for the title; by the original Latin title, with its full translation; and finally by the place and date of original publication if Swedenborg published it himself, or the approximate date of writing if he did not. The list is chronological, except for certain nontheological and posthumously published works, which are grouped separately.

Theological Works Published by Swedenborg

Secrets of Heaven
Traditional title: *Arcana Coelestia*
Original title: *Arcana Coelestia, Quae in Scriptura Sacra, seu Verbo Domini Sunt, Detecta: . . . Una cum Mirabilibus Quae Visa Sunt in Mundo Spirituum, et in Coelo Angelorum* [A Disclosure of Secrets of Heaven Contained in Sacred Scripture, or the Word of the Lord, . . . Together with Amazing Things Seen in the World of Spirits and in the Heaven of Angels]. London: 1749–1756.

Heaven and Hell
Traditional title: *Heaven and Hell*
Original title: *De Coelo et Ejus Mirabilibus, et de Inferno, ex Auditis et Visis* [Heaven and Its Wonders and Hell: Drawn from Things Heard and Seen]. London: 1758.

New Jerusalem
Traditional title: *New Jerusalem and Its Heavenly Doctrine*
Original title: *De Nova Hierosolyma et Ejus Doctrina Coelesti: Ex Auditis e Coelo: Quibus Praemittitur Aliquid de Novo Coelo et Nova Terra* [The New Jerusalem and Its Heavenly Teaching: Drawn from Things Heard from Heaven: Preceded by a Discussion of the New Heaven and the New Earth]. London: 1758.

Last Judgment
Traditional title: *The Last Judgment*
Original title: *De Ultimo Judicio, et de Babylonia Destructa: Ita Quod Omnia, Quae in Apocalypsi Praedicta Sunt, Hodie Impleta Sunt: Ex Auditis et Visis* [The Last Judgment and Babylon Destroyed, Showing That at This Day All the Predictions of the Book of Revelation Have Been Fulfilled: Drawn from Things Heard and Seen]. London: 1758.

White Horse
Traditional title: *The White Horse*
Original title: *De Equo Albo, de Quo in Apocalypsi, Cap. XIX: Et Dein de Verbo et Ejus Sensu Spirituali seu Interno, ex Arcanis Coelestibus* [The White Horse in Revelation Chapter 19, and the Word and Its Spiritual or Inner Sense (from *Secrets of Heaven*)]. London: 1758.

Other Planets
Traditional title: *Earths in the Universe*
Original title: *De Telluribus in Mundo Nostro Solari, Quae Vocantur Planetae, et de Telluribus in Coelo Astrifero, deque Illarum Incolis, Tum de Spiritibus et Angelis Ibi: Ex Auditis et Visis* [Planets or Worlds in Our Solar System, and Worlds in the Starry Heavens, and Their Inhabitants, as Well as the Spirits and Angels There: Drawn from Things Heard and Seen]. London: 1758.

The Lord
Traditional title: *Doctrine of the Lord*
Original title: *Doctrina Novae Hierosolymae de Domino* [Teachings for the New Jerusalem on the Lord]. Amsterdam: 1763.

Sacred Scripture
Traditional title: *Doctrine of the Sacred Scripture*
Original title: *Doctrina Novae Hierosolymae de Scriptura Sacra* [Teachings for the New Jerusalem on Sacred Scripture]. Amsterdam: 1763.

Life
Traditional title: *Doctrine of Life*
Original title: *Doctrina Vitae pro Nova Hierosolyma ex Praeceptis Decalogi* [Teachings about Life for the New Jerusalem: Drawn from the Ten Commandments]. Amsterdam: 1763.

Faith
Traditional title: *Doctrine of Faith*
Original title: *Doctrina Novae Hierosolymae de Fide* [Teachings for the New Jerusalem on Faith]. Amsterdam: 1763.

Supplements
Traditional title: *Continuation Concerning the Last Judgment*
Original title: *Continuatio de Ultimo Judicio: Et de Mundo Spirituali* [Supplements on the Last Judgment and the Spiritual World]. Amsterdam: 1763.

Divine Love and Wisdom
Traditional title: *Divine Love and Wisdom*
Original title: *Sapientia Angelica de Divino Amore et de Divina Sapientia* [Angelic Wisdom about Divine Love and Wisdom]. Amsterdam: 1763.

Divine Providence
Traditional title: *Divine Providence*
Original title: *Sapientia Angelica de Divina Providentia* [Angelic Wisdom about Divine Providence]. Amsterdam: 1764.

Revelation Unveiled
Traditional title: *Apocalypse Revealed*
Original title: *Apocalypsis Revelata, in Qua Deteguntur Arcana Quae Ibi Praedicta Sunt, et Hactenus Recondita Latuerunt* [The Book of Revelation Unveiled, Uncovering the Secrets That Were Foretold There and Have Lain Hidden until Now]. Amsterdam: 1766.

Marriage Love
Traditional title: *Conjugial Love*
Original title: *Delitiae Sapientiae de Amore Conjugiali: Post Quas Sequuntur Voluptates Insaniae de Amore Scortatorio* [Wisdom's Delight in Marriage Love: Followed by Insanity's Pleasure in Promiscuous Love]. Amsterdam: 1768.

Survey
Traditional title: *Brief Exposition*
Original title: *Summaria Expositio Doctrinae Novae Ecclesiae, Quae per Novam Hierosolymam in Apocalypsi Intelligitur* [Survey of Teachings for the New Church Meant by the New Jerusalem in the Book of Revelation]. Amsterdam: 1769.

Soul-Body Interaction
Traditional title: *Intercourse between the Soul and Body*
Original title: *De Commercio Animae et Corporis, quod Creditur Fieri vel per Influxum Physicum, vel per Influxum Spiritualem, vel per Harmoniam Praestabilitam* [Soul-body Interaction, Believed to Occur Either by a Physical Inflow, or by a Spiritual Inflow, or by a Preestablished Harmony]. London: 1769.

True Christianity
Traditional title: *True Christian Religion*
Original title: *Vera Christiana Religio, Continens Universam Theologiam Novae Ecclesiae a Domino apud Danielem Cap. VII:13–14, et in Apocalypsi Cap. XXI:1, 2 Praedictae* [True Christianity: Containing the Whole Theology of the New Church Predicted by the Lord in Daniel 7:13–14 and Revelation 21:1, 2]. Amsterdam: 1771.

Nontheological and Posthumously Published Works by Swedenborg Cited in This Volume

Joyous Accolade
Traditional title: *Festivus Applausus*
Original title: *Festivus Applausus in Caroli XII . . . in Pomeraniam Suam Adventum* [Joyous Accolade for Charles XII's . . . Arrival in His Own Pomerania]. Greifswald: [1714 or 1715].

Northern Muse
Traditional title: *Camena Borea*
Original title: *Camena Borea cum Heroum et Heroidum Factis Ludens* [The Northern Muse Amusing Herself with the Deeds of Heroes and Heroines]. Greifswald: 1715.

Dynamics of the Soul's Domain
Traditional title: *Economy of the Animal Kingdom*
Original title: *Oeconomia Regni Animalis in Transactiones Divisa* [Dynamics of the Soul's Domain: Divided into Treatises]. Amsterdam: 1740–1741.

Draft of a Rational Psychology
Traditional title: *Rational Psychology*
Original title: *[Psychologia Rationalis]* [Rational Psychology]. 1742.

The Soul's Domain
Traditional title: *The Animal Kingdom*
Original title: *Regnum Animale, Anatomice, Physice, et Philosophice Perlustratum* [The Soul's Domain Thoroughly Examined by Means of Anatomy, Physics, and Philosophy]. The Hague: 1744–1745.

The Old Testament Explained
Traditional title: *The Word Explained*
Original title: *Explicatio in Verbum Historicum Veteris Testamenti* [The Historical Word of the Old Testament Explained]. 1745–1747.

Spiritual Experiences
Traditional title: *The Spiritual Diary*
Original title: *Experientiae Spirituales* [Spiritual Experiences]. 1745–1765.

Revelation Explained
Traditional title: *Apocalypse Explained*
Original title: *Apocalypsis Explicata secundum Sensum Spiritualem, Ubi Revelantur Arcana, Quae Ibi Praedicta, et Hactenus Recondita Fuerunt* [The Book of Revelation Explained as to Its Spiritual Meaning, Which Reveals Secret Wonders That Were Predicted There and Have Been Hidden until Now]. 1758–1759.

Biblical Titles

Swedenborg referred to the Hebrew Scriptures as the Old Testament; his terminology has been adopted in this edition. As was the custom in his day, he referred to the Pentateuch (Genesis, Exodus, Leviticus, Numbers, and Deuteronomy) as the books of Moses; to the Psalms as the book of David; and occasionally to the Book of Revelation as John.

HEAVEN & HELL

[Author's Preface]

IN the twenty-fourth chapter of Matthew, we find the Lord[1] talking to [I]
his disciples about the close of the age, the last time of the church.[a],[*],[2]
At the end of his prophecies concerning the sequence of states of its love
and faith,[b],[3] he says:

> Immediately after the suffering of those days, the sun will be darkened
> and the moon will not give its light, and the stars will fall from heaven,
> and the powers of the heavens will be shaken. And then the sign of the
> Human-born One[4] will appear in heaven, and then all the tribes of the
> earth will lament. And they will see the Human-born One coming in
> the clouds of heaven with power and great glory. And he will send his
> angels with a trumpet and a loud voice, and they will gather his chosen
> ones from the four winds, from one end of the heavens all the way to
> the other end. (Matthew 24:29–31)[5]

When people understand these words according to their literal meaning, they can only believe that all these things are going to happen just as
this meaning describes them, at that end of time called the Last Judgment.[6] This does not mean only that the sun and moon will be darkened
and that the stars will fall from heaven, that the sign of the Lord will appear in heaven, and that he will be seen in the clouds with angels blowing
trumpets. It also includes matters prophesied elsewhere, statements that
the whole visible world is going to be destroyed and that afterward a new
heaven and a new earth will come into being.

---

a. On the close of the age as the last time of the church: 4535, 10672 *[10622]*.

b. For explanations of what the Lord said in Matthew 24 and 25 about the close of the age, his
coming, and thus the gradual destruction of the church and the Last Judgment, see the material
prefaced to chapters 5–24 *[26–40]* of Genesis. In particular, see 3353–3356, 3486–3489, 3650–3655,
3751–3759 *[3751–3757]*, 3897–3901, 4056–4060, 4129–4231 *[4229–4231]*, 4332–4335, 4422–4424,
[4535,] 4635–4638, 4661–4664, 4807–4810, 4954–4959, 5063–5071.

---

* Swedenborg's footnotes, indicated by superscript letters, comprise references to his previously
published *Secrets of Heaven* (1749–1756). Endnotes, containing information helpful to the reader,
are indicated by superscript numbers. Text citations in both series of notes refer to Swedenborg's
section numbers. See the list of short titles and other conventions on pages 79–84 above. [GFD]

Many people in the church these days are of this opinion.7 However, people who believe such things are not aware of the hidden depths that lie within the details of the Word.8 There is in fact spiritual meaning in these details, for they do not intend the outward and earthly events that we find on the literal level; instead they intend spiritual and heavenly events. This holds true not just for the meaning of phrases but even for each word.c

The Word is in fact written in pure correspondencesd,9 so that there may be deeper meaning in the details. Questions about the nature of this meaning can be resolved by all the things I have set forth about it in *Secrets of Heaven.*10 A selection of these may be found also in my explanation of the white horse in the Book of Revelation.11 It is in this deeper sense that we are to understand what the Lord said in the passage just cited about coming in the clouds of heaven. The sun that will be darkened means the Lord in respect to love,e the moon means the Lord in respect to faith.f The stars mean insights into what is good and true, or into love and faith.g The sign of the Human-born One in heaven means the appearing of divine truth. The wailing tribes of earth mean all the elements of what is true and good, or of faith and love.h The Lord's coming in the clouds of heaven with power and great glory means his presence in the Word, and revelation.i The clouds refer to the literal meaning of the Wordj and the glory to the Word's inner meaning.k The angels with a trumpet and a loud voice mean heaven, which is where divine truth comes from.l

c. There is deeper meaning in every detail of the Word: 1143, 1984, 2135, 2333, 2395, 2495, 4442, 9049, 9086.

d. The Word is composed using pure correspondences, so that its every detail points to something spiritual: 1404, 1408, 1409, 1540, 1619, 1659, 1709, 1783, 2900, 9086.

e. The sun in the Word means the Lord in respect to love, and therefore love for the Lord: 1529, 1837, 2441, 2495, 4060, 4696, 4996 *[4966]*, 7083, 10809.

f. The moon in the Word means the Lord in respect to faith, and therefore faith in the Lord: 1529, 1530, 2495, 4060, 4996 *[4696]*, 7083.

g. Stars in the Word mean insights into what is good and true: 2495, 2849, 4697.

h. Tribes mean all true and good elements in a single complex, or all elements of faith and love: 3858, 3926, 4060, 6335.

i. The Lord's coming is his presence in the Word, and revelation: 3900, 4060.

j. Clouds in the Word mean the Word in the letter or its literal meaning: 4060, 4391, 5922, 6343, 6752, 8106, 8781, 9430, 10551, 10574.

k. Glory in the Word means divine truth as it is in heaven and in the inner meaning of the Word: 4809, 5292 *[?]*, 5922, 8267, 8427, 9429, 10574.

l. The trumpet or horn means divine truth in heaven and revealed from heaven: 8815, 8823, 8915. "Voice" has the same meaning: 6971, 9926.

This enables us to see what these words of the Lord mean. They mean that at the end of the church, when there is no longer any love and therefore no longer any faith, the Lord will open the Word by disclosing its deeper meaning and will reveal the heavenly contents hidden[12] within it. The particular hidden contents to be disclosed in the pages that follow have to do with heaven and hell and with our own life after death.

Church people these days[13] know practically nothing about heaven and hell or their life after death, even though there are descriptions of everything available to them in the Word. In fact, many who have been born in the church deny all this. In their hearts they are asking who has ever come back to tell us about it.

To prevent this negative attitude—especially prevalent among people who have acquired a great deal of worldly wisdom—from infecting and corrupting people of simple heart and simple faith, it has been granted me to be with angels and to talk with them person to person. I have also been enabled to see what is in heaven and in hell, a process that has been going on for thirteen years. Now I am being allowed therefore to describe what I have heard and seen, in the hopes of shedding light where there is ignorance, and of dispelling skepticism.

The reason this kind of direct revelation is taking place today is that this is what the Coming of the Lord means.[14]

The Lord Is God of Heaven

FIRST and foremost, we need to know who the God of heaven is, since everything else depends on this. Throughout the whole of heaven, no one is acknowledged as God of heaven except the Lord.[15] Angels say what he himself taught, namely that he is one with the Father, that the Father is in him and he in the Father, that anyone who sees him sees the Father, and that everything holy emanates from him (John 10:30, 38; 14:9–11;[16] 16:13–15). I have often talked with angels about this, and their consistent testimony has been that in heaven they cannot divide the Divine[17] into three because they both know and perceive that

2

the Divine is one and that this "one" is in the Lord. They have also told me that when people arrive from earth with the idea of three divine beings they cannot be admitted to heaven. This is because their thinking vacillates between one opinion and the other, and in heaven they are not allowed[18] to think "three" and say "one."[a,19]

In heaven people actually speak directly from their thought, so that we have there a kind of thoughtful speech or audible thought. This means that if people have divided the Divine into three in the world and held a separate image of each one without gathering and focusing these three into one, they cannot be accepted. In heaven, there is a communication of all thoughts, so if people arrive who think "three" and say "one," they are recognized immediately for what they are and are sent away.

Still, it needs to be realized that in the other life any people who have not put "good" in one compartment and "true" in another—who have not separated faith from love—accept the heavenly concept of the Lord as God of the universe once they have been taught. It is different, though, with people who have separated their faith from their lives, that is, who have not lived by the guiding principles of true faith.

3 If people within the church have ignored the Lord and recognized only the Father and have closed their minds to other thoughts, they are outside heaven. Since they do not receive any inflow[20] from heaven, where the Lord alone is worshiped, they gradually lose their ability to ponder the truth of one thing after another. Eventually they either become speechless or inarticulate. They walk around aimlessly with their arms hanging down loosely as though all the strength had gone from their joints.

On the other hand, people who have denied the Lord's divine nature and have recognized only his human nature (like the Socinians)[21] are also excluded from heaven. They are taken a little way forward to the right[22] and are let down into the depths, which completely separates them from the Christian realm. Then too, there are people who claim to believe in an invisible Divine called the Being of the Universe and reject any faith in the Lord. When they are examined, it turns out that they do not believe in any god at all, since this invisible Divine of theirs is actually like the first principles of nature. This is incompatible with faith and love,

a. In the other life, Christians have been examined to find out what kind of concept of God they had, and it has turned out that they had a concept of three gods: 2329, 5256, 10736, 10738, 10821. On the recognition in heaven of a trinity within the Lord: 14, 15, 1729, 2005, 5256, 9303.

because it eludes [actual] thought.[b] These people are banished to the company of those called materialists.[23]

Things happen differently for people who are born outside the church, the ones we call non-Christians. We will discuss them later.[24]

All little children (and these make up a third part of heaven) are led **4** first into an acknowledgment and belief that the Lord is their father. Later they are brought into an acknowledgment and belief that he is Lord of all, which means God of heaven and earth. It will be made clear below that little children mature in heaven and by means of insights[25] are brought into full angelic intelligence and wisdom.[26]

There can be no doubt among church people that the Lord is God of **5** heaven, because he himself teaches that everything of the Father's belongs to him (Matthew 11:27; John 16:15; 17:2) and that he has all power in heaven and on earth (Matthew 28:18). It says "in heaven and on earth" because the ruler of heaven rules earth as well, the one actually depending on the other.[c] His "ruling heaven and earth" means our accepting from him everything good that is intrinsic to love and everything true that is intrinsic to faith. It therefore means accepting all intelligence and wisdom, and thus all happiness—in short, eternal life.

This too the Lord teaches when he says, "Whoever believes in the Son has eternal life; but whoever does not trust the Son will not see life" (John 3:36). Or again, he says, "I am the resurrection and the life. Whoever believes in me, even though he dies, will be alive, and whoever lives and believes in me will not die to eternity" (John 11:25–26).[27] Or again, "I am the way, the truth, and the life" (John 14:6).

There were some spirits who had acknowledged the Father but whose **6** only concept of the Lord had been that he was a human being like everyone else. This meant they did not believe that he was the God of heaven. As a result, they were allowed to travel here and there and to ask at will whether there was a heaven that did not belong to the Lord. They asked around for some days without finding any.

---

b. A Divine Being that cannot be grasped in any concept cannot be accepted by faith: 5110, 5633 [5663], 6982, 6996, 7004, 7211, 9359 [perhaps 9356], 9972, 10067.

c. The whole of heaven belongs to the Lord: 2751, 7086. Power in the heavens and on earth belongs to him: 1607, 10089, 10827. Because the Lord governs heaven, he also governs everything that depends on heaven, which means everything in this world: 2026, 2027, 4523, 4524. Only the Lord has the power to banish the hells, restrain people from evils, and keep them engaged in what is good—the power therefore to save: 10019.

They were people who placed happiness in glory and in being in control, and since they could not get what they craved and were told that such feelings were not part of heaven, they felt insulted. They wanted a heaven where they could lord it over others and excel in the kind of glory they had had in this world.

It Is the Lord's Divine Nature That Makes Heaven

7 WHILE we call the total assemblage of angels heaven because they do make it up, what really makes heaven overall and in every specific instance is the divine nature that emanates from the Lord, flowing into angels and accepted by them. The divine nature that emanates from the Lord is the good intrinsic to love and the truth intrinsic to faith. The amount angels accept from the Lord of what is good and what is true determines the extent to which they are angels and are heaven.

8 Everyone in the heavens knows, believes, and even perceives that nothing good is intended and done by the self and that nothing true is thought and believed by the self. Everything comes from the Divine, which means from the Lord. Anything good and true from the self is not good or true, because there is no life from the Divine within it. Angels of the central[28] heaven perceive and feel the inflow distinctly. The more they accept, the more they seem to be in heaven, because they are more fully absorbed in love and faith, in the light of intelligence and wisdom, and in the heavenly joy that results. Once we see that all these qualities emanate from the Lord's divine nature, we can see that the Lord's divine nature makes heaven. It is not anything the angels do with a sense of ownership.[a]

---

a. Angels recognize that everything good comes from the Lord and nothing from themselves, and that the Lord dwells within them in what is his own and not in anything that they can claim as their own: 9338, 10125, 10151, 10157. Consequently, "angels" in the Word mean something that belongs to the Lord: 1925, 2821, 3093, 4085, 8192, 10528. Because of their acceptance of the Divine from the Lord, angels are called gods: 4295, 4402, 7268, 7873, 8301, 8192. In fact, the Lord is the source of everything that is really good and everything that is really true—of all peace, love, thoughtfulness, and faith: 1614, 2016, 2751, 2882, 2883, 2891, 2892, 2904. He is also the source of all wisdom and intelligence: 109, 112, 121, 124.

This is why in the Word heaven is called the Lord's dwelling and his throne. It is why the people who live there are described as being "in the Lord."[b] We will explain later how the divine emanates from the Lord and fills heaven.[29]

In their wisdom, angels press on even further. They say that it is not just everything good and true that comes from the Lord, but every bit of life as well. They support this by pointing out that nothing can come into being from itself. Everything presupposes something prior. This means that everything has come into being from a First, which they call the essential reality of the life of everything. Everything endures in the same way, too, because enduring is a constant coming into being.[30] If anything were not kept in constant connection with the First,[31] through intermediate means, it would instantly collapse and disintegrate. They add that there is only one single wellspring of life, with human life as one stream flowing from it. If it were not constantly supplied from its wellspring, it would immediately peter out.

[2] Still further, they say that nothing flows from that unique wellspring of life, the Lord, that is not divinely good and divinely true. These affect every individual according to the way they are accepted. People who accept them into their faith and life are in heaven, while people who reject or stifle them transform them into hell. They actually change what is good into evil and what is true into falsity—life into death.

Angels also support their belief that the Lord is the source of every bit of life by observing that everything in the universe goes back to what is good and true. Our volitional life, the life of our love, goes back to what is good, while our cognitive life, the life of our faith, goes back to what is true. Since everything good and true comes to us from above, it follows that this is the source of all of our life.

[3] Because angels believe this, they decline any thanks offered them for the good they do. In fact they feel hurt and withdraw if anyone gives them credit for anything good. It bewilders them to discover that people can believe they are wise on their own or do good on their own. Doing good for one's own sake, in their language, cannot be called "good," because it stems from self. Doing good for its own sake is what they call "good from the Divine." This, they say, is the kind of good that makes heaven, because this kind of good is the Lord.[c]

b. People in heaven are described as being in the Lord: 3637, 3638.

c. Good from the Lord has the Lord within it, but good attributed to oneself does not: 1802, 3951, 8478.

10   Spirits who during their earthly lives had convinced themselves that they were the sources of the good they did and the truth they believed, or who had claimed these virtues as their own, are not accepted into heaven. This is the belief of all those who place merit in good deeds and claim to be righteous. Angels avoid them. They regard them as stupid and as thieves—stupid because they are constantly looking at themselves and not at the Divine, and thieves because they take from the Lord what is actually his. They stand in opposition to heaven's belief that the Lord's divine nature in angels is what makes heaven.

11   If people are in heaven or in the church, they are in the Lord and the Lord is in them. This is what the Lord taught when he said, "Abide in me, and I in you; as the branch cannot bear fruit by itself, unless it abides in the vine, neither can you unless you abide in me. I am the vine, you are the branches. Those who abide in me and I in them will bear much fruit; because without me you can do nothing" (John 15:4–7 [4–5]).

12   This allows us finally to conclude that the Lord dwells in angels in what belongs to himself, and therefore that the Lord is the sum and substance of heaven. This is because the good from the Lord is the Lord within and among them, since what comes from him is himself. Accordingly, the good from the Lord, and not anything of their own, is heaven for angels.

The Lord's Divine Nature in Heaven Is Love for Him and Thoughtfulness[32] toward One's Neighbor

13   IN heaven, the divine nature that emanates from the Lord is called divine truth, for reasons that will be given below. This divine truth flows into heaven from the Lord, out of his divine love. Divine love and the divine truth that derives from it are like the sun's fire and the light that comes from it in our world. The love is like the sun's fire, and the derivative truth is like the light from the sun. By reason of correspondence, fire means love and light means the truth that flows from it.[a]

This enables us to determine the character of the divine truth that emanates from divine love: in its essence, it is divine good united to divine truth, and because it is united, it gives life to everything in heaven the way the warmth of the sun, united to its light, makes everything fruitful on earth in spring and summer. It is different when the warmth is not united to light, when the light is therefore cold. Then everything slows down and lies there, snuffed out.

The divine good we have compared to warmth is the good of love within and among angels, and the divine truth we have compared to light is the means and the source of this good of love.

The reason the Divine in heaven (which in fact makes heaven) is love is **14** that love is spiritual union. It unites angels to the Lord and unites them with each other. It does this so thoroughly that in the Lord's sight they are like a single being.[33] Further, love is the essential reality of every individual life. It is therefore the source of the life of angels and the life of people here. Anyone who weighs the matter will discover that love is our vital core. We grow warm because of its presence and cold because of its absence, and when it is completely gone, we die.[b] We do need to realize, though, that it is the quality of our love that determines the quality of this life.[34]

There are two quite distinguishable loves in heaven—love for the **15** Lord and love for our neighbor. Love for the Lord is characteristic of the third or central heaven, while love for our neighbor is characteristic of the second or intermediate heaven.[35] Both come from the Lord, and each one makes a heaven.

In heaven's light, it is easy to see how these two loves differ and how they unite, but this can be seen only dimly in our world. In heaven, "loving the Lord" does not mean loving him for the image he projects[36] but loving the good that comes from him. Loving the good is intending and doing it from love. Further, "loving one's neighbor" does not mean loving companions for the images they project but loving the truth that

---

a. In the Word, fire means love in both senses [that is, love for good and for evil]: 934, 4906, 5215; holy and heavenly fire means divine love and every affection that belongs to it: 934, 6314, 6832; the derivative light means the truth that flows from the good of love, and light in heaven is divine truth: 3395 *[3195]*, 3485, 3636, 3643, 3993, 4302, 4413, 9548, 9684.

b. Love is the fire of life, and life itself actually comes from love: 4906, 5071, 6032, 6314.

comes from the Word. Loving the truth is intending and doing it. We can therefore see that these two loves differ the way "good" and "true" differ and unite the way these two unite.c

All this, though, will not conform to the notions of anyone who does not know what love is, what the good is, and what the neighbor is.d

16　　I have talked with angels about this on a number of occasions. They have expressed their astonishment that church people do not know that to love the Lord and to love one's neighbor is to love what is good and true and to do them intentionally. They should realize, though, that we demonstrate our love by intending and doing what someone else wants. This is how we become loved in return—not by "loving the other" and not doing what that other wants; in essence, that is not loving at all. They should also realize that the good that comes from the Lord is the Lord's own likeness because he is within it. We become likenesses of him and are united to him when we make what is good and what is true matters of our lives by doing them intentionally, since intending something is loving to do it. The Lord teaches that this is true when he says, "Those who have my commandments and do them are the ones who love me, and I will love them and make my dwelling with them" (John 14:21, 23);37 and again, "If you keep my commandments, you will abide in my love" (John 15:10, 12).38

17　　All my experience in heaven bears witness to the fact that the divine nature that comes from the Lord, affects angels, and constitutes heaven, is love. In fact, all the people there are forms of love and thoughtfulness. They look indescribably beautiful. Love radiates from their faces, from their speech, from every detail of their behavior.e

Further, there are surrounding auras39 of spiritual life that emanate from every angel and from every spirit and envelop them. By means of these auras one can recognize even from a distance the quality of the affections of their loves, since these auras flow out from the life of their affection and consequent thought—that is, from the life of their love and

---

c. Loving the Lord and our neighbor means living according to the Lord's laws: 10143, 10153, 10310, 10578, 10648.

d. Loving one's neighbor is not loving the image he or she projects but loving what is within one's neighbor and is therefore one's neighbor's source, namely the good and the true: 5025 [5028], 10336; if people love the individual and not what is within the individual and is therefore the source of the individual, they love the evil as much as the good: 3820; thoughtfulness is intending what is true and being influenced by things true for their own sake: 3876, 3877; thoughtfulness toward one's neighbor is doing what is good, fair, and honest in every task and in every office: 8120, 8121, 8122.

e. On angels as forms of thoughtfulness: 3804, 4735, 4797, 4985, 5199, 5530, 9879, 10177.

consequent faith. The auras that emanate from angels are so full of love that they touch the deepest reaches of life of the people they meet. I have been aware of them a number of times, and they have moved me deeply.[f]

I have been able to see that love was the source of angels' life because all the people in the other life turn in a direction determined by their own love. People engaged in a love for the Lord and a love for their neighbor are constantly turning toward the Lord, while people who are engaged in self-love are constantly turning their backs to the Lord. This holds true no matter which way they turn, since in the other life spatial relationships are determined by people's inner natures. These also determine geographical regions, whose boundaries are not drawn the way they are in the physical world but depend on which way people are facing. Actually, it is not angels who turn to the Lord but the Lord who turns toward himself the people who love to do whatever has its source in him.[g,40] But there will be more on this subject below, when we discuss geographical regions in the other life.[41]

The reason the Lord's divine nature in heaven is love is that love is what is receptive of every heavenly quality—that is, of peace, intelligence, wisdom, and happiness. Love is receptive of everything that is in harmony with it. It longs for such things, it seeks them out, it absorbs them spontaneously because it has the constant purpose of uniting itself with them and being enriched by them.[h] People actually recognize this fact, since the love within them surveys memory, so to speak, and draws out from it the items that agree with it. It gathers these together and arranges them within and beneath itself—within itself so that it may possess them and beneath itself so that they may serve it. It discards and eradicates, though, the items that do not agree with it.[42]

I have been able to see very clearly that love has a full, intrinsic ability to accept elements of truth that suit it and has also a desire of uniting them to itself. This has become clear from observing people who have

f. A spiritual aura that is an aura of life flows out in waves from every person, every spirit, and every angel and clings to them: 4464, 5179, 7454, 8630. It flows out from the life of their affection and consequent thought: 2489, 4464, 6206.

g. Spirits and angels are constantly turning in the direction of their loves, which means that people in the heavens are constantly turning toward the Lord: 10130, 10189, 10420, 10702. Geographical regions in the other life depend for particular individuals on the direction they are facing; this is what draws their boundaries, unlike the situation in the physical world: 10130, 10189, 10420, 10702.

h. Love includes countless elements, and welcomes into itself everything that is in harmony with it: 2500, 2572, 3078, 3189, 6323, 7490, 7750.

been transported into heaven. Even people who were simple folk in this world have arrived at angelic wisdom and heavenly happiness in the company of angels. This was because they loved what is good and true for the sake of what is good and true. They had grafted these qualities into their lives and had thereby become capable of accepting heaven and all its indescribable riches.

People caught up in love for themselves and for the world, however, have no such receptive ability. They turn away from such things, discard them, and at their first touch or inflow try to escape them. They ally themselves with people in hell who are caught up in loves like their own.

There were some spirits who doubted that love was so full and wanted to know whether this was really true. In order that they might find out, they were let into a state of heavenly love with all obstacles removed and were brought forward a considerable distance to an angelic heaven. They talked with me from there and told me that they felt deeper happiness than words could express, sorrowing that they would have to return to their former state. Other people as well have been raised into heaven, and the deeper or higher they have been taken, the deeper and higher they have penetrated into intelligence and wisdom, becoming able to grasp things that were incomprehensible to them before. We can see from this that the love that emanates from the Lord is open to heaven and all its riches.

19   We can conclude that love for the Lord and love for our neighbor embrace within themselves everything that is true from the Divine because this follows from what the Lord himself said about these two loves: "You shall love your God with all your heart and with all your soul: this is the greatest and first commandment. The second, which is like it, is that you should love your neighbor as yourself. On these two commandments depend the Law and the Prophets" (Matthew 22:37–40). The Law and the Prophets are the whole Word, which means all divine truth.

Heaven Is Divided into Two Kingdoms

SINCE there are infinite varieties in heaven—since no community and in fact no individual is just like any other[a]—heaven is therefore divided overall, more specifically, and in detail. Overall, it is divided into two kingdoms, more specifically into three heavens, and in detail into countless communities.[43] We will now discuss the details. They are called "kingdoms" because heaven is called "the kingdom of God."   **20**

There are angels who accept the divine nature that emanates from the Lord on a deeper level and angels who accept it less deeply. The ones who accept it more deeply are called heavenly angels, and the ones who accept it less deeply are called spiritual angels. Heaven is therefore divided into two kingdoms, one called the heavenly kingdom[44] and the other called the spiritual kingdom.[b]   **21**

Because the angels who make up the heavenly kingdom accept the Lord's divine nature on a deeper level, they are called more inward or higher angels. The heavens they constitute are therefore called more inward or higher heavens.[c] We use the words "higher" and "lower" as a way of referring to more inward things and more outward things.[d,45]   **22**

The love that envelops people in the heavenly kingdom is called heavenly love, and the love that envelops people in the spiritual kingdom is called spiritual love. Heavenly love is love for the Lord, and spiritual love is thoughtfulness toward one's neighbor. Further, since all "good" is   **23**

a. There is an infinite variety, and nothing can ever be identical to anything else: 7236, 9002. There is an infinite variety in heaven as well: 684, 690, 3744, 5598, 7236. The varieties in heaven are varieties of what is good: 3744, 4005, 7236, 7833, 7836, 9002. By this means all the communities in heaven and every angel in a community are distinguishable from each other: 690, 3241, 3519, 3804, 3986, 4067, 4149, 4263, 7236, 7833, 7836. Still, they all form one entity by means of love from the Lord: 457, 3986.

b. Overall, heaven is divided into two kingdoms, a heavenly kingdom and a spiritual kingdom: 3887, 4138. Angels of the heavenly kingdom accept the Lord's divine [nature] in their volitional side, and therefore more deeply than do spiritual angels, who accept it into their cognitive side: 5113, 6367, 8521, 9935 [9915], 9995, 10124.

c. The heavens that constitute the heavenly kingdom are called "higher," while those that constitute the spiritual kingdom are called "lower": 10068.

d. Deeper matters are expressed as higher, and higher matters as deeper: 2148, 3084, 4599, 5146, 8325.

a matter of love (since whatever we love is good in our estimation), the good of the one kingdom is called heavenly and the good of the other, spiritual. We can see from this the way in which these two kingdoms are distinguished from each other: namely, that it is like the way the good of love for the Lord is distinguished from the good of thoughtfulness toward our neighbor.[e] Since the former good is a deeper good and the former love is a deeper love, heavenly angels are more inward angels, and are called "higher."

24   The heavenly kingdom is also called the Lord's priestly kingdom—in the Word, "his dwelling"; and the spiritual kingdom is called his royal kingdom—in the Word, "his throne." The Lord in the world was called "Jesus" because of his heavenly divine nature, and "the Christ" because of his spiritual divine nature.

25   The angels in the Lord's heavenly kingdom far surpass the angels of the spiritual kingdom in regard to wisdom and splendor because they accept the Lord's divine nature on a deeper level. They live in love for him, and are therefore more intimately united to him.[f] The reason for their excellence is that they have accepted divine truths directly into their lives and continue to do so, rather than taking them into memory and thought first, the way spiritual angels do. This means they have them engraved on their hearts and grasp them, virtually see them, within themselves. They never calculate whether or not they are true.[g] They are like the people described in Jeremiah,

> I will put my law in their mind and engrave it on their heart: no longer
> will one person teach a friend or a brother, saying, "Know Jehovah";[46]
> from the smallest to the greatest, they will know me. (Jeremiah 31:33, 34)

In Isaiah, they are called "the people who have been taught by Jehovah" (Isaiah 54:13). In John 6:45–46, the Lord himself teaches that those who are taught by Jehovah are the ones who are taught by the Lord.

---

e. The good of the heavenly kingdom is the good of love for the Lord, and the good of the spiritual kingdom is the good of thoughtfulness toward one's neighbor: 3691, 6435, 9468, 9680, 9683, 9780.

f. Heavenly angels are far wiser than spiritual angels: 2718, 9995. On the nature of the difference between heavenly angels and spiritual angels: 2088, 2669, 2708, 2715, 3235, 3240, 4788, 7068, 8121 [8521], 9277, 10295.

g. Heavenly angels do not reason about truths of faith because they grasp them within themselves, while spiritual angels do reason about whether they are true or not: 202, 337, 597, 607, 784, 1121, 1387 [1384], 1398 [1385, 1394], 1919, 3246, 4448, 7680, 7877, 8780, 9277, 10786.

We have stated that they have more wisdom and splendor than others because they have accepted divine truths directly into their lives and continue to do so. The moment they hear them, they intend them and live them out. They do not refer them to memory and consider whether they are true. People like this know instantly, from an inflow from the Lord, whether the truth they are hearing is actually true. The Lord flows directly into our intentions, and indirectly, through our intentions, into our thinking. In other words, the Lord flows directly into what is good within us, and indirectly, through that good, into what is true.[h] That is, we call "good" whatever is a matter of intent and therefore of action, while we call "true" whatever is a matter of memory and therefore of thought. However, as long as any truth is in memory and therefore in thought, it is neither good nor living. It is not assimilated into the person, because a person is a person by virtue of intent primarily and cognitive abilities secondarily—not by virtue of cognitive abilities apart from volition.[i,47]

Since there is such a difference between angels of the heavenly kingdom and angels of the spiritual kingdom, they do not live together or associate with each other. They are granted communication only through intermediate angelic communities, communities called "heavenly-spiritual": it is through them that the heavenly kingdom flows into the spiritual kingdom.[j] The result of this is that while heaven is divided into two kingdoms, they still make a single whole. The Lord always provides intermediate angels like these through whom there can be communication and union.

h. The Lord's inflow is into the good and through the good into the true, and not vice versa. So it is into volition and through it into discernment, and not vice versa: 5482, 5649, 6027, 8685, 8701, 10153.

i. Our volition is the substance of our life and is what receives the good of love, while our cognitive ability is the consequent manifestation of life and is what receives true and good elements of faith: 3619, 5002, 9282. Therefore our volitional life is our primary life, and our cognitive life issues from it: 585, 590, 3619, 7342, 8885, 9285 *[9282]*, 10076, 10109, 10110. It is the things that are accepted into our volition that become matters of life and are assimilated to us: 3161, 9386, 9393. A person is a person by virtue of volition, and secondarily by virtue of cognitive abilities: 8911, 9069, 9071, 10076, 10106, 10110. People who intend good and think well are loved and valued by others, while people who think well but do not intend good are rejected and disparaged: 8911, 10076. After death, we continue to have the character of our volition and of the discernment that follows from it. Whatever is a matter of cognition only, and not of volition, disappears because it is not really within us: 9069, 9071, 9282, 9386, 10153.

j. There is a communication and union between the two kingdoms by means of angelic communities called "heavenly-spiritual": 4047, 6435, 8787 *[8796]*, 8881 *[8802]*. On the inflow of the Lord through the heavenly kingdom into the spiritual: 3969, 6366.

28   Since there will be a good deal of material on the angels of each kingdom in the pages that follow, I forego details at this point.

There Are Three Heavens

29   THERE are three heavens, very clearly distinguished from each other.
There is a central or third heaven, an intermediate or second one,
and an outmost or first.[48] These follow in sequence and are interdependent, like the highest part of the human body, the head; the middle, or
torso; and the lowest, or feet; or like the highest, middle, and lowest parts
of a house. The divine life that emanates and comes down from the Lord
is in this kind of pattern as well. It is this necessity of design that determines the tripartite arrangement of heaven.

30   The deeper levels of the human mind and disposition[49] are in a similar pattern as well. We have a central, intermediate, and outmost nature.
This is because when humanity was created the whole divine design was
gathered into it, to the point that as to structure, the human being is the
divine design and is therefore a heaven in miniature.[a] For the same reason we are in touch with heaven as to our inner natures and come into
the company of angels after death—of angels of the central or the intermediate or the outmost heaven depending on our acceptance of divine
good and truth from the Lord during our earthly lives.

31   The divine nature that flows from the Lord and is accepted in the
third or central heaven is called heavenly, and the angels there are

---

a. All the elements of the divine design are gathered into the human, and by creation the human
is, structurally, the divine design: 4219, 4220 *[4222]*, 4223, 4523, 4524, 5114, 5368 *[3628, 5168]*, 6013,
6057, 6605, 6626, 9706, 10156, 10472. Within the human individual, the inner person is structured in the likeness of heaven and the outer in the likeness of earth, which is why the ancients
called the human a microcosm: 4523, 5368 *[3628, 5115]*, 6013, 6057, 9279, 9706, 10156, 10472. So
by creation, the human being is a miniature heaven as to inward things, a mirror of the macrocosm, and so too is the person who has been created anew or regenerated by the Lord: 911, 1900,
1982 *[1928]*, 3624–3631, 3634, 3884, 4041, 4279, 4523, 4524, 4625, 6013, 6057, 9279, 9632.

consequently called heavenly angels. The divine nature that flows from the Lord and is accepted in the second or intermediate heaven is called spiritual, and the angels there are consequently called spiritual angels. The divine nature, though, that flows from the Lord and is accepted in the outmost or first heaven is called natural. However, since the "natural" of that heaven is not like the "natural" of our world, but has something spiritual and heavenly within it, that heaven is called "spiritual-natural" or "heavenly-natural," and the angels there are called "spiritual-natural" or "heavenly-natural."[b] The angels called spiritual-natural are the ones who accept an inflow from the intermediate or second heaven, which is the spiritual heaven, while the angels called heavenly-natural are the ones who accept an inflow from the central or third heaven, which is the heavenly heaven. Spiritual-natural and heavenly-natural angels are different from each other, but they constitute one heaven because they are all on the same level.

There is an outside and an inside to each heaven. The angels who are in the inner region are there called "inner angels," while the ones in the outer region are called "outer angels." The outside and the inside in the heavens (or in each particular heaven) are like our own volitional side and its cognitive aspect. Everything volitional has its cognitive side—neither occurs without the other. The volitional is like a flame and the cognitive like the light that it sheds.[50]

It needs to be quite clear that it is the inner nature of angels that determines which heaven they are in. The more the deeper levels have been opened, the more inward the heaven they are in. There are three inner levels of every angel and spirit, and of every person here as well. The people whose third level has been opened are in the central heaven, while the people whose second or first only has been opened are in the intermediate or the outmost heaven.

The deeper levels are opened by our acceptance of divine good and divine true gifts. People who are actually affected by divine true gifts and let them directly into their lives—into their intentions and therefore into act—are in the central or third heaven, located there according to their

---

b. There are three heavens, a central one, an intermediate one, and an outmost one, or a third, a second, and a first: 684, 8594 *[9594]*, 10270. The different kinds of good also follow in the same triple sequence: 4938, 4939, 9992, 10005, 10017. The good of the central or third heaven is called heavenly, the good of the intermediate or second is called spiritual, and the good of the outmost or first is called spiritual-natural: 4279, 4286, 4938, 4639, 9992, 10005, 10017, 10068.

acceptance of what is good in response to truth. People who do not let such gifts directly into their intentions, but into their memory and from there into their discernment, intending and doing them as a result of this process, are in the intermediate or second heaven. People who live good moral lives, though, and believe in the Divine with no particular interest in learning, are in the outmost or first heaven.[c] We may therefore conclude that the state of our inner natures is what constitutes heaven and that heaven is within each one of us, not outside us. This is what the Lord teaches in saying,

> The kingdom of God does not arrive when we are looking for it, nor do they say, "Here it is," or "There it is." Behold, you have the kingdom of God within you. (Luke 17:20–21)

34   All perfection increases as we move inward and decreases as we move outward, because more inward things are closer to the Lord and intrinsically purer, while more outward things are more remote from the Lord and intrinsically cruder.[d] Angelic perfection consists of intelligence, wisdom, love, and everything good, with happiness as their result. It does not consist in happiness without these former qualities, since happiness without them is merely superficial, with no depth.

Since the inner reaches of angels of the central heaven are opened at the third level, their perfection far surpasses that of angels in the intermediate heaven, whose inner reaches are opened at the second level. By the same token, the perfection of angels of the intermediate heaven surpasses that of angels of the outmost heaven.

35   Because of this difference, an angel of one heaven cannot gain admission to angels of another heaven: someone from a lower heaven cannot come up, nor can someone from a higher heaven come down. Anyone who comes up is seized by anxiety even to the point of pain and cannot

---

c. There are as many levels of life within the human individual as there are heavens, and these are opened after death depending on the way the individual has lived: 3747, 9594. Heaven is within us: 3884. So people who have accepted heaven within themselves in the world enter heaven after death: 10717.

d. More inward things are more perfect because they are closer to the Lord: 3405, 5146, 5147. There are thousands and thousands of things within that outwardly appear to be only a single generality: 5707. To the extent that we are raised from outer concerns toward more inward ones, we come into light and therefore into intelligence, and this ascent is like coming from the fog into clear air: 4598, 6183, 6333 [6313].

see the people who are there, let alone talk with them. Anyone who comes down from a higher heaven loses his or her wisdom, stammers, and loses confidence.

There were some people from the outmost heaven who had not yet been taught that heaven is a matter of angels' deeper qualities, but believed that they would find greater angelic happiness if only they were admitted to the heaven where these angels lived. They were allowed to visit them, but when they arrived, even though there were a great many angels there, they did not see anyone no matter where they looked. The deeper levels of the newcomers had not been opened at the level where the more inward angels lived, so they had no sight. Before long, they were seized by heart pain and eventually could scarcely tell whether they were still alive or not. So they quickly made their way back to the heaven they had come from, and were delighted to be among their own people. They vowed that they would never again crave conditions that were higher than the ones that suited their own way of life.

It is different when the Lord raises people from a lower heaven into a higher one so that they can see its splendor, which happens quite often. Then they are prepared in advance and provided with mediating angels who serve as agents of communication.

We can see from all this that the three heavens are quite distinct from each other.

However, people who live in the same heaven can associate with anyone there, and their delight in getting together is in proportion to the similarity of the values they are devoted to. There will be more about this, though, in later chapters.[51]   **36**

Even though the heavens are so distinct from each other that angels of one heaven cannot have regular dealings with angels of another, still the Lord unites all the heavens by means of a direct and an indirect inflow. The direct inflow is from him into all the heavens, and the indirect is through one heaven into another.[e] In this way, the Lord brings about a unity of the three heavens. They are all linked together, from the First[52] to the last, so that nothing exists that is not connected. Anything that is   **37**

e. The inflow from the Lord is directly from himself and also indirectly through one heaven into another, and the same holds true for us in regard to our more inward processes: 6063, 6307, 6472, 9682, 9683. On the direct inflow of divine [life] from the Lord: 6058, 6474–6478, 8717, 8728. On the indirect inflow through the spiritual world into the natural world: 4067, 6982, 6985, 6996.

not connected to the First by some intermediary does not endure, but disintegrates and becomes nothing.[f]

38   Anyone who does not know how the divine design is arranged in levels cannot grasp how the heavens are distinguished from each other, or for that matter, what the inner person and the outer person are (in an individual). The only idea most people in this world have about inner and outer things is one of continuity, or of a coherence along a continuum from the finer to the coarser. Inner and outer things are not arranged in a continuum, though, but with definite boundaries.

There are two kinds of levels, continuous and noncontinuous. Continuous levels are like decreasing levels of light from a flame, all the way to darkness, or like decreasing amounts of sight from objects in the light to objects in the shade, or like levels of density of the atmosphere from the lowest to the highest. These levels are measured by distance.

[2] Noncontinuous or distinct levels, though, are separated like prior and posterior, cause and effect, producer and product. Anyone who looks closely will discover that there are these kinds of stages of production and composition in everything in the world, no matter what, with one thing arising from another, and a third from that, and so forth.

[3] People who do not acquire a grasp of these levels have no way of knowing how the heavens are arranged or the arrangement of our own deeper and more outward abilities, or the difference between the spiritual world and the natural world, or the difference between our spirit and our body. This also means they cannot understand what correspondences[53] and images[54] are or what inflow is like. People who are attentive only to their physical senses do not grasp these differences, but regard them as instances of increase and decrease on the model of continuous levels.[55] As a result, they cannot think of the spiritual except as a kind of purer natural; so they stand outside, far removed from intelligence.[g]

---

f. All things come into being from things prior to them and therefore from a First. They are maintained in being in the same way, since continuance in being is constant coming into being. Therefore, nothing unconnected exists: 3626, 3627, 3628, 3648, 4523, 4524, 6040, 6056.

g. More inward and more outward realities are not on a continuum, but are arranged in distinct and discrete levels, with each level having a boundary: 3691, 4145 [5145], 5114, 8603, 10099. Each level is formed from another, and things formed in this way are not on a continuum from finer to cruder: 6326, 6465. Anyone who does not understand the difference between more inward and more outward realities according to levels of this kind cannot understand the inner and the outer person or the more inward and more outward heavens: 5146, 6465, 10099, 10181.

Lastly, let me disclose a particular secret about the angels of the three **39** heavens that people have not been aware of until now because they have not understood levels. It is this, that within every angel—and within every one of us here—there is a central or highest level, or a central and highest something, where the Lord's divine life flows in first and most intimately. It is from this center that the Lord arranges the other, relatively internal aspects within us that follow in sequence according to the levels of the overall design. This central or highest level can be called the Lord's gateway to the angels or to us, his essential dwelling within us.

It is this central or highest level that makes us human and distinguishes us from the lower animals, since they do not have it. This is why we, unlike animals, can be raised up by the Lord toward himself, as far as all the deeper levels of our mind and character are concerned. This is why we can believe in him, be moved by love for him, and therefore see him. It is why we can receive intelligence and wisdom, and talk rationally. It is also why we live forever.

However, what is arranged and provided by the Lord at this center does not flow into the open perception of any angel, because it is higher than angelic thought, and surpasses angelic wisdom.

These, then, are some of the general facts about the three heavens. **40** In the following pages, we will need to say more about each heaven in particular.[56]

The Heavens Are Made Up
of Countless Communities

THE angels of any given heaven are not all together in one place, but **41** are separated into larger and smaller communities depending on differences in the good effects of the love and faith they are engaged in. Angels engaged in similar activities form a single community. There is an infinite variety of good activities in heaven, and each individual angel is, so to speak, his or her own activity.[a]

42   The distances between angelic communities in the heavens also vary as their activities vary, in general and in detail. This is because the only cause of distance in the spiritual world is the difference of the state of our more inward natures—in the heavens, then, differences in the state of love. When communities are very different, the distance between them is great; when the difference is slight, the distance is slight. Likeness makes for unity.[b]

43   All the individuals in a single community are distanced from each other by the same principle. The better ones, that is, the ones who are more complete in goodness and therefore in love, wisdom, and intelligence, are in the center. Those who are less outstanding surround them at distances graded in proportion to their lessened perfection. It is like the way light decreases from a center toward a circumference. The ones who are in the middle are in the greatest light, while the ones who are toward the perimeter are in less and less.

44   Kindred souls gravitate toward each other spontaneously, as it were, for with each other they feel as though they are with their own family, at home, while with others they feel like foreigners, as though they were abroad. When they are with kindred souls, they enjoy the fullest freedom and find life totally delightful.

45   We can see from this that the good gathers everyone together in the heavens, and that angels are differentiated by what good they do. Still, it is not the angels who gather themselves, but the Lord, the source of all that is good. He leads them, unites them, differentiates them, and keeps them in freedom to the extent that they are engaged in what is good. So

a. There is an infinite variety, and there is never anything the same as anything else: 7236, 9002. There is an infinite variety in the heavens: 684, 690, 3744, 5598, 7236. The infinite varieties that exist in the heavens are varieties of the good: 3744, 4005, 7236, 7833, 7836, 9002. These varieties arise by means of truths, which are manifold, and which provide individuals with their good: 3470, 3804, 4149, 6917, 7236. As a result, all the communities in the heavens, and all the angels in the communities, are differentiated from each other: 690, 3241, 3519, 3804, 3986, 4067, 4149, 4263, 7236, 7833, 7836. Still, they all act in concert because of love from the Lord: 457, 3986.
b. All the communities of heaven have permanent locations depending on differences in their state of life, therefore depending on their differences in love and faith: 1274, 3638, 3639. Remarkable information about distance, location, place, space, and time in the other life or in the spiritual world: 1273–1277.

he keeps every individual in the life of his or her own love, faith, intelligence, and wisdom—and therefore in happiness.^c

Further, people of similar quality all recognize each other there just the way people in this world recognize their neighbors and relatives and friends, even though they may never have seen each other before. This happens because the only relationships and kinships and friendships in the other life are spiritual ones, and are therefore matters of love and faith.^d

I have often been allowed to see this when I was in the spirit and therefore out of body and in the company of angels. Then some of them looked to me as though I had known them from infancy, while others seemed totally unfamiliar. The ones who looked as though I had known them from infancy were the ones who were in a state like that of my own spirit, while the unfamiliar ones were in dissimilar states.[57]

All the individuals who make up a particular angelic community have a general facial resemblance, but differ in detail. I could grasp this general similarity and particular difference to some extent on the basis of similar situations in this world. We know that every race has a general similarity about the face and eyes that enables us to recognize it and distinguish it from other races, and that the same is even more true from one family to another. This holds true much more perfectly in the heavens, because there all the deeper feelings are visible and shine forth from the face, the face there being their outward and graphic form. It is not possible in heaven to have a face that differs from our feelings.[58]

I have also been shown how this general similarity is varied in detail in the individuals of a single community. There was a kind of angelic face that appeared to me, and this was varied according to the qualities of affections for the good and the true that were characteristic of the individuals in a particular community. These variations lasted quite a while, and through it all I noticed that the same general face remained

c. All freedom is a matter of love and attraction, because whatever we love we do freely: 2870, 3158, 8907 *[8987]*, 8990, 9585, 9591. Since freedom is a matter of love, it is the source of life and joy for every individual: 2873. Nothing seems to be our own unless it comes from freedom: 2880. The very essence of freedom is to be led by the Lord, because in this way we are led by a love for what is good and true: 892, 905, 2872, 2886, 2890, 2891, 2892, 9096, 9586–9591.

d. In heaven, all matters of proximity, family, kindred, and apparent blood relationship arise from what is good and depend on its affinities and differences: 695 *[685]*, 917, 1394, 2739, 3612, 3815, 4121.

constant as a basis, with everything else being simply derivations and elaborations from it. In this way, too, I was shown the affections of the whole community that occasioned the differences in the faces of its members, for as already noted, the faces of angels are their deeper qualities taking form, which means they are forms of the affections proper to their love and faith.

48   This is also why an angel of outstanding wisdom sees the quality of others instantly, from their faces. In heaven, no one can conceal inner character by facial expression and pretend, much less lie and deceive others by guile and hypocrisy.

It does sometimes happen that hypocrites steal into [heavenly] communities, hypocrites trained in hiding their inner nature and arranging their outward appearance in the benevolent form they present in public, thereby misleading angels of light. However, they cannot stay around very long. They begin to feel inner discomfort and torment, their faces start to turn blue, and they almost faint—changes caused by their opposition to the life that is flowing in and affecting them. So they promptly cast themselves back into the hell of people like themselves and no longer dare to climb up again. These are the people meant by the man who was discovered among the dinner guests without a wedding garment and was thrown out into outer darkness (Matthew 22:11[–14]).

49   All the communities communicate with each other, but not through open interaction. Actually, not many individuals leave their own community to go to another, because leaving their community is like leaving themselves or their life and crossing over into another that does not suit them. Rather, they all communicate by the outreach of the auras that emanate from the life of every individual.[59] An aura of life is an aura of affections based in love and faith. This reaches out far and wide into surrounding communities, farther and wider as the affections are deeper and more perfect.[e] Angels possess intelligence and wisdom in proportion to this outreach. The ones who are in the most inward heaven and therefore at the center have an outreach into all of heaven, so that there is a communication of everyone in heaven with each individual and of each

e. A spiritual aura, which is an aura of life, flows out from every person, every spirit, and every angel, and surrounds them: 4464, 5179, 7454, 8630. It flows out from the life of their affection and thought: 2489, 4464, 6206. In angelic communities, the outreach of these auras is proportional to the quality and intensity of their love: 6598–6613 *[6598–6612]*, 8063, 8794, 8797.

individual with everyone.[f] We will have more to say about this outreach below, though, when we discuss the heavenly form in which angelic communities are arranged (and also when we discuss the wisdom and intelligence of angels), for all the outreach of affections and thoughts follows this form.[60]

We have noted above that there are larger and smaller communities in the heavens. The larger ones consist of tens of thousands of individuals, the smaller of some thousands, and the smallest of hundreds. There are even people who live alone, house by house, so to speak, and family by family. Even though they live apart, they are still arranged in the same pattern as those who live in communities, with the wiser of them in the center and the simpler at the periphery. They are very closely under the Lord's guidance, and are the best of angels.

50

Each Community Is a Heaven in Smaller Form and Each Angel a Heaven in Smallest Form

THE reason each community is a heaven in smaller form and each angel a heaven in smallest form is that the activity of love and faith is what makes heaven. This good activity is in every community of heaven and in every angel of a community. It does not matter that this activity is different and distinctive everywhere, it is still the activity of heaven. The only difference is that heaven has one activity here and another there. So whenever anyone is raised into any community of heaven, they say that he or she has arrived in heaven. They say of those who are there that they are in heaven, each in his or her own. All the people who have arrived in the other life realize this; so individuals who are standing outside or below heaven and looking off into the distance where there is a gathering of angels say that heaven is there—and over there as well.

51

f. There is a sharing of everything good in heaven because heavenly love shares everything it has with others: 549, 550, 1390, 1391, 1399, 10130, 10723.

It is rather like the situation of officials and functionaries and servants in a royal palace or court. Even though they live individually in their dwellings or in their rooms, some higher than others, still they are in a single palace or a single court, each one involved in a particular function in the service of the king. We can see from this what is meant by the Lord's saying that "in my Father's house there are many dwellings" (John 14:2) and by "the stories of heaven" and the "heavens of heavens" in the prophets.[61]

52 We may also gather that a community is a heaven in lesser form from the fact that the heavenly form in each community is of the same nature as it is in heaven overall. In heaven overall (as noted above in §43), the most outstanding individuals are in the center, and around them, in decreasing order all the way to the circumference, are those who are less outstanding. It follows also from the fact that the Lord leads all the people in the whole of heaven as though they were a single angel, and does the same for those who are in any particular community. As a result, sometimes a whole angelic community appears as a single entity in the form of an angel, a sight that the Lord has allowed me to see. Further, when the Lord appears in the midst of angels, he does not appear surrounded by a crowd but as a lone individual in angelic form. This is why the Lord is called an angel in the Word, as is also a whole community: Michael, Gabriel, and Raphael are nothing but angelic communities that are given these names because of their functions.[a]

53 Just as a whole community is a heaven in lesser form, so too an angel is a heaven in least form. For heaven is not outside angels but within them. Their deeper levels, the levels of their minds, are arranged in the form of heaven and therefore are arranged to accept all the elements of heaven that are outside them. These elements they accept according to the quality of the goodness that is within them from the Lord. As a result, an angel is also a heaven.[62]

54 It can never be said that heaven is outside anyone. It is within; because every angel accepts the heaven that is outside in keeping with the heaven that is within. We can see, then, how mistaken people are who

a. In the Word, the Lord is called an angel: 6280, 6831, 8192, 9303. A whole community is called an angel, and Michael and Raphael are angelic communities so named because of their functions: 8192. Angelic communities and individual angels do not have particular names, but are identified by the quality of their goodness and by some concept of it: 1705, 1754.

think that getting into heaven is simply a matter of being taken up among the angels, regardless of the quality of their inner life, who believe that heaven is granted merely because of [the Lord's] mercy.[b] On the contrary, unless heaven is within an individual, nothing of the heaven that is outside flows in and is accepted.

There are many spirits who hold this opinion and who, because of their faith, have been taken up into heaven. However, once they arrived, because their inner life was contrary to the life angels are engaged in, they began to be blinded in their understanding to the point that they became virtually idiotic, while in regard to their self-control they began to be so tormented that they carried on like people gone mad. In short, people who have lived evil lives and who arrive in heaven bring their souls with them and are tormented like fish out of water, in the air, or like animals in the vacuum in air pumps once the air has been pumped out.[63] It stands to reason, then, that heaven is within us and not outside.[c]

Since everyone accepts the heaven that is outside according to the quality of the heaven that is within, angels accept the Lord in the same way, because it is the Lord's divine nature that constitutes heaven. Consequently, when the Lord renders himself present in any particular community, his appearance depends on the nature of the good activity that community is engaged in. It is therefore not exactly the same in one community as in another.[64] It is not that this difference is in the Lord: it is in the individuals who are seeing him from their own goodness and therefore in keeping with it. They are affected by the sight of him according to the quality of their own love. The ones who love him deeply are deeply moved, while the ones who love him less deeply are less deeply moved. Evil people, who are outside of heaven, find his presence intensely painful.

When the Lord does appear in any community, he appears there as an angel, but he is identified by the divine quality that shines through.

Further still, heaven is where the Lord is recognized, trusted, and loved. The different ways he is worshiped—in variations that stem from

55

56

---

b. Heaven is not granted out of sheer mercy, but according to our life; and every trace of the life through which we are led into heaven by the Lord is from mercy, which is what "mercy" means: 5057, 10659. If heaven were given by sheer mercy, it would be given to everyone: 2401. Information about some evil people who had been rejected from heaven, and who believed that heaven was granted to everyone out of sheer mercy: 4276 *[4226]*.

c. Heaven is within us: 3884.

the difference of activity from one community to another—do not cause harm but bring benefit, because they are a source of heaven's perfection.

It is hard to explain this in such a way that it can be grasped without resorting to expressions usually found in academic circles and using them to explain how a perfect whole is formed from a variety of elements. Every perfect whole arises from a variety of elements, for a whole that is not composed of a variety of elements is not really anything. It has no form, and therefore no quality. However, when a whole does arise from a variety of elements, and the elements are in a perfected form in which each associates with the next in the series like a sympathetic friend, then it has a perfect quality. Heaven is, then, a single whole composed of a variety of elements arranged in the most perfect form; for of all forms, the form of heaven is the most perfect.

We can see that this underlies all perfection from every instance of beauty, charm, and delight that moves both our senses and our spirits. Such instances arise and flow invariably from a harmonious agreement of many things that are in sympathetic concord, whether they are together simultaneously or follow in a sequence. They do not flow from a single unit that lacks plurality. So we say that variety delights, and recognize that the delight depends on the quality of the variety. We can see from this, as though in a mirror, how perfection stems from variety in heaven as well, since things that happen in the natural world offer us a reflection of things in the spiritual world.[d]

57   We can say the same of the church as we have of heaven, since the church is the Lord's heaven on earth. It also has many components, and yet each is called a church and is a church to the extent that the qualities of love and faith rule within it. In it, the Lord forms a single whole out of the varied elements, and therefore makes a single church out of many churches.[e]

Much the same can be said of the individual member of the church as has been said about the church in general, namely that the church is

d. Every whole arises from a harmony and agreement of many elements, and otherwise would have no quality: 457. The whole heaven is a single entity: 457. This is because all the people there are focused on a single goal, namely the Lord: 9828.

e. If goodness were the essential characteristic of the church and not truth apart from goodness, the church would be one: 1285, 1316, 2982, 3267, 3445, 3451, 3452. Further, all the churches constitute a single church in the Lord's sight because of their quality: 7395 *[7396]*, 9276.

within and not outside, and that anyone is a church in whom the Lord is present in the qualities of love and faith.[f]

Much the same can be said of the individual who has the church within as has been said about the angel who has heaven within, that such an individual is a church in least form as the angel is a heaven in least form. Even more, we can say that the individual who has the church within is a heaven just as much as an angel is, for we have been created to enter heaven and become angels. So anyone who has the quality of goodness from the Lord is an angel-person.[g]

It is worth noting what we have in common with angels and what we possess that they lack. We have in common with angels the fact that our deeper levels are formed in the image of heaven and that we also become images of heaven to the extent that we participate in the qualities of love and faith. What we have that angels lack is that our more outward levels are formed in the image of this world; and that to the extent that we are engaged in what is good, the world within us is subordinated to heaven and serves it;[h] and that then the Lord is present with us on both levels as he is in his heaven. He is actually present on both levels in his divine order, for God is order.[i]

It should be noted in closing that people who have heaven within themselves have heaven not only in their larger or shared aspects but also in their smallest or most specific ones, with the smallest ones in them

58

f. The church is within the individual and not outside, and the church in general is made up of people who have the church within themselves: 3884.

g. The individual who is a church is a heaven in least form, in the image of the greatest, because the deeper levels of his or her mind are arranged in the form of heaven and are therefore arranged for the acceptance of all the elements of heaven: 911, 1900, 1982 [1928], 3624–3631, 3634, 3884, 4041, 4279, 4523, 4524, 4625, 6013, 6057, 9279, 9632.

h. We have an inner and an outer nature, our inner formed from creation in the image of heaven, and our outer in the image of the world, which is why the ancients called the human being a microcosm: 4523, 4524, 5368 [3628], 6013, 6057, 9279, 9706, 10156, 10472. Consequently we have been so created that the world serves the heaven in us, which actually happens in good people: however, the opposite holds true for evil people, in whom heaven is subservient to the world: 9283, 9278.

i. The Lord is order because the divine good and truth that emanate from the Lord constitute order: 1728, 1919, 2201 [2011], 2258, 5110, 5703, 8988, 10336, 10619. Divine truths are laws of order: 2247, 7995. To the extent that we live according to order—that is, to the extent that we are engaged in what is good as determined by divine truths—to that extent we are human and have the church and heaven within us: 4839, 6605, 8067 [8513].

reflecting the largest. The reason for this is that as individuals we are our love and have a quality that depends on the quality of the love that is ruling. Whatever rules flows into the specifics and arranges them, and imposes everywhere an image of itself.ʲ In heaven, it is love for the Lord that rules, because the Lord is loved there above all else. As a result, the Lord is the sum and substance of everything there, flowing into absolutely everything, arranging everything, clothing everything with his likeness, and making heaven to be where he is. So an angel is a heaven in least form, a community a heaven in greater form, and all the communities together a heaven in greatest form. On the Lord's divine nature as constituting heaven, and on his being the sum and substance of heaven, see above, §§7–12.

The Whole Heaven, Grasped as a Single Entity, Reflects a Single Individual

59   IT is a secret not yet known in this world that heaven, taken in a single all-inclusive grasp, reflects a single individual. In heaven, though, nothing is better known. Knowing this, knowing particulars and details about it, is the hallmark of angelic intelligence there. In fact, many other things follow from it and do not come clearly and distinctly to mind without this as their general principle. Since angels do know that all the

---

j. The ruling or controlling love in every individual is found in every single detail of that individual's life and therefore in every single detail of thought and intent: 6159, 7648, 8067, 8853. The quality of each of us depends on the dominant quality of our life: 918, 1040, 1568, 1571 *[?]*, 3570, 6571, 6934 *[6935]*, 6938, 8854, 8856, 8857 *[8858]*, 10076, 10109, 10110, 10284. When love and faith rule, they are within the details of our lives, even though we are not aware of this: 8854, 8864, 8865.

heavens, like their communities, reflect a single individual, they refer to heaven as *the universal and divine human*[a]—"divine" because the Lord's divine nature constitutes heaven (see above, §§7–12).[65]

People who do not have an appropriate concept of spiritual and heavenly realities cannot grasp the fact that heavenly and spiritual realities are arranged and connected in this form and image. They think that the earthly and material elements that make up their outmost form[66] really make them what they are, and that without them they would not be human. Let them know, though, that they are not human beings because of these elements but because they are able to understand what is true and will what is good. These are the spiritual and heavenly realities that make them human.

People do recognize that the humanity of every individual depends on the quality of his or her understanding and intentions. They can also realize that the earthly body is formed to serve them in this world and to perform useful actions in a suitable manner in this outmost sphere of nature. This is also why the body does not do anything on its own, but acts in complete obedience to the bidding of our understanding and intentions. This holds true even to the point that our tongue and mouth say whatever we think, and the body and its limbs do whatever we intend. The actor is therefore our understanding and intention, not the body on its own. We can see from this that matters of our understanding and intention are what make us human, and that these are in a similar form because they act into the very details of the body just the way an inner reality acts into an outer one. It is because of these facts that we are called inner and spiritual humans. Heaven is this kind of person in the greatest and most perfect form.

This is the angelic concept of person, so angels never pay attention to what someone's body is doing, but rather to the intent from which the body is acting. They call this the essential person, together with the intellect to the extent that it is acting in unison with the intent.[b]

60

61

a. Heaven in a single grasp appears in the form of a person, and therefore heaven is called the universal human: 2996, 2998, 3624–3649, 3636–3643, 3741–3745, 4625.

b. Our intent is the essential reality of our life, and our intellect is the ensuing manifestation of that life: 3619, 5002, 9282. The life of our volition is our principal life, and the life of our intellect flows from it: 585, 590, 3619, 7342, 8885, 9282, 10076, 10109, 10110. A person is a person because of volition and consequent intellect: 8911, 9069, 9071, 10076, 10109, 10110.

62   Actually, angels do not see heaven in a single overview in this kind of form, since the entire heaven does not lie within the scope of any angel's sight. However, they do consistently see particular communities that are made up of many thousands of angels as single units in this kind of form; and from the community as a sample they draw their inference about the totality that is heaven. This is because in the most perfect form the greater elements are arranged like the parts, and the parts like the greater elements. The only distinction is between what is greater and what is lesser. Therefore they say that the entire heaven looks like this in the Lord's sight, because the Divine sees everything from the very center and summit.[67]

63   Since heaven is of this nature, it is also governed by the Lord as though it were a single individual and therefore a single unit. We ourselves consist of countless different things, both overall and in our parts. We are made up *overall* of our limbs, organs, and viscera, and *in our parts* of series of nerves, fibers, and blood vessels—made up of members within members, then, and parts within parts. Still, we do of course recognize that when we do anything, we do it as whole individuals. This is what heaven is like, too, under the Lord's guardianship and guidance.

64   The reason so many varied elements act as one in an individual is that there is nothing whatever there that does not contribute something to the common good and do something useful. The inclusive body serves its parts and the parts serve the inclusive body because the inclusive body is made up of parts and the parts make up the inclusive body. So they provide for each other respectively, they focus on each other mutually, and they are united in the kind of form that gives every single component a relationship to the inclusive entity and its well-being. This is what enables them to act as a unit.

[2] It is the same with assemblies in the heavens. People there unite in this kind of form in pursuit of any worthwhile activity. As a result any individuals who do not serve some use for the larger body are cast out of heaven because they are misfits. To "serve some use" is to intend well to others for the sake of the common good, while "not to serve some use" is to intend well to others not for the sake of the common good but for the sake of oneself. People who act in this latter fashion are people who love themselves above all, while people who act in the former fashion are the ones who love the Lord above all. This is why people in heaven act in unison not from themselves but from the Lord. They in fact focus on him as the unique source of all, and on his kingdom as the commonwealth[68] that

is to be cared for. This is the meaning of the Lord's words, "Seek first the kingdom of God and his righteousness, and everything will be given you in addition" (Matthew 6:33). To "seek his righteousness" is to seek his good.[c]

[3] There are people who in this world love the good of their country more than their own and the good of their neighbor as their own. They are the ones who love and seek the kingdom of the Lord in the other life, since there the kingdom of the Lord takes the place of one's country. Further, people who love to do good to others not for self-centered reasons but for the sake of the good itself are people who love their neighbor, since in the other life the good is one's neighbor.[d] All individuals who are of this quality are in the universal human—that is, in heaven.

Since heaven in its entirety does reflect a single individual, and is in fact the divine spiritual person in its greatest form and image, heaven is therefore differentiated into members and parts like a person, and these are given similar names. Angels know what member one community or another is in and say that this community is in the member or province of the head, that one in the member or province of the chest, that one in the member or province of the genitals, and so on.

In general, the highest or third heaven forms the head down to the neck, the middle or second forms the torso as far as the genitals and knees, and the lowest or first forms the feet to the very soles and also the arms all the way to the fingers, since the arms and hands are among our "lowest things" even though they are at our sides. We can see from this again why there are three heavens.

Spirits who are below heaven are amazed when they hear and see that heaven is both below and above them. They have had the faith and opinion common to people in this world that heaven is only overhead. They do not really know that the locations of the heavens are like the locations of the members and organs and viscera in a human being, with some above and some below, and that it is also like the locations of the parts

65

66

c. In the Word, "righteousness" refers to the good and "judgment" to the true, so "to do justice and judgment" is to do what is good and true: 2235, 9857.

d. In the highest sense, the Lord is our neighbor, and so loving the Lord is loving what comes from him, since he is present in everything that comes from him, and therefore what is good and true is also our neighbor: 2425, 3419, 6706, 6711, 6819, 6823, 8123. Therefore, everything good that comes from the Lord is our neighbor, and intending and doing that good is loving our neighbor: 5028, 10336.

within each member and outer or inner organ, with some within and some outside. This is the reason for their confusion about heaven.

67   We have presented these statements about heaven as the universal human because without them as preface there can be no comprehension whatever of the things about heaven that are to follow. No clear concept of heaven can be gained, either, no clear concept of the union of the Lord with heaven, of the union of heaven with us on earth, of the inflow of the spiritual world into the natural world, and none whatever of correspondence, all of which must be discussed in sequence in the pages that now follow. This material has been presented first, then, to shed light on these matters.

Each Community in the Heavens
Reflects a Single Individual

68   SEVERAL times I have been allowed to see that each community of heaven reflects a single individual and is in the likeness of a human being as well. There was one community that was infiltrated by a number of spirits who knew how to assume the guise of angels of light. They were hypocrites. As they were being set apart by some angels, I observed that the whole community first looked like something cloudy, then gradually took on a human form, though still a cloudy one, and finally appeared in the light as a person. The individuals who were in that person and made it up were the ones who participated in the benevolence of that community. The others, who were not in the person and did not make it up, were the hypocrites. These latter were cast out, while the former ones were retained. This is how the separation was accomplished.

Hypocrites are people who speak well and even behave well, but who are focused on themselves in specifics. They talk like angels about the Lord and heaven and love and heavenly life and they also behave well, so that their character seems to be in accord with their speech. However, they are thinking differently. They do not believe anything or will well to anyone but themselves. Any good they do is done in their own interests.

If it is in the interest of others, it is for the sake of appearance, and therefore in their own interest.

I have also been allowed to see that a whole angelic community appears as a single entity in human form when the Lord makes himself present. High up toward the east, there appeared something that looked like a cloud, white at first and then reddening, surrounded by little stars. It came down, and as it gradually did so, it became brighter and finally took on a perfect human form. The little stars that surrounded the cloud were angels, who looked like that because of the light from the Lord.

69

We do need to realize that even though all the individuals in a community of heaven look like a single entity in human likeness when they are all together, still one community is not the same person as any other. They are differentiated like the faces of individuals of one lineage. The reason for this is the same as that given in §47 above, namely that they differ depending on the various good activities that they participate in and that give them their form. Those communities that are in the central or highest heaven and are at its center appear in the most perfect and lovely human form.

70

It is worth noting that the more members there are in a single community and the more united they are in action, the more perfect is their human form. This is because variety arranged in a heavenly form makes perfection, as explained above in §56; and variety occurs where there are many individuals.

71

Every community in heaven is growing in numbers daily, and the more it grows, the more perfect it becomes. In this way, not only is the community perfected, but heaven in general is perfected as well, since the communities constitute heaven.

Since heaven is perfected by its numerical growth, we can see how mistaken people are who believe that heaven will be closed to prevent overcrowding. Actually, it is just the reverse. It will never be closed, and its ever increasing fullness makes it more perfect. So angels long for nothing more than to have new angel guests arrive there.

The reason each community appears in human likeness when it is seen all together as a unit is that heaven as a whole has this likeness, as may be seen in the preceding chapter; and in the most perfect form, like the form of heaven, there is a likeness of parts and whole, of lesser and greatest. The lesser elements and parts of heaven are the communities of which it consists, each of which is a heaven in lesser form, as may be seen above in §§51–58.

72

The reason for this constant likeness is that in the heavens all the qualities stem from a single love and therefore from a single source. The single love that is the origin of everything good in heaven is love for the Lord from the Lord. This is why all heaven is a likeness of him on the grand scale, every community a likeness on a less grand scale, and every angel in specific. See what has been said on this matter above in §58.

Therefore Every Angel Is in Perfect Human Form

73 IT has been explained in the two preceding chapters that heaven as a whole reflects a single individual and that the same holds true for each community in heaven. From the chain of causes presented there, it follows that each single angel reflects the same as well. As heaven is a person in greatest form and a community of heaven is a person in lesser form, so an angel is a person in least form; for in the most perfect form, like the form of heaven, there is a likeness of the whole in the part and of the part in the whole. The reason for this is that heaven is a commonwealth. In fact, it shares everything it has with each individual, and individuals receive everything they have from the commonwealth. An angel is a recipient and therefore a heaven in least form, as has been explained in the relevant chapter above.

To the extent that they accept heaven, people here too are recipients and heavens, and are angels (see §57 above).

This is described in the Book of Revelation as follows: "The wall of the holy Jerusalem was measured, a hundred and forty-four cubits, the measure of an individual, that is, of the angel" (Revelation 21:17). "Jerusalem" in this passage is the Lord's church, and in a more elevated sense, heaven.[a] The wall is the truth that protects it from the assault of false and evil things.[b] "A hundred and forty-four" refers to all good and

---

a. "Jerusalem" is the church: 402, 3654, 9166.
b. A wall is truth protecting from the assault of false and evil things: 6419.

true things as a whole.[c] "Measure" refers to its quality.[d] The human being is where all these things are found, in general and in specific, and therefore where heaven is found; and since an angel is a person as well because of these characteristics, it says "the measure of an individual, that is, of the angel." This is the spiritual meaning of these words. Apart from this meaning, who would understand that the measure of the wall of the holy Jerusalem would be the measure of an individual, which was the measure of the angel?[e]

But let us turn to experience now. As for angels being human forms, or people, this I have seen thousands of times. I have talked with them face to face, sometimes with just one, sometimes with several in a group, and as far as their form is concerned, I have seen in them nothing different from that of a human being. At times I have felt surprised that they were like this; and to prevent it being said that this was some illusion or hallucination, I have been allowed to see them while I was fully awake, or while I was in full possession of my physical senses and in a state of clear perception.

I have often told them that people in the Christian world are in such blind ignorance about angels and spirits that they think of them as minds without form, as mere thoughts, and can conceive of them only as something airy with something alive within it. Further, since they attribute to them nothing human except a capacity for thought, they believe angels cannot see because they have no eyes, cannot hear because they have no ears, and cannot talk because they have no mouths or tongues.

[2] Angels have replied that they know many people on earth have this kind of belief and that it is prevalent among the learned and— strangely!—among the clergy. They have told me that it is because some of the learned who were particularly eminent and who came up with this kind of concept of angels and spirits thought about them on the basis of the sensory faculties of the external person. If people think on this basis

74

---

c. Twelve refers to all true and good things taken together: 577, 2089, 2129, 2130, 3272, 3858, 3913. The same holds for seventy-two and for a hundred and forty-four, because a hundred and forty-four is twelve multiplied by itself: 7973. All the numbers in the Word mean something: 482, 487, 647, 648, 755, 813, 1963, 1988, 2075, 2252, 3252, 4264, 4495, 5265. Multiples have the same meaning as the simple numbers that produce them: 5291, 5335, 5708, 7973.

d. Measurement in the Word means the quality of an entity in regard to truth and good: 3104, 9603.

e. On the spiritual or inner meaning of the Word, see the expository work *The White Horse Described in the Book of Revelation,* and the appendix to *The New Jerusalem and Its Heavenly Doctrine.*

and not on the basis of a more inward light and the common idea native to everyone, they cannot help constructing images like this, because the sensory faculties of the external person grasp only matters that are within the bounds of nature and not things that are higher. So they do not grasp anything at all about the spiritual world.[f] From these eminent people as leaders, false thoughts about angels spread to people who did not think independently but relied on others; and people who let their thinking rely primarily on others and then form their faith, and later look into these matters with their minds, have a hard time giving these ideas up. As a result, many of them cooperate in confirming these false notions.

[3] Angels have also told me that people of simple faith and heart are not caught up in this concept of angels, but have an image of them as people in heaven. This is because they have not let erudition snuff out the image implanted in them from heaven and because they do not grasp anything unless it has some form. This is why the angels we see sculpted and painted in churches are invariably represented as human. As for this "image implanted in them from heaven," angels tell me that it is something divine that flows into people who are intent on goodness of faith and life.

75 On the grounds of all my experience, which has lasted for several years now,[69] I can say with full confidence that in their form, angels are completely human. They have faces, eyes, ears, chests, arms, hands, and feet. They see each other, hear each other, and talk to each other. In short, they lack nothing that belongs to humans except that they are not clothed with a material body. I have seen them in their own light, which is far, far greater than noonday on our earth, and in that light I have seen all the details of their faces more crisply and clearly than I have seen the faces of people here in the world.

I have also been allowed to see an angel of the central heaven. His face was more glorious, more radiant, than that of angels of the lower heavens. I looked at him very closely, and he had a human form in full perfection.

76 It does need to be realized, though, that we cannot see angels with our bodily eyes, only with the eyes of our spirit,[g] because they are in the

---

f. Unless we are raised above the sensory faculties of the outer person, we have little wisdom: 5089. A wise person thinks on a higher level than that of these sensory faculties: 5089, 5094. When we are raised above these sensory faculties, we are in a clearer light and ultimately in a heavenly light: 6183, 6313, 6315, 9407, 9730, 9922. Being raised above and freed from these sensory faculties was a familiar experience for the ancients: 6313.

g. As to our inner levels, we are spirits: 1594. The spirit is the essential person, and it is from the spirit that the body lives: 447, 4622, 6054.

spiritual world while everything bodily is in the natural world. Like sees like because it is of like substance. Further, the body's visual organ, the eye, is so crude that as everyone knows it does not even see the smaller elements of nature without a lens, much less things that are above the sphere of nature, as are all the realities of the spiritual world. These can be seen by us, though, when we are released from bodily sight and the sight of our spirit is opened. This happens instantly when it pleases the Lord that we should see. It then seems to us exactly as though we were seeing with our bodily eyes. This is how angels were seen by Abraham, Lot, Manoah, and the prophets. This is how the Lord was seen by the disciples after the resurrection. This is the same way, too, in which I have seen angels.

Because this was how the prophets saw, they are called "seers" and "ones whose eyes are opened" (1 Samuel 9:9; Numbers 23:3 *[24:3]*); and the act of enabling them to see this way is called "opening the eyes." This is what happened to Elisha's servant, of whom we read, "Elisha prayed, 'Jehovah,[70] open his eyes, I pray, so that he may see,' and as Jehovah opened the eyes of his servant, behold the mountain was full of horses and fiery chariots surrounding Elisha" (2 Kings 6:17).

Some honest spirits I talked with about this were distressed at heart that there was such ignorance in the church about the state of heaven and about spirits and angels. They kept insisting that I should take back the message that they were not formless minds or ethereal breath but human in form, and that they saw and heard and felt just as much as people in this world do.[h]

77

---

h. All angels, being recipients of divine order from the Lord, are in a human form whose perfection and beauty are proportional to their receptivity: 322, 1880, 1881, 3633, 3804, 4622, 4735, 4797, 4985, 5199, 5530, 6054, 9879, 10177, 10594. Divine truth is the means of order and divine good is the essence of order: 2451, 3166, 4390, 4409, 5232, 7256, 10122, 10555.

It Is Owing to the Lord's Divine Human
That Heaven, in Its Entirety and in Its Parts,
Reflects a Person

78 THIS conclusion—that it is owing to the Lord's divine human that heaven, in its entirety and in its parts, reflects a person—follows from all the things that have been presented in the preceding chapters: (1) the Lord is God of heaven [§§2–6]; (2) it is the Lord's divine nature that makes heaven [§§7–12]; (3) the heavens are made up of countless communities, and each community is a heaven in smaller form and each angel a heaven in smallest form [§§41–58]; (4) the whole heaven, grasped as a single entity, reflects a single individual [§§59–67]; (5) each community in the heavens reflects a single individual [§§68–72]; (6) therefore every angel is in perfect human form [§§73–77]. All these propositions lead to the conclusion that because the Divine is what makes heaven, the Divine is human in form.

It may be seen with somewhat greater clarity that this is the Lord's divine human from the references to *Secrets of Heaven* at the close of this chapter, since this collection provides a condensation. It can also be seen from these references that the Lord's human is divine, contrary to the belief in the church that it is not. This may be seen as well from the material about the Lord at the close of *The New Jerusalem and Its Heavenly Teaching*.[71]

79 The truth of this has been witnessed to me by an abundance of experiences, some of which now follow.

None of the angels in the heavens ever sees the Divine in any form except the human form. Even more remarkably, angels in the higher heavens cannot think about what is divine in any other way. They are led into the necessity of thinking this way because of the essential divine that is flowing into them and also because of the form of heaven, which determines how their thoughts reach out around them. In fact, all the thought that angels have spreads out in heaven, and they have intelligence and wisdom in proportion to this outreach. This is why everyone there acknowledges the Lord, since the divine human exists only in him. I have not only been told this by angels, I have been allowed to perceive it when I was raised into a more inward sphere of heaven.

We can see, then, that the wiser angels are, the more clearly they perceive this, which is why the Lord is visible to them. The Lord does appear in a divine angelic form, which is a human form, to people who acknowledge and trust in a visible Divine Being, but not to people who acknowledge and trust in an invisible Divine Being. The former can see the Lord's divine [form], but the latter cannot.

Since angels do not perceive an invisible Divine Being (which they call a formless Divine) but a visible Divine Being in human form, it is common practice for them to say that only the Lord is a person, and that they are people because of him. They also say that each of us is human in proportion to our acceptance of him. By "accepting the Lord" they understand accepting what is good and true that comes from him, because the Lord is present in everything good and true that comes from himself. Angels call this wisdom and intelligence. They say everyone knows that intelligence and wisdom are what make us human, not simply the outward form by itself.

The truth of this is actually visible to angels of the inner heavens. Since the Lord keeps them engaged in what is good and true and therefore in wisdom and intelligence, they are in the loveliest and most perfect human form; while the angels of lower heavens are in a less perfect and lovely form.

Everything is inverted in hell. In heaven's light, the people who are there hardly look human at all. They look like monsters. They are caught up in what is evil and false and not in what is good and true, and are therefore in the opposite of wisdom and intelligence. As a result, their life is not called life, but spiritual death.

Since heaven in its entirety and in its parts does reflect a person because of the Lord's divine human, angels say that they are "in the Lord" and even that they are "in his body," meaning that they are in the very substance of his love. This is also what the Lord is teaching us when he says, "Abide in me, and I in you. As the branch cannot bear fruit on its own unless it abides in the vine, so neither can you unless you abide in me; for without me you can do nothing. Abide in my love. If you keep my precepts, you will abide in my love" (John 15:4–10).

Since this is how the Divine Being is perceived in the heavens, it is instinctive in everyone who accepts any inflow from heaven to think of the Lord in a human guise. The ancients did so and even modern people do, both outside and inside the church. Simple people see him in thought as an ancient one, in glory.

But this instinct has been stifled by all the people who have distanced themselves from the heavenly inflow by pride in their own intelligence and by evil lives. The ones who have stifled it by pride in their intelligence prefer an invisible God, while the ones who have done so by evil lives prefer no God at all. Because this instinct is not in them, neither type knows that it even exists, although this is the essential heavenly divine nature that flows into us first and foremost from heaven because we are born for heaven; and no one enters heaven without some concept of the Divine Being.

83   This is why people who do not share in heaven's concept (that is, in the concept of the Divine Being who makes heaven) cannot be raised even to the first threshold of heaven. The moment any such individuals arrive, they feel a perceptible opposition and forceful resistance. This is because the deeper levels of such people, levels that are intended to accept heaven, are actually closed because they are not in heaven's form. In fact, the nearer such people come to heaven, the more tightly their deeper levels are closed.

This is the lot of people within the church who deny the Lord and who, like the Socinians, deny his divinity.[72] The lot of people who have been born outside the church and who have not acknowledged him or possessed the Word will be seen below.[73]

84   We can tell that the ancients had an image of the Divine as human from the way the Divine appeared to Abraham, Lot, Joshua, Gideon, Manoah and his wife, and others. Even though they saw God as a person, they still worshiped him as God of the universe, calling him "God of heaven and earth" and "Jehovah." In John 8:56, the Lord himself teaches that it was he whom Abraham had seen. We can see that it was the Lord whom others saw from the Lord's words, "No one has seen the Father or his appearance, or heard his voice" (John 1:18; 5:37).

85   But people who judge everything on the basis of their outward senses have great difficulty grasping the fact that God is a person. In fact, the only way sense-centered people can think about the Divine Being is on the basis of this world and what it contains, so they can think about a divine and spiritual person only as they do about a physical and natural one. This leads to the conclusion that if God is to be a person, he must be as big as the universe, and if he does rule heaven and earth, it must be through many underlings the way kings on earth rule. If such individuals are told that in heaven there is not the kind of extended space we have in this world, they do not grasp it at all. People who think on the basis of nature and of its light alone cannot help thinking in terms of the kind of extended space that lies before our eyes. However, they are sadly mistaken when they think the same way about heaven. The "extension" that

exists there is not like that in our world. In our world, it is fixed and therefore measurable, while in heaven it is not fixed and therefore not measurable. There will, though, be more about extension in heaven below, in the chapters on space and time in the spiritual world.[74]

Further, everyone knows how far our eyesight reaches—all the way to the sun and stars, which are so very far away. Anyone who thinks more deeply also knows that the inner sight that pertains to thought reaches even farther, and that still deeper sight reaches still farther. What must we say, then, of the divine sight, which is the deepest and highest of all?

Since thoughts do have this kind of extension, everything of heaven is communicated to everyone there. This means all of the divine nature that makes heaven and fills it, as I have explained in the preceding chapters.

People in heaven are amazed that people here believe they are intelligent when they think of something invisible in the process of thinking about God, something that cannot be comprehended in any form, and that they call people who think otherwise unintelligent and even simpleminded, when the opposite is in fact the case. They assert that if people who regard themselves as intelligent on this account would examine themselves, they would find nature in the place of God—for some, the nature in front of their eyes, for others, a nature they cannot see with their eyes. They would find that they are so blind that they do not know what God is, what an angel is, what a spirit is, what the soul is that will live after death, what the life of heaven is for us, or many other things that are matters of intelligence. Yet all the people whom they call simple know these things in their own way. They have an image of God as a Divine Being in human form, an image of an angel as a heavenly person, a concept of their soul that will live after death as being like an angel, and a concept of the life of heaven for us here as living by the divine commandments. Angels refer to these people as intelligent and fit for heaven, but the others they call unintelligent.

86

References to Passages in *Secrets of Heaven* Concerning the Lord and His Divine Human

[2] The Lord had a divine element from his very conception: 4641, 4963, 5041, 5157, 6716, 10125. Only the Lord had a divine seed: 1438. His soul was Jehovah: 1999, 2004, 2005, 2018, 2025. So the inmost of the Lord was the Divine itself, and its clothing was from his mother: 5041. The Divine itself was the very reality of the Lord's life, and his human nature then emerged and became the manifestation from that reality: 3194, 3210, 10270 *[10269]*, 10372.

[3] Within the church, where there is the Word and where the Lord is known through it, there must be no denial of the Lord's divine nature or of the holy emanation from him: 2359. People within the church who do not acknowledge the Lord have no union with the Divine; it is different for people outside the church: 10205. The essence of the church is to acknowledge the Lord's divine nature and his oneness with the Father: 10083, 10112, 10370, 10738 *[10728]*, 10730, 10816, 10817, 10818, 10820.

[4] The Word has a great deal to say about the Lord's glorification: 10828. This is everywhere in the inner meaning of the Word: 2249, 2523, 3245. The Lord glorified his human nature but not his divine nature, because the latter was intrinsically glorified: 10057. The Lord came into the world to glorify his human nature: 3637, 4286 *[4287]*, 9315. The Lord glorified his human nature by means of the divine love that was within him from conception: 4727. The Lord's love for the whole human race was the Lord's life in this world: 2253. The Lord's love transcends all human understanding: 2077. The Lord saved the human race by glorifying his human: 4180, 10019, 10152, 10655, 10659, 10828. Otherwise, the whole human race would have perished in eternal death: 1676. On the Lord's states of glorification and humiliation: 1785, 1999, 2159, 6866. When "glorification" is attributed to the Lord, it means his human becoming one with the Divine, and "glorifying" means "making divine": 1603, 10053, 10828. When the Lord glorified his human, he laid aside the human he had received from his mother so completely that he was no longer her son: 2159, 2574, 2649, 3036, 10829 *[10830]*.

[5] The Son of God from eternity was the divine truth in heaven: 2628, 2798, 2803, 3195, 3704. The Lord also made his human nature

divinely true from the divine good that was in him when he was in the world: 2803, 3194, 3195, 3210, 6716, 6864, 7014, 7499, 8127, 8724, 9199. The Lord then arranged everything within himself in the heavenly form that accords with divine truth: 1928, 3633. Therefore the Lord is called the Word, which is divine truth: 2533, 2818 *[2813]*, 2859, 2894, 3393, 3712. Only the Lord possessed perception and thought from himself and above all angelic perception and thought: 1904, 1914, 1915 *[1919]*.

The Lord made the divine truth that was himself one with the divine good that was in himself: 10047, 10052, 10076. This uniting was reciprocal: 2004, 10067. [6] When the Lord left this world, he also made his human divinely good: 3194, 3210, 6864, 7499, 8724, 9199, 10076. This is what is meant by "going out from the Father" and "returning to the Father": 3194, 3210. This is how he became one with the Father: 2751, 3704, 4766. Since this union, divine truth emanates from the Lord: 3704, 3712, 3969, 4577, 5704, 7499, 8127, 8241, 9199, 9398. Examples of the way divine truth emanates: 7270, 9407. The Lord united his human to his divine nature by his own power: 1616, 1749, 1753 *[1752]*, 1813, 1921, 2025, 2026, 2523, 3141, 5005, 5045, 6716. It therefore stands to reason that the Lord's human nature was not like the human nature of any other person, because it was conceived by the Divine itself: 10125, 10826. His union with the Father, who was the source of his soul, was not like a union between two entities, but like that between soul and body: 3737, 10824.

[7] The earliest people were not able to worship a divine reality but a divine manifestation, which is the divine human; so the Lord came into the world in order to become the divine manifestation from the divine reality: 4687, 5321. The early people acknowledged the Divine because it appeared to them in human form, and this form was the divine human: 5110, 5663, 6846, 10737. The infinite reality cannot flow into heaven among angels or into people on earth except through the divine human: 1646 *[1676]*, 1990, 2016, 2035 *[2034]*. In heaven, no other Divine is perceived except the divine human: 6475, 9303, 9267 *[9315, 9356]*, 10067. The divine human from eternity was the divine truth in heaven and the divine nature passing through heaven; so it was the divine manifestation, which later, in the Lord, became the divine reality in its own right, the source of the divine manifestation in heaven: 3061, 6280, 6880, 10579. What the state of heaven was like before the Coming of the Lord:[75] 6371, 6372, 6373. The Divine was not perceptible except as it passed through heaven: 6982, 6996, 7004.

[8] The inhabitants of all the planets worship the Divine in human form—therefore, the Lord: 6700, 8541–8547, 10736, 10737, 10738. They are overjoyed when they hear that the Lord actually became a human:

9361. The Lord accepts everyone who is involved in what is good and worships the Divine in human form: 9359. It is impossible to think about God except in human form, and what is incomprehensible does not accord[76] with any concept, so it does not accord with any faith: 9359, 9972. We can worship something of which we have some concept, but not something of which we have no concept: 4733, 5110, 5633 *[5663]*, 7211, 9267 *[10067]*, 10267. Therefore by most people worldwide the Divine is worshiped in human form; and this is the case because of an inflow from heaven: 10159. When people who are engaged in what is good in their behavior think about the Lord, they think about a divine human, and not about some human separated from the Divine. It is different for people who are not engaged in what is good in their behavior: 2326, 4724, 4731, 4766, 8878, 9193, 9198. The people nowadays who think about the Lord's human apart from the Divine are the ones in the church who are engaged in evil in their behavior and those who are in faith separated from thoughtfulness; also some reasons why they do not grasp what the divine human is: 3212, 3241, 4689, 4692, 4724, 4731, 5321, 6372 *[6872]*, 8878, 9193, 9198. The Lord's human was divine because he had his soul from the very reality of the Father; illustrated by the resemblance of a father in his children: 10270 *[10269]*, 10372, 10823. Also because it came from divine love, which was the very reality of his life from conception: 6872. The nature of every individual is determined by his or her deepest love; and each of us is his or her own deepest love: 6872, 10177, 10284. The Lord made his whole human nature divine—both its inward and its outward constituents: 1603, 1815, 1902, 1926, 2093, 2803 *[2083]*. So, unlike any other person, he rose with his whole body: 1729, 2083, 5078, 10825.

[9] The divinity of the Lord's human is recognized in his omnipresence in the Holy Supper: 2343, 2359. It is also recognized in his transfiguration before the three disciples; 3212, and also from the Word of the Old Testament, where he is called "God": 10154; and where he is called "Jehovah": 1603, 1736, 1815, 1902, 2921, 3035, 5110, 6281, 6303, 8864, 9194, 9315. In the literal meaning, a distinction is made between Father and Son or between Jehovah and the Lord, but this is not the case in the inner meaning of the Word that angels attend to: 3035. In the Christian world, the Lord's human is not recognized as divine, a situation that has come about in order that the pope might be recognized as his vicar: 3035 *[4738]*.

[10] Some Christians in the other life were examined to determine what kind of concept of the one God they had, and it was discovered that they had a concept of three gods: 2329, 5256, 10736, 10737, 10738,

10821. A trinity or divine trine in one person—and therefore a single God—is conceivable, but a trinity in three persons is not: 10738, 10821, 10824. A divine trine in the Lord is acknowledged in heaven: 14, 15, 1729, 2005 *[2004]*, 5256, 9303. The trine in the Lord is the essential divine nature called the Father, the divine human called the Son, the emanating[77] Divine called the Holy Spirit, and this divine trine is one: 2149, 2156, 2288, 2321 *[2319]*, 2329, 2447, 3704, 6993, 7182, 10738, 10822, 10823. The Lord himself teaches that the Father and he are one: 1729, 2004, 2005, 2018, 2025, 2751, 3704, 3736, 4766; and the holy Divine emanates from him and is his: 3969, 4673, 6788, 6993, 7499, 8127, 8302, 9199, 9228, 9229, 9270 *[9264]*, 9407, 9818, 9820, 10330.

[11] The divine human flows into heaven and makes heaven: 3038. The Lord is everything in heaven, and is heaven's life: 7211, 9128. The Lord dwells among angels in what is his: 9338, 10125, 10151, 10157. So people who are in heaven are in the Lord: 3637, 3638. The union of the Lord with angels takes place according to their acceptance of the quality of love and thoughtfulness from him: 904, 4198, 4206 *[4205]*, 4211, 4320 *[4220]*, 6280, 6832, 7042, 8819, 9680, 9682, 9683, 10106, 10811 *[10810]*. The whole heaven corresponds directly to the Lord: 551, 552. The Lord is the common center of heaven: 3633. Everyone there turns toward the Lord, who is above the heavens: 9828, 10130, 10189. However, angels do not turn themselves toward the Lord; rather, the Lord turns them toward himself: 10189. There is no presence of angels with the Lord, but there is a presence of the Lord with angels: 9415. There is no union with the essential Divine in heaven, but there is with the divine human: 4211, 4724, 5633 *[5663]*.

[12] Heaven corresponds to the Lord's divine human, and heaven overall is therefore like a single person; and therefore heaven is called the universal human: 2996, 2998, 3624–3649, 3636–3643, 3741–3745, 4625. The Lord is the only person, and only those who accept something divine from him are human: 1894. To the extent that they do so accept, they are human beings and images of him: 8547. Therefore angels are forms of love and thoughtfulness in human form, which is [given] by the Lord: 3804, 4735, 4797, 4985, 5199, 5530, 9879, 10177.

[13] The whole heaven belongs to the Lord: 2751, 7086. He has all power in the heavens and on earth: 1607, 10089, 10827. Because the Lord rules the entire heaven, he also rules everything that depends on it—therefore everything in the world: 2026, 2027, 4523, 4524. The Lord alone possesses the power to move the hells away from us, restrain us from evils and keep us in good, and thus to save us: 10019.

There Is a Correspondence of Everything in Heaven with Everything in the Human Being

87 PEOPLE today do not know what "correspondence" is. There are many reasons for this ignorance, the primary one being that we have moved away from heaven because of our love for ourselves and for the world. You see, people who love themselves and the world above all focus on nothing but earthly matters because these provide gratification to their more outward senses and pleasure to their moods. They do not attend to spiritual matters because these offer gratification to their deeper senses and pleasure to their minds. So they set such matters aside, saying that they are too lofty to think about.

The early people behaved differently. For them, knowledge about correspondences was the pearl[78] of all knowledge. By means of it, they gained intelligence and wisdom, and by means of it those who were of the church had a communication with heaven. Knowledge about correspondences is in fact angelic knowledge.

The earliest ones, who were heavenly people, did their thinking from correspondence like angels, so they could even talk with angels. Further, the Lord was quite often visible to them, and taught them. Nowadays, though, this knowledge has been so completely lost that people do not know what correspondence is.[a]

88 Now, without some grasp of what correspondence is, nothing can be known in clear light about the spiritual world or about its inflow into the natural world, nothing at all about what the spiritual is relative to the natural, nothing in clear light about the human spirit that is called "the soul" and how it affects the body inwardly, nothing about our state after death. Because of all this, I need to define it and explain what it is like. This will also pave the way for matters that are to follow.

89 First, I need to state what correspondence is. The whole natural world is responsive[79] to the spiritual world—the natural world not just in general, but in detail. So whatever arises in the natural world out of the

---

a. How superior a knowledge of correspondences is to other knowledge: 4280. The primary knowledge of the ancients was the knowledge of correspondences, but today this has been blotted out: 3021, 3419, 4280, 6749 *[4749]*, 4844, 4964, 4965 *[4966]*, 6004, 7729, 10252. The knowledge of correspondences flourished among those in the Near East and Egypt: 5702, 6692, 7097, 7779, 9391, 10407.

spiritual one is called "something that corresponds." It needs to be realized that the natural world arises from and is sustained in being by the spiritual world, exactly the way an effect relates to its efficient cause.

By "the natural world," I mean all that extended reality[80] that is under our sun[81] and that receives its light and warmth from it. All the things that are sustained in being from that source belong to that world. The spiritual world, in contrast, is heaven, and to that world belong all the things that are in the heavens.

Since a human being is a heaven *and* a world in least form in the image of the greatest (see §57 above), there is a spiritual world and a natural world within each of us. The deeper elements, which belong to our minds and relate to our intelligence and volition, constitute our spiritual world, while the outer elements, which belong to our bodies and relate to our senses and actions, constitute our natural world. Anything that occurs in our natural world (that is, in our bodies and their senses and actions) because of our spiritual world (that is, because of our minds and their intelligence and volition) is called something that corresponds. **90**

We can see in the human face what correspondence is like. In a face that has not been taught to dissimulate, all the affections of the mind manifest themselves visibly in a natural form, as though in their very imprint, which is why we refer to the face as "the index of the mind." This is our spiritual world within our natural world. Similarly, elements of our understanding are manifest in our speech, and matters of our volition in our physical behavior. So things that occur in the body, whether in our faces or in our speech or in our behavior, are called correspondences. **91**

We can also see from this what the inner person is and what the outer person is, namely, that the inner is the one that is called the spiritual person, and the outer the natural person. We can also see that they are as distinct from each other as heaven and earth, and that everything that happens and comes forth in the outer or natural person does so from the inner or spiritual one. **92**

We have been talking about the correspondence of our inner or spiritual person with our outer or natural one. In what follows, though, we need to discuss the correspondence of heaven in its entirety with the individual human being. **93**

It has already been explained that heaven in its totality reflects a single person, and that it is a person in image and is therefore called the universal human. It has also been explained that for this reason, the heavenly communities that make up heaven are arranged like the members, organs, and viscera in a human being. So there are communities that are located in the head, in the chest, in the arms, and in the particular parts of **94**

these members (see above, §§59–72). The communities that are in a particular member, then, correspond to the like member in a human being.
For example, the ones in the head in heaven correspond to our head, the
ones in the chest there correspond to our chest, the ones in the arms correspond to our arms, and so on for the rest. We continue in existence
because of this correspondence, for heaven is the only basis of our continued existence.

95 The differentiation of heaven into two kingdoms, one called the
heavenly kingdom and the other the spiritual kingdom, has been presented in its proper chapter above.[82] The heavenly kingdom in general
corresponds to the heart and to all the extensions of the heart throughout
the body. The spiritual kingdom corresponds to the lungs and to all their
extension throughout the body. Further, the heart and the lungs form
two kingdoms in us, the heart governing through the arteries and veins
and the lungs through the nerve and motor fibers, each involved in every
effort and action.

Within each one of us, in the spiritual world of ours that is called our
spiritual person, there are also two kingdoms. One is volitional and the
other is cognitive, the volitional governing through affections for what is
good and the cognitive through affections for what is true. These kingdoms also correspond to the kingdoms of the heart and lungs in the
body. The same holds true in the heavens. The heavenly kingdom is
heaven's volitional side, where the good that flows from love rules. The
spiritual kingdom is heaven's cognitive side, where truth rules. These are
what correspond to the functions of the heart and the lungs in us.

It is because of this correspondence that "the heart" in the Word
means volition and the good of love, while "the breath of the spirit"
means understanding and the truth of faith. This is also why we ascribe
feelings to the heart, even though they do not reside or originate there.[b]

96 The correspondence of heaven's two kingdoms with the heart and
lungs is the general correspondence of heaven with the human being.

b. On the correspondence of the heart and the lungs with the universal human that is heaven,
based on experience: 3883–3896. The heart corresponds to people who are in the heavenly kingdom, while the lungs correspond to people in the spiritual kingdom: 3685 [3885], 3886, 3887. In
heaven there is a pulse like that of the heart and a breathing like that of the lungs, but on a deeper
level: 3884, 3885, 3887. The heartbeat there varies depending on states of love, and the breathing
varies depending on states of charity and faith: 3886, 3887, 3889. "The heart" in the Word is volition, so what comes from the heart is what comes from volition: 2930, 7542, 8910, 9113, 10336. So
too, the heart in the Word means love, so what comes from the heart comes from love: 7542,
9050, 10336.

The less general correspondence, though, is with the specific members, organs, and viscera, and we need to note what this is like as well.[83]

People who are in the head in the universal human that is heaven are supremely involved in everything good. In fact, they are in love, peace, innocence, wisdom, intelligence, and therefore in delight and happiness. These flow into the head and into the components of the head in us, and correspond to them.

People who are in the chest of the universal human that is heaven are involved in the qualities of thoughtfulness and faith, and also flow into our chests and correspond to them. However, people who are in the groin of the universal human or heaven and in the organs dedicated to reproduction are in marriage love.[84]

People who are in the feet are in the outmost heaven, which is called "natural-spiritual good." People who are in the arms and hands are in the power of what is true because of what is good. People who are in the eyes are in understanding; people who are in the ears are in attentiveness and obedience; people who are in the nostrils are in perception; people in the mouth and tongue in conversing from discernment and perception.

People who are in the kidneys are in truth that probes and discriminates and purifies; people in the liver, pancreas, and spleen are in various aspects of purification of what is good and true; and so on. They flow into the like parts of the human being and correspond to them.

The inflow of heaven is into the functions and uses of these members, and since the uses originate in the spiritual world, they take form by means of elements characteristic of the natural world and thus make themselves known in their effects. This is the origin of correspondence.

This is why these same members, organs, and viscera in the Word mean similar things. Everything there actually has meaning according to its correspondence. The head there means intelligence and wisdom, the chest thoughtfulness, the groin marriage love, the arms and hands the power of truth, the feet what is natural, the eyes discernment, the nostrils perception, the ears obedience, the kidneys the probing of truth, and so on.[c]

97

---

c. The chest in the Word means charity: 3934, 10081, 10087. The loins and reproductive organs mean marriage love: 3021, 4280, 4462, 5050, 5051, 5052. The arms and hands mean the power of truth: 878, 3091, 4931–4937, 6947, 7205, 10017 [10019]. The feet mean the natural: 2162, 3147, 3761, 3986, 4280, 4938–4952. The eyes mean discernment: 2701, 4403–4421, 4523–4534, 6923, 9051, 10569. The nostrils mean perception: 3577, 4624, 4625, 4748, 5621, 8286, 10054, 10292. The ears mean obedience: 2542, 3869, 4523, 4653, 5017, 7216, 8361, 8990, 9311, 9396 [9397], 10061. The kidneys mean probing and purification of what is true: 5380–5386, 10032.

This is also why people commonly say that someone has a good head when they are talking about someone intelligent and wise, why they talk about a truly thoughtful person as a bosom friend, a particularly perceptive individual as having a keen nose, a discriminating one as sharp-sighted,[85] someone in power as having a long arm,[86] someone who acts intentionally from love as acting from the heart—these and many other expressions in human language come from correspondence. The expressions actually originate in the spiritual world, though people are unaware of it.

98 The reality of this kind of correspondence of everything in heaven with everything in us has been shown me by a great deal of experience—by so much, in fact, that I am as convinced of this as I am of anything that is so obvious as to be beyond doubt. There is no need to append all the evidence here, though, and there is too much to include. The reader may see some included in *Secrets of Heaven* where correspondences, representations, the inflow of the spiritual world into the natural, and the interaction of soul and body are dealt with.[d]

99 Even though we completely correspond physically to all of heaven, we are still not images of heaven in outward form, but only in inward form. Our deeper reaches are receptive of heaven, while our more outward ones are receptive of this world. To the extent, then, that those deeper reaches do accept heaven we are heavens in least form, in the image of the greatest; but to the extent that our deeper reaches are not receptive, we are not heavens or images of the greatest. Nevertheless, our more outward aspects, which are receptive of the world, may be in some form that is determined by the world, and therefore in more or less beauty. Outward, physical beauty has its origins in our parents and from our formation in the womb, and thereafter is maintained by a general inflow from the world. This is why our natural form differs markedly from our spiritual form.

I have been shown at times what a spiritual person is like in form, and I have seen that in some people who were lovely and attractive in physical appearance that inner form was misshapen, black, and grotesque—what you would call an image of hell rather than of heaven;

d. On the correspondence of all the members of our bodies with the universal human or heaven, in general and in detail, based on experience: 3021, 3624–3649, 3741–3751 *[3741–3750]*, 3883–3896, 4039–4051 *[4039–4054]*, 4218–4228, 4318–4331, 4403–4421, 4523–4534, 4622–4633, 4652–4660, 4791–4805, 4931–4953, 5050–5061, 5171–5189, 5377–5396, 5552–5573, 5711–5727, 10030. On the inflow of the spiritual world into the natural world, or of heaven into earth, and the inflow of the soul into all the elements of the body, based on experience: 6053–6058, 6189–6215, 6307–6327, 6466–6495, 6598–6626. On the interaction of the soul and the body, based on experience: 6053–6058, 6189–6215, 6307–6327, 6466–6495, 6598–6626.

while in some who were not beautiful, the inner form was graceful, radiant, and angelic. After death, our spirit looks the way it actually did within the body while we were living in it in this world.

Correspondence, though, extends to much more than human beings. **100** There is a correspondence of the heavens with each other. The second or intermediate heaven is responsive to the third or central one, the first or outmost heaven is responsive to the second or intermediate one, and this is responsive to the physical forms in us, the forms that are referred to as our members, organs, and viscera. So it is our bodily nature in which heaven finally comes to rest, on which it stands like a foundation. But this mystery will be explored further elsewhere.[87]

It is absolutely necessary to realize, though, that all correspondence **101** with heaven is correspondence with the Lord's divine human, because heaven is from him and because he is heaven, as has been explained in the preceding chapters. For unless the divine human flowed into every bit of heaven and, in accord with correspondences, into every bit of our world, there would be no angels and none of us.

Again then, we can see from this why the Lord became an individual on earth and clothed his divine nature with a human nature from first to last. This happened because the divine human on which heaven depended before the Coming of the Lord[88] was no longer adequate to sustain everything, since we, the foundation of heaven, had undermined and destroyed the design.

In the passages referred to at the close of the preceding chapter you may see what the divine human before the Coming of the Lord was and what its nature was, as well as the quality of the state of heaven then.

Angels are stunned when they hear that there are people who credit **102** everything to nature and nothing to the Divine, as well as people who believe that their bodies, in which so many wonders of heaven are gathered, are fashioned out of nature, and even that this is the source of our rational capacity. On the contrary, if people would just raise their minds a little, they could see that things like this come from the Divine and not from nature, and that nature was created simply to clothe the spiritual and responsively represent it on the lowest level of the design. They compare such people to owls, which see in darkness, but see nothing in the light.

There Is a Correspondence
of Heaven with
Everything Earthly

103   IN the preceding chapter, we have stated what correspondence is, and have explained as well that absolutely everything in the soul's body is a correspondence. Next in orderly sequence we need to explain that everything earthly and in general everything in our world is a correspondence.[89]

104   All earthly things are differentiated into three classes that we call "kingdoms," namely the animal kingdom, the vegetable kingdom, and the mineral kingdom. Members of the animal kingdom are correspondences[90] on the first level because they are alive. Members of the vegetable kingdom are correspondences on the second level because they merely grow. Members of the mineral kingdom are correspondences on the third level because they neither live nor grow.

The correspondences in the animal kingdom are the living creatures of various kinds, both those that walk and creep on the earth and those that fly in the air. We need not list them by name, because they are familiar. Correspondences in the vegetable kingdom are all the things that grow and bloom in gardens and forests and farms and meadows, which again are so familiar that they need not be listed by name. Correspondences in the mineral kingdom are metals noble and base, stones precious and common, and soils of various kinds, as well as bodies of water. Beyond these, things made from these elements by human industry for our use are correspondences, things such as foods of all kinds, garments, houses, major buildings, and so on.

105   Things that are above the earth are also correspondences, things like the sun, the moon, and the stars, and also things that occur in our atmospheres like clouds, mists, rainstorms, lightning bolts, and thunderclaps. The emanations of the sun in its presence and absence like light and shade, warmth and cold, are also correspondences; and so are such corollaries as the times of the year called spring, summer, fall, and winter, and the times of the day—morning, noon, evening, and night.

In a word, absolutely everything in nature, from the smallest to the **106** greatest, is a correspondence.[a] The reason correspondences occur is that the natural world, including everything in it, arises and is sustained from the spiritual world, and both worlds come from the Divine. We say that it also is sustained because everything is sustained from that from which it arose, enduring being in fact a perpetual arising;[91] and since nothing can endure independently, but needs something prior, it therefore needs a First, and if it were separated from that First, it would utterly perish and disappear.

Everything is a correspondent that arises and endures in nature ac- **107** cording to the divine design. What makes the divine design is the divine good that emanates from the Lord. It begins from him, emanates from him through the heavens in sequence into the world, and there comes to a close in things most remote. Things there that are in accord with the design are correspondences. The things that are in accord with the design are everything that is good and is perfected for some use, for everything good is good according to its usefulness. Its form reflects what is true because the true is the form of the good. This is why everything in the whole world and in the world of nature that is in the divine design goes back to what is good and what is true.[b]

The fact that everything in this world arises from the Divine and is **108** clothed with the kinds of elements in nature that enable it to be present there, serve some use, and therefore correspond, follows clearly from lit- tle things we can observe in both the animal and the vegetable kingdoms. In each there are things that anyone, with some deeper thought, can see must come from heaven. By way of illustration I may mention only a few out of the countless many.

First, some from the animal kingdom. In this field, many people real- ize what kind of knowledge is virtually instinctive in any creature you

---

a. Everything in the world and its three kingdoms corresponds to heavenly things that are in heaven; or things in the natural world correspond to things in the spiritual world: 1632, 1881, 2758, 2890–2893 *[2990–2993]*, 2897–3003 *[2987–3003]*, 3213–3227, 3483, 3624–3649 *[3624–3639]*, 4044, 4053, 4116, 4366, 4939, 5116, 5377, 5428, 5477, 9280. Through correspondences, the natural world is united with the spiritual world: 8615. So nature in its entirety is a theater portraying the Lord's kingdom: 2758, 2999, 3000, 3483, 4938, 4939, 8848, 9280.

b. Everything in both heaven and this world that is in accord with the design goes back to what is good and what is true: 2451, 3166, 4390, 4409, 5232, 7256, 10122; and to the union of the two, if it is actually to be anything: 10555.

choose. Bees know how to collect honey from flowers, build cells from wax in which they store their honey, and so provide food for themselves and their families for the coming winter. Their queen lays eggs, while the others cover them over and lead her around so that a new generation may be born. They live under a kind of government that all their members know instinctively, protecting their useful members and expelling the useless ones and clipping off their wings. There are even more marvels that are given them from heaven for their use. In fact, their wax serves the human race throughout the world for candles, and their honey for flavoring foods.

[2] Then what about caterpillars, the lowest creatures in the animal kingdom! They know how to nourish themselves with the sap of their leaves and in due time how to make a covering around themselves and virtually put themselves in a womb and so to hatch offspring of their own species. Some first turn into nymphs and chrysalides and make threads, and after exhausting labor grace themselves with new bodies and adorn themselves with wings. Then they fly in the air as though it were their heaven, celebrate their "weddings," lay their eggs, and so provide themselves with a posterity.

[3] Over and above these particular examples, all the fowl of the air know the foods that are good for them—not only what they are, but where they are. They know how to construct nests for themselves, each species differently from all others, how to lay their eggs there, incubate them, hatch and feed their chicks, and expel them from the nest when they can be on their own. They also know the particular enemies they must avoid and the allies they can associate with, all from earliest infancy. I will say nothing about the wonders in the eggs themselves, where everything necessary for the formation and nourishment of the embryonic chicks lies properly available, or countless other wonders.

[4] Will anyone who thinks with any rational wisdom say that such things arise from any source but a spiritual world, a world that the natural world serves by clothing what comes from it with a body, or presenting in effect that which is spiritual in origin?

The reason why earthbound animals and the fowl of the air are born into all this knowledge while we, who are actually superior, are not, is that animals are in the proper pattern of their life and cannot destroy what is within them from the spiritual world because they are not rational. It is different for us, who think from the spiritual world. Because we have corrupted ourselves by living contrary to the design that reason itself has recommended to us, we cannot escape being born into total ignorance, so that we can be led from there, by divine means, back into the pattern of heaven.

We can deduce how members of the vegetable kingdom correspond **109** from a multitude of instances—for example, from the fact that tiny seeds grow into trees, beget leaves, produce flowers and then fruits in which they place another generation of seeds, and that these things happen in a sequence and emerge all together in such a wondrous design that there is no way to describe it briefly. It would take volumes, and still there would be deeper mysteries suited to their uses that our knowledge could not compass.

Because these things stem from the spiritual world or heaven, which is in a human form (as was explained in the appropriate chapter above [§§78–86]), it is also true that the details of that kingdom have a kind of relationship to human characteristics—a fact that is recognized by some individuals in the learned world.

It has become clear to me from a great deal of experience that everything in that kingdom is also a correspondence. Very often, when I have looked over trees and fruits and flowers and vegetables in gardens, I have become aware of corresponding things in heaven. Then I have talked with nearby people there and have learned where these plants were from and what their characteristics were.

Nowadays, though, no one can know about the spiritual things in **110** heaven to which natural things in the world correspond except from heaven, because the knowledge of correspondence has now been completely lost. I should like to present a few examples to show what the correspondence of spiritual things with natural ones is like.

In general, earth's living creatures correspond to affections, the mild and useful ones to good affections, the fierce and useless ones to evil affections. Specifically, cattle and calves correspond to affections of the natural mind, sheep and lambs to affections of the spiritual mind. Flying creatures, species by species, correspond to cognitive activities of either level of the mind.[c] This is why various animals such as cattle, calves,

---

c. By reason of correspondence, animals refer to affections; mild and useful animals to good affections, fierce and useless ones to evil affections: 45, 46, 142, 143, 246, 714, 716, 719, 2179, 2180, 3519, 9280; illustrated by experience drawn from the spiritual world: 3218, 5198, 9090. On the inflow of the spiritual world into the lives of animals: 1633, 3646. By reason of correspondence, cattle and calves refer to affections of the natural mind: 2180, 2566, 9391, 10132, 10407. What birds mean: 4169, 4809. What lambs mean: 3994, 10132. Flying creatures mean cognitive activities: 40, 745, 776, 778, 866, 988, 993 [991], 5149, 7441; varied as indicated by their genera and species, based on experience in the spiritual world: 3219.

rams, sheep, male and female goats, male and female lambs, as well as pigeons and turtle doves were accepted for holy use in the Israelite church, which was a representative church.[92] They used them for their sacrifices and burnt offerings, and in these uses they did in fact correspond to spiritual realities that are understood in heaven in accord with their correspondence.

The reason animals are affections, according to their genera and species, is that they are alive, and the only source of the life of any creature is from affection and is in proportion to it. We humans are like animals as far as our natural person is concerned, which is why we are compared to them in colloquial usage. For example, we call a gentle person a sheep or a lamb, a violent one a bear or a wolf, a crafty one a fox or a snake, and so on.

111 There is a similar correspondence with things in the vegetable kingdom. A garden, in general terms, corresponds to heaven in respect to intelligence and wisdom, which is why heaven is called the garden of God and a paradise,[d] and why we call it a heavenly paradise.

Trees, species by species, correspond to perceptions and firsthand knowledge of what is good and true, which yield intelligence and wisdom. So the early people, who were absorbed in the knowledge of correspondences, held their holy worship in groves.[e] This is why trees are mentioned so often in the Word and why heaven, the church, and people are compared to them—to the vine, for example, the olive, the cedar, and others—and the good we do is compared to fruit.

Further, the foods we derive from them, especially the ones we get from crops planted in fields, correspond to affections for what is good and true because they nourish our spiritual life the way earthly foods nourish our natural life.[f]

Bread, generally speaking, corresponds to an affection for whatever is good because it is the mainstay of life and because it is used to mean all

d. By reason of correspondence, a garden or paradise means intelligence and wisdom: 100, 108; from experience: 3220. Everything that corresponds has the same meaning in the Word as well: 2890 [2896], 2987, 2989, 2990, 2971 [2991], 3002, 3225.

e. Trees mean perceptions and experiential knowledge: 103, 2163, 2682, 2722, 2972, 7692. So the early people held their divine worship in groves, under particular trees depending on their correspondence: 2722, 4552. On the inflow of heaven into members of the vegetable kingdom; for example, into trees and small plants: 3648.

f. By reason of correspondence, foods mean the kind of things that nourish our spiritual life: 3114, 4459, 4792, 4976, 5147, 5293, 5340, 5342, 5410, 5426, 5576, 5582, 5588, 5656 [5655], 5915, 6277, 8562, 9003.

food. It is because of this correspondence that the Lord calls himself the bread of life; and it is also because of this that bread was put to holy use in the Israelite church—they did in fact place bread on the table in the tabernacle and called it "the bread of presence."[93] Then too, all divine worship that they performed by sacrifices and burnt offerings was called "bread." Because of this correspondence too, the most sacred worship in the Christian church is the Holy Supper, in which bread and wine are shared.[g]

From these few examples, we can infer what correspondence is like.

We may note briefly how the union of heaven with the world occurs by means of correspondences. The Lord's kingdom is a kingdom of purposes that are functions[94] or—which amounts to the same thing—of functions that are purposes. For this reason, the universe has been so created and formed by the Divine that functions can clothe themselves in materials that enable them to present themselves in act or in results, first in heaven and then in this world, and so step by step all the way to the lowest things in nature. We can see from this that the correspondence of natural phenomena with spiritual ones, or of the world with heaven, takes place through functions, and that the functions are what unite them. We can also see that the forms that clothe the functions are correspondences and unions to the extent that they are forms of the functions.

In the three kingdoms of earthly nature, all the things that happen according to the design are [outward] forms of their functions or results formed by function for function. This is why the things that occur there are correspondences.

As for us, though, our acts are services in forms to the extent that we live according to the divine design—that is, in love for the Lord and in thoughtfulness toward our neighbor. To that extent, our acts are correspondences that unite us to heaven. In general terms, loving the Lord and our neighbor is being of service.[h]

112

---

g. Bread means everything good that nourishes our spiritual life: 2165, 2177, 3478, 3735, 3813, 4211, 4217, 4735, 4976, 9323, 9545, 10686. The loaves that were on the table in the tabernacle have a similar meaning: 3478, 9545. Sacrifices in general were called "bread": 2165. "Bread" includes all food: 2165. So it means all heavenly and spiritual food: 276, 680, 2165, 2177, 3478, 6118, 8410.

h. Everything good has its delight from its functions and in proportion to them, and this is also the source of its quality; so the nature of the function determines the nature of the good: 3049, 4984, 7038. Angelic life consists of good deeds of love and thoughtfulness, and therefore of being

We need to know as well that it is humankind through which the natural world is united to the spiritual world, that we are the means of the union. For there is within us a natural world and also a spiritual world (see above, §57); so to the extent that we are spiritual, we are a means of union. However, to the extent that we are natural and not spiritual, we are not a means of union. The Lord's inflow into the world and into the world's gifts within us continues even without our aid, but it does not come into our rational functioning.

113   Just as everything that is in accord with the divine design corresponds to heaven, everything that is contrary to the divine design corresponds to hell. Everything that corresponds to heaven reflects what is good and true, while what corresponds to hell reflects what is evil and false.

114   We may now say something about the knowledge of correspondences and its use. We have just stated that the spiritual world, which is heaven, is united to the natural world by means of correspondences; so it is through correspondences that we are given communication with heaven. Heaven's angels do not think in terms of natural phenomena the way we do, so when we are absorbed in the knowledge of correspondences we can be in the company of angels in respect to the thoughts of our minds. So we can be united to them in regard to our spiritual or inner person.

In order that there might be a union of heaven with humanity, the Word was written in pure correspondences. Absolutely everything in it corresponds.[i] So if we were steeped in a knowledge of correspondences, we would understand the Word in its spiritual meaning and be enabled to

---

of service: 453 [454]. The Lord—and this holds true for angels as well—focuses on nothing but purposes that are functions in regard to us: 1317, 1645, 5844 [5854]. The Lord's kingdom is a kingdom of functions and therefore of purposes: 453 [454], 696, 1103, 3645, 4054, 7038. To serve the Lord is to be useful: 7038. Absolutely everything in us is formed for some function: 3565 [3570], 4104, 5189, 9297; and everything comes from function; so function is prior to our organic forms through which the functions are exercised, because function arises from the inflow of the Lord through heaven: 4223, 4926. Further, the deeper structures of our mind are formed as we mature from function and for function: 1964, 6815, 9297. So the quality of an individual is determined by the quality of that individual's function: 1568, 3570, 4054, 6571, 6934, 6938, 10284. Functions are causative purposes: 3565, 4054, 4104, 6815. Function is our beginning and end, and therefore our whole humanity: 1964.

i. The Word was written in pure correspondences: 8615. Through the Word, there is a union of humanity with heaven: 2899, 6943, 9396, 9400, 9401, 10375, 10452.

know hidden treasures in it that we do not see at all in its literal meaning. The Word does in fact have a literal meaning and a spiritual meaning.[j] The literal meaning consists of the kind of things that are in our world, while the spiritual meaning consists of the kind of things that are in heaven; and since the union of heaven with our world is maintained by correspondences, we have been given a Word in which the details correspond, even down to the last jot.

I have been taught in heaven that the earliest people on our planet, who were heavenly people, thought on the basis of actual correspondences, and that the natural phenomena of the world that greeted their eyes served them as means for thinking in this way. Because they were of this character, they were in the company of angels and talked with them; and in this way heaven was united to the world through them. Therefore, that era was called the Golden Age. Classical authors described it as a time when the inhabitants of heaven dwelt with mortals and kept them company as friend with friend.[95]

After their era, though, a people came who did not think from actual correspondences but from a knowledge about correspondences. There was still a union of heaven with humanity, but not such an intimate one. Their era was called the Silver Age.

The people who came next were indeed familiar with correspondences but did not do their thinking on the basis of their knowledge of correspondences. This was because they were engrossed in what is good on the natural level and not, like their ancestors, on the spiritual level. Their era was called the Bronze Age.

I have been taught, lastly, that after that era humanity became more and more externally minded and at last physically minded. Then the knowledge of correspondences was completely lost, and with it any awareness of heaven and of its riches.

The names of these ages—Golden, Silver, and Bronze—also come from correspondence,[k] because gold, by reason of correspondence, means

115

---

j. On the spiritual meaning of the Word, see the booklet *The White Horse Described in the Book of Revelation.*

k. By reason of correspondence, gold means heavenly good: 113, 1551, 1552, 5658, 6914, 6917, 9510, 9874, 9881. Silver means spiritual good, or truth from a heavenly source: 1551, 1552, 2954, 5648 *[5658]*. Bronze means natural good: 425, 1551. Iron means truth on the lowest level of the design: 425, 426.

the heavenly goodness in which the earliest people lived. Silver, in contrast, means the spiritual goodness in which their successors, the early people, lived; while bronze means the natural goodness characteristic of their immediate followers. Iron, though, which gave its name to the last era, means a harsh truth, devoid of good.[96]

The Sun in Heaven

116   OUR world's sun is not visible in heaven, and neither is anything that is derived from it, since all that is natural. Nature, in fact, begins with that sun, and whatever is produced by it is called natural. The spiritual reality in which heaven exists, though, is above nature and completely distinct from anything natural. They communicate with each other only through correspondences.

The nature of the distinction can be gathered from what was said above about levels in §38, and the nature of the communication from the last two chapters about correspondences.

117   However, even though neither this world's sun nor anything derived from it is visible in heaven, there is a sun there; there is light and warmth, there are all the things we have in our world and many more—not from the same origin, though, since things in heaven are spiritual while things in our world are natural.

Heaven's sun is the Lord; light there is the divine truth and warmth the divine good that radiate from the Lord as the sun. Everything that comes into being and manifests itself in the heavens is from this source. We will discuss the light and warmth and the things that arise from them in subsequent chapters; here we restrict ourselves to the sun.

The reason the Lord in heaven appears as the sun is that he is the divine love from which all spiritual things come into being—and, through the agency of our world's sun, all natural things as well. That love is what shines like a sun.

118   As for the Lord's actually appearing in heaven as the sun, this is something I have not simply been told by angels but have also been

allowed to see a number of times; so I should like at this point to describe briefly what I have heard and seen[97] concerning the Lord as the sun.

The Lord does not appear as a sun *in* the heavens, but high above them, and not directly overhead but in front of angels at a middle elevation. He appears in two places, in one for the right eye and in another for the left, noticeably far apart. For the right eye he looks just like a sun, with much the same fire and size as our world's sun. For the left eye, though, he does not look like a sun but like a moon, with similar brilliance but more sparkling, and with much the same size as our earth's moon; but he seems to be surrounded by many apparent lesser moonlets, each similarly brilliant and sparkling.

The reason the Lord appears in two places, so differently, is that he appears to people according to their receptiveness. So he looks one way to people who accept him through the good of love and another way to people who accept him through the good of faith. To people who accept him through the good of love, he looks like a sun, fiery and flaming in response to their receptivity. These people are in his heavenly kingdom. To people who accept him through the good of faith, though, he looks like a moon, brilliant and sparkling in response to their receptivity. These people are in his spiritual kingdom.[a] This is because the good of love corresponds to fire, so that fire, in its spiritual meaning, is love; while the good of faith corresponds to light, so that light, in its spiritual meaning, is faith.[b]

The reason he appears to the eyes is that the deeper levels of the mind see through the eyes, looking from the good of love through the right eye and from the good of faith through the left eye.[c] You see, everything on

---

a. The Lord is seen in heaven as a sun, and is the sun of heaven: 1053, 3636, 3643, 4060. The Lord appears as a sun to people in the heavenly kingdom, where love for him reigns, and as a moon to people in the spiritual kingdom, where thoughtfulness toward one's neighbor and faith reign: 1521, 1529, 1530, 1531, 1837, 4696. The Lord as a sun appears at a medium elevation for the right eye, and as a moon for the left eye: 1053, 1521, 1529, 1530, 1531, 3636, 3643, 4321, 5097, 7078, 7083, 7173, 7270, 8812, 10809. The Lord has been seen as the sun and as the moon: 1531, 7173. The Lord's essential Divine is far above his Divine in the heavens: 7270, 8760.

b. Fire in the Word means love for either good or evil: 934, 4906, 5215. Sacred or heavenly fire means divine love: 934, 6314, 6832. Hellfire means love for oneself and the world, and all the craving that belongs to those loves: 1861, 5071, 6314, 6832, 7575, 10747. Love is the fire of life, and life itself actually comes from it: 4096 *[4906]*, 5071, 6032, 6314. Light means the truth of faith: 3395 *[3195]*, 3485, 3636, 3643, 3993, 4302, 4413, 4415, 9548, 9684.

c. The sight of the left eye corresponds to what is true in faith, and the sight of the right eye corresponds to what is good in it: 4410, 6923.

the right side of an angel or one of us corresponds to what is good and yields truth, while everything on the left side corresponds to that truth that comes from what is good.[d,98] "The good of faith" is, essentially, truth that comes from what is good.

119   This is why in the Word the Lord is compared to the sun when the focus is on love and to the moon when the focus is on faith. It is also why the sun means a love for the Lord that comes from the Lord, and the moon means a faith in the Lord that comes from the Lord. Compare the following passages.

> The light of the moon will be like the light of the sun, and the light of the sun will be sevenfold, like the light of seven days. (Isaiah 30:26)

> When I annihilate you, I will cover the heavens and blacken the stars. I will cover the sun with a cloud, and the moon will not make its light. I will blacken all the luminaries in the heavens above you and send darkness over your land. (Ezekiel 32:7–8)

> I will darken the sun in its rising, and the moon will not make its light shine. (Isaiah 13:10)

> The sun and the moon will be blackened and the stars will withdraw their shining; the sun will be turned into darkness, and the moon into blood. (Joel 2:2, 10, 31; 3:15)[99]

> The sun became black as hairy sackcloth,[100] and the moon became like blood, and the stars fell to earth. (Revelation 6:12[–13])

> Immediately after the affliction of those days, the sun will be darkened and the moon will not give its light and the stars will fall from heaven. (Matthew 24:29)

And elsewhere. In these passages, the sun means love and the moon faith, while the stars mean instances of recognizing what is good and true.[e] These are said to be darkened, to lose their light, and to fall from heaven when they no longer exist.

---

d. Things on our right side have reference to the good that yields truth, while things on our left have reference to the truth that comes from what is good: 9495, 9604.

e. In the Word, the lesser and greater stars mean instances of recognizing what is good and true: 2495, 2849, 4697.

The Lord's appearance as a sun in heaven may also be inferred from his transfiguration before Peter, James, and John, when "his face shone like the sun" (Matthew 17:2). This is how the Lord was seen by those disciples when they had been lifted out of their bodies and were in the light of heaven.

For this reason, when the early people (who constituted a representative church) were engaged in their divine worship, they faced the sun in the east. It is why they set their temples to face the east.

We can gather how great divine love is and what its quality is by comparison with the sun of our world—that love is most intense, far more intense, if you will believe it. So the Lord as the sun does not flow directly into the heavens; rather, the intensity of his love is by degrees tempered in its course. The stages of this tempering look like sparkling halos around the sun. Further, angels are shielded by a suitably thin cloud so that they will not be hurt by the inflow.[f] As a result, the heavens are distanced according to their receptiveness. The higher heavens, being in the good of love, are closest to the Lord as the sun. The lower heavens, though, being in the good of faith, are farther from him. People who are engaged in nothing good whatever, like the people in hell, are farthest away, their removal being in proportion to their opposition to what is good.[g]

However, when the Lord appears *in* heaven (which happens quite often) he does not appear clothed with the sun but in an angelic form, distinguishable from the angels by the divine quality that shines from his face. He is not actually there in person—since the Lord "in person" is always clothed with the sun—but is present in appearance. It is commonplace in heaven for things to be seen as though they were present in the

f. The quality and greatness of divine love, illustrated by comparison with the fire of our world's sun: 6834, 6844 *[8644]*, 6849. The Lord's divine love is a love for the whole human race, for its salvation: 1820, 1865, 2253, 6872. The love that emanates most closely from the fire of the Lord's love does not come into heaven, but appears around the sun like a sparkling halo: 7270. Further, angels are shielded by a suitably thin cloud, so that they will not be hurt by the inflow of the heat of love: 6849.

g. The manner of the Lord's presence with angels depends on their acceptance of the good of love and faith from him: 904, 4198, 4320, 6280, 6832, 7042, 8819, 9680, 9682, 9683, 10106, 10811. The Lord appears to every individual according to that individual's own quality: 1861, 2235 *[3235]*, 4198, 4206. The hells are distanced from the heavens by the fact that they cannot bear the presence of divine love from the Lord: 4299, 7519, 7738, 7989, 8157 *[8137]*, 8266 *[8265]*, 9327. So the hells are very far indeed from heaven, and this is the "great gulf": 9346, 10187.

place where their appearance is focused or delineated, even though this is very far from the place where they themselves actually are. This presence is called "a presence of inner sight," and will be discussed further below.[101]

Then too I have seen the Lord outside the sun in an angelic form overhead, a little below the sun, and also nearby in a similar form—once even among some angels, looking like a fiery ray of light.

122   To angels, our world's sun looks like something murky opposite to heaven's sun, and our moon like something dim opposite to heaven's moon, consistently. This is because our world's fire corresponds to a love for ourselves, and the light it emits corresponds to the distortion that arises from that love. Love for oneself is the absolute opposite of divine love, and the distortion that arises from it is the absolute opposite of divine truth.[102] Anything that is opposed to divine love and truth is darkness to angels.

This is why in the Word, worshiping our world's sun and moon and bowing down to them means loving oneself and the distortion that arises from self-love, and why these are to be abolished (Deuteronomy 4:19; 18:3–5 [17:3–5]; Jeremiah 8:1–2; Ezekiel 8:15, 16, 18; Revelation 16:8; Matthew 13:6).[h]

123   Since the Lord does appear in heaven as a sun because of the divine love that is in him and from him, all the people there constantly turn toward him. The inhabitants of the heavenly kingdom turn toward him as the sun, while the inhabitants of the spiritual kingdom turn toward him as the moon. In contrast, the inhabitants of hell turn toward the darkness and dimness that are on the opposite side, and therefore turn away from the Lord. This is because all the people who are in the hells are caught up in love for themselves and the world and are therefore opposed to the Lord. The ones who turn toward the darkness that stands for our world's sun are at the back of the hells and are called "demons," while the ones who turn toward the dimness that stands for our moon are in the front of hell and are called "spirits."[103] This is why people in the hells are described as being in darkness and people in the heavens as being in light. "Darkness" means falsity arising from evil, and "light" means truth arising from good.

h. Our world's sun is not visible to angels, but instead something dim behind them, opposite to heaven's sun or the Lord: 7078, 9755. In its opposite meaning, the sun means love for oneself: 2441; and in this meaning "worshiping the sun" means worshiping things that are contrary to heavenly love, or to the Lord: 2441, 10584. For people in the hells, heaven's sun is darkness: 2441.

The reason people turn in this way is that in the other life we all look toward what rules in our deeper natures—toward our own loves, then; and these deeper natures form the faces of angels and spirits. Further, in a spiritual world the cardinal points are not fixed the way they are in a natural world. Instead, they are determined by the way people face.

We ourselves, in spirit, are also turning in the same fashion—away from the Lord if we are caught up in self-love and love of the world, and toward him if we are in a love for him and for our neighbor. We are unaware of this, though, because we are in a natural world where the cardinal points are determined by the sun's rising and setting. Since it is hard for people to grasp this, examples will be given below where we deal with the cardinal points and with space and time in heaven.[104]

Since the Lord is the sun of heaven, and since everything that comes from him looks toward him, the Lord is the common center, the basis of all direction and orientation.[i] So too everything beneath is in his presence and under his control, everything in the heavens and everything on earth.   **124**

This enables us to see in clearer light the things that have been presented in the earlier chapters about the Lord, namely that he is the God of heaven (§§2–6), that his divine nature makes heaven (§§7–12), that the divine nature of the Lord in heaven is love for him and thoughtfulness toward our neighbor (§§13–19), that there is a correspondence of everything in our world with heaven, and through heaven with the Lord (§§87–115),[105] and that the sun of our world and its moon are correspondent entities (§105).   **125**

Light and Warmth in Heaven

PEOPLE who think solely on the basis of nature cannot grasp the fact that there is light in the heavens; yet in the heavens there is so much light that it is vastly greater than noonday light on earth. I have seen it often, even during our evenings and nights. At first I was amazed when I heard angels saying that our world's light was nothing but shadow in   **126**

i. The Lord is the common center toward which everything in heaven turns: 3633.

comparison to heaven's light, but now that I have seen it, I myself can bear witness. Its brightness and brilliance are beyond description. What I have seen in heaven I have seen in that light, and therefore more clearly and distinctly than what I have seen in this world.

127　　Heaven's light is not natural like the light of our world, but spiritual. It actually comes from the Lord as the sun, and that sun, as explained in the preceding chapter, is divine love. While what emanates from the Lord as the sun is called divine truth in the heavens, in essence it is divine good as one with divine truth. This is the source of light and warmth for angels: they get their light from the divine truth and their warmth from the divine good.

We can therefore conclude that heaven's light, in view of the nature of its source, is spiritual and not natural, as is its warmth.[a]

128　　The reason divine truth is light for angels is that angels are spiritual and not natural. Spiritual people see things from their sun, and natural people see from theirs. Divine truth is what provides angels with discernment; and discernment is their inner sight, which flows into their outer sight and produces it. So whatever is seen in heaven from the Lord as the sun is seen in the light.[b] Since this is the source of light in heaven, it varies depending on the acceptance of divine truth from the Lord or (which amounts to the same thing) depending on the intelligence and wisdom angels participate in. This means that it is different in the heavenly kingdom than in the spiritual kingdom, and different in each community. The light in the heavenly kingdom looks fiery because the angels who are there accept light from the Lord as the sun. The light in the spiritual kingdom, though, is white because the angels who are there accept light from the Lord as the moon (see above, §118). Further, the light is not the same in one community as in another. It even differs within each community. People in the middle are in more light, and people round about are in less (see §43).

In short, to the extent to which angels are open to divine truth (that is, participate in intelligence and wisdom from the Lord), they have light.[c] This is why heaven's angels are called angels of light.

a. All the light in the heavens is from the Lord as the sun: 1053, 1521, 3195, 3341, 3636, 3643, 4415, 9548, 9684, 10809. Divine truth emanating from the Lord appears in heaven as light, and constitutes all the light of heaven: 3195, 3222 [3223], 5400, 8644, 9399, 9548, 9684.

b. Heaven's light illuminates the sight and the discernment of angels and spirits: 2776, 3138.

c. Light in heaven is proportional to angels' intelligence and wisdom: 1524, 1529, 1530, 3339. There are as many variations of light in the heavens as there are communities, because there are constant variations in regard to what good and true, and therefore in regard to wisdom and intelligence: 684, 690, 3241, 3744, 3745, 4414, 5598, 7236, 7833, 7836.

Because the Lord in the heavens is divine truth and divine truth there   **129**
is light, the Lord is called "light" in the Word, as is the truth that comes
from him. Note the following passages:

> Jesus said, I am the light of the world. Whoever follows me will not
> walk in darkness, but will have the light of life. (John 8:12)

> As long as I am in the world, I am the light of the world. (John 9:15
> *[9:5]*)

> Jesus said, For a little while longer the light is with you; walk while you
> have the light, to prevent the darkness from overtaking you. While you
> have light, believe in the light, so that you may be children of light. I
> have come as a light into the world, so that anyone who believes in me
> may not remain in darkness. (John 12:35, 36, 40 *[46]*)

> Light has come into the world, but people loved darkness more than
> light. (John 3:19)

> John said of the Lord, his is the true light that enlightens everyone.
> (John 1:4, 9)

> The people that sit in darkness will see a great light, and for those who
> were sitting in the shadow of death, a light has risen. (Matthew 4:16)

> I will make you a covenant of the people, a light of the nations. (Isaiah
> 42:6)

> I have established you as the light of the nations, so that you may be
> my salvation to the end of the earth. (Isaiah 49:6)

> The nations that have been saved will walk toward his light. (Revela-
> tion 21:24)

> Send out your light and your truth; let them lead me. (Psalms 43:3)

In these and other passages, the Lord is called "light" by reason of the divine truth that comes from him, and that truth itself is called "light" as
well. Because the Lord as the sun is light in the heavens, when he was
transfigured before Peter, James, and John

> his face shone like the sun and his garments as light, sparkling and
> white as snow, as no fuller on earth could bleach them. (Mark 9:3;
> Matthew 17:2)

The reason the Lord's garments looked as they did was that they were images of the divine truth that comes from him in the heavens. Garments

in the Word mean truths as well,[d] so it says in David, "Jehovah, you clothe yourself with light as a garment" (Psalms 104:2).[106]

130 It stands to reason that the light in the heavens is spiritual and that that light is divine truth when we consider that we also have spiritual light and that we have enlightenment from it to the extent that we participate in intelligence and wisdom on the basis of divine truth. Our spiritual light is the light of our discernment, whose objects are things true that it arranges in order by a process of analysis and forms into relationships, and from which it draws a series of conclusions.[e]

Natural people are unaware that the light that enables us to see such things is a real light because they do not see it with their eyes or notice it with their thought. Still, many people do recognize it and also distinguish it from the natural light in which they find themselves when they are thinking naturally and not spiritually. People are thinking naturally when they are focusing solely on this world and attributing everything to nature. They are thinking spiritually, however, when they focus on heaven and attribute everything to the Divine.

I have often been allowed to perceive that the light that illumines the mind is a true light, quite different from the light that we call natural light. I have also been allowed to see it. I have been gradually elevated into that light inwardly, and as I was raised up, my discernment was enlightened to the extent that I could grasp what I had been unable to grasp before, ultimately things that could in no way be comprehended by thought from natural light. At times I have resented the fact that they were incomprehensible [in natural light] when they were so clearly and plainly perceived in the heavenly light.[f]

---

d. Garments in the Word mean the truths that clothe what is good: 1073, 2576, 5248, 5319, 5954, 9216, 9952, 10536. The garments of the Lord when he was transfigured meant the divine truth that emanates from his divine love: 9212, 9216.

e. Heaven's light illuminates our discernment, making us rational individuals: 1524, 3138, 3167, 4408, 6608, 8707, 9126 *[9128]*, 9399, 10659 *[10569]*. Discernment is enlightened because it is what is receptive of truth: 6222, 6608, 10659 *[10569]*. Discernment is enlightened to the extent that we accept what is true in what is good from the Lord: 3619. The quality of our discernment is determined by the quality of heartfelt truths out of which it is formed: 10064. Discernment has light from heaven the way sight has light from the world: 1524, 5114, 6608, 9128. Heaven's light from the Lord is always present with us, but flows in [only] to the extent that we are engaged in truth because of what is good: 4060, 4213 *[4214]*.

f. When we are lifted above the sensory level, we come into a gentler light, and eventually into a heavenly light: 6313, 6315, 9407. An actual raising into heaven's light occurs when we are engaged in intelligence: 3190. How much light I perceived when I was led out of my worldly concepts: 1526, 6608.

Since our mind does have light, we speak of it much as we do of our eyes—for example, that it sees and is in the light when it grasps something, and that it is in darkness and shadows when it does not; and there are many other similar sayings.

Since heaven's light is divine truth, that light is also divine wisdom and intelligence. Consequently "being raised into heaven's light" means the same thing as "being raised into intelligence and wisdom" and "being enlightened." So too, light among angels is at exactly the same level as their intelligence and wisdom.

131

Since heaven's light is divine wisdom, people are recognized in heaven's light for what they really are. Everyone's inner nature shines forth from the face just as it is, with nothing whatever concealed. Further, the more internally minded angels love to have everything within them visible because they do not intend anything but what is good. It is different for people who are below heaven and do not intend what is good. They are profoundly afraid of being seen in heaven's light. Remarkably, people in hell look human to each other, but in heaven's light they look like monsters, with frightful faces and bodies, in the exact form of their evil.g

We have a similar appearance as to our spirits when angels look at us. If we are good, we look like handsome individuals in accord with our goodness; if we are evil we look like monsters, misshapen in accord with our evil. We can see from this that everything is clear in heaven's light. It is clear because heaven's light is divine truth.

Since divine truth is the light in the heavens, all true things are luminous there wherever they occur—whether within an angel, outside of an angel, within the heavens, or outside of the heavens. Still, the truths outside the heavens do not shine the way the truths inside the heavens do. The truths outside the heavens shine coldly, like something snowy, without warmth, because unlike truths within the heavens, they do not derive their essence from what is good. So that cold light disappears at the touch of heaven's light; and if there is some underlying evil, it turns to darkness. I have seen this several times, along with many other remarkable things concerning luminous truths, which I forego for now.[107]

132

Something now needs to be said about heaven's warmth. In its essence, heaven's warmth is love. It emanates from the Lord as the sun,

133

g. People in the hells look human in their own light, which is like the light of glowing coals; but in heaven's light they look like monsters: 4532 [4531], 4533, 4674, 5057, 5058, 6605, 6626.

which is divine love for the Lord and from the Lord, as has been explained in the preceding chapter. We can therefore see that heaven's warmth is just as spiritual as its light, because they come from the same source.[h]

There are two things that emanate from the Lord as the sun, divine truth and divine good. Divine truth comes out in heaven as light and divine good as warmth. However, divine truth and divine good are so united that they are not two, but one. For angels, though, they are separated. There are angels who accept divine good more readily than divine truth, and there are angels who accept divine truth more readily than divine good. The ones who are more open to divine good are in the Lord's heavenly kingdom; the ones who are more open to divine truth are in the Lord's spiritual kingdom. The most perfect angels are the ones who are equally open to both.

134 Heaven's warmth, like heaven's light, is different in different places. It has one nature in the heavenly kingdom and another in the spiritual kingdom. It also differs in each community, not only in intensity but in quality. It is more intense and pure in the Lord's heavenly kingdom because the angels there accept more divine good. It is less intense and pure in the Lord's spiritual kingdom because the angels there accept more divine truth. In each community, it varies depending on people's receptivity. There is also warmth in the hells, but it is unclean.[i]

The warmth in heaven is meant by sacred and heavenly fire, and the warmth of hell by profane fire and hellfire. Both refer to love: heavenly fire to love for the Lord and love for one's neighbor, and hellfire to love for oneself and love of the world and all the craving that is associated with these loves.[j]

The fact that love is warmth of a spiritual origin can be seen from the way we grow warm in proportion to our love, even becoming inflamed and heated in proportion to its intensity and quality, with its full heat evident when we are attacked. This is why it is usual to talk about inflaming,

h. There are two sources of warmth and also two sources of light, our world's sun and heaven's sun: 3338, 5215, 7324. Warmth from the Lord as the sun is affection, which is a matter of love: 3636, 3643. So in its essence, spiritual warmth is love: 2146, 3338, 3339, 6314.

i. There is warmth in the hells, but it is unclean: 1773, 2757, 3340; and the smell that comes from there is like the smell of manure and excrement in our world—in the worst hells, like the smell of corpses: 814, 815 *[819]*, 817 *[820]*, 943, 944, 5394.

j. [Swedenborg's note at this point refers the reader back to the second note in §118 above.]

heating up, burning, boiling, and kindling when we are talking about either the affections of a good love or the cravings of an evil love.

The reason the love that emanates from the Lord as the sun is experienced as warmth in heaven is that the deeper levels of angels are involved in a love that comes from the divine good, which in turn comes from the Lord. Consequently, their more outward levels, which are warmed by this, are in warmth. This is why warmth and love are mutually responsive to each other in heaven, so that everyone is in the kind of warmth that accords with her or his love, as follows from what we have just been saying.

Our world's warmth does not enter heaven at all, because it is too crude, being natural and not spiritual. It is different for us, though, since we are in the spiritual world as well as in the natural world. As far as our spirits are concerned, we grow warm exactly according to our loves, but as far as our bodies are concerned, we respond to both—the warmth of our spirits and the warmth of the world. The former flows into the latter, because they correspond.

We can determine the nature of the correspondence of these two kinds of warmth by looking at animals, whose loves—the primary one being for the procreation of offspring of their own species—break forth and become active in response to the presence and touch of warmth from our world's sun, a warmth that comes primarily in spring and summertime.

People who believe that the inflow of our world's warmth arouses these loves are much mistaken. There is actually no inflow of what is natural into what is spiritual, but of what is spiritual into what is natural. This latter inflow is of the divine design, while the former would be contrary to the divine design.[k]

Like people on earth, angels have discernment and volition. Heaven's light produces their cognitive life because heaven's light is divine truth and the divine wisdom that comes from it; while heaven's warmth produces their volitional life because heaven's warmth is the divine good and the divine love that comes from it. The quintessential life of angels is from the warmth, but not from the light except to the extent that there is warmth in it. We can see that life comes from the warmth because when the warmth is taken away life dies. It is the same for faith without love or

k. There is a spiritual inflow and not a physical one, so the inflow is from the spiritual world into the natural and not from the natural into the spiritual: 3219, 5119, 5259, 5427, 5428, 5477, 6322, 9110 *[9109]*, 9111 *[9110]*.

for truth without goodness, since the truth that is attributed to faith is light and the goodness that is attributed to love is warmth.[l]

All this becomes even clearer from the warmth and light of our world, to which heaven's warmth and light correspond. From the warmth of our world, united to its light, all things on earth come to life and blossom. They are united in spring and summer. However, nothing comes to life or blooms from light separated from warmth—everything languishes and dies. They are disunited in winter, when the warmth is gone but the light remains. It is from this correspondence that heaven is called a paradise,[108] because there the true is united to the good, or faith to love, as light is united to warmth in springtime on earth.

This gives even clearer support to the truth discussed above in §§13–19, that the Lord's divine nature in heaven is love for him and thoughtfulness toward one's neighbor.

137   It says in John,

> In the beginning was the Word, and the Word was with God, and God was the Word: all things were made by means of him, and without him nothing was made that was made. In him was life, and the life was the light of humankind. He was in the world, and the world was made by means of him. And the Word was made flesh, and dwelt among us, and we saw his glory. (John 1:1, 3, 4, 10, 14)

It is clear that the Lord is the one who is meant by "the Word," since it says that the Word was made flesh. Precisely what is meant by "the Word," though, is not yet known and must therefore be stated. The Word in this passage is the divine truth that is in the Lord and from the Lord,[m] so here it is also called the light, which is divine truth, as has been shown earlier in this chapter. Now we need to explain the statement that all things were made and created by means of divine truth.

---

l. Truths apart from what is good are not truths intrinsically because they do not have any life; in fact, all the life of things true is from what is good: 9603; so they are like a body without a soul: 3180, 9454 [9154]. Truths without good are not accepted by the Lord: 4368. The nature of truth apart from goodness, and therefore the nature of faith without love; and the nature of heartfelt truth and therefore the nature of faith from love: 1949, 1950, 1951, 1964, 5830, 5951. It boils down to the same thing whether you say "truth" or "faith," "good" or "love," because truth is an attribute of faith and goodness is an attribute of love: 2839, 4353 [4352], 4997, 7178, 7623, 7624, 10367.

m. "The Word" in Sacred Scripture has various meanings—speech, the thought of the mind, every entity that actually comes into being, or anything at all, and in the highest sense divine truth and the Lord: 9987. "The Word" means divine truth: 2803, 2884 [2894], 4692, 5075, 5272, 7830 [7930], 9987. "The Word" means the Lord: 2533, 2859.

[2] In heaven, it is divine truth that possesses all power, and apart from it there is no power whatever.[n] All angels are called "powers" because of divine truth, and are powers to the extent that they are recipients or vessels of it. Through it they prevail over the hells and over all who oppose them. A thousand enemies there cannot bear one ray of heavenly light, which is divine truth. Since angels are angels because of their acceptance of divine truth, it follows that all heaven is from this source and no other, since heaven is made up of angels.

[3] People cannot believe that this kind of power is inherent in divine truth if the only concept of truth they have has to do with thought or speech, which have no power in them except to the extent that other people concede it by being obedient. There is an intrinsic power within divine truth, though, power of such nature that by means of it heaven, the world, and everything in them was created.

We can illustrate the fact that this kind of power is inherent in divine truth by two comparisons—by the power of what is true and good in us, and by the power of light and warmth from the sun in our world.

By the power of what is true and good in us: Everything we do, we do out of our discernment and intent. Out of our intent, we act by means of what is good, and out of our discernment by means of what is true. In fact, all the elements of our volition are related to what is good, and all the elements of our discernment are related to what is true.[o] On this basis, then, we set our whole body in motion and a thousand things there rush to do our bidding of their own accord. We can see from this that our whole body is formed for obedience to what is good and true and therefore from what is good and true.

[4] *By the power of light and warmth from the sun in our world:* Everything that grows in our world—things like trees, shrubs, flowers, grasses, fruits, and seeds—arises only by means of the warmth and light of the sun. So we can see what kind of productive power is inherent in that warmth and light. What about the divine light that is divine truth, then,

---

n. Divine truth emanating from the Lord is what possesses all power: 6948, 8200. All power in heaven belongs to the true from the good: 3091, 3563, 6344, 6413 *[6423]*, 8304, 9643, 10019, 10182. Angels are called powers, and are powers as a result of their acceptance of divine truth from the Lord: 9639. Angels are recipients of divine truth from the Lord, and are therefore often called "gods" in the Word: 4295, 4402, 8301, 8192, 9398 *[8988]*.

o. Discernment is the recipient of what is true, and volition is the recipient of what is good: 3623, 6125, 7503, 9300, 9930. Therefore, all the elements of our discernment are related to what is true, whether these things are actually true or whether we believe them to be so; and all the elements of our volition are similarly related to what is good: 803, 10122.

and the divine warmth that is divine good, the source from which heaven comes into being and consequently the world as well, since as we have shown above, it is through heaven that the world comes into being?

This enables us to determine how to understand the statement that all things were made by means of the Word, and that without him nothing was made that was made, and further that the world was made by means of him, namely that this was accomplished by means of divine truth from the Lord.p

This is also why in the book of creation it first mentions light and then the things that arise from light (Genesis 1:3, 4). It is also why everything in all heaven and earth has to do with what is good and true and to their union if it is to be anything at all.q

139 [109] It should be realized that the divine good and divine truth that come from the Lord as the sun in the heavens are not in the Lord but are from him. All that is in the Lord is divine love, which is the reality from which divine good and truth become manifest. Becoming manifest from reality is what "emanating" means.[110] This too can be illustrated by comparison with our world's sun. The warmth and light in our world are not in the sun but are from it. In the sun there is nothing but fire, and warmth and light become manifest and emanate from it.

140 Since the Lord as the sun is divine love, and divine love is the essential divine good, the divine that emanates from him—his divine nature in heaven—is called divine truth for the sake of clarity, even though it is divine good united to divine truth. This divine truth is what is called "the holy" that emanates from him.

The Four Quarters in Heaven

141 THERE are four quarters in heaven just as there are in the world—east, south, west, and north. These are determined in each world by its sun, in heaven by heaven's sun, which is the Lord, and on earth by

---

p. Divine truth emanating from the Lord is the only thing that is real: 6880, 7004, 8200. By means of divine truth all things were made and created: 2803, 2884, 5272, 7835 [7796].
q. [Swedenborg's note at this point refers the reader back to the note in §107 above.]

earth's sun. However, there are major differences. The first is that in our world we call "south" the direction in which the sun reaches its greatest height above the earth, and "north" where it is below the earth, in the opposite direction. East is where the sun rises at the equinoxes, and west is where it sets at that time. So on earth, all the directions are determined on the basis of the south.[111] In heaven, though, they call "east" where the Lord is seen as the sun. West is in the opposite direction, south in heaven on the right, and north on the left. This holds true wherever people turn their faces and their bodies. So in heaven, all the directions are determined on the basis of the east.

The reason they give the name "east" to the direction in which the Lord is seen as the sun is that the whole *source* of life is from him as the sun. Further, to the extent that warmth and light, or intelligence and wisdom from him, are accepted among angels, they say that the Lord has *risen* among them. This is also why the Lord is called the east in the Word.[a,112]

A second difference is that for angels, the east is always in front of them, the west behind them, south on the right, and north on the left. However, since this is hard to understand in this world, because we turn our faces in all different directions, it needs to be explained. | 142 |

All heaven turns toward the Lord as its common center, so all angels turn in the same direction. It is recognized that everything points to a common center on earth as well, but the orientation in heaven is different from that on earth. In heaven, it is the forward parts that are turned toward the common center, while on earth it is the lower parts. This orientation in our world is what we call centripetal, and also gravitational. The deeper levels of angels are effectively turned forward; and since these deeper levels manifest themselves in the face, it is the face that determines the orientation.[b]

But that east is always in front of angels *no matter which way they turn their faces and bodies*—this is even harder to understand in our world, since for us, the direction that is in front of us depends on which way we are facing; so this too needs to be explained. | 143 |

Angels turn and direct their faces and bodies in any direction just as we do, but still, the east is always before their eyes. The way angels turn is

a. The east in the highest sense is the Lord, because he is heaven's sun, which is always rising and never setting: 101, 5097, 9668.

b. All the people in heaven turn toward the Lord: 9828, 10130, 10189, 10219. Still, angels do not turn themselves toward the Lord; rather, the Lord turns them toward himself: 10189. There is no presence of angels with the Lord, but there is a presence of the Lord with angels: 9415.

not the way we turn, since it comes from a different origin. The two modes of turning look the same, but they are not. The origin [for angels] is a ruling love. It is the basis of all delimitation for angels and spirits; for, as noted just above, their deeper levels are actually turned toward their common center. So in heaven they are turned toward the Lord as the sun; and since love is constantly in front of their deeper levels, and their faces are manifestations of these levels (being their outward form), the love that is predominant is always in front of their faces. In heaven, then, this is the Lord as the sun, since he is the source of all their love.[c] Further, since the Lord himself is in his love among the angels, it is the Lord who causes them to be looking at him wherever they turn. These matters cannot be further clarified here, but they will be in subsequent chapters. In particular, where we deal with representations and appearances and with time and space in heaven, they will be presented to understanding more plainly.[113]

As for angels having the Lord constantly in front of them, this I have been granted to know through a great deal of experience. Sometimes when I have been in the company of angels, I have noticed the Lord's presence before my own face: even though I did not see him, I could tell he was there because of the light. Angels have often borne witness to the truth of this as well.

Since the Lord is constantly in front of angels, we say in our world that they have God before their eyes and faces, that people who believe in him and love him look to him and see him. Expressions like this come to us from the spiritual world, for this is the source of many of our expressions, though we are unaware that they come from there.

144 This kind of turning toward the Lord is one of heaven's wonders, for many individuals can be together in one place, turning faces and bodies toward each other, and yet all of them will have the Lord in front of them, and each will have the south on the right, the north on the left, and the west behind.

Another extraordinary fact is that even though angels are completely oriented toward the east, they still have an orientation to the other three directions. This orientation, though, involves their more inward sight, which is a function of their thinking.

c. All the people in the spiritual world turn toward what they love, and the directions there have their source and definition on the basis of the face: 10130, 10189, 10420, 10702. The face is formed to correspond to the deeper levels: 4791–4805, 5695. So the deeper levels shine forth from the face: 3527, 4066, 4796. For angels, the face is united to the deeper levels: 4796, 4797, 4799, 5695, 8250. On the inflow of the deeper levels into the face and its muscles: 3631, 4800.

A further extraordinary fact is that in heaven, no one is allowed to stand behind anyone else and look at the back of his or her head. This disturbs the inflow of what is good and true from the Lord.

Angels see the Lord in one way, and the Lord sees angels in another. **145** Angels see the Lord with their eyes, while the Lord sees angels through their foreheads. The reason for this is that the forehead corresponds to love, and it is through love that the Lord flows into their volition and makes himself visible to their minds, to which the eyes correspond.[d]

However, the regions in the heavens that make up the Lord's heav- **146** enly kingdom differ from those in the heavens that make up the Lord's spiritual kingdom. This is because to the angels in his heavenly kingdom the Lord looks like a sun, while to the angels in his spiritual kingdom he looks like a moon, and the east is where the Lord is seen.

The distance between the sun and the moon is thirty degrees,[114] and the same alignment therefore holds true for the directions. The division of heaven into two kingdoms called the heavenly kingdom and the spiritual kingdom has been presented in its own chapter above (§§20–28), as has the Lord's looking like the sun in the heavenly kingdom and like the moon in the spiritual kingdom (§118). Still, the directions are not rendered uncertain by this, since spiritual angels cannot rise up to the level of heavenly angels, nor the latter come down to the former (see §35 above).

We can see from this what the Lord's presence is like in the heavens: **147** it is everywhere, with every individual in the good and true qualities that emanate from the Lord. So he is in angels in what is actually his own (as noted in §12 above).

Their sense of the Lord's presence is in their deeper reaches. It is from these that their eyes see, so he seems to be outside them because there is a continuum. This enables us to see how we should understand the Lord's being in them and their being in the Lord, according to the Lord's words,

> Abide in me, and I in you (John 15:4),

and

> Those who eat my flesh and drink my blood abide in me and I in them. (John 6:56)

---

d. The forehead corresponds to heavenly love, so in the Word the forehead refers to that love: 9936. The eye corresponds to our discernment, because discernment is inner sight: 2701, 4410, 4526, 9051, 10569. So to lift one's eyes and see means to discern, to perceive, and to notice: 2789, 2829, 3198, 3202, 4083, 4086, 4339, 5684.

"The Lord's flesh" means what is divine and good, and his "blood" means what is divine and true.[e]

148 All the people in the heavens live in different areas according to the cardinal directions. People who are sensitive to the good that love does live along the east-west axis: the ones who have a clear perception of this, toward the east; and the ones who have a vague perception of it, toward the west. People who are sensitive to the issues of wisdom that result [from that good] live along the south-north axis: the ones in a clear light of wisdom, toward the south; and the ones in a dim light of wisdom, toward the north.

The dwelling arrangement for angels in the Lord's spiritual kingdom is like that of the ones in his heavenly kingdom, with a difference that depends on the good that love does and the light of truth that comes from the good. This is because the love in the heavenly kingdom is a love for the Lord, and the light of truth from that love is wisdom. On the other hand, the love in the spiritual kingdom is the love for our neighbor that is called thoughtfulness, and the light of truth that comes from it is intelligence, also called faith (see above, §23). They also differ according to the directions, since as just noted (§146), the directions in the two kingdoms are thirty degrees apart.

149 There is a similar dwelling arrangement for the angels in each particular community of heaven. The ones who are engaged in a greater degree of love and thoughtfulness are toward the east, and the ones in less toward the west; the ones who are in greater light of wisdom are toward the south, and the ones in less toward the north. The reason for this arrangement is that each community is a reflection of heaven and is a heaven in lesser form as well (see above, §§51–58). The same thing happens in meetings. They are brought into this arrangement by the form of heaven, which enables every individual to know his or her place.

It is also provided by the Lord that there shall be all kinds of people in each community, because heaven has a consistent form throughout. Still, the arrangement of heaven as a whole does differ from that of a community as a general entity differs from its details. That is, the communities that are located toward the east are superior to those toward the west, and those toward the south are superior to those toward the north.

e. In the Word, the Lord's "flesh" means his divine human and the divine good of his love: 3813, 7850, 9127, 10283; and "the Lord's blood" means divine truth and the holiness of faith: 4735, 4978 [6978], 7317, 7326, 7846, 7850, 7877, 9127, 9393, 10026, 10033, 10152, 10204 [10210].

This is why the cardinal directions in heaven mean the qualities of the people who live there. The east means love and its good clearly perceived, the west the same dimly perceived, the south wisdom and intelligence in clear light, and the north the same in dim light. Further, since the directions have these meanings, they mean similar things in the inner or spiritual meaning of the Word,[f] since the inner or spiritual meaning of the Word is in complete accord with the way things are in heaven.

150

The opposite holds for the people who are in the hells. The people there do not focus on the Lord as the sun or the moon, but look away from the Lord toward that dark object that occupies the place of our world's sun and the gloomy object that occupies the place of earth's moon. The ones called demons look toward the dark object in our sun's place, and the ones called spirits toward the gloomy object in our moon's place.[g] As explained in §122 above, the sun of our world and earth's moon are not visible in the spiritual world, but in place of our sun there is something dark opposite heaven's sun and something gloomy opposite heaven's moon. This means that hell's inhabitants have directions opposite to those of heaven. Their east is where they see that dark or gloomy object and their west is where heaven's sun is. Their south is to their right and their north to their left, no matter which way they turn their bodies. Nothing else is possible for them, because the whole tendency of their deeper natures, their whole orientation therefore, aims and strives in this direction. On the fact that love is what determines the tendency of our deeper natures and therefore the orientation of everyone's actions in the other life, see §143. The love of people in the hells is a love for oneself and for the world, these loves being what is meant by the sun of this world and earth's moon (see §122). Further, these loves are opposite to love for the Lord and love for one's neighbor.[h] This is why they turn toward the darkness, away from the Lord.

151

The people who are in the hells also live arranged according to the cardinal directions. The ones who are obsessed with evils that arise from love for themselves are along the east-west axis, and the ones who are

f. The east in the Word means love clearly perceived: 1250, 3708. The west means love dimly perceived: 3708, 9653. The south means a state of light of wisdom and intelligence: 1458, 3708, 5672; and the north means that state dimly perceived: 3708.

g. The identity and nature of the people called demons, and the identity and nature of the ones called spirits: 947, 5035, 5977, 8593, 8622, 8625.

h. People who are absorbed in love for themselves and for the world turn away from the Lord: 10130, 10189, 10420, 10702. Love for the Lord and thoughtfulness toward one's neighbor make heaven, and love for oneself and for the world make hell, because they are opposites: 2041, 3610, 4225, 4776, 6210, 7366, 7369, 7490, 8232, 8678, 10455, 10741–10745.

obsessed with falsifications for the sake of evil are along the south-north axis. There will be more about them later, though, where we discuss the hells.[115]

152   When an evil spirit comes into the company of good ones, it usually results in such a confusion of directions that the good spirits hardly know where their east is. This is an event I have often noticed, and I have heard about it from spirits who complained about it.

153   Evil spirits sometimes seem to be oriented to heaven's directions, at which time they have intelligence and a grasp of what is true, but no affection for what is good; so as soon as they turn back toward their own directions, they are without intelligence or any grasp of what is true. They then say that the true things they had heard and understood are not true but false, and even want false things to be true. I have been told about this kind of turning, specifically that for evil people the intellectual faculty can be turned in this way, but not the voluntary faculty. I have also been told that this is provided by the Lord to the end that everyone may have the ability to see and acknowledge what is true, but that no one will accept it except people who are focused on what is good, since the good—never the evil—is what accepts truths. Further, it is similar with us, so that we can be corrected by means of truths, though the extent to which we are corrected depends on our focus on what is good. This is why we can be turned toward the Lord in much the same way. However, if we are engaged in evil in the conduct of our lives, we immediately turn back again and justify within ourselves the false rationalizations of our evil over against the truths that we have understood and seen. This happens when we think within ourselves, on the basis of our deeper inclinations.

How the States of Angels in Heaven Change

154   BY "the changes of angels' states," we mean their changes in regard to love and faith and therefore in regard to wisdom and intelligence— to the state of their life, that is. States are attributes of life and of matters that pertain to life; and since angelic life is a life of love and faith and thereby of wisdom and intelligence, states are attributes of these, and we talk about states of love and faith and states of wisdom and intelligence. Now we need to describe how these states change for angels.

Angels are not constantly in the same state as to love, and consequently they are not in the same state as to wisdom, for all the wisdom they have is from their love and in proportion to it. Sometimes they are in a state of intense love, sometimes in a state of love that is not intense. It decreases gradually from its most to its least intense. When they are in the highest level of love, they are in the light and warmth of their lives, or in their greatest clarity and delight. Conversely, when they are in the lowest level they are in shadow and coolness, or in what is dim and unpleasant. From this latter state they return to the first, and so on. The phases follow each other with constant variety.

155

These states follow each other like variations of light and shade, warmth and cold, or like the morning, noon, evening, and night of individual days in our world, varying constantly throughout the year. Not only that, they correspond—morning to the state of their love in clarity, noon to the state of their wisdom in clarity, evening to the state of their wisdom in dimness, and night to a state of no love or wisdom. It should be known, though, that there is no correspondence of night with the states of life of people in heaven, but rather a correspondence of the half-light that comes before dawn. The correspondence of night is with people who are in hell.[a]

Because of this correspondence, "day" and "year" in the Word mean states of life in general, warmth and light mean love and wisdom, morning the first and highest level of love, noon wisdom in its light, evening wisdom in its shade, and the half-light the dimness that comes just before the morning. Night, though, means the loss of love and wisdom.[b]

As the states of the inner levels of angels' love and wisdom change, so too do the states of the various things that surround them and are visible to their eyes; for the things that surround angels are given their appearance

156

a. In heaven, there is no state that corresponds to night, but to the half-light that comes before dawn: 6110. The half-light means the state halfway between the last and the first: 10134.

b. The alternations of state as to enlightenment and perception are structured in heaven the way the times of day are in the world: 5672, 5962, 6310 *[6110]*, 8426, 9213, 10605. Days and years in the Word mean all states in general: 23, 487, 488, 493, 893, 2788, 3462, 4850, 10656. Morning means the beginning of a new state, and a state of love: 7216 *[7218]*, 8426, 8427, 10114, 10134. Evening means a state when light and love are vanishing: 10134, 10135. Night means a state without love or faith: 221, 709, 2353, 6000, 6110, 7870, 7947.

according to the things that are within them. We will describe what these are and what they are like in later chapters, where we discuss representations and appearances in heaven.[116]

157　　Each individual angel undergoes and passes through changes of state like this, and so too does each community collectively. Still, one individual does so differently from another because people vary in love and wisdom. There are people in the middle, in a more perfect state than those who are around them all the way to the borders (see above, §§23 *[43]* and 128). But it would take too long to recount the differences, since the quality of love and faith determines how each individual undergoes the changes. Consequently, one may be in clarity and delight when another is in dimness and discomfort, even at the same time, within the same community. It happens differently in one community than in another, too, and in communities of the heavenly kingdom differently than in communities of the spiritual kingdom.

Broadly speaking, the differences in their changes of state are like the variations of states of days in one climate and another on earth. There it is morning for some people while it is evening for others, and some have warmth while others are cold, and vice versa.

158　　I have been told from heaven why changes of state like this occur. Angels have said that there are many reasons. First, the delight of life and of heaven that angels enjoy because of the love and wisdom given them by the Lord would gradually pall if they were constantly engaged in it, the way it happens for people who are involved in pleasures and enjoyments without variety. A second reason is that angels have a sense of self or self-image [117] just as we do, and this involves loving themselves. All the people in heaven are kept free of their sense of self, and to the extent that the Lord does keep them free, they enjoy love and wisdom. To the extent that they are not kept free, however, they are caught up in love for themselves; and since all of them do love that sense of self and carry it with them,[c] these changes of state or successive alternations do occur. A third reason is that they are made more perfect in this way, since they become accustomed to being kept in love for the Lord and kept free from love for themselves. Further, by these alternations of delight and discomfort,

c. Our self-image is loving ourselves: 694, 731, 4317, 5660. This self-image must be detached from us in order for the Lord to be present: 1023, 1044. It is actually detached when we are being kept in what is good by the Lord: 9334, 9335, 9336, 9445 *[9447]*, 9452, 9453, 9454, 9938.

their perception of and sensitivity to what is good become more and more delicate.[d]

They have gone on to say that the Lord does not produce these changes of their states, since the Lord as the sun is always flowing in with warmth and light, that is, with love and wisdom. Rather, they themselves are the cause, since they love their sense of self and this is constantly misleading them. They illustrate this by comparison with our world's sun, which is not the cause of the changes of warmth and cold and of light and darkness, of distinct years and distinct days, because it stays motionless. The reason can be traced to our earth.

I have been shown how the Lord as the sun looks to angels in the heavenly kingdom in their first state, in their second state, and in their third. I saw the Lord as the sun, at first reddish and gleaming, so brilliant as to be beyond description. I was told that the Lord as the sun looks like this to angels in their first state. Later I saw a great, dim halo around the sun, because of which the reddish, gleaming quality that made the sun so brilliant began to dim. I was told that the sun looks like this to them in their second state. Then I saw the halo become darker so that the sun seemed less ruddy, step by step, until finally it looked quite pale. I was told that the sun looks like this to them in their third state. After this, I saw that pale [disk] move to the left toward heaven's moon and add its light to the light of the moon so that the moon shone exceptionally brightly. I was told that this was the fourth state of people in the heavenly kingdom and the first state of people in the spiritual kingdom. I was also told that the changes of state in each kingdom proceed alternately, not throughout, but in one community after another. I was also told that these alternations are not fixed, but happen more or less swiftly without people being aware of it.

Angels went on to say that the sun in and of itself neither changes nor moves, but that things look the way they do because of the ongoing progressions of state in themselves, since the Lord appears to each individual in keeping with that individual's state—reddish to people when they are in an intense love, less ruddy and ultimately pale as their love wanes. The quality of their state is pictured by the dim halo that imposes the apparent changes of flame and light on the sun.

159

d. Angels are being made more perfect to eternity: 4803, 6648. In heaven, there is never any state exactly like any other, which results in a perpetual process of perfecting: 10200.

160   When angels are in this last state, which is when they are involved in their sense of self, they begin to feel depressed. I have talked with them when they were in this state and witnessed their depression.[118] They kept saying, though, that they lived in hope that they would soon return to their earlier state and be in heaven again, so to speak, since heaven for them is being kept free from their sense of self.

161   There are also changes of state in the hells, but these will be described later, when I deal with hell.[119]

Time in Heaven

162   EVEN though things keep happening in sequence and progressing in heaven the way they do in the world, still angels have no notion or concept of time and space. The lack is so complete that they simply do not know what time and space are. Here we will discuss time in heaven, leaving space to be discussed in its own chapter.[120]

163   The reason angels do not know what time is (even though everything for them moves along in sequence just the way it does in our world, so much so that there is no difference) is that in heaven there are no years or days, but only changes of state. Where there are years and days there are times, and where there are changes of state, there are states.

164   The reason we have times in our world is that the sun seems to move sequentially from one zone to another and to make the times we call the seasons of the year. It also moves around the earth and makes the times we call times of day, and it does these by fixed periods.

It is different for heaven's sun. It does not make years and days by sequential motions and rotations, but makes apparent changes of state; and it does not make these by fixed periods, as explained in the preceding chapter. This is why angels are incapable of having any concept of time, but have a concept of state instead. What "state" is may be seen above in §154.

165   Since angels have no concept derived from time, as we in our world do, they have no concept of time or of the things that depend on time.

They do not even know what all these temporal things are, like a year, a month, a week, a day, an hour, today, tomorrow, or yesterday. When angels hear these expressions from one of us (angels are always kept in contact with us by the Lord), they perceive states instead, and things that have to do with state. So our natural concept is changed into a spiritual concept with the angels. This is why expressions of time in the Word mean states, and why things proper to time like the ones listed above mean the spiritual things that correspond to them.[a]

166　It is much the same for all the things that occur as a result of time, such as the four seasons of the year called spring, summer, autumn, and winter; the four times of day called morning, noon, evening, and night; our own four ages called infancy, youth, maturity, and old age; and with the other things that either occur as a result of time or happen in temporal sequence. When we think about them, it is from a temporal standpoint; but an angel thinks about them from the standpoint of state. Consequently, anything in them that is temporal for us changes into an idea of state for the angel. Spring and morning change into an idea of love and wisdom the way they are for angels in their first state; summer and noon change into an idea of love and wisdom as they are in the second state; autumn and evening, as they are in the third state; and night and winter into a concept of the kind of state that is characteristic in hell. This is why similar things are meant by these times in the Word (see above, §155). We can see from this how the natural concepts that occur in our thought become spiritual for the angels who are with us.

167　Since angels have no notion of time, they have a different concept of eternity than we earthly people do. By "eternity," angels perceive an infinite state, not an infinite time.[b]

I was thinking about eternity once, and using a concept of time I could grasp what "to eternity" entailed—namely, without end—but not what "from eternity" entailed and therefore not what God did before

---

a. Expressions of time in the Word mean states: 2788, 2837, 3254, 3356, 4816 [4814], 4901, 4916, 7218, 8070, 10133, 10605. Angels do their thinking without any concept of time or space: 3404. The reasons for this: 1274, 1382, 3356, 4882, 4901, 6110, 7218, 7381. What a "year" means in the Word: 487, 488, 493, 893, 2906, 7828, 10209. What a "month" means: 3814. What a "week" means: 2044, 3845. What a "day" means: 23, 487, 488, 6110, 7430 [7443], 8426, 9213, 10062 [10132], 10605. What "today" means: 2838, 3998, 4304, 6165, 6984, 9939. What "tomorrow" means: 3998, 10497. What "yesterday" means: 6983, 7124 [7114], 7140.

b. We have a concept of eternity that includes time, while angels have one without time: 1382, 3404, 8325.

creation, from eternity. As my anxiety mounted because of this, I was raised into the sphere of heaven and therefore into the perception of eternity shared by angels. This shed light for me on the fact that we ought not to think about eternity in temporal terms but in terms of state, and that when we do, we can grasp what "from eternity" entails, which was actually done for me.

168 The angels who talk with us never use the natural concepts that are proper to us, all of which derive from time, space, matter, and the like. They use spiritual concepts, all of which derive from states and their various changes in and around angels. However, when the angelic concepts, which are spiritual, flow into us, they change instantly and spontaneously into those natural concepts proper to us which exactly correspond to the spiritual ones. Neither the angels nor we are aware of this; but still, this is how all inflow of heaven occurs for us.

There were some angels who were let very intimately into my thoughts, all the way into natural ones that contained a mass of material from time and space. However, since at that point they could not understand anything at all, they promptly withdrew; and after they had withdrawn I heard them talking, saying that they had been in darkness.

[2] I have been allowed to know from experience what angels' ignorance of time is like. There was a particular individual from heaven whose nature did allow him to be let into natural concepts such as we have. I talked with him afterward, person to person, and at first he did not know what it was that I was calling "time." So I actually had to tell him how the sun seems to travel around our earth and make years and days, and that as a result, years are divided into four seasons and into months and weeks, and days into twenty-four hours, and that these times recur at fixed intervals. This gives rise to our expressions for time. He was astonished when he heard this, and said that he had not known that kind of thing, but only what states were.

[3] In the course of our conversation I mentioned that it was known in our world that there is no time in heaven. We do actually talk as though we knew, since when people die, we say that they have left temporal things and have passed beyond time, meaning that they have left our world. I also said that it is known by some that times are states in origin because they recognize that times are experienced in precise accord with the states of affection we are caught up in. They are short for us when we are engaged in pleasant and cheerful pursuits and long when we are engaged in distasteful and depressing ones, and variable when we are

in hope or expectation. As a result, scholars are asking what time and space are, and some of them even recognize that time is an attribute of the natural person.

A natural person may believe that we would have no thought if concepts of time, space, and matter were taken away from us, that all our thought is based on these foundations.[c] Let such people know, though, that thoughts are limited and constrained to the extent that they derive from time, space, and matter, and that they are freed and expanded to the extent that they do not derive from such things, because to that same extent the mind is raised above bodily and worldly considerations. This is the source of angels' wisdom, which is so great that we must call it incomprehensible, since it does not fit into ideas that are formed merely from these [lower] concerns.

169

Representations and Appearances in Heaven

ANYONE who thinks solely from natural light cannot understand that anything in heaven is like anything in our world. This is because such people, on the basis of this light, have both thought and decided that angels are nothing but minds, and that minds are like ethereal breath. This would mean that angels did not have the senses we do, so they would not have eyes; and if they did not have eyes there would be no objects [of sight]. However, angels do have all the senses we do—far more delicate ones, in fact—and the light in which they see is far brighter than the light in which we see.

170

On angels being people in a most perfect form with the use of all their senses, see §§73–77 above; and on light in heaven being far brighter than the light in our world, see §§126–132.

There is no way to describe briefly how things look to angels in the heavens. To a considerable extent, they look like the things we see on earth, but they are more perfect in form and also more abundant.

171

---

c. Unlike angels, we do not think without some concept of time: 3404.

We may conclude that there are things like this in the heavens because of what the prophets saw—for example what Ezekiel saw of the new temple and the new earth as described in chapters 40 to 48 [of his book], what Daniel describes in his chapters 7–12, what John saw as described from the first through the last chapter of Revelation, along with other visions presented in both the historical and the prophetic books of the Word.[121] They saw things like this when heaven was opened to them, and heaven is said to be opened when our inner sight, the sight of our spirit, is opened. For the things that exist in heaven cannot be seen with our physical eyes, but only with the eyes of our spirit; and when it pleases the Lord, these are opened. At such times we are led out of the natural light that our physical senses are in and raised into the spiritual light in which we dwell because of our spirit. This is the light in which I have seen the things that exist in the heavens.

172   But even though the things that are seen in the heavens are largely similar to things on earth, they are not alike in essence. The things that exist in the heavens come from heaven's sun, while earthly things come from our world's sun. Things that arise from heaven's sun are called spiritual, while things that arise from our world's sun are called natural.

173   Things that arise in the heavens do not arise in the same way as things on earth. In the heavens, everything comes into being from the Lord in response to the deeper natures of the angels. Angels do in fact have more inward and more outward natures. Everything that is deeper within them has to do with love and faith, and therefore with their intending and discernment, since their intending and discernment are the vehicles of their love and faith. Their more outward natures, though, are perfectly responsive to their inner natures (on the responsiveness of their outward natures to their more inward ones, see §§87–115 above). This can be illustrated by what we have said above about heaven's warmth and light, that angels have warmth in keeping with the quality of their love, and light in keeping with the quality of their wisdom (see §§128–134). The same holds true for the other things that impinge on angels' senses.

174   When I have been allowed to be in the company of angels, I have seen what was there exactly the way I see things in our world, so perceptibly that I did not know I was not in our world and in the court of some king here. I have also talked with angels just as one person here talks to another.

175   Since all the things that are responsive to angels' deeper natures also portray them, they are called *representations*. Since they vary depending on the states of the deeper natures for angels, they are called *appearances,*

even though the things that are visible to angels' eyes in the heavens and are perceived by their other senses appear and are sensed just as vividly as things are for us on earth, in fact far more clearly, crisply, and perceptibly. The appearances that arise in heaven in this way are called *real appearances* because they do actually come into being. There are also unreal appearances, things that seem to be present but do not correspond to deeper realities.[a] But more on this later.[122]

By way of illustration, I should like to offer one instance of the way things look to angels because of correspondences. To angels who are focused on intelligence there appear gardens and parks full of all kinds of trees and flowers. The trees there are laid out in the loveliest designs, joined into vaulted arches offering spaces for entrance, and with promenades around them. All this is so beautiful as to defy description. People who are focused on intelligence stroll there picking the flowers and weaving garlands to grace babies with. There are kinds of tree and flower there never seen, not even possible, in our world. In the trees, too, there are fruits in keeping with the quality of the love these intelligent angels are absorbed in. They see such things because a garden and a park, and the fruit trees and flowers, correspond to intelligence and wisdom.[b]

It is known on earth that things like this exist in the heavens, but it is known only to people who are engaged in what is good and who have not extinguished heaven's light within themselves by natural light and its deceptiveness. When the subject is heaven, people actually think and say that things are there *that ear has never heard, nor eye seen.*[123]

176

---

a. All the things that are visible to angels are representations: 1971, 3213–3226, 3457 *[3342]*, 3475, 3485, 9481, 9574 *[9457]*, 9576, 9577. The heavens are full of representations: 1521, 1532, 1619. The representations are lovelier as one moves more deeply into the heavens: 3475. The representations there are real appearances because they come from heaven's light: 3485. The divine inflow is changed into representations in the higher heavens, and consequently in the lower heavens as well: 2179, 3213, 9457, 9481, 9576, 9577. Things are called representations that appear to angels' eyes in forms like those in nature and therefore like things in our world: 9574 *[9457]*. Inner things change into outer ones in this way: 1632, 2987–3002. The nature of representations in heaven, illustrated by various examples: 1521, 1532, 1619–1628, 1807, 1973, 1974, 1977, 1980, 1981, 2299, 2601, 2761, 2762, 3217, 3219, 3220, 3348, 3350, 5198, 9090, 10278 *[10276]*. All the things that are visible in the heavens are in accord with correspondences and are called representations: 3213–3226, 3457 *[3342]*, 3475, 3485, 9481, 9574 *[9457]*, 9576, 9577. All the things that are responsive also portray and also mean what they respond to: 2890 *[2896]*, 2987, 2971 *[2991]*, 2989, 2990, 3002, 3225.
b. "Garden" and "park" mean intelligence and wisdom: 100, 108, 3220. The meaning of the garden of [literally, "from"] Eden and the garden of Jehovah: 99, 100, 1588. How magnificent the paradisal things in the other life are: 1122, 1622, 2296, 4528, 4529. Trees mean the perceptions and insights that give rise to wisdom and intelligence: 103, 2163, 2682, 2722, 2972, 7692. Fruits mean the good that love and thoughtfulness do: 3146, 7690, 9337.

The Clothes Angels Appear In

177 SINCE angels are people and live together the way people on earth do, they have clothes and homes and a great many other things: the difference, however, being that everything is more perfect for them because they are in a more perfect state. For just as angelic wisdom surpasses our wisdom so greatly as to be inexpressible, so too does everything that comes to their perception and sight, since everything perceived by and apparent to angels corresponds to their wisdom (see above, §173).

178 Like everything else, the clothes angels wear correspond, and since they do correspond they truly exist (see above, §175). Their clothes reflect their intelligence, so all the people in heaven are dressed according to their intelligence; and since one will surpass another in intelligence (see §§43 and 128), one will have better quality clothing than another. The most intelligent wear clothes that gleam as though aflame, some radiant as though alight. The less intelligent wear pure white and soft white clothes that do not shine, and those still less intelligent wear clothes of various colors. The angels of the inmost heaven, though, are naked.

179 Because angels' clothes correspond to their intelligence they also correspond to what is true, since all intelligence comes from divine truth. So it amounts to the same thing whether you say that angels are dressed according to their intelligence or according to divine truth. The reason the garments of some angels gleam as though aflame, while the garments of others shine as though alight, is that flame corresponds to what is good, and light to what is true because of that good.[a] The reason some garments are pure white and soft white and do not shine, while others are of various colors, is that divine good and truth are less dazzling and are also differently accepted among less intelligent people.[b]

a. Garments in the Word mean truths by reason of correspondence: 1073, 2576, 5319, 5954, 9212, 9216, 9952, 10536; because truths clothe what is good: 5248. A veil means something of intellect, since discernment is the vessel of what is true: 6378. White garments of linen mean truths from the Divine: 5319, 9469. Flame means spiritual good, and the light from it means truth from that good: 3222, 6832.
b. Angels and spirits are seen wearing clothes that accord with their truths and therefore with their intelligence: 165, 5248, 5954, 9212, 9216, 9814, 9952, 10536. Some garments of angels are radiant, and some are not: 5248.

Pure white and soft white correspond to what is true,[c] and colors correspond to different shadings of truth.[d] The reason angels in the inmost heaven are naked is that they are in innocence, and innocence corresponds to nudity.[e]

Since angels wear clothes in heaven, they have appeared clothed when they were seen in our world, like the ones seen by the prophets and the ones by the Lord's tomb, whose "appearance was like lightning and whose clothes were gleaming and white" (Matthew 28:3; Mark 16:5; Luke 22:4 *[24:4]*; John 20:11, 13 *[20:12]*) and the ones seen in heaven by John whose "garments were of linen and white" (Revelation 4:4; 19:11, 13). And since intelligence comes from divine truth, the Lord's garments, when he was transfigured, were "gleaming and white as light" (Matthew 17:2; Mark 9:3; Luke 9:29: on light as divine truth emanating from the Lord, see §129 above). This is why garments in the Word mean things true and the intelligence that results from them, as in John:[124] "Those who have not defiled their garments will walk with me in white, because they are worthy; whoever overcomes will be clothed with white garments" (Revelation 3:4, 5); and "Blessed are those who are watchful and take care of their garments" (Revelation 16:15).

Concerning Jerusalem, meaning the church as it is focused on what is true,[f] it says in Isaiah, "Rise up, put on your strength, O Zion; put on the garments of your beauty, O Jerusalem" (Isaiah 52:1); and in Ezekiel, "O Jerusalem, I have clothed you with linen, I have veiled you with silk, your garments are linen and silk" (Ezekiel 16:10, 13); and many other passages.

In contrast, someone who is not engaged with truths is said not to be wearing a wedding garment, as in Matthew: "When the king came in, he saw the one not wearing a wedding garment and said, 'Friend, how have you come in here without a wedding garment?' So that one was cast

***

c. Pure white and soft white in the Word mean what is true, because they come from light in heaven: 3301, 3993, 4001 *[4007]*.

d. Colors in heaven are variegations of the light there: 1042, 1043, 1053, 1624, 3993, 4530, 4742, 4922. Colors mean various things that are matters of intelligence and wisdom: 4530, 4922, 4677, 9466. The precious stones in the Urim and Thummim, depending on their colors, meant all the truths in the heavens that stem from what is good: 9865, 9868, 9905. To the extent that colors are derived from red, they mean what is good; while to the extent that they are derived from white, they mean what is true: 9476.

e. All the people in the inmost heaven are innocent, and therefore seem to be naked: 154, 165, 297, 2736, 3887, 8375, 9960. Innocence is manifested in heaven as nudity: 165, 8375, 9960. For innocent and chaste people, nudity is not a matter of shame because there is no occasion for offense: 165, 213, 8375.

f. Jerusalem means the church where there is genuine doctrine: 402, 3654, 9166.

out into the outer darkness" (Matthew 22:12–13 *[11–13]*). The wedding house means heaven and the church by virtue of the Lord's union with them through his divine truth. This is why in the Word the Lord is called the Bridegroom and Husband, and heaven and the church the bride and wife.

181   We can tell that angels' clothes do not merely look like clothes but really are because they not only see them, they feel them as well. Further, they have many garments that they take off and put on, and they put away the ones they are not using and put back on the ones they are. I have seen thousands of times that they wear different clothes.

I have asked them where they got their clothes, and they have told me that their clothes come from the Lord and are given to them, and that sometimes they are clothed without noticing it. They have also said that their clothes change depending on the changes of their state, that their clothes are radiant and gleaming white in their first and second state, while in the third and fourth states they are somewhat dimmer. This too is because of correspondences, because these changes of state have to do with their intelligence and wisdom, discussed above in §§154–161.

182   For everyone in the spiritual world, clothing depends on intelligence and therefore on the truths that constitute intelligence. Although people in the hells do seem to be clothed, because they lack truths their clothes are nothing but rags, dirty and foul, each individual in keeping with his or her own insanity. They cannot be clothed in any other way, either. The Lord allows them to wear clothes so that they will not appear naked.

Angels' Homes and Houses

183   SINCE there are communities in heaven, with people living there the way we do, they too have homes; and these vary depending on the state of the life of each individual. They are splendid for people who are especially deserving and less splendid for people who are of lower rank.

At times, I have talked with angels about homes in heaven, telling them that nowadays hardly anyone would believe that they have homes and houses—some because they do not see them, some because they do not realize that angels are people, some because they believe that the angelic heaven is the sky they see about them with their eyes. Since this appears to be empty and they think that angels are ethereal forms, they come to the conclusion that angels live in the ether. Further, they do not grasp the fact that the same kinds of thing exist in the spiritual world as in the natural, because they know nothing about the spiritual.

[2] Angels have told me that they were aware that this kind of ignorance was prevalent in the world nowadays and, remarkably enough, mainly within the church, and more among the intellectuals there than among the ones labeled simple. They have also said that people could know from the Word that angels are people because the ones that have been seen have been seen as people. So too was the Lord, who took on his full humanity. People could then realize that since angels are people, they have houses and homes and do not fly around in the air,[125] that even though they are called "spirits" they are not breezes, as the ignorance (which angels call insanity) of some would have it. They could also grasp this if when they thought about angels and spirits they would step outside their preconceptions, which happens when they are not constantly questioning and consciously pondering *whether this is so.* Everyone actually has a general notion that angels are in human form and that they have homes that are called heavenly dwellings, which are more splendid than earthly houses. But this general notion (which comes from an inflow from heaven), the angels said, promptly collapses into nothing when it becomes the center of conscious attention and is faced with the question *whether it is so.* This happens particularly among scholars who have used their self-generated intelligence to shut off from themselves both heaven and the passage of light from it.[126]

[3] Much the same happens in regard to faith in our life after death. People who talk about it without thinking at the same time from scholarly concepts of the soul or the doctrine of reunion with our physical bodies believe that after death we will live as people—among angels if we have lived well—and that then we will see magnificent sights and experience raptures. But the moment they focus on the doctrine of reunion with our bodies or some hypothesis about "the soul," and therefore begin to wonder whether the soul is really like this, whether it is all true, their former notion vanishes.

But it would be better to present some experiential evidence at this point. Whenever I have talked with angels face to face, I have been with them in their houses. Their houses were just like the houses on earth that

184

we call homes, but more beautiful. They have chambers, suites, and bedrooms in abundance, and courtyards with gardens, flower beds, and lawns around them. Where there is some concentration of people, the houses are adjoining, one near another, arranged in the form of a city with streets and lanes and public squares, just like the ones we see in cities on our earth. I have been allowed to stroll along them and look around wherever I wished, at times entering people's homes. This has happened when I was fully awake, with my inner sight opened.[a]

185　I have seen palaces in heaven that were so splendid as to be beyond description. Their upper stories shone as though they were made of pure gold, and their lower ones as though they were made of precious gems. Each palace seemed more splendid than the last. It was the same inside. The rooms were graced with such lovely adornments that neither words nor the arts and sciences are adequate to describe them. On the side that faced south there were parklands where everything sparkled in the same way, here and there the leaves like silver and the fruits like gold, with the flowers in their beds making virtual rainbows with their colors. On the horizon of sight there were other palaces that framed the scene. The architecture of heaven is like this, so that you might call it the very essence of the art—and small wonder, since the art itself does come to us from heaven.

Angels tell me that things like this and countless others even more perfect are presented to their view by the Lord; but that such sights actually delight their minds more than their eyes because they see correspondences in the details, and through their correspondences they see things divine.

186　On this matter of correspondences, I have also been told that not only the palaces and the homes but all the little things within and outside them correspond to the deeper qualities that they receive from the Lord. In general terms, their houses correspond to the good that occupies them and the items within their houses to the various things that constitute that good.[b] The items that are outside the homes refer to true

---

a. Angels have towns, palaces, and homes, described: 940, 941, 942, 1116, 1626, 1627, 1628, 1630, 1631, 4622.

b. Houses, and their contents, mean the things within us that are attributes of our minds, and therefore mean our more inward natures: 710, 2233, 2234 *[2231]*, 2719 *[2454]*, 3128, 3538, 4973, 5023, 6619 *[6639]*, 6690, 7353, 7848, 7910, 7929, 9150; and therefore matters of what is good and true: 2233, 2234 *[2231]*, 2559, 4982, 7848, 7929. Rooms and bedrooms mean the things that are deeper within: 3900, 5994 *[5694]*, 7353. The roof of a house means the inmost: 3652, 10184. A wooden house means matters of good, and a stone house matters of truth: 3720.

things that derive from the good, and also to experiences of perception and recognition.ᶜ Since these correspond to the good and true things they receive from the Lord, they correspond to their love and therefore to their wisdom and intelligence, because love is a matter of what is good, wisdom of what is both good and true, and intelligence of truth that stems from the good. This, they tell me, is the sort of thing angels perceive when they look at their houses; and this is why these sights delight and move their minds more than their eyes.

So I could see why the Lord calls himself the temple that is in Jerusalem (John 2:19, 21).ᵈ I could also see why the New Jerusalem appeared as a city of pure gold, with gates of pearl and foundations of precious gems (Revelation 21): it is because a temple offers an image of the Lord's divine human; the New Jerusalem refers to the church that was going to be founded; and the twelve gates are the truths that lead to what is good, and the foundations are the truths on which it is based.ᵉ

The angels who constitute the Lord's heavenly kingdom live for the most part in loftier places that look like mountains above the ground. The angels who constitute the Lord's spiritual kingdom live in less lofty places that look like hills, while the angels who live in the lowest regions of heaven live in places that look like rocky cliffs. These things also stem from correspondences, since the deeper things correspond to higher ones and the more outward to lower ones.ᶠ This is why mountains in the Word mean heavenly love, hills mean spiritual love, and rocks mean faith.ᵍ

c. [Swedenborg's note here refers the reader to the note in §176 above.]

d. In the highest sense, "the house of God" means the Lord's divine human in respect to divine good, and the temple means the same in respect to divine truth. In a relative sense, they mean heaven and the church in respect to what is good and true: 3720.

e. Jerusalem means the church where there is authentic doctrine: 402, 3654, 9166. The gates mean an introduction to the doctrine of the church, and through that doctrine, to the church itself: 2943, 4478 *[4477]*. The foundation means the truth on which heaven, the church, and the doctrine are based: 9643.

f. In the Word, more inward things are expressed by "higher," and higher things mean more inward ones: 2148, 3084, 4599, 5146, 8325. "High" means inner, and also heaven: 1735, 2148, 4210, 4599, 8153.

g. In heaven, one can see mountains, hills, rocks, valleys, and plains just as we can in this world: 10608. Angels who are in the good of love live on mountains, angels in the good of charity on hills, and angels in the good of faith on cliffs: 10438. Therefore mountains in the Word mean the good of love: 795, 4210, 6435, 8327, 8758, 10438, 10608. Hills mean the good of charity: 6435, 10438. Rocks mean the good and truth of faith: 8581, 10580. The stone from which rocks are made also means the truth of faith: 114, 643, 1298, 3720, 6426, 8608 *[8609]*, 10376. This is why mountains mean heaven: 8327, 8805, 9420; and why a mountaintop means the highest heaven: 9422, 9434, 10608. Therefore the early people held their holy worship on mountains: 796, 2722.

189   There are angels who do not live in communities but apart, home by home. They live in the center of heaven because they are the best angels.

190   The houses angels live in are not constructed as houses in our world are, but are given them by the Lord gratis, to each individual according to his or her acceptance of what is good and true. They also change slightly in response to the changes of state of their deeper natures (see above, §§154–160).

Whatever angels possess, they attribute to the Lord, and anything they need is given to them.

Space in Heaven

191   EVEN though everything in heaven appears to be located in space just like things in our world, still angels have no notion or concept of location and space. Since this can only seem like a paradox, and since it is highly significant, I should like to shed some light on it.

192   All motion in the spiritual world is the effect of changes of inner states, to the point that motion is nothing but change of state.[a] This is how I have been led by the Lord into the heavens and also to other planets in the universe.[127] This happened to my spirit, while my body remained in the same place.[b] This is how all angels move about, which

a. In the Word, places and spaces mean states: 2625, 2837, 3356, 3387, 7381, 10578 *[10580]*; from experience: 1274, 1277, 1376–1381, 4321, 4882, 10146, 10578 *[10580]*. Distances mean differences in state of life: 9104, 9967. Motion and changes of location in the spiritual world are changes of the state of life because that is their source: 1273, 1274, 1275, 1377, 3356, 9440. The same holds true of journeys: 9440, 10734; illustrated from experience: 1273–1277, 5606 *[5605]*. This is why journeying in the Word means living, and also the course of life, as does emigrating: 3335, 4554, 4585, 4882, 5493, 5606 *[5605]*, 5996, 8345, 8397, 8417, 8420, 8557. "To go with the Lord" is to live with him: 10567.

b. An individual can be led great distances in spirit by changes of state, with the body staying in the same place: from experience, 9440, 9967, 10734. What it means to be led by the spirit into another place: 1884.

means they do not have distances; and if they do not have distances, they do not have space. Instead they have states and their changes.

This being the nature of motion, we can see that drawing near is likeness of inner state and moving away is dissimilarity. This is why the people who are nearby are the ones in a similar state and the ones who are far away are in dissimilar states. It is why space in heaven is nothing but the outward states that correspond to the inner ones.

This is the only reason the heavens are differentiated from each other, as are the communities of each heaven and the individuals in each community. It is also why the hells are completely separate from the heavens: they are in an opposite state.

This is also why in the spiritual world one individual is present to another if only that presence is intensely desired. This is because one person sees another in thought in this way and identifies with that individual's state. Conversely, one person moves away from another to the extent that there is any sense of reluctance; and since all reluctance comes from an opposition of affections and disagreement of thoughts, there can be many people appearing together in one place as long as they agree, but as soon as they disagree, they vanish.

Whenever people move from one place to another, whether it is within their town, in their courtyards, in their gardens, or to people outside their own community, they get there more quickly if they are eager to and more slowly if they are not. The path itself is lengthened or shortened depending on their desire, even though it is the same path. I have often seen this, much to my surprise.

We can see from all this again that distance and space itself depend wholly on the inner state of angels;[c,128] and since this is the case, no notion or concept of space can enter their minds even though they have space just the way we do in our world.

We can illustrate this by our own thoughts, which are also devoid of space; for whatever we focus on intently in our thought is seemingly present. Then too, anyone who reflects on it realizes that our eyesight registers space only through the intermediate objects on earth that we see at the same time, or from our knowing from experience that things are a certain distance away. This is because we are dealing with a continuum, and in a continuum there is no apparent distance except by means of

193

194

195

196

c. Places and spaces are presented to view in response to the inner states of angels and spirits: 5604 [5605], 9440, 10146.

discontinuities. This is even more the case for angels because their sight acts in unison with their thought, and their thought in unison with their affection, and also because things seem near or remote, and things change, in response to the states of their deeper natures, as already noted.

197 This is why places and spaces in the Word (and everything that involves space) mean matters that involve state—distances, for instance, and nearness and remoteness, paths, journeys, emigrations, miles, stadia,[129] plains, fields, gardens, cities, streets, motion, various kinds of measurement, length, breadth, height, and depth, and countless other things—for so many things that enter our thought from our world derive something from space and time.

[2] I should like only to highlight what length, breadth, and height mean in the Word. In this world we call something long and broad if it is long and broad spatially, and the same holds true for "high." In heaven, though, where thinking does not involve space, people understand length as a state of good and breadth as a state of truth, while height is their difference in regard to level (discussed above in §38). The reason these three dimensions are understood in this way is that length in heaven is from east to west, which is where people live who are in the good of love. Breadth in heaven is from south to north, where people live who are in truth because of what is good (see above, §148); and height in heaven applies to both in regard to their level. This is why qualities of this sort are meant in the Word by length and breadth and height as in Ezekiel 40–48, where the measurements are given of the new temple and the new earth, with its courts, rooms, doors, gates, windows, and surroundings, referring to the new church and the good and true things that are in it. So too all the measurements elsewhere. [3] The New Jerusalem is similarly described in Revelation, as follows:

> The city was laid out foursquare, its length the same as its breadth; and [the angel] measured the city with the reed at twelve thousand stadia;[130] the length and breadth and height were equal. (Revelation 21:16)

Here the New Jerusalem means a new church, so its measurements mean attributes of that church, length referring to the good of its love, breadth to the truth that derives from that good, and height to both the good and the true in respect to their level. Twelve thousand stadia means everything good and true taken together. Otherwise, what would be the point of having its height be twelve thousand stadia like its length and its breadth?

We can see in David that breadth in the Word means truth:

Jehovah, you have not left me in the grasp of my enemy's hand; you have made my feet stand in a broad place. (Psalms 31:8)[131]

I called on Jah from my constraint; he answered me in a broad place. (Psalms 118:5)

There are other passages as well; for example, Isaiah 8:8 and Habakkuk 1:6. It also holds true elsewhere.

We can see from this that even though there is space in heaven as   198
there is in our world, nothing there is evaluated on the basis of space, but only on the basis of state. Also spaces there cannot be measured the way they can in our world, but only seen out of and in accordance with the state of their deeper natures.[d]

The essential first cause of all this is that the Lord is present to each in-   199
dividual according to that individual's love and faith,[e] and that everything looks near or remote depending on his presence, since this is what defines everything that exists in the heavens. This is what gives angels wisdom, since it provides them with an outreach of thoughts, which in turn affords them communication with everyone in the heavens. In a word, this is what enables them to think spiritually and not naturally, the way we do.

Heaven's Form, Which Determines How People Associate and Communicate There

TO some extent, we can determine what heaven's form is like on the   200
basis of what has been presented in the preceding chapters—that heaven has a basic similarity in its greatest and its smallest instances (§72);

---

d. In the Word, length means what is good: 1613, 9487. Breadth means what is true: 1613, 3433, 3434, 4482, 9487, 10179. Height means what is good and true in respect to their level: 9489, 9773, 10181.

e. The Lord's union and presence with angels depends on their acceptance of love and thoughtfulness from him: 290, 681, 1954, 2658, 2886, 2888, 2889, 3001, 3741, 3742, 3743, 4318, 4319, 4524, 7211, 9128.

that therefore each community is a heaven in lesser form, and each angel in least form (§§51–58); that as heaven as a whole resembles a single person, so every community of heaven resembles a person in lesser form and every individual angel in least form (§§59–77); that the wisest people are at the center, with the less wise around them all the way to the borders, and that the same holds true for each community (§43); and that people who are engaged in the good of love live along the east-west axis and people who are engaged in truths that derive from the good along the south-north axis, which also holds true for each community (§§148–149). All these things are determined by heaven's form, so we can figure out what that form is like in a general sense.[a]

201　We need to know what heaven's form is like because it determines not only how angels associate with each other but also how all their communication takes place; and since all their communication is also an outreach of their thoughts and affections, this means all their intelligence and wisdom. This is why the extent to which we are in heaven's form (are forms of heaven) determines how wise we are. It amounts to the same thing whether you say "in heaven's form" or "in heaven's design," since the form of any entity comes from its design and is determined by it.[b]

202　One thing needs to be said first, namely what it is to be in heaven's form. We have been created in the image of heaven and in the image of this world, our inner being in the image of heaven and our outer in the image of this world (see above, §57). Whether you say "in the image" or "according to the form," it amounts to the same thing. However, since by the evils of our intention and the distortions of our thinking we have destroyed the image and therefore the form of heaven within us, and in its place have imported the image and form of hell, our inner being is closed from the time of birth. This is why we, unlike all other kinds of animal, are born into utter ignorance. However, for the image or form of heaven to be restored for us, we need to be educated in the principles of the design; for the form, as explained above, depends on the design. The Word contains all the laws of the divine design, for the laws of the divine design are the precepts we find there. To the extent that we know them and live

a. The whole heaven—specifically all its angelic communities—is arranged by the Lord according to his divine order, since the Lord's divine [nature] in and around the angels constitutes heaven: 3038, 7211, 9128, 9338, 10125, 10151, 10157. On the heavenly form: 4040–4043, 6607, 9877.
b. Heaven's form is a form that follows from the divine design: 4040–4043, 6607, 9877.

by them, our inner being is opened, and in it the design or form of heaven is formed anew. We can see from this what it is to be in heaven's form—namely, it is living according to what is in the Word.[c]

To the extent that people are in heaven's form they are in heaven and are in fact a heaven in least form (§57). Further, they live in intelligence and wisdom to that same extent, for as already noted, all the thought of our intellect and all the affection of our volition reach out round about us in heaven according to its form and communicate wonderfully with the communities there, and they in turn communicate with us.[d]

[2] There are people who believe that their thoughts and affections do not really reach out around them but are inside them, because they see what they are thinking as inside themselves and not as remote from themselves. They are sadly mistaken, though; for just as our eyesight reaches out to remote objects and is affected in keeping with the patterns that it sees in that outreach, so our inner sight, which is an attribute of our intellect, has an outreach in the spiritual world even though (for reasons presented in §196 above) we do not perceive it. The only difference is that our eyesight is affected on the natural level because it is made of materials from the natural world, while the sight of our intellect is affected spiritually because it is made of materials in the spiritual world that all have to do with what is good and true. The reason we do not know that this is the case is that we do not know that there is a certain light that illumines our understanding. Yet without the light that illumines our understanding, we would be incapable of thinking anything. (On this light, see above, §§126–132.)

203

c. Divine truths are the laws of the design: 2247 [2447], 7995. To the extent that we live according to the design—to the extent, that is, that we are engaged in what divine truths tell us is good—we are human: 4839, 6605, 6626. The human is the creature in which all the elements of the divine order are brought together, and from creation we are the divine design in form: 4219, 4220 [4222], 4223, 4523, 4524, 5114, 5368 [4839], 6013, 6057, 6605, 6626, 9706, 10156, 10472. We are born not into what is good and true but into what is evil and false, into the opposite of the divine design, that is; and this is why we are born into utter ignorance, and why it is necessary for us to be born anew, that is, regenerated, which is accomplished by means of divine truths from the Lord, so that we may be brought into the design: 1047, 2307, 2308, 3518, 3812, 8480, 8550, 10283, 10284, 10286, 10731. When the Lord forms us anew (that is, regenerates us) he arranges everything within us according to the design, therefore in heaven's form: 5700, 6690, 9931, 10303.

d. Everyone in heaven has a communication of life, which we can call an outreach, into the surrounding angelic communities in accord with the amount and quality of his or her good: 8794, 8797. Thoughts and affections have this kind of outreach: 2475, 6598–6613. We are united and separated according to our dominant affections: 4111.

[3] There was one particular spirit who believed that he thought independently—that is, without any outreach beyond himself and therefore communication with the surrounding communities. So that he might learn that he was wrong, he was deprived of any communication with nearby communities. As a result, he not only lost the power of thinking but actually collapsed lifelessly, just flailing his arms like a newborn baby. In a little while the communication was restored, and bit by bit, as it was restored, he returned to his usual state of thinking.

[4] Some other spirits, who saw this, then admitted that all their thought and affection was flowing in according to this communication—and since this was true of all their thought and affection, it was true of their whole life as well, since all our life consists of our ability to think and to be affected, or in other words, to understand and intend.[e]

204 We need to realize, though, that intelligence and wisdom vary for individuals depending on the communication. For people whose intelligence and wisdom are formed from things genuinely good and true, there is a sharing with communities according to heaven's form; while for people whose intelligence and wisdom are not formed from things genuinely good and true but [only] from things that are in accord with them, the communication is intermittent and only partially coherent because it is not with communities in the sequence characteristic of heaven's form. However, because people who are not in intelligence and wisdom at all are caught up in false notions that stem from their evils, they have a sharing with communities in hell. The outreach depends on the extent to which their attitudes have been internalized.

It should also be known that this sharing with communities is not something that comes to the overt perception of the people involved in

---

e. There is only one life from which all the people in heaven and on earth live: 1954, 2021, 2536, 2658, 2886–2889, 3001, 3484, 3742, 5847, 6467. That life comes from the Lord alone: 2886–2889, 3344, 3484, 4319, 4320, 4524, 4882, 5986, 6325, 6468, 6469, 6470, 9276, 10196. It flows into angels, into spirits, and into us in a wondrous way: 2886–2889, 3337, 3338, 3484, 3742. The Lord flows in from his divine love, which by its very nature wants what is its own to be given to others: 3472 [3742], 4320. Therefore our life seems to be within us and not to be flowing in: 3742, 4320. On the joy of angels that I have perceived—and that has been confirmed by their testimony to me—at the fact that they do not live on their own but from the Lord: 6469. Evil people do not want to be convinced that their life is flowing in: 3743. Life from the Lord does flow in, even for evil people: 2706, 3743, 4417, 10196. However, they turn good into evil and truth into falsity, because our quality determines our acceptance; with examples: 4319, 4320, 4417.

it, but is a communication with the quality in which they participate and which reaches out from them.[f]

All the people in heaven are grouped according to spiritual affinities, which are matters of what is good and true in their pattern—the same way in the whole heaven as in each community and in each household. This is why angels who are involved in similar good and true activities recognize each other the way relatives and kindred spirits do on earth—just as though they had known each other from infancy.

The good and true elements that make up intelligence and wisdom are similarly arranged within each individual angel. They recognize each other in much the same way, and as they recognize each other, they unite.[g]

As a result, people in whom things good and true are united according to heaven's form see things that follow in their sequence and how things fit together far and wide around them. It is different for people in whom things good and true are not united according to heaven's form.

In each heaven, this is the form that determines communication and the outreach of thoughts and affections for angels and therefore determines their intelligence and wisdom. The communication of one heaven with another, though, is different—that of the third or inmost heaven with the second or intermediate, and of these two with the first or outmost. In fact, the communication between heavens should not be called "communication" but "inflow," which we now need to say something about. On the three heavens and their differentiation, see the appropriate chapter above (§§29–40).

We may conclude from the way the heavens are situated in relation to each other that there is not a communication of one heaven with another but an inflow. The third or inmost heaven is above, the second or intermediate is lower, and the first or outmost is still lower. It is much the same for all the communities of each heaven: for example there are some in lofty places that look like mountains (see §188), with people from the

205
206
207

f. Thought flows outward into surrounding communities of spirits and angels: 6600–6605. Still, it does not agitate or disturb the thoughts of the communities: 6601, 6603.

g. What is good recognizes its appropriate truth, and what is true recognizes its good: 2429, 3101, 3102, 3161, 3179, 3180, 4358, 5407 [5704], 5835, 9637. This is the source of the union of what is good and what is true: 3834, 4096, 4097, 4301, 4345, 4353, 4364, 4368, 5365, 7623–7627, 7752–7762, 8530, 9258, 10555; and this happens because of heaven's inflow: 9079.

inmost heavens living on their summits, people from the second heaven below them, and below them again people from the outmost heaven. It is like this everywhere, whether in lofty areas or in lowly ones. A community of a higher heaven does not have any communication with a community of a lower heaven except by means of correspondences (see above, §100), and communication by correspondences is what is called inflow.

208　　One heaven is united to another (or a community of one heaven with a community of another) by the Lord alone, through a direct and an indirect inflow. The direct is from himself, and the indirect is sequential through the higher heavens into the lower ones.[h]

Since the union of the heavens through inflow is accomplished by the Lord alone, the greatest possible precautions are taken to prevent any angel from a higher heaven from looking down into a community of a lower one and talking with anyone there. The moment this happens, the angel will lose intelligence and wisdom. The reason needs to be stated. Every angel has three levels of life, like the three levels of heaven. For the ones in the inmost heaven, the third or inmost level is opened and the second and first are closed. For people in the intermediate heaven the second level is opened and the first and third are closed; and for people in the outermost heaven the first level is opened and the second and third are closed. The moment an angel of the third heaven, then, looks down into a community of the second and talks with anyone there, the third level of that angel is closed; and when it is closed the angel is deprived of wisdom because her or his wisdom dwells on the third level, with none on the second and first.

This is the meaning of the Lord's words in Matthew:

> Let those who are on the roof not come down to take what is in the house; and let those who are in the field not turn back to take their garments. (Matthew 24:17–18)

And in Luke:

> Let those who are on the roof on that day while their belongings are in the house not go down to get them, and let those who are in the field

h. There is a direct inflow from the Lord and an indirect one through heaven: 6063, 6307, 6472, 9682, 9683. The Lord's direct inflow is into the smallest details of everything: 6058, 6474–6478, 8717, 8728. Concerning the Lord's indirect inflow through the heavens: 4067, 6982, 6985, 6996.

not turn back to what is behind them: remember Lot's wife. (Luke 17:31–32)

There is no inflow from lower heavens into higher ones because this goes against the design. Rather, inflow is from the higher ones into the lower. The wisdom of angels of a higher heaven surpasses the wisdom of angels of a lower one by a ratio of thousands to one. This is also why angels of a lower heaven cannot talk with angels of a higher one. In fact, when they look in their direction they do not see them; their heaven looks like something cloudy overhead. However, angels of a higher heaven can see people who are in a lower heaven, though they are not allowed to carry on conversations with them, to prevent them from losing their wisdom, as already mentioned.

209

The thoughts, the affections, and the conversations of angels of the inmost heaven are wholly beyond the perception of angels in the intermediate heaven because they are so transcendent; but when it pleases the Lord, they are visible in the lower heavens as something flamelike from the higher one, while conversations in the intermediate heaven are seen as something shining in the outmost heaven—sometimes as a bright, iridescent cloud. The lower angels can to some extent tell what the higher ones are saying from the way the cloud rises and descends and from its form.

210

This enables us to conclude what heaven's form is like, namely that it is most perfect of all in the inmost heaven, perfect in the intermediate heaven but less so, and still less so in the heaven below that. We can also conclude that the form of one heaven is maintained by another through the inflow from the Lord.

211

However, there is no way to understand what communication by inflow is like without knowing what vertical levels are like and what the difference is between these levels and degrees of length and breadth. The nature of both kinds of levels may be seen in §38.

As to heaven's form and how it works and flows, this is incomprehensible even to angels. It can be brought to some measure of conceptualization by comparison with the form of all the elements of the human body as explored and examined by someone who is both wise and experienced; for as explained above in the relevant chapters, heaven as a whole resembles a single person (§§59–72) and everything in the human [body] corresponds to the heavens (§§87–102). We can see in a general way how incomprehensible and intricate this form is simply by looking at our nerve fibers, which serve to weave absolutely everything [in us] together. There is no way their nature and how they work and flow in the brain can be presented to our

212

eyes, for the countless things involved are so intricate that viewed en masse they look like a soft, undefined lump. Yet actually each and every function of our volition and understanding flows into act through them with perfect definition. We can see how these fibers rejoin in the body by looking at the various plexuses—cardiac, mesenteric, and others—and the nodes called ganglia where many fibers from all over the body come together, combining within these nodes and then exiting in different arrangements to various functions, a pattern that is repeated over and over again. Further, there are similar arrangements in all our viscera, in each member and organ and muscle. Anyone who probes these and other wonders with the eye of wisdom will be utterly stunned; and yet these are the few things that the eye can see, and what it cannot see is more amazing still because it is more inward in nature.

It is abundantly clear that this form corresponds to heaven's form if we consider the way our volition and discernment work in it and according to it, because whatever we intend flows spontaneously into act and whatever we think travels along the fibers from their beginnings to their ends, giving rise to our senses. Further, since this is the form of our thought and intentions, it is the form of our intelligence and wisdom.

It is this form that corresponds to heaven's form. We can learn from this that it is this kind of form that determines the way all the affection and thought of angels reaches out, and that they enjoy intelligence and wisdom to the extent that they are in this form. It may be seen above (§§78–86) that this form of heaven comes from the Lord's divine human.

These matters have been included so that it may also be known that heaven's form by its very nature can never be fathomed even in a general way and is thus incomprehensible even to angels, as already stated.

Forms of Government in Heaven

213 SINCE heaven is differentiated into communities, and the larger communities consist of some hundreds of thousands of angels (§50), and since all the people in a given community are involved in similar good but not in similar wisdom (§43), it follows of necessity that there are forms of government. Good order needs to be kept, and all matters of good order seen to.

The actual forms of government in heaven vary, though. There is one kind in the communities that constitute the Lord's heavenly kingdom and another in the communities that constitute the Lord's spiritual kingdom. They even vary depending on the particular function of each community. However, in the heavens there is no government except the government of mutual love, and the government of mutual love is heavenly government.

The form of government in the Lord's heavenly kingdom is called justice, since all the people there are intent on the good the Lord's love does in and through us, and anything that results from this good is called just. This government belongs to the Lord alone. He leads them and teaches them in matters of life. The truths that we associate with judgment are engraved on their hearts. Everyone knows them, grasps them, and sees them.[a] So matters of judgment never come into dispute for them, only matters of justice that are matters of life. The less wise ask the wiser ones about them, and they in turn ask the Lord and bring back the responses. Their heaven—their deepest delight—is to live justly from the Lord.

214

Government in the Lord's spiritual kingdom is called judgment, since they are intent on that spiritual good that is the good of thoughtfulness toward their neighbor, and this good is in essence true.[b] What is true is a matter of judgment, and what is good is a matter of justice.[c]

215

These angels too are led by the Lord, but indirectly (§208); so they have officials, fewer or more depending on the needs of the community they live in. They also have laws that they observe in their life together. The officials manage everything according to the laws; they understand

---

a. Heavenly angels do not think and talk on the basis of truths the way spiritual angels do, because they enjoy a perception of all matters of truth from the Lord: 202, 597, 607, 784, 1121, 1387 [1384], 1398, 1442, 1919, 7680, 7877, 8780, 9277, 10336. Concerning truths, heavenly angels say, "Yes, yes," or "No, no," while spiritual angels consider whether they are true or not: 2715, 3246, 4446 [4448], 9166, 10786; where explanation is given of the Lord's words, "Let your conversation be 'Yes, yes,' 'No, no'; anything beyond this is from evil" (Matthew 5:37).

b. People in the Lord's spiritual kingdom are focused on what is true and people in the heavenly kingdom on what is good: 863, 875, 927, 1023, 1043, 1044, 1555, 2256, 4328, 4493, 5113, 9596. The good of the spiritual kingdom is the good of thoughtfulness toward one's neighbor, and this good is essentially truth: 8042, 10296.

c. Justice in the Word is associated with what is good and judgment with what is true, so to do justice and judgment is to do what is good and true: 2235, 9857. "Great judgments" [Exodus 6:6] are laws of the divine design and are therefore divine truths: 7206.

them because they are wise, and in matters of doubt they are enlightened by the Lord.

216   Since government on the basis of what is good (the kind in the Lord's heavenly kingdom) is called justice, and government on the basis of what is true (the kind in the Lord's spiritual kingdom) is called judgment, in the Word it says "justice and judgment" when it is talking about heaven and the church; "justice" meaning heavenly good, and "judgment" spiritual good—which latter good, as explained above, is in essence true. The following examples may serve:

> There will be no end to peace on the throne of David and on his kingdom, to establish it and to sustain it in *judgment and justice* from now on and even to eternity. (Isaiah 9:7)[132]

"David" here means the Lord,[d] and his kingdom means his heaven, as we can see from the next passage:

> I will raise up for David a just shoot and he will reign as king and act discerningly and make *judgment and justice* on earth. (Jeremiah 23:5)

> Let Jehovah be extolled because he lives on high and fills Zion with *judgment and justice.* (Isaiah 33:5)

Zion too means heaven and the church.[e]

> I, Jehovah, am he who makes *judgment and justice* on earth, because in them I take pleasure. (Jeremiah 9:24)[133]

> I will betroth you to myself for eternity, and I will betroth you to myself in *justice and judgment.* (Hosea 2:19)

> Jehovah, in the heavens your *justice* is like the mountains of God, and your *judgment* like the great deep. (Psalms 36:5–6)[134]

> They ask me for *judgments of justice,* they long for the approach of God. (Isaiah 58:2)

And elsewhere.

217   In the Lord's spiritual kingdom there are various forms of government, not the same in one community as in another but varying depending on the functions the communities fulfill. Their functions parallel those of the human [body], to which they correspond; and the variety of

---

d. In the prophetic books of the Word, David means the Lord: 1888, 9954.
e. Zion means the church, and specifically the heavenly church: 2362, 9055.

these is well known. The heart has one function, the lungs another, the liver another, the pancreas and spleen others, and so also for each sensory organ. Just as we have these various services going on in our bodies, so services are carried on in the universal human that is heaven, since it is its communities that correspond to them. (The reader may see in the appropriate chapter above, §§87–102, that everything in heaven corresponds to something in us.)

Still, all the forms of government share a central focus on the public good as their end, and within that good, the good of each individual.[f] This is because everyone in all heaven is under the guidance of the Lord, who loves everyone and who from his divine love arranges things so that it is the common good from which individuals receive what is good for them. Each individual receives benefit in proportion to his or her love of the whole, for to the extent that they love the whole they love all the individuals. Since this love is the Lord's they are proportionally loved by the Lord and are benefited.

We may conclude from this what the officials are like—namely, that they are the people who more than others enjoy love and wisdom and who therefore, out of that love, wish well to everyone and out of that wisdom know how to make sure it happens. People like this do not control and command but minister and serve, for doing good for others out of a love for what is good is serving, and making sure that it happens is ministering. They do not make themselves more important than other people but less so, for they put the welfare of the community and of their neighbor first and their own later. What is first is more important, and what is later is less.

They do have respect and renown, though. They live in the center of their communities, loftier than others, and in splendid mansions as well; and they accept this renown and respect. However, they do so not on their own account but for the sake of obedience. They all know that this respect and this renown are gifts from the Lord, so that they may be obeyed.

218

---

f. Every individual and community, including the country and the church and in a universal sense the Lord's kingdom, is our neighbor; and supporting them out of a love for their welfare, in keeping with the quality of their state, is "loving our neighbor"; so their welfare (which is the common good that is to be of primary concern) is our neighbor: 6818–6824, 8123. Further, civic good, which is what is just, is our neighbor: 2915, 4730, 8120–8123. So charity toward our neighbor reaches out to every single detail of our lives; and to love what is good and do what is good out of a love for what is good and true, to do what is just out of a love for what is just in every role and action is to love our neighbor: 2417, 8121–8124.

This is the meaning of the Lord's words to the disciples:

Whoever among you wants to be great needs to minister to you; and whoever among you wants to be first needs to serve you; just as the Human-born One did not come to be ministered to, but to minister. (Matthew 20:27–28 *[26–28]*)

Let the greatest among you be as the least, and the one who is your guide be as one who ministers. (Luke 22:26)

219 A similar form of government, on the smallest scale, is found in each household. There is a master and there are servants; and the master loves the servants and the servants love their master, so out of this love they serve each other. The master teaches how to live and says what needs to be done and the servants obey and fulfill their functions. Being useful is the essential delight of life for everyone. We can see from this that the Lord's kingdom is an organized structure of functions.[135]

220 There are forms of government in the hells as well; for unless there were, they would not be kept in restraint. However, the forms of government there are exact opposites of those in the heavens because they all derive from selfishness. All people there want to control others and to be preeminent. They hate the people who do not agree with them, and use vicious means to get even with them because this is what selfishness is like. So for them it is the more vicious ones who hold office, and who are obeyed out of fear.[g] But more on this later, where I discuss the hells.[136]

Divine Worship in Heaven

221 OUTWARDLY, divine worship in the heavens is not unlike divine worship on earth, but inwardly it is different. People there too have doctrines and sermons and church buildings. The doctrines agree in

g. There are two kinds of dominion, one from love for our neighbor and one from love for ourselves: 10814. Everything good and happy comes from dominion out of love for our neighbor: 10160, 10814. In heaven, no one wants to be in control because of self-love; all want to be helpful, and this is governing out of love for their neighbor and is the source of whatever power they possess: 5732. Everything evil comes from dominion out of self-love: 10038. Once love for oneself and for the world has begun to take control, people are forced into subjection to dictators simply in order to be protected: 7364, 10160, 10814.

essentials, but those in the higher heavens are of deeper wisdom than those of lower heavens. The sermons are in keeping with the doctrines; and just as they have homes and mansions (§§183–190), they also have church buildings where the instruction takes place.

The reason things like this exist in heaven is that angels are constantly being perfected in wisdom and love. They have volition and intellect just as we do, and their intellect, like their intentions, is by nature constantly striving toward perfection—their intellect by means of the truths that constitute intelligence and their intentions through the values that constitute love.[a]

However, the essential divine worship in the heavens does not consist of going to church regularly and listening to sermons but of a life of love, thoughtfulness, and faith in keeping with doctrine. The sermons in church serve only as means of instruction in how to live.

222

I have talked about this with angels and have told them that people in this world believe that divine worship consists solely of going to church and listening to sermons, taking communion three or four times a year, and observing other rituals according to the church's regulations, as well as making time for prayer and behaving devoutly. The angels have told me that these are outward matters that are worth doing but that they are ineffective unless there is something within from which they flow, and that this something within is a life according to the principles that doctrine teaches.

So that I could learn what their church services are like, I have occasionally been allowed to go in and hear sermons. The preacher in the pulpit is stationed in the east. Directly in front sit the people who are in greater light of wisdom than others, while to their right and left are the people in less light. The seating is laid out in a circular form so that everyone can be seen by the preacher. No one is off to the sides and out of the preacher's sight. Newcomers stand by the door at the eastern end of the church to the left of the pulpit. No one is allowed to stand behind the pulpit; if anyone is there, the preacher loses the train of thought. The same thing happens if anyone in the congregation disagrees, so anyone who does is obliged to look away.

223

The sermons there are given with such wisdom that their earthly counterparts cannot be compared to them: people in the heavens actually experience a more inward light.

a. Intellect is open to what is true and volition is open to what is good: 3623, 6125, 7503, 9300, 9930. Just as everything goes back to what is true and good, so everything about our life goes back to intellect and volition: 803, 10122. Angels are being perfected to eternity: 4803, 6648.

Churches in the spiritual kingdom seem to be made of stone, and those in the heavenly kingdom of wood. This is because stone corresponds to the truth that occupies people in the spiritual kingdom and wood to the good that occupies people in the heavenly kingdom.[b] The buildings in this latter kingdom are not called "churches" but "houses of God."

Buildings in the heavenly kingdom are devoid of splendor, but in the spiritual kingdom they are more or less ornate.

224 I also talked with one particular preacher about the holy state characteristic of people who are listening to preachers in church. He said that there is something reverent, devout, and holy in all of us depending on the deeper levels of our love and faith, since there is something holy within our love and faith because the Lord's divine [presence] is there. He added that he did not know what anything holy was apart from these. Further, he said that when he thought about something externally holy apart from these, it might possibly be something that mimicked holiness in outer appearance, something acquired either by skill or by hypocrisy. A deceptive fire arising from love for oneself and the world would generate and present this kind of appearance.

225 All preachers are from the Lord's spiritual kingdom and none from his heavenly kingdom. The reason they are from the spiritual kingdom is that people there are attuned to truths that stem from what is good, and all preaching comes from truths. The reason none is from his heavenly kingdom is that the people there are attuned to the good of love, and see and grasp truths on this basis, but do not talk about them.[c]

Even though the angels who are in the heavenly kingdom grasp and see truths, there are still sermons there because sermons are means of enlightenment in the truths that the angels already know and lead to further perfection by means of many things they have not known before. The moment they hear them, they acknowledge them and therefore grasp them. The truths they grasp they also love, and by living according to them they make them part of their life. They say that living by truths is loving the Lord.[d]

---

b. Stone means what is true: 114, 643, 1298, 3720, 6426, 8609, 10376. Wood means what is good: 643, 3720, 8354. So for the earliest people, who were attuned to heavenly good, buildings were wooden: 3720.

c. [Swedenborg's note at this point refers the reader to the note in §214 above.]

d. To love the Lord and our neighbor is to live by the Lord's precepts: 10143, 10153, 10310, 10578, 10645, 10648 *[10659]*.

All preachers are appointed by the Lord and therefore enjoy the gift **226** of preaching. No one else is allowed to teach in church.

They are called preachers rather than priests. The reason they are not called priests is that heaven's priesthood is the heavenly kingdom, priesthood meaning the good of love for the Lord that characterizes the people in that kingdom. In contrast, heaven's kingship is the spiritual kingdom, kingship meaning the truth from what is good that characterizes people in that kingdom (see above, §24).[e]

All the doctrines that govern the preaching focus on life as their end, **227** none on faith apart from life. The doctrine of the inmost heaven is more full of wisdom than that of the intermediate heaven, and this in turn is more full of intelligence than that of the outmost heaven. The doctrines are in fact suited to the grasp of the angels of each heaven.

The essential of all the doctrines is the recognition of the Lord's divine human.

The Power of Heaven's Angels

PEOPLE who do not know anything about the spiritual world and its **228** inflow into the natural world cannot grasp the fact that angels have power. They think that angels cannot have power because they are spiritual and so pure and insubstantial that they cannot even be seen by our eyes. People who probe more deeply into the causes of things, though, feel otherwise about it. They are aware that all the power we ourselves have comes from our intellect and volition, since without these we cannot move the slightest part of our bodies. Intellect and volition are our spiritual person. This person is what animates the body and its members at will, for the mouth and tongue say what it thinks and the body does

e. Priests represented the Lord in respect to divine good, kings in respect to divine truth: 2015, 6148. So a priest in the Word means people who are attuned to the good of love for the Lord, and priesthood means that good itself: 9806, 9809. A king in the Word means people who are attuned to divine truth, so kingship means what is true from the good: 1672, 2015, 2069, 4575, 4581, 4966, 5044.

what it intends. It even bestows energy at will. Our intention and discernment are governed by the Lord through angels and spirits; and since this is true of our intention and discernment, it is true of all aspects of our bodies because these latter come from the former. Believe it or not, we cannot move a step without the inflow of heaven.

I have been shown that this is true by a great deal of experience. Angels have been allowed to activate my walking, my actions, my tongue, and my conversation as they wished, by flowing into my intention and thinking, and I learned at first hand that I could do nothing on my own.[137] They told me later that everyone is governed in this way, and that we might learn this from the doctrine of the church and from the Word. We actually pray that God will send his angels who may lead us, guide our steps, teach us, and inspire us as to what we should think and say, and so on—this even though we talk and believe quite differently in our private thoughts apart from doctrine.

These things have been mentioned to illustrate the kind of power angels have with us.

229 In the spiritual world angels have so much power that if I were to highlight everything I have seen, it would strain credulity. If anything there is in the way and needs to be removed because it is opposed to the divine design, they raze and overturn it simply by an effort of will and a look. So I have seen mountains that were the abode of evil people leveled and overturned, sometimes shaken from end to end as happens in our earthquakes. I have seen cliffs split down the middle right to the bottom and the evil people on them swallowed up. I have also seen angels scatter some hundreds of thousands of evil spirits and cast them into hell. A vast multitude is powerless against them. The skills and wiles and alliances of evil spirits amount to nothing. Angels see everything and dispel it instantly. But there is more about this in the story of Babylon destroyed.[138] They do have this kind of power in the spiritual world.[139]

The Word, too, shows that angels have power like this in the natural world when it is granted them. For example, they are said to have brought death upon whole armies,[140] to have brought about a plague that killed seventy thousand people. We read of this latter angel:

> The angel stretched out a hand against Jerusalem to destroy it; but Jehovah, repenting of his evil, said to the angel who was destroying the people,[141] It is enough, now hold back your hand: and David saw the angel who was striking the people. (2 Samuel 24:15, 16, 17)

among other passages.

Because angels do have this kind of power they are called powers. It also says in David, "Bless Jehovah, you angels most powerful in strength" (Psalms 103:20).

It does need to be known, though, that angels have absolutely no power on their own, but that all the power they have comes from the Lord. Further, they are powers to the extent that they recognize this fact. Any of them who believe that their power comes from themselves immediately become so weak that they cannot resist even a single evil spirit. This is why angels take absolutely no credit to themselves and turn down any praise or admiration for anything they have done, but attribute it all to the Lord.

It is the divine truth emanating from the Lord that possesses all power in the heavens, because the Lord in heaven is divine truth united to divine good (see §§126–140). To the extent that angels are open to this truth, they are powers.[a]

Further, each individual angel is her or his own truth and own good, because the nature of each one is determined by her or his discernment and intent, discernment being a matter of what is true because all its functions originate in truths, and intent being a matter of what is good because all its functions originate in aspects of the good. You see, whatever we understand we call true and whatever we intend we call good. This is why each one of us is his or her own truth and own good.[b] Therefore, to the extent to which an angel is truth from the Divine and good from the Divine, that angel is a power because the Lord is with her[142] to that extent. Further, since no one enjoys exactly the same good and truth as anyone else (for in heaven and in this world there is constant variety, §20), one angel does not enjoy the same power as another.

The angels who constitute the arm in the universal human or heaven have the most power because they are the ones who more than any others are focused on things true, and good flows into their truths from the entire heaven. So too, all our strength is concentrated in our arms, and the

---

a. Angels are called powers, and they are powers because of their acceptance of divine truth from the Lord: 9639. Angels are open to divine truth from the Lord, and throughout the Word are therefore called "gods": 4295, 4402, 8301, 8192, 9398 *[8988]*.

b. Both people here and angels are their own good and their own truth, therefore their own love and their own faith: 10298, 10367. They are their own discernment and intent because all their life comes from this source; the life of the good is a matter of intent and the life of truth is a matter of discernment: 10076, 10177, 10264, 10284.

whole body expresses its powers through them. This is why "arms" and "hands" in the Word mean power.c

Sometimes a bare arm appears in heaven that has so much power that it could crush any obstacle, even if it were a boulder on earth. Once it moved toward me, and I saw that it could crush my bones to powder.

232 It may be seen in §137 above that all power belongs to the divine truth that emanates from the Lord and that angels are powers to the extent that they accept divine truth from the Lord. However, angels are open to divine truth to the extent that they are open to divine good, since all the power that truths have comes from good. Truths apart from good have none. Further, all the power good has is by means of truth; good has no power apart from truths. Power arises from the union of the two. The same holds true for faith and love, since it is all the same whether you say truth or faith, since everything that makes up faith is true, and whether you say good or love, since everything that makes up love is good.d

I have been able to see how much power angels have through truths from good from the fact that when angels simply look at them, evil spirits fall down in a faint and no longer look human, and that this lasts until the angel looks away. The reason this sort of thing results from the gaze of angels is that their sight comes from the light of heaven, and heaven's light is divine truth (see above, §§126–132). Eyes correspond to truths from good.e

233 Since all power belongs to truths from good, deliberate distortions have none.f All the people in hell are preoccupied with deliberate distortions, so they have no power against what is true and good. However, I will be describing later the kind of power they have among each other and the kind of power evil spirits have before they are thrown into hell.[143]

c. On the correspondence of the hands, arms, and shoulders with the universal human or heaven: 4931–4937. Hands and arms in the Word mean power: 878, 3091, 4931–4932 [4932–4933], 6947, 10017 [10019].

d. All power in the heavens is a property of truth from good, and therefore of faith from love: 3091, 3563, 6413 [6423], 8304, 9643, 10019, 10182. All power comes from the Lord, since he is the source of everything true that constitutes faith and everything good that constitutes love: 9327, 9410. This power is meant by the keys given to Peter: 6344. It is divine truth emanating from the Lord that possesses all power: 6948, 8200. This power of the Lord is what is meant by "sitting at the right of Jehovah": 3387, 4592, 4933, 7518, 7673, 8281, 9133. "The right" is power: 10019.

e. Eyes correspond to truths from good: 4403–4421, 4523–4534, 6923.

f. Falsity from evil has no power because truth from good has it all: 6784, 10481.

The Language of Angels

ANGELS talk with each other just the way we do in this world. They talk about various things—domestic matters, community concerns, issues of moral life, and issues of spiritual life. There is no difference except that they talk with each other more intelligently than we do because they talk from a deeper level of thought. **234**

I have often been allowed to be in their company and talk with them like one friend with another, or sometimes like one stranger with another; and since at such times I was in a state like theirs, it seemed exactly as though I were talking with people on earth.

Angelic language, like human language, is differentiated into words. It is similarly uttered audibly and heard audibly. Angels have mouths and tongues and ears just as we do; and they also have an atmosphere in which the sound of their language is articulated. However, it is a spiritual atmosphere that is adapted to angels, who are spiritual. Angels breathe in their atmosphere and use their breath to utter words just the way we do in ours.[a] **235**

All people in heaven have the same language. They all understand each other, no matter what community they come from, whether nearby or remote.[144] This language is not learned but is innate; it flows from their very affection and thought. The sound of the language corresponds to their affection and the articulations of the sound—the words, that is—correspond to the mental constructs that arise from their affections. Since their language corresponds to these [inner events], it too is spiritual, for it is audible affection and vocal thinking. **236**

[2] Anyone who reflects may realize that all thought comes from affection, which is a function of love, and that mental constructs are various forms into which the general affection is apportioned; for no thoughts or concepts whatever occur apart from affection. This is the source of their soul and life. This is why angels know simply from speech

---

a. There is a breathing in the heavens, but it is more inward: 3884, 3885; from experience: 3884, 3885, 3891, 3893. The ways they breathe differ and vary depending on their states: 1119, 3886, 3887, 3889, 3892, 3893. Evil people are utterly incapable of breathing in heaven and suffocate if they come there: 3893 *[3894]*.

what kind of person someone is—they know the quality of the affection from the sound and the quality of the mind from the articulations of the sound, or words. Wiser angels know from a single series of statements what someone's ruling affection is, since this is what they are primarily attentive to.

[3] It is recognized that all people have various affections or moods—one in times of happiness, another in times of sorrow, another in times of tenderness and compassion, another in times of honesty and truth, another in times of love and thoughtfulness, another in times of zeal or anger, another in times of pretense and guile, another in times of ambition for respect and adulation, and so on; but there is a dominant affection or love within all of these, so since the wiser angels perceive this, they know from conversation the whole state of another person.

[4] I have been granted knowledge of this through an abundance of experience. I have heard angels discover a person's life simply by listening. They have told me that they know everything about another person's life from a few individual ideas because these enable them to know the person's ruling love, which contains everything in a pattern. This is all that our "book of life" is.145

237   Angelic language has nothing in common with human language except with a few of our words whose sound reflects some feeling, and in this case not with the words themselves but with their sound, which will be further dealt with later.146

The fact that angelic language has nothing in common with human language is evidenced by angels' inability to pronounce a single word of a human language. It has been tried, and they could not. The only things they can utter are the ones that are in complete accord with their own affection. Anything that does not agree offends their very life, since their life is a matter of affection and their language flows from it.

I have been told that the first language of people on our earth shared this nature because it was given them from heaven, and that Hebrew resembles it in some respects.

238   Since angels' language corresponds to the affections of their love, and since heaven's love is love for the Lord and love for our neighbor (see above, §§13–19), we can see how elegant and delightful their conversation is. It affects not only the ears but also the deeper levels of the minds of those who hear it. There was one particular hard-hearted spirit with whom an angel talked, and eventually he was so moved by what the angel was saying that he burst into tears, saying that he couldn't help it, love was talking, and he had never cried before.

The language of angels is also full of wisdom, since it flows from the deeper levels of their thought and their deeper thought is wisdom the way their deeper affection is love. Their love and wisdom unite in speech. As a result, it is so full of wisdom that they can in a single word express what we cannot say in a thousand words; and the concepts of their thinking can encompass things the like of which we cannot grasp, let alone articulate.[147] This is why the things that have been heard and seen in heaven are called inexpressible, such as ear has never heard, nor eye seen.[148]

[2] I have been granted knowledge of this through experience as well. At times I have been conveyed into the state in which angels are and have talked with them in that state. At such times I understood everything, but when I returned to my original state and therefore into the normal thought processes of physical consciousness and wanted to recall what I had heard, I could not. There were a thousand things that would not fit into natural ideas and were therefore inexpressible except by subtle shifts of heavenly light, and not at all, then, in human words.

[3] The individual ideas of angels that give rise to their words are also variations in heaven's light; and the affections that give rise to the sounds of the words are variations of heaven's warmth. This is because heaven's light is divine truth or wisdom and heaven's warmth is divine good or love (see above, §§126–140), and angels receive their affection from divine love and their thought from divine wisdom.[b]

Because angels' language flows directly from their affection (since their individual ideas are various forms into which their affections are apportioned, as noted above in §236), angels can express in a minute more than we can say in half an hour, and can present in a few words things that would make many pages of writing. This too has been witnessed to me by a great deal of experience.[c]

Angels' individual ideas and the words of their language form a single whole the way an efficient cause does with an effect; for what is presented in the words as an effect is what is resident in the ideas as a cause.[149] This is why a single word contains so much within itself.

When the details of angels' thought and the consequent details of their language are presented in visual form, they look like a subtle wave

239

240

b. Angels' concepts, from which they speak, arise through wondrous shifts of heaven's light: 1646, 3343, 3693.

c. In their language, angels can express in a moment more than we can in half an hour in our language, and this includes things that by nature do not fit into the words of human language: 1641, 1642, 1643, 1645, 4609, 7089.

or flowing atmosphere in which there are countless elements in their own pattern, elements of their wisdom that enter into thought at a higher level and stir the affections. The individual ideas of anyone—whether an angel or one of us—can be presented visually in heaven's light when it so pleases the Lord.[d]

241 Angels who live in the Lord's heavenly kingdom talk much the same way as angels who are citizens of the Lord's spiritual kingdom. However, heavenly angels talk from a deeper level of thought than spiritual angels do. Further, since heavenly angels are attuned to the good of love for the Lord, they talk from wisdom, while spiritual angels—being attuned to the good of thoughtfulness toward their neighbor (which in its essence is truth, see §215)—talk from intelligence. For wisdom comes from what is good and intelligence from what is true.

The speech of heavenly angels is like a gentle stream, soft and virtually unbroken, while the speech of spiritual angels is a little more resonant and crisp. Then too, the vowels *U* and *O* tend to predominate in the speech of heavenly angels, while in the speech of spiritual angels it is the vowels *E* and *I*.[150] The vowels stand for the sound and in the sound there is the affection; for as already noted (§236), the sound of angels' speech is responsive to their affection, and the articulations of the sound, or the words, correspond to the individual ideas that stem from their affection. For this reason, the vowels do not belong to the language but to a raising of its words, by means of sounds, toward various affections according to the state of each individual. So in Hebrew the vowels are not written and are also pronounced variously.[151] This enables angels to recognize what someone's quality is in respect to affection and love.

Further still, the language of heavenly angels lacks any hard consonants and rarely puts two consonants together without inserting a word that begins with a vowel. This is why the little word *and*[152] is inserted so often in the Word, as can be determined by people who read the Word in

---

d. There are countless things within a single concept: 1008, 1869, 4946, 6613, 6614, 6615, 6617, 6618. Our concepts are opened in the other life, with a vivid visual presentation of their quality: 1869, 3310, 5510. What they look like: 6201 *[6200]*, 8885. The concepts of angels of the inmost heaven look like the light of a flame: 6615. The concepts of angels of the outmost heaven look like faint, bright clouds: 6614. An angel's concept was seen from which rays went forth toward the Lord: 6620. Concepts of thought reach out far and wide on all sides in angelic communities: 6598–6613.

Hebrew, in which language that word is soft and in either pronunciation is a vowel sound. We can also learn some of this from the vocabulary of the Hebrew Bible, since the words belong to either a heavenly or a spiritual category. That is, they involve either what is good or what is true, with the expressions involving what is good making ample use of the vowels *U* and *O* and to some extent *A,* and the expressions involving what is true making use of *E* and *I.*

Since affections are expressed primarily through sounds, words that use *U* and *O* are well loved in human language to express great matters like heaven and God. Musical sounds tend in this direction as they rise,[153] when they are dealing with such matters, but not when they are dealing with lesser things. This is why the art of music is so adept at expressing various kinds of affection.

There is a certain concord in angelic speech that is indescribable.[e] This concord stems from the fact that the thoughts and affections that give rise to speech flow forth and spread out in keeping with heaven's form, heaven's form being what determines how everyone there associates and communicates. (See above, §§200–212, on the way heaven's form determines how angels associate and the flow of their thoughts and affections.)

The same kind of speech we find in the spiritual world is innate in all of us, but in the deeper part of our intellect. However, since for us it does not come down into words that parallel our affections the way it does for angels, we are unaware that we possess it. Yet this is why we have access to the same language as spirits and angels when we arrive in the other life and know how to talk with them without being taught.[f] But more on this below.[154]

There is, as already noted, a single language for everyone in heaven; but it does vary, in that the language of wiser people is more profound and more full of shades of affections and specific concepts. The language of less wise individuals is less profound and not so full, and the language of simple people is still less profound, actually consisting of words that

242
243
244

e. In angelic speech there is a harmonic, descending concord: 1648, 1649, 7191.

f. The spiritual or angelic language is within us, even though we are not aware of it: 4014 *[4104]*. The concepts of our inner person are spiritual, but while we are living in this world, we perceive them in natural forms because we are thinking on the natural level: 10236, 10240, 10550. After death, we have access to our deeper concepts: 3226, 3342, 3343, 10568, 10604. These then constitute our language: 2470, 2478, 2479.

yield meaning only the way they do when we on earth talk with each other.

There is also a language of facial expressions that switch over to a sound modified by ideas, and a language in which images of heaven are combined with concepts and the concepts are presented visually. There is also a language of bodily movements responsive to affections and portraying the same things that their verbal expressions do. There is a language of shared affections and of shared thoughts; there is a thunderous language; and there are other languages as well.

245 The language of evil and hellish spirits is much the same, because it too stems from their affections, but it comes from evil affections and their foul concepts, which are utterly repugnant to angels. This means that the languages of hell are opposite to the languages of heaven. Evil people cannot stand angelic speech, and angels cannot stand hellish speech. To angels, hellish speech is like a rank odor that assaults the nostrils.

The language of hypocrites—people who can imitate angels of light—is like that of angels as far as its words are concerned, but exactly opposite in respect to its affections and their individual thoughts. So when the inner quality of their speech is perceived, as it is by wise angels, it sounds like a grinding of teeth and strikes horror into them.

How Angels Talk with Us

246 ANGELS who talk with us do not talk in their own language but in ours, or in other languages in which we may be fluent—not in languages of which we have no knowledge. The reason for this is that when angels talk with us they turn toward us and unite with us; and one consequence of this union is that the two parties have much the same thought processes. Since our thinking is closely allied with our memory, and our language flows from it, the two parties share the same language. Further, when angels or spirits come to us and unite with us by turning toward us, they enter into our whole memory so completely that it seems exactly as though they themselves know everything we know, including our languages.

[2] I have talked with angels about this and said that they might suppose they were talking with me in my own mother tongue simply because it seemed that way, when in fact it was not they talking but I. This follows from the fact that angels cannot utter a single word of our human language (§237). Then too, human language is natural and they are spiritual, and spiritual beings cannot produce anything natural. They have answered that they knew that when they were talking with us their union with us was with our spiritual thinking, but since this spiritual thinking flowed into our natural thought, and this natural thinking is so closely allied with our memory, it seemed to them as though our language were their own, along with all our acquired knowledge. This is because it has pleased the Lord that there should be this kind of union and inner presence of heaven with us. However, they said, the state of humanity is now such that this kind of union is no longer with angels but with spirits who are not in heaven.[155]

[3] I have talked with spirits about this matter, too; but they wanted to believe not that we were talking but that they were talking within us, so that we did not really know what we know, but they did, which meant that everything we knew came from them. I wanted to convince them by many arguments that this was not the case but failed.

We will explain later just who are meant by "angels" and who by "spirits," when we come to our description of the world of spirits.[156]

The reason angels and spirits are so intimately united to us that it seems to them as though our characteristics were their own is that there is such an intimate union within us of the spiritual and the natural worlds that they are virtually one. However, because we have separated ourselves from heaven, the Lord has provided that there should be angels and spirits with each of us and that we should be governed by the Lord through them. This is the reason there is such an intimate union.

It would have been different if we had not separated ourselves, because then we could have been governed by the Lord through a general inflow from heaven without having spirits and angels assigned to us.

There will be more on this later, though, where we describe how heaven is united to us.[157]

When angels and spirits talk with us, it sounds just as audible as when we talk with each other, but it is not audible to people who are nearby, only to ourselves. This is because the speech of an angel or spirit

247

248

flows first into our thought and then by an inner route into our organ of hearing so that it activates it from within. Our speech with each other flows first into the air and comes to our organ of hearing and activates it by an outward route. We can see from this that the speech of an angel or spirit with us is heard within us, and that since it activates our hearing mechanism just as much [as our speech with each other does], it is just as audible.

The fact that the speech of an angel or spirit flows down into the ear from within has been made clear to me from the way it flowed into my tongue as well and made it tremble slightly, though not with the actual motion involved when we are articulating the sounds of speech in the formation of words.

249   Talking with spirits is rarely allowed nowadays, though, because it is dangerous.[a] The spirits then actually know that they are with us, which otherwise they would not; and evil spirits by nature harbor a murderous hatred for us and crave nothing less than our total destruction, body and soul. This is what actually goes on in people who regularly lose themselves in delusions, even to the point that they lose touch with the pleasures appropriate to their natural person.

There are some people who lead solitary lives who sometimes hear spirits talking with them without risk; but the Lord keeps these spirits a little space away so that they do not know they are with these individuals. Most spirits, you see, are not aware that there is any other world than the one they are living in or therefore that there are people anywhere else. So we are not allowed to talk back to them, since if we did, they would know.

People who are constantly thinking about religious matters, so wrapped up in them that they practically see them within themselves, also begin to hear spirits talking with them. This is because when we voluntarily get wrapped up in religious matters, no matter what kind, without the interruption of various useful activities in the [external] world, these matters enter into us very deeply and take substance there so that they occupy our whole spirit, move into the spiritual world, and affect spirits there. However, people like this are visionaries or fanatics, and no

a. It is possible for us to talk with spirits and angels, and the early people often did talk with them: 67, 68, 69, 784, 1634, 1636, 7802. On some planets, angels and spirits appear in human form and talk with people: 10751, 10752. On our planet at present, though, it is dangerous to talk with spirits unless we are involved in true faith and are led by the Lord: 784, 9438, 10751.

matter what spirit they hear, they believe it is the Holy Spirit, even though the spirits they hear are fanatical. Spirits like this see false things as true; and because they see them as true they convince themselves and also convince the people into whom they flow. Further, since spirits like this who command obedience have also begun to urge people to do evil things, they have gradually been moved away. Fanatical spirits can be differentiated from other spirits by the fact that they believe they are the Holy Spirit and that what they are saying is divine. They do not harm us, because we offer them divine worship.

I have talked with them on occasion and the unspeakable things they instill into their worshipers have come to light. They live all together toward the left,[158] in a desert area.

Conversation with angels is not granted, though, except to people who are focused on truths that flow from good intent, especially people who acknowledge the Lord and the divine nature within his human nature, because this is the truth in which heaven exists. For as already noted, the Lord is heaven's God (§§2–6); the Lord's divine nature makes heaven (§§7–12); the Lord's divine nature in heaven is love for him and thoughtfulness from him toward one's neighbor (§§13–19); and the whole heaven, grasped as a single entity, reflects a single individual, as does each community of heaven; and each individual angel has a perfect human form because of the Lord's divine human nature (§§59–86). We can see from this that conversation with angels is not granted except to people whose deeper levels have been opened by divine truths all the way to the Lord, since it is into these that the Lord flows within us, and when the Lord flows in, so does heaven.

The reason divine truths open our deeper levels is that we have been so created that our inner person is an image of heaven and our outer an image of the world (§57); and our inner person is opened only by the divine truth that emanates from the Lord, because this is the light and the life of heaven (§§126–140).

The inflow of the Lord himself into us is into the forehead and from there into the whole face.[b] The inflow of the spiritual angels who are with us is into our head overall, from the forehead and temples to the

250

251

---

b. The forehead corresponds to heavenly love, and therefore means that love in the Word: 9936. The face corresponds to our deeper levels, which have to do with thought and affection: 1568, 2988, 2989, 3631, 4796, 4797, 4800, 5165, 5168, 5695, 9306. So too, the face is formed to be responsive to our more inward natures: 4791–4805, 5695. So the face in the Word means our deeper natures: 1999, 2434, 3527, 4066, 4796.

whole region that covers the cerebrum, because this area corresponds to our intelligence. In contrast, the inflow of heavenly angels is into the part of the head that covers the cerebellum and is called the occiput, from one ear to the other and down to the neck, since this area corresponds to our wisdom.

All the speech of angels comes into our thoughts by these two paths. This has enabled me to notice just which angels were talking with me.

252 People who talk with heaven's angels also see the things that are in heaven because they are seeing in that light of heaven that surrounds their inner levels. Not only that, through them angels see things that are on our earth.[c] For people who talk with angels, heaven is actually united to our world and our world to heaven; for as already noted (§246), when angels turn toward us they unite themselves with us so completely that it seems to them exactly as though whatever is ours is actually theirs. This applies not only to elements of our language but to what is involved in our sight and hearing. In addition, it seems to us exactly as though the things that are flowing in through the angels are really ours.

The earliest humans on our planet enjoyed this kind of union with heaven's angels, which is why their times are called the Golden Age. Because they acknowledged the Divine in human form and therefore were acknowledging the Lord, they talked with heaven's angels as they did with members of their own family, and heaven's angels talked with them in the same way; and in them heaven and this world were a single whole.

But after those times, people moved step by step away from heaven by loving themselves more than the Lord and the world more than heaven. So they began to feel the pleasures of self-love and love of the world separately from the pleasures of heaven, ultimately to the point where they did not know there was any other kind of pleasure. Then their deeper levels were closed, the levels that open into heaven, while their outer levels were open to the world. Once this has happened, we are in the light in respect to everything in this world and in darkness in respect to everything in heaven.

253 Since those times people have seldom talked with heaven's angels, though some have talked with spirits who are not in heaven. Our inner and outer levels can by their nature be turned toward the Lord as their

---

c. Spirits cannot see, through us, anything that is in this subsolar world; but they have seen through my eyes, and why: 1880.

common center (§124), or toward ourselves and therefore away from the Lord. The ones that are turned toward the Lord are also turned toward heaven, while the ones that are turned toward ourselves are also turned toward this world; and the ones that are turned in this latter direction are hard to raise up. Still, they are raised up by the Lord to the extent that they can be, through a turning of our love; and this is accomplished by means of truths from the Word.

254

I have been told how the Lord spoke to the prophets through whom the Word was written. He did not talk with them the way he did with the early people, by an inflow into their deeper natures, but through spirits sent to them whom the Lord filled with his appearance. In this way, he inspired them with the words that they in turn told to the prophets, so that it was not a case of inflow but of direct command. Since at that time the words were coming directly from the Lord, the very details are filled with the Divine and contain within themselves an inner meaning of such nature that heaven's angels take them in a heavenly and spiritual meaning while we are taking them in a natural meaning. In this way, the Lord unites heaven and earth through the Word.

I have also been shown how the Lord fills spirits with his divine nature by means of his appearance. Spirits filled with the Divine by the Lord have no sense whatever that they are not actually the Lord or that it is not the Lord who is speaking, which lasts as long as they are talking. Afterward they realize and admit that they are spirits and that they were not talking on their own, but from the Lord.

Because this was the state of the spirits who talked with the prophets, they themselves said that Jehovah was talking. The spirits actually called themselves "Jehovah," as can be seen not only in the prophetic books but also in the historical books of the Word.[159]

255

To illustrate what the union of angels and spirits with us is like, I may cite a few memorable instances that will serve to illuminate the subject and enable some conclusions to be drawn. When angels and spirits turn toward us, it seems to them exactly as though our language were their own and that they have no other. This is because they are involved in our language at such times, and do not even remember their own. The moment they turn away from us, though, they are back in their own angelic and spiritual language and have no knowledge whatever of ours. The same thing has happened with me when I have been in the company of angels and in a state like theirs. Then I have talked with them in their language and knew nothing of my own. I could not even remember it.

However, the moment I was no longer in their company I was back in my own language.

[2] It is also worth noting that when angels and spirits turn toward us, they can talk with us even from a great distance. They have talked with me from far off just as audibly as though they were nearby. Still, when they turn away from us and talk with each other, nothing of what they say is audible to us even though this is happening right next to our ears. This has enabled me to see that in the spiritual world, all union depends on the way people are facing.

[3] Again, it is worth noting that many of them can talk with one of us at the same time, and that person with them. They send some particular spirit from themselves to the individual with whom they want to talk, and this envoy spirit turns toward the person while the others turn toward their [envoy] spirit and so concentrate their thoughts, which the spirit then presents. It seems to such envoys entirely as though they were talking on their own, and to the others as though they themselves were. So a union of several with one is achieved by the way they face.d But we will say more later about these envoy spirits, called agents, and the communication that takes place through them.160

256   No angel or spirit is allowed to talk with one of us from the angel's or spirit's own memory, only from that of the individual in question. Angels and spirits actually have memory just as we do. If a spirit were to talk with us from his or her own memory, then it would seem to us entirely as though the thoughts were our own, when they would really belong to the spirit. It is like remembering something that we have never seen or heard. I have been granted knowledge of the truth of this by experience.

This is why some of the ancients were of the opinion that after some thousands of years they would return to their former life and all its deeds, and that they had in fact returned. They gathered this from the fact that sometimes a kind of memory would come up of things that they had never seen or heard. This happened because spirits had flowed from their own memory into the images of these people's thoughts.

257   There are also spirits called natural and physical spirits who do not unite with our thoughts when they come to us the way other spirits do but rather enter our bodies and take over all its senses, talking through

---

d. Spirits sent out by communities of spirits to other communities are called "agents": 4403, 5856. Communications in the spiritual world take place by means of such envoy spirits: 4403, 5856, 5983. Spirits who have been sent out and are serving as agents do not think on their own but from the spirits who sent them: 5985, 5986, 5987.

our mouths and acting through our limbs. It seems to them entirely as though everything of ours were theirs. These are the spirits that possess people; but they have been cast into hell by the Lord and moved decisively away; so possession like this no longer occurs nowadays.[e]

Written Materials in Heaven

SINCE angels do have language and their language is one of words, they also have written materials; and through those written materials just as through their conversation, they express what their minds are sensing. I have sometimes been sent pages covered with writing, just like pages handwritten or printed and published in our world. I could even read them in much the same way, but I was not allowed to get more out of them than a bit of meaning here and there. This was because it is not in keeping with the divine design to be taught by written materials from heaven, but [only] by the Word, since this is the sole means of communication and union between heaven and earth, and therefore between the Lord and humanity.

258

We gather from Ezekiel that pages written in heaven appeared to the prophets as well:

> When I looked, behold, a hand was stretched out to me by the spirit, and in it the scroll of a book that he unrolled in my sight. It was written on the front and on the back. (Ezekiel 2:9–10)[161]

And in John,

> I saw in the right hand of the one who was sitting on the throne a book written within and on the back, sealed with seven seals. (Revelation 5:1)

The occurrence of written materials in the heavens is provided by the Lord for the sake of the Word, for in its essence the Word is the divine

259

---

e. External or physical possession no longer occurs today the way it used to: 1983. Now, however, there is more internal, mental possession than there used to be: 1983, 4793. We are possessed more inwardly when we entertain filthy thoughts and libels against God and our neighbor and when we are kept from airing them only by the outward restraints imposed by our fear of losing reputation, respect, profit, legal standing, or life: 5990. On the diabolic spirits who primarily possess our deeper levels: 4793. On the diabolic spirits who want to possess our more outward levels, who are pent up in the hells: 2752, 5990.

truth from which both angels and people on earth get all their wisdom. It has in fact been spoken by the Lord, and what is spoken by the Lord passes through all the heavens in sequence and comes to rest with us. In this way it is adapted both to the wisdom that angels enjoy and to the intelligence that we do. As a result, angels have a Word that they read just as much as we do ours. They draw their doctrinal principles from it, and their sermons come from it (§221). It is the same Word; but its natural meaning, which to us is its literal meaning, does not exist in heaven. There is a spiritual meaning there instead, which is its inner meaning. The nature of this meaning may be seen in the booklet *The White Horse Described in the Book of Revelation.*[162]

260   Another time I was sent a small page from heaven with only a few words written on it in Hebrew letters. I was told that each letter enfolded treasures of wisdom, and that these were contained in the bends and curves of the letters and therefore in the sounds as well. I could see from this the meaning of the Lord's words, "I tell you in truth, until heaven and earth pass away, not one jot or one tittle shall pass away from the Law" (Matthew 5:18).[163] It is acknowledged in the church that the Word is divine right down to the smallest point, but where in each point the Divine lies hidden—that is not known as yet, so it needs to be explained. In the inmost heaven, the writing consists of various curving and bending forms, and these curves and bends are in keeping with the form of heaven. Through them, angels express the treasures of their wisdom, including many things that they cannot say in words. Believe it or not, the angels know this writing without practice or teachers. They are inwardly gifted with it as they are with the language itself (§236), so this writing is heavenly writing. The reason they are inwardly gifted with it is that all the outreach of angels' thoughts and affections and therefore all communication of their intelligence and wisdom takes place in keeping with heaven's form (§201). This is why their writing flows into that same form.

I have been told that before letters were invented, the earliest humans on our planet had this kind of writing, and that it was transferred into the Hebrew letters, which in early times were all curved, with none marked off by straight lines the way they are now. This is why there are divine things and treasures of heaven in the Word even in its jots and points and little horns.

261   This writing, which uses symbols of the heavenly form, is in use in the inmost heaven, whose inhabitants enjoy greater wisdom than others. It

expresses the affections from which their thoughts flow and which follow in sequence according to the substance of the matter under consideration. This is why these writings enfold treasures that cannot be completely drawn out by thought. I have also been allowed to see these writings.

In the lower heavens, though, there are no written materials of this sort. The written materials there are much like those in our world, with similar letters. However, they are still not intelligible to people on earth because they are written in an angelic language, and angelic language by nature has nothing in common with our languages (§237). They express affections through the vowels; with the consonants they express the particular concepts that derive from the affections, and with the words they express the meaning of the matter (§§236, 241).

Further, this writing enfolds in a few words more than we can describe in several pages. I have seen these written materials as well.

This means that they have a written Word in the lower heavens, and one expressed through heavenly forms in the inmost heaven.

262 It is worth knowing that in the heavens, writing flows spontaneously from thoughts. It is done with such ease that it is as though the thought projected itself. The hand does not pause over the choice of some particular word, because the words—both the spoken and the written ones— are responsive to their individual thoughts, and anything that is so responsive is natural and spontaneous.

There are also things written in the heavens without the use of hands, simply in response to thoughts; but these do not last.

263 I have also seen written materials in heaven comprising nothing but numbers arranged in a pattern and series, just like the writing of letters and words; and I have been told that these writings come from the inmost heaven, whose heavenly writing (described above in §§260–261) comes out as numbers for angels in the lower heavens when thought from the higher heaven flows down. I have also been told that this numerical writing enfolds mysteries, some of which cannot be grasped by thought or expressed in words. All numbers do in fact correspond and have meaning depending on their correspondence, just as words do,[a] but with the difference that numbers represent general entities and words

a. All the numbers in the Word mean particular things: 482, 487, 647, 648, 755, 813, 1963, 1988, 2075, 2252, 3252, 4264, 4674 *[4670]*, 6175, 9488, 9659, 10217, 10253; shown from heaven: 4495, 5265. Multiples mean the same thing as their factors: 5291, 5335, 5708, 7973. The early people conveyed heavenly mysteries by numbers—a kind of ecclesiastical algebra: 575.

specific ones. Since one general entity involves countless specific ones, numeric writing enfolds more mysteries than alphabetic writing does.

I could see from this that numbers in the Word mean things just the way words do. What the simple numbers mean, like 2, 3, 4, 5, 6, 7, 8, 9. 10, and 12, and what the composite ones mean, like 20, 30, 50, 70, 100, 144, 1000, 10,000, and 12,000 and others, may be seen in *Secrets of Heaven,* where such matters are dealt with.[164]

In this kind of writing in heaven the number on which the following numbers depend in sequence is always put first, as though it set their theme; for this number is a kind of title of the matter under consideration, and the numbers that follow serve to delimit the matter more specifically.

264   If people have no concept of heaven and do not want any concept of it other than one of some insubstantial atmosphere in which angels fly around like intellectual minds without the senses of hearing and sight, they cannot believe that angels have language and writing. They locate the entire presence of everything in matter. Yet the things that one finds in heaven occur with just as much reality as those in our world, and the angels who are there have everything they need for life, and everything they need for wisdom.

The Wisdom of Heaven's Angels

265   THE nature of the wisdom of heaven's angels is almost beyond comprehension because it so transcends human wisdom that there are no means of comparison, and anything transcendent seems to be nothing at all. Still, there are a few overlooked means that can be used for description, means which until they are recognized seem like shadows in the mind and actually obscure the nature of the matter as it is in itself. Yet they are the kinds of things that can be known, and can be understood once they are known, if only the mind takes delight in them; for since delight arises from love, it has a light with it; and for people who love matters of divine and heavenly wisdom, that light radiates from heaven and provides them with enlightenment.

We may gather what angels' wisdom is like from the fact that they **266** live in heaven's light, and in its essence heaven's light is divine truth or divine wisdom. This light illuminates at one and the same time both their inner sight, which is mental, and their outer sight, the sight of their eyes. (On heaven's light being divine truth or divine wisdom, see above, §§126–133.) Angels also live in heaven's warmth, which in its essence is divine good or divine love, and from this comes their affection and longing for wisdom. (On heaven's warmth being divine good or divine love, see above, §§133–140.)

Angels enjoy wisdom to the point that they might be called "wisdoms," as we may gather from the fact that all the elements of their thoughts and affections flow according to the heavenly form, which form is the form of divine wisdom, and further that their more inward levels, which are open to wisdom, are framed according to this form. (On angels' thoughts and affections, and therefore their intelligence and wisdom as well, flowing according to heaven's form, see above, §§201–212.)

[2] We may further infer the excellence of angels' wisdom from the fact that their speech is the speech of wisdom. It actually flows directly and[165] freely from their thought, which in turn comes from their affection, so that their speech is their thought from[166] affection in an external form. Consequently, nothing draws them away from the divine inflow: there is none of that external matter that for us keeps intruding into our speech from thoughts about other things. (On angels' speech being the speech of their thought and affection, see §§234–245.)

It also contributes to this kind of angelic wisdom that everything they see with their eyes and perceive with their senses is in harmony with their wisdom. This is because all these things are correspondences and therefore the objects of their senses are forms that portray elements proper to their wisdom. (On the fact that everything visible in heaven is in correspondence with the deeper levels of the angels and is representative of their wisdom, see above, §§170–182.)

[3] Further, angels' thoughts are not bounded and constrained by concepts drawn from space and time the way ours are; for space and time are properties of nature, and properties of nature distract the mind from spiritual things and deprive our intellectual sight of breadth. (On angels' concepts being devoid of time and space and therefore unlimited, relative to ours, see above, §§162–169 and 191–199.)

Angels' thoughts are not diverted to earthly and material concerns or interrupted by the cares and needs of life, so they are not distracted by such things from the joys of wisdom the way our thoughts are in this world. They are given everything by the Lord gratis: they are clothed gratis, fed gratis, housed gratis (§§181–190); and beyond this, they are provided with joys and pleasures in proportion to their acceptance of wisdom from the Lord.

All this has been presented to show where angels derive this kind of wisdom.[a]

267 The reason angels can accept so much wisdom is that their deeper levels are open, and wisdom, like any perfection, increases as one moves toward the deeper levels and as they are opened.[b]

In every angel there are three levels of life corresponding to the three heavens (see §§29–40). People whose first level has been opened are in the first or most remote heaven. People whose second level has been opened are in the second or intermediate heaven. People whose third level has been opened are in the third or inmost heaven. The wisdom of angels in heaven is according to these levels; so the wisdom of angels of the third heaven vastly transcends the wisdom of angels of the intermediate heaven, and their wisdom in turn transcends that of angels of the farthest heaven (see above, §§209–210, and on the nature of the levels, see §38).

The reason for these differences is that the elements of the higher levels are detailed, and those of the lower are general, the general ones being inclusive of the details. The ratio of details to generalizations is on the order of thousands or ten thousands to one, so this is the ratio between the wisdom of angels of a higher heaven and that of angels of a lower heaven.

However, the wisdom of these latter angels similarly transcends our wisdom, for we are engrossed in our bodies and their sensory operations,

a. On angels' wisdom—that it is incomprehensible and inexpressible: 2795, 2796, 2802, 3314, 3404, 3405, 9094, 9176.

b. To the extent that we are raised from more outward to more inward concerns, we come into the light and therefore into intelligence: 6183, 6313. This raising really happens: 7816, 10330. Being raised from outer to more inward concerns is like rising from a fog into the light: 4598. Our more outward levels are farther from the Divine and therefore relatively cloudy: 6451; and also relatively disorganized: 996, 3855. Our deeper levels are more perfect because they are nearer the Divine: 5146, 5147. In our inner nature there are thousands and thousands of things that outwardly look like a single generalization: 5707. So the deeper our thought and perception are, the clearer they are: 5920.

and these physical sensory faculties are on the lowest level of all. This fact enables us to see the nature of the wisdom of people who base their thinking on sensory information—that is, the ones we call sense-oriented people. Specifically, they have no access to wisdom, only to information.[c] It is different, though, for people whose thoughts are raised above sensory matters, and even more for people whose deeper levels have been opened all the way into heaven's light.

We may gather how great angels' wisdom is from the fact that in heaven there is a communication that involves everyone. The intelligence and wisdom of one individual is shared with another: heaven is where everyone shares everything of value. This is because the very nature of heavenly love is to want what is one's own to belong to another; so no one in heaven regards his or her good as authentically good unless it is someone else's as well. This is also the basis of heaven's happiness. Angels are led into it by the Lord, whose divine love has this same quality.

268

I have also been granted knowledge, by experience, of this kind of communication in the heavens. Once some simple people were taken up into heaven, and after they had arrived, they arrived also at an angelic wisdom. They understood things they could not grasp before and said things they could not express in their former state.

Words are not adequate to describe the quality of angels' wisdom—it can be suggested only by some generalizations. Angels can express in a single word what we cannot express in a thousand words. Further, in a single angelic word there are countless things that are beyond the capacity of human words to convey. In the details of angelic speech there are actually treasures of wisdom in unbroken connection, utterly beyond the reach of human knowledge. Then too, what angels cannot evoke with the words of their language they fill in with the sound, which embodies

269

c. The sensory level is the outmost level of our life, associated with and resident in our bodies: 5077, 5767, 9212, 9216, 9331, 9730. We call people sense-oriented if they base all their judgments and conclusions on their physical senses and believe nothing unless they see it with their eyes and touch it with their hands: 5094, 7693. People like this think on their outward level and not deeply within themselves: 5089, 5094, 6564, 7693. Their deeper levels are closed, so that they do not see any element of spiritual truth there: 6564, 6844, 6845. In short, they are people who live in the gross light of nature and therefore do not perceive anything that arises from heaven's light: 6201, 6310, 6564, 6844, 6845, 6598, 6612, 6614, 6622, 6624. Inwardly, they are opposed to the principles of heaven and the church: 6201, 6316, 6844, 6845, 6948, 6949. Scholars who have made up their minds against the truths of the church are like this: 6316. Sense-oriented people are especially wily and malicious: 7693, 10236. They reason acutely and skillfully, but on the basis of their physical memory, which for them is the location of all intelligence: 195, 196, 5700, 10236. However, this is based on sensory illusions: 5084, 6948, 6949, 7693.

their sensitivity to the proper arrangement of things; for as already noted (§§236, 241), they express their affections through the sounds and the concepts derived from their affections through the words. This is why the things that people have heard in heaven are called ineffable.

Angels can also state completely in a few words the details that are written in a whole volume, giving each word something that raises it toward a deeper wisdom. Their language by nature agrees with their affections, and every word agrees with their concepts. The words actually vary in infinite shadings depending on the way they express in sequence things that are simultaneous in their thought.

[2] The more inward angels can even tell a speaker's whole life from the tone of voice and a few words. From the way the sound is differentiated by concepts into words, they actually perceive the speaker's ruling love, in which, so to speak, the very details of life are engraved.[d]

We can see from all this what angels' wisdom is like. Relative to our wisdom, it is on the order of ten thousands to one. It is like the ratio between the motor energies of the body, which are countless, to some act that results from them, which to our senses seems like a single event. Or it is like the thousands of things we see through a perfect microscope compared to the one fuzzy thing we see with the naked eye.[167]

[3] I should also like to illustrate the matter with one example. An angel, out of his[168] wisdom, described the process of regeneration[169] and presented mysteries about it in their proper sequence, amounting to a hundred. He filled out each single mystery with concepts containing even deeper mysteries, and did this from beginning to end, explaining how the spiritual person is conceived anew; is carried in the womb, so to speak; is born; matures; and is gradually perfected. He said that he could multiply the number of mysteries into the thousands, and that the things he was talking about involved only the regeneration of the outer person. There were countless more about the regeneration of the inner person.

This and other things of the same sort that I have heard from angels have shown me how much wisdom they have and how much ignorance

---

d. The love that rules or governs throughout is present within us in the details of our life, so it is present in every detail of our thought and affection: 4459, 5949, 6159, 6571, 7648, 8067, 8853–8858. Our nature is determined by our ruling love: 918 *[917]*, 1040, 8858; illustrated by examples: 8854, 8857. Whatever rules throughout constitutes the life of our spirit: 7648. This is our essential intent, our essential love, and the goal of our life, because what we intend is what we love, and what we love is what we set as our goal: 1317, 1568, 1571, 1909, 3796, 5949, 6936. Therefore our intent, or our ruling love, or the goal of our life, determines the kind of person we are: 1568, 1571, 3570, 4054, 6571, 6934 *[6935]*, 6938, 8856, 10076, 10109, 10110, 10284.

we have by comparison, with hardly any knowledge of what regeneration is and no awareness of a single step when we are being regenerated.

I need now to say something about the wisdom of the angels of the third or inmost heaven, and about how much it surpasses the wisdom of the first or outmost heaven. **270**

The wisdom of angels of the third or inmost heaven is beyond comprehension, even for angels of the first or outmost heaven. This is because the inner natures of angels of the third heaven are opened at the third level, while those of angels of the first heaven are open only at the first level; and all wisdom increases as you move toward the deeper levels and is perfected as they are opened (§§208, 267).

[2] Since the inner levels of angels of the third heaven are opened at the third level, they have divine truths virtually engraved on them, for inner matters at the third level are more in heaven's form than those at the second and first level. Heaven's form arises from divine truth and therefore is in agreement with divine wisdom. This is why divine truths seem to these angels to be engraved, or to be instinctive and innate. Because of this, as soon as they hear genuine divine truths, they immediately acknowledge and grasp them and from then on virtually see them within themselves. Because this is characteristic of angels of this heaven, they never try to figure out[170] divine truths, much less argue whether some particular truth is true or not. They do not know what it is to believe or have faith, but say, "What is faith? I perceive and see that this is so." They offer a comparison by way of illustration. It would be like someone seeing a house and various things in and around it and telling someone with him that he ought to believe that they existed and that they were what they seemed to be. Or it would be like someone seeing a garden with trees and fruit in it and telling someone that she should have faith that it was a garden and that those were trees and fruit when she could see them plainly with her own eyes. So these angels never call "faith" by name and in fact have no concept of it. This is why they do not try to figure out divine truths, much less argue whether any particular truth is true or not.[e]

e. Heavenly angels know countless things and are vastly wiser than spiritual angels: 2718. Heavenly angels do not think and talk on the basis of faith the way spiritual angels do, because they are gifted by the Lord with a perception of everything that has to do with faith: 202, 597, 607, 784, 1121, 1387 *[1389]*, 1398, 1442, 1919, 7680, 7877, 8780, 9277, 10336. Concerning truths of faith, they simply say, "Yes, yes," or "No, no," whereas spiritual angels try to calculate whether it is true: 2715, 3246, 4448, 9166, 10786; an explanation of the Lord's words, "Let your speech be yes, yes, no, no": Matthew 5:36 *[5:37]*.

[3] In contrast, angels of the first or outmost heaven do not have divine truths engraved on their inner natures in this way because for them only the first level of life has been opened. So they do try to figure things out, and people who are calculating in this way see little more than the subject they are puzzling over. They do not go beyond that subject except to find support for their conclusions, and once they have decided, they say that these should be matters of faith and are to be believed.

[4] I have talked about this with angels, who have told me that the difference between the wisdom of angels of the third heaven and the wisdom of angels of the first heaven is like the difference between something bright and something dark. Or again, they have compared the wisdom of angels of the third heaven to a palace full of everything useful, surrounded far and wide by parklands, with all sorts of splendid things beyond. Since these angels enjoy truths of wisdom, they can enter the palace and see everything there. They can stroll anywhere in the parks and enjoy whatever they see. It is different for people who are trying to figure things out, though, and even more so for people who argue about them. These individuals do not see truths in the light of truth, but adopt them either from other people or from the literal meaning of the Word, which they do not understand in depth. So they say that truths must be believed or that people must have faith in things—things that they then do not want anyone looking into very deeply. The angels kept saying that these people could not get to the first threshold of the palace, much less enter it and stroll around in its parks, because they are stuck at the first step. It is different for people who are engaged in actual truths. Nothing keeps them from moving ahead without limit; for once truths have been seen they lead on wherever they are headed, even into spacious meadows, because every truth has an infinite outreach and is united to many, many others.

[5] They also said that the wisdom of angels of the inmost heaven consists primarily of their seeing divine and heavenly things in individual objects and wonders in series of objects, for everything that appears to their eyes has a correspondence. When they see palaces and gardens, for instance, their insight does not dwell on the things in front of their eyes but sees the deeper things they stem from, the things, that is, to which they correspond. This goes on with constant variety in keeping with the appearance of the objects; so at any given time there are countless things in a pattern and a connectedness so delightful to their minds that they seem to be transported. (Everything that is visible in the heavens corresponds to something divine that is from the Lord in angels, see §§170–176.)

The reason angels of the third heaven are like this is that they are **271** centered in love for the Lord, and that love opens the deeper levels of the mind to the third level and is open to and retentive of all wisdom. It should also be known that angels of the inmost heaven are constantly being even more perfected in wisdom and that this too happens differently than for angels of the outmost heaven. Angels of the inmost heaven do not store up divine truths in their memory or translate them into information. Rather, as soon as they hear them, they grasp them and apply them to their lives. This is why divine truths for them are virtually engraved, because anything that is committed to life is to that extent internalized. It is different, though, for angels of the outmost heaven. They first assign divine truths to their memory and store them in the form of information. Then they retrieve them and use them to perfect their understanding; and without any deeper grasp of their truth, they intend them and commit them to life. Consequently, things are relatively cloudy for them.

It is worth noting that angels of the third heaven are perfected in wisdom through hearing rather than through seeing. What they hear through preaching does not go into their memory but directly into their perception and intention and becomes a matter of their life. What they see with their eyes, though, does go into their memory, and they think and talk about it. This has enabled me to see that the path of hearing is the path of wisdom for them. This too is because of correspondence, since the ear corresponds to obedience, and obedience has to do with the way we live; while the eye corresponds to intelligence, and intelligence is a matter of doctrine.[f] The state of these angels is described in many places in the Word; for instance in Jeremiah:

> I will put my law in their mind and write it on their heart. No longer will anyone teach a friend or a brother by saying "Know the Lord," for all the people there are will know me, from the least of them to the greatest of them. (Jeremiah 31:33–34)

And in Matthew,

> Let your conversation be "Yes, yes; no, no," for anything beyond this comes from evil. (Matthew 5:36 [5:37])

---

f. On the correspondence of the ear and hearing: 4652–4660. The ear corresponds to perception and obedience and therefore refers to them: 2542, 3869, 4653, 5017, 7216, 8361, 9311, 9397, 10065 [10061]. It means the acceptance of truths: 5471, 5475, 9926. On the correspondence of the eye and its sight: 4403–4421, 4523–4534. Eyesight therefore means the intelligence of faith and also faith itself: 2701, 4410, 4526, 6923, 9051, 10569.

The reason anything beyond this comes from evil is that it is not from the Lord; for the truths that are resident within angels of the third heaven are from the Lord because they are centered in a love for him. Love for the Lord in that heaven is intending and doing divine truth, for divine truth is the Lord in heaven.

272   There is still another reason, beyond the ones already given, why angels can accept so much wisdom, a reason that in heaven is actually the primary one. It is that they are free of any selfishness;[171] for to the extent that people are free of selfishness they can be wise in divine matters. Selfishness is what closes off our deeper natures from the Lord and heaven and opens our outer natures and turns them toward ourselves. So all people in whom that selfish love predominates are in the depths of darkness as far as heavenly realities are concerned, no matter how much light they may enjoy in regard to worldly matters. In contrast, since angels are free of that love, they enjoy the light of wisdom. The heavenly loves in which they are centered—love for the Lord and love for their neighbor—open the deeper levels because these loves come from the Lord and the Lord himself is within them. (These loves constitute heaven in general and form heaven in individuals in particular: §§13–19.)

Since heavenly loves open our deeper levels toward the Lord, all the angels turn their faces toward the Lord (§142): in the spiritual world love is what turns the deeper levels of every individual toward itself, and what turns the deeper levels turns the face, since the face there acts in unison with the deeper levels and is actually their outward form. Further, because love does turn the deeper levels and the face toward itself, it also unites itself to them, since love is spiritual union. Therefore it also shares what it has with them. It is from this turning and the consequent union and sharing that angels get their wisdom (all union in the spiritual world takes place according to the way people are facing, §255).

273   Angels are constantly being perfected in wisdom,[g] but still they cannot to eternity be so perfected that there is any ratio between their wisdom and the Lord's divine wisdom. For the Lord's divine wisdom is infinite and the angels' is finite, and there is no ratio between the infinite and the finite.

274   Since wisdom perfects angels and makes their life, and since heaven with its blessings flows into individuals according to their wisdom, all the people there long for it and seek it, much the way a hungry person

g. Angels are being perfected to eternity: 4803, 6648.

seeks food. In fact, information, intelligence, and wisdom are spiritual nourishment the way food is natural nourishment. They correspond to each other.

The angels in any given heaven—even the angels in any given community—do not enjoy the same wisdom, but differ. Those in the center have the most wisdom, while those who have less are around them all the way to the borders. The decrease of wisdom according to the distance from the center is like the decrease in light as it tends toward darkness (see above, §§43, 128). Further, the light for them is on a consistent level, since heaven's light is divine wisdom and each individual is in light in proportion to his or her acceptance of it. (On heaven's light and the different ways it is accepted, see above, §§126–132.)

275

The State of Innocence of Angels in Heaven

NOT many people in our world know what innocence is or what its quality is, and people involved in evil do not know at all. It is, of course, visible to our eyes—something about the face and the voice and the gestures, especially of infants—but still we do not know what it is, much less that it is where heaven lies concealed within us. To make it known, I should like to proceed in order and talk first about the innocence of infancy, and then about the innocence of wisdom, and finally about the state of heaven in respect to innocence.

276

The innocence of infancy, or of little ones, is not real innocence, since it is solely a matter of outward form and not internal. Still, we can learn from it what innocence is like, since it does radiate from their faces and from some of their gestures and from their first efforts at speech and affects [the people around them. The reason it is not real innocence is]¹⁷² that they do not have any internal thought—they do not yet know what good and evil are, or what true and false are, and this knowledge is the basis of our thinking. [2] As a result, they do not have any foresight of their own, no premeditation, and therefore no intent of evil. They have no self-image acquired through love for themselves and the world. They

277

do not claim credit for anything, but attribute everything they receive to their parents. They are content with the few little things given them as gifts and enjoy them. They are not anxious about food and clothing or about the future. They do not focus on the world and covet[173] much from it. They love their parents, their nurse, and their little friends and play innocently with them. They are willing to be led, they listen and obey; [3] and since they are in this state, they accept everything as a matter of life. So they have suitable habits, language, and the beginnings of memory and thought without knowing where these gifts come from; and their state of innocence serves as a means of accepting and absorbing them. However, since this innocence is strictly a matter of the body and not of the mind,[a] as already noted, it is external. Their mind is not yet formed, since the mind is our discernment and volition and the thought and affection that come from them.

[4] I have been told from heaven that infants are especially in the Lord's care, and that there is an inflow from the central heaven, where the state is one of innocence, that passes through infants' deeper natures, affecting those natures in its passage only through innocence. This is the source of the innocence they present to our view in their faces and in some of their gestures. It is what deeply affects their parents and creates the love called *storge*.[174]

278   The innocence of wisdom is real innocence because it is internal, being a property of the mind itself and therefore of our volition itself and our consequent understanding. When there is innocence in these, then there is wisdom as well, because wisdom is a property of volition and understanding. That is why they say in heaven that innocence dwells in wisdom and why angels have as much wisdom as they do innocence. They support the truth of this by observing that people in a state of innocence do not take credit for anything good, but ascribe and attribute everything to the Lord. They want to be led by him and not by themselves, they love everything that is good and delight in everything that is true because they know and perceive that loving what is good—that is,

a. The innocence of infants is not real innocence—real innocence dwells in wisdom: 1616, 2305, 2306, 3495 [3494], 4563, 4797, 5608, 9301, 10021. The good of infancy is not spiritual good; that comes into being through the implanting of truth: 3504. Still, the innocence of infancy is a means through which intelligence is sown: 1616, 3183, 9301, 10110. Without the good of innocence in infancy, we would be wild: 3494. Whatever is absorbed in infancy seems to be part of our nature: 3494.

intending and doing good—is loving the Lord, and loving what is true is loving their neighbor. They live content with what they have, whether it is little or much, because they know that they receive as much as is useful—little if little is good for them and much if much is good for them. They do not know what is best for themselves—only the Lord knows; and in his sight everything he supplies is eternal. [2] So they have no anxiety about the future, but refer to anxiety about the future as "care for the morrow,"[175] which they say is pain at losing or not getting things that are not needed for their life's useful activities. They never collaborate with friends from evil intent, but only from good, fair, and honest intent. To act from evil intent, they say, is guile, which they avoid like the poison of a snake because it is diametrically opposed to innocence. Since their greatest love is to be led by the Lord, and since they ascribe everything to him, they are kept away from their self-centeredness, and to the extent that they are kept away from their self-centeredness, the Lord flows in. This is why they do not store in their memory what they hear from him, whether through the Word or through preaching, but immediately heed it, that is, intend and do it. Their intention itself is their memory. They appear extraordinarily simple in outward form, but they are wise and provident inwardly. They are the ones the Lord was referring to when he said, "Be wise as serpents and simple as doves" (Matthew 10:16). This is the nature of the innocence called the innocence of wisdom.

[3] Since innocence does not take credit for anything good but ascribes it all to the Lord, and since innocence loves to be led by the Lord, giving rise to that acceptance of everything good and true that leads to wisdom, we have been so created as to be in an outward innocence when we are little, but in an inward innocence in old age, to come to the latter through the former. So when we do get old, our bodies deteriorate and we become like little children again—but like wise little children or angels, for in the highest sense, a wise infant is an angel. This is why "infant" in the Word means one who is innocent, and "elderly one" means a wise person full of innocence.[b]

It is much the same for everyone who is being regenerated. Regeneration is rebirth as a spiritual person. [When we are being regenerated,] we

279

---

b. Infants in the Word mean innocence: 5608; and so do nursing babies: 3183. An old person means a wise one, or abstractly, wisdom: 3183, 6523 *[6524]*. We have been so created as to become like infants as we approach old age, but with wisdom in our innocence. This is so that we may cross over into heaven in this state and become angels: 3183, 5608.

are brought first into the innocence of infancy, which is realizing that we know nothing of truth and are capable of nothing of good on our own, but only from the Lord, and that we long for and seek what is true and good simply because it is true and good. These gifts are granted by the Lord as we advance in age. We are led first into knowledge about them, then from knowledge into intelligence, and finally from intelligence into wisdom, always hand in hand with innocence, which is, as already noted, the recognition that we know nothing of truth and are capable of nothing of good on our own, but only from the Lord. No one can accept heaven without this belief and this perception. It is the prime component of the innocence of wisdom.

280   Since innocence is being led by the Lord and not by ourselves, all the people who are in heaven are in innocence, since all the people who are there love to be led by the Lord. They know that to be led by oneself is to be led by one's self-centeredness, and self-centeredness is loving oneself. People who are in love with themselves are not willing to be led by anyone else. This is why angels are in heaven to the extent that they are in innocence; that is, to that extent they are absorbed in divine good and divine truth, for being absorbed in these is being in heaven. Consequently, the heavens are differentiated according to their innocence. People who are in the outmost or first heaven are in innocence of the first or outmost level. People who are in the intermediate or second heaven are in innocence of the second or intermediate level. People who are in the inmost or third heaven, though, are in innocence of the third or inmost level; so they are the very innocent of heaven, since they above all others want to be led by the Lord the way infants are led by their father. This is why they accept divine truth directly into their intent and do it, making it a matter of life, whether they receive it directly from the Lord or mediately through the Word and sermons. This is why they have so much more wisdom than angels of the lower heavens (see §§270–271). Because this is the nature of these angels, they are closest to the Lord, who is the source of their innocence, and they are also distanced from their self-centeredness so much that they seem to live in the Lord. In outward form they look simple—even like infants or little children in the eyes of angels of the lower heavens. They look like people who do not know very much, even though they are the wisest of angels. They are in fact aware that they have no trace of wisdom on their own and that to be wise is to admit this and to admit that what they do know is nothing compared to what they do not know. Knowing, recognizing, and perceiving this is what they call the first step toward wisdom. These angels are also naked, because nakedness corresponds to innocence.[c,176]

I have talked a lot with angels about innocence and have been told that innocence is the inner reality of everything good and that therefore anything good is good to the extent that there is innocence within it. Consequently wisdom is wisdom to the extent that it derives from innocence, and the same is true of love, thoughtfulness, and faith.[d] This is why no one can enter heaven unless he or she has innocence. This is what the Lord meant by saying,

> Let the little ones come to me, do not forbid them, for of such is the kingdom of the heavens. I tell you in truth, whoever will not accept the kingdom of the heavens like a little child will not enter into it. (Mark 10:14–15; Luke 18:16–17)

Little ones in this passage, as elsewhere in the Word, mean the innocent.[e] The state of innocence is described by the Lord in Matthew 6:24–25 [25–34], but in pure correspondences.[177] The reason good is good to the extent that there is innocence in it is that all good comes from the Lord, and innocence is being willing to be led by the Lord.

I have also been told that truth cannot be united to good or good to truth except by means of innocence. This is also why angels are not angels of heaven unless there is innocence in them, since heaven is not within anyone until the truth has been united with the good within. So the union of the true and the good is called the heavenly marriage, and the heavenly marriage is heaven.

I have also been told that true marriage love[178] derives its origin from innocence because it comes from the union of the good and the true that engages the two minds, the minds of husband and wife. When this union descends, it takes on the appearance of marriage love because the

---

c. All the people in the inmost heaven are innocents: 154, 2736, 3887; and therefore they look to others like infants: 154. They are also naked: 165, 8375, 9960. Nakedness is innocence: 165, 8375. Spirits have a practice of witnessing to their innocence by taking off their clothes and standing naked: 8375, 9960.

d. All the good of love and the truth of faith need to have innocence within them if they are to be good and true: 2526, 2780, 3111, 3994, 6013, 7840, 9262, 10134. Innocence is the essential element of what is good and true: 2780, 7840. No one is allowed into heaven unless she or he has some innocence: 4797.

e. [Swedenborg's note at this point refers the reader to the note in §278 above.]

spouses, like their minds, love each other. This is the source of the child-like and innocent play in marriage love.[f]

282 Since innocence, for heaven's angels, is the very essence of what is good, we can see that the divine good emanating from the Lord is innocence itself, inasmuch as it is this good that flows into angels, moves their deepest natures, and aligns and adapts them to accept all the blessings of heaven. Much the same happens with infants, whose deeper natures are not only formed by the passage of innocence from the Lord but are also constantly adapted and aligned to accept the good of heavenly love, because the good of innocence acts from deep within, being, as already noted, the very essence of all good. This shows that all innocence is from the Lord, which is why the Lord is called the Lamb in the Word, since a lamb means innocence.[g]

Because innocence is the very heart of all the good of heaven, it also affects minds so strongly that people who feel it—which happens at the approach of an angel of the inmost heaven—feel as though they are not under their own control. They are moved by such a joy, so taken out of themselves, so to speak, that it seems as though all the pleasure of the world is nothing by comparison. I speak of this from having experienced it.

283 Anyone who is in the goodness of innocence is moved by innocence, and is moved by innocence to the extent that she or he is in that good. However, people who are not in the good of innocence are not moved by it. Consequently, all the people in hell are absolutely opposed to innocence. They do not know what innocence is. Their nature is such that the more innocent people are, the more they burn with desire to cause them harm. This is why they cannot stand to see little children. The moment they do, they are consumed with a vicious desire to inflict harm.

---

f. True marriage love is innocence: 2736. Marriage love is intending what the other intends, mutually and reciprocally: 2731. People who are in marriage love are living together in the inmost aspects of life: 2732. There is a union of two minds, so effective that they become one from love: 10168, 10169. True marriage love derives its origin and essence from the marriage of the good and the true: 2728, 2729. About some angelic spirits who could perceive whether a true inclination toward marriage existed from the image they perceived of the union of the good and the true: 10756. Marriage love works exactly like the union of the good and the true: 1094 *[1904]*, 2173, 2429 *[2729]*, 2503 *[2508]*, 3101, 3102, 3155, 3179, 3180, 4358, 5407 *[5807]*, 5835, 9206, 9207, 9495, 9637. So in the Word, "marriage" means the union of the good and the true as it is in heaven and as it should be in the church: 3132, 4434, 4834.
g. A lamb in the Word means innocence and the good it does: 3994, 10132.

This has shown me that our self-image and the self-love it fosters are opposed to innocence, for all the people who are in hell are caught up in their own self-image and therefore in self-love.[h]

The State of Peace in Heaven

284 ANYONE who has not experienced heaven's peace cannot know what the peace is that angels enjoy. As long as we are in our bodies, we cannot accept heaven's peace, so we cannot perceive it, our perception being on the natural level. In order to perceive it, we need to be the kind of person who as to thought can be raised and taken out of the body and brought into the spirit so as to be with angels. Since I have perceived heaven's peace in this way, I can describe it, but not in words as it really is, because human words are not adequate. Using words, I can only describe what it is like compared to that peace of mind that people have who are content in God.[179]

285 There are two things at the heart of heaven, innocence and peace. We say that they are at the heart because they come straight from the Lord. From innocence comes everything good about heaven and from peace comes all the delight of that good. Everything good has its own delight, and both—the good and the delight—are matters of love. This is because what is loved is what is called good and also is perceived as delightful. It follows from this that these two inmost qualities, innocence and peace, emanate from the Lord's divine love and move angels to their very core.

In the previous chapter on the state of innocence of heaven's angels, it was shown that innocence is the very heart of good. Now I need to

---

h. The human "ego" [Latin *proprium,* literally, "that which is one's own"] is loving oneself more than God, and the world more than heaven, and regarding one's neighbor as nothing compared to oneself; which means that it is love for oneself and for the world: 694, 731, 4317, 5660. Evil people are so completely opposed to innocence that they cannot stand its presence: 2126.

explain that peace is the very heart of the delight that comes from the goodness of innocence.

286   First, we need to say where peace comes from. Divine peace is within the Lord, arising from the oneness of his divine nature and the divine human nature within him.[180] The divine quality of peace in heaven comes from the Lord, arising from his union with heaven's angels, and specifically from the union of the good and the true within each angel. These are the sources of peace. We may therefore conclude that peace in the heavens is the divine nature intimately affecting everything good there with blessedness. So it is the source of all the joy of heaven. In its essence, it is the divine joy of the Lord's divine love, arising from his union with heaven and with every individual there. This joy, perceived by the Lord in the angels and by the angels from the Lord, is peace. It flows down from there to provide angels with everything that is blessed and delightful and happy—what is called "heavenly joy."[a]

287   Because these are the origins of peace, the Lord is called the Prince of Peace and says that peace comes from him and that peace is in him. So too angels are called angels of peace and heaven the dwelling place of peace, as in the following passages:

> A child is born to us, a son is given to us, on whose shoulder the government [shall rest], and his name shall be called Wonderful, Counselor, God, Hero, Eternal Father, *Prince of Peace;* of the increase of government and *peace* there shall be no end. (Isaiah 9:5–6 *[6–7]*)

> Jesus said, "*Peace* I leave with you, my *peace* I give you, not as the world gives do I give to you." (John 14:27)

> I have told you these things so that you might have *peace* in me. (John 16:33)

> May Jehovah lift his face to you and give you *peace.* (Numbers 6:26)

> *The angels of peace* weep bitterly, the highways are ruined. (Isaiah 33:7–8)

---

a. In the highest sense, peace means the Lord, because he is the source of peace; and in the inner sense it means heaven, because people there are in a state of peace: 3780, 4681. Peace in the heavens is the divine nature profoundly touching everything good and true there with a blessedness that is beyond our comprehension: 92, 3780, 5662, 8455, 8665. Divine peace occurs in what is good, but not in what is true apart from what is good: 8722.

The work of justice will be *peace,* and my people will live in a *dwelling place of peace.* (Isaiah 32:17–18)

[2] We may also gather that "peace" in the Word means divine and heavenly peace from other passages where it is mentioned, as for example in Isaiah 52:7; 54:10; 59:8; Jeremiah 16:5; 25:37; 29:11; Haggai 2:9; Zechariah 8:12; Psalms 37:37; and elsewhere.

Because peace means the Lord and heaven and also heavenly joy and the delight of good, greetings in ancient times were—and consequently still are—"Peace be with you." The Lord confirmed this, too, when he sent out his disciples and told them, "When you enter a house, first say '*Peace* be upon this house'; and if a child of *peace* is there, let your *peace* rest upon it" (Luke 10:5–6). Further, the Lord himself said "*Peace* be with you" when he appeared to the apostles (John 20:19, 21, 26).

[3] A state of peace is also meant in the Word when it says that "Jehovah smelled an odor of quietness," as in Exodus 29:18, 25, 41; Leviticus 1:9, 13, 17; 2:2, 9; 6:8, 14 *[6:15, 21];* 23:12, 13, 18; Numbers 15:3, 7, 13; 28:6, 8, 13; 29:2, 6, 8, 13, 36. "An odor of quietness," in the heavenly sense, means a perception of peace.[b]

Since peace means the oneness of the Divine itself and the divine human in the Lord and the union of the Lord with heaven and with the church and with everyone in heaven, and also with everyone in the church who accepts him, the Sabbath was instituted as a reminder of these matters and was named for quietness and peace. It became the holiest symbol of the church, which is why the Lord called himself the Lord of the Sabbath (Matthew 12:8; Mark 2:27–28; Luke 6:5).[c]

Since heaven's peace is a divine blessedness that profoundly affects the essential good within angels, it does not come to their open perception

288

b. An odor in the Word means a perception of something pleasant or unpleasant, depending on the quality of the love and faith of the entity described: 3577, 4626, 4628, 4748, 5021 *[5621],* 10292. An odor of quietness, in relation to Jehovah, means a perception of peace: 925, 10054. So frankincense, various kinds of incense, and the fragrances in oils and salves came to be representative: 925, 4748, 5621, 10177.

c. In the highest sense, the Sabbath means the oneness of the Divine itself with the divine human in the Lord; and in the inner sense the union of the Lord's divine human with heaven and the church. In a general sense it means the union of the good and the true and therefore the heavenly marriage: 8495, 10356, 10730. So the rest on the Sabbath day meant the state of that oneness, because then the Lord has rest, through which peace and salvation come to the heavens and to earth; and in a relative sense it means the union of the Lord with us, because then we have peace and salvation: 8494, 8510, 10360, 10367, 10370, 10374, 10668, 10730.

except through a heartfelt delight when they are involved in the good of their life, a pleasure when they hear something true that is in accord with their good, and a gaiety of mind when they perceive the union of the two. Still, it does flow into all the acts and thoughts of their life and makes itself known as joy, even in outward form.

[2] Peace varies in quality and quantity in the heavens, though, in proportion to the innocence of the people in any given location, because innocence and peace walk hand in hand. For as already noted, innocence is the source of everything good in heaven and peace is the source of all the joy of that good. We may conclude, then, that we can say much the same about the state of peace as has already been said about the state of innocence in the preceding chapter, since innocence and peace are united the way anything good and its delight are. Whatever is good is in fact sensed by its delight, and whatever is delightful is recognized by virtue of its goodness. This being the case, we can see that angels of the inmost or third heaven are in the third or inmost level of peace because they are in the third or inmost level of innocence, and that angels of the lower heavens are in lesser levels of peace because they are in lesser levels of innocence (see above, §280).

[3] If we look at little children, we can see that innocence and peace occur together in the same way that anything good and its delight do. Because they are in innocence, they are at peace as well; and because they are at peace, everything associated with them has a playful quality. However, their peace is an outward peace. Inner peace, like inner innocence, is found only in wisdom; and since it does dwell in wisdom, it is found in the union of the good and the true, since this is the origin of wisdom.

Heavenly or angelic peace occurs in us when we are attuned to wisdom because of the union of the good and the true and therefore see ourselves as contented in God. However, as long as we are living in this world, that peace lies hidden in our depths. Still, it is unveiled when we leave our bodies behind and enter heaven, because then those depths are opened.

289 Since divine peace arises from the Lord's union with heaven—and in particular with each individual angel by virtue of the union of the true and the good—when angels are in a state of love they are in a state of peace, because this is when the good within them is united to what is true (it has been explained above that angels' states change periodically, §§154–160). Much the same is true of us when we are being regenerated. When a union of the good and the true takes place within us, which happens principally after trials by temptation, we come into a state of delight that arises from heavenly peace.[d]

That peace is like the morning time or dawn in spring, when, once the night has passed, all things of earth begin to take new life from the rising of the sun; the dew that falls from heaven spreads a leafy fragrance far and wide, and springtime's gentle warmth makes meadows fertile and instills its charm in human minds as well. This is because morning or dawn in springtime corresponds to the state of peace of angels in heaven (see §155).[e]

I have talked with angels about peace as well, and have told them that on earth they call it peace when wars and conflicts between nations are over, or enmities and disagreements between individuals, and that they think inner peace is simply the peace of mind we have when anxieties are banished, or especially the relief and delight when things turn out well for us. The angels have responded, though, that this peace of mind, this relief and delight when anxieties are banished and things turn out well for us, may look like effects of peace; but they do not come from real peace except in people who are focused on heavenly good. This is because peace occurs only in that good. Peace actually flows in from the Lord into the very core of such individuals, and from that core comes down and spreads into their lower natures, causing peace of mind, relief of the spirit, and a consequent joy.

For people engrossed in evil, though, there is no peace.[f] There is an apparent calm, tranquillity, and pleasure when they get their way, but this is outward only, with no inward substance. Inside there is raging hostility, hatred, vengefulness, cruelty, and all kinds of evil cravings. Their spirits rush into these feelings the moment they see anyone who is not on their side, and it bursts forth whenever there is no fear [to restrain it]. This is why their delight is at home in insanity, while the delight of people involved in good is at home in wisdom. It is like the difference between hell and heaven.

290

d. The union of the good and the true in people who are being regenerated takes place in a state of peace: 3696, 8517.

e. The state of peace in heaven is like the state of morning or spring on earth: 1726, 2780, 5662.

f. The cravings that arise from love for oneself and for the world totally destroy peace: 3170, 5662. Some people find peace in restlessness and in other such things that are the opposite of peace: 5662. There is no peace until the cravings of evil have been taken away: 5662.

The Union of Heaven with the Human Race

291 IT is acknowledged in the church that everything good comes from God and nothing of it from us, and therefore that we should never take personal credit for anything good. It is also recognized that evil comes from the devil. This is why people who talk from the doctrine of the church describe people who are acting well and who are talking devoutly and preaching as being led by God, and say the opposite about people who are acting maliciously and speaking blasphemously.[181] None of this could happen unless we had a union with heaven and a union with hell, and unless those unions were with our volition and our understanding, since it is from these that the body acts and the mouth speaks. We need now to describe what this union is like.

292 There are good spirits and evil spirits with every individual. We have our union with heaven through the good spirits and our union with hell through the evil ones. These spirits are in the world of spirits, which is intermediate between heaven and hell and will be specifically treated later.[182]

When these spirits come to us, they come into our whole memory and from there into all our thinking—evil spirits into the matters of memory and thought that are evil, and good spirits into the matters of memory and thought that are good. These spirits are totally unaware that they are with us. Rather, as long as they are, they believe that all these matters of our memory and thought are actually theirs. They do not see us, either, because their sight does not extend to things in our subsolar world.[a,183]

The Lord takes the greatest care to prevent spirits from knowing whom they are with.[184] If they did know, they would talk with them, and then the evil spirits would destroy them; for evil spirits, being united to hell, want nothing more than to destroy us not only as to spirit (that is, as to our love and faith) but as to our bodies as well. It is different when

a. There are angels and spirits with every individual, and through them we have communication with the spiritual world: 697, 2796, 2886, 2887, 4047, 4048, 5846–5866, 5976–5993. Apart from these spirits with us, we could not live: 5993. We are not visible to the spirits, nor are they to us: 5885 *[5862]*. Spirits cannot see anything in our subsolar world of humanity except things [visible] to the individual they are talking to: 1880.

they do not talk with us. Then they do not know that we are the source of what they are thinking—and what they are saying to each other, since they talk to each other just the way we do—but believe that these matters are their own. They value and love whatever is their own, so these spirits are constrained to love and value us, even though they do not know it.

This kind of union has become so familiar to me through years of constant experience as to be commonplace.

The reason spirits who are in touch with hell are attached to us as well is that we are born into all kinds of evil, so that our first life is made up of nothing else. Unless spirits of the same kind were associated with us, then, we could not live or be led out of our evils and reformed. So we are kept in our own life by evil spirits and restrained from it by good spirits. Through the two kinds, we are kept in a balance; and since we are in a balance we enjoy an appropriate measure of freedom and can be led out of our evils and turned toward good.[185] This good can be sown in us as well, which could never happen except in our freedom; and the freedom could not be granted us unless spirits from hell were acting on the one side and spirits from heaven on the other, with us in the middle.[186]

I have been shown that to the extent that we exist from our hereditary nature and from ourselves, we could have no life at all if we were not allowed to engage in evil. We would also have no life if we were not in some freedom, and we cannot be compelled to good: anything compelled does not become part of us. I have also been shown that anything good that we accept in freedom is sown in our intentions and becomes virtually our own.[b] This is why we have a communication with hell and a communication with heaven.

I also need to describe the nature of the communication of heaven with good spirits, the nature of the communication of hell with evil spirits, and the nature of the consequent union of heaven and hell with us. All the spirits who are in the world of spirits are in communication with

293

294

---

b. All freedom is a matter of love and affection, because what we love, we do freely: 2870, 3158, 8907 [8987], 8990, 9585, 9591. Freedom is a matter of love, which is its life: 2873. Nothing seems to be ours unless it comes from our freedom: 2880. We need to have some freedom in order to be reformed: 1937, 1947, 2876, 2881, 3145, 3146, 3158, 4031, 8700. Otherwise, the love for what is good and true could not be sown in us and given to us as though it were ours: 2877, 2879, 2880, 2888 [2883], 8700. Nothing that is forced upon us is united to us: 2875, 8700. If we could be reformed by force, then everyone would be reformed: 2881. The use of force in reformation is harmful: 4031. The state of some people who had been compelled: 8392.

heaven or with hell, the evil ones with hell and the good ones with heaven. Heaven is differentiated into communities, and so is hell. Every spirit is a member of some community, is sustained by an inflow from it, and therefore acts in harmony with it. This is why we are united with heaven or hell just as we are united with spirits. We are actually united to some community there, the community we belong to in respect to our affection or our love; for all heaven's communities are differentiated according to their affections for what is good and true and all hell's communities according to their affections for what is evil and false (on heaven's communities, see above, §§41–45 and 148–151).

295   The kind of spirit that is associated with us is determined by the kind of person we are in respect to affection and love, though good spirits are assigned to us by the Lord while we ourselves summon the evil ones. The spirits with us change, however, as our own affections change. This means we have one kind with us in infancy, another kind during our childhood, another kind as we are growing up and in early adulthood, and still another kind in old age. During our earliest years, spirits who are in innocence are with us, that is, spirits who are in touch with the heaven of innocence, the inmost or third heaven. In later childhood we are in the company of spirits who are engaged in an affection for knowledge and who are in touch with the ultimate or first heaven. As we are growing up, during our early adulthood, spirits who are responsive to affections for what is true and good and therefore with intelligence are with us. They are spirits who are in touch with the second or intermediate heaven. In old age, though, spirits who are in wisdom and innocence are with us, spirits therefore who are in touch with the inmost or third heaven.

Still, this association is arranged by the Lord for people who can be reformed and regenerated. It is different for people who cannot be reformed or regenerated. Good spirits are assigned to them as well in order to restrain them from evil as much as possible, but their direct connection is with the evil spirits who are in touch with hell. This means that the spirits are of the same nature as the people they are associated with. Whether they love themselves or money or revenge or adultery, the same kind of spirits are with them and are, so to speak, taking up residence in their evil affections. To the extent that we cannot be restrained from evil by good spirits, they inflame us, and to the extent that an evil affection is in control, they cling to us and will not back off.

In this way, evil people are united to hell and good people to heaven.[187]

The reason we are controlled by the Lord through spirits is that we are not in the pattern of heaven. We are in fact born into evils that are from hell and are therefore exactly opposite to the divine pattern. This means that we need to be brought back into the pattern, and we cannot be brought back except through the agency of spirits. It would be different if we were born into the good that accords with heaven's pattern. Then we would not be controlled by the Lord through the agency of spirits but through the pattern itself and therefore through a general inflow.[188]

This [general] inflow determines the way things move from thought and intent into act and therefore determines our speech and actions, since these both do flow according to a natural pattern. So the spirits who are with us have nothing to do with these processes.

Animals are also controlled through a general inflow from the spiritual world because they are in the pattern proper to their life, a pattern that they can neither distort nor destroy, because they do not have a rational faculty.[c] (On the difference between humans and animals see above, §39.)

To continue with the general topic of the union of heaven with the human race, we need to be aware that the Lord flows into each one of us according to heaven's design, into our inmost natures as well as into our outmost, and disposes us to accept heaven. He controls our outmost natures from the inmost and the inmost from the outmost at the same time, and in this way keeps everything about us in coherent connection. This inflow from the Lord is called a direct inflow, while a second inflow that happens through the agency of spirits is called an indirect inflow. The latter is sustained by the former. The direct inflow, an action of the Lord himself, is from his divine human. It comes into our intentions, and through our intentions into our understanding. This means it comes into what is good in us and through that good into what is true in us, or (which amounts to the same thing) into our love and through our love into our faith. It does not happen the other way around, much

c. The difference between us and animals is that we can be raised by the Lord to himself, can think about the Divine and love it, and so can be united to the Lord and have eternal life, which is not true of animals: 4525, 6323, 9231. Animals are in the pattern proper to their lives and are therefore born into things that are suited to their natures; but we are not, so we need to be led into the pattern proper to our lives by cognitive means: 637, 5850, 6323. Thought descends into speech and intention into actions for us according to a general inflow: 5862, 5990, 6192, 6211. On the general inflow of the spiritual world into the lives of animals: 1633, 3646.

less into faith apart from love or into truth apart from good or into understanding apart from volition.

This divine inflow is unceasing and is accepted in what is good in good people, but not in evil ones. In them it is either rejected or stifled or distorted. So they have an evil life that spiritually understood is a death.[d]

298   The spirits who are with us—both those united to heaven and those united to hell—never flow into us from their own memory and consequent thought. If they did flow into us from their own thought it would seem to us exactly as though their character was our own (see above, §256). However, there does flow into us through them an affection from a love of what is good and true from heaven and an affection from a love of what is evil and false from hell. So to the extent that our own affection agrees with what is flowing in, we accept its influence in our thinking. This is because our more inward thought is in complete accord with our affection or love. To the extent that our own affection does not agree, we do not accept [the influence]. We can see from this that thoughts are not instilled into us by spirits but only an affection for what is good or an affection for what is evil. This gives us a choice because it gives us freedom. It means that in our thought we can accept what is good and reject what is evil, since we know from the Word what is good and what is evil. What we accept in thought from affection becomes part of us, while what we do not accept in thought from affection does not become part of us. This enables us to determine the nature of the inflow into us of the good from heaven and of the evil from hell.

299   I have been enabled to learn where we get the anxiety, distress of mind, and inward sadness called depression.[189] There are spirits who are not yet united with hell because they are still in their first state (which will be described later when we talk about the world of spirits).[190] They

d. There is a direct inflow from the Lord and also an indirect inflow through the spiritual world: 6063, 6307, 6472, 9682, 9683. The Lord's direct inflow is into the most minute details of all: 6058, 6474–6478, 8717, 8728. The Lord flows into our first and our last things at the same time [see Swedenborg's note to §304:3 below], and how this happens: 5147, 5150, 6473, 7004, 7007, 7270. The Lord's inflow is into the good within us and through that good into the truth, and not the reverse: 5482, 5649, 6027, 8685, 8701, 10153. The life that flows in from the Lord varies according to our state and according to our openness: 2069 [1909], 5986, 6472, 7343. In evil people, the good that flows in from the Lord is turned into evil and the truth into falsity; from experience: 3643 [3642], 4632. We accept the good and the consequent truth that are unceasingly flowing in from the Lord to the extent that evil and its consequent falsity do not block the way: 2411, 3142, 3147, 5828.

love half-digested and noxious substances like the foods that are becoming excrement in the stomach, so they attach themselves to the same sort of matter in us, because they find delight in it; and they talk with each other there out of their evil affection. The emotional tone of their conversation flows into us, and since it is contrary to our affection, it brings about a sadness and an anxious depression; while if it agrees with our affection, it brings about a sense of happiness and exhilaration. These spirits can be seen in the neighborhood of the stomach, some on the left and some on the right, some lower and some higher, nearer or farther away—variously depending on the affections they are involved in.[191] A great deal of experience has convinced me that they are the source of our anxiety of spirit. I have seen them, heard them, felt the anxieties that well up from them.[192] I have talked with them, they have been driven off and the anxiety has ceased, they have come back and the anxiety has returned, I have observed its increase and decrease as they drew near and moved away. It has become clear to me, then, where that anxiety originates that is blamed on a stomachache by people who do not know what conscience is because they do not have any.[e]

Heaven's union with us is not like the union of one person with another, but is a union with the deeper levels of our minds and therefore with our spiritual or inner person. There is, though, a union with our natural or outer person by correspondences, which union will be discussed in the next chapter when I deal with heaven's union with us by means of the Word.   300

I will also explain in the next chapter that heaven's union with us and our union with it are of such a nature that each relies on the other.   301

I have talked with angels about the union of heaven with the human race and have told them that church people actually do say that everything good is from the Lord and that there are angels with us, but few people really believe that angels are so close to us, much less that they are   302

e. People who do not have a conscience do not know what a conscience is: 7490, 9121. There are even people who laugh at conscience when they hear that it exists: 7217. Some people believe that conscience is nothing, some that it is a kind of natural, distressing sadness that arises either from events in the body or events in the world, and some that it is something common people get from their religion: 950. There is a true conscience, an imitation conscience, and a false conscience: 1033. Pangs of conscience are an anxiety of mind because of anything unjust, dishonest, and evil that we believe to be contrary to God and contrary to the welfare of our neighbor: 7217. People who are in love for God and charity toward their neighbor have conscience, but not people who are not: 831, 965, 2380, 7490.

in our thought and affection. The angels have told me that they knew this kind of [empty] belief and talk occurred in the world, and especially (which astonished them) in the church, where people have the Word that teaches them about heaven and its union with them. Yet in fact the union is so vital that we could not think the least thought apart from the spirits who are with us. Our spiritual life depends on this. They said that the reason for this ignorance was that people believe they live on their own, without any connection with the Ultimate Reality of life,[193] and do not know that there is this connection through the heavens. Yet if that connection were severed, we would instantly drop down dead. If we believed the way things really are, that everything good comes from the Lord and everything evil from hell, then we would not take credit for the good within us or blame for the evil. Whenever we thought or did anything good, we would focus on the Lord, and any evil that flowed in we would throw back into the hell it came from. But since we do not believe in any inflow from heaven or from hell and therefore believe that everything we think and intend is in us and from us, we make the evil our own and defile the good with our feeling that we deserve it.

Heaven's Union with Us through the Word

303 PEOPLE who think from their deeper rationality can see that there is a connection of all things, through intermediate ones, with a First,[194] and that anything that is not so connected will disintegrate. When they think about it, they know that nothing can exist on its own, but requires something prior to itself, which means that everything goes back to that First. They know that the connection with what is prior is like that of an effect with its efficient cause,[195] since when the efficient cause is removed, the effect comes apart and collapses. Since this has been the thought of the learned, they have both seen and pronounced that existence is a constant becoming,[196] so that all things are constantly coming into being—that is, existing—from that First from which they originated.

But there is no way to explain briefly the nature of that connection of everything with what is prior and therefore with the First that is the source of everything, because it is varied and diverse. We can say generally only that there is a connection of the natural world with the spiritual world that results in a correspondence between everything in the natural world and everything in the spiritual world. (On this correspondence, see §§103–115, and on the connection and consequent correspondence of everything in us with everything in heaven, see §§87–102.)

We have been so created that we have a connection and a union with the Lord, while with angels we have only an association. The reason we have only an association, not a union, with angels is that we are from creation like angels in respect to the deeper levels of our minds. We have a similar purposefulness and a similar capacity to understand. This is why we become angels after death if we have lived according to the divine pattern, and why we then, like the angels, have wisdom. So when we talk about our union with heaven, we mean our union with the Lord and our association with angels, since heaven is not heaven because of anything that really belongs to the angels but because of the divine nature of the Lord. (On the fact that the Lord's divine nature makes heaven, see §§7–22 [7–12] above.)

304

[2] Over and above what angels have, though, there is the fact that we are not just in a spiritual world by virtue of our inner natures but are at the same time in a natural world by virtue of our outward natures. These outward things that are in the natural world are all the contents of our natural or outer memory and the thinking and imaging we do on that basis. In general, this includes our insights and information together with their delights and charm to the extent that they have a worldly flavor, and all the pleasures that derive from our physical senses. Then too, there are those senses themselves and our words and actions. All these are ultimate things in which the Lord's divine inflow comes to rest, since it does not stop in the middle but goes on to its very limit.

We may gather from this that the ultimate form of the divine pattern is in us, and since it is the ultimate form, it is the basis and foundation.

[3] Since the Lord's divine inflow does not stop in the middle but goes on to its very limit, as just stated, and since the intermediate region it crosses is the angelic heaven and the limit is in us, and since nothing disconnected can exist, it follows that there is such a connection and union of heaven with the human race that neither can endure without the other. If the human race were cut off from heaven, it would be like a

chain with a link removed, and heaven without the human race would be like a house without a foundation.[a]

305 However, since we have broken this connection by turning our inward natures away from heaven and toward the world and ourselves through our self-love and love of the world and have so pulled away that we no longer serve heaven as its basis and foundation, the Lord has provided a medium to serve in place of that basis and foundation and to maintain the union of heaven with humanity. That medium is the Word.

Just how the Word serves as that medium, though, has been shown at length in *Secrets of Heaven,* with pertinent material collected in the booklet *The White Horse Described in the Book of Revelation* and also in the "Appendix to the Heavenly Teaching."[197] Some of these references are cited in the footnote below.[b]

306 I have been told from heaven that the earliest people had direct revelation because their inner natures were turned toward heaven, and that

a. Nothing arises from itself, but only from something prior to itself; so all things come from a first, and endure by connection with what they originated from, so that existing is a constant becoming: 2886, 2888, 3627, 3628, 3648, 4523, 4524, 6040, 6056. The divine pattern does not stop in the middle but keeps on to its limit, and its limit is in us; so the divine pattern ends in us: 634, 2853, 3632, 5897, 6239, 6451, 6465, 9216, 9217 [9215], 9824, 9828, 9836, 9905, 10044, 10329, 10335, 10548. The inner elements flow sequentially into the outer all the way to the end or limit, and there they take form and endure: 634, 6239, 6465, 9216, 9217 [9215]. The inner elements take form and endure in the outer in a simultaneous arrangement, which is described: 5897, 6451, 8603, 10099. So all the inner elements are kept connected together from the First to the ultimate: 9828. For this reason, "the First and the Last" means everything in detail, the whole: 10044, 10329, 10335; and for this reason, strength and power are in ultimate things: 9836.
b. The Word in its literal sense is natural: 8783; because the natural level is the ultimate level in which spiritual and heavenly things (which are more inward) come to rest, and on which they rest like a house on its foundation: 9430, 9433, 9824, 10044, 10436. In order to be of this nature, the Word was written in pure correspondences: 1404, 1408, 1409, 1540, 1615 [1619], 1659, 1709, 1783, 8615, 10687. Since the Word is like this in its literal meaning, it is a vessel for spiritual and heavenly meaning: 9407; and it is adapted to us and to angels at the same time: 1769–1772, 1887, 2143, 2157, 2275, 2333, 2396 [2395], 2540, 2541, 2545, 2553, 7381, 8862, 10322. It is what unites heaven and earth: 2310, 2495, 9212, 9216, 9357, 9396, 10375. The Lord's union with us through the Word by means of its inner meaning: 10375. This union takes place by means of every detail in the Word, so it is more marvelous than any other writing: 10632, 10633, 10634. Now that the Word has been written, the Lord speaks to us through it: 10290. Relative to people outside the church, who do not have the Word and know the Lord, the church where the Word is and where the Lord is known is like the human heart and lungs relative to the other parts of the body, which derive their life from the heart and lungs as from a wellspring: 637, 931, 2054, 2853. The whole church throughout the world is like a single person in the Lord's sight: 7395 [7396], 9276. This is why the human race would perish if there were not a church in our world where the Word was found and the Lord was known: 468, 637, 931, 4545, 10452.

this was the source of the Lord's union with the human race at that time. After those times, though, there was not the same kind of direct revelation, but an indirect revelation through correspondences. All their divine worship consisted of these; so the churches of those times were called symbolic churches. They knew what correspondences and representations were and that everything on earth answered to spiritual things in heaven and the church (or represented them, which amounts to the same thing). In this way, the natural elements that constituted their outward worship served them as means for thinking spiritually and therefore thinking with angels.

Once all knowledge of correspondences and representations had been lost, then a Word was written in which all the words and the meanings of the words are correspondences and therefore contain that spiritual or inner meaning in which angels are engaged. So when we read the Word and grasp it in its literal or outward meaning, angels grasp it in its inner or spiritual meaning. In fact, all the thought of angels is spiritual, while ours is natural. These two kinds of thought do seem different, but they are one because they correspond.

This is why, after we had moved away from heaven and broken the connection, the Lord provided that there should be a means of union of heaven with us through the Word.

I should like to use a few passages to show how heaven is united with us through the Word. The New Jerusalem is described in the Book of Revelation as follows:

307

> I saw a new heaven and a new earth, and the former heaven and former earth had passed away. And I saw the holy city Jerusalem coming down from God out of heaven. The city was foursquare, its length equal to its breadth. And the angel measured the city with the reed at twelve thousand stadia;[198] the length, breadth, and height were equal; and he measured its wall, 144 cubits, the measure of a human being, which was that of the angel. The construction of the wall was jasper, but the city itself was pure gold and like pure glass; and the foundation of the wall was decorated with every precious stone. The twelve gates were twelve pearls, and the street of the city was pure gold like transparent glass. (Revelation 21:1, 2, 16, 17, 18)[199]

People who read this understand it simply according to its literal meaning, namely that this visible sky and earth are going to perish and that a new heaven is going to be established, that on a new earth the holy city

Jerusalem is going to descend, and that all its measurements will be as described. But the angels who are with us understand it very differently, understanding spiritually what we take in a natural sense. [2] For them, the new heaven and the new earth mean a new church; the city Jerusalem descending from God out of heaven means its heavenly doctrine revealed by the Lord; its length, breadth, and height, which are equal at twelve thousand stadia, mean all the good and true elements of that doctrine grasped as a single whole; the wall means the truths that protect it; the measure of the wall being 144 cubits, which was the measure of a human being, that is, of the angel, means all those protective truths grasped as a single whole, and their quality; the twelve gates made of pearls mean introductory truths (pearls mean that kind of truth); the foundations of the wall that were of precious stones mean the acknowledgments on which that doctrine is based; and the gold like pure glass of which the city and its streets were made means the good of love that makes doctrine and its truths transparent. This is how angels understand all these things, so it is not the way we do. This is how our natural concepts are transformed into spiritual concepts among angels without their knowing anything about the literal meaning of the Word—about the new heaven and the new earth, for example, or the new city Jerusalem, its wall, the foundations of the wall, and its measurements. Still, the angels' thoughts form a unity with ours because they correspond. They form a single whole almost like the words of a speaker and the understanding of those words by a listener who is focused not on the words themselves but on understanding them. This may enable us to see how heaven is united to us through the Word.

[3] For another example from the Word,

> In that day there will be a highway from Egypt to Assyria, and Assyria will come into Egypt and Egypt into Assyria, and the Egyptians will serve the Assyrians. In that day Israel will be a third for Egypt and Assyria, a blessing in the middle of the land, whom Jehovah of hosts will bless, saying, "Blessed is my people Egypt, and the work of my hands Assyria, and my inheritance Israel." (Isaiah 19:23, 24, 25)

We can see how people on earth think and how angels think when they read this if we look at the literal meaning of the Word and at its inner meaning. We think, on the basis of its literal meaning, that Egypt and Assyria are going to be converted to God and received, and that they will become united to the Israelite nation. The angels, though, think on the basis of its inner meaning about people of the spiritual church, who are being described here in that inner meaning. Their spiritual level is Israel, their natural level is Egypt, and their rational level, which is the intermediate level, is Assyria.[c] Still, these two meanings are one because they correspond. Consequently, when angels are thinking spiritually like this and we are thinking naturally the way we do, we are united almost like a soul and a body. The inner meaning of the Word is its soul, and the literal meaning is its body.

The Word is like this throughout; so we can see that it is a means of heaven's union with us and that the literal meaning serves as its basis and foundation.

There is also a union of heaven through the Word with people who are outside the church, where the Word is not found; for the Lord's church is everywhere and exists with everyone who acknowledges something divine and lives considerately. People like this are taught by angels after their decease and accept divine truths.[d] There will be more on this below in its proper chapter, where we discuss non-Christians.[200]

In the Lord's sight, the universal church on earth is like a single individual just as heaven is (as noted above in §§59–72). However, the church where the Word is and the Lord is known through it is like the heart and lungs of that person. It is common knowledge that the viscera and members of the whole body get their life from the heart and lungs by various routes. So too the human race that is outside the church where the Word is gets its life in the same way and constitutes the members of that person. Heaven's union through the Word with people who are at a distance can be compared to light that spreads in all directions from a center. The divine light is in the Word, and the Lord is present there with his heaven. People who are far off also receive light from that presence. It would be different if there were no Word, which can be more fully

308

---

c. Egypt and Egyptian in the Word mean what is natural, and therefore what has to do with information: 4967, 5079, 5080, 5095, 5460 [5160], 5799, 6015, 6147, 6252, 7353 [7355], 7648, 9340, 9319 [9391]. Assyria means the rational level: 119, 1186. Israel means the spiritual level: 5414, 5801, 5803, 5806, 5812, 5817, 5819, 5826, 5833, 5879, 5951, 6426, 6637, 6862, 6868, 7035, 7062, 7198, 7201, 7215, 7223, 7956 [7957], 8234, 8805, 9340.

d. The church in specific is where the Word is and where the Lord is known because of it, so it is where divine truths from it have been revealed from heaven: 3857, 10761. The Lord's church exists throughout the whole world with all people who live in good according to their religions: 3263, 6637, 10765. All people who live in good according to their religions and acknowledge something divine are accepted by the Lord, wherever they are: 2589–2604, 2861, 2863, 3263, 4190, 4197, 6700, 9256; and especially all infants, wherever they may have been born: 2289–2309, 4792.

understood by reference to what has been presented above about the form of heaven that determines its gatherings and communications.[201]

Still, this arcanum is understandable to people who are in spiritual light but not to people who are only in natural light. People who are in spiritual light, that is, see quite clearly countless things that people who are in natural light alone either do not see at all or see only as a single vague entity.

309 If there had not been this kind of Word on our earth, the humanity of our earth would have separated itself from heaven, and once separated from heaven would no longer have had any rational ability. Our human rational ability in fact arises from an inflow of light from heaven.

We on this earth are by nature incapable of accepting any direct revelation and being taught about divine truths by that means, unlike the inhabitants of other planets ([whose abilities] have been dealt with in their own separate booklet).[202] We more than they are engrossed in worldly concerns and therefore in superficial matters,[203] while it is the deeper levels that are open to revelation. If the outer levels were receptive, we still would not understand the truth.

This nature of people on our earth is clearly visible in members of the church. Even though they know from the Word about heaven, hell, and life after death, they still deny these things at heart. This includes people who have made a name for themselves for outstanding learning, who you would think would therefore be wiser than others.

310 I have talked with angels about the Word on occasion, and have told them that it is looked down on by some people because of its pedestrian style.[204] They know absolutely nothing about its deeper meaning and therefore do not believe that this kind of wisdom lies hidden within. The angels have told me that even though the style of the Word may appear pedestrian in its literal meaning, it is qualitatively incomparable because divine wisdom lies hidden not just in the overall meaning but in every word, and that this wisdom shines out in heaven. They have wanted to declare that because it is divine truth, it is heaven's light, since divine truth in heaven is radiant (see above, §132). They have added that without this kind of Word there would be no light of heaven among the people of our earth and consequently no union with heaven for them; for the amount of heaven's light there is among us determines the union and therefore the extent to which we have any revelation of divine truth through the Word. The reason people do not know this union exists (through the spiritual meaning of the Word corresponding to its natural meaning) is that the people of our earth do not know anything about angels' spiritual thinking and conversation. They do not know that this is different from our natural thinking and conversation; and anyone who does not know this cannot possibly know what the inner meaning is and therefore cannot know that it can make this kind of union possible.

They have also said that if we knew that this kind of meaning existed and when we read the Word did our thinking with any knowledge of it, we would come into a deeper wisdom and be more closely united to heaven, because in this way we would have access to concepts like those of angels.

Heaven and Hell Come from the Human Race

PEOPLE in the Christian world are totally unaware that heaven and hell come from the human race. They actually believe that angels were created in the beginning and constitute heaven, and that the devil or Satan was an angel of light who became rebellious and was cast out together with his faction, and that this gave rise to hell. **311**

Angels are utterly amazed that there can be this kind of belief in the Christian world, and even more so that people know absolutely nothing about heaven, even though this is a primary doctrine of the church. Knowing that this kind of ignorance is prevalent, they are profoundly delighted that it has now pleased the Lord to reveal to us so much about heaven—and about hell as well—and so as much as possible to dispel the darkness that is rising daily because this church is drawing to a close. [2] So they want me to testify on their behalf that in all heaven there is not a single angel who was created as such in the beginning, nor is there in all hell a devil who was created as an angel of light and cast out. Rather, all the people in heaven and in hell are from the human race—in heaven the ones who have lived in heavenly love and faith, and in hell the ones who have lived in hellish love and faith. Hell as a whole is what is called the devil and Satan. The hell at the back, where the people called evil demons live, is the devil, and the hell that is in front, where the people live who are called evil spirits, is Satan.ª We will describe later what each hell is like.²⁰⁵ [3] They insisted that the reason the Christian world has adopted this kind of belief about people in heaven and people in hell is that they have taken a few passages of the Word, understanding them only in their literal meaning, with no enlightenment or instruction based on genuine doctrine from the Word. Yet the literal meaning of the Word, without the light of genuine doctrine, leads the mind astray in all directions, giving rise to ignorance, heresy, and error.ᵇ

312 This belief among church people is also the cause of their belief that no one will arrive in heaven or hell before the time of the Last Judgment, which they have come to believe will be a time when everything they can see perishes and new things come into being, when souls will return into their bodies and then begin once more to live as people because of this reunion. This faith implies the other, about angels having been created in the beginning, for it is not possible to believe that heaven and hell come from the human race when you believe that no one is going to get there until the end of the world.

[2] So to convince people that this is not the case, I have been allowed to associate with angels and to talk with people in hell for several years now, sometimes constantly from morning until evening, and so to learn about heaven and about hell. The purpose of all this is that church people should remain no longer in their mistaken beliefs about a resurrection on Judgment Day and about the state of their souls in the meanwhile, or about angels and the devil. Because this faith is a mistaken one, it brings darkness with it; and for people who think about such things on the basis of their own intellect, it leads to doubt and eventually to denial. They are actually saying in their hearts, "How can such a vast heaven and so many

a. The hells as a whole, or hellish people en masse, are called the devil and Satan: 694. People who were devils in the world are devils after death: 968.
b. The church's doctrine must be derived from the Word: 3464, 5402, 6832 *[6822]*, 10763, 10765 *[10764]*. Without doctrine, the Word is not understood: 9021 *[9025]*, 9409, 9424, 9430, 10324, 10431, 10582. True doctrine is a lamp for people who read the Word: 10401 *[10400]*. Genuine doctrine must be provided by people who have enlightenment from the Lord: 2510, 2516, 2519, 9424, 10105. People engaged in the literal meaning apart from any doctrine do not attain any understanding of divine truths: 9409, 9410, 10582; and are carried off into many errors: 10431. The nature of the difference between people who teach and learn from the doctrine of the church derived from the Word and people who do so solely from the Word's literal meaning: 9025.

stars be destroyed and disappear, along with the sun and the moon? How can stars that are larger than the earth fall on the earth? How can bodies that have been eaten by worms and destroyed by decay and scattered to the four winds be reunited to their souls? Where have these souls been in the meanwhile, and what have they been like without any of the senses they had in their bodies?" [3] There are many other questions like these, which do not accord with belief because they are incomprehensible, and for many people they are destroying any belief in a life after death, in heaven and hell, and along with these the rest of the contents of the faith of the church.²⁰⁶ This destruction can be observed in people who say, "Who has come back from heaven and told us that it exists, or from hell, to say that it exists? What is this business about people being tortured by fire to eternity? What is this Judgment Day? Haven't we been waiting for it for centuries, all in vain?" along with any number of other things that imply a denial of everything. [4] Many people who are particularly skilled in worldly affairs think like this; so to prevent them from further disturbing and misleading people of simple faith and simple heart and bringing on a hellish darkness concerning God, heaven, eternal life, and the other matters that follow from them, the deeper reaches of my spirit have been opened by the Lord, enabling me to talk after their death with all the people I have ever known during their physical lives. I have talked with some for days, with some for months, and with some for a year. I have talked with so many others that it would be no exaggeration to talk in terms of a hundred thousand, many in heaven and many in hell. I have talked with some just two days after their deaths and told them that now their funerals and burial rites were being performed so that they could be interred; to which they have responded that it was a good thing they had cast off what had served them as a body for their functions in our world, wanting me to say that they were not dead at all. They were just as alive and just as human as ever, having simply crossed over from one world to another. They were not aware of having lost anything, since they were just as much in a body as before, enjoyed volition and understanding just as before, and had thoughts and affections, sensation, and desires similar to the ones they had in our world.

[5] Many people who have just died, when they have discovered that they are living persons just as they were before, and in a similar state (for our first state after death is like the one we were in on earth, although this changes gradually for us either toward heaven or toward hell), have been moved by a newfound joy at still being alive. They have said they would not have believed it. They were absolutely amazed that they had

been in such ignorance and blindness about the state of life after death, all the more so that this is true of people within the church, who could be in more light about such matters than all the rest of the whole world.[c] Now for the first time they were seeing the reason for this blindness and ignorance, namely, that their outward concerns, their concerns for worldly and bodily matters, preoccupied and filled their minds so completely that they could not be raised into heaven's light and look into ecclesiastical subjects beyond the formalities of doctrine. When bodily and worldly matters are loved as much as they are today, nothing flows in from them but darkness when the mind tries to press further.

313   Many of the scholars of the Christian world are dumbfounded when they find themselves after death in bodies, wearing clothes, and in houses the way they were in this world. When they call to mind what they had thought about life after death, the soul, spirits, and heaven and hell, they are embarrassed and say that they had been thinking nonsense. They say that people of simple faith had been far wiser than they. Some scholars were examined who had completely convinced themselves in this kind of belief and attributed everything to nature. It turned out that their inner natures were completely closed off, while their more outward natures were open. This meant that they were not looking toward heaven but toward the world, and therefore toward hell; for to the extent that our deeper natures are opened, we look toward heaven, while to the extent that they are closed and our more outward natures are open, we look toward hell. Our deeper levels are formed for the acceptance of heaven and our more outward ones for acceptance of the world; and if we accept the world without accepting heaven at the same time, we are accepting hell.[d]

c. Not many people in today's Christianity believe that we will rise again immediately after death: Genesis 16 preface, 4622, 10758; but only at the time of the Last Judgment, when the visible world will perish: 10594 [10595]. The reason for this belief: 10594 [10595], 10758. The fact is, though, that we do rise again immediately after death, and are then completely human in all respects: 4527, 5006, 5078, 8939, 8991, 10594, 10758. The soul that lives after death is our spirit, which is the essential person within us and is in a perfect human form in the other life as well: 322, 1880, 1881, 3633, 4622, 4735, 5883, 6054, 6605, 6626, 7021, 10594; from experience: 4527, 5006, 8939; from the Word: 10597. An explanation of the meaning of the dead who were seen in the holy city in Matthew 27:53: 9229. How we are revived from death, from experience: 168–189. Our state after we have been revived: 317, 318, 319, 2119, 5079, 10596. False notions about the soul and its resurrection: 444, 445, 4527, 4622, 4658.

d. The spiritual world and the natural world are united in us: 6057. The inner person is formed on the model of heaven, while the outer is formed on the model of the world: 3628, 4523, 4524, 6057, 6314 [6013], 9706, 10156, 10472.

We may conclude that heaven is from the human race from the fact that angelic minds and our minds are very much alike. Both enjoy abilities to understand, perceive, and intend. Both are formed for the acceptance of heaven. In fact, our minds are just as wise as angelic minds; but they are not as wise in this world because we are in an earthly body, and in an earthly body our spiritual mind thinks in a natural manner. It is different, though, when it is freed from its tie to the body. Then we no longer think naturally, but spiritually, and when we think spiritually, we think thoughts that are incomprehensible and inexpressible to a natural person. This means we are as wise as angels. We may gather from this that our own inner person, what we call our spirit, is essentially an angel (see above, §57).^e Once it is freed from the earthly body it is in a human form just like that of an angel. (On angels being in perfect human form, see §§73–77 above.) However, when our inner person has not been opened upward but only downward, then we are in a human form after we are freed from this body, but it is a frightening and diabolical form because it cannot look upward toward heaven, only downward toward hell.

Once we have learned about the divine design, we can understand that we were created to become angels because the ultimate boundary of that design is found in us (§304), which means that in us the substance of heavenly and angelic wisdom can take form and can be restored and multiplied. The divine design never comes to rest part way, forming something without a boundary: that is not the design in its fullness and perfection. Rather, it presses on to its ultimate boundary,^f and when it has reached that limit it takes form; and then by means that it gathers on that level it restores itself and produces more, which is accomplished by procreation. This is why the seedbed of heaven is on this lowest level.

The reason the Lord rose not only in respect to his spirit but in respect to his body as well is that when the Lord was in the world, he glorified his whole human nature—that is, he made it divine. In fact, his soul, which he received from the Father, was essentially the Divine itself, and his body became an image of that soul (that is, of the Father) and therefore also

314

315

316

e. There are as many levels of life in a human being as there are heavens, and these are opened after death depending on how we have lived: 3747, 9594. Heaven is within us: 3884. People who are living lives of love and thoughtfulness have an angelic wisdom within them, but it is hidden; and they come into the use of it after death: 2494. In the Word, anyone who accepts the good of love and faith from the Lord is called an angel: 10528.

f. [Swedenborg's note here refers the reader back to the note in §303 above.]

divine. This is why he, unlike anyone else, rose in both spirit and body.g He showed this to his disciples—who believed they were seeing a spirit when they saw him—by saying, "Look at my hands and my feet, that it is I myself. Touch me and see, for a spirit does not have flesh and bones as you see that I do" (Luke 24:36–38 *[24:39]*). In this way he pointed out that he was not a person in spirit only, but in body as well.

317   To let people know that we live after death, and that then we come into either heaven or hell depending on our lives, I have been shown a great deal about our state after death that will be presented in sequence below when we come to a description of the world of spirits.[207]

Non-Christians, or People outside
the Church, in Heaven

318   THE general opinion is that people who have been born outside the church, the people called "the nations" or "non-Christians,"[208] cannot be saved because they do not have the Word and therefore do not know the Lord; and without the Lord there is no salvation.[209] They could know, however, that these people too are saved simply from the fact that the Lord's mercy is universal, that is, it is extended to all individuals. Non-Christians are born just as human as people within the church, who are in fact few by comparison. It is not their fault that they do not know the Lord. So anyone who thinks from any enlightened reason at all can see that no one is born for hell. The Lord is actually love itself, and his love is an intent to save everyone. So he provides that everyone shall have some religion, an acknowledgment of the Divine Being through that religion, and an inner life. That is, living according to one's religious principles is an inner life, for then we focus on the Divine; and to the

g. We rise again as to our spirits: 10593, 10594. Only the Lord rose as to his body as well: 1729, 2083, 5078, 10825.

extent that we do focus on the Divine, we do not focus on the world but move away from the world and therefore from a worldly life, which is an outward life.[a]

People can realize that non-Christians as well as Christians are saved if they know what constitutes heaven in us; for heaven is within us, and people who have heaven within them come into heaven. The heaven within us is our acknowledgment of the Divine and our being led by the Divine. The beginning and foundation of every religion is its acknowledgment of the Divine Being; a religion that does not acknowledge the Divine Being is not a religion at all. The precepts of every religion focus on worship, that is, on how the Divine is to be honored so that we will be acceptable in its sight; and when this fully occupies the mind (or, to the extent that we intend this or love this) we are being led by the Lord.

It is recognized that non-Christians live lives that are just as moral as the lives of Christians—many of them, in fact, live more moral lives. A moral life may be lived either to satisfy the Divine or to satisfy people in this world. A moral life that is lived to satisfy the Divine is a spiritual life. The two look alike in outward form, but inwardly they are totally different. One saves us, the other does not. This is because if we live a moral life to satisfy the Divine we are being led by the Divine; while if we live a moral life to satisfy people in this world, we are being led by ourselves.

[2] This may be illustrated by an example. If we do not do harm to our neighbor because that is against our religion and therefore against the Divine, our refraining from evil stems from a spiritual source. But if we refrain from doing harm to others simply because we are afraid of the law or of losing our reputation or respect or profit—for the sake of self and the world, that is—then this stems from a natural source and we are being led by ourselves. This latter life is natural, while the former is spiritual. If our moral life is spiritual, we have heaven within ourselves; but if our moral life is merely natural, we do not have heaven within ourselves. This is

319

a. Non-Christians are saved just as Christians are: 932, 1032, 1059, 2284, 2589, 2590, 3778, 4190, 4197. On the lot of non-Christians and people outside the church in the other life: 2589–2604. The church specifically defined is where the Word is and where the Lord is known through it: 3857, 10761. This does not mean, though, that people belong to the church by being born where the Word is and where the Lord is known, but rather by living a life of thoughtfulness and faith: 6637, 10143, 10153, 10578, 10645, 10829. The Lord's church is found among all the people in the whole world who live intent on what is good as their own religion defines it and who acknowledge a divine being; they are accepted by the Lord and enter heaven: 2589–2604, 2861, 2863, 3263, 4190, 4197, 6700, 9256.

because heaven flows in from above, opens our deeper natures, and flows through those deeper natures into our more outward natures; while the world flows in from below and opens our more outward natures but not our deeper natures. No inflow occurs from the natural world into the spiritual, only from the spiritual world into the natural; so if heaven is not accepted at the same time, the deeper levels are closed. We can see from this who accept heaven into themselves and who do not.

[3] However, the heaven in one individual is not the same as the heaven in another. It differs in each according to the affection for what is good and true. If people are absorbed in an affection for what is good for the sake of the Divine, they love divine truth because the good and the true love each other and want to be united.[b] Consequently, non-Christian people who have not had access to genuine truths in the world still accept them in the other life because of their love.[210]

320   There was one spirit from a non-Christian country who had lived a good and thoughtful life according to his religion in this world. When he heard some Christian spirits discussing their creeds (spirits talking to each other reason much more exhaustively and acutely than people on earth, especially about what is good and true), he was astonished to find that they quarreled. He said he did not want to listen, since they were arguing on the basis of deceptive appearances. His advice to them was, "If I am a good person, I can know what is true simply from its goodness, and I can be open to what I do not know."

321   I have been taught by a great many instances that if non-Christians have lived decent lives, intent on obedience and appropriate deference and in mutual thoughtfulness as their religion requires so that they have acquired a measure of conscience, they are accepted in the other life and are taught by angels about matters of goodness and truth with most sensitive care. Once they have been taught, they behave unpretentiously, intelligently, and wisely and readily accept and absorb truths. This is because no false principles have taken form to oppose truths of faith, principles that would need to be ousted, let alone slanders against the Lord, as is the case for many Christians whose treasured concept of the Lord is simply of an ordinary human being. It is different for non-Christians. When they

b. There is a likeness of a marriage between what is good and what is true: 1094 *[1904]*, 2173, 2503 *[2508]*. What is good and what is true are engaged in a constant effort toward union, with what is good longing for what is true and for union with it: 9206, 9207, 9495. How and in whom this union of what is good and what is true takes place: 3834, 3843, 4096, 4097, 4301, 4345, 4353, 4364, 4368, 5365, 7623–7627, 9258.

hear that God became a person here and made himself known in the world, they acknowledge it immediately and revere the Lord. They say that of course God made himself known; after all, he is the God of heaven and earth, and the human race belongs to him.[c]

It is a divine truth that there is no salvation apart from the Lord, but this needs to be understood as meaning that there is no salvation that does not come from the Lord. There are many planets in the universe, all full of inhabitants. Hardly any of them know that the Lord took on a human nature on our planet. Still, though, since they do revere the Divine Being in human form, they are accepted and led by the Lord. On this matter, see the booklet *Other Planets*.[211]

There are wise and simple people among non-Christians just as there are among Christians. To show me what they were like, I have been allowed to talk with both kinds, sometimes for hours and even for days. Nowadays, though, there are not wise ones like those of ancient times, especially in the early church[212] (this covered much of the Near East[213] and was the source from which religion spread to many non-Christian peoples). I have been allowed to carry on personal conversations with some of them in order to find out what they were like.

One particular individual was with me who had been one of the wise at one time and who was therefore well known in the scholarly world. I talked with him about various subjects and was given to believe that he was Cicero. Since I knew that he was wise, we talked about wisdom, intelligence, the pattern of reality, the Word, and finally about the Lord. [2] On wisdom, he said that there was no wisdom that was not a matter of life, and that wisdom could not be an attribute of anything else. On intelligence, he said that it came from wisdom. On the pattern of reality, he said that the pattern comes from the Supreme Deity, and that living in accord with this pattern is being wise and intelligent. As to the Word, when I read him something from the prophets he was utterly enchanted,

322

---

c. The difference between the good that non-Christians are engaged in and the good that Christians are engaged in: 4189, 4197. On truths among non-Christians: 3263, 3778, 4190. The deeper levels are not as closed in non-Christians as they are in Christians: 9256. Neither can there be such dense clouds for non-Christians who have lived by their religions in mutual thoughtfulness as there are for Christians who have lived in no thoughtfulness at all, and the reasons this is so: 1059, 9256. Non-Christians cannot profane the holy matters of the church the way Christians can, because they do not know them: 1327, 1328, 2051. They are afraid of Christians because of the way Christians live: 2596, 2597. The ones who have lived well according to their religious principles are taught by angels and readily accept truths of faith and confess the Lord: 2049, 2595, 2598, 2600, 2601, 2603, 2661 *[2861]*, 2863, 3263.

especially at the fact that the individual names and the individual words referred to deeper realities. He was quite astonished that modern scholars take no pleasure in this pursuit. I could sense very clearly that the deeper levels of his thought or mind were open. He said that he could not remain present because he felt something too holy for him to bear, it affected him so deeply.

[3] Finally, our conversation turned to the Lord—on his birth as a person here, but one conceived from God; on his putting off the maternal human nature and putting on a divine human nature; and on his being the One who rules the universe. He said that he knew a great deal about the Lord that he grasped in his own way, and that there was no other way the human race could have been saved. All this time, some evil Christians were showering us with libels of various kinds; but he paid no attention to them. He said it was not surprising. It was because during their physical lives they had soaked up notions on these subjects that were not fitting, and that until these were ousted they could not let in notions that supported [the truth] the way people who were simply ignorant could.

323 I have also been allowed to talk with some others who lived in early days and were among the wiser ones of their times. They first appeared in front of me at some distance, and from there they could observe the deeper levels of my thinking. This meant they could observe me very completely, learning a whole series of thoughts from just one of my mental concepts and filling it with delightful elements of wisdom and charming images. I could tell from this that they were among the wiser ones; and I was told that they were from early times. At this point they came nearer, and when I read them something from the Word, they were totally enchanted. I could sense their very delight and pleasure, which stemmed especially from the fact that every least detail of what they were hearing from the Word was an image and indicator of heavenly and spiritual things. They said that in their own day, when they were living in our world, their mode of thinking and speaking and even writing was like this, and that this was the focus of their wisdom.

324 As for today's non-Christians, they are not that wise; but many of them are simple-hearted. However, in the other life they do accept wisdom from others who have lived lives of thoughtfulness together. I may offer a couple of examples.

When I read chapters 17 and 18 of Judges about Micah (whose idol, household gods, and Levite were stolen by the Danites),[214] there was one non-Christian spirit who had revered an idol during his physical life. He listened intently to what happened to Micah and was deeply pained because of the idol that the Danites stole. His distress overcame him and moved him so deeply that he scarcely knew what he was thinking because of the depth of his pain. I sensed his pain and at the same time the innocence within his particular affections. There were some Christian spirits present who were surprised that this idolater was moved by such mercy and such an affection of innocence.

Later some good spirits talked with him and told him that he should not revere idols and that he could understand this because he himself was a human being. Rather, his thought should reach beyond the idol to the God who was creator and ruler of the whole heaven and the whole earth, and who was the Lord. When he was told this, I could sense his deep feeling of reverence. It was communicated to me as something much holier than what could be found among Christians. I could gather from this that non-Christians come into heaven more readily than Christians nowadays, in keeping with the Lord's words in Luke:

> Then they will come from the east and the west and the north and the south and will recline in the kingdom of God; and indeed there will be many of the last who will be first, and of the first who will be last. (Luke 13:29–30)

Because of the state he was in, that is, he could absorb all matters of faith and could accept them with a deep inner affection. There was a loving mercy about him and in his ignorance an innocence; and when these are present, all matters of faith are accepted spontaneously, so to speak, and with joy. After this, the non-Christian spirit was accepted among the angels.

One morning I heard a far off chorus. I could tell from images of the chorus that they were Chinese, since they presented to view a kind of woolly goat and a cake of millet and an ebony spoon, as well as an image of a floating city.[215] They were eager to come closer to me, and when we were together they said that they wanted to be alone with me in order to disclose their thoughts. They were told, however, that we were not alone, and that the others were offended that they wanted to be alone, since they were guests. When they perceived this feeling of offense in their thoughts, their mood changed, since they had transgressed against a neighbor, and since they had claimed as their own something that belonged to others (in the other life, all our thoughts are shared). I was enabled to perceive their distress of mind. It involved a recognition that they might have injured them, and a sense of shame on that account,

325

along with other emotions characteristic of honest people, so that you could tell they were endowed with thoughtfulness.

I talked with them shortly afterward, and eventually mentioned the Lord. When I called him "Christ," I could sense a kind of resistance in them. The reason for this was uncovered, though. This derived from their experience in the world, from their having known that Christians lived worse lives than they did, lives devoid of thoughtfulness. When I simply mentioned "the Lord," though, they were deeply moved. Later they were taught by angels that Christian doctrine more than any other in the whole world demands love and thoughtfulness, but that there are not many people who live up to it.

There are non-Christian individuals who during their earthly lives have learned by hearsay that Christians live evil lives—lives of adultery, hatred, bickering, drunkenness, and the like—which appalled them because things like this are contrary to their religion. In the other life they are particularly hesitant about accepting truths of faith. However, they are taught by angels that the Christian doctrine and the faith itself teach something very different, but that Christians do not live up to their doctrines as much as non-Christian people do. When they grasp this, they accept truths of faith and worship the Lord, but only after quite a while.

326   It often happens that when non-Christians come into the other life, if they have worshiped some god in the form of an image or statue or idol, they are introduced to people who take on the roles of those gods or idols in order to help rid them of their illusions. After they have been with these people for a few days, they are taken away.

If they have worshiped particular individuals, then they are introduced either to those people themselves or to individuals who play their parts. Many Jews, for example, are introduced to Abraham, Jacob, Moses, or David; but when they realize that they are just as human as anyone else and that they have nothing special to offer them, they are embarrassed, and are taken off to whatever place is in keeping with their lives.

Of non-Christians, the Africans are especially valued in heaven. They accept the good and true things of heaven more readily than others do. They want especially to be called obedient, but not faithful. They say that Christians could be called "faithful," since they have a doctrine of faith, but only if they accept the doctrine—or, as the Africans say, if they *can* accept it.[216]

327   I have talked with some people who were in the early church.[217] (By "the early church," we mean the religious culture [that prevailed] after the flood over many kingdoms, throughout Assyria, Mesopotamia, Syria, Ethiopia, Arabia, Libya, Egypt, Philistia as far as Tyre and Sidon, and the land of Canaan on both sides of the Jordan.)[d] People then knew about the Lord who was going to come, and they absorbed the good qualities of faith; but nevertheless they did fall away and become idolaters. They are in the front toward the left[218] in a dark area, and are in a sorry state. They have piping, monotone voices, and practically no rational thought. They said they had been there for centuries and that sometimes they were let out in order to be of some menial service to others.

This led me to reflect on the many Christians who are not idolaters outwardly but are inwardly because they actually worship themselves and the world, and at heart deny the Lord. This is the kind of lot that awaits them in the other life.

It has been explained in §308 above that the Lord's church is spread throughout the whole world. It is universal, then, and consists of all individuals who have lived in the virtue of thoughtfulness according to the principles of their religions. In relation to the people outside it, the church where the Word is and the Lord is known through it is like the heart and lungs of the human body, which give life to all the organs and members of the body according to their forms, locations, and connections.

328

Children in Heaven

SOME people believe that only children born in the church get into heaven, not children born outside the church. They say this is because children born in the church are baptized and are introduced into the

329

d. The first or earliest church on this planet was the one described in the opening chapters of Genesis, and this church was above all heavenly: 607, 895, 920, 1121, 1122, 1123, 1124, 2896, 4493, 8891, 9942, 10545. What those people are like in heaven: 1114–1125. There were various churches after the flood, referred to as the early church; together with some description: 1125, 1126, 1127, 1327, 10355. What the people of the early church were like: 609 *[607]*, 895. The early churches were symbolic churches: 519, 521, 2896. There was a Word in the early church, but it has been lost: 2897. What the early church was like as it began to decline: 1128. The difference between the earliest church and the early church: 597, 607, 640, 641, 765, 784, 895, 4493. The statutes, judgments, and laws that were obligatory in the Jewish church were to some extent like those of the early church: 4288, 4449, 10149. The Lord was the God of the earliest church and of the early church, and was known as Jehovah: 1343, 6846.

faith of the church by this baptism. They do not realize that no one gets either heaven or faith by baptism. Baptism serves only as a sign and reminder that we need to be reborn, and that people born in the church can be reborn because the Word is there, the Word that contains the divine truths that make regeneration possible. The church is where the Lord, who is the source of rebirth, is known.[a]

May it be known, therefore, that every child who dies, no matter where he or she was born, within the church or outside it, of devout or irreverent parents, is accepted by the Lord after death, brought up in heaven, taught according to the divine design and filled with affections for what is good and through them with direct knowledge of the truth; and then, being continually perfected in intelligence and wisdom, all such individuals are led into heaven and become angels.

Anyone who thinks rationally can realize that no one is born for hell—everyone is born for heaven. We ourselves are to blame if we arrive in hell, but children are not yet liable for any blame.

330 Children who die are still children in the other life. They have the same kind of childlike mind, the same innocence in their ignorance, the same total delicateness—they are only in the rudiments of becoming angels; for children are not angels in being but only angels in becoming. Actually everyone who leaves this world stays in the same state of life—a baby is in the state of a baby, a child in the state of a child, an adolescent or adult or senior in the state of an adolescent, an adult, or a senior. However, this state eventually changes. A child's state is better than the others, though, in regard to innocence, and in regard to the fact that children have not yet let evils take root in them by actually living them. The quality of innocence is such that everything heavenly can be sown in it, because innocence is the vessel of the truths of faith and the good affections of love.

331 The condition of children in the other life is vastly better than that of children in our world because they are not clothed with an earthly body. Instead, they have an angelic one. An earthly body is inherently heavy. It does not receive its primary sensations and primary impulses from the inner or spiritual world but from the outer or natural one; so children in this world learn by practice to walk, to do things, and to talk—even their

---

a. Baptism means regeneration by the Lord by means of truths of faith from the Word: 4255, 5120, 9089 [9088], 10239, 10386, 10387, 10388, 10392. Baptism is a sign that a person belongs to the church where the Lord, the source of rebirth, is acknowledged: 10386, 10387, 10388. Baptism does not give either faith or salvation, but bears witness to the fact that the people who will be accepted [into heaven] will be the ones who have been reborn: 10391.

senses, such as sight and hearing, are developed by use. It is different for children in the other life. Because they are spirits, their actions are impelled directly by their inner natures. They walk without practice and even talk, though at first this is just a matter of general affections as yet undifferentiated into mental concepts. However, they are very soon introduced into these latter as well, since their outer natures are in such concord with their inner natures. Then too, angels' speech flows from their affections, varied by the concepts of their thought, so that their speech is in perfect agreement with the thoughts that arise from their affections (see §§234–245 above).

As soon as children are reawakened (which happens immediately after their death), they are taken to heaven and given to female angels who had loved children tenderly during their physical lives and had loved God as well. Since in this world they had loved all children with a kind of maternal tenderness, they accept these new ones as their own, and the children love them as their mothers as though this were inborn in them. Each such angel has as many children as her spiritual maternal nature wants. 332

This heaven can be seen in the forward part of the forehead, directly on the line or radius along which angels look at the Lord.[219] The reason for this location is that children are under the direct care of the Lord. Into them flows the heaven of innocence, which is the third heaven.

Children have different natures. Some have the nature of spiritual angels, some the nature of heavenly angels. The children of a heavenly nature appear on the right in heaven, and the ones of a spiritual nature on the left. All the children in the universal human that is heaven are in the province of the eyes, with the ones of a spiritual nature in the province of the left eye and the ones of a heavenly nature in the province of the right eye. This is because to angels of the spiritual kingdom, the Lord appears to be in front of the left eye and to angels of the heavenly kingdom he appears to be in front of the right eye (see §118 above). Since children are in the province of the eye in the universal human or heaven, we can see that they are under the Lord's direct view and care. 333

We need to explain briefly how children are brought up in heaven. They learn to talk from their nurse. Their first speech is only the sound of their affection, which gradually becomes more articulated to the extent that the concepts they are thinking enter in, since such concepts arising from affections make up the whole angelic language, as may be seen in §§234–245. 334

The first things instilled into these affections (which all stem from their innocence) are the kinds of thing they see with their eyes that particularly delight them; and since these are from a spiritual origin, aspects of heaven flow into them that serve to open their deeper natures. In this way they become more perfect every day. Once this first age has been completed, they are taken to another heaven where they are taught by instructors, and so on.

335   Children are taught especially by images suited to their natures, images that are unbelievably lovely and full of wisdom from within. In this way, there is gradually instilled into them an intelligence that derives its essence from goodness. I may cite at this point two examples I have been allowed to see that will serve to suggest the nature of the rest.

At first, the Lord was pictured rising from the tomb, and along with this, the uniting of his human nature with his divine nature. This was done in such a wise manner as to surpass all human wisdom, but at the same time with a childlike innocence. The idea of a tomb was presented, but with the Lord present only so remotely that one could hardly tell that it was the Lord, as though he were far off. This was because there is a sense of death in the notion of a tomb, which they were removing by this means. Then something ethereal, something that looked faint and watery was carefully let into the tomb, referring to the spiritual life represented by baptism, again from a proper distance.

Then I saw a representation of the Lord coming down to the captives and rising with the captives into heaven, presented with incomparable care and reverence. The childlike aspect of this was that little cords were let down, almost invisible, as soft and delicate as possible, which supported the Lord in his ascent. Throughout it all, there was a holy fear lest anything in the images should touch on a matter in which there was not something spiritual and heavenly.

There were other representations that engaged the children as well—for example, plays suited to the minds of children—through which they were led into awareness of truth and affections for what is good.

336   I was also shown the nature of their delicate understanding. When I was saying the Lord's Prayer and they were flowing into my concepts from their own comprehension, I noticed that their inflow was so delicate and gentle that it was almost nothing but a feeling. At the same time, I noted that their understanding had been opened to the Lord, for it was as though what was coming from them was flowing through them. In fact, the Lord flows into children's concepts, primarily from the deepest ones. Nothing has closed these off, as happens with adults—no principles of falsity closing them off from true understanding, no life of evil closing them off from accepting what is good and thus from being wise.

We may gather from all this that children do not become angels immediately after their death but are gradually led [into heaven] through awareness of what is good and true, all according to the design of heaven. This is because the least details of their nature are known to the Lord, so they are led, in cooperation with every least impulse of their inclinations, toward the acceptance of truths that arise from good and the good that is done from truth.

I have also been shown how all these things are instilled using delightful and charming means that are suited to their natures. I have in fact been allowed to see children clothed most becomingly, with garlands of flowers around their chests glowing with the most charming and heavenly colors, and similar ones around their slender arms. Once I was even allowed to see some children with their nurses, in the company of some young women in a paradisal garden—not a garden of trees, but one with vaulted arches of something like laurels making the most intricate doorways with paths offering access inward—and the children themselves dressed with like beauty. When they entered, the flowers over the entrance radiated the most joyous light imaginable. This enabled me to gather what their delights were like and how they were led into the blessings of innocence and thoughtfulness by things charming and delightful, with the Lord constantly instilling blessings by means of these charming and delightful gifts.

337

By a means of communication that is common in the other life, I have been shown what children's concepts are like when they are looking at various objects. It is as though everything were alive; so in the smallest concepts of their thought there is an inherent life. I gathered that children on earth have concepts that are much the same when they are involved in their play, for they do not yet have the kind of reflective thought that grownups have about what is inanimate.

338

I mentioned earlier that children have either a heavenly or a spiritual nature. You can tell the ones of a heavenly nature from the ones of a spiritual nature very clearly. The former think and talk and act more gently, so that hardly anything is perceptible but something flowing from a love of what is good, a love for the Lord and for other children. The latter do not think and talk and act so gently. Instead, there is something like fluttering wings that shows in them in small ways. Then too, it can be seen in their annoyance, as well as in other things.

339

Many people think that children remain children in heaven and are like children among the angels. People who do not know what an angel is can corroborate this opinion because of the images here and there in churches, where angels are represented as children. However, things are actually very different. Intelligence and wisdom make an angel, qualities that they do not have as long as they are children. Children are with the

340

angels, but they themselves are not angels yet. Once they are intelligent and wise they are angels for the first time. In fact—something that has surprised me—then they no longer look like children but like adults, because they no longer have a childlike nature but a more grown-up angelic nature. This goes with intelligence and wisdom.

The reason children look more grown-up as they are perfected in intelligence and wisdom—that is, like adolescents and young adults—is that intelligence and wisdom are the essential spiritual food.[b] So the things that nourish their minds also nourish their bodies, which is a result of correspondence, since the form of the body is nothing but an outward form of their inner natures.

It does need to be known that children in heaven do not grow up beyond the prime of youth, but remain at that age forever. To assure me of this, I have been allowed to talk with some who had been raised as children in heaven and had grown up there, with some while they were still children, and then later with the same ones when they had become youths; and I have heard from them about the course of their life from one age level to another.

341 We may gather from what has been presented above (§§276–283) about the innocence of angels in heaven that innocence is the vessel of everything heavenly and therefore that children's innocence is a matrix for all the affections for what is good and true. We explained there that innocence is wanting to be led by the Lord and not by oneself, so that the extent to which we are in innocence determines the extent to which we are freed from preoccupations with our self-image. To the extent that we are freed from this self-image, we gain an identity given by the Lord. The Lord's identity is what is called the Lord's righteousness and worth.

Children's innocence, though, is not real innocence, because it still lacks wisdom. Real innocence is wisdom because to the extent that we are wise we want to be led by the Lord; or what amounts to the same thing, to the extent that we love being led by the Lord, we are wise.

[2] So children are brought through from the outward innocence that characterizes them at first, which is called the innocence of infancy, to the inner innocence that is the innocence of wisdom. This latter innocence is

---

b. Spiritual food is information, intelligence, and wisdom, and therefore the goodness and the truth that are their source: 3114, 4459, 4792, 5147, 5293, 5340, 5342, 5410, 5426, 5576, 5582, 5588, 5656 [5655], 8562, 9003. So "food" in a spiritual sense is whatever comes forth from the mouth of the Lord: 681. "Bread" means all food in general, so it means all heavenly and spiritual good: 276, 680, 2165, 2177, 3478, 6118, 8410. This is because they nourish the mind, which belongs to the inner person: 4459, 5293, 5576, 6277, 8418 [8410].

the goal of their whole process of instruction. Consequently, when they arrive at the innocence of wisdom, the innocence of infancy that had served them as a matrix in the interim is united to them.

[3] The nature of children's innocence was portrayed to me as something woody and almost lifeless that was brought to life as the children were brought toward fulfillment by discoveries of truth and the effects of what is good. Afterward the nature of real innocence was portrayed as a supremely beautiful child, naked and very much alive. The actual innocent people who are in the inmost heaven look to the eyes of other angels simply like children, some of them naked, since innocence is portrayed as a nakedness without embarrassment, as we read concerning the first man and his wife in the garden (Genesis 2:25). So too, when they lost their innocence they were ashamed of their nakedness and hid themselves (Genesis 3:7, 10, 11).

In short, the wiser angels are, the more innocent they are; and the more innocent they are, the more they look like children. This is why infancy in the Word means innocence (see above, §278).

I have talked with angels about children, wondering whether they were free from evils because they did not have any realized evil the way adults do. I was told, though, that they are equally involved in evil, even to the point that they too are nothing but evil.[c,220] However, they, like all angels, are withheld from their evils by the Lord and kept focused on what is good to the point that it seems to them as though they were focused on what is good of their own accord. So to prevent children from having a false notion about themselves after they have grown up in heaven—a belief that the good that surrounds them is from them and not from the Lord—they are let back into their hereditary evils from time to time and left in them until they know and recognize and believe the way things really are.

342

---

c. We are all born in evils of every kind, to the point that our own identity is nothing but evil: 210, 215, 731, 874, 875, 876, 987, 1047, 2307, 2308, 3518, 3701, 3812, 8480, 8550, 10283, 10284, 10286, 10731 *[10732]*. So we need to be reborn—that is, regenerated: 3701. The evil we inherit is loving ourselves more than God and the world more than heaven, and regarding our neighbor as nothing compared to ourselves, except for our own benefit and therefore for ourselves; so that inheritance is love for oneself and for the world: 694, 731, 4317, 5660. It is from love for oneself and for the world, when they rule, that all evils come: 1307, 1308, 1321, 1594, 1691, 3413, 7255, 7376, 7480 *[7489]*, 7488, 8318, 9335, 9348, 10038, 10742; which evils are a contempt for others, hostility, hatred, vengefulness, cruelty, and deceit: 6667, 7372, 7373, 7374, 9348, 10038, 10742; and from these evils comes everything that is false: 1047, 10283, 10284, 10286. These loves rush in to the extent that they are given free rein, and love for oneself aspires even to the throne of God: 7375, 8678.

[2] There was one individual who had died in infancy and grown up in heaven who had this kind of opinion. He was the son of a particular king; so he was let back into his own innate life of evil. I could tell then from the aura of his life that he had a drive to lord it over others and regarded adultery as of no concern whatever—evils that were part of his heredity from his parents. Once he recognized that he was like this, though, he was again accepted among the angels he had been with before.

[3] In the other life, none of us suffers any punishment for inherited evil, because it is not ours. We are not at fault for our hereditary nature. We suffer punishment for any actualized evil that is ours—that is, for whatever hereditary evil we have claimed as our own by acting it out in our lives.[221]

The reason grown-up children are let back into the state of their hereditary evil is not to punish them. It is to make sure they know that on their own they are nothing but evil and that they are borne from hell into heaven by the Lord's mercy, that they are in heaven not because they deserve it but as a gift from the Lord. This prevents them from inflating themselves over others because of the good that attends them, for this is in opposition to the blessing of mutual love just as it is against the truth of faith.

343   Several times a number of children have been with me in groups, before they had learned to talk at all.[222] They made a soft, formless sound, as though they were not yet able to act together the way they would when they were older. What surprised me was that the spirits who were with me could not keep from trying to get them to talk—this kind of impulse is innate in spirits. Every time, though, I noticed that the children resisted, not wanting to talk like that. I often picked up a reluctance, a distaste, that had a kind of resentment in it. Once they did have some power of speech, all they said was "That isn't so." I was told that this is a kind of testing of the children not only to accustom and introduce them to resisting whatever is false and evil but to keep them from thinking or speaking or acting at the bidding of someone else, so that they will not let themselves be led by anyone but the Lord.

344   We may gather from this what the upbringing of children is like in heaven—through an understanding of truth and a wisdom about what is good, they are led into an angelic life, which consists of love for the Lord and a mutual love in which there is innocence.

An example may serve to illustrate how different the upbringing of children on earth is in many instances. I was on the street of a large city and saw some boys fighting with each other. A crowd gathered and watched this with great delight, and I was told that the parents themselves urged their children into fights like these. The good spirits and angels who were seeing all this through my eyes were so repelled that I could feel them shudder, especially at the fact that the parents were encouraging this kind of behavior. They said that by doing this they would at the very earliest age stifle all the mutual love and all the innocence that little ones receive from the Lord and lead them into hatred and vindictiveness. So by their own deliberate practices they would shut their children out of heaven, where there is nothing but mutual love. Let any parents who wish well for their children beware of things like this.

We need also to describe the difference between people who die as children and people who die as adults. People who die as adults have a plane[223] acquired from the earthly, material world, and they take it with them. This plane is their memory and its natural, physical sensitivity. This stays fixed and then goes dormant; but it still serves their thought after death as an outmost plane because their thinking flows into it. This is why the nature of this plane and the way their rational activity answers to its contents determines the nature of the individual after death.   **345**

People who have died in childhood and have been raised in heaven, though, do not have this kind of plane. They have a natural-spiritual plane because they bring with them nothing from the material world or their earthly bodies. This means that they cannot be engrossed in such crude affections and consequent thoughts. They actually derive everything from heaven.

Not only that, little children are unaware that they were born on earth, so they think they were born in heaven. This means they do not know what any birth is other than the spiritual birth that is accomplished through familiarity with what is good and true and through the intelligence and wisdom that make people truly human. Since these come from the Lord, they believe that they belong to the Lord himself, and love to have it so.

However, the state of people who have grown up on earth can become just as perfect as the state of children who have grown up in heaven if they move away from the physical and earthly loves, love for themselves and love for the world, and accept spiritual loves in their stead.

Wise and Simple People in Heaven

346   PEOPLE think that wise individuals will have more glory and renown in heaven than simple people because it says in Daniel, "The intelligent will shine like the radiance of the firmament, and those who have justified many,[224] like stars forever" (Daniel 12:3). However, not many people know who are meant by "the intelligent" and "those who justify." The common opinion is that these are the people we call scholarly and learned, especially the ones who have had teaching roles in the church and have surpassed others in doctrine and in preaching—even more so if they are among those who have converted many to the faith. People like this are all considered "intelligent" in the world; but still, the people this verse is about are not intelligent in heaven unless their intelligence is the heavenly intelligence that we are about to describe.

347   Heavenly intelligence is a deeper intelligence arising from a love of what is true—not for the sake of any praise in the world or any praise in heaven, but simply for the sake of the truth itself, because it is profoundly moving and delightful. People who are moved and delighted by the truth itself are moved and delighted by heaven's light; and if so, then they are also moved and delighted by divine truth and actually by the Lord himself, since heaven's light is divine truth, and divine truth is the Lord in heaven (see above, §§126–140).

This light enters the deeper levels of the mind only, since the deeper levels of the mind are formed to accept it; and to the extent that it enters, it moves and delights because anything that flows in from heaven and is accepted has delight and pleasure within it. This is the source of a genuine affection for what is true—an affection for what is true for its own sake. People who are caught up in this affection (or in this love, which amounts to the same thing), enjoy heavenly intelligence and shine in heaven like the radiance of the firmament. The reason they shine is that wherever divine truth occurs in heaven, it shines (see above, §132); and by reason of correspondence, the firmament of heaven means the deeper intelligence, both in angels and in us, that is in heaven's light.

[2] However, people who are engaged in a love for what is true for the sake of praise in this world or praise in heaven cannot possibly shine in heaven, because they are not delighted and moved by heaven's light,

only by the world's light; and this latter light without the heavenly one is pure darkness.[a] Their own praise is actually in control because it is the goal they have in view, and when that praise is our goal, then we are focused primarily on ourselves; and the truths that are useful as means to our praise are regarded solely as means to an end and as slaves. This is because whenever we love divine truths for the sake of our own praise, we are focusing on ourselves in the divine truths and not on the Lord. This switches our sight (which is an activity of our understanding and faith) from heaven to the world and from the Lord to ourselves. This is why we are in the world's light and not in heaven's light.

[3] Outwardly, in each other's sight, they look just as intelligent and wise as people who are in heaven's light, because they talk in much the same way. They may even seem wiser outwardly, because they are energized by their self-love and have learned to imitate heavenly affections. Inwardly, though, as angels see them, they are totally different.

We may gather in some measure from this just who are meant by "the intelligent, who will shine like the radiance of the firmament." Now we need to explain who are meant by "the ones who justify many, who will shine like stars."

"The ones who justify many" means the ones who are wise. In heaven people are called wise if they are engaged in what is good, and people are engaged in what is good when they involve divine truths directly in their lives, since divine truth becomes good when it becomes a matter of life. Then it truly becomes a matter of intent and love; and anything that belongs to our intent and love is called good. This is why these individuals are called wise, since wisdom is a matter of life. In contrast, people are called intelligent if they do not involve divine truths directly in their lives but consign them first to their memories and then draw them out and apply them to life. The nature and extent of the difference between these two kinds of people in the heavens has been presented in the chapter on heaven's two kingdoms, the heavenly and the spiritual (§§20–28), and in the chapter on the three heavens (§§29–40).

348

---

a. The world's light is for the outer person, heaven's light for the inner: 3222, 3223 *[3224]*, 3337. Heaven's light flows into our natural illumination, and as natural people we are wise to the extent that we accept heaven's light: 4302, 4408. Looking from the world's light, which is called natural illumination, things that are in heaven's light cannot be seen, but the reverse can happen: 9754 *[9755]*. So people who are solely in the world's light cannot see things that are in heaven's light [reading *luce*, "light," for the nonsensical *lude* of the first edition]: 3108. The world's light is darkness to angels: 1521, 1783, 1880.

People who are in the Lord's heavenly kingdom, especially the ones in the third or inmost heaven, are called the just because they do not ascribe any justice to themselves, but all justice to the Lord. The Lord's justice in heaven is the good that comes from the Lord,[b] so these are the people meant by "those who justify." They are also the ones the Lord was talking about when he said, "The righteous shall shine like the sun in my Father's kingdom" (Matthew 13:43). The reason they shine like the sun is that they are caught up in love for the Lord from the Lord, and this love is what the sun means (see above, §§116–125). Further, the light they have is fiery, and their individual thoughts have something flamelike about them because they are receiving the good of love directly from the Lord as the sun in heaven.

349 All the people who have acquired intelligence and wisdom in the world are received in heaven and become angels, according to the quality and amount of their individual intelligence and wisdom. Whatever we have acquired in this world stays with us. We take it with us after death, where it is increased and filled out, all within the level of our own affection and desire for what is true and good, and not beyond that level. People who have had little affection and desire accept little, but still as much as they can accept on their own level. People who have had great affection and desire accept much. The actual level of affection and desire is like a measure that is filled to the brim. This means more for people whose measure is great and less for people whose measure is small. This is because the love to which affection and desire belong accepts everything that suits it, so the amount of love determines the amount of receptivity. This is the meaning of the Lord's words, "To all who have, it will be given, and they will have more abundantly" (Matthew 13:12; 25:29); "Into your lap will be given a good measure, pressed down, shaken, and overflowing" (Luke 6:38).

350 Everyone is accepted into heaven who has loved what is true and good for the sake of what is true and good. People who have loved a great deal are the ones who are called "wise," and people who have loved less are the ones who are called "simple." The wise ones in heaven are in

b. The Lord's worth and justice are the good that rules in heaven: 9486, 9986. Just people, or justified ones, are people to whom the Lord's worth and justice have been allotted, and unjust people are people who have their own justice and self-worth: 5069, 9263. The nature in the other life of people who have claimed righteousness for themselves: 942, 2027. Justice in the Word is ascribed to what is good and judgment to what is true, so to do justice and judgment is [to do] what is good and true: 2235, 9857.

abundant light, while the simple in heaven are in less light, all according to their level of love of what is good and true.

To love what is true and good for the sake of what is true and good is to intend and to do them, for the people who intend and act are the ones who love, not the ones who do not intend and act. The former are the ones who love the Lord and are loved by the Lord, because what is good and what is true are from the Lord; and since they are from the Lord, the Lord is within them (within what is good and what is true, that is); so he is also with people who accept what is good and what is true into their lives by intending and doing them.

Seen in our own right, we are nothing but our good and our truth, because the good is the substance of our volition and the true is the substance of our understanding, and the quality of our volition and understanding determines our own quality as persons. We can see from this that we are loved by the Lord to the extent that our volition is formed from what is good and our understanding is formed from what is true.

To be loved by the Lord is to love the Lord as well, because love is reciprocal. The Lord enables the beloved to love.

In this world, it is believed that people who are full of information— whether concerning the doctrines of the church and the Word or the arts and sciences—see truths more deeply and sharply than others, and are therefore more intelligent and wiser. These people believe the same about themselves. We need to explain below, though, what true intelligence and wisdom are, and what the counterfeit and false versions are.

[2] True intelligence and wisdom are seeing and grasping what is true and good; on that basis seeing what is false and evil, and distinguishing accurately between them; and doing this from insight and an inner perception. There are deeper and more external levels to every individual, the deeper comprising what belongs to the inner or spiritual person and the outer what belongs to the outer or natural person. The way the deeper levels are formed and unite with the outer ones determines the way we see and perceive. Our deeper levels can be formed only in heaven, while the outer ones are formed in this world. When the inner levels have been formed in heaven, then whatever occurs there flows into the outer levels that are derived from this world and forms them to be responsive—that is, to act as one with the inner levels. Once this has been accomplished, we see and perceive from within.

The only way these inner levels can be formed is by our focusing on the Deity and on heaven, for as already noted, the deeper levels are formed in heaven. We focus on the Deity when we believe the Deity and believe that it is the source of everything true and good and therefore of all intelligence and wisdom. We believe the Deity when we want to be led by the Deity. This is the only way our deeper levels are opened.

[3] When we are devoted to this faith and are in a life in keeping with it, we enjoy the ability to understand and to be wise. However, in order to be intelligent and wise, it is fitting that we learn a great deal not only about heavenly matters but also about earthly ones. We learn about heavenly matters from the Word and the church and about earthly ones from the arts and sciences. To the extent that we learn and apply our learning to our lives, we become intelligent and wise, for to that extent our deeper vision, the sight of our understanding, and our deeper affection, which is the affection of our intentions, are perfected.

Of people like this, the simple ones are the ones whose deeper levels have been opened but have not been so much developed through spiritual, moral, civil, and natural truths. They grasp truths when they hear them, but do not see them within themselves. In contrast, the wise ones are the ones whose deeper levels have been not only opened but also developed. They both see truths within themselves and grasp them.

We can see from all this what true intelligence and wisdom are.

352   By pseudo-intelligence and wisdom we mean not seeing and grasping what is true and good (and therefore what is false and evil) from within oneself, but only believing that things are true and good or false and evil because someone else says so, and then ratifying it. Since such people are not seeing what is true on the basis of its truth but only on someone's authority, they can just as well latch onto something false as something true and believe it, and even rationalize it until it actually seems to be true. Whatever is rationalized takes on the appearance of truth, and there is nothing that cannot be rationalized. Their deeper levels are open only downward, and their outer levels are opened to the extent that they have made up their minds. So the light they see from is not heaven's light but the world's light, which is called "natural illumination."[225] In this light, false things can shine as though they were true. In fact, once they have become matters of complete conviction, they can even glow, though not in heaven's light.

The less intelligent and wise people of this sort are those who have convinced themselves of a great many opinions, and the more intelligent and wise are the ones who have convinced themselves of fewer.

We can see from all this what pseudo-intelligence and wisdom are.

[2] However, this category does not include people who as children believed as true what they heard from their teachers, if in later youth, when they began to think on their own, they did not hang on to these

opinions but had a longing for truth, sought it because of their longing, and were moved inwardly when they found it. Because they are moved by truth for its own sake, they see what is true before they make it a matter of conviction.[c]

[3] An example may serve to illustrate this. Some spirits were engaged in a conversation about the reason why animals are born into all the knowledge that is appropriate to their natures, while humans are not. They were told that this is because animals are wholly engaged in the pattern appropriate to their lives, while we are not; so we have to be led into that pattern by means of insights and information. If we were born into the pattern of our lives, which is loving God above all and our neighbor as ourselves, we would be born into intelligence and wisdom and therefore into a trust in everything true to the extent that our insights built up. The good spirits immediately saw and grasped that this was so, simply from the light of truth. However, some spirits who had convinced themselves of faith alone and had therefore pushed love and thoughtfulness aside could not understand it, because the light of false convictions obscured the light of truth for them.

By false intelligence and wisdom we mean any intelligence and wisdom that is devoid of acknowledgment of the Divine. In fact, people who do not acknowledge the Divine Being but put nature in place of the Divine all think on the basis of their physical bodies. They are merely sense-centered, no matter how scholarly and learned they are considered in this world.[d] Their learning, though, does not rise any higher than the things in front of their eyes in this world, things that they keep in their memory

353

---

c. The part of wisdom is to see and grasp whether something is true before one ratifies it, not to ratify what we are told by others: 1017, 4741, 7012, 7680, 7950. Seeing and grasping what is true before it is ratified is granted only to people who are moved by truth for its own sake and for the sake of their lives: 8521. The light of ratification is a natural and not a spiritual light; it is a sensory light that can be found among evil people as well: 8780. Anything can be rationalized, even false things, so as to appear to be true: 2482 [2477], 2490 [2480], 5033, 6865, 8521.

d. The sensory level is the outmost level of our life, attached to and embedded in our bodies: 5077, 5767, 9212, 9216, 9331, 9730. We call people sense-centered if they evaluate and decide about everything on the basis of their physical senses and do not believe anything unless they see it with their eyes and touch it with their hands: 5094, 7693. People like this do their thinking in their most external minds, and not more inwardly within themselves: 5089, 5094, 6564, 7693. Their deeper levels are closed, so that they can see nothing of divine truth: 6564, 6844, 6845. In short, they are in a crude natural illumination and can see nothing that comes from heaven's light: 6201, 6310, 6564, 6844, 6845, 6598, 6612, 6614, 6622, 6624. So they are profoundly opposed to whatever involves heaven and the church: 6201, 6316 [6310], 6844, 6845, 6948, 6949. Scholars who have convinced themselves in opposition to the truths of the church are sense-centered: 6316. A description of the nature of sense-centered people: 10236.

and inspect almost physically. This is the case even though the very same branches of knowledge serve truly intelligent people as a means of forming their understanding. By "branches of knowledge" we mean the various experimental disciplines such as physics, astronomy, chemistry, mechanics, geometry, anatomy, psychology, philosophy, and political history, as well as the realms of literature and criticism and language study.

[2] There are church dignitaries who deny the Divine. They do not raise their thoughts any higher than the sensory concerns of the outer person. They look on the contents of the Word as no different from knowledge about anything else; they do not treat those contents as subjects of thought or of any thorough consideration by an enlightened rational mind. This is because their own deeper levels are closed off, and along with them, the more outward levels that are next to these deeper ones. The reason they are closed is that they have turned their backs on heaven and reversed the things that they could see there, things that are proper to the deeper levels of the human mind, as we have noted before. This is why they cannot see what is true and good—because these matters are in darkness for them, while what is false and evil is in the light.

[3] Nevertheless, sense-centered people can think logically, some of them actually with more skill and penetration than other people. However, they rely on deceptive sensory appearances bolstered by their own learning, and since they can think logically in this fashion, they think they are wiser than other people.[e] The fire that fuels their reasoning is the fire of love for themselves and the world.

These are the people who are devoted to false intelligence and wisdom, the ones meant by the Lord in Matthew: "Seeing they do not see, and hearing they do not hear, nor do they understand" (Matthew 13:13–15); and again, "Things are hidden from the intelligent and wise and revealed to children" (Matthew 11:25–26).

354　　I have been allowed to talk with many scholars after their departure from our world, with some who were quite renowned and celebrated throughout the learned world for their publications, as well as with some who were not so well known but who still had within themselves a hidden wisdom.

---

e. The logical thinking of sense-centered people is both keen and skillful because they place all intelligence in talking from their physical memory: 195, 196, 5700, 10236. However, all this relies on deceptive sensory appearances: 5084, 6948, 6949, 7693. Sense-centered people are more canny and vicious than others: 7693, 10236. The ancients called people like this "serpents of the tree of knowledge": 195, 196, 197, 6398, 6949, 10313.

The ones who at heart denied the Deity, whether or not they acknowledged the Deity out loud, had become so stupid that they could
scarcely understand any civic truth, let alone any spiritual truth. I could
both comprehend and see that the inner levels of their minds were so
shut off that they looked inky black (things like this are made visible in
the spiritual world), and that this meant they could not bear any heavenly light or let in any inflow from heaven. The blackness that enveloped
their deeper levels was greater and more extensive for people who had
convinced themselves of their opposition to the Divine by means of their
secular scholarship.

In the other life, people like this gladly accept anything false. They
soak it up like a sponge soaking up water; and they repel anything true
the way something bony and springy repels anything that falls on it. It is
also said that if people convince themselves of their opposition to the Divine and their advocacy of nature, their deeper levels actually become
bony. Their heads even look callused, as though they were made of
ebony, and this reaches all the way to their noses, a sign that they no
longer have any perception.

People like this are sunk in quagmires that look like swamps, where
they are pestered by the hallucinations that their falsities turn into. Their
hellfire is their craving for glory and fame, which leads them to denounce
each other and to torment with hellish zeal anyone who does not worship them as gods. They do this to each other by turns.

This is what becomes of all earthly learning that does not accept light
from heaven into itself by our acknowledgment of the Divine.

We might gather that they are like this when they arrive in the spir- **355**
itual world after death simply from the fact that at that point everything in their natural memory becomes dormant, everything that is
directly united to their physical senses, like the academic disciplines we
listed just above. All that remain are the rational abilities that now serve
as a basis for thinking and talking. We actually take with us our entire
natural memory, but its contents are not open to our inspection and do
not enter into our thought as when we were living in this world. We
cannot retrieve anything from it and present it to spiritual light because
the contents are not matters of that light. However, the rational or cognitive abilities we acquired through the arts and sciences while living in
the flesh do square with the light of the spiritual world. So to the extent that our spirit has become rational by means of our insights and
learning in this world, we are rational after our departure from the

body. For then we are spirits, and it is the spirit that thinks within the body.[f]

356   It is different for people who have acquired intelligence and wisdom by means of their insights and information, people who have applied everything to the service of their lives and have at the same time acknowledged the Divine Being, loved the Word, and led a life both spiritual and moral (as described above in §319). For them, learning served as a means to being wise and for substantiating matters of faith. The deeper levels of their minds are perceived and even seen as transparent to the light, with a bright color, fiery or azure, like that of clear diamonds or rubies or sapphires, depending on the support they derived, from their learning, for the Divine and for divine truths. True intelligence and wisdom look like this when they are presented visually in the spiritual world. This comes from heaven's light, which is divine truth emanating from the Lord, the source of all intelligence and wisdom (see above, §§126–133). [2] The focal planes of this light in which the shadings stand forth like colors are the deeper levels of the mind; and it is the validations of divine truths through what we find in nature—that is, by learning—that produce these shadings.[g] Actually, our inner mind probes the material in our natural memory and uses the fire of heavenly love to refine (so to speak) the things there that support it, to draw them off and purify them to the point that they become spiritual concepts. We are not aware that this is going on as long as we are in our physical bodies because in this state, though we are thinking both spiritually and naturally, we still do not notice what we are thinking spiritually but only what we are thinking naturally. However, once we have arrived in the spiritual world we are not aware of what we once thought naturally, in this world, only what we were thinking spiritually. This is how our state changes. [3] We can see from this that we become spiritual by means of our insights and learning and that these are means of becoming wise only for people who acknowledge the Divine Being in both faith and life.

These people are received into heaven before others and live there with the ones who are in the center (§43) because they are in more light

f. Information is a matter of our natural memory, which we have while we are in the body: 5212, 9922. We take our entire natural memory with us after death: 2475; from experience: 2481–2486; but for many reasons, we cannot pull things out of it the way we could in this world: 2476, 2477, 2479.

g. The loveliest colors can be seen in heaven: 1053, 1624. The colors in heaven come from the light that is there, and are modifications or shadings of it: 1042, 1043, 1053, 1624, 3993, 4530, 4922, 4742. They are appearances of truth from good, and refer to aspects of intelligence and wisdom: 4530, 4922, 4677, 9466.

than others. In heaven they are the intelligent and wise ones who shine like the radiance of the firmament and gleam like stars. The simple people there, though, are the ones who have acknowledged the Divine Being and have loved the Word and led a spiritual moral life, but who have not developed the deeper levels of their minds through insights and learning in the same way. The human mind is like soil whose quality depends on the way it is tilled.

References to Passages in *Secrets of Heaven* Concerning Different Types of Knowledge

[4] We should saturate ourselves with information and knowledge, because it is through them that we learn to think, then to sort out what is true and good, and ultimately to be wise: 129, 1450, 1451, 1453, 1548, 1802. Factual information constitutes the elemental basis on which our civic and moral lives as well as our spiritual lives are built and grounded; and it is learned with a view to using it: 1489, 3310. Real knowledge opens a path to the inner person, and then unites that person with the outer in proportion to useful action: 1563, 1616. Our rational functioning is born through information and knowledge: 1895, 1900, 3086. This does not happen through knowledge itself, however, but through the affection of putting it to use: 1895.

[5] There are facts that are open to divine truths and facts that are not: 5213. Empty information should be destroyed: 1489, 1492, 1499, 1580 *[1581]*. Information is "empty" if it aims at and strengthens love for ourselves and love for the world, and if it leads us away from love for God and our neighbor. This is because such influences close off the inner person, even to the point that we cannot accept anything from heaven: 1563, 1600. Facts may be a means to wisdom or a means to insanity. Through them the inner person is either opened or closed, and rational functioning either nurtured or destroyed: 4156, 8628, 9922.

[6] The inner person is opened and is progressively completed by means of information if we have constructive activity as our goal—especially

activity that focuses on our eternal life: 3086. Then the heavenly and spiritual characteristics of our spiritual person reach out to the information that is in our natural person, and adopt whatever is suitable: 1495. Then the Lord draws out whatever is useful for heavenly life from the information in our natural person, by way of the inner person, and elaborates and exalts it: 1895, 1896, 1900, 1901, 1902, 5871, 5874, 5901. Facts that do not fit, or that oppose, are banished to the sides and eliminated: 5871, 5886, 5889.

[7] The sight of the inner person selects from the information of the outer person only those items that suit its love: 9394. In the view of the inner person, the items that suit its love are in full light, in the center, while those that do not suit are off to the sides, in the shadows: 6068, 6085 *[6084]*. Suitable facts are grafted onto our loves step by step, and, so to speak, dwell in them: 6325. We would be born into discernment if we were born into love for our neighbor, but since we are born into love for ourselves and the world, we are born into complete ignorance: 6323, 6325. Information, discernment, and wisdom are children of love of God and our neighbor: 1226, 2049, 2116.

[8] It is one thing to be wise, another to be discerning, another to be well informed, and another to act; still, to the extent that we are alive spiritually, these follow in a sequence and are all together at once when we act, or in our deeds: 10331. Further, it is one thing to be well informed, another to acknowledge, and another to have faith: 896.

[9] The factual knowledge of the outer or natural person is in the world's light, while the truths that have become matters of faith and love, and have thus come to life, are in heaven's light: 5212. Truths that are suited to spiritual life are grasped through natural ideas: 5510. Spiritual inflow is from the inner or spiritual person into the information that is in the outer or natural person: 1940, 8005. Facts are receptacles and, so to speak, vessels of the good and the true elements of the inner person: 1469, 1496, 3068, 5489, 6004, 6023, 6052, 6071, 6077, 7770, 9922. They are like mirrors in which the good and true elements of the inner person appear as in an image: 5201. They are all there together in their most concrete form: 5373, 5874, 5886, 5901, 6004, 6023, 6052, 6071.

[10] Inflow is spiritual and not physical: that is, there is an inflow from the inner person into the outer and therefore into its information, but not from the outer into the inner and therefore not from information into the truths of faith: 3219, 5119, 5259, 5427, 5428, 5478, 6322, 9110, 9111 *[9401]*. We are to start from the truths of the church's teaching, which are drawn from the Word, and this teaching should first be acknowledged: it is legitimate to consider facts on this basis: 6047. This

means that for people who are affirmatively disposed toward the truths of faith, it is legitimate to use facts intellectually to confirm them, but not for people who are negatively disposed: 2568, 2588, 4760, 6047. People who will not believe divine truths unless they are convinced by the facts will never believe: 2094, 2832. To enter into the truths of faith from factual information is disorderly: 10236. People who do this become insane in matters that concern heaven and the church: 128–130. They fall into the distortions of evil: 232, 233, 6047. In the other life, when they think about spiritual matters, they seem to become drunk: 1072. More on their nature: 196. Examples illustrating that spiritual matters cannot be grasped if they are entered from factual information: 233, 2094, 2196, 2203, 2209. Many of the learned are more insane in spiritual matters than simple people because they are negatively disposed, confirming [their opinions] by the information that is constantly and abundantly in their view: 4760, 8629.

[11] People who argue against the truths of faith on the basis of information argue keenly because they depend on sensory illusions, which captivate and convince because they are hard to dispel: 5700. What sensory illusions are and what they are like: 5084, 5094, 6400, 6948. People who understand nothing of the truth and who are also involved in evil can argue about what is true and good in matters of faith without understanding them: 4213 *[4214]*. It is not a matter of intelligence simply to confirm a dogma, but to see whether it is true or not before one confirms it: 4741, 6047.

[12] After death, factual knowledge makes no difference—[what make a difference are] the things we have drawn out for understanding and life: 2480. Everything we have learned still endures after death; it merely becomes dormant: 2476–2479, 2481–2486.

[13] The same facts are false for evil people, because they are applied to evil ends, that are true for good people because they are applied to good ends: 6917. True information is not true for evil people, even though things seem true when they say them, because there is evil within them: 10331.

[14] An example of the kind of craving for knowledge spirits have: 1993 *[1973]*. Angels have a tremendous desire to know and to be wise, because information, intelligence, and wisdom are spiritual food: 3114, 4459, 4792, 4976, 5147, 5293, 5340, 5342, 5410, 5426, 5576, 5582, 5588, 5656 *[5655]*, 6277, 8562, 9003. The knowledge of the ancients was a knowledge of symbols and images, through which they led themselves into a familiarity with spiritual matters; but at the present time this knowledge has been totally effaced: 4844, 4749, 4964, 4965.

[15] Truths on a spiritual level cannot be grasped without a knowledge of the following universal principles:

1. Everything in the universe goes back to the good and the true and their union in order to be anything—that is, to love and faith and their union.

2. People have discernment and volition: discernment is the receptacle of what is true, and volition the receptacle of what is good. Everything in us goes back to these two and to their union just as everything [in the universe] goes back to the good and the true and their union.

3. There is an inner and an outer person, as distinct from each other as heaven and the world; yet they must become one if the person is to be truly human.

4. Heaven's light is the light the inner person is in, and the world's light is the light the outer person is in. Heaven's light is what is essentially divine and true, the source of all intelligence.

5. There is a responsiveness between the things in the inner person and those in the outer, so that things from either side appear in a different guise on the other side—so different that they cannot be identified without a knowledge of correspondences.

Without knowledge of these and many other matters, only incongruous concepts can be grasped and formed of truths on the spiritual and heavenly levels. This means that without these universal principles, the information and insights of the natural person can scarcely serve for the discernment and development of the rational person. This shows how necessary elementary information is.

Rich and Poor People in Heaven

357   THERE are various opinions about acceptance into heaven. Some people think that the poor are accepted but not the rich; some think that rich and poor alike are accepted; some think that rich people cannot

be accepted unless they give up their assets and become like the poor—and all of them support their opinions from the Word. However, as far as heaven is concerned, people who differentiate between the rich and the poor do not understand the Word. At heart, the Word is spiritual, though it is natural in the letter; so if people take the Word only in its literal meaning and not in some spiritual meaning they go astray in all kinds of ways, especially regarding the rich and the poor. They believe that it is as hard for rich people to enter heaven as it is for a camel to go through the eye of a needle and that it is easy for the poor by reason of their poverty, since it says, "Blessed are the poor, because theirs is the kingdom of the heavens" (Luke 6:20–21).

However, people who know something about the spiritual meaning of the Word think differently. They know that heaven is for everyone who lives a life of faith and love, whether rich or poor. We will explain below who are meant by "the rich" in the Word and by "the poor."

Out of a great deal of conversation and living with angels, I have been granted sure knowledge that rich people enter heaven just as easily as poor people do, and that no one is shut out of heaven for having abundant possessions or accepted into heaven because of poverty. There are both rich and poor people there, and many of the rich are in greater splendor and happiness than the poor.

By way of preface, we may note that it is all right to acquire wealth and accumulate any amount of assets, as long as it is not done by fraud or evil devices.[226] It is all right to eat and drink with elegance, as long as we do not invest our lives in such things. It is all right to be housed as graciously as befits one's station, to chat with others like ourselves, to go to games, to consult about worldly affairs. There is no need to walk around looking pious with a sad, tearful face and a bowed head. We can be happy and cheerful. There is no need to give to the poor except as the spirit moves us. In short, we can live to all appearances just like worldly people. This is no obstacle to our acceptance into heaven as long as we keep God appropriately in mind and act honestly and fairly toward our neighbors. Our quality is actually that of our affection and thought, or our love and faith. Everything we do outwardly derives its life from these, since acting is intending and speaking is thinking. We act, that is, from our intent, and we speak from our thought. So when it says in the Word that we are judged according to our deeds and rewarded according to our works,[227] it means that we are judged and rewarded according to the thought and affection that give rise to our deeds or that are within our

358

deeds. This is because deeds have no meaning apart from these contents. Their quality is wholly determined by them.[a]

We can see from this that our outer nature accomplishes nothing. It is our inner nature, which gives rise to the outer.

Take for example people who behave honestly and do not cheat others solely out of fear of the law and loss of reputation, leading to loss of respect or profit. If that fear did not restrain them, they would cheat others as often as they could. Their thought and intent are fraudulent, even though their actions look honest in outward form. Because they are dishonest and fraudulent inwardly, they have hell within themselves. But if people behave honestly and do not cheat others because this is against God and against their neighbor, then even if they could cheat someone they would not want to. Their thought and intent are their conscience, and they have heaven within themselves. In outward form, the actions of the two kinds look alike, but inwardly they are totally different.

359 One person can live like another in outward form. As long as there is an inward acknowledgment of the Deity and an intent to serve our neighbor, we can become rich, dine sumptuously, live and dress as elegantly as befits our station and office, enjoy pleasures and amusement, and meet our worldly obligations for the sake of our position and of our business and of the life of both mind and body. So we can see that it is not as hard to follow the path to heaven as many people believe. The only difficulty is finding the power to resist love for ourselves and love of the world and preventing those loves from taking control, since they are the source of all our evils.[b] The fact that it is not so hard as people believe is what is meant by these words of the Lord: "Learn of me that I am

a. It often says in the Word that we will be judged and requited according to our deeds and works: 3934. "Deeds and works" in the Word do not mean deeds and works in their outward form but in their inner form, because even evil people can do outwardly good deeds, while only good people can do things that are good both outwardly and inwardly: 3934, 6073. Our works, like all actions, derive their reality, their form, and their quality from our deeper levels, which pertain to our thought and intent, because they emanate from there; so the quality of the deeper levels determines the quality of the works: 3934, 8911, 10331. This means they depend on the quality of our deeper levels in respect to love and faith: 3934, 6073, 10331, 10333 [10332]. It also means that our works contain these qualities and in fact are these qualities in practice: 10331. To be judged and requited according to our deeds and works, then, is to be judged and requited according to these qualities: 3147, 3934, 6073, 8911, 10331–10333. To the extent that our works focus on ourselves and the world, they are not good—only as they focus on the Lord and our neighbor: 3147.

b. From love for oneself and for the world come all evils: 1307, 1308, 1321, 1594, 1691, 3413, 7255, 7376, 7480 [7490], 7488, 8318, 9335, 9348, 10038, 10742; which are contempt for others, hostility, hatred, vengefulness, cruelty, and deceit: 6667, 7372, 7373, 7374, 9348, 10038, 10742. We are born into these loves, so our hereditary evils are in them: 694, 4317, 5660.

gentle and lowly of heart, and you will find rest for your souls: for my yoke is easy and my burden light" (Matthew 11:29–30). The reason the Lord's yoke is easy and his burden light is that to the extent that we resist the evils that well up from love for ourselves and the world, we are led by the Lord and not by ourselves. Then the Lord resists those things within us and removes them.

I have talked after their death with some people who during their earthly lives had renounced the world and devoted themselves to a virtually solitary life, wanting to make time for devout meditation by withdrawing their thoughts from worldly matters. They believed that this was the way to follow the path to heaven. In the other life, though, they are gloomy in spirit. They avoid others who are not like themselves and they resent the fact that they are not allotted more happiness than others. They believe they deserve it and do not care about other people, and they avoid the responsibilities of thoughtful behavior that are the means to union with heaven. They covet heaven more than others do; but when they are brought up to where angels are, they cause anxieties that upset the happiness of the angels. So they part company; and once they have parted, they betake themselves to lonely places where they lead the same kind of life they had led in the world.

[2] The only way we can be formed for heaven is through the world. That is the ultimate goal by which every affection must be defined. Unless affection manifests itself or flows into action, which happens in sizeable communities, it is stifled, ultimately to the point that we no longer focus on our neighbor at all, but only on ourselves. We can see from this that the life of thoughtfulness toward our neighbor—behaving fairly and uprightly in all our deeds and in all our responsibilities—leads to heaven, but not a life of piety apart from this active life.[c] This means that the practice of thoughtfulness and the benefits that ensue from this kind of life can occur only to the extent that we are involved in our occupations, and that they cannot occur to the extent that we withdraw from those occupations.

[3] But let me say something about this from experience. Many people who devoted their energies to business and trade in the world, many who became rich, are in heaven. There are not so many, though, who made a name for themselves and became rich in public office. This is

360

---

c. Thoughtfulness toward our neighbor is doing what is good, fair, and upright in all our deeds and in all our responsibilities: 8120, 8121, 8122. So thoughtfulness toward our neighbor extends to every least thing we think and intend and do: 8124. Without a life of thoughtfulness, a life of piety is of no use, but with it, it is immensely productive: 8252, 8253.

because these latter were led into love for themselves and the world by the profits and the positions they were given because of their administration of justice and morality and of profits and positions. This in turn led them to deflect their thoughts and affections from heaven and direct them toward themselves; for to the extent that we love ourselves and the world and focus on ourselves and the world exclusively, we estrange ourselves from the Divine and move away from heaven.

361 Broadly speaking, what lies in store for rich people in heaven is this. They live more elegantly than others, some in palaces where everything within gleams like gold and silver. They have everything they need for a useful life. However, they do not set their hearts on such things but on their useful activities. These they see clearly and in full light, while the gold and silver are relatively hazy and shadowy. The reason is that in the world they had loved being useful and had loved gold and silver only as subservient means. This is how useful things gleam in heaven—what works for good like gold, what works for truth like silver.d The quality of the useful functions they served in the world determines their wealth, their pleasure, and their happiness.

Good and useful activities include providing the necessities of life for oneself and one's own, wanting ample resources for the sake of one's country and one's neighbor, whom a rich person can benefit in far more ways than a poor person can. [These activities are useful also] because they lead the mind away from an idle life, which is destructive, since in that kind of life our thoughts turn to evil because of our inborn evil nature.

These useful activities are good to the extent that the Divine is within them—that is, to the extent that we focus on the Divine and on heaven and invest ourselves in these as good, investing in wealth only as a subservient means.

362 What awaits rich people who do not believe in the Divine Being and reject matters of heaven and the church from their minds is quite the opposite. They are in hell, where they find filth and wretchedness and want. When wealth is loved as an end, it turns into things like these, and not

d. It is from use and in proportion to use that everything good derives its delight: 3049, 4984, 7038; and its quality as well; so the quality of the use determines the quality of the good: 3049. All the happiness and delight of life comes from use: 997. In general, life is a life of useful activities: 1964. Angelic life consists of the good fruits of love and thoughtfulness, and therefore of being useful: 453 [452]. The Lord, and therefore the angels as well, focuses on nothing in us except our goals, which are useful activities: 1317, 1645, 5844. The Lord's kingdom is a kingdom of useful functions: 453 [454], 696, 1103, 3645, 4054, 7038. To serve the Lord is to be useful: 7038. Our quality is determined by the uses we fulfill: 4054, 6815; with examples: 7038.

only the wealth itself but also what it is used for—the pampered living, the indulgence in pleasures, the wider and freer dedication to amorality, the self-exaltation over people they belittle. Because these riches and these functions have nothing spiritual in them, only earthly qualities, they turn to filth. The spiritual aspect of wealth and its uses is like the soul in a body and like the light of heaven in moist earth. So a body without a soul becomes putrid, as does moist earth without the light of heaven. These are the people whom wealth has seduced and drawn away from heaven.

After death, our ruling affection or love awaits each one of us. This is never rooted out to eternity because our spirit is exactly like our love; and (what has not been known before) the body of every spirit and angel is an outward form of her or his love that is completely responsive to the inner form that is the character and mind of that spirit or angel. That is why you can recognize the quality of spirits from their faces, their postures, and their speech. That is why our own spirits are recognized in this world if we have not learned how to pretend with our faces and postures and speech. We may gather from this that our own eternal quality is that of our ruling affection or love. 〔363〕

I have been allowed to talk with people who lived more than seventeen centuries ago, people whose lives are known from the literature of their own times; and I have been convinced that the same love they had then is still sustaining them.

We may also gather from this that a love of wealth and the usefulness it affords also remains with us forever, with exactly the quality it acquired in this world. There is this difference, though: for people whose wealth served them as means to useful lives, it is turned into delights in keeping with their usefulness, while for people whose wealth served them as means to evil activities, it is turned into filth—filth that they enjoy just as much as they enjoyed their ill-used wealth in the world. The reason they enjoy the filth is that the foul pleasures and pursuits that were their practices in the world, and their greed (which is a love of wealth with no thought of use), correspond to filth. Spiritual filth is nothing else.

Poor people do not get into heaven because of their poverty but because of their lives. Our lives follow us whether we are rich or poor. There is no special mercy for the one any more than for the other.[e] People who have lived well are accepted; people who have lived badly are rejected. 〔364〕

e. There is no direct mercy, only mercy through means—that is, for people who live according to the Lord's commandments, whom he in his mercy is constantly leading in this world, and afterwards to eternity: 8700, 10659.

Poverty can actually seduce people and lead them away from heaven just as much as wealth can. There are many people among the poor who are not content with their lot, who covet much more, and who believe that wealth is a blessing;[f] so when they do not get what they want, they are enraged and harbor evil thoughts about divine providence. They envy other people their assets, and given the chance would just as soon cheat them and live in their own foul pleasures.

It is different, though, for poor people who are content with their lot, are conscientious and careful in their work, prefer work to idleness, behave honestly and reliably, and lead Christian lives. I have sometimes talked with rural and common people who had believed in God while they lived in this world and had behaved honestly and righteously in their jobs. Because they were impelled by a desire to know what was true, they kept asking what thoughtfulness and faith were, since they had heard a lot about faith in this world and were hearing a lot about thoughtfulness in the other life. So they were told that thoughtfulness is all about living and faith is all about doctrine. This means that thoughtfulness is intending and doing what is fair and right in every task, while faith is thinking what is fair and right; so faith and thoughtfulness go together like doctrine and a life according to it, or like thought and intent. Faith becomes thoughtfulness, then, when we intend and do the fair and right things that we think. When this happens, they are not two but one. They understood this perfectly well and were overjoyed, saying that in the world they had not understood believing to be any different from living.

365   We may gather from this that rich people arrive in heaven just as much as poor people do, one as easily as the other. The reason people believe that it is easy for the poor and hard for the rich is that the Word is misunderstood when it talks about the rich and the poor. In the spiritual meaning of the Word, "the rich" means people who are amply supplied with understandings of what is true and good, that is, people in the church where the Word is. "The poor" means people who lack these understandings but who long for them, or people outside the church, where the Word is not found.

[2] The rich person dressed in purple and fine linen who was cast into hell means the Jewish nation. Because they had the Word and were

f. High rank and wealth are not real blessings, so both evil and good people have them: 8939, 10755, 10776. Real blessing is the acceptance of love and faith from the Lord and a consequent union [with him], because these bring us happiness forever: 1420, 1422, 2846, 3017, 3408 [3406], 3504, 3514, 3530, 3565, 3584, 4216, 4981, 8939, 10495.

therefore amply supplied with understandings of what is good and true, they are called "rich." The garments of purple actually mean understandings of what is good, and the fine linen means understandings of what is true.g The poor person who was lying in the gateway and who longed to feast on the crumbs that were falling from the rich person's table, who was carried up into heaven by angels, means the non-Jews²²⁸ who did not have understandings of what is good and true but who still longed for them (Luke 16:19, 31).

The rich who were invited to the great feast but who excused themselves also mean the Jewish nation, and the poor who were brought in to replace them mean the non-Jews who were outside the church (Luke 12:16–24 [14:16–24]).

[3] We need also to explain who are meant by the rich of whom the Lord said, "It is easier for a camel to go through the eye of a needle than for a rich person to enter the kingdom of God" (Matthew 19:24). "The rich person" here means the rich in both senses, natural and spiritual. Rich people in the natural sense are people who have abundant wealth and set their hearts on it, while in a spiritual sense they are people who are amply supplied with insights and knowledge (for these are spiritual wealth) and who want to use them to get themselves into heavenly and ecclesiastical circles by their own intellect. Since this is contrary to the divine design, it says that it is easier for a camel to get through the eye of a needle. On this level of meaning, a camel means our cognitive and informational level in general, and the eye of a needle means spiritual truth.h

Nowadays people do not know that this is the meaning of the camel and the eye of a needle because there has not yet been any access to the

---

g. Garments mean things that are true, and therefore insights: 1033 [1073], 2576, 5319, 5954, 9212, 9216, 9952, 10536. Purple means heavenly good: 9467. Linen means truth of a heavenly origin: 5319, 9469, 9744.

h. A camel in the Word means our cognitive and informational level in general: 3048, 3071, 3143, 3145. What embroidery, embroidering, and therefore needles are: 9688. To start from outward facts in order to gain access to truths of faith is contrary to the divine design: 10236. People who do this become insane in matters of heaven and the church: 128, 129, 130, 232, 233, 6047; and in the other life, when they think about spiritual things, they become virtually drunk: 1072. More about their nature: 196. Examples to illustrate the fact that spiritual things cannot be grasped if they are approached on this basis: 233, 2094, 2196, 2203, 2209. It is all right to go from spiritual truth into the knowledge appropriate to our natural level, but not the other way around, because there is an inflow of the spiritual into the natural but not an inflow of the natural into the spiritual: 3219, 5119, 5259, 5427, 5428, 5478, 6322, 9110, 9111 [10199]. We need first to acknowledge the truths of the Word and the church, and then it is all right to take our secular learning into account; but not the other way around: 6047.

knowledge that teaches what is meant spiritually by the things that the
Word says literally. There is spiritual meaning in the details of the Word,
and natural meaning as well; because the Word was written in pure correspondences of natural realities with spiritual ones in order to effect a
union of heaven and the world, or of angels with us, once the direct
union had ceased. We can see from this exactly who are meant by the
rich in the Word.

[4] We may gather from a number of passages that on the spiritual
level "the rich" in the Word refers to people who enjoy insights into what
is good and true and that wealth means those insights themselves, which
are spiritual riches: see Isaiah 10:12, 13, 14; 30:6, 7; 45:3; Jeremiah 17:3;
47:7 *[48:7]*; 50:36–37; 51:13; Daniel 5:2–4; Ezekiel 26:7, 12; 27:1–36;
Zechariah 9:3–4; Psalms 45:12;[229] Hosea 12:9; Revelation 3:17–18; Luke
14:33; and elsewhere. On the poor in the spiritual sense as people who
do not have insights into what is good and true but who long for them,
see Matthew 11:5; Luke 6:20–21; 14:21; Isaiah 14:30; 29:19; 41:17–18;
Zephaniah 3:12, 18 *[13]*. An explanation of the spiritual meaning of all
these passages may be found in §10227 of *Secrets of Heaven*.

Marriages in Heaven

366 SINCE heaven comes from the human race, which means that there
are angels of both sexes there, and since by creation itself woman is
for man and man for woman, each for the other, and since this love is inborn in both sexes, it follows that there are marriages in the heavens just
as there are on earth. However, the marriages in the heavens are very different from earthly ones. In the following pages I will be explaining how
marriages in the heavens do differ from earthly ones and in what respects
they agree.

367 Marriage in the heavens is the union of two people into one mind.
First, I need to explain the nature of this union. The mind consists of
two parts, one called intellect and the other called volition.[230] When
these two parts are acting as one, we call them one mind. In heaven, the
husband plays the role labeled intellect and the wife the role called volition. When this union—a union of their deeper natures—comes down

into their lower, bodily natures, it is perceived and felt as love. That love is marriage love.[231]

We can see from this that marriage love finds its source in the union of two people in one mind. In heaven, this is called "living together," and they are not called "two" but "one." Consequently two spouses in heaven are not called two angels but one angel.[a]

The reason for this kind of union of husband and wife on the deepest levels of their minds goes back to creation itself. The male is born to focus on cognitive processes, and therefore bases his thinking on his intellect. In contrast, the woman is born to focus on intentions, and therefore bases her thinking on her volition. We can see this from the tendency or innate nature of each as well as from their form. As to innate nature, men do act on the basis of reason, while women act on the basis of their feelings. As to form, the man has a rougher and less attractive face, a deeper voice, and a stronger body, while the woman has a softer and more attractive face, a gentler voice, and a softer body. This is like the difference between intellect and volition or between thought and affection. It is also like the difference between what is true and what is good or between faith and love, since truth and faith are matters of intellect, while good and love are matters of volition.

This is why a boy or a man, in the spiritual sense of the Word, means the discernment of truth, while a girl or woman means an affection for what is good. It is also why the church is called a woman or a girl on the basis of its affection for what is good and true and why everyone who is absorbed in an affection for what is good is called a young woman, as in the Book of Revelation 14:4.[b]

Both man and woman are endowed with intellect and volition, but for men intellect tends to take the lead, while for women it is volition that does so; and people are characterized by what is in control. There is

368

369

a. The nature and source of marriage love are unknown at the present time: 2727. Marriage love is willing what the other wills—mutually, then, and reciprocally: 2731. People who are immersed in marriage love are living together at the deepest level of their lives: 2732. It is a union of two minds so that they become one because of their love: 10168, 10169; since the love of minds, which is a spiritual love, is a union: 1594, 2057, 3939, 4018, 5807, 6195, 7081–7086, 7501, 10130.

b. Boys in the Word mean the understanding of what is true, or discernment: 7668; and men mean much the same: 158, 265, 749, 915, 1007, 2517, 3134, 3236, 4823, 9007. A woman means an affection for what is good and true: 568, 3160, 6014, 7337, 8994; and the church: 252, 253, 749, 770; and so does a wife: 252, 253, 409, 749, 770; with some difference: 915, 2517, 3236, 4510, 4822 [4823]. In the highest sense, "husband and wife" describes the Lord and his union with heaven and the church: 7022. A young woman means an affection for what is good: 3067, 3110, 3179, 3189, 6731, 6742; and also the church: 2362, 3081, 3963, 4638, 6729, 6775, 6778 [6788].

no controlling, though, in marriages in the heavens. The volition of the wife actually belongs to the husband and the intellect of the husband belongs to the wife. This is because each wants to intend and think like the other, mutually, that is, and reciprocally. This is how the two are united into one.

This is a truly effective union. The intent of the wife actually enters into the thinking of the husband, and the thinking of the husband enters into the intent of the wife, especially when they look each other in the face, since as already noted there is a sharing of thoughts and affections in the heavens. There is all the more sharing between a wife and a husband because they love each other.

We may gather from this what the union of minds is like that makes a marriage and that gives birth to marriage love in the heavens—it is that each wants his or her blessings to belong to the other, and that this is mutual.

370 I have been told by angels that the more two spouses are engaged in this kind of union, the more they are caught up in marriage love and, at the same time, in intelligence, wisdom, and happiness. This is because divine truth and divine good, the source of all intelligence, wisdom, and happiness, flow primarily into marriage love. This means that marriage love is the essential matrix for the divine inflow because it is itself a marriage of the true and the good. This in turn is because the nature of the union of intellect and volition determines the nature of the union of the true and the good because the intellect is a receptor of divine truth, being formed from truths, while volition is a receptor of divine good and is actually formed from things good. In fact, whatever we intend is good in our estimation, and whatever we understand is true for us. This is why it is all the same whether you talk about the union of intellect and intent or the union of the true and the good.

The union of the true and the good makes an angel, and also makes angels' intelligence, wisdom, and happiness. The actual nature of angels depends on how what is true in them is united to what is good, and what is good is united to what is true. In other words, the nature of angels depends on the way their love is united to their faith and their faith to their love.

371 The reason the divine nature that emanates from the Lord flows primarily into marriage love is that marriage love flows down from the union of the good and the true, for as already noted, it does not matter whether you talk about the union of intellect and volition or the union of the good and the true. The union of the good and the true finds its origin in the Lord's divine love for everyone in the heavens and on earth.

Divine good emanates from this divine love, and divine good is accepted by angels and by us in divine truths, truth being the only vessel for the good. So nothing from the Lord and heaven can be accepted by people who are not interested in truth. To the extent that true elements are united to what is good within us, then, we are united to the Lord and heaven. This is the actual source of marriage love, which means that it is the actual matrix for the inflow of the Divine.

This is why the union of the good and the true in the heavens is called the heavenly marriage and why heaven is compared to a marriage in the Word and is even called "a marriage." It is why the Lord is called the Bridegroom and Husband, and heaven and the church are called the bride and wife.[c]

When the good and the true are united in an angel or in one of us, they are not two entities but one, since the good then follows from the true and the true from the good. This union is like the one that occurs when we think what we intend and intend what we think. Then our thought and our intention form a unity; the thought forms or presents in a form what our volition intends, and our volition gives it its appeal. This is also why two spouses in heaven are not called two angels, but one.

372

Again, this is the meaning of the Lord's words,

> Have you not read that the One who made them from the beginning made them male and female and said, "For this reason a man shall leave his father and mother and cling to his wife, and the two will become[232] one flesh." So they are no longer two, but are one flesh. What God has united, let no one sever. Not everyone accepts this word, only those to whom it is given. (Matthew 19:4–6, 11; Mark 10:6–9; Genesis 2:24)

Here we have a description of the heavenly marriage angels are in and at the same time the marriage of the good and the true. "Let no one sever what God has united" means that the good is not to be severed from the true.

---

c. True marriage love finds its origin, its means, and its essence in the marriage of what is good and what is true, so it comes from heaven: 2728, 2729. About angelic spirits who can tell whether there is a marital quality present from people's concepts of the union of what is good and what is true: 10756. Marriage love precisely parallels the union of what is good and what is true, with some description: 1094 *[1904]*, 2173, 2429, 2503 *[2508]*, 3101, 3102, 3155, 3179, 3180, 4358, 5407 *[5807]*, 5835, 9206, 9495, 9637. How and for whom the union of what is good and what is true takes place: 3834, 4096, 4097, 4301, 4345, 4353, 4364, 4368, 5365, 7623–7627, 9258. Only people who are focused by the Lord on what is good and true know what real marriage love is: 10171. In the Word, a marriage refers to a marriage of what is good and what is true: 3132, 4434, 4834 *[4835]*. It is in real marriage love that the kingdom of the Lord and heaven is found: 2737.

373   We can now see from the foregoing where true marriage love comes from, namely that it first takes form in the minds of the individuals in the marriage and then comes down and flows into their bodies, where it is perceived and felt as love. Actually, everything that is perceived and felt in the body finds its origin in its spiritual counterpart because it comes from our intellect and volition. Intellect and volition make up our spiritual person. Everything that comes down into the body from our spiritual person comes to view there in some other guise; but there is still a similarity and agreement like that between the soul and the body, like a cause and its effect, as can be gathered from what was presented in the two chapters on correspondences.[233]

374   I once heard an angel describe true marriage love and its heavenly pleasures along these lines: It is the Lord's divine nature in the heavens, that is, divine good and divine truth, united in two individuals to the point that they are no longer two but one. The angel said that two spouses in heaven *are* that love because each is her or his own good and truth in both mind and body. This is because the body is the outward model of the mind, having been formed as its image. It follows that the Divine is imaged in two people who are immersed in true marriage love; and because the Divine is imaged, so is heaven, since the totality of heaven is divine good and divine truth emanating from the Lord. This is why everything heavenly has this love engraved upon it, along with so many blessings and pleasures that they cannot be numbered. Expressing the number with a word that suggested ten thousands times ten thousands, the angel was astonished that church people do not know anything about this when the church is the Lord's heaven on earth and heaven is a marriage of the good and the true; and the angel described being dumbfounded at the thought that adultery was practiced and even rationalized more within the church than outside it, because spiritually understood (and therefore in the spiritual world), the pleasure of adultery is essentially nothing but the pleasure of a love of the union of what is false and what is evil. This is a hellish pleasure, because it is diametrically opposed to the pleasure of heaven, which is the pleasure of a love of what is true united to the good.

375   Everyone knows that two spouses who love each other are intimately united, and that the essence of marriage is the union of spirits or minds. People might therefore realize that the essential nature of the spirits or minds determines the nature of the union and the nature of the love the two have for each other. The mind is formed from nothing but things that are true and things that are good, since everything in the universe goes back to the good and the true and also to their union. So the quality of the union of minds depends entirely on the quality of the true and good elements that constitute those minds. This means that the most perfect union is a union of minds formed from things that are genuinely true and good.

It does need to be realized that there is no greater love than the love between the true and the good, which is why real marriage love comes down from that love.[d] What is false and what is evil also love each other, but this love later turns into hell.

We may conclude from what has been said thus far about the origin of marriage love just which people are actually involved in it and which people are not. People who are focused on divinely good realities because of divine truths are in marriage love; and marriage love is genuine to the extent that the truths that are united to the good are themselves more genuine. Further, since everything good that is united to truths comes from the Lord, it follows that no one can be in real marriage love who does not acknowledge the Lord and his divine nature, since apart from this acknowledgment the Lord cannot flow in and be united to the truths within us.

376

We can see from this that people who are caught up in false thoughts are not involved in marriage love, especially if those false thoughts stem from evil. In people who are engaged in evil and consequently in false thoughts, the deeper levels of their minds are closed. This means that there cannot be any source of marriage love within them. However, on a lower level, in the outer or natural person divorced from the inner, there is a union of the false and the evil, a union that is called a hellish marriage.

377

I have been allowed to see what marriage is like between people who are caught up in false thoughts of an evil origin, which is called hellish marriage. They do talk to each other and even cohabit out of lust, but inwardly they burn with a mutual hatred so murderous as to be beyond description.

Marriage love does not occur between people of different religions, either, because the truth of one is not in harmony with the good of the

378

d. Everything in the universe, both in heaven and on earth, goes back to what is good and what is true: 2451 *[2452]*, 3166, 4390, 4409, 5232, 7256, 10122; and to their union: 10555. There is a marriage between what is good and what is true: 1094 *[1904]*, 2173, 2503 *[2508]*. What is good loves what is true, and from its love desires it and desires its union with itself, so it is in an unceasing effort toward union: 9206, 9207, 9495. The life of the true comes from the good: 1589, 1997, 2579 *[2572]*, 4070, 4096, 4097, 4736, 4757, 4884, 5147, 9667. The true is the form of the good: 3049, 3180, 4574, 9154. The true is to the good as water is to bread: 4976.

other, and two unlike and discordant entities cannot make one mind out of two. This means that the source of their love has nothing spiritual in it. If they do live together in harmony, it is strictly for natural reasons.[e]

For this reason, marriages in the heavens are contracted with people within their own community because they are focused on similar kinds of good and truth, and they do not associate with people outside their community. It may be seen in §§41–45 above that all the people who are within a given community are focused on similar good and truth, and that they differ from people who are outside the community. This was also represented in the Israelite nation by the fact that they contracted marriages within their tribes and even within their clans, and not outside them.[234]

379   Genuine marriage love is not possible between one husband and more than one wife. Polygamy in fact destroys the spiritual source of marriage love, whose purpose is to form one mind out of two. It therefore destroys the deeper union of the good and the true that is the very essence of that love. Marriage with more than one is like an intellect divided among more than one will or like a person pledged to more than one church. This actually pulls faith apart so that it becomes no faith at all.[235]

Angels say that taking more than one wife is absolutely contrary to the divine design and that they know this for many reasons, including the fact that the moment they think about marriage with more than one, they are estranged from their inner blessedness and heavenly happiness. They become virtually drunk because the good is severed from the true within them; and since the deeper levels of their minds come into this kind of state when they simply think about this with some slight intent, they perceive clearly that marriage with more than one woman closes their own inner nature and makes lust invade where there should be marriage love. Lust leads away from heaven.[f]

---

e. Marriages between people of divergent religions are not permitted because there is no union of like good and truth on the inner levels: 8998.

f. Since husband and wife are to be one and are to live together at the very deepest level of life, and since the two together make one angel in heaven, genuine marriage love cannot exist between one husband and more than one wife: 1907, 2740. Taking more than one wife at the same time is contrary to the divine design: 10835 [10837]. It is clearly perceived by people in the Lord's heavenly kingdom that there is no marriage except between one husband and one wife: 865, 3246, 9902 [9002], 10172; because angels there are in a marriage of what is good and what is true: 3246. The Israelites were allowed to take more than one wife and to take concubines in addition to their wives, but this is not allowable for Christians. This is because the former nation was focused on outward things apart from deeper ones, while Christians can be intent on deeper ones and therefore on the marriage of what is good and what is true: 3246, 4837, 8809.

They added that people on earth have a hard time understanding this because so few do experience true marriage love, and if people are not intent on this, they have absolutely no knowledge of the inner delight that dwells within that love. They are aware only of the delight of lust, a delight that turns disagreeable after people have lived together for a little while. The delight of real marriage love, though, not only lasts into old age on earth but even becomes heavenly delight after death, when it is filled with a deeper delight that becomes better and better to eternity.

The angels even said that the blessings of real marriage love could be listed in the thousands, with not a single one known to people here or comprehensible to the understanding of anyone who is not in a marriage of the good and the true from the Lord.

Any love of control of one over the other utterly destroys marriage love and its heavenly pleasure, for as already noted, marriage love and its pleasure consist of the intent of one belonging to the other, and of this being mutual and reciprocal. A love of being in control in a marriage destroys this because the dominant partner simply wants his or her will to be in the other, and does not want to accept any element of the will of the other in return. So it is not mutual, which means that there is no sharing of any love and its pleasure with the other, and no accepting in return. Yet this sharing and the union that follows from it is the very inward pleasure that is called blessedness in marriage. Love of being in control stifles this blessedness, and with it absolutely everything heavenly and spiritual about the love, to the point that even all knowledge of its existence is lost. One could even say that it is held so cheaply that the mere mention of [marriage] blessedness makes people laugh or flare up in anger.

380

[2] When one partner wants or loves what the other does, then there is a freedom for both, because all freedom stems from love. However, there is freedom for neither one when there is control. One is the servant; and so is the one in control, because he or she is being driven like a servant by a need to be in control. However, people who do not know what the freedom of a heavenly love is do not understand this at all. They might find out from the things just said about the origin and essence of marriage love, that as control comes in the door, minds are not united but severed. Control subjugates, and a subjugated mind either has no purpose or is of opposite purpose. If it has no purpose it has no love, and if it is of opposite purpose there is hatred in the place of love.

[3] The deeper natures of people who live in this kind of marriage clash and struggle with each other, as is normal for two things that are opposed to each other, no matter how their outer natures are restrained

and tranquilized for the sake of peace. The clash and struggle of their inner natures comes out after their death. They usually get together and then battle each other like enemies and tear each other apart. They are in fact acting in accord with the state of their own deeper natures. I have occasionally been allowed to see how they fight and tear one another; some instances are full of spite and savagery. Everyone's deeper levels are allowed a certain freedom in the other life, being no longer constrained by outward considerations, for their worldly purposes. Then people are outwardly what they are inwardly.

381   There is a kind of image of marriage love in some people, but it is not marriage love unless they are focused on a love of the good and the true. It is a love that looks like marriage love for a number of reasons—we want to be taken care of at home, to feel secure, to be at peace or at leisure, to be taken care of when we are ill or elderly, or [to work together] for the sake of beloved children. In some cases it arises from a fear of the spouse, because of what people will think, or for evil ends; and for some it is lust that causes it.

Marriage love also differs between spouses. It may be more or less in one, little or none in the other; and since it may differ, it may be heaven for one and hell for the other.

382a [236]   Genuine marriage love is found in the inmost heaven because the angels there are absorbed in the marriage of the good and the true and are in innocence as well. Angels of lower heavens are in marriage love too, but only to the extent that they are in innocence; because seen in its own right, marriage love is a state of innocence. So between partners who are in marriage love there are heavenly pleasures almost like games of innocence to their minds, like those of babies, because there is nothing that does not delight them. Heaven flows into the smallest details of their lives with its joy. This is why marriage love is pictured in heaven by the loveliest things of all. I have seen it represented by an indescribably lovely young woman enveloped by a white cloud. I was told that all the beauty of angels in heaven comes from marriage love. The affections and thoughts that flow from it are represented by gleaming auras, like those of fiery gems[237] or rubies, all this accompanied by feelings of delight that move the deeper levels of the mind.

In a word, heaven portrays itself in marriage love because heaven for angels is the union of the good and the true, and it is this union that constitutes marriage love.

382b   Marriages in the heavens differ from marriages on earth in that earthly marriages are also for the purpose of having children, while this is not the case in the heavens. In place of the procreation of children there is the procreation of what is good and true. The reason for this replacement is that their marriage is a marriage of the good and the true, as presented above, and in this marriage what is good and true is loved above all, as is their union; so these are what are propagated by the marriages in the heavens. This is why in the Word births and generations mean spiritual births and generations, births of what is good and true. The mother and father mean the true united to the good that is prolific, the sons and daughters the good and true things that are born, and the sons-in-law and daughters-in-law mean the unions of these [descendants], and so on.[g]

We can see from this that marriages in the heavens are not the same as marriages on earth. In the heavens there are spiritual weddings that should not be called weddings but unions of minds, because of the union of the good and the true. On earth, though, there are weddings, because they concern not only the spirit but the flesh as well. Further, since there are no weddings in the heavens, two spouses there are not called husband and wife, but because of the angelic concept of the union of two minds into one, each spouse is identified by a word that means "belonging to each other."

This enables us to know what is meant by the Lord's words about marriages in Luke 21:35–36 [20:35–36].

I have also been allowed to see how marriages are entered into in the heavens. Throughout heaven, people who are similar gather together and people who are dissimilar part company. This means that every community consists of like-minded people. Like are drawn toward like not by their own will but by the Lord (see above, §§41–45). In the same way, spouse is drawn toward spouse when their minds can be united into one. So at first sight they love each other most deeply, see each other as married partners, and enter into their marriage. This is why all of heaven's

383

g. Conception, giving birth, being born, and generations mean spiritual events that are matters of what is true and what is good, or of love and faith: 613, 1145, 1755 [1255], 2020, 2584, 3860, 3868, 4070, 4668, 6239, 8042, 9325, 10197 [10249]. Begetting and being born mean regeneration and rebirth by means of faith and love: 5160, 5598, 9042, 9845. A mother means the church in regard to truth and therefore the truth of the church as well; a father means the church in regard to good and therefore the good of the church as well: 2691, 2717, 3703, 5580 [5581], 8897. Sons mean affections for what is true and therefore truths: 489, 491, 533, 2623, 3373, 4257, 8649, 9807. Daughters mean affections for what is good and therefore things that are good: 489, 490, 491, 2362, 3963, 6729, 6775, 6778, 9055. A son-in-law means something true connected with an affection for the good: 2389. A daughter-in-law means something good connected with its truth: 4843.

marriages are the work of the Lord alone. They also hold a feast in celebration with many people gathered; these feasts differ from community
to community.

384   Marriages on earth are the seedbed of the human race and also of the
angels of heaven, for as already noted in its own chapter, heaven is from
the human race. For this reason, and because they do have a spiritual origin (from the marriage of the good and the true), and because the Lord's
divine nature flows especially into this love, these earthly marriages are
seen as most holy by heaven's angels. Correspondingly, adultery, as the
opposite of marriage love, is seen by them as unholy; for as angels see in
marriages a marriage of the good and the true, which is heaven, so in
adultery they see a marriage of the false and the evil, which is hell. So if
they even hear adultery mentioned, they turn away. This is why heaven is
closed to people if they commit adultery because they enjoy it. Once it is
closed, the Divine Being is no longer acknowledged, nor is anything of
the faith of the church.[h,238]

I could tell that everyone in hell is opposed to marriage love from the
aura that emanated from hell. It was like a ceaseless effort to break up
and destroy marriages. This showed that the dominant pleasure in hell is
the pleasure of adultery, and that the pleasure of adultery is also the pleasure of destroying the union of the good and the true, the union that
makes heaven. It follows from this that the pleasure of adultery is a hellish pleasure, diametrically opposed to the pleasure of marriage, which is a
heavenly pleasure.

385   There were some spirits who plagued me with particular ingenuity
because of their practice during their physical life. They did this by a
rather subtle inflow, almost wavelike, a kind that is characteristic of honest spirits; but I could tell that there were elements of deception and the
like within them, intended to ensnare and deceive. Eventually I talked
with one of them who had been in command of an army when he lived
in the world, so I was told. Since I could tell that there was something li-
centious in what he was processing mentally, I talked with him about
marriage in a spiritual language, using images—many of them very

h. Acts of adultery are unholy: 9961, 10174. Heaven is closed to adulterers: 275 *[2750]*. People who
feel pleasure in acts of adultery cannot enter heaven: 539, 2733, 2747, 2748, 2749, 2751, 10175.
Adulterers are merciless and have no religion: 824, 2747, 2748. Adulterers' ideas are filthy: 2747,
2748. In the other life they love filth and are in that kind of hell: 2755, 5394, 5722. Acts of adultery
in the Word mean adulterations of what is good, and prostitution means the distortion of what is
true: 2466, 2729, 3399, 4865, 8904, 10648.

brief—that expressed my sentiments fully. He said that during his physical life he had thought nothing of acts of adultery.

It occurred to me to tell him, though, that acts of adultery are unspeakable, no matter how different and even permissible they may look to people like him because of the pleasure they are grasping and their consequent rationalizations. He might realize this simply because marriages are the seedbed of the human race and therefore the seedbed of the kingdom of heaven. Because of this, they should never be violated but should be regarded as holy. He might also realize this because he must know that he was now in the other life and in a state to perceive that marriage love was coming down from the Lord through heaven, and that mutual love, the foundation of heaven, was derived from that love as from a parent. There was also the fact that when adulterers merely approach heavenly communities they become aware of their own stench and dive down toward hell. He should at least know that violation of marriage is against divine laws and against the civil laws of all kingdoms as well as contrary to genuine rational light because, among many other things, it is contrary to both divine and human order.

However, he answered that he had not thought that way during his physical life. He wanted to quibble about whether this was true or not; but he was told that there is no quibbling about the truth. Quibbling favors whatever pleases us, and therefore supports what is evil and false. He should first think about what he had been told, because it was true. Or again, he could start from the principle widely acknowledged in the world that we should not do anything to others that we do not want them to do to us. So if anyone had practiced this kind of deception on his own wife, whom he loved (as is the case in the early stages of every marriage), then when he was at the peak of his blazing rage about it and gave voice to his feelings, wouldn't he himself hold adultery to be detestable and, being intellectually gifted, wouldn't he of all people defend his condemnation to the point of damning adultery to hell?

386 I have been shown how the pleasures of marriage love lead to heaven and how the pleasures of adultery lead to hell. The path of marriage love toward heaven led into constantly increasing blessings and delights until they were beyond number or description. The deeper they were, the more of them there were and the more indescribable they were, all the way to the delights of the inmost heaven, the heaven of innocence. All this was accomplished with the greatest freedom, because all freedom stems from love; so the greatest freedom comes from marriage love, which is the essential heavenly love.

On the other hand, the path of adultery led toward hell, step by step to the very lowest where there is nothing that is not grim and terrifying. This is the kind of fate that awaits adulterers after their life in the world. By "adulterers," we mean people who find pleasure in acts of adultery and not in marriage.

What Angels Do in Heaven

387 THERE is no way to list all the functions that people have in the heavens or to describe them in detail, though it is possible to say something on the subject in general terms; they are innumerable and vary depending on the roles of the communities as well. In fact, each community plays a unique role, since the communities differ depending on their virtues (see above, §41) and therefore on their function. This is because virtues for everyone in the heavens are virtues in act, which are functions. Everyone there does something specifically useful, for the Lord's kingdom is a kingdom of uses.[a,239]

388 There are many services in the heavens just as there are on earth, since there are ecclesiastical, civic, and domestic affairs there. The existence of the ecclesiastical ones follows from what was presented above about divine worship in §§221–227, the existence of civic ones from what was presented about forms of government in heaven in §§213–220, while the existence of domestic ones follows from the material on angels' homes and houses (§§183–190) and on marriages in heaven (§§366–386). We can therefore see that the roles and services in any given heavenly community are multiple.

389 Everything in the heavens is arranged according to the divine design, which is managed everywhere by the oversight of angels, with the wiser ones tending to matters of the common good or use and the less wise to

a. The Lord's kingdom is a kingdom of uses: 453 *[454]*, 696, 1103, 3645, 4054, 7038. Serving the Lord is being useful: 7038. Everyone needs to be useful in the other life: 1103; even evil and hellish people, but in a different manner: 696. Everyone's quality is determined by the use that individual fulfills: 4054, 6815; with examples: 7038. Angelic blessedness consists of good, thoughtful deeds, and therefore of fulfilling uses: 454.

smaller details, and so on. These matters are ranked just as uses are ranked in the divine design. This also means that importance is attributed to each role in keeping with the importance of its use. Angels, however, do not claim any importance for themselves but ascribe it all to the use; and since the use is the good that it serves and everything good comes from the Lord, they ascribe it all to the Lord. This means that if people think about respect for themselves first and for their use secondarily instead of for the use first and for themselves secondarily, they cannot hold any office in heaven because they are looking away from the Lord, putting themselves first and their use second. To say "use" is to mean the Lord as well, since as just noted use is something good, and good comes from the Lord.

This enables us to determine what rankings in the heavens are like, namely that we love, value, and respect the functionaries the way we love, value, and respect the functions that are associated with them, and also that these functionaries are loved, valued, and respected to the extent that they do not attribute their use to themselves but to the Lord. To that extent they are wise, and to that extent they fulfill their uses from good motives. Spiritual love, value, and respect are nothing but love, value, and respect for the use in the role, respect for the role because of the use and not for the use because of the role. If we look at people from a spiritually true perspective, this is the only way to see them. Then we see one person as much like another, whether their rank is great or small. The only difference we see is a difference in wisdom, and wisdom is loving use, which means loving the welfare of our fellow citizens, our community, our country, and the church.

This is also what constitutes love for the Lord, since everything good that is effectively good comes from the Lord. It also constitutes love for our neighbor, since our neighbor is the welfare that is to be loved in our fellow citizens, our community, our country, and our church, and that is to be fostered for their sakes.[b,240]

390

b. Loving our neighbor is loving not the role but what is in our neighbor and is the source of our neighbor: 5025, 10336. People who love the role rather than the substance and source of the person love the evil just as much as the good: 3820; and help evil and good people equally even though helping evil people is hurting good ones, which is not loving one's neighbor: 3820, 6703, 8120. Judges who punish evildoers in order to correct them and to keep them from corrupting and harming good people are loving their neighbor: 3820, 8120, 8121. Every individual and community, the country and the church, and in the widest sense the Lord's kingdom, are all "our neighbor," and helping them out of a love for their welfare and according to their state is loving our neighbor: this means that their welfare, which is to be focused on, is our neighbor: 6818–6824, 8123.

391   All the communities in the heavens are differentiated according to their forms of service because they are differentiated according to their virtues, as has been noted above (§§41–45). Their virtues are virtues in action or acts of thoughtfulness, which are services. There are some communities whose tasks are to take care of babies; there are other communities whose tasks are to teach and lead children while they are growing up; there are other communities that look after young boys and girls who are well disposed because of the way they were raised in this world and have come [straight] to heaven, where they are taught and raised in much the same way. There are some that teach simple people from the Christian world and lead them on the way to heaven, and there are some that do the same for various non-Christian peoples. There are some that protect new spirits, just arrived from the world, from the attacks of evil spirits; and there are some who attend to people in the lower earth.[241] Then there are some who attend to people in the hells and control them so that they do not torture each other beyond set limits. There are also some who tend to people who are being awakened from their death.

Broadly speaking, angels of all communities are assigned to us to protect us, to lead us away from evil feelings and the evil thoughts that these cause and to instill good feelings to the extent that we are freely open to them. These serve to control our deeds or works by removing our evil intentions to the extent that this can be done. When angels are with us they seem to dwell in our affections, near us to the extent that we are engaged in something good because of truth, and distant to the extent that our life is removed from such engagement.[c]

However, all these tasks are things the Lord does by means of angels, since angels do them not on their own but from the Lord. This is why in the deeper meaning of the Word "angels" does not mean angels but something of the Lord; and this is why angels are called gods in the Word.[d]

392   These are general categories of angels' activities, but each individual has her or his own specific contribution to make. This is because every

---

c. On angels with babies and then with children, and thereafter: 2303. We are awakened from death by angels; from experience: 168–189. Angels are sent to people in hell to prevent them from tormenting each other excessively: 967. On the services angels provide to people who are arriving in the other life: 2131. Spirits and angels are with us all, and the Lord is leading us through spirits and angels: 50, 697, 2796, 2887, 2888, 5847–5866, 5976–5993, 6209. Angels have power over evil spirits: 1755.

d. "Angels" in the Word means something divine from the Lord: 1925, 2821, 3039, 4085, 6280, 8192. Angels are called gods in the Word because of their openness to divine truth and good from the Lord: 4295, 4402, 8301, 8192.

general service is made up of countless elements that are called mediate or subservient or supporting services. All of these are arranged and ranked according to the divine design, and taken together they make up and complete an overarching function that is the common good.

The people in heaven who are involved in church affairs are the ones who loved the Word in the world and looked for truths in it with lively interest, not for the sake of eminence or profit but for the service of their own life and the lives of others. In proportion to their love and eagerness for service, they are enlightened there and are in the light of wisdom, attaining it because of the Word in the heavens, which is not natural the way it is in the world, but spiritual (see §259 above). They have the gift of preaching; and in keeping with the divine design, the ones who are more highly placed there are the ones who surpass others in the wisdom they derive from their enlightenment.

[2] The people who are involved in civic affairs are the ones who loved their country and its welfare more than their own, who behaved honestly and fairly out of a love for what is honest and fair. To the extent that they sought out laws of justice because of the urging of this love and thereby became discerning they enjoy the ability to fill governing offices in heaven. They perform these duties in the place or on the level appropriate to their discernment, which in turn is equivalent to their love of service in the common good.

[3] Further, there are so many offices and departments in heaven, so many tasks, that there are simply too many to list. There are relatively few in the world. No matter how many people are involved, they are all caught up in a love of their work and tasks out of a love of service—no one out of selfishness or a love of profit. In fact, there is no love of profit for the sake of livelihood, since all the necessities of life are given them gratis. They are housed gratis, clothed gratis, and fed gratis. We can see from this that people who have loved themselves and the world more than service have no place in heaven. In fact, our love or affection invariably stays with us after our life in the world. It is not uprooted to eternity (see above, §363).

Everyone in heaven is engaged in his or her work according to its correspondence, and the correspondence is not with the work itself but with the use of each particular task (see above, §112); and everything has a correspondence (§106). When we are engaged in an activity or a task in heaven that does answer to its use, then we are in a state of life very much like the one we were in in this world. This is because what is spiritual and what is natural act as one by means of their correspondence, but with the difference that [after death] we enjoy a deeper delight because we are engaged in a spiritual life. This is a deeper life, and therefore more open to heavenly blessedness.

Heavenly Joy and Happiness

395 HARDLY anyone nowadays knows what heaven is or what heavenly joy is. People who think about either subject come up with such pedestrian and crude notions that they scarcely amount to anything at all. I have had a wonderful opportunity to learn from spirits who were coming from this world into the other life what kind of idea they had about heaven and heavenly joy, for when they are left on their own, as they were in the world, they still think the same way.[242]

The reason they do not know about heavenly joy is that people who think about it at all base their judgments on the external joys of the natural person. They do not know what the inner or spiritual person is, so they do not know what that person's pleasure and blessedness are. So even if they were told by people involved in spiritual or inner joy what heavenly joy is and how it feels, they would not be able to grasp it. It would have descended into an unfamiliar concept and therefore not into their perception, so it would have become one of those things that the natural person casts aside.

Everyone is capable of knowing that when we leave our outer or natural person we enter our inner or spiritual one; so we can also know that heavenly pleasure is an inner and spiritual pleasure and not an outer or natural one. Since it is inner and spiritual, it is purer and finer and moves our deeper levels, the levels of our soul or spirit.

We may also conclude from this that the quality of our pleasure follows from the quality of the pleasure of our spirit, and that the pleasures of our bodies, called "the pleasures of the flesh," have nothing to do with heaven by comparison. Whatever is in our spirit when we leave the body remains with us after death, for we then live as human spirits.

396 All pleasures flow from love, because what we love we feel as pleasant. There is no other source of any pleasure. It follows, then, that the quality of the love determines the quality of the pleasure. Pleasures of the body or of the flesh flow from love for ourselves and from love of the world, and these are also the source of our urges and their gratifications. The pleasures of the soul or spirit, though, all flow from love for the Lord and love for our neighbor, which are also the source of affections for what is good and true and of our deeper bliss. These loves and their pleasures flow in from the Lord and from heaven by an inner path, from above, and move our deeper natures. The other loves and their pleasures, though, flow in from the flesh and the world by an outer path, from below, and move our outer natures.

To the extent that the two loves of heaven[243] are accepted and affect us, then, our deeper levels—levels of our souls or spirits—are opened; and they look away from the world toward heaven. To the extent that the two loves of the world[244] are accepted and affect us, though, our outer levels—levels of the body or the flesh—are opened; and they look away from heaven toward the world. As loves flow in and are accepted, so their pleasures flow in, pleasures of heaven into our deeper natures and pleasures of the world into our outer natures, because as already noted all pleasure comes from love.

By its very nature, heaven is full of pleasures, even to the point that if we see it as it really is, it is nothing but bliss and pleasure. This is because the divine good that emanates from the Lord's divine love constitutes heaven both overall and in detail for everyone there; and divine love is the intent that everyone should be saved and should be most profoundly and fully happy. This is why it is all the same whether you say "heaven" or "heavenly joy." 397

Heaven's pleasures are both indescribable and innumerable; but no one can realize or believe anything about their multitude who is wholly wrapped up in pleasures of the body or the flesh. This, as I have already said, is because their deeper levels are looking away from heaven toward the world, which is backward. For no one who is wholly involved in pleasures of the body or the flesh (or in love for oneself and the world, which is the same thing) feels any pleasure except in eminence or profit or in physical and sensory gratification. These stifle and smother deeper pleasures of heaven so completely that people do not even believe such pleasures exist. So they would be quite bewildered if they were so much as told that any pleasures remain once the pleasures of eminence and profit have been taken away; and they would be even more bewildered if they were told that the pleasures that take their place are countless and simply defy comparison with pleasures of the body and the flesh, especially pleasures of eminence and profit. We can see, then, why people do not know what heavenly joy is. 398

399 We may gather the magnitude of heaven's pleasure simply from the fact that for everyone there it is delightful to share their pleasure and bliss with someone else; and since everyone in the heavens is like this, we can see how immense heaven's pleasure is. For as I explained above (§268), there is in heaven a sharing by everyone with each individual, and by each individual with everyone.

This kind of sharing flows from the two loves of heaven, which as noted are love for the Lord and love for our neighbor. These loves by nature want to share their pleasures. The reason love for the Lord is like this is that because the Lord's love is a love of sharing everything it has with everyone, it intends the happiness of everyone. Much the same love exists in individuals who love him, because the Lord is in them. So there is a mutual sharing of angels' pleasures with each other. We shall see later that love for our neighbor is like this as well. We may gather from all this that these loves by nature want to share their pleasures.

It is different for love for oneself and love for the world. Love for oneself takes away and carries off all the pleasure of others and diverts them to itself because it has only its own welfare in mind. Love of the world wants the possessions of the neighbor to be its own. So these loves by nature want to destroy pleasures for other people. If they have any tendency to share, it is for their own interests and not for others; so in relation to others (except insofar as they can appropriate and embody the pleasures of those others) they do not tend to share but to destroy.

I have very often been shown by vivid experience that this is what love for oneself and love for the world are like when they are in control. Whenever spirits who were engrossed in these loves when they lived as people in the world have come up to me, my own pleasure has waned and vanished. I have also been told that if people like these so much as move toward any heavenly community, the pleasure of the members of that community decreases in direct proportion to their presence. Remarkably, too, the evil people are then delighted. I could see from this what the state of the human spirit in the body is like, for it is much the same as it is after separation from the body. Specifically, they crave and covet the pleasures or assets of others, and to the extent that they acquire them they themselves are pleased. We can see from this that love for oneself and love for the world are destructive of heavenly joy and are therefore diametrically opposed to heavenly loves, whose nature is to share.

400 However, we do need to realize that if people are engrossed in love for themselves and love for the world, the pleasure they are feeling when they move toward some heavenly community is the pleasure of their own cravings. So it is diametrically opposed to the pleasure of heaven. They attain the pleasure of their cravings when they succeed in stealing and taking away heavenly pleasure from people who are absorbed in it. It is different when no theft or removal occurs. Then they cannot get nearer because to the extent that they do, they are plunged into pain and torment. This is why they rarely dare to approach. This too I have been shown by an abundance of experience, some of which I should like to present.

[2] There is nothing spirits want more when they are arriving in the other life from this world than to get into heaven. Almost all of them expect to because they believe that heaven is simply a matter of being let in and accepted. Because this is what they want, then, they are taken to some community of the outmost heaven. If they are devoted to love for themselves and the world, then the moment they reach the first border of that heaven they begin to feel pain and to be so tormented within that they feel as though they were in hell rather than in heaven. So they themselves dive down headlong and are not at rest until they are with their own kind in the hells.

[3] It has also often happened that spirits like this have wanted to find out what heavenly joy is, and when they have heard that it is within the deeper nature of angels, they have sought to share in it for themselves. So this too was done, because when spirits are not yet in heaven or in hell, whatever they want is granted if it may do any good. Once communication was established, they began to feel such agony that they did not know how to control their bodies because of the pain. It looked as though they pushed their heads down to their feet and threw themselves on the ground and twisted themselves into loops like snakes, all because of their inner agony. This was the effect that heavenly pleasure had on people whose pleasures stemmed from love for themselves and love for the world. The reason is that these loves are diametrically opposed, and when a love meets its opposite this kind of pain results. Further, since heavenly pleasure comes in by an inner path and flows into an opposing pleasure, it twists the deeper levels that are engrossed in that pleasure backward, in the opposite direction. This results in this kind of agony.

[4] As I have already noted, the reason these loves are contrary to each other is that love for the Lord and love for our neighbor want to share everything with others. This is in fact their delight. But self-love and love for the world want to take things away from others for themselves, and find pleasure to the extent that they can succeed.

This also enables us to realize why hell is separated from heaven. It is because all the people who are in hell, while they lived in the world, were wholly focused on pleasures of the body and the flesh because of their love for themselves and love for the world; while all the people who are in heaven, while they lived in the world, were focused on pleasures of the soul and the spirit because of their love for the Lord and their love for their neighbor. Since these loves are opposed to each other, the hells and the heavens are completely separated, even to the point that spirits who are in hell do not dare stick out a single finger or raise the top of their heads, for the moment they do so, even the slightest bit, they are in torment and agony. This too I have often seen.

401   As long as people who are caught up in the love for themselves and the world are living in the body, they feel the pleasure that stems from those loves and the pleasure of the gratifications that result from those loves. As long as people who are focused on love for God and love for their neighbor are living in the body, though, they have no obvious sense of the pleasure that stems from those loves and from the good affections that arise from them. All they feel is a sense of well-being that is barely perceptible because it is hidden away in their deeper natures, veiled by the outer sensations of their bodies and dulled by the cares of this world. Our state changes completely after death, however. Then the pleasures of love for ourselves and the world turn into painful and fearful sensations because within them is what we call hellfire, and also into foul and unclean things that answer to their filthy gratifications—all of which, remarkably enough, are now quite delightful to them.

In contrast, the faint sense of pleasure, the almost imperceptible sense of well-being that was found in people who were focused on love for God and love for their neighbor in the world, turns into the pleasure of heaven, perceptible and palpable in countless ways. That sense of well-being that had been lying hidden in their deeper natures while they lived in the world is now unveiled and released into open sensation, because now they are in the spirit, and this was the delight of their spirit.

402   All the pleasures of heaven are united to forms of service and dwell within them, because forms of service are the good effects of the love and thoughtfulness that angels are immersed in. Consequently, the nature of each individual's pleasures depends on the nature of that individual's service, and its intensity depends on the intensity of the affection for service.

We can be assured that heaven's pleasures are pleasures of service by comparing them with our own five physical senses. Each sense has its own pleasure in accord with the service it performs. Sight has its pleasure, hearing its own, smell its own, taste its own, and touch its own. The pleasure of sight derives from beauty and forms, that of hearing from harmonies, of smell from fragrances, of taste from flavors. Anyone who reflects knows what services the individual senses perform, and people familiar with correspondences know this even more fully. The reason sight has the kind of pleasure it does lies in the service it performs for our discernment, which is an inner sight. The reason hearing has the kind of pleasure it does lies in the service it performs for our discernment and our volition by its attentiveness. The reason smell has the kind of pleasure it does lies in the service it performs for the brain and for the lungs. The reason taste has the kind of pleasure it does lies in the service it performs for the stomach and indirectly for the whole body by nourishing it. Marital pleasure, which is a purer and more delicate pleasure of touch, surpasses all others because of its service, the procreation of the human race and thus of the angelic heaven.

These pleasures are inherent in the senses because of the inflow of heaven, where all pleasure belongs to service and depends on service.

On the basis of an opinion formed in the world, some spirits have **403** believed that heavenly happiness consisted of a life of leisure, being waited on by others; but they were informed that there is never any happiness in idling around in order to be content. This would mean wanting the happiness of others for oneself, in which case no one would have any at all. This kind of life would be idle, not active, a life that would lead to atrophy. They might in fact have known that apart from an active life, a life has no happiness, and that idleness serves that life only for refreshment, in order to return them to the active life with more energy. Then they were shown in many ways that angelic life consists of worthwhile, thoughtful actions, actions that are useful to others, and that all the happiness angels have is found in service, derives from service, and is proportional to service.

So that these people might feel shame (people who have had the notion that heavenly joy consists of a life of leisure, inhaling eternal bliss) they are enabled to perceive what kind of life this would be. They see that it is thoroughly miserable; and once all their delight therefore dies away, they are very soon disgusted and nauseated.

Some spirits who thought themselves better informed than others **404** claimed that in the world they had held to the belief that heavenly joy consisted solely in praising and glorifying God, and that this was an active life. They have been told, though, that praising and glorifying God is not an appropriate kind of active life, since God has no need of praise and glorification.[245] Rather, God wants us to be useful to each other, to do the worthwhile things that are called works of charity. However, they could not connect any notion of heavenly joy with thoughtful good deeds, only a notion of slavery. The angels, though, bore witness that it was the freest life of all because it stemmed from a deep affection and was invariably accompanied by an indescribable pleasure.

405   Almost all the people who arrive in the other life think that hell is the same for everyone and that heaven is the same for everyone, when in fact there are infinite variations and differences in each. Hell is never the same for any two people, nor is heaven. In the same way, no one of us, no spirit, and no angel is ever exactly like any other, even facially. When I even thought about two identical or equal beings, the angels were aghast. They said that every unity is formed by a harmonious agreement of many constituents and that the nature of the unity depends on the nature of the agreement. This is how every community of heaven forms a unity and how all the communities form a single heaven, which is accomplished solely by the Lord, by means of love.[a,246]

Useful activities in the heavens occur in similar variety and diversity. The function of one individual is never exactly the same as that of any other, so the delight of one is never the same as another's. Not only that, the delights of each function are countless, and these countless delights are equally varied, yet they are united in a design that enables them to focus on each other as do the functions of the individual members and organs and viscera in the human body; or even more, like the functions of every vessel and fiber in those members and organs and viscera. These are all interconnected in such a way that they focus on what they can contribute to the other and therefore to all, with all mindful of the individual members. They act as one because of this regard for the whole and for the individual.

406   I once talked with some spirits who had just arrived from the world about the state of eternal life. I emphasized the fact that it is important to know who the lord of a kingdom is, what the government is like, and what the forms of government are. It is the same when people are visiting a foreign country in this world. Nothing is more critical for them than to know who the king is and what his character is, what the government is like, and a great many more details about the nation. How much more important must this be in the kingdom where they are going to live forever! They should realize, then, that it is the Lord who governs heaven—and the universe, for whoever rules the one rules the other as well. This means that the

---

a. A unity consists of different constituents and derives its form and quality from them, and it derives its perfection from the way they harmonize and agree: 457, 3241, 8003. There is an infinite variety, and nothing is ever the same as anything else: 7236, 9002. It is the same in the heavens: 5744 *[3744]*, 4005, 7236, 7833, 7836, 9002. Consequently all the communities in the heavens and all the individual angels in a community differ from each other because they are engaged in different virtues and services: 690, 3241, 3519, 3804, 3986, 4067, 4149, 4263, 7236, 7833, 3986. The Lord's divine love arranges them all in a heavenly form and unites them as though they were a single individual: 457, 3986, 5598.

kingdom where they now find themselves belongs to the Lord and that the laws of this kingdom are eternal truths all based on the law that they should love the Lord above all and their neighbor as themselves. Not only that, but if they wanted to be like angels, they needed to love their neighbor more than themselves.

When they heard this last point they were unable to respond, because they had heard something like this during their physical lives but had not believed it. They wondered whether there was that kind of love in heaven, whether it was possible for anyone to love her or his neighbor more than herself or himself. They were told, though, that in the other life everything good increases immensely. Life in a physical body cannot by nature progress beyond loving one's neighbor as the self, because it is immersed in physical concerns. Once these are removed, though, the love becomes purer and ultimately angelic, which is loving one's neighbor more than oneself. This is because in the heavens doing good for someone else is a delight and doing good for oneself is not unless it is to give to another and therefore for the sake of the other. This is loving one's neighbor more than oneself.

As for the possibility of this love, it was said that in this world it might be gathered from the marriage love some people have for each other, people who would rather die than allow their spouse to be hurt. Or they might consider the love of parents for their children, the mother who would rather starve than see her children go hungry; or the true friendship that leads people to face peril for the sake of their friends. They might even consider the simulated friendship of formal courtesy, in which people try to imitate the real thing by offering the better portions to people they claim to want to help and then make noise about it, though it is not from their hearts. Lastly, they might consider the nature of love, whose nature is to find joy in serving others for their sake and not for its own.

However, the ones who loved themselves more than others could not grasp this, nor could the ones who had been keen on profit taking during their physical lives; and least of all, misers.

There was one man who had been particularly powerful during his physical life, and who in the other life still had his desire to be in control. He was told that he was in another kingdom now, an eternal one, and that his own dominion was in the land of the dead. Here no one was valued for anything but their virtue and truth, and for the Lord's mercy they had enjoyed through their earthly lives. He was also told that this kingdom was like earthly ones where people were valued for their wealth and their standing with the leadership. Here wealth was virtue and truth, and standing with the leadership was the mercy the individual had enjoyed

407

from the Lord through life in the world. If he wanted to rule on any other basis he was a revolutionary, since he was in someone else's kingdom. He was embarrassed when he heard this.

408   I talked with some spirits who thought that heaven and heavenly joy consisted of being important; but I told them that in heaven the greatest is the one who is least. This is because people are called "least" when they have no ability or wisdom and do not want any ability or wisdom on their own, but only from the Lord. This kind of "least person" has the greatest happiness. And because such people do have the greatest happiness, it follows that they are the most important, because this is how they have all their capability and the most wisdom of all—from the Lord. Further, what is being the greatest if not being the happiest? The greatest happiness is what powerful people are seeking with their power and what rich people are seeking with their wealth.

I went on to say that heaven did not consist of wanting to be least in order to be greatest. People who do this pant and long for greatness. Rather, it means a heartfelt wishing better for others than for oneself, and serving others for the sake of their happiness with no thought of reward, simply out of love.

409   Actual heavenly joy as it is in and of itself is beyond description because it dwells in the deepest natures of angels. It flows from there into the details of their thought and affection and from these into the details of their speech and action. It is as though their deeper levels were wide open and freed to accept a delight and bliss that spreads out through all their fibers and therefore through their whole being, giving them a kind of perception and feeling that simply cannot be described. Anything that arises from the deepest levels flows into the details that derive from those deepest levels and proliferates toward the outer levels, constantly gaining strength.

When good spirits who have not yet experienced this pleasure (not having been raised into heaven yet) perceive it from the aura of love from some angel, they are filled with such pleasure that they find themselves in a kind of sweet faint. This often happens to people who want to know what heavenly joy is.

410   Some spirits wanted to know what heavenly joy was, so they were allowed to feel it to the point that they could not bear any more. Still, this was not angelic joy, but only the slightest trace of the angelic quality that they were allowed to observe and share. It was so slight that it was almost cool, yet they called it most heavenly because it was so deep within them. I could tell from this not only that there are levels of heavenly joy, but also that the deepest level of one individual barely touches the outmost or some median level of another. I could also see that when we do reach our own deepest level we are in our own heavenly joy and that we could not bear anything deeper because it would become painful for us.

Some spirits who were not evil settled down into a peaceful state, **411** rather like sleep, and in this way were taken into heaven in respect to the deeper levels of their minds; for before the deeper levels of their minds are opened, spirits can be taken into heaven and taught about the happiness of the people who live there. I saw them rest quietly for half an hour and then return to the outer consciousness they had been in before, but with a memory of what they had seen. They said that they had been with angels in heaven and had seen and perceived stunning things all gleaming like gold and silver and precious gems, in amazing forms that varied bewilderingly. They said that the angels took no particular delight in these outward things but in what they represented—unutterable, divine things of infinite wisdom; these were their real joy. There were countless other things that human language could not describe, not a ten-thousandth part, things that would not fit into any concepts that had anything material about them.

Almost all the people who arrive in the other life are ignorant of the **412** nature of heavenly bliss and happiness. This is because they do not know what inner joy is or what its quality is except on the basis of their grasp of physical and worldly good cheer and pleasure. Since they do not know about it they think it is not real, when in fact physical and earthly pleasures are nothing in comparison. So in order that they may know and recognize it, honest people who do not know what heavenly joy is are first taken to parks that surpass every image of their imagination. Just when they think that this is a heavenly paradise, they are told that this is not real heavenly happiness. So they are allowed to recognize deeper states of joy as these are perceptible to their deepest natures; and then they are transported into a state of peace that reaches their very inmost nature. They confess that no part of this can be expressed or even comprehended. Then they are taken into a state of innocence, again all the way to their own deepest feeling. In this way they are enabled to realize what real spiritual and heavenly goodness are.

To enable me to know what heaven and heavenly joy are and what **413** their quality is, though, the Lord has allowed me to feel the pleasures of heavenly joy often and at length. Because this was living experience, I may indeed know about them, but there is no way to describe them. Still, something should be said in order to provide at least some notion about them. There is an effect of countless pleasures and joys that unite to present a single something, a unity or united affection that contains a harmony of countless affections that do not come through to consciousness individually, only vaguely, because the consciousness is so very general. It was still possible to perceive that there were countless elements within it, so beautifully arranged as to defy description. The qualities of those countless elements flow from the very design of heaven; and this kind of design is resident in the very least affections, affections that are manifest and perceived only as a very general unity, depending on the perceptive ability of the subject. In a word, there are infinite elements in a most intricate form in every general entity, and there is nothing that is not alive and does not affect everything even at the very center, since heavenly joys emanate from the very center.

I have also noticed that heavenly joy and delight seemed to be coming from my heart, spreading very subtly through all my inner fibers and from there into the gatherings of fibers with such a profound sense of pleasure that my fibers seemed to be nothing but joy and delight, and everything I perceived and felt was alive with bliss. Next to these joys, the joy of physical pleasures is like crude and irritating dust compared to a pure and gentle breeze.

I noticed that when I wanted to convey all my pleasure to someone else, a deeper and fuller pleasure flowed in ceaselessly in its place. The more I wanted to convey it, the more it flowed in; and I perceived that this was from the Lord.

414   People in heaven are continually progressing toward the springtime of life. The more thousands of years they live, the more pleasant and happy is their springtime. This continues forever, increasing according to the growth and level of their love, thoughtfulness, and faith.

As the years pass, elderly women who have died of old age—women who have lived in faith in the Lord, thoughtfulness toward their neighbor, and in contented marriage love with their husbands—come more and more into the flower of growing youth and into a beauty that surpasses any notion of beauty accessible to our sight. Their goodness and thoughtfulness is what gives them their form and gives them its own likeness, making the pleasure and beauty of thoughtfulness radiate from every least corner of their faces so that they become actual forms of thoughtfulness. Some people have seen them and have been stunned. The form of thoughtfulness that is open to view in heaven is like this because it is thoughtfulness itself that both gives and is given visible form. In fact, it does this in such a way that the whole angel, especially her face, is virtually thoughtfulness itself appearing to open perception. When people look at this form, its beauty is unutterable, affecting the very inmost life of the mind with thoughtfulness. In a word, to grow old in heaven is to grow young. People who have lived in love for the Lord and in thoughtfulness toward their neighbor are forms like this, or beauties like this, in the other life. All angels are forms like this, in infinite variety. This is what makes heaven.

The Vastness of Heaven

THE vastness of the Lord's heaven follows from many of the things that have been presented above, especially from the fact that heaven is from the human race (see §§311–317), not only that portion of it born within the church but also the portion born outside it (§§318–328). This means that heaven includes everyone who has lived a good life since the very beginning of our planet. **415**

Anyone familiar with the continents and regions and nations of this world may gather what a multitude of people there are on our whole globe. Anyone who goes into the mathematics of it will discover that thousands and thousands of people die on any given day, making hundreds of thousands or millions every year; and this has been going on since the earliest times, thousands of years ago.[247] All of these people have arrived in the other world, called the spiritual world, after their decease, and they are still arriving.

I cannot say how many of these are or are becoming angels of heaven. I have been told that most of the earliest people became angels, because they thought more deeply and spiritually and were therefore enveloped in heavenly affection; while for later ages it was not so many because as time passed we became more externally minded and began to think more on the natural level, which meant that we were enveloped in more earthly affection.

This enables us to gather at the outset that heaven is huge simply from the inhabitants of this planet.

The immensity of the Lord's heaven may also be gathered simply from the fact that all children, whether born within or outside the church, are adopted by the Lord and become angels, and their number amounts to a quarter or a fifth of the whole human race. **416**

It may be seen above (§§329–345) that every child—wherever born, whether within the church or outside it, whether of devout or irreverent parents—is accepted by the Lord at death. Every child is raised in heaven, is taught and is permeated with affections for what is good according to the divine design and thereby with firsthand knowledge of things true, and is then perfected in intelligence and wisdom, so to speak, and admitted into heaven to become an angel. You can gather what a vast multitude of heaven's angels has come from this source alone from the beginning of creation to the present day.

417   The vastness of the Lord's heaven also follows from the fact that all the planets we can see in our solar system are earths, and especially that there are untold more in the universe, all inhabited, as discussed in a special booklet entitled *Other Planets,* from which I should like to cite the following.

[2] It is common knowledge in the other life that there are many planets with people on them and therefore angels and spirits from them, since anyone who wants to talk with spirits from other planets because of a love of the truth and a desire to be useful is allowed to do so to be convinced of the plurality of worlds, to learn that the human race is not just from one earth but from countless planets.

[3] I have talked about this on occasion with spirits from our earth, noting that intellectually gifted people could know, on the basis of much that is familiar to them, that there are many earths with people on them. That is, they could come to the rational conclusion that masses as big as the planets, some of which are larger than our earth, are not empty lumps created only to meander around the sun and radiate their feeble light for just one planet, but that their function must be more worthwhile than this.

People who believe (as they should) that the Divine created the universe for the sole purpose of the emergence of the human race and a heaven from it (for the human race is the seedbed of heaven) cannot help but believe that there are people wherever there is a planet.

It is abundantly clear that the planets visible to our eyes, the ones in our solar system, are earths, because they are material bodies, since they reflect the sun's light; and when we look at them through a telescope they do not look like ruddy, fiery stars but like earths with blurry bands of color. There is also the fact that they are borne around the sun, through the stations of the Zodiac, just like our earth, which must cause years and the seasons of the year called spring, summer, fall, and winter. Similarly, they rotate on their axes like our earth, which makes days and the times of day called morning, noon, evening, and night. Not only that, some of them have moons called satellites, which have their own periodic orbits around their sphere the way the moon orbits our earth. The planet Saturn, which is very far from the sun, has also a huge luminous belt that gives a great deal of light to that planet, even though it is reflected light. How could anyone who knows all this and thinks rationally say that these are empty bodies?

[4] Then too, I have talked with spirits about the fact that people could realize that there is more than one earth in the universe from the fact that the starry heaven is so immense. There are so incomprehensibly many stars in it, each one a sun in its own place and its own system, like our sun, of different magnitudes. If people think this through carefully, they will come to the conclusion that this whole vast universe cannot be anything but a means to an end, which is the goal of creation, a heavenly kingdom in which the Divine can dwell with angels and with us. The visible universe, the heaven spangled with so incomprehensibly many stars that are all suns, is in fact simply a means for the production of planets with people on them who can make up a heavenly kingdom.

Given all this, rational people cannot help thinking that such a vast means toward such an end did not come into being for the sake of a human race on one earth. What would that be for a divine being, an infinite being, for whom thousands or tens of thousands of planets, all fully inhabited, would be so slight as to be practically nothing?

There are spirits whose special passion is to learn at first hand, because this is the only kind of knowledge that gives them any pleasure. [5] These spirits are therefore allowed to travel around and even to leave this solar system and visit others, to gather firsthand knowledge there. They have told me that there are inhabited planets not only in our solar system but also outside it in the starry sky—a vast number of them. These spirits are from the planet Mercury.

[6] By a preliminary calculation, if there were a million planets in the universe with three hundred million people on each one, and two hundred generations over six thousand years, and if each person or spirit were allotted three cubic cubits, and if all these people or spirits were gathered into one place, they would not even fill the volume of our earth, hardly more than a satellite of one of the planets. This would be such a small space in the universe as to be barely visible, since we can scarcely see those satellites with the naked eye. What would this be for the Creator of the universe, for whom it would not be enough if the whole universe were filled? For the Creator is infinite.

I have talked about this with angels, who have told me that they have much the same idea about how small the number of the human race is in comparison to the infinity of the Creator. However, they do not think in terms of space but of states, and to their minds, no matter how many tens of thousands of planets you could conceive of, it would still be simply nothing to the Lord.[248]

[7] Information on the planets in the universe, their inhabitants, and the spirits and angels who come from them may be found in the booklet mentioned earlier.[249] What you will find there has been revealed and shown to me to let people know that the Lord's heaven is vast and that it is all from the human race, and also that our Lord is recognized everywhere as the God of heaven and earth.

418 We may also gather how vast the Lord's heaven is from the fact that heaven in a single complex resembles a single human being and also corresponds to everything within us. This relationship can never be completely filled in because there is a correspondence not only with the particular members and organs and viscera of the body but also, in most minute detail, with all the tiny organelles and viscera within them, even with the individual vessels and fibers—and not only with these, but with the organic substances that receive the inflow of heaven from within, the inflow that gives us the inner processes that support the workings of our spirits. In fact, everything that happens within us happens in the forms of our substance; anything that does not happen in substances as agents is nothing. There is a correspondence of all these substances with heaven, as you may gather from the chapter on the correspondence of everything in heaven with everything in the human being (§§87–102). This correspondence can never be completely filled in because the more assemblies of angels there are that answer to each member, the more complete heaven is. In the heavens, all forms of perfection increase as numbers increase. This is because there is one goal for everything there and a unanimous focus of everyone on that goal. That goal is the common good; and when this rules, there is benefit to individuals from the common good and from the good of individuals to the good of the whole. This happens because the Lord turns everyone in heaven toward himself (see above, §123) and in this way makes them one with himself.

Anyone with a little rational enlightenment can figure out that the unanimous harmony of many people, especially from such a source and with such intimacy, brings forth perfection.

419 I have been allowed to see the extent of the inhabited heaven and also the extent of the uninhabited heaven; and I have seen that the uninhabited heaven is so vast that it could never be filled to all eternity even if there were thousands of thousands of planets with as many people on each one as there are on ours. On this subject, see *Other Planets,* §168.

Because they take a few passages from the Word literally, some people think that heaven is not vast but small. For example, there are places where it says that only the poor will be accepted into heaven, or only the elect, or only people in the church and not people from outside, or only people for whom the Lord makes intercession, or that heaven will be closed when it is full, and that the time for this is foreordained.[250] These people do not realize that heaven will never be closed; that there is no foreordained time, no fixed number; and that "the elect" are people who live lives of goodness and truth;[a] that "the poor" are people who have not found out what is good and true but who long to (they are also called "the hungry" because of this longing).[b]

People who think that heaven is small because they have misunderstood the Word can only be thinking that heaven is in a single place where everyone is gathered together. Yet in fact heaven consists of countless communities. (See above, §§41–50.) Further, they can only be thinking that heaven is granted to individuals out of direct mercy and therefore consists simply of admission and acceptance out of good will. They do not realize that the Lord, out of his mercy, leads everyone who accepts him, and that the people who accept him are the people who live according to the laws of the divine design, which are precepts of love and faith. They do not realize that being led by the Lord from infancy to the end of earthly life and then on to eternity is what mercy really means. If only they knew that everyone is born for heaven, that people are accepted into heaven who accept heaven into themselves in this world, and that people who do not accept it are shut out!

420

a. The elect are people who lead lives of goodness and truth: 3755, 3900. There is no election and acceptance into heaven out of mercy as this is commonly understood, only in keeping with one's life: 5057, 5058. There is no direct mercy of the Lord, only an indirect mercy, that is, for people who live by his precepts, whom he, out of mercy, is constantly leading while they are in the world and afterward to eternity: 10659, 8700.

b. The poor in the Word means people who are spiritually poor, people who do not know what is true but still long to learn: 9209, 9253, 10227. When it says that they are hungry and thirsty, it is referring to their longing to encounter what is good and true and to be led in this way into the church and heaven: 4958, 10227.

THE WORLD OF SPIRITS
AND
OUR STATE AFTER DEATH

What the World of Spirits Is

THE world of spirits[251] is neither heaven nor hell but a place or state between the two. It is where we first arrive after death, being in due time either raised into heaven or cast into hell from it depending on our life in this world.

The world of spirits is a place halfway between heaven and hell, and it is also our own halfway state after death. I have been shown that it is a halfway place by seeing that the hells were underneath it and the heavens above it, and that it is a halfway state by learning that as long as we are in it, we are not yet in either heaven or hell.

A state of heaven for us is the union of what is good and true within us, and a state of hell is a union of what is evil and false within us. When the good in a spirit-person is united to the true, then that individual arrives in heaven, because as already stated that union is heaven within us. On the other hand, when the evil is united to the false within us, then we arrive in hell, because that union is hell within us. The process of union takes place in the world of spirits because then we are in a halfway state. It amounts to the same thing whether you say the union of intellect and will or the union of the true and the good.

First I need to say something about the union of intellect and will and its resemblance to the union of the good and the true, because this union does take place in the world of spirits.[252] Each of us has an intellect and a will, the intellect being open to truths and formed from them and the will being open to things that are good and formed from them. So whatever we understand and therefore think, we call true; and whatever we intend and therefore think, we call good. We are capable of thinking from our intellect and thus observing what is true and also what is good, but we still do not think from our will unless we intend and do it. When we intend it and do it intentionally, then it is in both our intellect and our will and therefore in us. This is because the intellect alone is not what makes a person, nor the will alone, but the intellect and the will together. This means that anything that is in both intellect and will is in us and is therefore attributed to us. Whatever is only in the intellect is associated with us but is not in us. It is only a matter of our memory, an item of information in our memory that we can think about when we are not in private but are with other people. So it is something we can talk and argue about and even something we can imitate with our affections and behavior.

424   Our ability to think from our intellect and not at the same time from our will is provided us so that we can be reformed, for we are reformed by means of truths; and truths, as already noted, are matters of intellect. We are actually born into total evil as far as our wills are concerned, wishing well to no one but ourselves; if we wish well to ourselves alone, we are delighted when harm comes to others, especially when it is to our advantage. We actually want to channel everyone else's assets to ourselves, whether those assets are high rank or wealth, and are happy to the extent that we succeed. To correct and reform this kind of intent, we are given the ability to understand things that are true and to use them to control the evil urges that well up from our will. This is why we can think true things from our intellect and talk about them and do them even though we cannot think them from our will until we have changed in nature so that on our own, that is, from the heart, we intend them and do them. When we have this nature, then the things we think from our intellect are matters of our faith and the things we think from our will are matters of our love. This means that faith and love are now united within us, just as intellect and will are.

425   To the extent that truths of the intellect are united to good things of the will, then, or to the extent that we intend and therefore do truths, we have heaven within us, because as already noted the union of the good and the true is heaven. However, to the extent that false elements of intellect are united to evil elements of will, we have hell within us, because the union of the false and the evil is hell. Still, to the extent that truths of intellect are not united to good elements of will, we are in the halfway state. Almost all of us nowadays are in a state in which we know things that are true and think about them on the basis of our information and also from our intellect. We act on either a lot of them or a few of them or none of them or act contrary to them because of our love of evil and consequent trust in what is false. So in order that we may gain either heaven or hell, after death we are first taken to the world of spirits, where either the union of the good and the true takes place for people who are to be raised into heaven, or the union of the evil and the false for people who are to be cast into hell. This is because no one in heaven or in hell is allowed to have a divided mind, to understand one thing and intend something else. What we intend we understand and what we understand we intend. Consequently, anyone in heaven who intends what is good understands what is true, and anyone in hell who intends what is evil understands what is false. So for good people, the false elements are taken away and they are given truths suited and fitted to their virtue, while for evil people truths are taken away and they are given false elements suited and fitted to their vice. This enables us to see what the world of spirits is.

There is a vast number of people in the world of spirits, because that is where everyone is first gathered, where everyone is examined and prepared. There is no fixed limit to our stay there. Some people barely enter it and are promptly either taken up into heaven or cast down into hell. Some stay there for a few weeks, some for a number of years, though not more than thirty. The variations in length of stay occur because of the correspondence or lack of correspondence between our deeper and our more outward natures.

426

In the following pages I will be explaining just how we are led from one state into another and prepared.

After we die, just as soon as we arrive in the world of spirits, we are carefully sorted out by the Lord. Evil people are immediately connected with the hellish community their ruling love had affiliated them with in the world, and good people are immediately connected with the heavenly community their love and thoughtfulness and faith had affiliated them with in the world.

427

Even though we are sorted out in this way, we are still together in that world and can talk to anyone when we want to, to friends and acquaintances from our physical life, especially husbands and wives, and also brothers and sisters. I have seen a father talking with his six sons and recognizing them. I have seen many other people with their relatives and friends. However, since they were of different character because of their life in the world, they parted company after a little while.

However, people who are coming into heaven from the world of spirits and people who are coming into hell do not see each other any more. They do not even recognize each other unless they are of like character because of a likeness in love. The reason they see each other in the world of spirits but not in heaven or hell is that while they are in the world of spirits they are brought into states like the ones they were in during their physical lives, one after another. After a while, though, they settle into a constant state that accords with their ruling love. In this state, mutual recognition comes only from similarity of love, for as we explained above (§§41–50), likeness unites and difference separates.

Just as the world of spirits is a state halfway between heaven and hell within us, it is a halfway place. The hells are underneath it and the heavens above it.

428

All the hells are closed on the side that faces that world, accessible only through holes and crevices like those in rocks and through broad gaps that are guarded to prevent anyone from coming out without permission, which happens in cases of real need, as will be discussed later.[253] Heaven too is bounded on all sides, and the only access to any heavenly community is by a narrow way whose entry is also guarded. These exits and entrances are what are called the doors and gates of hell and heaven in the Word.

429   The world of spirits looks like a valley surrounded by mountains and cliffs, with dips and rises here and there. The doors and gates to heavenly communities are visible only to people who are being readied for heaven. No one else finds them. There is one entrance to each community from the world of spirits with a single path beyond it; but as the path climbs, it divides into several.

The doors and gates to the hells are visible only to the people who are going to enter them. They open for them, and once they are opened you can see dark, sooty caves slanting downward into the depths, where there are still more gates. Rank, foul stenches breathe out from them, stenches that good spirits flee because they are repelled by them, while evil spirits are drawn toward them because they find them delightful. In fact, just as we find delight in our own evil in this world we find delight after death in the stench that corresponds to our evil. We might compare this with the delight of carrion birds and beasts like crows and wolves and pigs who fly or run toward rotting corpses as soon as they get wind of them. I heard one man who screamed aloud in utter torment at a breath of air from heaven, but was calm and happy when a breath from hell reached him.

430   There are two doors in each of us as well, one facing hell and open to evil and false things from hell, the other facing heaven and open to good and true things from heaven. The door of hell is opened for people who are involved in what is evil and its consequent falsity, though just a little light from heaven flows in through the cracks, which enables us to think, reason, and talk. On the other hand, the door of heaven is opened for people who are focused on what is good and therefore on what is true. There are actually two paths that lead to our rational mind, one from above or within, through which the good and the true enter from the Lord, and one from below or outside through which the evil and the false infiltrate from hell. The rational mind itself is at the intersection of these two paths, so to the extent that light from heaven is let in, we are rational; but to the extent that it is not let in, we are not rational even though we seem so to ourselves.

I have mentioned these things so that our correspondence with heaven and with hell may be known. While our rational mind is in the process of being formed, it is responsive to the world of spirits. What is above it belongs to heaven, and what is beneath it belongs to hell. The higher things open, and the lower close against the inflow of evil and falsity, for people who are being readied for heaven; while the lower things open, and the higher close against the inflow of goodness and truth, for people who are being readied for hell. As a result, these latter can only look downward, toward hell, and the former can only look upward, toward heaven. Looking upward is looking toward the Lord, because he is the common center that everything in heaven faces. Looking downward, though, is looking away from the Lord toward the opposite center, the center toward which everything in hell faces and gravitates (see above, §§123 and 124).

In the preceding pages, where it said "spirits," it meant people in the world of spirits; while "angels" meant people in heaven.   431

Each of Us Is Inwardly a Spirit

ANYONE who thinks things through carefully can see that it is not   432
the body that thinks, because the body is material. Rather, it is the soul, because the soul is spiritual. The human soul, whose immortality has been the topic of many authors, is our spirit; it is in fact immortal in all respects, and it is also what does the thinking in our bodies.[254] This is because it is spiritual and the spiritual is open to the spiritual and lives spiritually, through thought and intention. So all the rational life we can observe in our bodies belongs to the soul and none of it to the body. Actually, the body is material, as just noted, and the matter that is proper to the body is an addendum and almost an attachment to the spirit. Its purpose is to enable our spirit to lead its life and perform its services in a natural world that is material in all respects and essentially lifeless. Since matter is not alive—only spirit—we may conclude that whatever is alive in us is our spirit and that the body only serves it exactly the way a tool serves a live and activating force. We may of course say that a tool works or moves or strikes, but it is a mistake to believe that this is a property of the tool and not of the person who is wielding it.

433 Since everything that is alive in the body—everything that acts and feels because of life—belongs to the spirit alone and none of it belongs to the body, it follows that the spirit is the actual person. In other words, we are essentially spirits and have much the same form as well. You see, everything that is alive and sensitive within us belongs to our spirit, and there is nothing in us, from head to toe, that is not alive and sensitive. This is why when our bodies are separated from our spirits, which is called dying, we still continue to be human and to be alive.

I have heard from heaven that some people who die, while they are lying on the slab, before they have been revived, are still thinking in their cold bodies, and cannot help but feel that they are alive, but with the difference that they cannot move a single part of the matter that makes up their bodies.

434 We could not think or intend if there were no agent,[255] no substance as the source and focal point of thought and intent. Anything we may imagine happening apart from a substantial agent is nothing. We can tell this from the fact that we could not see without an organ serving as the agent of our sight or hear without an organ as the agent of our hearing. Apart from these, sight and hearing would be nothing, would not exist. The same holds true for thought, which is inner sight, and for attention, which is inner hearing. Unless these happened in and from agents that are organic forms, as subjects, they would not happen at all. We may gather from this that our spirit is also in a form and that it is in human form, that it enjoys sensory organs and senses when it is separated from the body just as it did when it was in it. We may gather that all of the eye's life, all of the ear's life, in fact all of our sensory life belongs not to the body but to the spirit that is in these functions and even in their least details. This is why spirits see and hear and feel just as much as we do, though after we have left the body this does not happen in the natural world but in the spiritual one. The reason the spirit was sensitive on the natural level when it was in the body is that it worked through the material part that was appended to it. However, it was still spiritually sensitive in its thinking and intending.

435 I have presented this to convince rational people that, seen in our own right, we are spirits, and that the physical nature appended to us so that we can function in the natural and material world is not the real person but only the tool of our spirit.

But some supporting instances from experience would be better, because rational arguments are beyond many people, and the ones who have convinced themselves of opposite opinions make these arguments grounds for their skepticism by arguing on the basis of sensory illusions.

People who have convinced themselves of an opposite opinion tend to think that animals live and sense just the way we do, so that they too have a spiritual nature like ours; yet this dies along with their bodies. However, the spiritual nature of animals is not the same as ours. We have an inmost nature that animals do not, a nature into which the Divine flows and which it raises toward itself, in this way uniting us to itself.[256] So we, unlike animals, can think about God and about divine matters of heaven and the church. We can love God because of these matters and by engaging with them; and can so be united to him; and anything that can be united to the Divine cannot be destroyed. Anything that cannot be united to the Divine, though, does disintegrate. In §39 above, I discussed this inmost that we have and animals do not. The reason for mentioning it again here is that it is important to dispel the illusions many people get from [believing that animals are just like humans], people who cannot draw rational conclusions about these subjects because they lack information or because their intellect is not open. What I said there was as follows:

> I should like to disclose a particular secret about the angels of the three heavens that people have not been aware of until now because they have not understood the levels discussed in §38. It is this, that within every angel—and within every one of us here—there is a central or highest level, or a central and highest something, where the Lord's divine life flows in first and most intimately. It is from this center that the Lord arranges the other, relatively internal aspects within us that follow in sequence according to the levels of the overall design. This central or highest level can be called the Lord's gateway to angels or to us, his essential dwelling within us.
>
> It is this central or highest level that makes us human and distinguishes us from the lower animals, since they do not have it. This is why we, unlike animals, can be raised up by the Lord toward himself, as far as all the deeper levels of our mind and character are concerned. This is why we can believe in him, be moved by love for him, and therefore see him. It is why we can receive intelligence and wisdom, and talk rationally. It is also why we live forever.
>
> However, what is arranged and provided by the Lord at this center does not flow into the open perception of any angel, because it is higher than angelic thought, and surpasses angelic wisdom.[257]

A great deal of experience has taught me that we are spirits inwardly, experience that would fill whole volumes, as they say, if I were to include

436

it all. I have talked with spirits as a spirit and I have talked with them as a person in a body. When I have talked with them as a spirit, they could not tell that I was not a spirit myself, in just as human a form as theirs. That is how my inner nature looked to them, because when I talked with them as a spirit, they could not see my material body.

437 We may gather that inwardly we are spirits from the fact that after we depart from our bodies, which happens when we die, we are still alive and just as human as ever. To convince me of this, [the Lord] has allowed me to talk with almost all the people I had ever met during their physical lives, with some for a few hours, with some for weeks and months, and with some for years. This was primarily so that I could be convinced and could bear witness.

438 I may add here that even while we are living in our bodies, each one of us is in a community with spirits as to our own spirits even though we are unaware of it. Good people are in angelic communities by means of [their spirits] and evil people are in hellish communities. Further, we come into those same communities when we die. People who are coming into the company of spirits after death are often told and shown this.

Actually, we are not visible as spirits in our [spiritual] communities while we are living in the world because we are thinking on the natural level. However, if our thinking is withdrawn from the body we are sometimes visible in our communities because we are then in the spirit. When we are visible, it is easy to tell us from the spirits who live there because we walk along deep in thought, silent, without looking at others, as though we did not see them; and the moment any spirit addresses us, we disappear.

439 To illustrate the fact that we are spirits inwardly, I should like to explain from experience what happens when we are *taken out of the body* and how we are *led by the spirit into another place*.

440 The first experience, being taken out of the body, is like this. We are brought into a particular state that is halfway between sleep and waking.[258] When we are in this state, it seems exactly as though we were awake; all our senses are as alert as they are when we are fully awake physically— sight, hearing, and strange to say, touch. These senses are more perfect than they can ever be during physical wakefulness. This is the state in which people have seen spirits and angels most vividly, even hearing them and, strange to say, touching them, with hardly anything physical interfering. It is the state described as *being taken out of the body* and *not knowing whether one is in the body or outside it*.

I have been admitted to this state three or four times, simply to let me know what it was like, and also to teach me that spirits and angels enjoy all the senses and that we do too, as to our spirits, when we are taken out of the body.[259]

As for the second kind of experience, being led by the spirit into an-other place, I have been shown by firsthand experience what happens and how it happens, but only two or three times.[260] I should like to cite just one experience. While I was walking through city streets and through the countryside, absorbed in conversation with spirits, it seemed exactly as though I were just as awake and observant as ever, walking without straying, though all the while I was in visions. I was seeing groves, rivers, mansions, houses, people, and more. After I had been walking for some hours, though, I suddenly found myself back in con-sciousness of my physical sight and realized that I was somewhere else. I was utterly stunned by this, and realized that I had been in the state of people described as *being led by the spirit into another place;* for as long as it lasted I was not thinking about my route, even though it might have been many miles, or about the time, though it might have been many hours or even days. I was not conscious of any fatigue, either. This is how we can be led by ways we know nothing of all the way to some predeter-mined place, without straying. 441

These two states, though, which are states we have when we are awake to our deeper nature or (which is the same thing) our spirit, are out of the ordinary. They were shown me simply to teach me what they were like be-cause they are known in the church. But talking with spirits, being with them as one of them—this is something I have been granted when I was fully awake physically, and it has been going on now for years. 442

There is further support of our being spirits inwardly in the material presented in §§311–317 above, where I discussed the fact that heaven and hell are from the human race. 443

Our being spirits inwardly has reference to our capacities for thinking and intending because these are our actual inner natures. They are what make us human, and the quality of our humanity depends on their quality. 444

Our Revival from the Dead and
Entry into Eternal Life

445 WHEN someone's body can no longer perform its functions in the natural world in response to the thoughts and affections of its spirit (which it derives from the spiritual world), then we say that the individual has died. This happens when the lungs' breathing and the heart's systolic motion have ceased.[261] The person, though, has not died at all. We are only separated from the physical nature that was useful to us in the world. The essential person is actually still alive. I say that the essential person is still alive because we are not people because of our bodies but because of our spirits. After all, it is the spirit within us that thinks, and thought and affection together make us the people we are.

We can see, then, that when we die we simply move from one world into another. This is why in the inner meaning of the Word, "death" means resurrection and a continuation of life.[a]

446 The deepest communication of our spirit is with our breathing and our heartbeat; thought connects with our breathing, and affection, an attribute of love, with our heart.[b] Consequently, when these two motions in the body cease, there is an immediate separation. It is these two motions, the respiratory motion of the lungs and the systolic motion of the heart, that are essential ties. Once they are severed, the spirit is left to itself; and the body, being now without the life of its spirit, cools and decays.

The reason the deepest communication of our spirit is with our breathing and our heart is that all our vital processes depend on these, not only in a general way, but in every specific.[c]

a. Death in the Word means resurrection because when we die, our life still goes on: 3498, 3505, 4618, 4621, 6036, 6222 *[6221]*.

b. The heart corresponds to our volition and therefore to affection of love as well, while the breathing of the lungs corresponds to our intellect and therefore to thought: 3888. In the Word, then, the heart means volition and love: 7542, 9050, 10336; and the soul means intellect, faith, and truth, so that "from the soul and from the heart" means what comes from intellect, faith, and truth, and what comes from intent, love, and good: 2930, 9050. On the correspondence of the heart and lungs [Latin *anima*, "soul," also means "breath"] with the universal human or heaven: 3883–3896.

c. The heartbeat and the breathing of the lungs are regulative throughout the body and flow in together everywhere: 3887, 3889, 3890.

After this separation, our spirit stays in the body briefly, but not after the complete stoppage of the heart, which varies depending on the cause of death. In some cases the motion of the heart continues for quite a while, and in others it does not. The moment it does stop, we are awakened, but this is done by the Lord alone. "Being awakened" means having our spirit led out of our body and into the spiritual world, which is commonly called "resurrection."

The reason our spirit is not separated from our body until the motion of the heart has stopped is that the heart answers to affection, an attribute of love, which is our essential life, since all of us derive our vital warmth from love.[d] Consequently, as long as this union lasts there is a responsiveness, and therefore the life of the spirit is [still] in the body.

447

I have not only been told how the awakening happens, I have been shown by firsthand experience. The actual experience happened to me so that I could have a full knowledge of how it occurs.[262]

448

I was brought into a state in which my physical senses were inoperative—very much, then, like the state of people who are dying. However, my deeper life and thought remained intact so that I could perceive and retain what was happening to me and what does happen to people who are being awakened from death. I noticed that my physical breathing was almost suspended, with a deeper breathing, a breathing of the spirit, continuing along with a very slight and silent physical one.

449

At first then a connection was established between my heartbeat and the heavenly kingdom, because that kingdom corresponds to the human heart.[e] I also saw angels from that kingdom, some at a distance, but two sitting close to my head. The effect was to take away all my own affection but to leave me in possession of thought and perception. [2] I remained in this state for several hours.

Then the spirits who were around me gradually drew away, thinking that I was dead. I sensed a sweet odor like that of an embalmed body, for when heavenly angels are present anything having to do with a corpse smells sweet. When spirits sense this, they cannot come near. This is also how evil spirits are kept away from our spirit when we are being admitted into eternal life.

---

d. Love is the very being of human life: 5002. Love is spiritual warmth and is therefore our own vital essence: 1589, 2146, 3338, 4906, 7081–7086, 9954, 10740. Affection is a corollary of love: 3938.
e. The heart corresponds to the Lord's heavenly kingdom and the lungs to his spiritual kingdom: 3635, 3886, 3887.

The angels who were sitting beside my head were silent, simply sharing their thoughts with mine (when these are accepted [by the deceased], the angels know that the person's spirit is ready to be led out of the body). They accomplished this sharing of thoughts by looking into my face. This is actually how thoughts are shared in heaven.

[3] Since I had been left in possession of thought and perception so that I could learn and remember how awakening happens, I noticed that at first the angels were checking to see whether my thoughts were like those of dying individuals, who are normally thinking about eternal life. They wanted to keep my mind in these thoughts. I was later told that as the body is breathing its last, our spirit is kept in its final thought until eventually it comes back to the thoughts that flowed from our basic or ruling affection in the world.

Especially, I was enabled to perceive and even to feel that there was a pull, a kind of drawing out of the deeper levels of my mind and therefore of my spirit from my body; and I was told that this was being done by the Lord and is what brings about our resurrection.

450 When heavenly angels are with people who have been awakened they do not leave them, because they love everyone. But some spirits are simply unable to be in the company of heavenly angels very long, and want them to leave. When this happens, angels from the Lord's spiritual kingdom arrive, through whom we are granted the use of light, since before this we could not see anything but could only think.

I was also shown how this is done. It seemed as though the angels rolled back a covering from my left eye toward the center[263] of my nose so that my eye was opened and able to see. To the spirit, it seems as though this were actually happening, but it is only apparently so. As this covering seemed to be rolled back, I could see a kind of clear but dim light like the light we see through our eyelids when we are first waking up. It seemed to me as though this clear, dim light had a heavenly color to it, but I was later told that this varies. After that, it felt as though something were being rolled gently off my face, and once this was done I had access to spiritual thought. This rolling something off the face is an appearance, for it represents the fact that we are moving from natural thinking to spiritual thinking. Angels take the greatest care to shield the awakening person from any concept that does not taste of love. Then they tell the individual that he or she is a spirit.

After the spiritual angels have given us the use of light, they do everything for us as newly arrived spirits that we could ever wish in that state. They tell us—at least to the extent that we can grasp it—about the realities of the other life. However, if our nature is such that we do not want to be taught, then once we are awakened we want to get out of the company of angels. Still, the angels do not leave us, but we do leave them. Angels really do love everyone. They want nothing more than to help people, to teach them, to lead them into heaven. This is their highest joy.

When spirits leave the company of angels, they are welcomed by the good spirits who are accompanying them and who also do all they can for them. However, if they had led the kind of life in the world that makes it impossible for them to be in the company of good people, then they want to get away from these as well. This happens as long and as many times as necessary, until they find the company of people their earthly life has fitted them for. Here they find their life; and remarkable as it may sound, they then lead the same kind of life they had led in the world.

This first stage of our life after death does not last more than a few days, though. In the following pages I will be describing how we are then brought from one state into another until finally we arrive either in heaven or in hell. This too is something I have been allowed to learn from a great deal of experience. **451**

I have talked with some people on the third day after their death, when the events described in §§449 and 450 have been completed. I talked with three whom I had known in the world and told them that their funeral services were now being planned so that their bodies could be buried. When they heard me say it was so that *they* could be buried, they were struck with a kind of bewilderment. They said that they were alive, and that people were burying what had been useful to them in the world. Later on, they were utterly amazed at the fact that while they had been living in their bodies they had not believed in this kind of life after death, and particularly that this was the case for almost everyone in the church. **452**

Some people during their earthly lives have not believed in any life of the soul after the life of the body. When they discover that they are alive, they are profoundly embarrassed. However, people who have convinced themselves of this join up with others of like mind and move away from people who had lived in faith. Most of them link up with some hellish community because such people reject the Divine and have no use for the truths of the church. In fact, to the extent that we convince ourselves in our opposition to the ideal of the eternal life of the soul, we also convince ourselves in opposition to the realities of heaven and the church.

After Death, We Are in a Complete Human Form

453 THE fact that the form[264] of a spirit-person is the human form or that a spirit is a person as far as form is concerned follows from what has been presented in a number of the earlier chapters, especially where I explained that every angel is in a perfect human form (§§73–77), that everyone is a spirit inwardly (§§432–444), and that the angels in heaven are from the human race (§§311–317).

[2] This may be grasped even more clearly from the fact that we are human because of our spirit, not because of our body, and because our physical form is appended to the spirit in keeping with its form, not the other way around, since a spirit is clothed with a body that suits its form. As a result, the human spirit acts upon the individual parts of the body, even the smallest ones, even to the point that any part that is not activated by the spirit, any part in which there is no spirit acting, is not alive. Anyone may realize this by considering that thought and intent activate absolutely everything in the body and are so completely in control that nothing dissents, and that if anything does not consent it is not part of the body. It is actually expelled as something with no life in it. Thought and intent are attributes of our spirit, not of the body.

[3] The reason we cannot see the human form of spirits who have left the body and spirits still within the people we meet is that our physical organ of sight, the eye, is material to the extent that it can see in this world, and what is material sees only what is material. What is spiritual, though, does see what is spiritual; so when the material eye is covered over and loses its coordination with the spirit, then spirit is visible in its own form. This is a human form not only for spirits who are in the spiritual world but also for spirits in people we meet while they are still in their bodies.

454 The reason the form of a spirit is a human one is that in regard to our spirits we have been created in the form of heaven, since all the elements of heaven and its design are summed up in the elements of the human mind.[a]

a. In us all the elements of the divine design are gathered together, and by virtue of creation we are the divine design in form: 4219, 4220, 4223, 4523, 4524, 5114, 5368, 6013, 6057, 6605, 6626, 9706, 10156, 10472. To the extent that we live according to the divine design, in the other life we look like complete and lovely people: 4839, 6605, 6626.

This is the source of our ability to accept intelligence and wisdom. It makes no difference whether you talk about our ability to accept intelligence and wisdom or our ability to accept heaven, as you may gather from what has been presented concerning heaven's light and warmth (§§126–140), heaven's form (§§200–212), angels' wisdom (§§265–275), and from the chapter titled "The Whole Heaven, Grasped as a Single Entity, Reflects a Single Individual" (§§59–77). This is caused by the Lord's divine human nature, which is the source of heaven and its form (§§78–86).

Rational individuals can understand what has been said so far because they can see this from the chain of causes and from truths in their pattern. However, people who are not rational do not understand these things. There are several reasons why they do not understand. The primary one is that they do not want to understand because these things contradict the false opinions that they have made their truths. People who do not want to understand for this reason close off the path of heaven into their rational ability. Even so, it can still be opened if only their will does not offer resistance (see above, §424). A great deal of experience has shown me that people can understand what is true and be rational if only they are willing. Quite often, evil spirits who have become irrational by denying the Divine and the truths of the church in this world (and convincing themselves in their denial) have by divine compulsion been faced toward people who were in the light of truth. Then they understood everything like angels and admitted that they were true and that they understood everything. However, the moment they turned back toward the love proper to their own intentions, they did not understand anything and said just the opposite. [2] I have even heard some hellish people saying that they knew and recognized that what they were doing was evil and what they were thinking was false, but that they could not resist the gratification of their love and therefore of their will. This moved their thoughts to see evil as good and falsity as true. I could see from this that people who are immersed in false notions because of their malice could understand and could therefore be rational, but that they did not want to. The reason they did not want to was that they loved false notions more than true ones because the former supported the evil pursuits they were engaged in. Loving and intending are the same thing because we love what we intend and intend what we love.

[3] Since we are by nature able to understand what is true if we are willing to, I have been granted the privilege of supporting spiritual truths, truths of the church and heaven, by rational considerations. This is to the end that the false notions that have obscured the rational functioning of

455

many people may be dispelled by rational considerations and their eyes perhaps opened a little. If people are focused on truths, it is granted them to support spiritual truths by rational ones. Who would possibly understand the Word simply from its literal meaning unless they saw some truths in it by enlightened reason? What else is the cause of the many heresies drawn from the same Word?[b]

456   Years and years of daily experience have witnessed to me that after separation from the body the human spirit is a person and is in a similar form. I have seen this thousands of times, I have heard such spirits, and I have talked with them even about the fact that people in the world do not believe that they are what they are, and that scholars think people who do believe are simpletons. Spirits are heartsick over the fact that this kind of ignorance is still common in the world and especially in the church. [2] They say, however, that this belief stems especially from academics who have thought about the soul on the basis of physical sensory reality. The only concept this can yield is one of pure thought, and when this lacks any medium in which and on the basis of which it is examined, it is like some volatile form of pure ether that can only dissipate when the body dies. Since the church believes in the immortality of the soul on the basis of the Word, though, they cannot help but attribute something vital to it, something thoughtlike. However, they do not attribute to it any sensory capacity like ours until it is reunited with its body. Their doctrine of the resurrection is based on this notion, as is their belief that there will be a reunion [of soul and body] when the Last Judgment comes. The result is that when people think about the soul on the basis of both doctrine and speculation, they do not at all grasp the fact that it is the spirit and that it is in human form. There is also the fact that hardly anyone nowadays knows what the spiritual is, let alone that people who are spiritual, as all spirits and angels are, have a human form.

[3] This is why almost all the people who arrive from this world are as astonished as they can be to find that they are alive and that they are just as

---

b. A starting point should be derived from the truths of church doctrine drawn from the Word, and these should be acknowledged first; then it is all right to take factual knowledge into account: 6047. So if people have an affirmative attitude toward truths of faith, it is all right for them to support them rationally with factual knowledge; but this is not appropriate for people who have a negative attitude: 2568, 2588, 4760, 6047. It is in accord with the divine design to work rationally from spiritual truths into factual knowledge, natural truths, but not from the latter into the former, because there is an inflow of spiritual things into natural ones but not from natural or physical things into spiritual ones: 3219, 5119, 5259, 5427, 5428, 5478, 6322, 9110, 9111.

human as ever, that they are seeing and hearing and talking, that their bodies are still endowed with the sense of touch, and that nothing at all has changed (see §74 above). Once they get over their amazement, though, then they are amazed that the church does not know anything about this state of ours after death and therefore does not know anything about heaven or hell, even though all the people who have lived in this world are in the other life and are living people. Since they do keep wondering why this has not been made plain to people on earth through visions, inasmuch as it is essential to the faith of the church, they have been told from heaven that such visions could happen whenever it pleased the Lord—nothing could be easier. However, people would not believe even if they were to see, because they have convinced themselves of the opposing false notions. Further, it is dangerous to use visions to convince people of anything if they are immersed in false opinions, because they will believe at first and then deny. In this way they will desecrate the truth itself, since desecration is believing and then denying. People who desecrate truths are forced down into the lowest and direst hell of all.c

[4] This is the danger meant by the Lord's words, "He has blinded their eyes and hardened their hearts lest they see with their eyes and understand with their heart and turn themselves and I might heal them" (John 12:40); and the fact that people immersed in false opinions still would not believe is meant when it says, "Abraham said to the rich man in hell, They have Moses and the prophets, let them heed them. But he said, No, Father Abraham, but if someone from the dead were to come to them, they would change. But Abraham said, If they do not heed Moses and the prophets, then even if someone were raised from the dead, they would not believe" (Luke 16:29–31).

---

c. Desecration is the mingling of the good and the evil and of the true and the false within us: 6348. The only people who can desecrate what is true and good, or the holy things of the Word and the church, are people who have first acknowledged them, all the more if they have lived by them, and later fall away from their faith, deny them, and live for themselves and the world: 593, 1008, 1010, 1059, 3398, 3399, 3898, 4289, 4601, 10284, 10287. If we fall back into prior evils after heartfelt repentance, we commit desecration; and then our later state is worse than our former one: 8394. People cannot desecrate holy things if they have not acknowledged them, and still less if they have not even known about them: 1008, 1010, 1059, 9188, 10284. Non-Christians who are outside the church and do not have the Word are incapable of desecration: 1327, 1328, 2051, 2081. This is why deeper truths were not disclosed to the Jews, because if they had been disclosed and acknowledged, they would have desecrated them: 3398, 3489 [3479], 6963. The fate of desecrators in the other life is the worst of all because the good and truth they acknowledged is still there and so is what is evil and false; and since these coexist, there is a wrenching of their very life: 571, 582, 6348. So the Lord takes the greatest care to prevent desecration: 2426, 10384.

457   When we first enter the world of spirits (which happens shortly after the reawakening just described), our spirit has a similar face and tone of voice as it did in the world. This is because at that point we are in the state of our external concerns, with our deeper concerns not yet uncovered. This is our initial state after decease. Later, though, our face changes and becomes quite different. It comes to look like the ruling affection in which the deeper reaches of our minds were engaged in the world, the kind of affection characteristic of the spirit within our body, because the face of our spirit is very different from the face of our body. We get our physical face from our parents and our spiritual face from our affection, which it images. Our spirit takes on this face after our physical life is over, when the outer coverings have been removed. This is our third state.[265]

I have seen some newcomers from the world and have recognized them by their faces and voices; but when I saw them later, I did not recognize them. People who were engaged in good affections had lovely faces, while people who were engaged in evil affections had ugly ones. Seen in its own right, our spirit is nothing but our affections, whose outward form is our face.

The reason our faces change is that in the other life no one is allowed to pretend to affections they do not really have, so we cannot put on a face that is contrary to the love we are engaged in. We are all refined down to a state in which we say what we think and manifest in expression and act what we intend. This is why our faces all become forms and images of our affections; and this is why all the people who have known each other in the world still recognize each other in the world of spirits, but not in heaven or hell, as already noted (§427).[d]

458   The faces of hypocrites change more slowly than those of other people, because by constant practice they have formed the habit of arranging their inner minds into a counterfeit of good affections. So for a long time they look fairly attractive. However, since this false front is gradually

---

d. Our faces are formed to be responsive to our inner natures: 4791–4805, 5695. On the correspondence of our faces and their expressions with the affections of our minds: 1568, 2988, 2989, 3631, 4796, 4797, 4800, 5165, 5168, 5695, 9306. For heaven's angels, the face forms a single whole with the deeper levels of the mind: 4796, 4797, 4798, 4799, 5695, 8250. So in the Word, "the face" means the deeper levels of the mind, or of affection and thought: 1999, 2434, 3527, 4066, 4796, 5102, 9306, 9546. How the inflow from the brains into the face changed in the course of time, and with it the face itself in regard to its responsiveness to our deeper natures: 4326, 8250.

stripped off and the deeper elements of their minds are arranged in the form of their affections, eventually they are uglier than other people.

Hypocrites are people who talk like angels but who inwardly respect only nature, not the Divine Being, and who therefore deny the realities of the church and of heaven.

It does need to be known that our human form is lovelier after death to the extent that we have more deeply loved divine truths and have lived by them, since our deeper levels are opened and formed according to both our love of these truths and our life. So the deeper the affection and the more it accords with heaven, the lovelier the face. This is why the angels who are in the inmost heaven are the loveliest—because they are forms of heavenly love. On the other hand, people who have loved divine truths more outwardly and have therefore lived by them more outwardly are less lovely, since only the more outward aspects radiate from their faces, and the deeper heavenly love—which means the form of heaven as it is in its own right—does not shine through these more outward forms. You can see something relatively dim in their faces, not enlivened by a light of their inner life shining through. In short, all perfection increases as you move inward and lessens as you move outward. As the perfection increases or lessens, so does the beauty. **459**

I have seen faces of angels of the third heaven so beautiful that no painters, with all their skill, could render a fraction of their light with their pigments or rival a thousandth part of the light and life that show in their faces. The faces of angels of the outmost heaven, though, can be mirrored to some extent.

Finally, I should like to offer a secret no one has ever known before, namely that everything good and true that comes from the Lord and makes heaven is in the human form. This is true not only of the greatest whole but also of every least part. This form influences everyone who accepts what is good and true from the Lord, and causes everyone in heaven to be in a human form according to that acceptance. This is why heaven is consistent with itself in general and in particular, why the human form is the form of the whole, of each community, and of each angel, as explained in the four chapters from §59 to §80. I need to add here that this is also the form of the details of thought that come from heavenly love in angels. **460**

This secret may not fit well into the understanding of anyone on earth, but it is clear to the understanding of angels because they are in heaven's light.

After Death, We Enjoy Every Sense, Memory, Thought, and Affection We Had in the World: We Leave Nothing Behind except Our Earthly Body

461 REPEATED experience has witnessed to me that when we move from the natural world into the spiritual, which happens when we die, we take with us everything that pertains to our character except our earthly body. In fact, when we enter the spiritual world or our life after death, we are in a body as we were in this world. There seems to be no difference, since we do not feel or see any difference. This body is spiritual, though, so it has been separated or purified from earthly matter. Further, when anything spiritual touches and sees something spiritual, it is just like something natural touching and seeing something natural. So when we have become a spirit, we have no sense that we are not in the body we inhabited in the world, and therefore do not realize that we have died.

[2] As "spirit-people," we enjoy every outer and inner sense we enjoyed in the world. We see the way we used to, we hear and talk the way we used to; we smell and taste and feel things when we touch them the way we used to; we want, wish, crave, think, ponder, are moved, love, and intend the way we used to. Studious types still read and write as before. In a word, when we move from the one life into the other, or from the one world into the other, it is like moving from one [physical] place to another; and we take with us everything we owned as persons to the point that it would be unfair to say that we have lost anything of our own after death, which is only a death of the earthly body. [3] We even take with us our natural memory, since we retain everything we have heard, seen, read, learned, or thought in the world from earliest infancy to the very end of life. However, since the natural objects that reside in our memory cannot be reproduced in a spiritual world, they become dormant the way they do when we are not thinking about them. Even so, they can be reproduced when it so pleases the Lord. I will have more to say soon, though, about this memory and its condition after death.[266]

Sense-centered people are quite incapable of believing that our state after death is like this because they do not grasp it. Sense-centered people can think only on the natural level, even about spiritual matters. This means that anything they do not sense—that is, see with their physical eyes and touch with their hands—they say does not exist, as we read of Thomas in John 20:25, 27, 29. The quality of sense-centered people has been described above in §267, and in note c there.

Nevertheless, the difference between our life in the spiritual world and our life in the natural world is considerable, in regard both to our outer senses and the way they affect us and to our inner senses and the way they affect us. People who are in heaven have far more delicate senses. That is, they see and hear and also think more discerningly than when they were in this world. This is because they are seeing in heaven's light, which vastly surpasses the world's light (see above, §126), and they hear by way of a spiritual atmosphere that vastly surpasses the atmosphere of the earth (see §235). The difference in their outer senses is like that between something clear and something hidden by a cloud, or like noonday light and the dimness of evening. Because it is divine truth, heaven's light enables angels' sight to notice and differentiate the slightest things. [2] Further, their outer sight is responsive to their inner sight or discernment, since for angels the one sight flows into the other and they act as a single faculty. This is why they are so keen. Their hearing is similarly responsive to their perception, which is a function of both discernment and volition. So they pick up in the tone and words of speakers the slightest shadings of their affection and thought—shadings of affection in the tone, and shadings of thought in the words (see above, §§234–245).

462a ²⁶⁷

However, the other senses are not as delicate for angels as their senses of sight and hearing, because sight and hearing serve their intelligence and wisdom, while the others do not. If the other senses were as sensitive, they would take away the light and pleasure of angels' wisdom and interject a pleasure of motivations centering in various physical appetites, appetites that obscure and weaken the intellect to the extent that they flourish. This happens to people in the world as well, who become dull and mindless in regard to spiritual truths to the extent that they pander to their taste and to the sensual allurements of the body.

[3] What was presented in the chapter on the wisdom of heaven's angels (§§265–275) may suffice to indicate that the deeper senses of heaven's angels, the senses of their thought and affection, are more delicate and perfect than the ones they had in the world.

As for the difference in state of people who are in hell from their state in the world, this too is substantial. The perfection and wonder of the outer and inner senses of angels in heaven is paralleled by their imperfection for people in hell. However, we need to deal with their state later.²⁶⁸

462b   As for our keeping our whole memory when we leave the world, I have been shown this by many examples and have seen and heard a great deal worth talking about. I should like to cite a few examples in a sequence. There have been people who denied the crimes and transgressions they had committed in the world. To prevent them from believing they were blameless, everything was disclosed and drawn out of their own memory in sequence from the beginning of their life to the end. Most of these transgressions were acts of adultery and promiscuity.

[2] There were people who had deceived others with malicious skill and had stolen from them. Their deceptions and thefts were also recounted one after the other, many of them known to practically no one in the world other than themselves. They even admitted them because they were made plain as day, along with every thought, intention, pleasure, and fear that mingled in their minds at the time.

[3] There were people who had taken bribes and made money from judicial decisions. They were similarly examined from their own memories, and everything was recounted from their first taking office to the end. The details of amount and value, of the time, and of their state of mind and intention, all consigned to their remembrance together, were brought to view, a hundred or more instances. In some cases, remarkably enough, the very diaries in which they had recorded these deeds were opened and read to them, page by page.

[4] There were men who had lured virgins to dishonor and violated their chastity. They were summoned to a similar judgment, and the details were drawn out of their memory and listed. The actual faces of the virgins and other women were presented as though they were there in person, along with the places, the words, and the thoughts. It was done as instantaneously as when something is actually being witnessed firsthand. Sometimes these presentations lasted for hours.

[5] There was one man who thought nothing of slandering others. I heard his slanders recounted in sequence as well as his blasphemies, along with the actual words, the people they were about, and the people they were addressed to. All these were presented together as lifelike as could be even though he had very carefully kept them hidden from his victims while he was living in the world.

[6] There was one man who had defrauded a relative of his legacy by some devious pretext. He was exposed and judged in the same way. Remarkably, the letters and documents they exchanged were read aloud

to me, and he said that not a word was missing. [7] This same man had also secretly killed a neighbor by poison just before his own death, which was disclosed in the following way. A trench seemed to open under his feet, and as it was opened, a man came out as though from a tomb and screamed at him, "What have you done to me?" Then everything was disclosed—how the poisoner had talked amicably with him and offered him a drink, what he had thought beforehand, and what happened afterward. Once this was uncovered, the murderer was condemned to hell.

[8] In a word, all their evils, crimes, thefts, wiles, and deceptions are made clear to every evil spirit. They are drawn from their own memories and exposed. There is no room for denial because all the circumstances are presented together.

I also heard that angels have seen and displayed from the memory of one individual everything he had thought one day after another over the course of a month, with never an error, recalled as though he himself were back in those very days.

[9] We may gather from these instances that we take our whole memory with us, and that nothing is so concealed in this world that it will not be made known after death, made known in public, according to the Lord's words, "Nothing is hidden that will not be uncovered, and nothing concealed that will not be known. So what you have said in darkness will be heard in the light, and what you have spoken in the ear will be proclaimed from the rooftops" (Luke 12:2–3).

When we are being faced with our deeds after death, angels who have been given the task of examining look searchingly into the face and continue their examination through the whole body, beginning with the fingers first of one hand and then of the other and continuing through the whole. When I wondered why this was so, it was explained to me. The reason is that just as the details of our thought and intention are inscribed on our brains because that is where their beginnings are, so they are inscribed on the whole body as well, since all the elements of our thought and intention move out into the body from their beginnings and take definition there in their outmost forms. This is why the things that are inscribed on our memory from our intention and consequent thought are inscribed not only on the brain but also on the whole person, where they take form in a pattern that follows the pattern of the parts of the body. I could therefore see that our overall nature depends on the nature of our intention and consequent thought,

463

so that evil people are their own evil and good people are their own good.ª

We may also gather from this what is meant by our book of life, mentioned in the Word.[269] It is the fact that all our deeds and all our thoughts are written on our whole person and seem as though they are read from a book when they are called out of our memory. They appear in a kind of image when our spirit is looked at in heaven's light.

I should like to add to this something noteworthy about the memory that we keep after death, something that convinced me that not just the general contents but even the smallest details that have entered our memory do last and are never erased. I saw some books with writing in them like earthly writing, and was told that they had come from the memories of the people who had written them, that not a single word was missing that had been in the book they had written in the world. I was also told that all the least details could be retrieved from the memory of someone else, even things the person had forgotten in the world. The reason for this was explained as well; namely, that we have an outer and an inner memory, the outer proper to our natural person and the inner proper to our spiritual person. The details of what we have thought, intended, said, and done, even what we have heard and seen, are inscribed on our inner or spiritual memory.ᵇ There is no way to erase anything there, since everything is written at once on our spirit itself and on the members of our body, as noted above. This means that our spirit is formed in accord

a. Good people, spirits, and angels are their own good and their own truth: that is, the nature of the whole person depends on the nature of that good and truth: 10298, 10367. This is because the good constitutes our volition and the true constitutes our intellect, and volition and intellect constitute the entire life for a person here, for a spirit, and for an angel: 3332, 3623, 6065. This is the same as saying that people here, spirits, and angels are their love: 6872, 10177, 10284.

b. We have two memories, an outer and an inner, or a natural one and a spiritual one: 2469–2494. We are not aware that we have this inner memory: 2470, 2471. How much better the inner memory is than the outer one: 2473. The contents of our outer memory are in the world's light, while the contents of our inner memory are in heaven's light: 5212. It is because of our inner memory that we can think and talk intelligently and rationally: 9394. Absolutely everything we have thought, said, done, seen, and heard is inscribed on our inner memory: 2474, 7398. That memory is our book of life: 2474, 9386, 9841, 10505. In our inner memory are the true things that have become matters of our faith and the good things that have become matters of our love: 5212, 8067. Things that have become second nature to us and part of our life and therefore have been erased from our outer memory are in our inner memory: 9394, 9723, 9841. Spirits and angels talk from their inner memory, which is why they have a universal language: 2472, 2476, 2490, 2493. Languages in the world are matters of the outer memory: 2472, 2476.

with what we have thought and what we have done intentionally. I know these things seem paradoxical and hard to believe, but they are true nevertheless.

Let no one believe, then, that there is anything we have thought or done in secret that will remain hidden after death. Believe rather that absolutely everything will come out into broad daylight.

While our outer or natural memory is still part of us after death, still the merely natural things that are in it are not recreated in the other life, only spiritual things that are connected to the natural ones by correspondence. Still, when they are presented visually, they look just the same as they did in the natural world. This is because everything we see in the heavens looks as it did in the world, even though in essence it is not natural but spiritual, as has been explained in the chapter on representations and appearances in heaven (§§170–176).

[2] As for our outer or natural memory, though, to the extent that its contents are derived from matter, time, space, and everything else proper to nature, it does not fulfill the same function for the spirit that it fulfilled in the world. This is because in the world, when we thought on the basis of our outer sensitivity and not at the same time on the basis of our inner or intellectual sensitivity, we were thinking on the natural level and not on the spiritual one. However, in the other life, when our spirit is in the spiritual world, we do not think on the natural level but on the spiritual one. Thinking on the spiritual level is thinking intelligently or rationally. This is why our outer or natural memory then goes dormant as far as material things are concerned. The only things that come into play are what we have gained in the world through those material things and have made rational. The reason our outer memory goes dormant as far as material things are concerned is that they cannot be recreated. Spirits and angels actually talk from the affections and consequent thoughts of their minds, so they cannot utter anything that does not square with these, as you may gather from what was said about the language of angels in heaven and their communication with us (§§234–257). [3] This is why we are rational after death to the extent that we have become rational by means of languages and the arts and sciences in this world, and emphatically not to the extent that we have become skilled in them.

I have talked with any number of people who were regarded as learned in the world because of their knowledge of such ancient languages as Hebrew and Greek and Latin, but who had not developed their rational functioning by means of the things that were written in those

464

languages. Some of them seemed as simple as people who did not know anything about those languages; some of them seemed dense, though there still remained a pride, as though they were wiser than other people.

[4] I have talked with some people who had believed in the world that wisdom depends on how much we have in our memory and who had therefore filled their memories to bursting. They talked almost exclusively from these items, which meant that they were not talking for themselves but for others; and they had not developed any rational function by means of these matters of memory. Some of them were dense, some silly, with no grasp of truth whatever, no sense of whether anything was true or not. They seized on every false notion sold as true by people who called themselves scholars. They were actually incapable of seeing anything as it actually was, whether it was true or not, so they could not see anything rationally when they listened to others.

[5] I have talked with some people who had written a great deal in the world, some of them in all kinds of academic fields, people who had therefore gained an international reputation for learning. Some of them could quibble about whether truths were true or not. Some of them understood what was true when they turned toward people who were in the light of truth; but since they still did not want to understand what was true, they denied it when they focused on their own false opinions and were therefore really being themselves. Some of them did not know any more than the illiterate masses. So they varied depending on the way they had developed their rational ability through the treatises they had written or copied. Still, if people had opposed the truths of the church, had based their thinking on the arts and sciences, and had used them to convince themselves of false principles, they had not developed their rational ability but only their skill in argumentation—an ability that is confused with rationality in the world, but is in fact a different ability from rationality. It is an ability to prove anything one pleases, to see false things rather than true ones on the basis of preconceptions and illusions. There is no way people like this can be brought to recognize truths because it is impossible to see truths from false principles, though it is possible from true principles to see what is false.

[6] Our rational faculty is like a garden or flower bed, like newly tilled land. Our memory is the soil, information and experiential learning are the seeds, while heaven's light and warmth make them productive. There is no germination without these latter. So there is no germination in us unless heaven's light, which is divine truth, and

heaven's warmth, which is divine love, are let in. They are the only source of rationality.

Angels are profoundly grieved that scholars for the most part keep attributing everything to nature and therefore close the deeper levels of their minds so that they can see no trace of truth from the light of truth, the light of heaven. As a result, in the other life they are deprived of their ability to reason so that they will not use reason to spread false notions among simple people and mislead them. They are dismissed to desert areas.

One particular spirit resented the fact that he could not remember much of what he had known during his physical life. He was grieving over the pleasure he had lost because it had been his chief delight. He was told, though, that he had not lost anything at all and that he knew absolutely everything. In the world where he was now living he was not allowed to retrieve things like that. It should satisfy him that he could now think and talk much better and more perfectly without immersing his rational functioning in dense clouds, in material and physical concerns, the way he had before, in concerns that were useless in the kingdom he had now reached. Now he had whatever he needed for his functioning in eternal life, and there was no other way he could become blessed and happy. So it was the counsel of ignorance to believe that the removal and dormancy of material concerns in the memory led to the disappearance of intelligence,[270] when in fact the more the mind can be led out of the sensory concerns that are proper to the outer person or the body, the more it is raised up to spiritual and heavenly concerns.

In the other life, people are sometimes shown what memories are like by having them presented visually in forms that are merely appearances (many things are presented visually there that for us here are strictly conceptual). The outer memory there looks like a callus, while the inner looks like the medullary substance found in the human brain. This also enables us to recognize their quality.

For people who have focused solely on memorization during their physical lives, without developing their rational ability, their memory has a callused quality that looks hard and streaked with tendons inside. For people who have filled their memories with false notions it looks shaggy because of the random mass of disorganized stuff. For people who have focused on memorization with themselves and the world first in mind, it looks stuck together and bony. For people who have tried to probe divine secrets through acquired information, especially philosophical information, without believing anything before they are convinced by the information, their memory looks dark, with a quality that actually absorbs rays of light and turns them into darkness. For people who have been guileful and hypocrites it looks bony and hard as ebony that reflects light rays.

However, for people who have focused on the good of love and truths of faith, no such callus is visible. This is because their inner memory is transmitting rays of light into their outer memory, and those rays find definition in its objects or concepts as though it were their foundation or their soil, and find congenial vessels there. This is because the outer memory is the outmost element of the design, where spiritual and heavenly matters come gently to rest and dwell when there are good and true contents in it.

467 While we are living in the world, if we are engaged in a love for the Lord and in thoughtfulness toward our neighbor, we have with and within us an angelic intelligence and wisdom, but it is hidden away in the depths of our inner memory. There is no way this intelligence and wisdom can become visible before we leave our bodies. Then our natural memory is put to sleep and we are awakened into consciousness of our inner memory and eventually of our actual angelic memory.

468 I do need to explain briefly how our rational ability is developed. A genuine rational ability is made up of true elements and not of false ones. Anything made up of false elements is not rational. There are three kinds of true elements: civic, moral, and spiritual. Civic truths have to do with judicial matters and the governmental affairs of nations—in general, with what is fair and equitable. Moral truths have to do with matters of personal life in its societal and social contexts, in general with what is honest and upright, and in particular with all kinds of virtues. Spiritual truths, however, have to do with matters of heaven and the church, in general with what is good in respect to love and what is true in respect to faith.

[2] There are three levels of life in every individual (see above, §267). Our rational ability is opened at the first level by means of civic truths, at the second level by moral truths, and at the third level by spiritual truths.

We need to realize, though, that our rational ability is not formed and opened simply by virtue of our knowing these truths, but by virtue of our living by them. Living by them means loving them out of a spiritual affection; and loving them out of a spiritual affection means loving what is fair and equitable because it is fair and equitable, what is honest and upright because it is honest and upright, what is good and true because it is good and true. On the other hand, living according to them and loving them out of a physical affection is loving them for the sake of oneself, one's repute, prestige, or profit. Consequently, to the extent that we love these truths out of a carnal affection, we do not become rational because we do not love them; we love ourselves, with the truths serving us the way slaves serve their master. When truths become slaves, they do not become part of us or open any level of our life, not even the first. Rather, they stay in our memory like information in material form and unite with love for ourselves there, which is a physical love.

[3] We may gather from this how we become rational, namely that at the third level it is through a spiritual love of what is good and true in regard to heaven and the church; at the second level it is through a love of what is honest and upright; and on the first level it is through a love of what is fair and equitable. The latter two loves also become spiritual from a spiritual love of what is good and true that flows into them and unites itself to them and forms its own face in them, so to speak.

Spirits and angels have memory just as we do. What they hear and see and think and intend and do stays with them; and through their memory they are constantly developing their rational ability forever. This is why spirits and angels are being perfected in intelligence and wisdom through experiences of what is true and good just the way we are.

469

I have been shown that spirits and angels have memory by a great deal of experience as well. I have seen everything they had thought and done called up from their memory both in public and in private, when they were with other spirits. I have also seen people who had been focused on some truth from simple virtue become steeped in insights and in a consequent intelligence and then taken up into heaven.

It should be realized, though, that they are not steeped in insights and a consequent intelligence beyond the level of the affection for what is good and true that engaged them in the world.[271] In fact, each spirit and angel retains the amount and kind of affection she or he had in the world, and this is afterward perfected by being filled in. This too goes on forever, since everything is capable of infinite variation and enrichment by different means, so it can be multiplied and can bear fruit. There is no end to any instance of goodness, since its source is the Infinite.

The fact that spirits and angels are constantly being perfected in intelligence and wisdom by means of insights into what is true and good has been presented in the chapters on the wisdom of heaven's angels

(§§265–275); on non-Christians or people outside the church in heaven (§§318–328); and on infants in heaven (§§329–345). This happens at the level of the affection for the good and the true that engaged them in the world, and not beyond it (§349).

Our Nature after Death Depends on the Kind of Life We Led in the World

470
ANY Christian knows from the Word that our life is still with us after death, since it says in many places that we will be judged according to our deeds and works and rewarded accordingly. Further, anyone who thinks on the basis of what is good and from real truth cannot help but see that people who live well enter heaven and people who live evil lives enter hell. However, people who are intent on evil do not want to believe that their state after death depends on their life in the world. They think rather, especially when their health begins to fail, that heaven is granted to all on the basis of mercy alone no matter how people have lived, and that this depends on a faith that they keep separate from life.

471
It does say in many places in the Word that we will be judged and requited according to our deeds and works. I should like to cite a few passages here.

The Human-born One is to come in the glory of the Father with his angels, and then he will render to everyone according to his or her works. (Matthew 16:17 [16:27])

Blessed are the dead who die in the Lord. Truly, says the spirit, so that they may rest from their labors, their works follow them. (Revelation 14:11 [14:13])

I will give to all according to their works. (Revelation 2:23)

I saw the dead, small and great, standing in the presence of God, and books were opened, and the dead were judged according to what was written in the books, according to their works; the sea gave up those who had died in it, and death and hell gave up the people who were in them, and they were all judged according to their works. (Revelation 20:13, 15 [20:12, 13])

See, I am coming; and my reward is with me, and I will give to all according to their works. (Revelation 22:12)

Everyone who hears my words and does them I will compare to a prudent person, but everyone who hears my words and does not do them is like a foolish person. (Matthew 7:24, 26)

Not everyone who says to me, "Lord, Lord," will enter into the kingdom of the heavens, but the one who does the will of my Father who is in the heavens. Many people will say to me on that day, "Lord, Lord, have we not prophesied through your name, and through your name cast out demons, and in your name done many powerful deeds?" But then I will confess to them, "I do not recognize you. Get away from me, workers of iniquity." (Matthew 7:22, 23)

Then you will begin to say, "We have eaten in your presence and drunk, and you have taught in our streets." But he will say, "I tell you, I do not recognize you, workers of iniquity." (Luke 13:25–27)

I will repay them according to their work, and according to the deeds of their hands. (Jeremiah 25:14)

Jehovah, whose eyes are open upon all our paths, to give to us all according to our ways and according to the fruit of our works. (Jeremiah 32:19)

I will visit upon their ways and repay them their works. (Hosea 4:9)

Jehovah deals with us according to our ways and according to our works. (Zechariah 1:6)

Where the Lord is predicting the Last Judgment, he recounts only deeds, and [says] that the people who have done good works will enter eternal life, and that the people who have done evil works will enter damnation (Matthew 25:32–46). There are many other passages as well that deal with our salvation and damnation.

We can see that our outward life consists of our works and deeds, and that the quality of our inner life is manifested through them.

472   "Works and deeds," though, does not mean works and deeds solely the way they look in outward form. It also includes their deeper nature. Everyone knows, really, that all our deeds and works come from our intention and thought, for if they did not come from there they would be no more than motions like those of machines or robots.[272] So a deed or work in its own right is simply an effect that derives its soul and life from our volition and thought, even to the point that it is volition and thought in effect, volition and thought in an outward form. It follows, then, that the quality of the volition and thought that cause the deed or work determines the quality of the deed or work. If the thought and intent are good, then the deeds and works are good; but if the thought and intent are evil, then the deeds and works are evil, even though they may look alike in outward form. A thousand people can behave alike—that is, can do the same thing, so much alike that in outward form one can hardly tell the difference. Yet each deed in its own right is unique because it comes from a different intent.

[2] Take for example behaving honestly and fairly with an associate. One person can behave honestly and fairly with someone else in order to seem honest and fair for the sake of self and to gain respect; another person can do the same for the sake of worldly profit; a third for reward and credit; a fourth to curry friendship; a fifth out of fear of the law and loss of reputation and office; a sixth to enlist people in his or her cause, even if it is an evil one; a seventh in order to mislead; and others for still other reasons. But even though all of their deeds look good (for behaving honestly and fairly toward a colleague is good), still they are evil because they are not done for the sake of honesty and fairness, not because these qualities are loved, but for the sake of oneself and the world, because these are loved. The honesty and fairness are servants of this love, like the servants of a household whom their lord demeans and dismisses when they do not serve.

[3] People behave honestly and fairly toward their colleagues in a similar outward form when they are acting from a love of what is honest and fair. Some of them do it because of the truth of faith, or obedience, because it is enjoined in the Word. Some of them do it for the sake of the goodness of faith or conscience, because they are moved by religious feeling. Some of them do it out of the good of thoughtfulness toward their neighbor, because one's neighbor's welfare is to be valued. Some of them do it out of the goodness of love for the Lord, because what is good should be done for its own sake; so too what is honest and fair should be

done for the sake of honesty and fairness. They love these qualities because they come from the Lord, and because the divine nature that emanates from the Lord is within them. So if we see them in their true essence, they are divine. The deeds or works of these people are inwardly good, so they are outwardly good as well; for as already noted, the nature of deeds and works is entirely determined by the nature of the thought and intent from which they stem, and apart from such thought and intent they are not deeds and works but only lifeless motions.

We may gather from this what is meant by works and deeds in the Word.

Since deeds and works are matters of intention and thought, they are also matters of love and faith to the point that their quality is the quality of their love and faith. That is, it amounts to the same thing whether you talk about our love or about our intentions, whether you talk about our established faith or about our thought, since what we love we also intend, and what we believe we also think. If we love what we believe, we intend it as well and do it to the extent that we can. Anyone can realize that love and faith dwell within our intentions and thought and not outside them, since intent is what is kindled by love and thought is what is enlightened in matters of faith. This means that only people who can think wisely are enlightened; and depending on their enlightenment they think what is true and intend what is true, they believe what is true and love what is true.[a]

473

We do need to recognize, though, that volition makes us who we are. Thought does so only to the extent that it arises from our volition, while deeds and works come from both. Or in other words, love is what makes us who we are; faith does so only to the extent that it arises from love, and deeds and works come from both. It follows from this that love or intent is the actual person, for the things that come forth belong to the

474

a. Just as everything in the universe that occurs in an orderly fashion goes back to what is good and true, so everything in us goes back to volition and intellect: 803, 10122. This is because it is our volition that receives what is good and our intellect that receives what is true: 3332, 3623, 5332, 6065, 6125, 7503, 9300, 9930. It amounts to the same thing whether you talk about what is true or faith, since faith is a matter of truth and truth is a matter of faith; and it also amounts to the same thing whether you talk about what is good or love, since love is a matter of what is good, and what is good is a matter of love: 4353, 4997, 7178, 10122, 10367. So it follows that intellect is the recipient of faith and volition the recipient of love: 7178, 10122, 10367; and since our intellect can accept faith in God and our volition love for God, we can be united to God by faith and love; and anyone who can be united to God by faith and love cannot die forever: 4525, 6323, 9231.

person they come forth from. To come forth is to be produced and presented in a form suited to observation and sight.[b]

We may gather from this what faith is apart from love—no faith at all, only information with no spiritual life in it. The same holds true for deeds apart from love. They are not deeds or works of life at all, only deeds or works of death containing some semblance of life derived from a love of evil and a faith in what is false. This semblance of life is what we call spiritual death.

475   We should realize as well that we present our whole person in our works and deeds and that our volition and thought, or the love and faith that are our inner constituents, are not complete until they are [embodied] in the deeds and works that are our outer constituents. These latter are in fact the outmost forms in which the former find definition; and without such definitions they are like undifferentiated things that do not yet have any real presence, things that are therefore not yet in us. To think and intend without acting when we can is like a flame sealed in a jar and stifled, or it is like seed sown in the sand that does not grow but dies along with its power to reproduce. Thinking and intending and doing, though, is like a flame that sheds its light and warmth all around, or like seed sown in the soil, that grows into a tree or a flower and becomes something. Anyone can see that intending and not acting when we can is not really intending, and loving and not doing good when we can is not really loving. It is only thinking that we intend and love; so it is a matter of isolated thought that disintegrates and vanishes. Love and intent are the very soul of the deed or work. It forms its own body in the honest and fair things that we do. This is the sole source of our spiritual body, the body of our spirit; that is, our spiritual body is formed entirely from what we have done out of love or intent (see above, §463). In a word,

b. Our volition is the essential reality of our life, since it is the vessel of love or what is good; and our intellect is the consequent manifestation of life because it is the vessel of faith or what is true: 3619, 5002, 9282; so our voluntary life is our primary life and our intellectual life is secondary to it: 585, 590, 3619, 7342, 8885, 9282, 10076, 10109, 10110. It is like light from a fire or flame: 6032, 6314. It follows from this that we are human because of our volition and our consequent intellect: 8911, 9069, 9071, 10076, 10109, 10110. Every individual is loved and valued by others in proportion to the virtue of her or his intentions and the consequent thought. We are loved and valued if we intend well and understand well, rejected and demeaned if we understand well but do not intend well: 8911, 10076. After death we retain the quality of our intentions and our consequent understanding: 9069, 9071, 9386, 10153. This means that after death we retain the quality of our love and faith. Any elements that are matters of faith but not at the same time of love vanish then because they are not within us and therefore are not part of us: 553, 2364, 10153.

everything of our character and our spirit is [embodied] in our works or deeds.[c]

We may gather from this what is meant by the life that stays with us after death. It is actually our love and our consequent faith, not only in theory but in act as well. So it is our deeds or works because these contain within themselves our whole love and faith. 476

There is a dominant love that remains with each of us after death and never changes to eternity. We all have many loves, but they all go back to our dominant love and form a single whole with it, or compose it in the aggregate. All the elements of our volition that agree with our dominant love are called loves because they are loved. There are deeper and more superficial loves, loves that are directly united and loves that are indirectly united; there are closer and more distant ones; there are loves that serve in various ways. Taken all together they make a kind of kingdom. They are actually arranged in this way within us even though we are utterly unaware of their arrangement. However, the arrangement becomes visible to some extent in the other life because the outreach of our thoughts and affections there depends on it. The outreach is into heavenly communities if our dominant love is made up of loves of heaven, but it is into hellish communities if our dominant love is made up of loves of hell. 477

On the outreach into communities of all the thought and affection of spirits and angels, see the previous chapters on the wisdom of heaven's angels and on heaven's form, which determines its gatherings and communications [§§265–275, 200–212].

What I have said so far, though, is addressed only to our rational thought. In order to present the matter to sensory observation, I should like to add some experiences that may serve to illustrate and support the claims that *first,* we are our love or intention after death; *second,* we remain the same forever in regard to our volition or dominant love; *third,* we come into heaven if our love is heavenly and spiritual, and into hell if 478

---

c. Deeper things flow sequentially into more outward ones and ultimately into what is outmost or final, which is where they find presence and permanence: 634, 6239, 6465, 9216, 9217. They not only flow in, they form a simultaneous whole on that outmost level, in a particular design: 5897, 6451, 8603, 10099. This is why all our deeper elements are held in connection and are stable: 9828. Deeds or works are the final forms in which our deeper elements exist: 10331; so being repaid and judged according to our works is [being repaid and judged] according to everything that pertains to our love and faith or our intentions and thought, since these are the deeper realities within our works: 3147, 3934, 6073, 8911, 10331, 10333.

our love is carnal and worldly without any heavenly and spiritual dimension; *fourth,* our faith does not stay with us unless it comes from a heavenly love; and *fifth,* love in action, and therefore our life, is what remains.

479   A great deal of my experience has testified to the fact that *we are our love or intention after death.* All heaven is differentiated into communities on the basis of differences in the quality of love, and every spirit who is raised up into heaven and becomes an angel is taken to the community where her or his love is. When we arrive there we feel as though we are in our own element, at home, back to our birthplace, so to speak. Angels sense this and associate there with kindred spirits. When they leave and go somewhere else, they feel a constant pull, a longing to go back to their kindred and therefore to their dominant love. This is how people gather together in heaven. The same applies in hell. There too, people associate according to loves that oppose heavenly ones. On the fact that both heaven and hell are made up of communities and that they are all differentiated according to differences of love, see §§41–50 and 200–212 above.

[2] We may also gather that we are our love after death from the fact that anything that does not agree with our dominant love is then removed and apparently taken away from us. For good people, what is removed and apparently taken away is everything that disagrees and conflicts, with the result that they are admitted to their love. It is much the same for evil people, except that what is taken away from them is everything true, while for good people everything false is taken away. Either way, the result is that ultimately everyone becomes his or her own love. This happens when we are brought into our third state, which will be discussed below.

Once this has happened, we constantly turn our faces toward our love and have it constantly before our eyes no matter which way we face (see above, §§123–124).

[3] All spirits can be led wherever you want as long as they are kept in their dominant love. They cannot resist even though they know what is happening and think that they will refuse. Spirits have often tried to do something in opposition, but without success. Their love is like a chain or rope tied around them, with which they can be pulled and which they cannot escape. It is the same for people in this world. Our love leads us as well, and it is through our love that we are led by others. It is even more so when we become spirits, though, because then we are not allowed to present a different love or pretend to a love that is not ours.

[4] It is obvious in every gathering in the other life that our spirit is our dominant love. To the extent that we act and talk in keeping with

someone else's love, that individual looks whole, with a face that is whole, cheerful, and lively. To the extent that we act and talk against someone else's dominant love, though, that individual's face begins to change, to dim, and to be hard to see. Eventually it disappears as though it were not even there. I have often been amazed at this because this kind of thing cannot happen in the world. However, I have been told that the same thing happens to the spirit within us, in that when we turn our attention away from someone, that individual is no longer in our sight.

[5] I have also seen that our spirit is our dominant love from the fact that every spirit seizes and claims whatever suits his or her love and rejects and repels whatever does not suit it. Our love is like a spongy, porous wood that absorbs whatever liquids prompt its growth, and repels others. It is like animals of various kinds. They recognize their proper foods, seek out the ones that suit their natures, and avoid the ones that disagree. Every love actually wants to be nourished by what is appropriate to it—an evil love by falsities and a good love by truths. I have occasionally been allowed to see that some particular simple and good people wanted to teach evil people things that were true and good. Faced with this teaching, though, the evil people fled far away; and when they reached their own kind, they seized on whatever falsities suited their love with great delight. I have also been allowed to see good spirits talking with each other about truths, which other good spirits in attendance listened to eagerly, while some evil ones who were there paid no attention, as though they did not hear anything.

In the world of spirits you can see paths, some leading to heaven and some leading to hell, each one leading to some specific community. Good spirits travel only the paths that lead to heaven, and to the community engaged in their own quality of love. They do not see paths that lead anywhere else. On the other hand, evil spirits travel only the paths that lead to hell and to that community there which is engaged in the evil of their own love. They do not see paths that lead anywhere else; and if they do see them, they still do not want to follow them.

Paths like this in the spiritual world are "real appearances" that correspond to true and false [understandings]; so this is what "paths" in the Word mean.[d]

---

d. A way, road, track, lane, or street means things that are true and that lead to something good, as well as false things that lead to something evil: 627, 2333, 10422. To sweep a path is to prepare to accept what is true: 3142. To make a path known, when it is said of the Lord, is to teach people about the truths that lead to what is good: 10564.

These proofs from experience support what was said above on rational grounds, namely that after death we are our own love and our own intent. I say "intent" because for each of us, our intent is our love.

480   A great deal of experience has also convinced me that *after death we remain the same forever in regard to our volition or dominant love.* I have been allowed to talk with some people who lived more than two thousand years ago, people whose lives are described in history books and are therefore familiar. I discovered[273] that they were still the same, just as described, including the love that was the source and determinant of their lives.

There were others who had lived seventeen centuries ago, also known from history books, and some who had lived four centuries ago, some three, and so on, with whom I was also allowed to talk and to learn that the same affection still governed within them. The only difference was that the pleasures of their love had been changed into corresponding ones.

Angels have told me that the life of our dominant love never changes for anyone to all eternity because we are our love, so to change it in any spirit would be to take away and snuff out his or her life.

They have also told me that this is because after death we can no longer be reformed by being taught the way we could in this world, since the outmost level, made up of natural insights and affections, is then dormant and cannot be opened because it is not spiritual (see above, §464). The deeper functions of our mind or spirit rest on this level the way a house rests on its foundation, which is why we do stay forever like the life of our love in the world. Angels are utterly amazed that people do not realize that our nature is determined by the nature of our dominant love and that many people actually believe they can be saved by instantaneous mercy, simply on the basis of their faith alone, regardless of the kind of life they have led, not realizing that divine mercy operates through means. The means involve being led by the Lord in the world as well as afterward in heaven, and the people who are led by mercy are the ones who do not live in evil. People do not even know that faith is an affection for what is true, an affection that comes from a heavenly love that comes from the Lord.

481   *We come into heaven if our love is heavenly and spiritual and into hell if our love is carnal and worldly without any heavenly and spiritual dimension.* My evidence for this conclusion is all the people I have seen raised into heaven and cast into hell. The ones who were raised into heaven had lives of heavenly and spiritual love, while the ones who were cast into hell had lives of carnal and worldly love. Heavenly love is loving what is good, honest, and fair because it is good, honest, and fair, and doing it because of that love. This is why they have a life of goodness, honesty, and fairness, which is a heavenly life. If we love these things for their own sakes and do or live them, we are also loving the Lord above all because they come from him. We are also loving our neighbor, because these things are our neighbor who is to be loved.[e] Carnal love, though, is loving what is good and honest and fair not for their own sakes but for our own sake, because we can use them to gain prestige, position, and profit. In this case we are not focusing on the Lord and our neighbor within what is good and honest and fair but on ourselves and the world, and we enjoy deceit. When the motive is deceit, then whatever is good and honest and fair is actually evil and dishonest and unfair. This is what we love within [the outward appearance].

[2] Since these loves define our lives, we are all examined as to our quality immediately after death, when we arrive in the world of spirits, and we are put in touch with people of like love. If we are focused on heavenly love, we are put in touch with people in heaven; and if we are focused on carnal love, we are put in touch with people in hell. Further, once the first and second states have been completed the two kinds of people are separated so that they no longer see or recognize each other. We actually become our own love not only as to the deeper levels of our minds but outwardly as well, in face, body, and speech, since we become images of our love even in outward things. People who are carnal loves look coarse, dim, dark, and misshapen; while people who are heavenly loves look lively, clear, bright, and lovely. They are completely different in

---

e. In the highest sense, the Lord is our neighbor because he is to be loved above all; however, loving the Lord is loving what comes from him because he is in everything that comes from him, so [our neighbor is] whatever is good and true: 2425, 3419, 6706, 6711, 6819, 6823, 8123. Loving what is good and true, which come from him, is living by them, and this is loving the Lord: 10143, 10153, 10310, 10336, 10578, 10648. Every individual and community, our country and church, and in the broadest sense the Lord's kingdom, is our neighbor; and loving our neighbor is helping them from a love for their good in keeping with their state. This means that their welfare, which we are to value, is the neighbor: 6818–6824, 8123. Moral good, or what is honest, and civic good, or what is fair, are our neighbor as well; and acting honestly and fairly out of a love for what is honest and fair is loving the neighbor: 2915, 4730, 8120, 8121, 8122, 8123. Consequently, thoughtfulness toward our neighbor includes all aspects of our lives, and doing what is good and fair, and acting honestly from the heart in every position we hold and in everything we do, is loving our neighbor: 2417, 8121, 8124. The doctrine of the early church was a doctrine of charity, and this was the source of their wisdom: 2417, 2385, 3419, 3420, 4844, 6628.

spirit and in thought as well. People who are heavenly loves are intelligent and wise, while people who are carnal loves are dense and rather silly.

[3] When leave is given to examine the inner and outer aspects of the thoughts and affections of people engaged in heavenly love, the inner reaches look as though they were made of light, in some cases like the light of a flame; and their outer manifestations are of various lovely colors, like a rainbow. In contrast, the inner reaches of people who are engaged in carnal love look gloomy because they are closed in, in some cases like a smoky fire for people who were inwardly maliciously deceptive. Their outer manifestations have an ugly color, depressing to look at (both the inner and outer aspects of the mind and spirit are presented visually in the spiritual world whenever it so pleases the Lord).

[4] People who are engaged in carnal love do not see anything in heaven's light. Heaven's light is darkness to them, while hell's light, which is like the light of glowing embers, is like daylight to them. In fact, in heaven's light their inner sight is deprived of light to the point that they become insane. As a result, they run away from it and hide in caves and caverns of a depth that corresponds to the false convictions that stem from their evil intentions. Exactly the reverse is true for people who are engaged in heavenly love, though. The deeper or higher they enter into heavenly light, the more clearly they see everything and the lovelier it all looks, and the more intelligently and wisely they grasp what is true.

[5] There is no way that people who are engaged in carnal love can live in heaven's warmth, because heaven's warmth is heavenly love. They can live in hell's warmth, though, which is a love of cruelty toward people who do not support them. The pleasures of this love are contempt for others, hostility, hatred, and vengefulness. When they are absorbed in these they are in their very life, with no knowledge whatever of what it means to do good for others out of sheer goodness and for the sake of the good itself. All they know is how to do good out of malice and for the sake of malice.

[6] People who are engaged in carnal love cannot breathe in heaven either. When evil spirits are taken there, they draw breath like someone who is struggling painfully. On the other hand, people who are engaged in heavenly love breathe more freely and feel more alive the deeper into heaven they come.

We may gather from this that a heavenly and spiritual love is heaven for us because everything heavenly is written on that love; and that carnal and worldly love apart from heavenly and spiritual love is hell for us because everything hellish is written on that love.

We can see, then, that people come into heaven who have a heavenly and spiritual love, and people come into hell who have a carnal and worldly love without a heavenly and spiritual one.

The fact that *our faith does not stay with us unless it comes from a heavenly love* has been brought home to me by so much experience that if I were to relate what I have seen and heard about it, it would fill a book. I can attest to this: that there is no faith whatever and there can be none for people who are engrossed in carnal and worldly love apart from heavenly and spiritual love. There is only information, or a secondhand belief[274] that something is true because it serves their own love. Further, a number of people who thought they had had faith were introduced to people of real faith; and once communication was established they perceived that they had no faith at all. They even admitted later that simply believing the truth or the Word is not faith; but faith is loving what is true from a heavenly love and intending and doing it from a deep affection. I was also shown that the secondhand belief they called faith was only like the light of winter in which everything on earth lies dormant, bound by the ice and buried in snow because there is no warmth to the light. As a result, the moment it is touched by rays of heaven's light, the light of their secondhand faith is not only extinguished but actually becomes a dense darkness in which people cannot even see themselves. At the same time, too, their deeper reaches are so darkened that they cannot discern anything and ultimately go mad because of their false convictions.

The result is that all the truths such people have learned from the Word and from the teaching of the church are taken away from them, all the things they claimed were part of their faith, and in their place they are filled with everything false that accords with the evil of their life. They are actually all plunged into their loves and into the false notions that support them as well. Then, since truths contradict the false, malicious notions they are absorbed in, they hate the truths, turn their backs on them, and reject them.

I can bear witness from all my experiences of what happens in heaven and in hell that people who have confessed faith alone as a matter of doctrine and have engaged in evil as regards their lives are all in hell. I have seen thousands of them sent there and have described them in the booklet *The Last Judgment and Babylon Destroyed.*[275]

The fact that *love in action, and therefore our life, is what remains* follows logically from what I have presented from experience and what I have just said about deeds and works. Love in action is the work and the deed.

482

483

484   We do need to know that all works and deeds are matters of moral and civic life and therefore focus on what is honest and right and what is fair and equitable. What is honest and right is a matter of moral life, and what is fair and equitable is a matter of civic life. The love these come from is either heavenly or hellish. The works and deeds of our moral and civic life are heavenly if we do them from a heavenly love, because things that we do from a heavenly love we do from the Lord, and everything we do from the Lord is good. On the other hand, the deeds and works of our moral and civic life are hellish if they come from a hellish love, since whatever[276] we do from this love, which is a love for ourselves and the world, we do from ourselves, and whatever we do from ourselves is intrinsically evil. In fact, seen in our own right, or in terms of what is actually ours, we are nothing but evil.[f]

After Death, the Pleasures of Everyone's Life Are Turned into Things That Correspond

485   I explained in the last chapter that our dominant affection or predominant love stays with us forever. Now, though, I need to explain that the pleasures of that affection or love change into things that correspond. "Changing into things that correspond" means changing into spiritual things that answer to the natural ones. We may gather that they change

---

f. Our own nature is to love ourselves more than God and the world more than heaven, and to regard the neighbor as nothing in comparison to ourselves, so it is a love for oneself and for the world: 634 *[694]*, 731, 4317. This is the self into which we are born, and it is solid evil: 210, 215, 731, 874, 875, 876, 987, 1047, 2307, 2318 *[2308]*, 3518, 3701, 3812, 8480, 8550, 10283, 10284, 10286, 10731 *[10832]*. From our self-image comes not only everything evil but also everything false: 1047, 10283, 10284, 10286. The evils that come from our self-image are contempt for others, hostility, hatred, vengefulness, cruelty, and deceit: 6667, 7372, 7373, 7374, 9348, 10038, 10742 *[10743]*. To the extent that our self-image rules, we either reject or stifle or pervert the goodness of love and the truth of faith: 2041, 7491, 7492, 7643, 8487, 10455, 10743. Our self-image is hell for us: 694, 8480. Anything good that we do because of our self-image is not good but is essentially evil: 8478 *[8480, 8487]*.

into spiritual things from the fact that as long as we are in our earthly bodies we are in the natural world; but once we leave that body behind, we arrive in the spiritual world and put on a spiritual body. (On angels having perfect human forms and being people after death, and on the bodies they wear being spiritual, see above, §§73–77 and 453–460; and for a description of the correspondence of spiritual things with natural ones, see §§87–115.)

All our pleasures stem from our dominant love, for the only things that feel pleasant to us are the ones that we love; so the most pleasant of all is what we love above all. Whether you say "our dominant love" or "what we love above all," it amounts to the same thing.

486

There are different pleasures—as many, generally speaking, as there are different dominant loves, which means as many as there are of us, and of spirits and angels, since no one's dominant love is entirely like that of anyone else. This is why no one's face is exactly like that of anyone else, since the face is the image of the mind, and in the spiritual world is an image of the dominant love. The pleasures of any specific individual are infinitely varied as well, with no pleasure ever entirely like any other. This applies both to the pleasures that come in sequence and to the ones that occur simultaneously. No two are ever alike. However, the specific pleasures of any given individual go back to that single love which is that individual's dominant love. In fact, they constitute it and therefore become one with it. In much the same way, all pleasures overall go back to one love that is universally dominant—in heaven, a love for the Lord, and in hell, a love for oneself.

The only way to know the kinds and qualities of the spiritual pleasures into which natural pleasures turn after death is through a knowledge of correspondences. This teaches in general that there is nothing natural to which something spiritual does not answer, and it teaches specifically the identity and nature of whatever does so correspond. This means that people who are engaged in this knowledge can recognize and know their state after death provided they know their love and how it relates in its nature to the universally dominant love to which, as we have just stated, all loves go back.

487

However, people who are involved in self-love cannot know what their dominant love is because they love whatever is theirs and call their evils good. They also call false things true, the false notions that support them and that they use to rationalize their evils. If they were willing, though, they could still know [their dominant love] from other people who are wise, because these latter see what they themselves do not. This does not happen, though, in the case of people who are so enmeshed in their self-love that they have nothing but contempt for any teaching of the wise.

[2] On the other hand, people who are in heavenly love do accept instruction and do see the evils into which they were born when they are led into them. They see them from truths because truths make evils obvious. Anyone can in fact see what is evil and the distortion it causes by seeing from the truth that arises from what is good; but no one can see what is good and true from an evil standpoint. This is because the false notions that arise from evil are darkness and correspond to it. So people who are caught up in false notions that arise from evil are like blind people who do not see things that are in the light, and they avoid them the way owls avoid daylight.ª On the other hand, the true perceptions that arise from good are light and correspond to light (see above, §§126–134). So people who are focused on the true perceptions that arise from good are sighted and open-eyed and can differentiate between things that are in light and shade.

[3] I have been granted confirmation of this too by experience. The angels who are in the heavens both see and grasp the evil and false promptings that well up in them from time to time; and they can also see the evil and false promptings that engage the spirits in the world of spirits who are in touch with the hells, though the spirits themselves cannot see their own evil and false promptings. They do not grasp what the virtue of heavenly love is, what conscience is, what is honest and fair (except as it is to their own advantage), or what it means to be led by the Lord. They say these things do not exist and therefore make no difference whatever.

All this has been presented to encourage people to examine themselves and to identify their dominant love on the basis of their pleasures, so that according to their grasp of the knowledge of correspondences, they may know their state of life after death.²⁷⁷

488   It is possible to know from a knowledge of correspondences how our life pleasures are changed after death into what corresponds to them; but

---

a. By reason of correspondence, darkness in the Word means falsities, and dense darkness or gloom means falsities that stem from evil: 1839, 1860, 7688, 7711. Heaven's light is darkness to evil people: 1861, 6832, 8197. People who are in the hells are said to be in darkness because they are engrossed in false notions that stem from evil; with some discussion: 3340, 4418, 4531. In the Word, "the blind" means people who are engrossed in false convictions and do not want to be taught: 2383, 6990.

since this is not common knowledge, I should like to shed some light on the matter from experience.

People who are caught up in evil and who have formed fixed false convictions against the truths of the church, especially people who have rejected the Word, flee from heaven's light. They plunge into cellars that look murky through their openings and into crevices in the rocks and hide themselves there. This is because they have loved their false notions and hated true ones. Cellars like this, and crevices in the rocks as well,[b] and false things, correspond to darkness;[c,278] and light corresponds to things that are true. They find it pleasant to live there, and painful to live out in the open.

[2] People who took delight in covert plotting and in manufacturing deceptive schemes in secret also live in these cellars and move into rooms so dark that people can barely see each other. They whisper in each other's ears in the corners. This is what becomes of the pleasures of their love.

If people have loved the academic disciplines only in order to sound learned, without using them to develop their ability to reason, taking delight in their pride at the contents of their memories, they love sandy areas and prefer them to meadows and gardens because sandy areas correspond to these kinds of study.

[3] People who are wrapped up in knowing the doctrines of churches, their own and others', without applying them to life, love stony areas and live among rock piles. They avoid cultivated land because it is repulsive to them.

If people have given nature—and their own prudence—credit for everything and have used various devices to gain high office and a great deal of wealth, in the other life they study magical arts that are misuses of the divine design, and find in them the greatest pleasure of their life.

[4] People who have adapted divine truths to their own loves and have therefore falsified them love urinary things because urinary things correspond to the pleasures of this kind of love.[d]

People who were filthy misers live in cubicles and love the filth of pigs and the foul odors they breathe out from half-digested food in their stomachs.

---

b. In the Word, rocky crevices and fissures mean what is dim and false in faith: 10582; because rocks mean faith from the Lord: 8581, 10580; and stone means truth of faith: 114, 643, 1298, 3720, 6426, 8608, 10376.

c. [Swedenborg's note at this point refers the reader back to the note in §487:2.]

d. Defilement of truth corresponds to urine: 5390.

[5] If people have devoted their lives wholly to pleasure, living elegantly, pandering to the gullet and the belly, loving this as the greatest good of life, in the other life they love feces and latrines and find them delightful. This is because pleasures like these are spiritual filth. They avoid places that are clean and free from filth because they find them distasteful.

[6] People who took pleasure in adultery pass their time in brothels where everything is filthy and foul. They love these places and avoid chaste homes. The moment they come near such homes they feel faint. Nothing pleases them more than to break up marriages.

People who have been bent on revenge and have therefore taken on a savage and sadistic nature love places like morgues, and are in hells of that sort.

Others fare differently.

489 In contrast, the life pleasures of people who have lived in heavenly love in the world change into the kinds of corresponding things that exist in the heavens, things that come into being from heaven's sun and from its light. The things which that light renders visible have hidden within them divine realities. What comes to view from this source moves the deeper reaches of angels' minds and the outer levels of their bodies as well; and since a divine light (which is divine truth emanating from the Lord) is flowing into their minds, which have been opened by heavenly love, it presents in outward form things that answer to the pleasures of their love. In the chapter that dealt with representations and appearances in heaven (§§170–176) and the chapter on the wisdom of heaven's angels (§§265–275), I have explained that the things presented to angels' sight in the heavens answer to their own deeper natures or to elements of their faith and love, and therefore to their intelligence [and] wisdom.

[2] Since I have begun supporting this general proposition by examples drawn from my experience, to shed light on what has been said so far on the basis of the causes of things, I should also like to bring in at this point something about the heavenly pleasures into which the natural pleasures turn for people who live in heavenly love in the world.

People who have loved divine truths and the Word from a deep affection, or from an affection for the truth itself, live in the light, in uplands that look like mountains, and are constantly bathed in the light of heaven there. They know nothing of the kind of darkness we have at night in the world, and they live in a springtime climate as well. Their scenery offers them views like fields ripe for harvest and vineyards. Everything in their houses gleams as though it were made of precious stones. Looking through their windows is like looking through pure crystal.

These are their visual pleasures; but they are actually deeper pleasures because of their correspondence with divine heavenly qualities, since the truths from the Word that they have loved correspond to the harvest fields, vineyards, precious stones, windows, and crystals.[e]

[3] People who have applied the teachings of the church from the Word directly to their lives are in the inmost heaven and more than anyone else are absorbed in the pleasures of wisdom. They see divine realities in particular objects. They actually do see the objects, but the corresponding divine realities flow directly into their minds and fill them with a sense of blessedness that affects all their sensory functions. As a result, everything they see seems to laugh and play and live (on this, see above, §270).

[4] If people have loved learning and have developed their rational ability accordingly and thereby gained intelligence, and if they have acknowledged the Divine Being at the same time, their delight in knowledge and pleasure in reasoning changes in the other life into a spiritual pleasure that is the delight of firsthand knowledge of what is good and true. They live in gardens where you can see flower beds and lawns beautifully marked off, surrounded by rows of trees with arcades and promenades. The trees and flowers change from day to day. Looking at all this brings pleasure to their minds generally, and the specific changes make it constantly new. Further, since all this corresponds to divine qualities, and since these people are drawn to their knowledge of correspondences, they are constantly being filled with new insights and thereby having their spiritual rational faculty perfected. They enjoy these pleasures because gardens, flower beds, lawns, and trees correspond to information, insights, and the intelligence that ensues.[f]

[5] If people have given the Divine credit for everything and regarded nature as relatively dead, simply subservient to spiritual concerns, and if they have convinced themselves of this, they are in heavenly light; and everything that presents itself to their eyes derives a kind of translucence from that light. In that translucency they see

e. A harvest in the Word means a state of acceptance and growth of what is true because of the good: 9291. Standing grain means truth being conceived: 9146. Vineyards mean the spiritual church and the truths of that church: 1069, 9139. Precious stones mean truths of heaven and of the church translucent from the good: 114, 9863, 9865, 9868, 9873, 9905. Windows mean the intellectual function of our inner sight: 655, 658, 3391.

f. Gardens, groves, and parks mean intelligence: 100, 103, 3220. Therefore the early people held their holy worship in groves: 2722, 4552. Flowers and flower beds mean truths of information and insight: 9553. Small plants, grasses, and lawns mean true information: 7571. Trees mean perceptions and insights: 103, 2163, 2682, 2722, 2972, 7692.

innumerable shadings of light that their inner sight seems to drink directly in. This is how they perceive deeper pleasures. The objects in their houses look like diamonds with similar variegations of light. I have been told that their walls look like crystal and are therefore also translucent, and that within them one can see what looks like fluid forms representative of heavenly things, again with constant variety. This is because this kind of translucence corresponds to an intellect that has been enlightened by the Lord, with the shadows that arise from faith in and love of natural things taken away. Things like this—and infinitely more—are what people who have been in heaven are talking about when they say that they have seen what the eye has never seen, and that from the grasp of divine things conveyed to them in this connection, they have heard what the ear has never heard.[279]

[6] If people have not acted covertly but have wanted everything they were thinking to be out in the open to the extent that civil law allows, then since they have thought nothing but what was honest and fair because of the Deity, in heaven their faces are radiant. Because of that radiance, the details of their thoughts and affections are visible in their faces as though presented in a form; and in both speech and action they are virtual images of their feelings. They are more beloved than others. When they are talking, their faces dim a little, but after they have spoken, then the very things they have said can be fully and plainly seen in their faces. Further, since everything around them answers to their deeper natures, everything takes on a countenance that enables others to see clearly what they represent and mean. Spirits who have found pleasure in covert activity get as far from them as they can, and seem to themselves to slither away from them like snakes.

[7] People who have regarded adultery as unspeakable and have lived in chaste love of their marriage are more in the pattern and form of heaven than anyone else. This gives them a total beauty and a constant flower of youth. The pleasures of their love are indescribable, and increase to eternity. This is because all the joys and delights of heaven flow into that love; and this in turn is because that love comes down from the Lord's union with heaven and with the church and in general from the union of the good and the true that is heaven in general and in every individual angel in particular (see above, §§366–386). Their external pleasures are so wonderful that they cannot be described in human words.

Still, what I have said about the correspondences of pleasures for people who are involved in heavenly love is only a little.

490   This enables us to know that after death our pleasures do change into corresponding ones, but that the love itself remains the same forever, especially marriage love, the love of what is fair, honest, good, and true, the love of information and insights, the love of intelligence and wisdom, and the rest. The things that flow from these loves like streams from their spring are pleasures that not only last but are raised to a higher level when they are changed from natural pleasures into spiritual ones.

Our First State after Death

THERE are three states that we pass through after death before we arrive in either heaven or hell. The first state is one of more outward concerns, the second is one of more inward concerns, and the third is one of preparation. We go through these states in the world of spirits.

491

Some people, however, do not go through these states but are either raised into heaven or cast into hell immediately after their death. The people immediately raised into heaven are ones who have been regenerated and thus prepared for heaven in this world. People who have been regenerated and prepared to this extent need only to slough off their natural uncleanness along with their bodies and are immediately taken into heaven by angels. I have seen people taken up an hour after their death.

On the other hand, people who have been profoundly malicious but have outwardly worn a guise of goodness, people who have therefore filled their malice with guile and used goodness as a means of deception are cast directly into hell. I have seen people like this cast into hell immediately after their death. One of the most deceitful went head first and feet last; for others it is different.

There are also people who are sent off into caves right after their death and in this way are segregated from people in the world of spirits. They are alternately brought out and sent back in. These are people who have treated their neighbors maliciously under the pretext of civic behavior.

There are few such people, though, compared to the number of people who are kept in the world of spirits and prepared there for either heaven or hell according to the divine plan.

As to the first state, the state of more outward concerns, we arrive in this immediately after our death. Everyone has more outward and more inward aspects of the spirit. We use the outer aspects of our spirit to

492

adapt our bodies in the world—especially our faces, speech, and behavior—
to our interactions with other people. The more inward aspects of our
spirit are the ones proper to our intentions and consequent thought,
which rarely show in our faces, speech, and behavior. We are trained
from infancy to present ourselves as friendly, benevolent, and honest, and
to conceal the thoughts of our own intentions. So we acquire a habitual
lifestyle that is outwardly moral and civil no matter what we are like inwardly. As a result of this habitual behavior, we scarcely know our own
inner natures and pay no attention to them.

493   Our first state after death is like our state in this world, since we are
then similarly involved in outward concerns. We have similar faces,
voices, and character; we lead similar moral and civil lives. This is why it
still seems to us as though we were in this world unless we notice things
that are out of the ordinary and remember that angels told us we were
spirits when we were awakened (§450). So the one life carries on into the
other, and death is only a passage.

494   Since this is what we are like as spirits immediately after our life in
the world, our friends and people we had known in the world then recognize us. Spirits perceive who we are not only from our faces and voices
but also from the aura of our life when they come near. In the other life,
whenever we think about someone, we call up that individual's face in
our thought along with many details about her or his life; and when we
do this, the other is called to us. Things like this happen in the spiritual
world because thoughts are shared there and because space is not what it
is in the natural world (see above, §§191–199). This is why as soon as we
arrive in the other life, we are all recognized by our friends and relatives
and by people we have known in one way or another. Further, we talk
with each other and continue to see each other in keeping with our
friendship in the world. I have heard many people who had just come
from the world overjoyed to see their friends again, and their friends
overjoyed that they had arrived.

It often happens that married partners meet and welcome each other
joyfully. They stay together as well, but for a longer or shorter time depending on how happily they had lived together in the world. Ultimately, unless they had been united by real marriage love (which is a
union of minds from heavenly love), they separate after having been together for a while.

If the minds of the partners disagreed, however, and if they were inwardly repellent to each other, they break out into open hostility and
sometimes actually fight with each other. Still, they are not separated until they enter the second state, which will be described shortly.

Since the life of newly arrived spirits is not unlike their life in the world, and since they do not know anything about life after death, heaven, or hell except what they have learned from the literal meaning of the Word and some sermons drawn from it, once they get over their astonishment at being in a body and enjoying all the senses they had in the world, seeing familiar things around them, they find themselves wanting to know what heaven and hell are like and where they are. Consequently, their friends tell them about the state of eternal life and take them around to various places, into the company of different people. They go to different cities, to gardens and parks, often to gorgeous ones because things like this appeal to the outward concerns they are involved in. Then from time to time they are led into the thoughts they had had during their physical lives about the state of the soul after death and about heaven and hell. This brings them to the point of resentment that they had been so ignorant about such matters, and also that the church had been so ignorant.

Almost all of them want to know whether they will make it into heaven. Many of them think they will because they led moral and civic lives in the world, not reflecting that both evil and good people lead similar outward lives, being similarly helpful to others, going to church, listening to sermons, and praying similarly, utterly unaware that outward behavior and outward worship accomplish nothing whatever; only the inner realities that give rise to these outward ones are effective. Scarcely one in thousands even knows what the inner realities are or that they are the focal point of heaven and the church for us. Even fewer realize that the quality of our outward actions is determined by the quality of our intentions and thoughts and the love and faith within them, from which our actions arise. Even when they are told, they do not grasp the fact that thinking and intending actually make a difference. They attach importance only to speaking and acting. Many of the people who are coming into the other life from the Christian world are like this nowadays.

Eventually, good spirits examine them to determine their nature. This is done in various ways because in this first state evil people can say true things and do good things just the way good people do. As I have already explained, this is because they have lived just as morally in outward form because they were living under governments and laws, and because this gained them a reputation for fairness and honesty, won people over to them, and raised them to high office and wealth. However, one can tell evil spirits from good ones particularly by the fact that the evil ones pay close attention when the conversation is about external concerns and little attention when it is about more inward matters, about the true and good principles of the church and heaven. They do hear such things, but without any real attention or pleasure. One can also identify them by the fact that they consistently turn toward certain regions, and when they are left to themselves follow paths that lead to them. One can tell what love is leading them from the regions they face and the paths they follow.

497   All the spirits who arrive from the world are put in touch with some community in heaven or some community in hell. However, this applies only to their deeper natures, and their deeper natures are not apparent to them as long as they are focused on their outward concerns. This is because their outward concerns cloak their inner ones, especially for people more deeply involved in evil. However, they come out in the open when they arrive in the second state because there their deeper levels are opened and their outer ones become dormant.

498   This first state after death lasts a few days for some people, months for some, and a year for some, but rarely more than a year for anyone. The difference for particular individuals depends on the harmony or discord between their inner and outer natures. These inner and outer natures must act as one and correspond for everyone. No one is allowed to think and intend one way and speak and act another way in the spiritual world. Everyone must be an image of his or her affection or love, which means we must be outwardly what we are inwardly. This is why the outer concerns of a spirit are first stripped off and brought into order: so that they may serve as a plane[280] responsive to the inner ones.

Our Second State after Death

499   OUR second state after death is called a state of our deeper interests because then we are given access to the deeper reaches of our minds, or of our intentions and thoughts, while the more outward interests that engaged us in the first state become dormant.

Anyone who is observant of our life and our words and actions can recognize that we all have more outward and more inward natures, or more outward and more inward thoughts and intentions. We can recognize this from the fact that if we are involved in civic life, we think about other people in terms of their reputation, or of what we have picked up about them when they were the subjects of conversation. However, we do not talk with them the way we think about them, and even if the others are evil people, we still behave courteously toward them. This is particularly noticeable in pretenders and sycophants whose words and deeds are wholly at odds with their thoughts and intentions, and in hypocrites who talk about God, heaven, the salvation of souls, the truths of the church, the welfare of the country, and their neighbor as though they were motivated by faith and love when at heart they believe otherwise and love no one but themselves.

[2] We may gather from this that we have two thought processes, one more outward and one more inward, and that we talk on the basis of our more outward thinking and feel differently on the basis of our more inward thinking. Further, these two thought processes have been separated to prevent the inner from flowing into the outer and becoming somehow visible.

We have been so created that our inner thought may act in unison with our outer by means of correspondence; and it does act as one when we are involved in something constructive, since we do not think anything that is not good, and what we say is good. But if we are involved in something evil, our deeper thought does not act as one with our outer thought, because we are thinking something evil and saying something good. This means that the pattern is inverted, since the good is on the outside for us and the evil lies within. As a result, the evil controls the good and suppresses it like a slave, to make it serve as a means to securing its own ends, the objects of its love. Since this kind of purpose is latent in the good we say and do, we can see that now the good is not really good but is infected with evil, no matter how good it may look in outward form to people who are not aware of deeper matters. [3] It is different for people who are involved in something good. For them, the pattern is not inverted; rather, the good flows from their deeper thought into their more outward thought and therefore into their words and deeds. This is the pattern into which we were created. In this way, our deeper reaches are in heaven and in the light there, and since heaven's light is divine truth emanating from the Lord and is in fact the Lord in heaven (see §§126–140), the Lord is leading us.

I mention this to show that each of us has a more inward thought and a more outward thought, and that these are distinguishable. When I say "thought," I mean volition as well, since thought comes from volition. No one can actually think without intent.

We can see from this what our states of outer concerns and of inner concerns are.

500　　When I speak of volition and thought, "volition" means affection and love as well as every delight and pleasure that derives from affection and love, since these go back to volition as their basis. Whatever we intend, we love, and it feels delightful and pleasant to us; and in turn, whatever we love and find pleasant and delightful, we intend. Thought, though, also means everything we use to support our affection or love, for thought is nothing but the form of our intention or the means by which what we intend comes to light. This form is constructed by various rational analyses that have their source in the spiritual world and are integral functions of our spirit.

501　　We need to know that our basic quality is determined entirely by the quality of our inner natures, not by what we are like outwardly apart from that inner nature. This is because our inner reaches are our spirit, and since it is from the spirit that the body lives, our life is the life of our spirit. Consequently, whatever we are like in our inward natures, that is what we are like to eternity. Since our more outward natures belong to the body they are separated after death, and any elements of them that cling to the spirit become dormant, serving only as a plane[281] for deeper concerns, as I explained above in describing the memory that we retain after death.[282]

We can see from this what really belongs to us and what does not. For evil people the contents of the outer thought that gives rise to their words and the outer intent that gives rise to their actions do not really belong to them. What belongs to them is the contents of their deeper thought and intentions.

502　　Once the first state has been completed—the state of more outward concerns described in the preceding chapter—we as spirits are brought into the state of our deeper concerns, or into the state of those deeper intentions and consequent thoughts we engaged in when we were left to ourselves in this world and our thinking was free and unfettered. We slip into this state without realizing it much as we did in the world when we drew the thought nearest to our speech, the immediate source of our speech, back toward our inner thought, and let it pause there a while. So when we as spirits are in this state, we are being ourselves and living our real life, since thinking freely from our own affection is our very life and our very self.

503　　Spirits in this state think from their own intent and therefore from their own affection or love; and then their thought forms a unity with their intention, such a unity that they scarcely seem to be thinking, only intending. It is almost the same when they talk, except that there is some fear that the thoughts of their intention might appear naked, since their civic life in the world had planted this fear in their intention.

All of us, without exception, are brought into this state after death **504** because it is the proper state of our spirits. The earlier state was characteristic of our spirit when we were in public, and that is not its very own state. As for the latter state, which is the state of the outer concerns that we find ourselves in immediately after death (as described in the previous chapter), there are many reasons to conclude that it is not the proper state of our spirits. For example, spirits not only think but even talk from their own affection, since that is the source of their language, as is implied in what was presented in the chapter on the language of angels (§§234–245). We thought the same way in the world when we were turned inward, because at such times we did not think on the basis of our physical language but simply surveyed it, and could think more things in a minute than we could say in half an hour. We can also see that this state of relatively outward concerns is not the proper state of ourselves or our spirits from the fact that when we were in public in the world, we talked in keeping with the laws of moral and civic life. Then our deeper thought controlled our outer thought the way one person controls another, to see that it did not cross the bounds of propriety and decency. It is also evidenced by the fact that when we do think privately, we think about what we will say and do in order to please people and to gain friendship, good will, and gratitude by devious means—that is, differently than if we were acting from our actual intent.

We can see from all this that the state of more inward concerns that spirits are led into is their proper state, which means that it was also the proper state of the individuals when they were living in the world.

When spirits are in this state of their deeper concerns, then it is obvi- **505** ous what kind of people they really were in the world. They actually behave in accord with their own nature. People who were inwardly devoted to the good in the world then behave sanely and wisely, more wisely than when they were living in the world, in fact, because they have been freed from any connection with the body and therefore with the earthly things that darken and cover with a kind of cloud.

In contrast, people who were focused on evil in the world then behave foolishly and insanely, more insanely than when they were in the world, in fact, because they are in freedom and are no longer constrained. As long as they were living in the world, they were outwardly sensible, because this was how they imitated rational people. So when the outer layers are stripped off, their inner insanity is unveiled.

An evil person who outwardly pretends to be good can be compared to a brightly polished jar with a cover on, with all kinds of filth hidden inside, just as the Lord said: "You are like whitewashed sepulchers that look lovely on the outside but are inwardly full of the bones of the dead and all uncleanness" (Matthew 23:27).

506   All the people who have lived lives in the world focused on what is good and have acted in accord with their consciences—that is, people who have acknowledged the Divine Being and loved divine truths, and especially people who have applied them to their lives—seem to themselves to have awakened from sleep when they are let into this state of their more inward concerns, like people who have come from darkness into light. They are actually thinking from heaven's light and therefore from a deeper wisdom; and they are acting from what is good and therefore from a deeper affection. Heaven is flowing into their thoughts and affections with a profound feeling of blessedness and pleasure that they had never known before. This is because they are in touch with heaven's angels. Then too, they acknowledge the Lord and worship him with their very lives, because they are engaged in their own lives when they are in this state of more inward concerns (as noted just above in §505). They are also acknowledging and worshiping him in freedom, since freedom is a matter of our deeper affection. In this way they move away from an outward holiness and into the inner holiness that is the essence of real worship. This is the state of people who have lived a Christian life in accordance with the precepts of the Word.

[2] Quite the opposite, though, is the state of people who in the world lived lives focused on evil, who had no conscience and therefore denied the Divine Being; for all the people who live in evil deny the Divine Being inwardly, no matter how convinced they are outwardly that they are not denying but acknowledging. This is because acknowledging the Divine Being and living in evil are opposites. When people like this come into the state of their deeper concerns in the other life, they seem foolish when people hear them talk or see them act, because their evil impulses impel them to break out into wicked deeds—into contempt for others, into derision and blasphemy, hatred, and vengefulness. They cook up plots, some of them with such ingenuity and malice that you would scarcely believe anything like this existed in any human being. They are then free to act in accord with the thoughts of their intentions because they are separated from the more outward

factors that constrained them in the world. In short, they lose their rationality because in the world their rationality did not dwell in their deeper natures but in their outer ones. Still, they seem to themselves to be wiser than anyone else.

[3] Once people like this are in the second state, they are let back into the state of their more outward concerns for brief periods of time. They then retain a memory of how they behaved when they were in the state of their more inward concerns. Some of them are embarrassed, and admit that they were insane. Some of them are not embarrassed at all. Some of them resent the fact that they are not allowed to be in the state of their more outward concerns all the time, but they are shown what they would be like if they were constantly in this state. They would be constantly trying to do the same things covertly, misleading people of simple heart and faith with simulations of goodness, honesty, and fairness. They would destroy themselves completely, because eventually their outer natures would be ablaze with the same fire as their inner natures; and this would consume their whole life.

When spirits are in this second state, they actually look exactly the way they were inwardly in the world. The things they had done and said in secret are made public, too, because now, since outward factors are not restraining them, they say the same things openly; and they keep trying to do the same things without any of the fear for the reputations that they had in the world. Further, they are then led into many states of their evils, so that they look to angels and good spirits like the people they really are. This is how hidden things are opened and covert things are uncovered according to the Lord's words, "Nothing is hidden that will not be disclosed or concealed that will not be recognized. What you have said in darkness will be heard in the light, and what you have spoken in the ear in closets will be proclaimed on the rooftops" (Luke 12:2–3); and again, "I tell you, every idle word people have spoken, they will give an account of it on the day of judgment" (Matthew 12:36).   **507**

There is no way to describe briefly what evil people are like in this state because their insanity depends on their urges, and these vary. So I should like to mention just a few particular cases that will enable you to draw conclusions about the rest.   **508**

Some people have loved themselves above all else. They have focused on their own prestige in their duties and positions, they have done constructive things not for the sake of doing them or from finding pleasure in them but for the sake of their reputation, to be ranked above other people on that account, therefore finding pleasure in their reputation for

eminence. When they arrive in the second state, they are supremely stupid because the more they love themselves the farther they move from
heaven, and the farther they move from heaven, the farther they move
from wisdom.

[2] There are people caught up in self-love and in guile at the same
time, people who have used devious means to raise themselves to positions of esteem. They take up company with the worst people of all and
study magical arts that are abuses of the divine design, using them to ha-
rass everyone who does not defer to them. They hatch plots, cherish
hatred, breathe out vengeance, and long to savage everyone who does not
submit to them. They plunge into all these behaviors to the extent that
the malevolent horde supports them. Eventually, they start mulling over
how they can climb up to heaven and destroy it, or how they can be worshiped there as gods. Their madness carries them all the way to this.

[3] Catholics like this are more insane than others.[283] They cherish
the thought that heaven and hell are in their power and that they can for-
give sins at will. They claim everything divine for themselves and call
themselves Christ. Their belief that this is true is so strong that wherever
it flows in it disturbs minds and brings on a darkness to the point of
pain. They are much the same in both states, though in the second they
lack rationality. There will be particular information about their forms of
insanity and their lot after this state in the booklet *The Last Judgment and
Babylon Destroyed.*[284]

[4] There are people who have attributed creation to nature and have
therefore denied the Divine Being at heart, though not out loud, thus
denying everything about the church and heaven. They gather with people like themselves in this state and call everyone God who is particularly
guileful, even honoring such individuals with divine worship. I have seen
people like this in a meeting worshiping a magician, discussing nature,
and behaving like idiots—as though they were animals in human form.
Some of them had been appointed to high office in the world and some
had been considered learned and wise. The details may vary.

[5] You may gather from these few cases what people are like whose
deeper levels of mind are closed toward heaven. This is what happens for
everyone who does not accept any inflow from heaven by acknowledging
the Divine Being and by a living life of faith. People may judge for themselves what they would be like if this were their nature, if they were allowed to behave with no fear of the law or fear for their lives, without
any outward restraints—threats to their reputation or to their rank, their
profit, and the pleasures that attend them.

[6] However, the Lord controls their madness so that it does not transgress the bounds of usefulness, for there is some use for every such individual. Good spirits see in them what evil is and what its nature is, and what people are like if they are not led by the Lord. Openly evil individuals also serve to gather people of similar evil and separate them from good people, to remove from evil people the true and good elements that they presented and feigned outwardly, and to lead them into the evils of their life and the falsities of their malice and thus prepare them for hell. [7] This is because people do not get into hell until they are immersed in their malice and in the falsities that stem from it, because no one is allowed to have a divided mind, to think and say one thing and intend something else. Every evil person there must think what is false out of malice and talk out of that malicious falsity there, both from intent and therefore from his or her own love and pleasure and gratification. This is how they behaved in the world when they were thinking in their spirit—that is, when they were thinking within themselves, from their deeper affection. This is because intent is the essential person, not thought except as it is derived from intent; and volition is the essential nature or character of the human being. So being remanded to our own intentions is being remanded to our own nature or character and to our own life as well, since it is through life that we acquire our nature. After death, we retain the nature we had gained by our life in the world, which for evil people can no longer be changed for the better by the path of thought or of understanding what is true.

Since evil spirits plunge into all kinds of evils when they are in this second state, it is normal for them to be punished often and severely. There are many kinds of punishments in the world of spirits, and there is no respect for rank, for whether someone was a king or a servant in the world. Every evil brings its own punishment with it. They are united; so whoever is involved in something evil is involved in the punishment of the evil as well. Still, no one suffers any punishment for evil things done in the world, only for current evil deeds. It boils down to the same thing, though, and makes no difference whether you say that we suffer punishments because of our evil deeds in the world or that we suffer punishments because of our evil deeds in the other life, because after death we all return to our life, which means that we are involved in the same kinds of evil. This is because our nature is determined by the kind of physical life we led (§§470–484).

The reason they are punished is that fear of punishment is the only means of taming their evils in that state. Encouragement does not work

509

any more, or teaching or fear of the law or fear for their reputation, because they are acting from their nature, which cannot be compelled or broken by anything but punishments.

Good spirits are never punished, though, even though they have done bad things in the world. This is because their evils do not come back. I have also been granted a knowledge that their evils are of a different kind or nature. They do not stem from any deliberate resistance to what is true, and they are not from any evil heart except the one they acquired by heredity from their parents, which blind pleasure drove them into when they were involved in outward concerns separated from inner ones.

510   Every individual comes to the community where her or his spirit was in the world. Each of us, as to spirit, is actually united to some community, either heavenly or hellish, evil people to hellish communities and good people to heavenly ones. (See §438 on the fact that we are brought to our own communities after death.) Spirits are brought there gradually, and ultimately get in. When evil spirits are in the state of their deeper concerns, they gradually turn toward their own communities and eventually face them directly, before this state is completed. When the state is completed, then the evil spirits themselves plunge into a hell where there are people of like mind. To the eye, this plunge looks like someone falling backward headfirst. The reason it looks like this is that such people are in an inverted order. They have loved hellish things and spurned heavenly ones. During this second state, some evil people go in and out of various hells; but they do not seem then to go headlong the way people do when they have been completely undone.

The actual community where their spirits were in the world is shown to them, too, while they are in the state of their outer concerns, so that they know from this that they were in hell during their physical life; but still they are not in the same state as the people who are in hell itself. Rather, they are in a state like that of people in the world of spirits. I will explain later what this state is like compared to that of people in hell.[285]

511   The separation of evil spirits from good spirits takes place in this second state, since in the first state they were all together. The reason is that as long as spirits are focused on their outward concerns it is like the situation in the world—evil people together with good ones and good ones with evil ones. It is different when people have been brought into their inner natures and are left to their own nature or intentions.

There are various means used for this separation of good people from evil ones. Often it is by having them led around to the communities they had been in touch with through their good thoughts and affections during the first state. This brings them to communities they had misled by outward appearance into believing that they were not evil. Often they are led around through a great arc, and their intrinsic quality is displayed to good spirits everywhere. The good spirits turn away as soon as they see them; and as they turn away, so the evil spirits who are being led around turn away as well, facing the hellish community that is their destination. I forbear to mention other modes of separation; there are many of them.

Our Third State after Death, Which Is a State of Instruction for People Who Are Entering Heaven

OUR third state after death, or the third state of our spirits, is one of instruction. This state is for people who are entering heaven and becoming angels, but not for people who are entering hell, because these latter cannot be taught. As a result, their second state is also their third, and ends in their turning straight toward their own love and therefore toward the hellish community that is engaged in a love like their own. Once this has happened, their intentions and thinking flow from that love; and since it is a hellish love, they intend only what is evil and think only what is false. These are their pleasures because they are matters of their love. Further, this results in their rejecting everything that is good and true that had served their love as means.

[2] Good people, though, are brought from the second state into a third, which is a state of preparation for heaven by means of instruction. In fact, no one can be prepared for heaven except by knowing at first hand what is good and true, and therefore only by being taught. This is because without being taught, no one can know what spiritual good and truth are and what the evil and falsity that oppose them are. We can know in the world what civil and moral good and truth are, what is called fair and honest, because there are civil laws there that teach what is fair, and there are also social situations where we learn to live by moral laws, which all deal with what is honest and equitable. Spiritual good and truth, however, are not learned from the world but from heaven. We can in fact know them from the Word and from the church's doctrine from the Word, but this still cannot flow into life unless we are in heaven in

regard to the deeper levels of our minds. We are in heaven when we acknowledge the Divine Being and at the same time act fairly and honestly, recognizing that we should because it is commanded us in the Word. In this way we live fairly and honestly for the sake of the Divine and not for the sake of ourselves and the world as our primary goals. [3] However, no one can behave like this without first having been taught things like the fact that God exists, that heaven and hell exist, that there is a life after death, that God is to be loved above all and our neighbor as ourselves, and that we are to believe what it says in the Word because the Word is divine. Without recognizing and admitting these principles we cannot think spiritually, and without thought about such matters we cannot intend them; for what we do not know we cannot think, and what we do not think we cannot intend. However, when we do intend such things, heaven flows in—that is, the Lord flows into our lives through heaven, for he flows into the will and through that into the thought, and through both of these into the life, since they are where our whole life comes from. We can see from this that spiritual good and truth are not learned from the world but from heaven, and that no one can be prepared for heaven except by instruction.

[4] Then too, to the extent that the Lord flows into our life he does teach us, since to that same extent he kindles our intentions with a love of learning what is true and enlightens our thought so that we know what is true. To the extent that this happens, our deeper reaches are opened and heaven is sown in them. Even beyond this, to that same extent what is divine and heavenly flows into the honest deeds of our moral life and the fair deeds of our civic life and makes them spiritual, since then we are doing them from the Divine because we are doing them for the sake of the Divine. The honest and fair deeds of our moral and civic life that we do from this source are actual effects of spiritual life; and an effect derives all its being from its efficient cause,[286] because the quality of the cause determines the quality of the effect.

513   The teaching is done by angels from a number of communities, mainly ones in the northern and southern regions, because these angelic communities are focused on intelligence and wisdom based on firsthand knowledge of what is good and true. The teaching sites are in the north; and there are different ones, differentiated and arranged according to the genera and species of heavenly virtues so that everyone can be taught there in a manner suited to his or her character and receptivity. The sites are spread out over a large area there.

Good spirits who need to be taught are taken there by the Lord after their time in the world of spirits has been fulfilled. This does not apply to everyone, though, since people who have been taught in the world have already been prepared for heaven by the Lord and are taken up into heaven by a different route. For some, this happens immediately after death. For others, it happens after a short stay with good spirits for the removal of the cruder elements of their thoughts and affections (acquired because of concerns for rank and wealth in the world), and their consequent purification. Some people are shattered first, which happens in sites under the soles of the feet called the lower earth, where they suffer harsh treatment. These are people who have convinced themselves of false principles but still have lived good lives. False convictions cling hard, and until they are dispelled, truths cannot be seen and therefore cannot be accepted. These shattering experiences and the different ways they happen have been treated in *Secrets of Heaven,* though, and some references to that work are appended in the note.[a]

The people who are at these instructional sites live in different places. As individuals, they are inwardly in touch with the communities of heaven they are headed for; so since heaven's communities are arranged in a heavenly form (see above, §§200–212), so too are the places where the teaching takes place. As a result, when you look at these sites from

514

a. Shattering experiences do happen in the other life—that is, some people who arrive there from the world are shattered there: 698, 7122, 7474, 9763. Upright people are shattered as regards false elements, and evil people as to true ones: 7474, 7541, 7542. Shattering experiences happen to upright people so that they can shed the earthly and worldly preoccupations they acquired while they were living in the world: 7186, 9763; and so that evil and false things may be removed, providing room for the inflow of good and true things out of heaven from the Lord, and providing the ability to accept them: 7122, 9331 *[9330]*. We cannot be raised into heaven before things like this are removed because they get in the way and do not agree with heavenly values: 6928, 7122, 7136 *[7186]*, 7541, 7542, 9763. This is how people who are to be raised into heaven are prepared: 4728, 7090. It is dangerous for people to enter heaven before they have been prepared: 537, 538. On the state of enlightenment and the joy of people who are emerging from shattering experiences and being raised into heaven, and on how they are accepted there: 2699, 2701, 2704. The area where shattering experiences take place is called "the lower earth": 4728, 7090. A description of this area under the soles of the feet, surrounded by hells: 4940–4951, 7090; from experience: 699. The particular hells that attack and shatter more than the others: 7317, 7502, 7545. People who attack and shatter upright souls later fear and flee and avoid them: 7768. These attacks and shattering experiences take different forms depending on the stubbornness of the evil and false elements and the manner and mode in which they persist: 1106–1113. Some people undergo shattering experiences willingly: 1107. Some people are shattered by fears: 4942; some by being assailed by evil things they had done in the world and false things they had thought in the world, which gives rise to anxiety and pangs of conscience: 1106. Some are shattered by spiritual imprisonment, which is ignorance and deprivation of truth yoked to a longing to know what is true: 1109, 2694; some by dreams [reading *somnium;* the first edition has *somnum,* "sleep"], some by a state halfway between waking and sleep, with a description: 1108. People who have claimed credit for their deeds seem to be chopping wood: 1110. And so on, with a wide range of variety: 699.

heaven, they look like a heaven in lesser form. In length they stretch from east to west, and in breadth from south to north; but the breadth seems to be less than the length.

The general arrangement is like this. Toward the front are people who have died in childhood and are being educated in heaven up to the age of early adolescence. After having spent their infancy with women educators, they are brought to this location by the Lord and taught.

Behind them are the places where people are taught who died as adults and who in the world were drawn to truth because of the goodness of their lives.

Behind these again are people who were devoted to Islam and had led a moral life in the world, acknowledged one God, and recognized the Lord as the essential prophet. When they let go of Muhammad because he cannot do anything for them, they turn to the Lord and worship him, recognizing his divine nature; and then they receive instruction in the Christian religion.

Behind these, and farther to the north, there are sites for the instruction of various non-Christian people who in the world lived good lives in accord with their own religion, acquired a kind of conscience, and behaved fairly and honestly not because of the laws of their nation but because of the laws of their religion, believing these laws to be holy and not to be violated by their actions in any way. All of them are readily led to recognize the Lord when they have been taught, because at heart they have held that God is not invisible but visible in human form. There are more of these than of any other kind, and the best of them are from Africa.

515 Not everyone is taught in the same way or by the same communities of heaven. People who have been raised in heaven from infancy are taught by angels of the inner heavens because they have not absorbed false notions from distortions of religion or befouled their spiritual life with impurities drawn from rank and wealth in the world.

Most people who have died as adults are taught by angels of the outmost heaven because these angels are better adapted to them than are angels of the more inward heavens. These latter focus on a deeper wisdom that the deceased cannot yet accept.

Muslims, though, are taught by angels who once adhered to that religion but have turned to Christianity. Other non-Christians too are taught by their own angels.

516 All the teaching there is from doctrine drawn from the Word, and not from the Word apart from doctrine. Christians are taught on the basis of a heavenly doctrine that is in complete agreement with the inner meaning of the Word. The others, like the Muslims and non-Christians, are taught on the basis of doctrines suited to their grasp. These differ from heavenly doctrine only in that spiritual life is taught through a moral life in accord with the good tenets of their own religion, which was the basis of their life in the world.

Teaching in the heavens differs from teaching on earth in that [there] information is not consigned to memory but to life, since spirits' memory is in their life. They actually accept and absorb whatever agrees with their life and do not accept, much less absorb, what does not agree. This is because spirits are affections, and therefore have a human form that resembles their affections.

517

[2] Since this is their nature, they are constantly breathing in a desire to know what is true, for the sake of constructive living. The Lord in fact sees to it that we love the constructive activities that suit our gifts. This love is intensified by our hope of becoming angels. Further, since all the activities of heaven focus on a common use, which is the welfare of the Lord's kingdom (which now is our country), and since we fulfill our distinctive individual functions to the extent that they focus directly and intimately on that common use, all the countless distinctive and individual functions are good and heavenly. This means that for each of us an affection for what is true is united to an affection for usefulness to the point that they act as one. A true understanding of use is sown in this way, so that the truths we learn are true perceptions of what is useful. This is how angelic spirits are taught and prepared for heaven.

[3] There are various ways in which an affection for the truth suited to usefulness is instilled, many of them unknown in the world, primarily by depictions of useful activities. These can be presented in thousands of ways in the spiritual world, with such grace and charm that they permeate spirits all the way from the deeper levels of their minds to the outer levels of their bodies and therefore affect the whole person. As a result, spirits virtually become their constructive lives; so when they arrive in the communities their instruction has prepared them for, they are in their own life when they are engaged in their useful activities.[b]

---

b. Everything good has its delight from constructive activities and in keeping with them; this is also the source of its quality, so the nature of the activity determines that of the good: 3049, 4984, 7038. Angelic life consists of the virtues of love and thoughtfulness, and therefore in constructive actions: 453 [454]. For the Lord and therefore for angels, nothing matters in people except goals that are useful activities: 1317, 1645, 5844 [5854]. The Lord's kingdom is a kingdom of useful activities: 453 [454], 696, 1103, 3645, 4054, 7038. Serving the Lord is living constructively: 7038. Our character is determined by the uses we have: 1568, 3570, 4054, 6571, 6934 [6935], 6938, 10284.

We may gather from this that awareness, which is an outward form of truth, does not get anyone into heaven. Rather, what gets us in is the useful life that is granted through knowledge.

518 There were some spirits who while they were in the world had thought their way into the conviction that they would get into heaven and would be accepted before anyone else because they were well educated and knew a lot about the Word and the doctrine of the churches. They believed that they were wise, that they were the people meant by the prophecy in Daniel 12:3 that "they will shine like the glory of the firmament and like the stars."[287] However, they were examined to see whether their learning was lodged in their memories or in their life. The ones who had a real affection for truth—that is, for the sake of constructive acts apart from merely physical and worldly motives, acts that were essentially spiritual—once they had been instructed, were accepted into heaven. They were then granted knowledge of what does shine in heaven. It is the divine truth (which is heaven's light there) in constructive living, this being the facet that receives that light and turns it into various kinds of radiance.

For others, though, the learning was lodged only in their memories. They had thereby acquired an ability to reason about truths and to prove the ones they accepted as fundamental, notions that looked true once they were proved, even though they were false. These people were not in heaven's light at all, but were wrapped up in a faith based on the pride that characterizes so many people of like intelligence, a pride in being especially erudite and therefore destined for heaven where they will be waited on by angels. Because of all this, to extract them from their conceited faith, they were taken up to the first or outmost heaven to be admitted into one particular angelic community. Even as they were entering it, though, their sight began to darken at the inflow of heaven's light. Then their intellects began to be confused, and eventually they began to labor for breath as though they were dying. Not only that, when they began to feel heaven's warmth, which is heavenly love, they began to feel profound agonies. So they were expelled, and then were taught that knowledge does not make an angel, only the actual life that people have gained through their knowledge. This is because in and of itself, knowledge is outside of heaven; but a life gained through knowledge is inside heaven.

519 After spirits have been prepared for heaven in these learning sites (which does not take long, because they are surrounded by spiritual concepts that comprehend a great deal at once), they are dressed in angelic

clothing, usually white as linen, taken to a path that leads up toward heaven, and turned over to guardian angels there. Then they are accepted by other angels and put in touch with their communities and with a host of blessings. The Lord then takes each angel to her or his community. This happens in various ways, sometimes with detours. No angel knows the paths along which they are taken, only the Lord. When they arrive at their own communities, their inner natures are opened, and since they are in harmony with the inner natures of the angels who are members of that community, they are recognized instantly and accepted with joy.

I should like to add here something remarkable about the paths that lead from these sites to heaven, the paths by which newly arrived angels are admitted. There are eight paths, two from each teaching site. One leads up toward the east and the other toward the west. People who are entering the Lord's heavenly kingdom are admitted by the eastern path, while people who are entering the Lord's spiritual kingdom are admitted by the western path.

The four paths that lead to the Lord's heavenly kingdom are graced by olive trees and various fruit trees, while the ones that lead to the Lord's spiritual kingdom are graced by grapevines and laurel. This is because of correspondence, since vines and laurel correspond to an affection for truth and its uses, while olive and fruit trees correspond to an affection for what is good and its uses.

No One Enters Heaven on the Basis of Mercy Alone

IF people have not been taught about heaven, the way to heaven, and the life of heaven for those on earth, they think that acceptance into heaven comes from a pure mercy extended to people of faith, people for whom the Lord intercedes, so that admission depends solely on grace.[288] They therefore think that anyone at all can be saved out of good will; and some people even think that this includes the inhabitants of hell.

However, they do not know anything about human beings, that our quality depends on our lives and our lives on our loves. This applies not only to the deeper levels of our volition and intellect but even to the outer aspects of our bodies, with the physical form being nothing but an outward form in which our deeper natures manifest themselves in practice. This means that our love is our whole person (see above, §363). Nor do they realize that the body does not live on its own but from its spirit, and that our spirit is our actual affection, with our spiritual body being nothing more than our affection in the kind of human form it presents after death (see above, §§453–460). As long as these facts are not known, people can be led to believe that salvation is nothing more than the divine pleasure that we call mercy and grace.

522 First, though, let me state what divine mercy is. Divine mercy is a pure mercy toward the whole human race with the intent of saving it, and it is constant toward every individual, never withdrawing from anyone. This means that everyone who can be saved is saved. However, no one can be saved except by divine *means,* the means revealed by the Lord in the Word. Divine means are what we refer to as divine truths. They teach how we are to live in order to be saved. The Lord uses them to lead us to heaven and to instill heaven's life into us. The Lord does this for everyone; but he cannot instill heaven's life into anyone who does not refrain from evil, since evil bars the way. So to the extent that we do refrain from evil, the Lord in his divine mercy leads us by divine means, from infancy to the end of life in the world and thereafter to eternity. This is the divine mercy that I mean. We can therefore see that the Lord's mercy is pure mercy, but not unmediated: that is, it does not save people whenever it feels like it, no matter how they have lived.

523 The Lord never does anything contrary to his design because he himself is the design. The divine truth that emanates from him is what establishes the design, and divine truths are the laws of the design by which the Lord is leading us. Saving people by unmediated mercy is contrary to the divine design, and anything contrary to the divine design is contrary to the divine nature.

The divine design is heaven for us. We have distorted it by living contrary to its laws, which are divine truths. The Lord brings us back into the design out of pure mercy, through the laws of the design; and to the extent that we are brought back, we accept heaven into ourselves. Whoever accepts heaven enters heaven.

This shows again that the Lord's divine mercy is pure mercy but not unmediated.[a]

If we could be saved by nothing but mercy then everyone would be saved, even the people in hell. In fact, there would not be any hell because the Lord is mercy itself, love itself, goodness itself. So it goes against his essential divine nature to say that all people can be saved directly and that he does not save them. We know from the Word that the Lord intends the salvation of all and the damnation of no one.

Many people who arrive in the other life from the Christian world bring with them a faith that they are going to be saved out of straight mercy, because they plead for it. When they are examined, though, it turns out that they have believed that getting into heaven was simply a matter of being let in, and that people who had been admitted were in heavenly joy. They have had no notion of what heaven is or what heavenly joy is. So they are told that the Lord does not deny heaven to anyone. They can be let in if they wish and even stay there. Some who wanted to were actually let in; but at the very threshold, at the touch of heaven's warmth (that is, of the love angels are engaged in) and the inflow of heaven's light (which is divine truth), they were seized with such pain in the heart that they felt themselves in the torments of hell rather than in the joys of heaven. Struck by this, they plunged down headlong. In this way they were taught by firsthand experience that no one can enter heaven out of straight mercy.

524

525

---

a. Divine truth emanating from the Lord is the source of his design, and divine good is the essence of the design: 1728, 2258, 8700, 8988. As a result, the Lord is the design: 1919, 2011, 5110, 5703, 10336, 10619. Divine truths are the laws of the design: 2247 [2447], 7995. The whole heaven is arranged by the Lord according to its divine pattern: 3038, 7211, 9128, 9338, 10125, 10151, 10157. So heaven's form is a form in accord with the divine design: 4040–4043, 6607, 9877. To the extent that we live according to the design, that is, to the extent that we live intent on what is good according to divine truths, we accept heaven into ourselves: 4839. The human being is where all the elements of the divine design are gathered together, and by creation we are the divine design in form because we are its vessels: 4219, 4220, 4223, 4523, 4524, 5114, 5368 [4839], 6013, 6057, 6605, 6626, 9706, 10156, 10472. We are not born into what is good and true but into what is evil and false, and therefore not into the divine design but into a pattern contrary to it, which is why we are born into pure ignorance and need to be born again or regenerated; the Lord effects this through divine truths, in order to bring us back into the design: 1047, 2307, 2308, 3518, 3812, 8480, 8550, 10283, 10284, 10286, 10731. When the Lord is forming us afresh or regenerating us, he arranges everything in us according to the design, or into heaven's form: 5700, 6690, 9931, 10303. Evil and false things are contrary to the design, but still people who are absorbed in them are governed by the Lord, not according to the design but from it: 4839, 7877, 10778 [10777]. It is impossible for someone who is living in evil to be saved out of pure mercy, because this goes against the divine design: 8700.

526   I have at times talked with angels about this and have said that many people in the world who have lived intent on evil and have talked with others about heaven and eternal life say only that getting into heaven is simply a matter of being let in on the basis of pure mercy. This is true especially of people who make faith the only means of salvation, since from this fundamental tenet of their religion they do not focus on life or on the deeds of love that make up one's life. As a result, they do not focus on the other means the Lord uses to instill heaven into us and render us open to heavenly joy. So since they reject all the actual means, the necessary corollary of their premise is that we enter heaven on the basis of pure mercy, believing God the Father to be moved to it through the intercession of the Son. [2] Angels have responded that they know this kind of dogma follows necessarily from acceptance of the principle of salvation by faith alone and that this dogma is the head of the others, a head into which no light from heaven can flow, because it is not true. It is therefore the source of the ignorance the church is mired in nowadays—ignorance about the Lord, heaven, life after death, heavenly joy, the essential nature of love and thoughtfulness, and in general about what is good and its union with what is true. This results in ignorance about human life, its source, and its quality. Life is never gained by mere thought, but only by intent and consequent deeds. It is the result of thought to the extent that the thought derives from intent, so it is from faith only to the extent that faith derives from love. Angels grieve that these people do not realize that faith alone cannot exist in anyone because faith apart from its source, which is love, is only information, or for some a secondhand belief that counterfeits faith (see above, §482). This belief is not part of our life but is outside it, since it is separated from us if it is not coherent with our love.

[3] Angels have also said that people who are caught up in this kind of principle concerning the essential means of our salvation cannot help believing in straight mercy because they can tell from natural light and from visual experience that faith by itself does not constitute human life—people who are leading evil lives can think and convince themselves of the same principles. This is why they believe that evil people can be saved just like good ones, provided in the hour of their death they talk about intercession and mercy obtained by it.

The angels kept insisting that they have never yet seen people who lived an evil life accepted into heaven out of straight mercy, no matter how fervently they had spoken in the world from faith, or from the trust that is meant by *faith* in its primary sense.

[4] When they have asked about Abraham, Isaac, Jacob, and David, about the apostles, whether they were not accepted into heaven out of straight mercy, angels have answered that none of them was. Each one was accepted on the basis of his life in the world. They should realize where they were. No one had more prestige than anyone else. They said that the reason these individuals were mentioned in the Word with such respect was that they referred in the deeper meaning to the Lord— Abraham, Isaac, and Jacob to the Lord in respect to his divine nature and his divine human nature, David to the Lord as to the regal divine nature, and the apostles to the Lord as to divine truths. The angels do not pay any attention to these individuals when the Word is being read by people on earth because their names do not cross over into heaven. They are conscious of the Lord instead, as just noted. So the Word that is in heaven (described above in §259) never mentions them, since that Word is the inner meaning of the Word that exists in the world.[b]

I can testify on the grounds of abundant experience that it is impossible to grant the life of heaven to people who have led lives opposed to it in the world. There have actually been people who believed that they would readily accept divine truths after death when they heard them from angels, that they would become believers and lead different lives, so that they could be accepted into heaven. However, this has been tried with any number of individuals (though only with people who shared this same kind of belief), granted them so that they could learn that there is no repentance after death. Some of them did understand truths and seemed to accept them; but the moment they turned back to the life of their own love they rejected them and even argued against them. Some rejected them on the spot, unwilling even to listen to them. Some wanted the life of the love they had acquired in the world to be taken

527

b. In the inner meaning of the Word, Abraham, Isaac, and Jacob mean the Lord in regard to his divine nature and his divine human nature: 1893, 4615, 6098, 6185, 6276, 6804, 6847. Abraham is unknown in heaven: 1834, 1876, 3229. David means the Lord in regard to his divine kingship: 1888, 9954. The twelve apostles represented the Lord in regard to all the elements of the church, and therefore to matters of faith and love: 2129, 3354, 3488, 3858, 6397. Peter represented the Lord in respect to faith, James in respect to thoughtfulness, and John in respect to thoughtful works: 3750, 10087. The statement that the twelve apostles would sit on twelve thrones and judge the twelve tribes of Israel means that the Lord will judge according to the true and good elements of faith and love: 2129, 6397. The names of people and places in the Word do not make their way into heaven, but change into things and states; and in fact the names cannot even be pronounced in heaven: 1876, 5225, 6516, 10216, 10282, 10432. Further, angels think without reference to roles: 8343, 8945 [8985], 9007.

away from them and an angelic life or the life of heaven poured in to re-place it. Permission was given for even this to be done for them; but once the life of their own love was taken away, they lay there like corpses, with no control over themselves.

These and other similar kinds of experience teach simple good peo-ple that there is no way to change anyone's life after death, no way to rewrite an evil life into a good one or a hellish life into an angelic one. This is because the nature of every spirit from head to toe is determined by his or her love and consequently by his or her life. To change this into its opposite would mean the total destruction of the spirit. Angels insist that it is easier to change one owl into a dove or another[289] into a bird of paradise than to change a hellish spirit into an angel of heaven.

The reader may see in the appropriate chapter above (§§470–484) that our nature after death is determined by the quality of our life in the world. We can gather from this that no one can be accepted into heaven on the basis of pure mercy.

It Is Not So Hard to Lead a Heaven-Bound Life as People Think It Is

528 SOME people believe it is hard to lead the heaven-bound life that is called "spiritual" because they have heard that we need to renounce the world and give up the desires attributed to the body and the flesh and "live spiritually."[290] All they understand by this is spurning worldly inter-ests, especially concerns for money and prestige, going around in con-stant devout meditation about God, salvation, and eternal life, devoting their lives to prayer, and reading the Word and religious literature. They think this is renouncing the world and living for the spirit and not for the flesh. However, the actual case is quite different, as I have learned from an abundance of experience and conversation with angels. In fact, people who renounce the world and live for the spirit in this fashion take

on a mournful life for themselves, a life that is not open to heavenly joy, since our life does remain with us [after death]. No, if we would accept heaven's life, we need by all means to live in the world and to participate in its duties and affairs. In this way, we accept a spiritual life by means of our moral and civic life; and there is no other way a spiritual life can be formed within us, no other way our spirits can be prepared for heaven. This is because living an inner life and not an outer life at the same time is like living in a house that has no foundation, that gradually either settles or develops gaping cracks or totters until it collapses.

If we look critically at human life with rational insight, it turns out to be threefold—spiritual life, moral life, and civic life. These lives are distinguishable: some people live a civic life but not a moral or spiritual one, some live a moral life but not a spiritual one, and some live a civic and a moral life and a spiritual life as well. These last are the ones who are leading heaven's life, while the former are leading the world's life, divorced from heaven's life. 529

To begin with, then, we may gather that a spiritual life is not separate from a natural life or the world's life but is united to it like a soul to its body; and if they were separated, it would be like a house without a foundation, as just stated.

In fact, moral and civic living is what spiritual life does, for intending well is the essence of spiritual life and behaving well is the essence of moral and civic life. If these are separated from each other, spiritual life consists solely of thinking and talking, and the intent ebbs away because it has no support. Yet intent is our actual spiritual substance.

What follows will make it possible to see that it is not all that hard to lead a heaven-bound life. 530

Who *can't* lead a civic and moral life? After all, we are introduced to it in infancy and know it from living in the world. We do in fact lead this kind of life whether we are evil or good, since no one wants to be called dishonest or unfair. Almost everyone practices honesty and fairness outwardly, even to the point of seeming genuinely honest and fair, or seeming to act from genuine honesty and fairness. Spiritual people have to live in much the same way and can do so just as easily as natural people, the difference being that spiritual people believe in the Divine Being and act honestly and fairly not just because it follows civil and moral laws but also because it follows divine laws. In fact, since they are thinking about divine [laws] when they act, they are in touch with heaven's angels; and to the extent that they are, they are united to them, and their inner person—which is essentially a spiritual person—is opened. When this is our nature, the Lord adopts and leads us without our realizing it, and whatever things we do that are honest and fair—the deeds of our moral and civil life—come from a spiritual source. Doing what is honest and fair from a spiritual source is doing it from genuine honesty and fairness, or doing it from the heart.

[2] Outwardly, such honesty and fairness look just like the honesty and fairness of natural people or even evil and hellish people, but inwardly they are totally different. Evil people do what is fair and honest solely for the sake of themselves and the world. If they were not afraid of the law and its penalties, of losing their reputation, their wealth, and their life, they would act with utter dishonesty and unfairness. Since they have no fear of God or of any divine law, they have no inner restraint that keeps them in check; so to the extent that they can, they cheat and rob and plunder others just for the pleasure of it. Their inner nature is especially clear from people like them in the other life, when all people's outer natures are stripped away and their inner natures disclosed, the natures in which they will go on living to eternity (see above, §§499–511). Since they are then acting without external restraints, which are (as just noted) fears of the law and of losing reputation, prestige, profit, and life, they act wildly and scoff at honesty and fairness.

[3] In contrast, people who have lived honestly and fairly because of divine laws act wisely when their outer natures are stripped away and they are left to their inner natures, because they are united to heaven's angels, who share their wisdom with them.

This enables us to gather initially that spiritual people can behave much the same as natural people in their civil and moral life, provided they are united to the Deity in their inner person, in their intent and thought (see above, §§358, 359, 360).

531 The laws of spiritual life, the laws of civil life, and the laws of moral life are handed down to us in the Ten Commandments. The first three commandments contain the laws of spiritual life, the next four the laws of civil life, and the last three the laws of moral life. Outwardly, purely natural people live by these same commandments just the way spiritual people do. They worship the Divine, go to church, listen to sermons, wear devout faces, do not kill or commit adultery or steal or bear false witness, do not cheat their colleagues of their goods. However, they behave this way solely in their own interest, in order to look good in the world. Inwardly, these same people are exactly the opposite of what they seem to be outwardly. Because at heart they deny the Divine, they play the hypocrite in their worship. In their private thinking they scoff at the holy rites of the church, believing that they serve only to restrain the simple masses. [2] This is why they are wholly cut off from heaven. So since they are not spiritual, they are not moral or civic people either; for even though they do not kill, they hate everyone who gets in their way and burn with vengefulness because of their hatred. So if they were not constrained by civil laws and the outward restraints exercised by their fears, they would kill. Because this is what they crave, it follows that they are constantly killing. Even though they do not commit adultery, still because they believe there is nothing wrong with it they are constantly adulterous, and actually do commit it as much as they can and as often as they have the opportunity. Even though they do not steal, still since they do covet other people's assets and regard cheating and malicious devices as legally justifiable, they are constantly stealing in their minds. The same applies to the other commandments of moral life—not bearing false witness or coveting the goods of others. All who deny the Divine are like this, all who do not have some conscience based on religion. Their nature shows obviously in similar people in the other life when they are let into their inner nature after their outer nature has been stripped away. Since they are separated from heaven at that point, they act in unison with hell; so they keep company with the people who live there.

[3] It is different for people who at heart have acknowledged the Deity and have attended to divine laws in the deeds of their lives, living both by the first three commandments of the Decalogue and by the others as well.[291] When they are let into their inner nature, after their outer nature is stripped away, they are wiser than they were in the world. Coming into their inner natures is like coming from darkness into light, from ignorance into wisdom, from a sad life into a blissful one, because they are in the Divine and therefore in heaven.

I have mentioned this to let it be known what each kind of person is like, though both may lead the same kind of outward life.

Anyone may recognize that thoughts tend to follow where intentions lead, or to go where we aim them. Thought is actually our inner sight and behaves like our outward sight. It turns and dwells where it is directed and aimed. If our inner sight or thought is turned toward the world and dwells there, it follows that our thought becomes worldly. If it is turned toward self and our prestige, it becomes carnal. However, if it is turned toward heaven, it becomes heavenly. So if it is turned toward heaven, it is raised up; if it is turned toward self, it is pulled away from heaven and immersed in the physical; if it is turned toward the world, it

532

is also turned away from heaven and spread out among whatever items meet our eyes.

[2] It is our love that creates our intentions and that focuses our inner sight or our thought on its objects. So love for ourselves directs our thought toward ourselves and what we claim as our own, love of the world directs it toward worldly matters, and love of heaven directs it toward heavenly matters. This can enable us to know what state the inner reaches of our minds are in once we identify our love. That is, if we love heaven, the inner reaches are raised up toward heaven and open upward. If we love the world and ourselves, our inner reaches are closed upward and open outward. So we may gather that if the higher reaches of our minds are closed to what is above them, we can no longer see the objects that pertain to heaven and the church. These are in darkness for us, and whatever is in darkness we either deny or do not understand. This is why people who love themselves and the world above all, since the higher levels of their minds are closed, deny divine truths at heart; and if they do say anything about them from their memory, they still do not understand it. They have the same attitude toward these matters as toward worldly and physical interests; and since they are like this, they cannot think about anything except what comes in through their physical senses, which are their sole delight. Their sensory experience also includes much that is foul, obscene, irreligious, and criminal. They cannot be distracted from these obsessions because there is no inflow from heaven into their minds, since as already noted their minds are closed to what is above them.

[3] The purpose that focuses our inner sight or thought is our volition, since our intentions determine our aims and our aims determine our thoughts. So if we aim for heaven, we focus our thinking on it, and with our thinking, our whole mind, which is therefore in heaven. This means it looks at the concerns of the world as below itself, like someone on the roof of a house. This is why people in whom the deeper levels of the mind are open can see the evil and false elements in themselves, since these are below their spiritual mind. Conversely, if people's inner reaches are not open, they cannot see their evil and false elements because they are in them and not above them. We may gather from this where our wisdom comes from and where our insanity comes from, and what we will be like after death when we are left to intend and think and then to act and speak in keeping with our inner nature.

Again, this has been presented to show what we are like inwardly, no matter how much alike we may seem outwardly.

We can now see that it is not so hard to lead the life of heaven as people think, because it is simply a matter of recognizing, when something attractive comes up that we know is dishonest or unfair, that this is not to be done because it is against the divine commandments. If we get used to thinking like this, and from this familiarity form a habit, then we are gradually united to heaven. To the extent that we are united to heaven, the higher levels of our minds are opened, and to the extent that they are opened, we see what is dishonest and unfair; and to the extent that we see this, these qualities can be dispelled. For no evil can be banished until it has been seen. This is a state we can enter because of our freedom, since everyone is free to think in this way. However, once the process has started, the Lord works his wonders within us, and causes us not only to see evils but to refuse them and eventually to turn away from them. This is the meaning of the Lord's words, "My yoke is easy and my burden light" (Matthew 11:30).

It is important to realize, though, that the difficulty of thinking like this and also of resisting evils increases to the extent that we deliberately do evil things—in fact, to that extent we become used to doing them until ultimately we no longer see them. Then we come to love them and to excuse them to gratify our love and to rationalize them with all kinds of self-deceptions and call them permissible and good. This happens, though, to people who in early adulthood plunge into all kinds of evil without restraint and at the same time at heart reject everything divine.

I was once shown the way to heaven and the way to hell. There was a broad path leading off to the left or north. There seemed to be a great many spirits traveling along it. In the distance, though, I could see a fairly large boulder where the broad path ended. Then two paths led off from the boulder, one to the left and the other, on the other side, to the right. The path to the left was narrow and confined, leading around through the west to the south, and therefore into the light of heaven. The path to the right was broad and open, leading obliquely down toward hell.

At first, everyone was clearly following the same path as far as the large boulder at the fork; but at that point they parted company. The good turned to the left and started along the confined path that led to heaven. The evil did not even see the boulder at the fork but fell over it and hurt themselves. When they got up, they rushed along the broad path to the right that led toward hell.

[2] Later, the meaning of all this was explained to me. The first path, the broad one where so many good and evil people were traveling

together, chatting with each other like friends with no visible difference between them, pictured people who live similarly honest and fair outward lives, with no visible difference between them. The stone at the fork or corner where the evil people stumbled, from which they rushed along the path to hell, pictured divine truth, which is denied by people who are focusing on hell. In the highest sense this stone meant the Lord's divine human nature. However, people who acknowledge divine truth and the divine nature of the Lord as well were taken along the path that led to heaven.

This showed me again that both evil and good people live the same life outwardly, or travel the same path, one as readily as the other. Yet the ones who at heart acknowledge the Divine, especially those within the church who acknowledge the Lord's divine nature, are led to heaven; while those who do not acknowledge it are led to hell.

[3] Paths in the other life picture the thoughts that flow from our aims or intentions. The paths that are presented to view there answer exactly to the thoughts of our aims, and our course follows the thoughts that flow from our aims. This is why you can tell the quality of spirits and of their thoughts from their paths. This also showed me the meaning of the Lord's words, "Enter through the narrow gate, for broad is the gate and open the way that leads to destruction, and there are many who walk along it; confined is the path and narrow the gate that leads to life, and there are few who find it" (Matthew 7:13–14). The way that leads to life is not narrow because it is difficult but because so few people find it, as stated.

The boulder I saw at the corner where the broad, common path ended and the two ways seemed to lead in opposite directions showed me the meaning of the Lord's words, "Have you not read what is written, 'The stone that the builders rejected has become the head of the corner'? Whoever falls over this stone will be shattered" (Luke 20:17–18).[292] The stone means divine truth, and the rock of Israel means the Lord in regard to his divine human nature. The builders are the people of the church. The head of the corner is where the fork is, and to fall and be shattered is to deny and perish.[a]

---

a. A stone means truth: 114, 643, 1298, 3720, 6426, 8609, 10376. So the law was written on stone tablets: 10376. The rock of Israel is the Lord as to divine truth and as to his divine human nature: 6426.

I have been allowed to talk with some people in the other life who **535** had distanced themselves from the affairs of the world in order to live in devotions and sanctity, and also with some who had mortified themselves in various ways because they thought this was renouncing the world and taming the desires of the flesh. However, most of them had wound up with a gloomy kind of life from this and had distanced themselves from that life of active thoughtfulness that can be led only in the world, so they could not associate with angels. The life of angels is cheerful and blessed. It consists of worthwhile activities that are deeds of thoughtfulness. Particularly, people who have led a life withdrawn from worldly concerns are aflame with a sense of their own worth and constantly crave heaven. They think of heavenly joy as their reward, with no knowledge whatever of what heavenly joy actually is. When they are with angels and are let into that joy—which has no sense of merit and consists of activities and public duties and in bliss at the good that is accomplished through them—they are as bewildered as though they were seeing something totally alien to their faith. Since they are not open to these joys, they move off and associate with people who have led the same kind of life in the world.

[2] There are other people who have lived outwardly devotional lives, constantly in churches and at prayer there. They have mortified their souls while constantly thinking about themselves, how they are worthier and more estimable than others and will be regarded as saints after their death. They are not in heaven in the other life because they have done all this with themselves first in mind. Since they have polluted divine truths by the self-love they immersed them in, some of them are so deranged that they think they are gods. So they are with similar people in hell. Some of them are ingenious and crafty and are in hells for the crafty people who used their skills and wiles to construct outward appearances that would lead the masses to believe them possessed of a divine sanctity.

[3] This includes many of the Catholic saints. I have been allowed to talk with some of them and have had their lives clearly described, both the lives they had led in the world and what they were like afterward.

I have mentioned all this to let it be known that the life that leads to heaven is not one of withdrawal from the world but a life in the world, and that a life of piety apart from a life of thoughtfulness (which is possible only in the world) does not lead to heaven at all. Rather, it is a life of thoughtfulness, a life of behaving honestly and fairly in every duty, every affair, every task, from our deeper nature and therefore from a heavenly source. The source of this life is within us when we act honestly and fairly because doing so is in accord with divine laws. This life is not hard, but a life of piety apart from a life of thoughtfulness is hard. Still, this latter life leads away from heaven as surely as people believe it leads to heaven.[b]

b. A life of piety apart from a life of thoughtfulness accomplishes nothing, but together they accomplish everything: 8252, 8253. Thoughtfulness toward our neighbor is doing what is good, fair, and upright in every task and in every duty: 8120, 8121, 8122. Thoughtfulness toward our neighbor includes absolutely everything we think, intend, and do: 8124. A life of thoughtfulness is a life by the Lord's commandments: 3249. Living by the Lord's commandments is loving the Lord: 10143, 10153, 10310, 10578, 10648 *[10645]*. True thoughtfulness is not for credit because it comes from a deeper affection and a consequent deeper pleasure: 2340 *[2380]*, 2373 *[2371]*, 2400, 3887, 6388–6393. Our abiding character after death is determined by the quality of our life of thoughtfulness in the world: 8256. Heavenly bliss flows from the Lord into a life of thoughtfulness: 2363. No one is let into heaven simply by thinking, but by intending and doing together with thinking: 2401, 3459. Unless doing what is good is united to intending what is good and thinking what is good, there is no salvation and no union of our inner person with our outer: 3987.

HELL

The Lord Governs the Hells

IN the earlier discussion of heaven, it was made clear throughout (particularly in §§2–6) that the Lord is the God of heaven and that the whole government of the heavens is in the Lord's hands. Since the relationship of heaven to hell and of hell to heaven is like that of two opposites that act against each other, with the action and reaction yielding the state of equilibrium within which everything exists, in order for absolutely everything to be kept in this balance, it is necessary that the ruler of the one be the ruler of the other as well. That is, unless the same Lord controlled the attacks of the hells and restrained their madness, the balance would be destroyed; and if the balance were destroyed, everything else would go.

536

First, though, I need to say something about the balance. It is recognized that when two forces act against each other and when one reacts and resists as much as the other acts and pushes, neither has any force because each has the same amount of power. Then either can be moved by a third force at will, since when the two have no force because of their equal resistance, the force of the third has total control and acts as easily as if there were no resistance at all.

537

[2] There is this kind of equilibrium between heaven and hell. However, it is not the kind of equilibrium that occurs between two people who are fighting physically, with one just as strong as the other; it is rather a spiritual balance, one of the false against the true and the evil against the good. Malicious falsity constantly breathes forth from hell and benevolent truth constantly breathes forth from heaven. This is the spiritual balance that provides us with our freedom for thinking and intending, since everything we think and intend depends either on evil and its consequent falsity or on good and its consequent truth. [3] So when we are in this state of equilibrium, we are in freedom either to let in and accept what is evil from hell and its consequent falsity or to let in and accept what is good from heaven and its consequent truth. Each of us is kept in this equilibrium by the Lord, who governs both heaven and hell.[293]

I will explain later, in a separate chapter, why we are kept in this freedom by means of the balance, and why the evil and the false are not taken away from us by divine power and the good and true instilled.[294]

538 I have sometimes been allowed to sense the aura of malevolent falsity flowing out of hell. It was like a constant effort to destroy everything good and true, united to an anger, a kind of rage at not being able to do so. Especially, it was an effort to destroy the divine nature of the Lord because this is the source of everything good and true.

I have sensed an aura of benevolent truth from heaven, though, that served to restrain the rage of the effort rising up from hell, which yielded an equilibrium. I perceived that the sole source of this aura was the Lord, even though it seemed to be coming from angels in heaven. The reason it comes solely from the Lord and not from angels is that every angel in heaven admits that nothing of what is good and true comes from herself or himself, but that it all comes from the Lord.

539 All the power in the spiritual world belongs to benevolent truth and none whatsoever to malevolent falsity.

The reason all power belongs to what is good and true is that the essential divine nature in heaven is divine good and divine truth, and all power belongs to the Divine. Malevolent falsity has no power because all power belongs to benevolent truth, and there is no benevolent truth in malevolent falsity. This is why all the power is in heaven, and none in hell. Everyone in heaven is focused on what is true for the sake of the good, and everyone in hell is focused on what is false for the sake of what is evil. This is because no one is let into heaven until she or he is focused on what is true for the sake of good, and no one is cast into hell until she or he is focused on what is false for the sake of what is evil. In support of this, see the chapters where I dealt with our first, second, and third states after death (§§491–520); and on benevolent truth possessing power, see the chapter on the power of heaven's angels (§§228–233).

540 This, then, is the balance between heaven and hell. People in the world of spirits are in this balance, since the world of spirits is halfway between heaven and hell. So too we in the world are kept in the same kind of balance, since the Lord governs us in the world by means of spirits in the world of spirits, a subject I shall deal with below in a separate chapter.[295]

This kind of balance would not be possible unless the Lord ruled both heaven and hell and regulated both. Otherwise, malicious falsity would cross the boundaries and affect the simple, good people who are in the outmost parts of heaven, people who are more easily misled than actual angels. This would destroy the balance, and with the balance would go our freedom.

Like heaven, hell is differentiated into communities. In fact, there are just as many communities in hell as there are in heaven, since each heavenly community has an opposite number in hell, for the sake of the balance.

However, the communities in hell are differentiated according to their evils and consequent falsities because the communities in heaven are differentiated according to their good will and consequent truths. We may be sure that there is some evil opposite to everything good and some falsity opposite to everything true from the fact that nothing exists without a relationship to its opposite. The opposite enables us to know its actual nature and level. Opposition is the source of all perception and sensation.[296]

This is why the Lord is constantly taking care that every community of heaven has its opposite in some community of hell and that there is a balance between them.

Because hell is differentiated into as many communities as heaven is, there are also as many hells as there are communities of heaven. As each community of heaven is a heaven in smaller form (see §§51–58), so each community of hell is a hell in smaller form.

Because there are three heavens overall, there are also three hells overall. There is a deepest hell that is opposite to the inmost or third heaven; there is a middle hell that is opposite to the middle or second heaven; and there is a highest hell that is opposite to the outmost or first heaven.

I need to explain briefly how the hells are governed, though. Overall, the hells are governed by a general impingement of divine good and divine truth from the heavens through which the general effort that flows out of the hells is restrained and controlled. There is also a specific impingement from each heaven and from each community of heaven.

Specifically, the hells are governed by means of angels who are given the ability to look into the hells and check the insanities and riots there. Sometimes angels are sent there, and their very presence brings matters under control.

In general, though, all the people in the hells are governed by their fears, some by fears sown and still in place from the world. However, since these fears are not adequate and gradually weaken, they are governed through fears of punishment, which are the primary means of preventing them from doing evil. There are many kinds of punishment there, milder or more severe depending on the evil [they are restraining]. Most of the time, the relatively malevolent spirits are in power, having gained control by their experience and skill; and they are able to keep the rest in servile obedience by punishments and the fears that these give birth to. These dominant spirits do not dare go beyond fixed limits.

We do need to realize that the only way of controlling the violent rages of people in the hells is through fear of punishment. There are no other means.

544 People in the world still believe that there is a devil who rules the hells and that he was created as an angel of light but was cast into hell with his gang after he led a rebellion. The reason for this belief is that the Word talks about the devil and Satan, and about Lucifer as well; and in these cases the Word is understood literally. However, in these passages the devil and Satan mean hell. The devil means the hell toward the rear where the worst people live, the people called evil demons; and Satan means the hell that is toward the front where the less malevolent people live, the people called evil spirits. Lucifer means the people who are from Babel or Babylon, the ones who extend their control all the way into heaven.

We can also see that there is no devil to whom the hells are subject from the fact that all the people who are in the hells, like all the people in the heavens, are from the human race (see §§311–317), that there are millions there from the beginning of creation to the present day, and that everyone there is the kind of devil he or she became by opposition to the Deity while in the world (see above, §§311–312).

The Lord Does Not Cast Anyone into Hell: Spirits Cast Themselves In

545 SOME people cherish the notion that God turns his face away from people, spurns them, and casts them into hell, and is angry against them because of their evil. Some people even go so far as to think that God punishes people and does them harm. They support this notion from the literal meaning of the Word where things like this are said, not realizing that the spiritual meaning of the Word, which makes sense of the letter, is wholly different. So the real doctrine of the church, which is from the spiritual meaning of the Word, teaches something else. It teaches that the Lord never turns his face away from anyone or spurns anyone, never casts anyone into hell or is angry.[a]

Anyone whose mind is enlightened perceives this while reading the Word simply from the fact that the Lord is goodness itself, love itself, and mercy itself.[297] Good itself cannot do harm to anyone. Love itself and mercy itself cannot spurn anyone, because this is contrary to mercy and love and is therefore contrary to the divine nature itself. So people who are thinking with an enlightened mind when they read the Word perceive clearly that God never turns away from us, and that because he does not turn away from us, he behaves toward us out of goodness and love and mercy. That is, he wills well toward us, loves us, and has compassion on us.

Enlightened minds also see from this that the literal meaning of the Word where things like this are said has a spiritual meaning concealed within it, a meaning needed to explain expressions that in the letter are adapted to human comprehension, things said in accord with our primary and general conceptions.

Enlightened people also see that good and evil are two opposite things, as opposite as heaven and hell, and that everything good is from heaven and everything evil from hell. Further, since the Lord's divine nature constitutes heaven (see §§7–12), nothing flows into us from the Lord but what is good, and nothing from hell but what is evil. So the Lord is constantly leading us out of evil and toward good, while hell is constantly leading us into evil. Unless we were in between, we would have neither thought nor intention, much less any freedom or choice. We have all these gifts because of the balance between good and evil. So if the Lord were to turn away and we were left to our own evil, we would no longer be human.

546

---

a. Blazing wrath is attributed to God in the Word, but it is the wrath in us; and the Word says such things because it seems that way to us when we are being punished and condemned: 798 *[5798]*, 6997, 8284, 8483, 8875, 9306, 10431. Even evil is attributed to the Lord, though nothing comes from the Lord but what is good: 2447, 6073 *[6071]*, 6992 *[6991]*, 6997, 7533, 7632, 7677 *[7679]*, 7926, 8227, 8228, 8632, 9306. Why the Word says such things: 6073 *[6071]*, 6992 *[6991]*, 6997, 7643, 7632, 7679, 7710, 7926, 8282, 9009 *[9010]*, 9128. The Lord is pure mercy and clemency: 6997, 8875.

We can see from this that the Lord is constantly flowing into every individual with good, just as much into the evil person as into the good. The difference is that he is constantly leading evil people away from evil, while he is constantly leading good people toward the good. The reason for this difference lies in us, since we are the ones who accept.[298]

547   We can gather from this that we do evil from hell and good from the Lord. However, since we believe that whatever we do comes from ourselves, the evil we do clings to us as though it were our own. This is why we are at fault for our evil, never the Lord. The evil within us is hell within us, for it makes no difference whether you say "evil" or "hell." Since we are at fault for our evil, it is we, not the Lord, who lead ourselves into hell. Far from leading us into hell, the Lord frees us from hell to the extent that we do not intend and love to be absorbed in our evil. Our whole volition and love stays with us after death (see §§470–484). People who have intended and loved what is evil in the world intend and love what is evil in the other life, and then they no longer allow themselves to be led away from it. This is why people who are absorbed in evil are connected to hell and actually are there in spirit; and after death they crave above all to be where their evil is. So after death, it is we, not the Lord, who cast ourselves into hell.

548   I need to mention how this happens. When we arrive in the other life, we are first taken up by angels who do everything for us and also tell us about the Lord, heaven, and angelic life and offer us lessons in what is good and true. However, if we as spirits are the kind of people who have been familiar with things like this in the world but have denied or rejected them at heart, then after some conversation we want to get away from them and try to leave. When the angels notice this, they leave us. After spending some time with various other people, we eventually take up with people who are devoted to similar evils (see above, §§445–452). When this happens, we are turning away from the Lord and turning our faces toward the hell we were united to in the world, where people live who are engaged in a similar love of evil.

We can see from this that the Lord is leading every spirit toward himself through angels and through an inflow from heaven, but that spirits who are absorbed in evil resist strenuously and virtually tear themselves away from the Lord. They are drawn by their evil—by hell, that is—as though it were a rope; and because they are drawn and want to follow because of their love of evil, it follows that they freely cast themselves into hell.

This is hard to believe in the world because of people's notions about hell. In fact, it does not even look that way in the other life. It looks different for people who are outside of hell, though not to the people who are actually casting themselves in. They are entering voluntarily, and the ones who are doing so out of a burning desire for evil look as though they were diving in headfirst. This is why it looks as though they were being thrown into hell by divine power. There will be more on this below (see §574).[299]

We can now see that the Lord does not throw anyone into hell. We throw ourselves in, not only while we are living in this world but after death as well, when we arrive among spirits.

The reason the Lord cannot treat everyone alike from his divine essence, which is goodness, love, and mercy, is that our evil and false preoccupations stand in the way, not only blunting his divine inflow but even rejecting it. These evil and false proclivities are like black clouds that stand between the sun and our eyes and deprive us of the clear sunlight. All the while, the sun is trying to dispel the clouds. It is behind them, working away, and in the meantime a little hazy light does get through to our eyes by various detours. It is much the same in the spiritual world. The sun there is the Lord and divine love (see §§116–140), the light there is divine truth (§§126–140). The black clouds there are falsities from evil, the eye there is our ability to discern. To the extent that we are absorbed in malevolent falsity, there is a cloud around us whose blackness and density depends on the level of our evil. We can see from this simile that the Lord's presence with everyone is constant, but that our acceptance varies. 549

Evil spirits are punished severely in the world of spirits to keep them terrified of doing evil. This too seems to come from the Lord, but still no punishment there does come from the Lord. It comes from the evil itself, since an evil is so closely united to its punishment that they cannot be separated. The hellish mob craves and loves nothing more than inflicting harm, especially punishing and torturing, and they do inflict harm and punishment on anyone who is not being protected by the Lord. So when something evil is being done from an evil heart, since this rejects any protection by the Lord, evil spirits assail the evildoer and inflict punishment. 550

To some extent, this can be illustrated by evil deeds and their punishments in the world, where they are also united. The laws here set penalties for each crime, so anyone who plunges into evil is plunging into its punishment as well. The only difference is that in the world, evil can be hidden, which cannot happen in the other life.

We can therefore conclude that the Lord does not do harm to anyone. It is like this in the world as well. It is not the king or the judge or the law that is responsible for the punishment of the guilty, because they are not responsible for the evil of the criminal.

All the People Who Are in the Hells Are Absorbed in Evils and Consequent Falsities because of Their Love for Themselves and the World

551 ALL the people who are in the hells are devoted to evil goals and the distortions that result. There is no one there devoted to evil goals and interested in true perceptions. Many evil people in the world know about spiritual truths, the truths of the church, since they have learned them first in childhood and later from sermons and from reading the Word and have gone on to take them for granted in their conversations. Some of them have even led others to believe that they were Christians at heart because they had learned from these truths how to talk with apparent affection and to behave honestly as though motivated by a spiritual faith. As for the ones who inwardly thought the opposite, though, and who carefully refrained from doing the evil things they were thinking of simply because of civil laws and for the sake of their reputation and rank and profit, they are all evil at heart, involved in what is true and good only physically, not in spirit. So when their outer layers are stripped off in the other life and the inner natures that constituted their spirits are unveiled, they are wholly absorbed in evil and false concerns, unconcerned with anything true and good. Then one can see that the true and good values simply dwelt in their memories as things they had learned about, and that they retrieved them from memory when they were talking and imitated good deeds as though they were motivated by a spiritual love and faith.

When people like this are let into their inner natures—into their evils, that is—they can no longer say anything true. They can only say what is false because their speech arises from their evil intentions. It is impossible to say anything true for evil ends because by then their spirits are made up of nothing but their own evil, and falsity emanates from evil.

Every evil spirit is distilled to this state before he or she is thrown into hell (see above, §§499–512). This is called being stripped down as to what is true and good.ª The stripping down is simply the process of being let into their own inner natures, into what they have claimed as spirits, then, or into their spirits themselves. See also §425 above on these matters.

When we are like this after death, then we are no longer "spirit-persons" the way we were in the first state (described above, §§491–498); we are truly spirits, since people who are truly spirits have faces and bodies responsive to the inner natures of their minds. So they are in an outward form that is the imprint or image of their inner natures. Spirits are like this once the first and second states described above have been completed. This means that when they are seen by [spiritual] eyes, one can tell instantly what their nature is not only from their faces but also from their bodies, and especially from their speech and behavior. Further, because they are now their essential selves,[300] they can only be where kindred souls are. [2] There is a complete sharing of affections and consequent thoughts in the spiritual world; so spirits move spontaneously toward kindred spirits because they are motivated by what attracts and delights them. In fact, they actually turn in that direction because that is how they breathe in their life, or draw their breath[301] freely, and not when they turn elsewhere. We need to realize that in the spiritual world, communication depends on which way we face, and that the people in front of us are always the ones who are in a love like our own. This applies no matter which way we turn our bodies (see above, §151).

[3] This is why hellish spirits all turn away from the Lord toward the gloomy and dark objects there that are in the location of earth's sun and

552

a. Before evil people are thrown down into hell they are stripped of what is true and good, and once these elements have been taken away, they move voluntarily into hell: 6977, 7039, 7795, 8210, 8232, 9330. The Lord does not strip them [of good and truth]—they do it to themselves: 7642 [7643], 7926. Every evil has something false within it; so people who are intent on evil are intent on what is false, even though some of them do not realize it: 7577, 8094. People who are intent on evil cannot help but think falsely when they are thinking on their own: 7437. All the people who are in hell say what is false, with evil intent: 1695, 7351, 7352, 7357, 7392, 7698 [7689].

moon, while heaven's angels all turn toward the Lord as the sun and the moon of heaven (see above, §§123, 143, 144, 151).

This leads us to the conclusion that all the people in the hells are absorbed in evils and consequent falsities, and also that they turn toward their loves.

553 Seen in any of heaven's light, all the spirits in the hells appear in the form of their own evil. Each one is in fact an image of her or his evil, since for each individual the inner and outer natures are acting as a unit, with the deeper elements presenting themselves to view in the outer ones—in the face, the body, the speech, and the behavior. So you can tell what they are like by looking at them. In general, they are forms of contempt for others, threats against people who do not revere them; they are forms of various shadings of hatred, of various forms of vengefulness. Savagery and cruelty show through from within. When others praise them, though, or revere and worship them, their faces compose themselves and look almost happy and gratified. [2] There is no way to describe briefly all the ways these forms look, since no one is just like any other. There is only a general likeness among people who are absorbed in similar evils and are therefore in the same hellish community, a similarity that acts like a common background that gives the individual faces a kind of overall resemblance. In general, their faces are frightful, as lifeless as corpses. Some of their faces are black, some like little torches, some pimply, with huge ulcerated sores. In many cases there is no visible face, only something hairy or bony in its place, while with others only the teeth show. Their bodies are equally misshapen, and their speech seems to embody wrath or hatred or vengeance, since all their articulation comes from their false perception and all the tone comes from their evil intent. In a word, they are all images of their hell.

[3] I have not been allowed to see what form hell itself is in overall. I have only been told that in the same way that all heaven as a single entity resembles a single human being (§§59–67), so all hell as a single entity resembles a single devil and can be manifested as a likeness of a single devil (see above, §544). However, I have often seen what form particular hells or hellish communities have, since at their entrances (which are called the gates of hell), there often appears a monstrous figure that in a general way represents the form of the people who live there. The savagery of these inhabitants is then imaged by frightful horrors that I forbear to mention.

[4] It does need to be known, though, that hellish spirits look like this in heaven's light, but that they look human to each other. This is a

gift of the Lord's mercy, so that they do not look as repulsive to each other as they do to angels. However, this appearance is deceiving, since the moment a ray of light from heaven is let in, these human forms turn into the monstrous ones that they are essentially, the forms just described, because in heaven's light everything appears as it really is. This is also why they avoid heaven's light and dive into their own illumination, an illumination like that of glowing coals or, in places, like burning sulfur. This light, though, turns into pure darkness when any ray of light from heaven flows in. This is why the hells are described as being in gloom and darkness, and why the gloom and darkness mean the kinds of malevolent distortions characteristic of hell.

Having examined the misshapen forms of spirits in the hells, forms **554** that as noted are all forms of contempt for others, of threats against people who do not respect and revere them, and of hatred and vengeance against people who do not support them, it has become clear to me that in general they are all forms of love for oneself and the world and that the evils that give rise to individual forms can all be traced back to these two loves. I have also been told from heaven, and it has been witnessed to me by an abundance of experience, that these two loves, love for oneself and love of the world, do rule in the hells and actually constitute the hells, and that love for the Lord and love for one's neighbor rule in the heavens and actually constitute the heavens. I have also learned that the two loves that are hell's loves and the two loves that are heaven's loves are absolute opposites.

At first I wondered why love for oneself and love of the world are so **555** diabolic, why people who are absorbed in them look so frightful. After all, in the world we scarcely give love for ourselves a second thought. We focus only on that outward inflation of spirit called pride, which we believe is the only self-love because it is so visible. Not only that, if love for oneself does not express itself in pride, then we in the world think it is the vital fire that rouses us to work for high position and to do constructive things. We believe that if we saw no prospect of esteem and glory in these efforts, our spirits would become sluggish. People ask, "Who would do anything decent or useful or remarkable except to be praised and respected by others, [openly] or in their thoughts; and where does this come from except from the fire of a love for glory and esteem—that is, for the sake of self?" This is why people in the world do not realize that in its own right love for oneself is the love that rules in hell and that makes hell within us.

Since this is in fact the case, I should like first to describe what love for oneself is, and then explain that everything evil and false wells up from this love.[302]

556   Love for oneself is intending well to oneself alone, not to others except for the sake of oneself—not the church, the country, or any human community. It is helping them solely for the sake of one's own reputation and rank and glory. Unless these can be seen in the services we offer, we are saying at heart, "What difference does it make? Why should I? What's in it for me?" So we forget it. We can see from this that people who are absorbed in a love for themselves do not love their church or country or community or any constructive activity. They love only themselves. Their only pleasure lies in self-gratification; and since the pleasure that stems from love constitutes human life, their life is a life of self. A life of self is a life that depends on what we claim as our own, and in its own right what we claim as our own is nothing but evil.

People who love themselves do love their own as well, their own being specifically their children and grandchildren and more broadly all who ally with them, whom they call "their own people." Loving both the former and the latter is actually loving themselves, because they regard the others as though they were in themselves, and focus on themselves in others. These "others" who are claimed as their own include everyone who praises and reveres and worships them.

557   We can gather what love for oneself is like by comparing it to heavenly love. Heavenly love is loving constructive activity for its own sake, or loving for their own sake the worthwhile things we do for our church, our country, the human community, and our fellow citizens. This is really loving God and loving our neighbor, since all constructive activities and all worthwhile actions come from God and *are* the neighbor whom we are to love. In contrast, people who love these activities for the sake of self love them only as slaves who wait on them. It follows that people devoted to a love for themselves want their church, their country, the human community, and their fellow citizens to be their servants rather than wanting to serve them. They station themselves above these neighbors and put them down. So to the extent that people are devoted to a love for themselves, they move themselves away from heaven because they move themselves away from heavenly love.

558a [303]   Further, to the extent that we are engaged in heavenly love—which is loving constructive and worthwhile activities and being moved by heartfelt pleasure when we provide them to our church, our country, the human community, and our fellow citizens—we are being led by the Lord because this is the love he is in and the love that comes from him. However, to the extent that we focus on love for ourselves—doing constructive and worthwhile things for our own sakes—we are leading ourselves; and to the extent that we lead ourselves, we are not being led by the Lord. Again, then, it follows that the more we love ourselves, the more we move away from the Divine and also from heaven.

Being led by self is being led by what we claim as our own, and what we claim as our own is nothing but evil. It is actually our evil heredity, which involves loving ourselves more than God and the world more than heaven.[b]

We are completely absorbed in our self-image and therefore in our hereditary evil whenever we focus on ourselves in anything worthwhile we are doing, for we are focusing on ourselves and away from what is good and not on what is good and away from ourselves. So in the worthwhile activities we set up an image of ourselves and not an image of the Divine. I have been assured of this by experience as well. There are evil spirits who live halfway between the north and the west, underneath the heavens, who are particularly skilled at getting upright spirits involved in their self-image and therefore focused on various kinds of evil. They do this by getting them absorbed in thinking about themselves, either openly by words of praise and esteem or covertly by focusing their feelings exclusively on themselves. To the extent that they succeed, they turn the faces of the upright people away from heaven and also becloud their understanding, calling up evils from their self-concern.

If you look at their origins and essences, you can see that love for oneself and love of one's neighbor are opposites. In people who are wrapped up in love for themselves, love of their neighbor begins from self. They claim that everyone is her or his own neighbor; and from this as a center

558b

b. The self-image that we get from our parents by heredity is nothing but condensed evil: 210, 215, 731, 876, 987, 1047, 2307, 2318 [2308], 3518, 3701, 3812, 8480, 8550, 10283, 10284, 10286, 10731 [10732]. Our self-centeredness involves loving ourselves more than God and the world more than heaven, and regarding our neighbor as nothing compared to ourselves except when it benefits us; so it is loving ourselves and is a love for oneself and for the world: 694, 731, 4317, 5660. From love for oneself and for the world when they are put first come all evils: 1307, 1308, 1321, 1594, 1691, 3413, 7255, 7376, 7480 [7490], 7488, 8318, 9335, 9348, 10038, 10742; which are contempt for others, hostility, hatred, vengefulness, savagery, and deceit: 6667, 7372 [7370], 7374, 9348, 10038, 10742; and from these evils, everything false flows: 1047, 10283, 10284, 10286.

they reach out to all who ally with them, with progressively less intensity depending on the love that unites the others with them. They regard people outside this group as worthless, and people who offer opposition to them and their evildoing they regard as enemies. It does not matter what they are actually like, whether they are wise or upright or honest or fair.

A spiritual love of their neighbor, though, begins with the Lord, and spreads out from him as its center to all who are united to him by love and faith. Its spread depends on the quality of their love and faith.[c]

We can see from this that a love of our neighbor that begins with ourselves is the opposite of a love of our neighbor that begins with the Lord. The former comes from evil because it comes from what we claim as our own; while the latter comes from what is good because it comes from the Lord, who is good itself. We can also see that a love of our neighbor that comes from us and from our self-image is a physical love, while a love of our neighbor that comes from the Lord is heavenly.

In a word, when we are absorbed in love for ourselves it constitutes our head, and heavenly love constitutes the feet we stand on. If heavenly love does not serve us, we trample it underfoot. This is why people who are being thrown into hell look as though they are diving in headfirst, with their heads down and their feet toward heaven (see above, §548).

559 By nature, self-love runs wild to the extent that its reins are loosened, that is, to the extent that the outward restraints constituted by fears of the law and its penalties, fears of losing reputation, esteem, profit, position, and life are taken away. It runs wild even to the extent of wanting to

c. People who do not know what loving their neighbor is think that everyone is their neighbor and that everyone who is in need ought to be helped: 6704. They also believe that we are our own neighbor, and that love toward our neighbor therefore begins with us: 6933. People who love themselves above all, who therefore are ruled by love for themselves, also begin their love for their neighbor with themselves: 8120 [6710]. An explanation of the way in which we are our own neighbors: 6933–6938. However, people who are Christians and who love God above all begin their love toward their neighbor with the Lord, because he is to be loved above all: 6706, 6711, 6819, 6824. There are as many different kinds of neighbor as there are different kinds of good from the Lord, and good is to be done differently toward each individual depending on the quality of that individual's state, which is a matter of Christian prudence: 6707, 6709, 6710 [6711], 6818. There are countless such differences; so the pre-Christian people, who knew what the neighbor is, sorted thoughtful acts into classes and gave them names that enabled them to know in what way one or another person was their neighbor and how they were to be helped prudently: 2417, 6629 [6628], 6705, 7259–7262. The doctrine in the pre-Christian churches was a doctrine of thoughtfulness toward one's neighbor, which was the source of their wisdom: 2417, 2385, 3419, 3420, 4844, 6628 [6629].

rule not only over the whole globe but even over all heaven and the Lord himself. It knows no bound or limit. This is latent in everyone who is focused on self-love even though it may not show in the world, where the restraints we have mentioned hold it back.

We cannot fail to see this in people in power and kings who are not held back by any such restraints. They run wild and conquer as many territories and kingdoms as they can and aspire to boundless power and glory.[304] This is even clearer in the modern Babylon,[305] which extends its control into heaven and transfers all the Lord's divine power to itself and even craves more.

The reader may see in the booklet *Last Judgment*[306] that people like this are diametrically opposed to the Divine and to heaven and that they favor hell when they arrive in the other life after death.

Picture a community made up of people like this, all totally in love with themselves, not caring about others unless they are allies, and you will see that their love is no different from that of thieves for each other. To the extent that they are acting in concert, they embrace each other and call each other friends; but once they stop cooperating, once anyone resists their control, they attack and butcher each other. If their deeper natures—their minds—are probed, it will be clear that they are full of virulent hatred for each other, that at heart they ridicule anything fair and honest and even ridicule the Deity, tossing it aside as worthless. This comes out even more clearly from their communities in the hells, which will be described below.

The deeper levels of the thoughts and affections of people who love themselves above all are turned toward themselves and the world—and are turned away, therefore, from the Lord and heaven. This is why such people fall prey to all kinds of evil and why the divine nature cannot flow in. It is because the moment it does flow in, it is submerged in thoughts about self and polluted, and is saturated with evils that arise from their self-centeredness. This is why they all look away from the Lord in the other life, toward the gloom that occupies the site of our world's sun there and is directly across from heaven's sun, which is the Lord (see §123 above). Darkness means evil, and our world's sun means self-love.[d]

---

d. Our world's sun means love for oneself: 2441. How "worshiping the sun" [Deuteronomy 4:19, 17:3] means worshiping things that are contrary to heavenly love and the Lord: 441, 10584. The warming sun [Exodus 16:21] means the rising up of cravings for evil: 8487.

562   In broad terms, the evils characteristic of people focused on love for themselves are contempt for others; envy; enmity toward anyone who is not on their side, and a consequent hostility; various kinds of hatred; vengefulness; craft; deceit; callousness; and cruelty. In religious matters, this extends not only to a contempt for the Divine and for the divine gifts that are the true and good elements of the church; it extends also to anger at such things, an anger that turns into hatred when we become spirits. Then not only can we not stand hearing about these matters, we blaze with hatred against everyone who acknowledges and worships the Divine.

I talked with one man who had been in power in the world and loved himself far too much. When he simply heard the Divine mentioned— especially when he heard the Lord named—he was so struck by angry hatred that he was consumed with thoughts of murder. When the reins of his love were loosened, he even wanted to be the devil himself in order to satisfy his love by ceaseless attacks on heaven. Many individuals of the papal religion feel this desire in the other life when they realize that the Lord has all power and that they have none.

563   Some spirits appeared to me in the western region, toward the south, who said they had been granted high honor in the world and deserved to be promoted over others and to lord it over them. They were examined by angels to discover what they were like inwardly, and it turned out that in their earthly offices they had paid no attention to service but only to themselves, which meant that they had put themselves before service. Still, since they were aflame with ambition to be promoted, they were allowed to join a group of people who were discussing some rather important matters. You could tell, though, that they were unable to pay any attention to the real issues that were being discussed and could not see the matters in any depth. They did not say anything on the basis of the constructive effects of the discussion, but talked only on the basis of their own self-image. Their behavior was motivated by a desire to ingratiate themselves; so they were dismissed from the task and left to seek office elsewhere. So they went farther westward, where they were accepted here and there; but in every case they were told that they were not thinking about anything but themselves, that they were not thinking about the business at hand except in terms of themselves. This meant that they were stupid, just like sensual, carnal spirits. Wherever they arrived, then, they were rejected. After a while they were utterly bankrupt and were asking for handouts.[307]

Once more I could see from this that no matter how wisely people may seem to talk in the world from the fire of self-love, still it is just a matter of rote memory and not of any rational light. So in the other life, when they are no longer allowed to retrieve things from their natural memory, they are more stupid than other people because they are cut off from the Divine.

There are two ways of being in power. One comes from love for our neighbor and the other from love for ourselves. In essence, these two kinds of power are exact opposites. People who are empowered by love for their neighbor intend the good of everyone and love nothing more than being useful—that is, serving others (serving others means willing well and helping others, whether that is one's church, country, community, or fellow citizen). This is their love and the delight of their hearts. As such people are raised to high positions they are delighted; but the delight is not because of the honor but because of the constructive things they can now do more abundantly and at a higher level. This is what empowerment is like in the heavens. **564**

[2] In contrast, people whose self-love leads them to take power intend good to no one but themselves. Any services they perform for others are actually for their own esteem and renown, since only this is of any use to them. Helping others is for them simply a means to being waited on and respected and deferred to. They strive for high office not for the good they ought to do for their country and their church but to be prominent and praised and therefore in their heart's delight.

[3] A love of power does stay with all of us after death. However, people whose authority rested on their love for their neighbor are entrusted with power in the heavens. Actually, it is not they who have power but the services that they love, and when service rules, the Lord is ruling. However, people whose authority rested on their self-love in the world arrive in hell after their life in this world and are miserable slaves there. I have seen powerful people whose authority had rested on their self-love in the world abandoned among the most miserable, some of them living in outhouses.

As for love of the world, it is not so intensely opposed to heavenly love, because there are not so many evils latent in it. **565**

Love of the world is wanting to divert the wealth of others to ourselves by any means available. It is setting our heart on wealth and allowing the world to distract us from the spiritual love that is love for our neighbor and therefore from heaven and the Divine.

This love takes many forms, though. We may love wealth in order to be raised to exalted rank simply because we love exalted rank. We may love exalted rank and high position for the sake of wealth. We may love wealth for the sake of the various pleasures it offers in the world. We may love wealth simply for the sake of wealth, which is avarice, and so on. The purpose of being wealthy is called its use, and purpose or use is what gives a love its quality. That is, the quality of a love is determined by the goal it aims at. Everything else serves it as means.

Hellfire and Gnashing of Teeth

566   UNTIL now, hardly anyone has known the meaning of the eternal fire and gnashing of teeth ascribed to people in hell in the Word.[308] This is because people think materialistically about statements in the Word, in ignorance of its spiritual meaning. So some of them understand the fire to be material fire, some think it is torment in general, some the pangs of conscience, some that it is just words meant to strike a terror of evil into us. Some understand the gnashing of teeth to be a kind of grinding, some only the kind of shudder we feel when we hear this kind of clash of teeth.

Anyone familiar with the spiritual meaning of the Word, though, can realize what eternal fire and gnashing of teeth are, since there is spiritual meaning in every expression and in the meaning of every expression in the Word. At heart, that is, the Word is spiritual, and spiritual meaning can be expressed to us only in natural terms because we are in a natural world and think on the basis of what we encounter in it.

In the following pages, then, I shall explain what the eternal fire and gnashing of teeth are that evil people find after death, or that their spirits experience once they are in the spiritual world.

567   There are two sources of warmth. One is the sun of heaven, which is the Lord, and the other is our world's sun. The warmth that comes from heaven's sun or the Lord is spiritual warmth, which in its essence is love (see above, §§126–140). The warmth that comes from our world's sun, though, is a natural warmth that in its essence is not love but serves

spiritual warmth or love as a vessel. We may gather that love in essence is warmth from the fact that our minds and then our bodies become warmer because of love and according to its intensity and quality. This happens to us just as much in winter as in summer. We may also notice the warming of our blood. As for the fact that natural heat arising from the world's sun serves spiritual heat as a vessel, this we may gather from the warmth of the body that is stimulated by the warmth of its spirit and abets it. We may look particularly at what the warmth of spring and summer does for all kinds of animals with their annual love cycles. [2] It is not that the [natural] warmth *makes* this happen, but that it disposes their bodies to be receptive to the warmth that flows into them as well from the spiritual world. You see, the spiritual world flows into the natural the way a cause flows into its effect. People who believe that natural warmth creates these loves are quite mistaken, since the inflow is of the spiritual world into the natural world and not of the natural world into the spiritual; and all love is spiritual because it is the essence of life itself. [3] Further, people who believe that anything happens in the natural world apart from the inflow of the spiritual world are also mistaken, since natural phenomena arise and persist only from spiritual ones. Even the members of the vegetable kingdom get their power to sprout from this kind of inflow. The natural warmth of spring and summer simply disposes their seeds into their natural forms by swelling and opening them so that the inflow from the spiritual world can have its causative effect.

I mention all this to make it clear that there are two kinds of warmth, spiritual and natural, and that spiritual warmth comes from heaven's sun and natural warmth from the world's sun, and that inflow and cooperation set up the effects that we see before us in the world.[a]

For us human beings, spiritual warmth is the warmth of life, because as already noted it is essentially love. This love is what fire means in the Word. Heavenly fire means love for the Lord and love for our neighbor, and hellish fire means love for ourselves and love of the world.   **568**

Hellish fire or love has the same source as heavenly fire or love, namely heaven's sun or the Lord. However, it is changed into hellfire by the people who receive it, for all inflow from the spiritual world varies   **569**

a. There is an inflow of the spiritual world into the natural world: 6053–6058, 6189–6215, 6307–6327, 6466–6495, 6598–6626. There is also an inflow into the lives of animals: 5850; and into the members of the vegetable kingdom as well: 3648. This inflow is a constant effort to act in keeping with the divine design: 6211–6212.

depending on how it is received or depending on the forms into which it flows. The same thing happens with the warmth and light from the world's sun. Warmth flowing from this source into woods and flower beds produces vegetation and pleasant, soft aromas. The same warmth flowing into manure or carrion produces decay and foul stenches. Similarly light from the same sun on one object produces lovely, charming colors, while on another it produces ugly and unpleasant ones. It is the same with the warmth and light from heaven's sun, which is love. When that warmth or love flows into good recipients, like good people and spirits or angels, it makes their goodness fertile; whereas when it flows into evil people it has the opposite effect. Their evils either stifle it or distort it. Similarly, when heaven's light flows into the true perceptions of good will, it yields intelligence and wisdom; but when it flows into malicious distortions, it changes there into insanity and various kinds of illusion. Everything depends on reception.

570   Because hellfire is love for oneself and the world, it is also all the craving of those loves, since craving is love reaching out. Whatever we love we constantly crave, and it is our delight, since we feel delight when we get what we love or crave. There is no other source of our heart's delight. So hellfire is the craving and pleasure that well up from these two loves as its sources. These evils[309] are contempt for others, enmity and hostility toward people who do not support us, envy, hatred, and vengefulness; and savagery and cruelty as a result. In respect to the Divine, they are denial and a consequent contempt, derision, and blasphemy of the sacred values of the church. After death, when we become spirits, these turn into rage and hatred against such values (see above, §562).

Further, since these evils are constantly breathing out the death and destruction of everyone we see as the enemy, of everyone who is the target of this blazing hatred and vengefulness, the delight of our lives is the intent to destroy and kill, or to the extent that we cannot do this, to inflict harm, to wound, and to savage.

[2] These are the meanings of fire in the Word when it deals with evil people and the hells. I should like to cite a few passages in support.

> Everyone who is hypocritical and malicious, every mouth that utters folly, because it is aflame with malice as with fire, shall eat briars and brambles and kindle the thickets of the forest, and will rise up with the rising of smoke; and the inhabitants have become the food of fire, a man and his brother do not spare each other. (Isaiah 9:17–18 *[9:17–19]*)

> I will make great portents in heaven and on earth—blood and fire and columns of smoke; the sun will turn into darkness. (Joel 2:30, 31)[310]

The earth will become burning pitch, night and day it will not be put out, its smoke will rise up forever. (Isaiah 34:9–10)

Behold, the day is coming that will burn like an oven, and all the proud and all that do wickedness will be stubble, and the coming day will burn them up. (Malachi 4:1)[311]

Babylon has become the dwelling of demons, those who saw the smoke of her burning cried aloud, the smoke rose up forever and ever. (Revelation 18:2, 18; 19:2 [19:3])

He opened the pit of the abyss and smoke came up out of the pit like the smoke of a huge furnace, and the sun was darkened, and the air, by the smoke from the pit. (Revelation 9:2)

From the mouth of the horses came forth fire and smoke and sulfur; and a third part of the people were killed by the fire and the smoke and the sulfur. (Revelation 11:17–18 [9:17–18])

Whoever worships the beast will drink the wine of the wrath of God mixed with myrrh in the cup of his wrath and will be tortured with fire and sulfur. (Revelation 14:9–10)

The fourth angel poured out his vial on the sun, and it was allowed to burn people by fire with its heat, and so it scorched people with intense heat. (Revelation 16:[8–]9)

They were thrown into a swamp burning with fire and sulfur. (Revelation 19:20; 20:14–15, 21:8)

Every tree that does not produce good fruit will be cut down and thrown into the fire. (Matthew 3:10; Luke 3:9)

The Human-born One will send his angels, and they will gather from his kingdom everything that gives offense and everyone who does iniquity and consign them to a furnace of fire. (Matthew 13:41–42, 50)

The king will say to those on his left, "Leave me, cursed ones, for the eternal fire prepared for the devil and his angels." (Matthew 25:4 [25:41])

And they will be sent off into eternal fire, into a Gehenna of fire, where their worm does not die and their fire is not quenched. (Matthew 18:8–9; Mark 9:43–49)

The rich man in hell said to Abraham that he was being tormented in flame. (Luke 16:24)

In these and many other passages fire means the craving of love for one-self and love of the world, and the smoke from the fire means the falsity that comes from this evil.

571   Because hellfire means the urge to do the evils prompted by love for oneself and the world, and because this kind of urge is characteristic of everyone in hell (see the preceding chapter), when the hells are opened one sees the kind of smoky fire you get in conflagrations. An intense fire rises from the hells where love for oneself rules, and a flickering one from the hells where love of the world rules.

When the hells are closed, though, this fire is not visible. Instead, there is something dark, as though made from thickened smoke. Still, that fire is raging inside, as you can tell from the radiating heat. It is like the heat of ruins after a conflagration, or in some instances like the heat of an active furnace, or in others like that of a hot bath. When this heat flows into us it rouses our cravings—hatred and vengefulness in evil people, and dementia in the ill.

This kind of fire or heat is characteristic of people who are engrossed in the aforementioned loves because in spirit they are in touch with these hells even while they are still living in their bodies.

It does need to be known, though, that the people in the hells are not actually in fire. The fire is an appearance. They do not actually feel any burning, only the kind of warmth they knew in the world. The reason there seems to be fire is correspondence, since love corresponds to fire, and everything we see in the spiritual world has its visible form from its correspondence.

572   We should bear in mind that this hellish fire or heat changes into an intense cold when warmth flows in from heaven. Then the people there shiver as though they had feverish chills and are in inner torment. This is because of their absolute opposition to the Divine; and heaven's warmth, which is divine love, snuffs out the warmth of hell, which is love for one-self, and along with it the very fire of their life. This is what causes the cold, the shivering, and the pain. It also then brings about darkness there, and folly and confusion.

This does not happen very often, though; only when there is need to quell rebellions that are getting out of hand.

573   Since hellfire means all the craving to do evil that flows from love for oneself, that same fire also means the kind of torment that occurs in the hells. This is because the impulses that arise from that love are urges to wound people who do not offer respect and deference and reverence. To the extent that rage takes charge, and the hatred and vengefulness that come from rage, people are driven to attack others viciously. When this impulse is inherent in everyone in a community where there are no external restraints, no fears of the law or of loss of reputation or position or profit or life, everyone attacks everyone else out of sheer malice. The strong conquer and subject the rest to their tyranny, cheerfully torturing any who do not surrender. This latter delight is integral to the delight in tyranny to the point that they are of equal intensity. This is because sadism is inherent in hostility, envy, hatred, and vengefulness, which as already noted are the evils of a love of cruelty.

All the hells are communities like this, so everyone there cherishes hatred toward others in her or his heart and bursts out in savagery whenever there is the strength to do so.

These acts of savagery and torture are what are meant by hellfire, because they are the results of their obsessions.

I explained above (§548) that evil spirits voluntarily throw themselves into hell, so I need to state briefly why this happens when there is such torment in hell.

574

From each hell there breathes forth an aura of the cravings that obsess its inhabitants. When this aura is sensed by people who are obsessed with a similar craving, it touches their hearts and fills them with delight because the craving and the delight are inseparable—whatever we crave is delightful to us. This is why spirits turn in that direction and are impelled there by their hearts' delight. They do not yet realize what kind of torment there is in hell, and the ones who do know still feel the craving. In the spiritual world we are all incapable of resisting our impulses because the impulses come from our love and the love comes from our intent and the intent comes from our nature, and we all act from our nature there.

[2] So when spirits voluntarily or freely arrive at their hell and go in, they are accepted cordially at first and think they have arrived among friends. This lasts only a few hours, though. All the while they are being probed to find out how crafty they are, and therefore how powerful. Once this probing is complete the attacks begin in various ways, getting more and more severe and intense. The intensification is effected by their being taken farther and deeper into hell, since the farther and deeper you go there, the more malevolent are the spirits. After these attacks, the malevolent spirits begin to torment the newcomers with punishments until finally they are reduced to slavery.

[3] However, since rebellious movements are always arising (everyone there wants to be greatest and burns with hatred against everyone else, which keeps generating new attacks), the scene is constantly changing.

The people who were enslaved are released and offer their support to some new devil for the subjugation of others. Then the ones who do not surrender and yield their obedience are tortured in various ways, and so on and so on.

Torments like this are the torments of hell that are referred to as hellfire.

575 The gnashing of teeth, though, is the constant clash and strife of false convictions with each other (and therefore the warfare of the individuals who hold the false convictions) united to contempt for others, hostility, derision, mockery, and blasphemy. These even break out into various kinds of butchery. Everyone there is defending his or her own false convictions and calling them true. From outside the hells, these clashes and battles sound like gnashing teeth, and they turn into the gnashing of teeth when truths from heaven flow into hell.

In these hells dwell all the people who acknowledged nature and denied the Divine. The people who deliberately convinced themselves are in the deeper hells. Since they cannot accept any ray of light from heaven and can therefore not see anything within themselves, most of them focus on their senses and their bodies. These are people who do not believe anything they cannot see with their eyes and touch with their hands. So for them, all sensory illusions are the truths on which they base their arguments. This is why their arguments sound like the gnashing of teeth. It is because in the spiritual world all false statements grate, and teeth correspond to the outmost aspects of nature and to our own outmost natures, which have to do with our senses and our bodies.[b]

On the gnashing of teeth in the hells, see Matthew 8:12; 13:42, 50; 22:13; 24:51; 25:30; and Luke 13:28.

b. On the correspondence of teeth: 5565–5568. People who are merely sensory correspond to teeth and have hardly any spiritual light: 5565. In the Word, a tooth [reading *dens* for the obviously erroneous *Deus,* "God"] refers to the sensory level that is the outmost level of human life: 9052, 9062. Gnashing of teeth in the other life comes from people who give nature credit for everything and credit the Divine with nothing: 5568.

The Malice and Unspeakable
Skills of Hellish Spirits

ANYONE who thinks deeply and knows anything about the workings
of the human mind can see and understand how significantly superior spirits are to other people. In a minute, we can consider and turn over and decide in our minds more than we can express in speech or writing in half an hour. This shows how much better we are when we are in the spirit and therefore when we become spirits, since it is the spirit that thinks and the body is what the spirit uses to express its thoughts in speech or writing.

576

This is why people who become angels after death have access to indescribable intelligence and wisdom relative to the intelligence and wisdom they had while they were living in the world. While they were living in the world, their spirits were confined in a body and by that means were in the natural world. So when the spirit did think spiritually, the thoughts flowed into natural concepts that are relatively general, crude, and hazy. This means they are[312] not open to the countless elements characteristic of spiritual thought. They also immerse them in the thickets of the cares of the world. It is different once the spirit has been freed from the body and has arrived at its own spiritual state, which happens when it crosses from the natural world to the spiritual world that is appropriate to it. We can see from what has already been said that its state in regard to thoughts and affections is far better than its former state. This is why angels think thoughts that are unutterable and indescribable, things that cannot come through to our natural thoughts. Yet in fact, every angel was born a person on earth and lived as such, and then seemed to himself or herself to be no wiser than anyone else.

The level of wisdom and intelligence for angels is also the level of malice and craft among hellish spirits. The issue is much the same because once the human spirit is freed from its body it devotes itself wholly to its virtue or to its vice. An angelic spirit devotes itself to its virtue and a hellish spirit to its vice. This is because every spirit actually is its own good or its own evil because it is its own love, as has often been stated and explained above. This means that just as angelic spirits think and intend and speak and act from their good, so hellish spirits do the same from their evil. Thinking and intending and speaking and acting from evil itself is doing so on the basis of everything implicit in evil. [2] It was

577

different while they were living in the flesh because then the evil of their spirits was under the restraints that apply to all because of the law, or because of money, position, reputation, and their fears of losing these things. So the evil of their spirits could not break out and show itself in its true colors. Further, the evil of their spirit then lurked hidden by veils of outward integrity, honesty, fairness, and affection for what is true and good, qualities that such people presented and simulated in their speech for worldly reasons. All the while, the evil remained so hidden and veiled that they themselves scarcely knew that there was so much malice and craft in their spirits, that they were therefore intrinsically the very devils they would become after death when their spirits would come into their own and display their own nature.

[3] The kind of malice that surfaces then defies all belief. There are thousands of things that burst forth from the evil itself then, including some that are beyond the words of any language to describe. I have been allowed to learn and even to observe what they are like by many experiences because the Lord has granted me to be in the spiritual world as to my spirit while I was in the natural world as to my body. This I can testify: their malice is so great that scarcely a thousandth part of it can be described. Further, if the Lord did not protect us we would never be able to escape from hell; for with each of us there are both spirits from hell and angels from heaven (see §§292–293). Further, the Lord cannot protect us unless we acknowledge the Divine and live faithful, thoughtful lives. Otherwise, we are turning away from the Lord and toward hellish spirits and are therefore in spirit absorbing the same kind of malice. [4] Still, the Lord is constantly leading us away from the evils that we assimilate and attract by associating with these spirits, leading us if not by the inner restraints of conscience (which we do not accept if we deny the Divine), then by the outer restraints already listed, the fears of the laws and their penalties, of the loss of money and the forfeiture of rank and reputation. People like this can be led away from evils through the delights of their love and the fear of losing and forfeiting these delights, but they cannot be led into spiritual virtues. To the extent that they are led into them, you see, they convert them into guile and craft by pretending to be good and honest and fair-minded with a view to persuading and deceiving others. This guile is added to the evil of their spirits and gives it form, lending its own nature to the evil.

578 The worst people of all are the ones who have been absorbed in evil pursuits because of their love for themselves and whose inward behavior has been deceitful throughout. This is because the deceit wholly permeates their thoughts and intentions and infects them with venom, destroying all their spiritual life. Most of them are in the hells toward the rear and are called demons. They take particular delight in making themselves unnoticeable and floating around others like ghosts, doing their harm covertly, spraying it around like the venom of snakes. They are tortured more severely than others.

In contrast, if people have not been guileful but have been taken in by the craft of the malicious and still are engaged in evils because of their self-love, they find themselves toward the rear as well, but not so deep down. People engaged in evils because of their love of the world are in the hells toward the front, though, and are called spirits. They do not have the same kinds of evil, the same kinds of hatred and vengefulness, as people involved in love for themselves, so they do not have the same kind of malice and craft. As a result, their hells are milder.

I have been allowed to find out from experience the nature of the **579** malice of the people referred to as demons. Demons do not flow into people's thoughts but into their affections. They observe them and sniff them out the way dogs sniff out wild animals in the woods. When they notice good affections, they change them instantly into evil ones by using delights in something else to lead them astray in quite amazing fashion. They do this so subtly and with such malign skill that the victim does not notice anything. They take the greatest care to prevent anything from obtruding into thought because this would bring it into the open. In our case, they settle near the back of the head.

These are people who, in the world, enticed the minds of others deceptively, using the delights of their affections or their impulses to mislead and persuade them.

However, the Lord keeps these spirits away from anyone for whom there is any hope of reformation because they are the kind of spirit who can not only destroy conscience but also stir up our inherited evils that would otherwise lie hidden. So to prevent them from leading us into those evils, the Lord makes sure that these hells are completely closed off. When people of this nature arrive in the other life after death, they are instantly thrown into their hell. When they are examined as to their guile and craft, they look like snakes.

You can gather from their unspeakable arts what the malice of these **580** hellish spirits is like. There are so many of these arts that listing them would fill a book, and describing them would take volumes. Most of these arts are unknown in the world. One kind has to do with the misuse of correspondences; a second kind has to do with the misuse of the most superficial features of the divine design; a third kind with the sharing and instilling of thoughts and affections by distractions, focusing inward, and the use of decoy spirits as well as by emissaries; a fourth kind with manipulation by hallucinations; a fifth kind with external projections that enable the spirits to be present outside their bodies; a sixth kind with various types of imitation and persuasion and pretense.[313]

The spirits of evil people come into these arts spontaneously when they are freed from their bodies. These arts are inherent in the evil they are then absorbed in.

They use these arts to torture each other in the hells. However, since with the exception of the different varieties of imitation and persuasion and pretense these arts are unknown in the world, I do not want to describe them in detail, both because they would not be understood and because they are unspeakable.

581   The reason tortures are permitted by the Lord in the hells is that there is no other way evils can be restrained and tamed. Fear of punishment is the only means of controlling and taming evils and keeping the hellish mob in restraints. There is no other way, for if it were not for the fear of punishment and torture, evil would plunge into rage and destroy everything, as would happen in a kingdom on earth where there was neither law nor punishment.

The Appearance, Location, and Number of the Hells

582   IN the spiritual world, the world where spirits and angels live, things look much the same as they do in the natural world where we live—so similar that at first glance there seems to be no difference. You see plains there, mountains, hills, and cliffs with valleys between them, you see bodies of water and many other things that we find on earth. However, they all come from a spiritual source, so they are visible to the eyes of spirits and angels but not to our eyes because we are in a natural world. Spiritual people see things that come from a spiritual source, and natural people see things that come from a natural source. This means that there is no way for our eyes to see things in the spiritual world unless we are allowed to be in the spirit, or until we become spirits after death. On the other hand, angels and spirits are utterly incapable of seeing anything in the natural world unless they are with some one of us who has been allowed to talk with them. Our eyes are adapted to receive the light of the natural world, and the eyes of angels and spirits are adapted to receive the light of the spiritual world; yet the two kinds of eyes look exactly alike.

Natural people cannot understand that the spiritual world is like this, and sense-centered people even less so, being people who believe nothing unless they can see it with their physical eyes and touch it with their hands. This means they believe only what they glean through their sight and touch and that they think on this basis; so their thought is material and not spiritual.

Because of this resemblance between the spiritual world and the natural world, it is hard for people after death to realize that they are not in the world where they were born, the world they have just left; so they actually call death nothing but a crossing from one world into another like it.

On this kind of resemblance between the two worlds, see the discussion above of representations and appearances in heaven (§§170–176).

The heavens there are on the higher ground, the world of spirits there is in the lower areas, and beneath both lie the hells.

The heavens are not visible to spirits in the world of spirits unless their inner sight has been opened. Sometimes they do appear, looking like gleaming white clouds. This is because heaven's angels are in a more inward state as regards their intelligence and wisdom, so they are beyond the sight of people in the world of spirits.

The spirits who are in the plains and valleys can see each other, though when they are being sorted out (which happens when they are being let into their inner natures), then evil spirits do not see the good ones. The good ones can still see the evil ones, but they turn away from them, and spirits who turn away become hard to see.

The hells themselves, though, are not visible, because they are closed. All one can see are the entrances, called gates, when they open to admit spirits like the ones already there. All the gates into the hells open from the world of spirits, none from heaven.

584 There are hells everywhere. They are under the mountains and hills and cliffs and under the plains and valleys. The openings or gates to the hells that are under the mountains and hills and cliffs look at first sight like crevices or fissures in the rocks. Some of them are quite broad and open, some narrow and confined, full of rough places. All of them seem dim and gloomy when you look in, although the hellish spirits who live there have the kind of illumination you get from glowing coals. Their eyes are adjusted to the reception of this kind of light. This is because when they were living in the world they were in darkness about divine truths owing to their denial of them. They were in a kind of light as to their false convictions because they affirmed them, which gave their eyesight the form it has. This is also why heaven's light is darkness to them, so when they come out of their caves, they cannot see anything. This makes it abundantly clear that we come into heaven's light to the extent that we have acknowledged the Divine and affirmed within ourselves the values of heaven and the church. We come into the darkness of hell to the extent that we have denied the Divine and affirmed within ourselves values contrary to those of heaven and the church.

585 The entrances or gates to the hells that are under the plains and valleys have different forms. Some of them are like the ones under the mountains, hills, and cliffs; some of them are like caves and caverns; some are like large chasms and quagmires, some like swamps; and some like stagnant ponds. All of them are covered over and are visible only when evil spirits are being cast in there from the world of spirits. When they are opened, something breathes out like the smoky fire we see in the air from conflagrations, or like flame without smoke, or like the kind of soot that comes from a hot chimney, or like a dark storm cloud. I have heard that evil spirits neither see nor feel this because when they are in it, they are in their element and therefore in the delight of their life. This is because these appearances correspond to the evils and distortions they are absorbed in, the fire corresponding to their hatred and vengefulness and the smoke and soot to their consequent distortions, the flame to the evils of their self-love, and the dark storm cloud to the distortions that follow from it.

586 I have been allowed to look into the hells and see what they were like inside, for when it pleases the Lord, a spirit or angel who is overhead can probe visually into the depths and examine their nature with no coverings in the way. I have also been allowed to explore them in this fashion. Some of the hells looked to me like caves and caverns leading into cliffs and then slanting downward or off at an angle.

Some of these hells looked like the lairs or dens of wild animals in the woods, some like the vaulted chambers and crypts found in mines, with caverns leading downward. Many of the hells are threefold. The higher ones look gloomy inside because the people there are fond of malicious distortions. The lower ones look fiery, though, because their inhabitants are devoted to malice itself. Darkness in fact corresponds to malicious distortions, and fire to the actual malice. That is, the people in the deeper hells are the ones who acted from evil on a deeper level, while the people in the hells that are not so deep acted from evils on a more superficial level—that is, on the basis of their malicious distortions.

In some hells you can see what look like the ruins of houses and cities after a fire, where hellish spirits live and hide out.

In the milder hells you can see crude huts, sometimes grouped in something like a city, with alleyways and streets. There are hellish spirits in these homes, with constant quarrels, hostility, beating, and violence. The streets and alleys are full of thieves and robbers.

In some hells there are nothing but brothels, foul to look at and full of all kinds of filth and excrement.

There are also dark forests where hellish spirits roam like wild beasts; and there are underground caves there where they flee when they are being threatened by others. Then there are desert areas where everything is barren and sandy, with rugged cliffs here and there with caves in them, and huts scattered around as well. People are exiled from the hells into these desert places if they have suffered to the limit, especially people who in the world were craftier than others in the skills of deliberate manipulation and deceit. This kind of life is their final lot.

As to the location of specific hells, no one can know this, not even an angel in heaven—only the Lord. Roughly, though, their location is recognized by the quarter where they are found. Like the heavens, the hells are differentiated into regions; and in the spiritual world, regions are marked off according to loves because all regions in heaven start from the Lord as the sun, who is the east. So since the hells are the opposite of the heavens, their regions start from the opposite direction, the west. On this subject, see the chapter on the four quarters in heaven (§§141–153). [2] This is why the hells in the western quarter are the worst and most fearful of all, worse and more fearful incrementally the farther they are from the east. The people in these hells are people who were absorbed in self-love in the world and therefore in contempt for others, hostility toward people who did not support them, and hatred and vengefulness against people who did not admire and revere

587

them. In the farthest regions live people from the so-called Catholic religion who wanted to be worshiped as gods and who therefore burned with hatred against anyone who did not acknowledge their power over human souls and over heaven. They have the same kind of animus—the same kind of hatred and vengefulness—toward people who oppose them, as they did in the world. They take particular delight in cruelty, but in the other life this is turned against them; for in their hells (and the western quarter is full of them) they rage against each other because everyone is claiming divine power. There is more about this, though, in my booklet on *The Last Judgment and Babylon Destroyed.*[314]

[3] Still, we cannot know how the hells are arranged in this region, only that the most horrifying are off to the side toward the northern quarter and the less horrifying toward the southern quarter. That is, the horror of the hells decreases between the northern region and the southern, and also, successively, toward the east. The people toward the east there are the ones who were foolish and did not believe in the Divine, but still were not given to the same kind of hatred and vengefulness or trickery as the people who are deeper in the western quarter.

[4] At present, there are no hells in the eastern region. The people who were there have been transferred to the front of the western quarter.

There are a good many hells in the northern and southern regions. The people there were absorbed in love of the world during their lives and therefore in various kinds of evil such as enmity, hostility, thievery, robbery, fraud, avarice, and callousness. The worst hells of this sort are in the northern quarter and the milder ones in the south. Their dreadfulness increases the nearer they are to the western region and the farther they are from the south, and decreases toward the east and also toward the south.

Behind the hells in the western region lie dense forests where malevolent spirits roam like wild animals, and much the same is true of the hells in the northern quarter. Behind the hells in the southern quarter, though, lie the deserts just described. So much for the location of the hells.

588 As for the number of the hells, there are just as many hells as there are angelic communities in the heavens, because there is a hellish community that corresponds inversely to each heavenly one. I explained in the chapter on the communities that constitute heaven (§§41–50) and the chapter on the vastness of heaven (§§415–420) that there are countless heavenly communities, all differentiated according to their virtues of love, thoughtfulness, and faith. The same holds true for the hellish communities, which are differentiated according to the evils opposite to those virtues.

[2] There is an infinite variety to everything evil just as there is to everything good. People do not grasp this if they have only simplistic concepts of particular evils like contempt, hostility, hatred, vengefulness, deceit, and the like; but they should realize that each of these contains so many distinctive forms, each of which also contains distinctive or particular forms, that a whole volume would not be adequate to list them. The hells are so clearly arranged according to the distinctive features of everyone's evil that nothing could be more definitely and clearly arranged. We can gather from this that they are beyond counting, some near each other and some far removed according to the general, specific, and particular differences of their evils.

[3] Further, there are hells below hells. Some communicate by traffic to and fro, many by emanations, all in strict accord with the affinities of each genus and species of evil with others.

I have been given some knowledge of the number of the hells from the fact that they are underneath every mountain, hill, and cliff, every plain and valley, and that they stretch out there far and wide and deep. In short, it is as though the whole heaven and the whole world of spirits are hollowed out with one continuous hell under them. So much for the number of the hells.

The Equilibrium between Heaven and Hell

FOR anything to happen, there needs to be an equilibrium of everything involved. If there is no equilibrium, there is no action and reaction because the equilibrium occurs between two forces, one acting and the other reacting. The state of rest arising from equal agents and reagents is called an equilibrium. 589

In the natural world there is equilibrium throughout, in general in the atmospheres, with the lower layers reacting and resisting to the extent that the upper layers act and bear down. In the natural world there are also states of equilibrium between warmth and cold, light and darkness, dry and wet. Their median blend is the balance point. There is also an equilibrium in the members of all three of earth's kingdoms—mineral, vegetable, and animal; for nothing would occur in those kingdoms if it were not for the equilibrium. Everywhere, there is a kind of effort acting from one side and another reacting from the other.

[2] Every event, or every result, happens in an equilibrium, or happens by one force acting and another allowing itself to be acted upon, or by one force actively flowing in and the other accepting and yielding appropriately.

In the natural world, what acts and reacts is called force or energy,[315] but in the spiritual world what acts and reacts is called life and volition. Life there is a living force and volition is a living energy, and the actual equilibrium is called a state of freedom. This spiritual balance or freedom occurs, then, between the good acting from the one side and the evil reacting from the other, or from the evil acting on the one side and the good reacting from the other. [3] The balance between active good and reactive evil applies to good people, and the balance between active evil and reactive good applies to evil people. The reason the spiritual balance is between good and evil is that all human life has to do with good and evil, and our volition is their recipient vessel.

There is also a balance between what is true and what is false, but this is secondary to the balance between good and evil. The balance between the true and the false is like the balance between light and darkness, whose effect on members of the vegetable kingdom depends on the amount of warmth or cold there is in the light or darkness. You can tell that the light and shade themselves do not accomplish anything, only the warmth they bring, from looking at like amounts of light and darkness in winter and in spring.

The comparison of truth and falsity to light and darkness rests in their correspondence, since truth corresponds to light and falsity to darkness, and warmth corresponds to the goodness of love. Further, spiritual light is truth, spiritual darkness is falsity, and spiritual warmth is the goodness of love (on this, see the chapter on light and warmth in heaven, §§126–140).

590 There is a constant balance between heaven and hell. An effort to do evil is constantly emanating upward from hell, and an effort to do good is constantly emanating down from heaven. The world of spirits is in this equilibrium (on its location halfway between heaven and hell, see §§421–431 above).

The reason the world of spirits is in this equilibrium is that after death we first enter the world of spirits and are kept in the same state we were in in the world. This could not happen unless there were a perfect balance there. This allows everyone to be examined there as to quality, since we keep the same kind of freedom we had in the world. Spiritual equilibrium is a state of freedom for us and for spirits, as just noted (§589).

Angels in heaven can tell the kind of freedom people have by a communication of affections and consequent thoughts. It also becomes visible to angelic spirits from the paths people follow, with good spirits following paths that lead to heaven and evil spirits following paths that lead to hell. These paths are actually visible in that world, which is why paths in the Word mean truths that lead to what is good, or in an opposite sense, falsities that lead to what is evil. This is also why going, walking, and traveling in the Word mean processes of life.[a] I have often been allowed to see paths like these, with spirits walking along on them freely, in accord with their own affections and consequent thoughts.

The reason evil is constantly emanating up from hell and good emanating down from heaven is that everyone is surrounded by a spiritual aura, an aura that flows out in waves from the life of our affections and their thoughts.[b] Further, since this kind of aura flows out from every individual, it also flows out from every heavenly community and every hellish community, therefore from everyone at once, or from all heaven and all hell. The reason good flows out from heaven is that everyone there is involved in what is good, and the reason evil flows out from hell is that everyone there is involved in what is evil.[316] All the good that comes from heaven is from the Lord, since the angels who are in the heavens are all kept out of their self-image and kept in the Lord's image, which is goodness itself. On the other hand, all the spirits who are in the hells are in their own self-image and everyone's own self-image is nothing but evil; and since it is nothing but evil, it is hell.[c]

591

a. Traveling in the Word means a process of life, as does going: 3335, 4375, 4554, 4585, 4882, 5493, 5606 *[5605]*, 5996, 5181 *[8181]*, 8345, 8397, 8417, 8420, 8557. Going and walking with the Lord is accepting spiritual life and living with him: 10567. Walking is living: 519, 1794, 8417, 8420.

b. A spiritual aura flows out in waves from every human being, spirit, and angel, and surrounds them: 4464, 5179, 7454, 8630. It flows out from the life of our affections and their thoughts: 2489, 4464, 6206–6207. The quality of spirits can be discerned from a distance by their auras: 1048, 1053, 1316, 1504. The auras of evil people clash with those of good people: 1695, 10187, 10312. These auras have a wide outreach in angelic communities, depending on the kind and amount of their good: 6598–6613, 8063, 8794, 8797; and in hellish communities depending on the kind and amount of their evil: 8794, 8797.

c. Our own self-image is nothing but evil: 210, 215, 731, 874, 875, 876, 987, 1047, 2307, 2318 *[2308]*, 3518, 3701, 3812, 8480, 8550, 10283, 10284, 10286, 10731 *[10732]*. Our self-image is hell for us: 694, 8480.

We may gather from this that the equilibrium angels in the heavens and spirits in the hells are kept in is not like the balance that obtains in the world of spirits. The equilibrium of angels in the heavens depends on how much they had wanted to be involved in good or had lived in goodness in the world—how opposed they were to evil; while the equilibrium of spirits in hell depends on how much they had wanted to be involved in evil or had lived in evil in the world—that is, how resistant they had been to the good, in heart and in spirit.

592 If the Lord were not in control of both the heavens and the hells, there would be no equilibrium; and if there were no equilibrium, there would be no heaven or hell. Absolutely everything in the universe, everything in both the natural world and the spiritual world, is constituted by an equilibrium. Any rational person can grasp this. Let one side outweigh the other, with no resistance offered, and will not both be destroyed? This is what would happen in the spiritual world if the good did not react against the evil and constantly suppress its rebellions. Unless the divine power, and nothing else, did this, heaven and hell would perish, and the whole human race along with them. I refer to the "divine power and nothing else" because the selfhood of every angel, every spirit, and every one of us is nothing but evil (see above, §591). This means that no angel or spirit can ever resist the evil influences that are constantly breathed out of the hells since we all incline toward hell because of our self-concern. We can see from this that if the Lord alone were not in control of both the heavens and the hells, there would be no salvation for anyone.

Not only that, all the hells act in unison because the evil energies of the hells are all interconnected the way the good energies are in the heavens; and nothing but the only divine power can resist all the countless hells acting in concert against heaven and everyone there. That one divine power emanates from the Lord.

593 The balance point between the heavens and the hells shifts down and up depending on the number of people entering heaven and entering hell, which amounts to thousands every day. Knowing and grasping this, adjusting and centering the pointer of the scales, is something no angel can do, only the Lord, since the emanating divine nature is everywhere present and is everywhere watching every deviation. Angels see only what is around them, and do not even sense within themselves what is happening in their own community.

594 Everything in the heavens and the hells is so arranged that each individual there is in a personal equilibrium. We can to some extent gather this from what has already been presented concerning the heavens and the hells. That is, all the communities of heaven are very precisely differentiated according to the genera and species of their goodness, and all the communities of hell according to the genera and species of their evils. Further, there is a corresponding community of hell underneath every community of heaven, and this opposing correspondence yields an equilibrium. So the Lord is constantly making sure that the hellish community under any heavenly one does not get too strong. To the extent that one begins to get too strong, it is brought under control by various means and returned to its proper balanced relationship. I shall mention only a few of the many means. Some involve a stronger presence of the Lord. Some involve closer communication and union of one or more communities with others. Some involve the exile of extra hellish spirits into desert places, some the transfer from one hell to another, some the reorganization of the people in the hells, which also is accomplished in various ways. Some involve concealing some of the hells under thicker and heavier coverings, some sending them down deeper. Then there are other means, some involving the heavens overhead.

I mention this so that there may be some grasp of the fact that only the Lord provides that there shall be a balance between good and evil everywhere, and therefore between heaven and hell. On this kind of equilibrium depends the salvation of everyone in the heavens and everyone on earth.

It needs to be realized that the hells are constantly attacking heaven and trying to destroy it and that the Lord is constantly protecting the heavens by restraining the people there from the evils that arise from their self-concern and by keeping them involved in the good that comes from him. I have often been granted a sense of the aura that radiates from the hells—an aura of nothing but efforts to destroy the divine nature of the Lord and therefore heaven as well. At times I have also perceived forces boiling up from certain hells, made up of efforts to break free and wreak destruction. On the other hand, the heavens never attack the hells, since the divine aura that emanates from the Lord is a constant effort to save everyone. Since the people in the hells cannot be saved (all the people there being engrossed in evil and opposed to the Lord's divine nature), the attacks within the hells are kept as subdued as possible, and mutual viciousness is held within bounds. This too is accomplished by countless exercises of divine power.

The heavens are differentiated into two kingdoms, the heavenly kingdom and the spiritual kingdom (see above, §§20–28). Similarly, the hells are differentiated into two kingdoms, one opposite to the heavenly kingdom and one opposite the spiritual kingdom. The one opposite to the heavenly kingdom is in the western quarter, and the people who live there are called demons; while the one that is opposite to the spiritual kingdom is in the northern and southern quarter, and the people who live there are called spirits.

All the people in the heavenly kingdom are involved in a love for the Lord, and all the people in the hells opposite to that kingdom are involved in love for themselves. All the people who are in the spiritual kingdom are involved in love for their neighbor, and all the people who are in the hells opposite to that kingdom are involved in love of the world. This has enabled me to see that love for the Lord and love for oneself are opposites, as are love for our neighbor and love of the world.

The Lord is constantly taking care that nothing should flow out from the hells opposite to the Lord's heavenly kingdom toward the people who are in the spiritual kingdom. If this were to happen, the spiritual kingdom would be destroyed, for the reasons given in §§578–579 above.

These are the two general balances that the Lord is constantly keeping intact.

Our Freedom Depends on the Balance between Heaven and Hell

597 I have just described the balance between heaven and hell and have shown that the balance is between what is good from heaven and what is evil from hell, which means that it is a spiritual balance that in essence is a freedom.[317]

The reason this spiritual balance is essentially a freedom is that it exists between what is good and what is evil and between what is true and what is false, and these are spiritual realities. So the ability to intend either good or evil and to think either truth or falsity, the ability to choose one instead of the other, is the freedom I am dealing with here.

The Lord grants this freedom to every individual, and it is never taken away. By virtue of its source it in fact belongs to the Lord and not to us because it comes from the Lord; yet still it is given us along with our life as though it were ours. This is so that we can be reformed and saved, for without freedom there can be no reformation or salvation.

Anyone who uses a little rational insight can see that we have a freedom to think well or badly, honestly or dishonestly, fairly or unfairly, and that we can talk and act well, honestly, and fairly but not badly, dishonestly, and unfairly because of the spiritual, moral, and civil laws that keep our outward nature in restraint.

We can see from this that the freedom applies to our spirit, which does our thinking and intending, but not to our outer nature, which does our talking and acting, except as this follows the aforementioned laws.

The reason we cannot be reformed unless we have some freedom is that we are born into evils of all kinds, evils which need to be taken away if we are to be saved. They cannot be taken away unless we see them within ourselves, admit that they are there, then refuse them and ultimately turn away from them. Only then are they taken away. This cannot happen unless we are exposed to both good and evil, since it is from good that we can see evils, though we cannot see what is good from evil. We learn the good spiritual things we can think from infancy from the reading of the Word and from sermons. We learn the moral and civic values from our life in the world. This is the primary reason we need to be in freedom.

[2] The second reason is that nothing becomes part of us except as a result of some affection of love. True, other things can enter us, but no deeper than into our thought, not into our volition; and anything that does not enter our volition is not ours. This is because thinking is derived from our memory, while volition is derived from our life itself. Nothing is ever free unless it comes from our volition, or what amounts to the same thing, from a particular affection that stems from our love. Whatever we intend or love, we do freely. This is why our freedom and the affection of our love or intentions are one. So we also have freedom in order to be able to be moved by what is true and good, or to love them, so that they do become part of us. [3] In a word, anything that does not enter us in freedom does not stay with us, because it does not belong to our love or intentions; and anything that does not belong to our love or intentions does not belong to our spirit. The actual reality[318] of our spirit is love or volition— using the phrase "love or volition" because whatever we love, we intend. This is why we cannot be reformed except in a state of freedom.

598

But there is more on our freedom in the extracts from *Secrets of Heaven* below.

599 So that we can be in freedom for the sake of our reformation, we are united in spirit with heaven and with hell. With each of us there are spirits from hell and angels from heaven. By means of the spirits from hell we encounter our evil, and by means of the angels from heaven we encounter the good we have from the Lord. As a result, we are in a spiritual equilibrium—that is, in a freedom.

On the presence with us of angels from heaven and spirits from hell, see the chapter on the union of heaven with the human race (§§291–302).

600 We need to be aware that our union with heaven and with hell is not directly with them but is mediated by spirits who are in the world of spirits. These spirits are with us, none from hell itself or heaven itself. We are united to hell through evil spirits in the world of spirits and with heaven through the good spirits there. Because of this arrangement, the world of spirits is halfway between heaven and hell and is at the point of balance.

On the location of the world of spirits halfway between heaven and hell, see the chapter on the world of spirits (§§421–431); and on its being at the point of balance between heaven and hell, see the last chapter (§§589–596).

We can see from this where we get our freedom.

601 I need to say something else about the spirits associated with us. A whole community can establish communication with another community or with another individual in any location through a spirit emissary. This spirit is called the "agent" of the group. Much the same holds true for our union with communities in heaven and with communities in hell, through spirits associated with us in the world of spirits. On this matter too, see the references to *Secrets of Heaven* at the close of the chapter.

602 One last note, about our instinct concerning life after death that results from heaven's inflow into us. There were some common people who had lived in the virtues of their faith in the world. They were brought back into a state like the one they had in the world (which can happen to anyone when the Lord allows it), and then shown what kind of notion they had had about our state after death. They said that in the world, some intelligent people had asked them what they thought about their soul after their life in the world, and they said they did not know what a soul was. Then the questioners asked them what they believed about their state after death, and they said they believed they would live as spirits. Next they were asked what kind of belief they had about spirits, and they said that spirits were people. Their questioners kept asking how they knew this, and they kept saying that they knew it because it was true. The intelligent people were amazed that simple people had this kind of faith when they themselves did not.

I could see from this that everyone who is united to heaven has an instinctive notion about life after death. The sole source of this instinctive notion is the inflow from heaven, that is, through heaven from the Lord, by means of spirits who are assigned to us from the world of spirits. This instinctive notion is possessed by people who have not stifled their freedom of thought by assumptions about the human soul that they have seized on and confirmed by various means, assumptions that the soul is either pure thought or some animate principle whose seat they seek in the body.[319] However, the soul is nothing more nor less than our life, while the spirit is the actual person, and the body is an earthly thing we carry around in the world. It is only an agent through which our spirit, the actual person, acts in a way that is adapted to the natural world.

What I have been saying in this book about heaven, the world of spirits, and hell will be obscure to people who find no delight in knowing about spiritual truths; but it will be clear to people who do have this delight, especially to people involved in an affection for truth for its own sake—that is, people who love truth because it is true. Anything that is loved enters into the concepts of our minds with light, especially when what is loved is true, because all truth is in the light.

603

References to Passages in *Secrets of Heaven* Concerning Our Freedom, Inflow, and the Spirits Who Are the Means of Communication

[2] ON FREEDOM. All freedom is a matter of love or affection, because whatever we love, we do freely: 2870, 3158, 8907 *[8987]*, 8990, 9585, 9591. Since freedom is a matter of love, it is the life of every individual: 2873. Nothing seems to be part of us unless it comes from freedom: 2880. There is a heavenly freedom and a hellish freedom: 2870, 2873, 2874, 9589, 9590.

Heavenly freedom comes from heavenly love, or a love of what is good and true: 1947, 2870, 2872, and since a love of what is good and true comes from the Lord, we are truly free only when we are led by the Lord: 892, 905, 2872, 2886, 2890, 2891, 2892, 9096, 9586, 9587, 9589, 9590, 9591. The Lord brings us into heavenly freedom through regeneration: 2874, 2875, 2882, 2892. We need freedom in order to be regenerated: 1937, 1947, 2876, 2881, 3145, 3146, 3158, 4031, 8700. Otherwise the love of what is good and true could not be sown in us and become so much a part of us as to seem to be our own: 2877, 2879, 2880, 2888. Nothing is united to us that happens under compulsion: 8700, 2875. If we could be forcibly reformed, everyone would be saved: 2881. Compulsion in matters of reformation is destructive: 4031. All worship offered in freedom is worship, but not what is offered under compulsion: 1947, 2880, 7349, 10097. Repentance needs to happen in a state of freedom, and if it happens in a state of compulsion, it does not work: 8392. Just what a state of compulsion is: 8392.

[3] We are allowed to act from the freedom we have as rational beings, so that good may be provided to us; we therefore have a freedom of thinking and intending evil as well, and even of doing it to the extent that the laws do not prevent it: 10777. The Lord holds us between heaven and hell and therefore in a balance so that we can be in freedom for the sake of our reformation: 5982, 6477, 8209, 8907 *[8987]*. What is sown in freedom stays with us, but not what is sown under compulsion: 9588. So freedom is never taken away from anyone: 2876, 2881. The Lord does not compel anyone: 1937, 1947.

To compel oneself stems from freedom, but being compelled does not: 1937, 1947. We ought to compel ourselves to resist evil: 1937, 1947, 7914; and to do good as well, apparently on our own, but still recognizing that it comes from the Lord: 2883, 2891, 2892, 7914. We become more solidly free in those temptation struggles in which we win, because then we are inwardly compelling ourselves to resist, even though it does not seem that way: 1937, 1947, 2881.

[4] Hellish freedom is being led by love for oneself and love for the world and by their cravings: 2870, 2873. This is the only freedom people in hell know: 2871. Heavenly freedom is as remote from hellish freedom as heaven is from hell: 2873, 2874. Hellish freedom, which is being led by love for oneself and love for the world, is not freedom but slavery: 2884, 2890. So slavery is being led by hell: 9586, 9589, 9590, 9591.

[5] On Inflow. Everything we think and intend flows in; [learned] from experience: 904, 2886, 2887, 2888, 4151, 4319, 4320, 5846, 5848,

6189, 6191, 6194, 6197, 6198, 6199, 6213, 7147, 10219. Our ability to look into things, think, and draw analytic conclusions comes from inflow: 1288 *[1285]*, 4319, 4320. We could not live for a moment if we were deprived of the inflow from the spiritual world, [from] experience: 2887, 5849, 5854, 6321. The life that flows in from the Lord varies depending on our state and our openness to it: 2069, 5986, 6472, 7343. In evil people, the good that flows in from the Lord is turned into evil, and the truth into falsity; from experience: 3643 *[3642 or 3743]*, 4632. We accept the good and true things that flow in from the Lord to the extent that what is evil and false does not bar the way: 2411, 3142, 3147, 5828.

[6] Everything good flows in from the Lord and everything evil from hell: 904, 4151. Nowadays people believe that everything is in themselves and from themselves, when actually everything is flowing in, as they might learn from the doctrine of the church, which teaches that everything good comes from the Lord and everything evil from the devil: 4249, 6193, 6206. If our belief were in accord with doctrine, we would not claim evil as our own or make good our own: 6206, 6324, 6325. How happy our state would be if we believed that everything good flows in from the Lord and everything evil from hell: 6325. People who deny heaven or know nothing about it do not realize that there is any inflow from it: 4322, 5649, 6193, 6479. What inflow is, illustrated by comparisons: 6428 *[6128]*, 6480 *[6190]*, 9407.

[7] All of life flows in from the first wellspring of life because this is its source; and it is constantly flowing in, so it comes from the Lord: 3001, 3318, 3237 *[3337]*, 3338, 3344, 3484, 3619, 3741, 3742, 3743, 4318, 4319, 4320, 4417, 4524, 4882, 5847, 5986, 6325, 6468, 6469, 6470, 6479, 9276, 10196. The inflow is spiritual and not physical, which means that the inflow is from the spiritual world into the natural and not from the natural into the spiritual: 3219, 5119, 5259, 5427, 5428, 5477, 6322, 9110, 9111 *[9109]*. The inflow comes through the inner person into the outer, or through the spirit into the body, and not the other way around, because our spirit is in the spiritual world and our body in the natural world: 1702, 1707, 1940, 1954, 5119, 5259, 5779, 6322, 9380 *[9110]*. The inner person is in the spiritual world and the outer in the natural world: 978, 1015, 3628, 4459, 4523, 4524, 6057, 6309, 9701–9709, 10156, 10472. It seems as though there were an inflow from our outer natures into our inner, but this is an illusion: 3721. There is an inflow into our rational workings and through these into our information processing, and not the other way around: 1495, 1707, 1940. What the pattern of inflow is like: 775, 880, 1096, 1495, 7270. The inflow comes directly from the Lord and indirectly

through the spiritual world or heaven: 6063, 6307, 6472, 9682, 9683. The inflow from the Lord comes into what is good in us and through that good into what is true, but not the other way around: 5483 *[5482]*, 5649, 6027, 8685, 8701, 10153. What is good enables us to accept the inflow from the Lord, but not what is true apart from that good: 8321. Nothing that flows into our thought harms us, only what flows into our volition, because this becomes part of us: 6308.

[8] There is a general inflow: 5850. This is a constant energy favoring action in keeping with the design: 6211. This is what flows into the lives of animals: 5850; and also into the members of the vegetable kingdom: 3648. Further, our thought descends into speech and our intentions into actions and modes of behavior according to this general inflow: 5862, 5990, 6192, 6211.

[9] On Agents. The spirits who are sent out from communities of spirits to other communities or to individual spirits are called "agents": 4403, 5856. Communications in the other life take place by means of emissary spirits like these: 4403, 5856, 5983. Spirits who are sent out to act as emissaries do not think for themselves but think from the spirits who commissioned them: 5985, 5986, 5987. More about these spirits: 5988, 5989.

The End

NOTES & INDEXES

Notes

Notes to §1 (Author's Preface)

1. "The Lord" here refers to Jesus. Although Swedenborg's theology is thoroughly monotheistic, to denote God he uses many names and terms from philosophical and biblical backgrounds (God, the Divine Being, the Divine, the Divine Human, the One, the Infinite, the First, the Creator, the Redeemer, the Savior, Jehovah, God Shaddai, and many more). The most frequently occurring term, however, is "the Lord" (Latin *Dominus*), a title rather than a name, meaning "the one in charge," and referring to Jesus Christ as the visible manifestation of the one only God. For Swedenborg's brief explanation of his reasons for using "the Lord," see *Secrets of Heaven* 14. [JSR]

2. Swedenborg often used *ecclesia,* "church," to refer to the whole religious belief and practice of a given nation or era. [GFD]

3. Elsewhere Swedenborg explains the Lord's prediction as four sequential degenerative stages in the church's attitude toward love and faith: disputing about them, despising them, devastation of them, and profanation of them (see *Secrets of Heaven* 3754). [JSR]

4. The Latin phrase here translated "the Human-born One," *Filius hominis,* has traditionally been translated "Son of man." [GFD]

5. Swedenborg's Scripture citations often closely follow the Latin translation of the Bible by Sebastian Schmidt (1617–1696); sometimes—as here—they vary from it in the direction of greater literalism (see Schmidt 1696). Swedenborg also had access to the interlinear version of the Bible of the Spanish theologian and linguist Benedict Arias Montanus (1527–1598), and may agree with it against Schmidt (see Montanus 1657). The actual copy of Schmidt's translation used by Swedenborg, with his marginal notes, has been preserved in codices 89–90 in the library of the Royal Academy of Sciences, Stockholm. A photolithograph reproduction, edited by Rudolph Leonard Tafel, is also available (see Swedenborg 1872). [GFD]

6. As in the case of many other biblical concepts, Swedenborg's interpretation of the Last Judgment is quite different from that of most theological traditions of his time. Opposing suggestions that our earth and our life will be destroyed in a final battle between good and evil, or that history will come to some sort of cosmic conclusion, he presents the Last Judgment as a symbol. In *Secrets of Heaven* 3353, he writes: "The Last Judgment is nothing else than the end of the church [true religion] in one nation and its beginning in another . . . when there is no longer any acknowledgment of the Lord, . . . no faith, . . . and no thoughtfulness." For further discussion, see the introduction to this volume, as well as Swedenborg's 1758 work *Last Judgment.* [RHK]

7. As examples of some of the "many people" to which Swedenborg refers, two of the dominant figures in New Testament scholarship during Swedenborg's time might be cited. These were the Germans Johann Albrecht Bengel (1687–1752) and Johann August Ernesti (1707–1781), who can be said to have helped lay the basis for methodical textual criticism of the Bible. Both were passionate advocates of the *sensus literalis,* or

literal sense of the Bible, particularly in regard to the Last Judgment. Ernesti's review of Swedenborg's *Secrets of Heaven,* which appeared in the prestigious *Neue Theologische Bibliothek* (Ernesti 1760, 1:6 515–527), was vehemently critical of Swedenborg's assigning multiple meanings to single words of biblical text, which he considered a regression to nonscientific "allegorical and mystical" methods of commentary. Another influential German theologian of the period, the Pietist Friedrich Christoph Oetinger (1702–1782), who published reviews of Swedenborg that were favorable in other respects, sided with Bengel and Ernesti on the issue of Bible interpretation, complaining in one letter that "he [Swedenborg] places more trust in his analogy of history or his *scientiam correspondentiarum* [knowledge of correspondences] than in the clear [Bible] that needs no interpretation" ("daß er auf seine Ähnlichkeit der Geschichte, oder auf seine *scientiam correspondentiarum* mehr Vertrauen setzt, als auf das klare Wort, welches keiner Auslegung bedarf"; Ehman 1859, 750; attributed to Oetinger by Benz [1947, 166–181]). It should be noted, too, that Swedenborg's statement about "many people in the church" can be accepted as his assessment of contemporary religious opinion—a credible one, since his closest and most influential relatives included a current and a future bishop. (For more on Oetinger, see note 206 below.) [RHK]

8. "The Word" (Latin *Verbum*) was the preferred Lutheran designation of the Bible as revealed truth, the "Word of God." In his use of this term, however, Swedenborg meant specifically the books of the Bible that he identifies as having a spiritual meaning throughout, namely the Pentateuch (Genesis, Exodus, Leviticus, Numbers, Deuteronomy), the historical books (Joshua, Judges, 1 and 2 Samuel, 1 and 2 Kings), the Book of Psalms, the major and minor prophets (Isaiah, Jeremiah, Lamentations, Ezekiel, Daniel, Hosea, Joel, Amos, Obadiah, Jonah, Micah, Nahum, Habakkuk, Zephaniah, Haggai, Zechariah, Malachi), the Gospels (Matthew, Mark, Luke, John), and the Book of Revelation. See *Secrets of Heaven* 10325; and two other 1758 works of Swedenborg, *New Jerusalem* 266, and *White Horse* 16. It should be noted that in his 1771 work *True Christianity* he seems to use the term in the full Lutheran sense, including passages from the epistles of the apostles among citations from "the Word." For his explanation as to why he did not generally include the works of the apostles and Paul, see his letter to Beyer (April 15, 1766), cited in Acton 1955, 612–613. [GFD, JSR]

9. Swedenborg saw the material world as caused by the spiritual world and as therefore reflecting it; that is, physical phenomena and events *offer images of*—that is, are "responsive to" or "correspond to"—spiritual phenomena and events. As noted by Swedenborg himself in *Secrets of Heaven* 4, the primary purpose of that work (his largest) was to demonstrate that the Bible contains levels of spiritual meaning that could at least in part be discovered by a knowledge of specific correspondential relationships. [GFD, RHK]

10. *Secrets of Heaven* (1749–1756) had been published anonymously, as were the works published in 1758 (*Heaven and Hell, New Jerusalem, Last Judgment, White Horse,* and *Other Planets).* Swedenborg was not identified as their author until his clairvoyant experience of the Stockholm fire in 1759. On this topic, see Hjern 1990, 8–9. A shorter account of the event, in English, may be found in Dole and Kirven 1992, 50. [GFD, RHK]

11. See *White Horse,* one of the works published by Swedenborg in 1758 along with *Heaven and Hell.* [GFD]

12. The Latin phrase here translated "heavenly contents hidden" is *arcana coeli,* a phrase that evokes the title of Swedenborg's major published theological work, *Arcana Coelestia* (Secrets of Heaven), by expressing the same meaning in a slightly different grammatical form. [GFD]

13. "Church people these days" *(homo ecclesiae hodie)* describes Swedenborg's primary and consistent concern, distinguishable from "many people in the church" *(plerique hodie intra ecclesiam)*—the scholars referred to above (see note 7 above). His reported encounters with the spirits of recently deceased church people (see, for example, his 1771 work *True Christianity* 160:3, 692, 693, 694, 731:2, 738) convinced him that widespread ignorance of biblical teachings (his concern here), and distortions of the church's theological traditions (see, for example, note 18 below) were threatening people's ability to live well and to prepare themselves for heaven. Here he cites this circumstance as the explanation for his call and his revelation, and as the motive for his work. [RHK]

14. "The Coming of the Lord," or "the Lord's Advent," refers here to any instance of the Lord's renewed presence among people—any spiritual analog of the Lord's Incarnation. In his late works, Swedenborg began to speak explicitly of the "Second Advent," a term he used to describe the cosmic spiritual events that included the revelation he felt the Lord was accomplishing through Swedenborg's own spiritual experiences. See, for example, his 1771 work *True Christianity* 115, 121, 123; and his handwritten inscription on the inside cover of a copy of his 1769 publication *Survey:* "This work is part of the Coming of the Lord (written by command)." (On this inscription, see Tafel 1890, 757, and Sigstedt 1981, 375.) Swedenborg's spiritual experiences—which had lasted for thirteen years as of the time he wrote this passage, and comprised a total of twenty-nine years in his lifetime—are the main source on which he drew for his writing. Since he felt these experiences were provided him by the Lord, they also are his primary authority. In *Secrets of Heaven* 68 he wrote, "Many will claim, I realize, that no one can talk to spirits and angels as long as bodily life continues, or that I am hallucinating, or that I circulate such stories in order to play on people's credulity, and so on. But none of this worries me; I have seen, I have heard, I have felt." [GFD, RHK]

Notes to §§2–6

15. Swedenborg here refers to the Christian concept of the Trinity: Father (God), Son (Christ), and Holy Ghost. The unity of these triune essentials of divine nature, together with the theological preeminence of the Lord *(Dominus),* constitutes one of Swedenborg's most frequent and prominent emphases. (His teachings on the Word and on the inseparability of faith and works are the only comparably important issues for him.) He saw the trinitarianism of his day as essentially and disastrously tritheistic, leading to the worship of three gods instead of one. He viewed Jesus as having from conception an inner divine nature and an outer human nature. By a process of "temptation combats" analogous to our own struggles against temptation, the divine nature progressively transformed or "glorified" the human nature. The term "the Lord," as used by Swedenborg, consistently refers either to the inner divine nature (see note 17 below) or to the risen and ascended Christ, as the fullest possible self-disclosure of the infinite Divine, which in itself is utterly beyond our knowing. It is distinct from, and yet one with, the Father/Creator and the Holy Spirit. This definition is presented in *Secrets of Heaven* 14

and obtains consistently thereafter. His most complete continuous passages on trinitarian theology are in his 1763 work *The Lord* and the first three chapters of his 1771 work *True Christianity* (§§5–184). [GFD, RHK]

16. The first edition cites verses 10 and 11 of John chapter 14, but verse 9 is also clearly meant. [JSR]

17. Swedenborg used the substantive adjective "the Divine" *(Divinum)* to denote the three-in-one deity in all its aspects, almost exclusively in preference to "God" *(Deus)*, and as a consistent alternative to "the Trinity." "The Divine" also designates that quality in each "person" of the Trinity that unites it to the Trinity, as in §3, "the Lord's divine nature" *(Divinum Domini)*. [RHK]

18. In a major restructuring of traditional views of judgment in Christian eschatology and belief about salvation, Swedenborg describes judgment in the spiritual world as an internally directed process of aligning the reality of our character and most fundamental motivations with the objective realities of spiritual life. In §§510 and 511 below he describes the separation of evil spirits from good ones, showing the "spirits themselves diving" into hell. The chapter in §§545–550 below is headed "The Lord Does Not Cast Anyone into Hell: People Cast Themselves In," and he develops the notion in many contexts. Here in §2, "not allowed" *(non licet)*, and "sent away" *(rejiceretur)*, refer to self-judgment. The same applies to "let down" *(demittuntur)*, and "banished" *(relegantur)* in §3. Such terms, reflecting the appearance of external judgment, are not common in the work. [RHK]

19. We may suspect here an oblique reference to a statement in the work Swedenborg identified as the Athanasian Creed to the effect that while "we are obliged by Christian verity to acknowledge each Person in his own right as God and Lord, we are forbidden by the Catholic faith from saying that there are three Gods or three Lords." See, in his later works, *The Lord* 55, *Survey* 35, and especially *True Christianity* 173:2: "Beware, then, that the concept of three gods does not take root in your mind while your mouth—which has no concepts in it—pronounces one god. Would not the part of the mind that is above the memory thinking three gods, and the mind below the memory that makes the mouth say one god, be like a comedian on a stage who can play two parts, switching back and forth, saying one thing in one role and the opposite in the other, and in his argument calling himself wise one moment and demented the next?" [GFD]

20. "Inflow" (Latin *influxus*) is central to Swedenborg's concept of human nature. Both truth and the ability to identify truth "flow in" from the Lord through heaven to human understanding from moment to moment continuously. Thus knowledge—like life (and being itself)—is not a static "gift" but an ongoing dynamic relationship between a person and his or her context in spiritual reality. See §228 below, and §340 of Swedenborg's 1763 work *Divine Love and Wisdom*. Inflow between the heavens is discussed in §§207–209 below. [RHK]

21. This is a reference to the followers of the Italian theologian Faustus Socinus (1539–1604) and his uncle Laelius Socinus (1525–1562), who denied the divinity of Christ. For references to Swedenborg's position on Christ's divinity, see note 19 above. [RHK]

22. In describing locations in the spiritual world Swedenborg often uses phrases relating to three-dimensional space that either lack a clear frame of reference—"a little

forward to the right" (§3), "in the front" (§327), "moved away," and "toward the left" (§249)—or that have reference to some organ of the human body—"these spirits can be seen in the neighborhood of the stomach, some on the left and some on the right, some lower and some higher, nearer or farther away" (§299). In the latter case it is not clear whether the body is that of Swedenborg himself, or of the universal human (see §§59, 65, 66), or even of the Lord (see §81); perhaps it is the result of a perceptual overlap of the three. Swedenborg later points out that directions in the spiritual world are constant regardless of the turning of one's spirit-body. For angels east is always in front, west behind, south on the right, and north on the left (see §§141–142). "Front" and "back" are presumably then farther east and west respectively, that is, closer to and farther from the Lord as visible in the sun of heaven. "Higher" and "lower" presumably denote different levels, as described in §38 (see also §§22, 197). [JSR]

23. The Latin word here translated "materialists" is *naturalistae,* used by Swedenborg to mean those who worship the natural world in place of God. In §310 of the 1764 work *Divine Providence,* Swedenborg writes: "Every appearance that is confirmed as a truth becomes a fallacy. To the extent that people confirm themselves in fallacies they become materialists. And to that extent they believe nothing but what they can at the same time perceive by one of the bodily senses." [RHK]

24. See §§318–328 below. While Swedenborg was careful to refer back to relevant passages by section number, his references ahead are rarely specific. Where we do find such specific references (in §207 of *Secrets of Heaven,* for example, he refers to §265) we may assume that he added the number on the basis of his first draft when he wrote out his fair copy. [GFD]

25. The Latin word here translated "insights" is *cognitiones.* In *Secrets of Heaven* 24, Swedenborg assigns *scientifica,* "data" or "information about," to the outer person *(homo externus)* and *cognitiones* to the inner person *(homo internus).* The term *cognitiones* seems consistently to refer to direct, experiential awareness. "Insights" is here used in translation more for its compactness than for its precision. [GFD]

26. See §§334–337 below. [GFD]

27. The first edition reads 24–25. [JSR]

Notes to §§7–12

28. Swedenborg regularly equates "highest" with "inmost" or "central," and "lowest" with "outmost" or "most external." For further discussion, see note 45 below. [GFD]

29. See §§139–140 below. [GFD]

30. The Latin phrase here translated "enduring is a constant coming into being" *(subsistere est perpetuo existere)* was a philosophical maxim in Swedenborg's day (see *Secrets of Heaven* 3483, 5084:3; *Soul-Body Interaction* 4) on which Swedenborg frequently built (see *Secrets of Heaven* 775, 3648, 4322, 4523:3, 5116:3, 5377:1, 6040:1, 6482, 9502, 9847, 10076:5, 10152:3, 10252:3, 10266; *Heaven and Hell* 107, 303; *Divine Love and Wisdom* 152; *Divine Providence* 3:2; *Marriage Love* 380:8; *Soul-Body Interaction* 9; *True Christianity* 46, 224:1). The point of the maxim is this: although a given animal may have descended from its ancestors, and a given rock may have stood where it stands for millennia, in another way of looking at it the animal and the rock are created anew by

God each moment. Their enduring can also be seen as a perpetual arising or coming into existence. [JSR]

31. By "the First" here Swedenborg means God as the origin of all things; see also §§37, 303. [JSR]

Notes to §§13–19

32. The Latin word here translated "thoughtfulness" is *charitas,* traditionally translated "charity." At this point and in the following chapter the term denotes the practice of learning, wanting, and doing what one's neighbor wants. In other contexts—for example, the discussion below of the rich and the poor (see especially §364)—it refers to the concept of desiring what is good for one's neighbor. One of Swedenborg's most urgent concerns was the contemporary debate over the relative primacy of faith and charity (which can be considered thoughtfulness toward others, or "works," what one does for others) in practice and concept, which he felt had brought the religious life of the age into peril. For him, faith and charity were inseparable except in concept, and their relationship was that of thought and intent (see §364 below). [RHK]

33. The phrase "single being" here introduces Swedenborg's idea—developed at greater length in §§94–101 below—that the entire heaven has the form of a single human spirit patterned after the form of the Lord, and can be called the "universal human." This is a far-reaching concept informing his ontology, christology, anthropology, and eschatology. Its complete formulation appears in a series of twenty essays interspersed among certain passages of *Secrets of Heaven* (specifically, following Swedenborg's exegesis of Genesis chapters 23 through 43). For these essays, excerpted and translated, see Swedenborg 1984. [RHK]

34. The idea of love that is offered here is most fully defined in Swedenborg's 1763 work *Divine Love and Wisdom* 1–46. [RHK]

35. For an overview of the three heavens see §§29–40. [JSR]

36. The Latin here translated "for the image he projects" is *quoad personam.* It is probable that Swedenborg uses *persona* here in its classical sense of "mask." Note his citation of *Secrets of Heaven* 3820, with its contrast between the *persona* and the inner source of the *persona.* In *Divine Providence* 217:3 *persona* is also associated with *functio et honor,* "role and status," a meaning which is often applicable elsewhere and may be intended here. [GFD, RHK]

37. The present translation follows Swedenborg's practice of not indicating ellipses. [GFD]

38. John 15:12, here referred to but not cited, reads, "This is my commandment, that you love one another as I have loved you." [GFD]

39. The Latin word here translated "auras" is *sphaerae,* a word Swedenborg often uses to refer to regions or extents of influence. [GFD]

40. In Swedenborg's note at this point, it seems likely that the first list of references was intended to be 10130, 10420, and 10702, and the second to be 10130, 10189, and 10420, but that due to the substantial similarity the lists were conflated. [GFD]

41. See §§141–153 below. [GFD]

42. This general theme is explored in some detail in the references to *Secrets of Heaven* at the end of §356 below. [GFD]

Notes to §§20–28

43. For a mapping of the two kingdoms onto the human body see §95; for a mapping of the three heavens onto the human body, see §§29, 65. [JSR]

44. The Latin term here translated "heavenly kingdom" is *regnum coeleste.* Some translations render this "celestial kingdom." However, such a translation obscures a clearly intentional symmetry: *coelestis*/heavenly is to *coelum*/heaven as *spiritualis*/spiritual is to *spiritus*/spirit and *naturalis*/natural is to *natura*/nature. [GFD, RHK]

45. Throughout his theological works, Swedenborg relates "high" to inwardness and "low" to externality; that is, the higher something is said to be, the more inward it is; the lower something is said to be, the more outward or external it is. (The relationship is so close in each case that the terms involved seem interchangeable.) See the introduction to this volume; and for further development of the relational concept, see Swedenborg's 1763 work *Divine Love and Wisdom* 184–263, especially 205. [GFD, RHK]

46. Following the general Christian practice of his times, Swedenborg often renders the tetragrammaton of Hebrew Scriptures as "Jehovah." [JSR]

47. Since faith is an intellectual faculty, and thoughtfulness is a particular form of volition, Swedenborg's statement here constitutes a more generalized affirmation of the unity of faith and charity, or thoughtfulness toward one's neighbor (see note 32 above). [RHK]

Notes to §§29–40

48. The Latin words here translated "outmost or first," *ultimum seu primum,* could also be rendered "last or first"—a paradoxical description that may be one of the touches of rather dry wit visible in Swedenborg from time to time, alongside instances of a broader humor. The alternative meaning, equating "outmost" with "lowest" ("first" in this ascending series) is discussed in notes 28 and 45 above. [GFD, RHK]

49. The Latin word here translated "disposition" is *animus.* Swedenborg had a broad concept of "mind" with three components: (1) *anima,* "the soul" (also translated "higher mind," or "spiritual consciousness"); (2) *mens,* "rational mind" (also translated "conscious mind"); and (3) *animus,* "lower mind" (which we might call neuro-consciousness). For a discussion of these components, see his earlier work *Draft of a Rational Psychology* (= Swedenborg 1950, §§462–476). [RHK]

50. Since thoughtfulness toward others (charity) is a volition (as something we do) and faith a cognition (as something of which we are aware) this passage provides another perspective on Swedenborg's thoughtfulness/faith emphasis (see notes 32 and 47 above). [RHK]

51. See especially §§200–212 below. [GFD]

52. By "the First" here Swedenborg means God as the origin of all things; see also §§9, 303. [JSR]

53. See note 9 above. [GFD]

54. The Latin word here translated "images" is *repraesentationes,* sometimes translated "representations." While a correspondence *(correspondens)* necessarily changes to reflect changes in its inner cause, a representation *(repraesentatio)* may not necessarily do so. In *Secrets of Heaven* 2988, Swedenborg uses as an example of a correspondence a face that expresses actual, present feelings. An example of a representation would be an

outward appearance of courtesy that is at odds with one's feelings. See also the definition of *representation* in §175 below. [GFD, RHK]

55. Swedenborg's concept of levels *(gradus)* is presented most completely in *Divine Love and Wisdom* 179–263. [RHK]

56. There is little if any further mention of the lowest or natural heaven in the remainder of the work. Some mention of the spiritual heaven may be found in §§65:2, 100, 207–210, 280, and 295. The highest or third heaven receives the most attention, with information in §§49:2, 65:2, 70, 75, 178, 206–211, 227, 260:2, 267, 277:4, 295, 382, 459, and 489. [GFD]

Notes to §§41–50

57. "States" (Latin *status),* a term frequently employed by Swedenborg in the meaning "conditions," is defined in §154 below as "attributes of life and of matters that pertain to life." [RHK]

58. Swedenborg found the relationship between visible facial expressions and inner mental or spiritual states to be an excellent illustration of his key concepts of representations and correspondences (see notes 9 and 54 above). He develops the symbolism more thoroughly in *Secrets of Heaven* 2987–2990. [RHK]

59. See note 39 above. [RHK]

60. See §§200–212 below. [GFD]

Notes to §§51–58

61. The Latin phrase here translated "stories of heaven" is *habitacula coeli,* probably a reference to the "stories [Hebrew מַעֲלוֹת, *ma'ălôt*] of heaven" in Amos 9:6. The phrase "the heaven of heavens" occurs in Deuteronomy 10:14, 1 Kings 8:27 (= 2 Chronicles 6:18), 2 Chronicles 2:6, and Nehemiah 9:6. [GFD]

62. Swedenborg's references to the macrocosm/microcosm relate to his most inclusive image, the "universal human," mentioned in note 33 above. Here, the individual angel is a microcosm of her or his community, which is a microcosm of heaven, in turn a microcosm of the Lord *(Dominus),* who is the most we can know of the triune God. Swedenborg saw the microcosm as functionally derived from the macrocosm in the consistent and necessary pattern of creation, a more complex and comprehensive relationship than earlier Christian developments of the concept, such as that of Hildegard of Bingen (1098–1179). [RHK]

63. The Latin expression here translated "in the vacuum" is *in aethere*—strictly, "in the ether." Swedenborg shared the belief of his times that there is an atmosphere rarer than air, called "ether," that would not be exhausted by an air pump. He was convinced that there could be no absolute vacuum, since this would mean a total break in the seamless fabric of reality. See, for example, his 1763 work *Divine Love and Wisdom* 82. [GFD]

64. See note 33 above. The notion of the one Lord appearing differently in different communities presages Swedenborg's distinctive teaching that all people regardless of their religion have access to salvation: see his 1764 work *Divine Providence* 325. [RHK]

Notes to §§59–67

65. Before writing *Heaven and Hell,* Swedenborg had explained in detail the idea of heaven as a universal human in the sequential interchapter sections of *Secrets of Heaven* that are listed in Swedenborg's note to §98 below. See also note 33 above. [GFD]

66. The Latin word here translated "outmost form" is *ultimum.* Swedenborg consistently uses the adjective *ultimus* ("end" or "last" of any series) to mean farthest from the Divine, and therefore most external. The term is not always derogatory: for example, he writes in *Secrets of Heaven* 7337: "divine truth flowing from the Lord contains all power, so there is power even in the lowest details *[in ultimis]*"; and in *True Christianity* 212, "The last sense *[sensus ultimus]*, the natural one called the literal sense, is the container, basis, and support of the two interior senses." See also §§209–221 of his 1763 work *Divine Love and Wisdom.* [GFD, RHK].

67. See note 28 above [RHK]

68. The Latin word here translated "commonwealth" is *commune,* "common thing." [RHK]

Notes to §§73–77

69. By the time *Heaven and Hell* was actually published, some thirteen years would have elapsed from the beginning of Swedenborg's experiences in the spiritual world, as Swedenborg himself notes in §1 above. [GFD]

70. For this use of "Jehovah," see note 46 above. [JSR]

Notes to §§78–86

71. The reference is to Swedenborg's 1758 work referred to as *New Jerusalem* in this edition. [JSR]

72. On the Socinians see note 21 above. [RHK]

73. See §§318–328 below. [GFD]

74. Time is discussed in §§162–169 and space in §§191–199. See note 80 below for a discussion of extension. [GFD]

Notes to References to Passages in *Secrets of Heaven* at the end of §86

75. On "the Coming of the Lord," see note 14 above. [RHK]

76. The translation "does not accord" depends on reading *cadat* for the *cedat* of the first edition. Swedenborg elsewhere uses *cadere in ideam/intellectum,* literally "to fall into a concept/understanding," in the sense of "fitting into" or agreeing with. (See *Secrets of Heaven* 2896:2, 4096:2; *Divine Love and Wisdom* 5, 202). He uses *cedere,* "to yield," only in the sense of "giving way." (See *Secrets of Heaven* 1951, 8321:2; *Marriage Love* 218.) [GFD]

77. The Latin word here translated "emanating" is *procedens,* "going forth from." See note 110 below. [GFD, RHK]

Notes to §§87–102

78. The Latin word here translated "the pearl" is *praecipua,* literally "the chief features." [RHK]

79. The Latin word here translated "is responsive" is *correspondet,* "corresponds." [GFD]

80. The philosophically-minded reader of the eighteenth century would undoubtedly take the term "extended" here as a reference to Descartes's contrast between the extension *(extensio)* of matter and the thought *(cogitatio)* of the mind. In Descartes's

system, *extensio* refers to measurable spatial extent, while *cogitatio* denies that dimensionality and asserts (only) mental reality. [GFD]

81. Swedenborg's colloquial use of *omne . . . sub sole est,* "all . . . that is under our sun," does not imply that he was limited by a pre-Copernican cosmology. In the same year that he published *Heaven and Hell* (1758), he also published *Other Planets,* a work devoted to descriptions of life on other planets of our solar system and in distant galaxies. In fact, Swedenborg was among the first theologians to incorporate a post-Copernican perspective into a theological system. See Kirven 1988, 361–370, especially 368–369; and see Swedenborg's explicit description of the sun as standing still while the earth moves, §158 below. [RHK]

82. See §§20–28. [GFD]

83. See note 33 above. [GFD]

84. In his 1768 work on marriage love, Swedenborg provides a definition of that concept that covers both the abstract and the personal: "True marriage love is nothing but a union of love and wisdom. Two married partners who have this love between them and in them at the same time are a reflection and image of it" (*Marriage Love* 65). See also note 178 below. [JSR]

85. The Latin expression here translated "sharp-sighted" is *acutae aciei,* "of a sharp edge," with ellipsis of *oculorum,* "of the eyes." The full phrase occurs in *Marriage Love* 13:3, the elliptical in *True Christianity* 40 and 697:1. [GFD]

86. The Latin here translated "a long arm" is *extensas manus;* literally, "stretched-out hands." [GFD]

87. See §§291–302, especially §302. [GFD]

88. On "the Coming of the Lord," see note 14 above. [RHK]

Notes to §§103–115

89. The contents of §§103–115 are especially remarkable for having been written by a man of the Enlightenment, a time in which the movement to analyze nature with the tools of reason was gaining momentum. In prefaces to the scientific works that preceded his theological writing, Swedenborg displayed many of the goals and perspectives of Deists such as Matthew Tindal (1655–1733), including a confidence in the power of human reason and a belief in God as the architect of an ordered world. However, Swedenborg's perspective differed radically from that of the Deists in his acceptance of empirical revelation. (The Deists were generally suspicious of any beliefs that rested on an appeal to supernatural revelation, whether in the Bible or elsewhere.) Swedenborg's reliance upon revelatory experiences allowed him to combine scientific method with pervasive religious sensibility in a way that turned the Enlightenment goal on its head: instead of pursuing science in the hope of understanding spirit and God, in this passage and elsewhere he advocated a spiritual pursuit of God as a means of understanding nature and the material universe. For a discussion of Swedenborg's relationship with Deist thought, see Kirven 1965. [RHK]

90. While it might be expected that Swedenborg would use the more concrete *correspondentia,* "things that correspond," he uses the abstract *correspondentiae,* "correspondences," consistently in this section. [GFD]

91. See note 30 above. [JSR]

92. On Swedenborg's use of *ecclesia,* "church," see note 2 above. By *ecclesia repraesentativa,* here translated "a representative church," he meant a "church," or religious culture, that focused on the careful performance of prescribed actions whether or not its members had a sense of the spiritual realities those actions reflected. [GFD]

93. The Latin phrase here translated "the bread of presence" is *panes facierum,* "breads of faces," which follows the reading of Schmidt 1696 (see note 5 above) and very literally reflects the Hebrew לֶחֶם הַפָּנִים, *leḥem happānîm.* [GFD]

94. The Latin word here translated "functions" is *usus,* which is sometimes also translated "uses." Swedenborg employs this noun as at least a partial synonym for "good." When "use" is synonymous with "action" (as in the notion of "performing a use") it refers to an action that is helpful to—does good for—someone. When indicating an aspect of an activity or the person who performs it (as in "the use of a judge") it refers to the help that the activity or person provides. Swedenborg's notion of "use" is explored in Van Dusen 1981. [RHK, GFD]

95. The unusual Latin word *coelicolae* for inhabitants of heaven suggests that Swedenborg is alluding specifically to Catullus 64:409–411. For discussion and background see Frazier 1998. [JSR]

96. For an extensive report on Swedenborg's visits to the heavens of these ages, see his 1768 work *Marriage Love* 74–78. [JSR]

Notes to §§116–125

97. The Latin words here translated "I have heard and seen" are *audivi et vidi,* recalling the phrase *ex auditis et visis,* "from things heard and seen," in the title of the book. [GFD]

98. In more than twenty passages in his theological works, Swedenborg appears to have anticipated modern brain research in recognizing differing functions for the left and right hemispheres of the brain. For example, *Secrets of Heaven* 644 reads in part: "The will and the understanding are most distinct from each other. . . . The human brain is divided into two parts, called hemispheres; to its left hemisphere pertain the intellectual faculties, and to the right those of the will"—a distinction not incompatible with modern attributions of intellectual, detailed, literate, and mathematical functions to the left brain; and emotional and aesthetic functions to the right. [RHK]

99. The versification of Joel differs in Latin and English Bibles. Swedenborg's first edition reads 4:15 here, following Latin versification; in English versions this passage is 3:15. [JSR]

100. Reading *saccus,* "sackcloth," for the *succus,* "sap, juice," of the first edition; the Greek original has σάκκος *(sákkos),* "sackcloth." [GFD]

101. See §147 below. The subject of presence by way of inner sight is developed further in *Secrets of Heaven* 6849: "The Lord becomes present to people in no other way than by an inner looking, which is made possible by the person's faith derived from love for others." [GFD]

102. "Love for oneself"—described here as the opposite of divine love, in *Secrets of Heaven* 1675:6 as opposite to "the Lord's human essence," and in §558 below as the opposite of love of one's neighbor—is for Swedenborg the essence of human evil. The only "love" that might be worse is the love of dominating others, but that, too, is a form

of the love for oneself. A major discussion of love for oneself appears below in §§556–565. Also see note 171. [RHK]

103. In §311 below, Swedenborg associates the names "the devil" and "satan" with these two classes, respectively. He very frequently uses "spirits" to refer to people who after death are in the process of preparation for either heaven or hell. [GFD]

104. See §§141–153, 162–169, and 191–199. [GFD]

105. This reference differs from the others in the list in that it does not reflect the wording of the title of the chapter referred to; the appropriate point is made in §§101 and 103. [GFD]

Notes to §§126–140

106. As was the custom in his day, Swedenborg referred to the Psalms as the Book of David, and to the Pentateuch (Genesis, Exodus, Leviticus, Numbers, and Deuteronomy) as the books of Moses. [GFD]

107. Years later Swedenborg recorded memorable occurrences of truth shining in the spiritual world. He reports that if spirits rub the Word on their face or clothing, they shine as brightly as the moon or a star (*Divine Providence* 256:4)—even as brightly as if the spirits themselves were standing in a star (*True Christianity* 209:2). He writes that spirits cut paper into decorative shapes and write phrases from the Word on them because they become shining shapes in the air (*True Christianity* 209:2). He recounts a memorable occurrence in which he sees a table in great light where a truth written on paper shines like a star, but a falsified truth causes an explosion, rendering a spirit unconscious. In the same account he sees a room in which the Word is surrounded by gems that produce a rainbow with different colored backgrounds depending on what kind of angel is looking on (*Revelation Unveiled* 566:5–7). See also *Revelation Unveiled* 540; *Marriage Love* 77:2, 533. [JSR]

108. Swedenborg's *paradisus,* "paradise," includes the meaning "park." [GFD]

109. There is no §138 in the Latin edition. [GFD]

110. "Becoming manifest" (Latin *existere,* whose root meaning is "to stand out from"), "reality" (*esse,* literally, "to be"), and "emanating" (*procedere,* meaning literally "to come or go forth, to appear") are key terms in Swedenborg's ontology. Though simple Latin words, they present translation difficulties because of their metaphysical implications. Two classic passages for further study of Swedenborg's development of them are *True Christianity* 210: "[God] is Reality *[Esse]* itself and Manifestation *[Existere]* itself, and at the same time, Emanation *[Procedere]* itself"; and *Divine Love and Wisdom* 14: "Reality *[Esse]* and Manifestation *[Existere]* are distinguishably one in the God-Human. Where there is Reality *[Esse],* there is Manifestation *[Existere]:* one does not occur without the other." [RHK]

Notes to §§141–153

111. This discussion clearly and not surprisingly reflects Swedenborg's perspective as a lifelong resident of the northern hemisphere and his interest in astronomy, in which he had been intensely involved in earlier years. [GFD]

112. The statements in this paragraph play on the relationship between *oriens,* "east"; *origo,* "source"; and *exoriri,* "to rise." [GFD]

113. For treatment of representations and appearances, see §§170–176; for treatment of time and space in heaven, see §§162–169, 191–199. [GFD]

114. One possible interpretation of the statement that the distance between the sun and the moon is thirty degrees is that the heavenly angels see the Lord (in solar form) at a location in the sky thirty horizontal degrees from where the spiritual angels see the Lord (in lunar form). As a result east in the heavenly kingdom is pointing thirty degrees on the compass from where east points in the spiritual kingdom; if both were put on the same map, there would be two sets of each cardinal direction a twelfth of a rotation away from each other. Both kingdoms then are oriented in roughly but not exactly the same direction. There is no resulting confusion, however, because the two kingdoms are separate and no angel has to live with both sets of directions at once. [JSR]

115. See especially §587. [GFD]

Notes to §§154–161

116. See §§170–176. [GFD]

117. The Latin word here translated "self-image" is *proprium* (all that is one's own, whatever is proper to oneself). Swedenborg uses this adjective as a substantive to designate all that makes up our personal identity, self-image, or sense of self. [RHK]

118. The Latin word here translated "depression" is *maestitia*. [JSR]

119. While the subject of changes of state in hell is not given explicit attention, it is clearly implicit in §§562, 574, and 594. [GFD]

Note to §§162–169

120. See §§191–199. [GFD]

Notes to §§170–176

121. By "historical books" Swedenborg means Genesis, Exodus, Leviticus, Numbers, Deuteronomy, Joshua, Judges, 1 and 2 Samuel, and 1 and 2 Kings; by "prophetical" books he means Isaiah, Jeremiah, Lamentations, Ezekiel, Daniel, Hosea, Joel, Amos, Obadiah, Jonah, Micah, Nahum, Habakkuk, Zephaniah, Haggai, Zechariah, and Malachi. See also note 8 above. [JSR]

122. While there are many subsequent references to the way things "appear," the most explicit further attention to the topic is found in §479:5. [GFD]

123. The conclusion of this sentence is a quotation from Isaiah 64:4, cited in 1 Corinthians 2:9. [GFD]

Note to §§177–182

124. Following the custom in his day, Swedenborg occasionally referred to the Book of Revelation simply as John. [GFD]

Notes to §§183–190

125. The emphasis here is on flying or floating around bodiless *in the physical air* (compare §264). Elsewhere Swedenborg portrays angels, although wingless, as having the ability to fly (*Marriage Love* 2:1; *True Christianity* 134:5; compare Revelation 8:13, 14:6). [JSR]

126. Swedenborg often warns against using learning and self-generated intelligence to determine the truth of a proposition. On the other hand, he frequently suggests rational standards by which the truth of a proposition can be recognized. Both his warnings against learning and his encouragement to use reason arise from his fundamental conviction that the origin of all sin—as symbolized by Adam eating from the "fruit of the tree of knowledge of good and evil" in Genesis 3:1–13—consists of people "not believing the Lord or the Word, but believing themselves" (*Secrets of Heaven* 231). That is, he maintains that if people believe in the Lord or the Word, their reasoning is led by the Lord to recognize what is good and what is true; but if they believe only in themselves, their reasoning leads them into selfish or worldly errors. See also note 20 above regarding "inflow." [RHK]

Notes to §§191–199

127. See especially Swedenborg's 1758 work *Other Planets*. [JSR]

128. At this point, the first edition omits the superscript letter that indicates Swedenborg's footnote, but it is clear that it is appropriately placed here. [GFD]

129. A stadium (plural: stadia) was an ancient Greek unit of distance equal to about 185 meters or 607 English feet. [JSR]

130. For the unit of measure called a stadium, see note 129 above. A distance of 12,000 stadia is approximately 2220 kilometers, or 1380 miles. [JSR]

131. The versification of Psalm 31 differs in Latin and English Bibles. Swedenborg's first edition reads 31:9 here, following Latin versification; in English versions this passage is verse 8. [JSR]

Notes to §§213–220

132. The versification of Isaiah 9 differs in Latin and English Bibles. Swedenborg's first edition reads 9:6 here, following Latin versification; in English versions this passage is verse 7. [JSR]

133. The versification of Jeremiah 9 differs in Latin and English Bibles. Swedenborg's first edition reads 9:23 here, following Latin versification; in English versions this passage is verse 24. [JSR]

134. The versification of Psalm 36 differs in Latin and English Bibles. Swedenborg's first edition reads 36:6–7 here, following Latin versification; in English versions this passage is verses 5–6. [JSR]

135. The Latin phrase here translated "organized structure of functions," is *regnum usuum,* literally "a kingdom of uses." Swedenborg frequently gives evidence of a vivid sense of the interactive and interdependent nature of human society. See, for example, *Divine Providence* 4:4. [GFD]

136. See §§536–581, especially §543. [GFD]

Notes to §§228–233

137. Swedenborg records experiences of this nature early in his theological period. See *The Old Testament Explained* (= Swedenborg 1927–1951) §§943, 1149–1150. [GFD]

138. The reference is to Swedenborg's 1758 work *Last Judgment.* [GFD]

139. Most of the instances of the use of angelic power mentioned here are included in Swedenborg's account of the Last Judgment, which he reports as having occurred in 1757 C.E. For his description, see his 1758 work *Last Judgment;* for discussion, see pages 24–28 in the introduction to the present volume, and note 6 above.[JSR]

140. See 2 Kings 19:35 (= Isaiah 37:36). [GFD]

141. Swedenborg here renders the unusual Hebrew הַמַּשְׁחִית בָּעָם, *hammašḥît bāʿām* ("the destroyer among the people"?), with extreme literalism as *qui perdidit de populo,* "who destroyed from/of the people." [GFD]

142. The first edition here has *illam,* a feminine form of the third-person singular pronoun; this is perhaps a typographical error for *illum,* a gender-inclusive alternative that means "her or him." [GFD, JSR]

143. See §§299, 577–580. [GFD]

Notes to §§234–245

144. Swedenborg's statement here that there is a single language in heaven seems contradicted by his earlier statements that angels from higher and lower heavens cannot verbally communicate with one another (§§35, 208–209). Noting this apparent contradiction, King (1999, 30–35) proposes as a solution that what Swedenborg means by "language" and what he means by "speech" may not be identical: heaven's universal language may be "the nearly infinite system of possible uses of words to convey meaning, whereas speech involves one person's enactment of language" (King 1999, 33). See also §§241 and 244 below. [JSR]

145. For more on the book of life, see §463 and the Bible passages referred to in note 269 below. [JSR]

146. See §269 below. [GFD]

147. In *Spiritual Experiences* (= Swedenborg 1983–1997 = Swedenborg 1998–2000) §155, Swedenborg notes that in order to express angelic ideas at all in human language, the countless things angelic language simultaneously contains "need to be unfolded in a sequence, and with many digressions, at great length" *(successive et per plures ambages prolixe explicanda essent).* This diary entry offers a rare glimpse of his view of the problem he faced as a writer. It has no date, but a nearby entry (§165) is dated August 2, 1747. [GFD]

148. The reference is to Isaiah 64:4, which is cited in 1 Corinthians 2:9. [GFD]

149. Aristotle proposed four primary categories of cause: material, formal, efficient, and final; referring respectively to the substance of a thing, its form, the agency by which it was produced, and the purpose of its production. Swedenborg's employment of the Aristotelian terminology of "causes" and "First [cause]" may have more to do with the pervasive influence of Aristotle on the vocabulary and syntax of Western philosophical thought than with any dependence on Aristotle per se. His ontology, for one conspicuous example, includes Aristotle's without being limited by it. See Kirven 1988, 361–364. [RHK]

150. Swedenborg presumably intended Latin pronunciations of these vowels, but it cannot be precisely stated what the modern phonetic equivalents are. Several circumstances might have affected his pronunciation of the Neo-Latin of his times: his native language was Swedish; he knew a wide range of languages; he traveled and studied in Holland, England, and Italy; and he learned Latin from teachers whose idiosyncrasies of pronunciation are unknown to us. Furthermore, each of these letters may have more

than one Latin pronunciation; and *U* and *I* also represent semivowels. The pronunciation of the Latin *U* alone has exercised scholars for generations. A rough conjecture, avoiding any pretension to phonetic transcription, is that by *U* Swedenborg meant the vowel sounds in *boot* and *foot;* by *O* the sounds in *snow, oar,* and *not;* by *E* the sounds in *gate* and *get;* and by *I* the sounds in *sheen* and *pit.* [JSR]

151. Originally only the consonants of Hebrew were written. As Hebrew ceased to be a commonly spoken language, indications of vowels were added as pronunciation guides. By late in the first millennium, a western Palestinian system for vowel representation had become normative. Swedenborg's comment that the vowels are "pronounced variously" presumably reflects the fact that the system faithfully represented the slight shifts in vowel pronunciation occasioned by shifts of accent. [GFD]

152. In his discussion of the Hebrew word *and,* Swedenborg refers to the proclitic ו, *və;* or ו, *û.* It may be worth noting that Schmidt 1696 (see note 5 above) uses a variety of devices to avoid the repetition of Latin *et,* "and"; and that in these instances Swedenborg consistently uses *et.* [GFD]

153. This may be a reference to the vocal technique of "covering" back vowels, shifting them toward an "ah" sound, when they are sung in the upper register. [GFD]

154. See §§255, 334, and 463. [GFD]

Notes to §§246–257

155. This assertion is significant in relation to Swedenborg's warning of the danger of spiritualistic practices undertaken in order to establish communication with the dead. The current passage suggests that in his view there is a normal and salutary communication between spirits and people; the danger arises when the motivation for such communication is idle curiosity, thrill-seeking, or avarice, to which nonangelic spirits are attracted. See §§249–250 below, and Swedenborg's posthumous work *Revelation Explained* (= Swedenborg 1994–1997) §§1182:4–1183. [RHK]

156. See §431. [GFD]

157. See §§291–310 below. [GFD]

158. On Swedenborg's method of referring to locations in spiritual space see note 22 above. [JSR]

159. For a list of the historical and prophetical books of the Word see note 121 above. [JSR]

160. See §§601 and 603:9 below. [GFD]

Notes to §§258–264

161. The first edition has "11:9.10." Presumably the printer misread Swedenborg's "ii." [GFD]

162. See *White Horse,* one of the books published by Swedenborg in 1758 along with *Heaven and Hell.* [GFD]

163. The word "jot" is the traditional translation of the Greek word ἰῶτα, *iota,* referring ultimately to the Hebrew letter י, *yôd,* which was in the time of Jesus the smallest letter of the Aramaic and Hebrew alphabets. The word "tittle" is the traditional translation of the word κεραία, *keraía,* in the Greek text, represented by *corniculum* in the

Latin text of Schmidt 1696 (see note 5 above) and in Swedenborg. Both the Latin and Greek mean "horn-like projection," referring to the apical brush-stroke of the "square" script used for Hebrew sacred texts after the fifth century B.C.E. The modern English equivalent would be "the dots on the *i*'s and the crosses on the *t*'s." [GFD]

164. Obviously Swedenborg does not use "composite" here in the modern sense of "factorable into two or more prime numbers other than one and itself," any more than he means "prime" when he says "simple." "Simple" means twelve or under, and "composite" a number greater than twelve resulting from the multiplication of two or more simple numbers (see *Secrets of Heaven* 487, 575). Perhaps Swedenborg skips eleven in this list because, as he says elsewhere, it has an inner meaning similar to that of ten (*Secrets of Heaven* 9616). For Swedenborg's explanations of the inner meaning of numbers in general, see *Secrets of Heaven* 482, 487, 647, 648, 755, 813, 1963, 1988, 2075, 2252. In *Secrets of Heaven,* for the meaning of two see §§720, 900; three §§482, 720, 900; four §1686; five §§649, 798, 1686; six §§62, 84–85; seven §§395, 433, 813:2; eight §2044; nine §§1987, 2025, 2075:2; ten §468:4; twelve §§575, 577, 648:2; one hundred forty-four §7973:2–3; one thousand §§482, 2588:4; twelve thousand §7973:2–3. This and many earlier manuscripts and publications are evidence of Swedenborg's lifelong interest in numbers and mathematics. [JSR]

Notes to §§265–275

165. Reading *et,* "and," for *ex,* "from." [GFD]

166. Reading *ex,* "from," for *et,* "and." [GFD]

167. On his first trip outside Sweden after graduation from Uppsala in 1709, Swedenborg either had made or made for himself in Leiden a forty-two power microscope that seems to have been a particular treasure for him. See Kirven and Larsen 1988, 15. [GFD]

168. The Latin of this account actually contains no gender-specific pronouns, but it is highly likely that if the interlocutor had been a female angel, Swedenborg would have noted that fact—as he does, for example, in *Marriage Love* 293. [GFD]

169. By regeneration Swedenborg means in general the process of human spiritual rebirth, and in specific, the last stage of that process in which the individual gains a new heart or will and a new mind or intellect. The process mirrors gestation, birth, infancy, and childhood. Although Swedenborg has much to say about it in *Secrets of Heaven,* for a succinct introduction to the process see the chapter in *True Christianity* on reformation and regeneration (§§571–620). [JSR]

170. The Latin word here translated "try to figure out" is *ratiocinantur,* which Swedenborg rarely uses in an affirmative or even a neutral sense. It often has the connotation of rationalization. [GFD]

171. The Latin phrase here translated "selfishness" is *amore sui,* literally "love for oneself," but clearly meaning "regarding oneself as of supreme importance." *Amor sui* is in fact defined in §65 of another of Swedenborg's 1758 works, *New Jerusalem,* as "willing well to ourselves alone, and not to others except for the sake of ourselves." In the subsequent §99 there, Swedenborg makes it clear that we are obliged to provide for our own welfare first in order to be capable of service to others. See also note g to §283 below. [GFD]

Notes to §§276–283

172. It appears that something has been omitted at this point, probably amounting to a full line of Swedenborg's fair copy. Ager's translation (Swedenborg [1758] 1995) seems to assume a similar minimal restoration. [GFD]

173. Reading *cupiunt,* "covet," for the first edition's *capiunt,* "take, grasp." [GFD]

174. "Storge" (pronounced "stór-gay") is a Latinized (and Anglicized, as its presence in the *Oxford English Dictionary* attests) version of the Greek word στοργή, *storgé,* which in Swedenborg's time denoted the powerful, indiscriminate, almost instinctive love parents have for their offspring, especially for the recently born. [JSR]

175. The Latin for the phrase quoted here is *curam pro crastino.* The reference is to Matthew 6:34: in the translation of Schmidt 1696 (see note 5 above), *Ne sitis igitur soliciti in crastinum,* "Therefore do not be anxious about tomorrow." [GFD]

176. See above, §§177–179. [RHK]

177. The passage cited refers to not worrying about food and clothing—correspondences that are illustrated in §§103–115 above under the heading, "There Is a Correspondence of Heaven with Everything Earthly," particularly in §108. [RHK]

178. The Latin for "true marriage love" is *amor vere conjugialis,* which in some other versions has been translated "love truly conjugial." Swedenborg's ongoing interest in the subject of marriage love is witnessed by over five hundred references to it in his *Secrets of Heaven,* including a brief survey of its principles in §§10167–10175; in §§366–386 of the present work (under the heading "Marriages in Heaven"); in index and draft material in his manuscripts; and in his published work of 1768 titled *Delitiae Sapientiae de Amore Conjugiali: Post Quas Sequuntur Voluptates Insaniae de Amore Scortatorio* (Wisdom's Delight in Marriage Love: Followed by Insanity's Pleasure in Promiscuous Love). The latter has appeared in a number of English translations, whose various titles include *Conjugial Love, Marital Love, Married Love,* and *Love in Marriage;* the short title *Marriage Love* is used in the present edition. See note 84 above and 231 below. [GFD, RHK]

Notes to §§284–290

179. This section provides one of the clearest of many passages in which Swedenborg expresses the difficulty of providing verbal images, descriptions, and explanations of his spiritual experiences. His attitude appears to derive from his longtime interest in the physical sciences and his devotion to what would come to be known as "scientific method": he seems to be aware that his descriptive methodology is itself part of his message. See also note 147 above. [GFD, RHK]

180. See note 15 above. "The oneness of his divine nature and the divine human nature within him" here refers to the first "Person" (the Divine) and the second "Person" (the divine human nature, the Lord) of the "Trinity"—emphasizing oneness or unity over "threeness" or trinity in the godhead. [RHK]

Notes to §§291–302

181. This section displays one of Swedenborg's central focuses, namely his interest in identifying what was true (and good) in church doctrine and popular piety, and using those truths to call people away from distortions that he saw in contemporary church teachings. See note 13 above. [RHK]

182. See especially §§421–431. [GFD]

183. See §§246–257 above, under the heading "How Angels Talk with Us," especially §247. [RHK]

184. An evident exception to this principle may be found in §137:8 of Swedenborg's *True Christianity*, and a highly probably one in §137:12 of the same work. While the individuals in those passages are not named, the geographical references make it clear that Johann August Ernesti (1707–1781; see note 7 above) and Bishop Eric Lamberg (1719–1780) of the Gothenburg diocese are intended. [GFD]

185. This is the focus of the closing chapters of the book, §§589–603. [GFD]

186. This notion of "balance" or "equilibrium" is central to Swedenborg's teaching on "regeneration," the process of rebirth or salvation by which the Lord prepares us for heaven. Two key passages developing the idea are *Divine Love and Wisdom* 21–24 and *True Christianity* 475–478. [RHK]

187. This section and the preceding one provide important context for one of Swedenborg's key statements about human nature: "The Lord created us in such a way that we could talk with spirits and angels while still living in our bodies, as people actually did in the earliest times. After all, we are united with spirits and angels, being ourselves spirits clothed in flesh. Eventually, though, people immersed themselves so deeply in bodily and worldly concerns that almost nothing else could interest them, and so the path of communication closed. But as soon as the bodily concerns that absorb us drop away, the path opens and we find ourselves among spirits, living life together with them" (*Secrets of Heaven* 69). [RHK]

188. While Swedenborg maintains that "everyone is born for heaven, and no one is born for hell" (for example, §329 below), he also says that "we are born into every kind of evils, and thus of ourselves we are condemned to hell. . . . Therefore we need to be regenerated" (*Secrets of Heaven* 10367). This section refers to divine response to that need. Swedenborg claims that if the Lord ever left us alone with our own evils, we would no longer be human (§546 below); so the human condition is one of being saved if we are willing. [RHK]

189. The Latin word here translated "depression" is *melancholia*. [GFD]

190. See §§491–498. [GFD]

191. On Swedenborg's method of referring to locations in spiritual space see note 22 above. [JSR]

192. The phrasing is reminiscent of *Secrets of Heaven* 68, where Swedenborg acknowledges that though his claims to spiritual experience will strain belief, this does not deter him; because as he says, "I have seen, I have heard, I have felt." [GFD]

193. The Latin phrase translated "with the Ultimate Reality of life," is *cum primo Esse vitae*—literally, "with the first 'to be' of life." [GFD]

Notes to §§303–310

194. By "a First" here Swedenborg means God as the origin of all things; see also §§9, 37. [JSR]

195. See note 149 above. [RHK]

196. See note 30 above. [JSR]

197. The works mentioned here were both published by Swedenborg in 1758. The first is referred to in this edition by the short title *White Horse*. The "Appendix to the Heavenly Teaching" is presumably a reference to the material in §§255–266 of *New Jerusalem*. [GFD]

198. See note 130 above. [JSR]

199. The citation also includes material from verses 19 and 21. [GFD]

200. The term here translated "non-Christians" is a form of the Latin noun *gentes.* There does not seem to be any English word that fairly represents what Swedenborg intends by this usage. In *Secrets of Heaven* 367, the term clearly means "gentiles" (non-Jews) in contrast to Jews; in §516 of the present work, it means certain unspecified non-Christians in contrast to Muslims. There does not seem to be any passage in which Swedenborg specifically includes Jews among the *gentes,* so it seems safe to conclude that by this term he generally meant people who were neither Christians nor Jews. The translation "non-Christians" has been adopted primarily to avoid the derogatory connotations of the words "heathen" and "pagan," it being clear from the passage as a whole that Swedenborg intended no derogation whatever. Though the term "non-Christian" might seem inaccurate on the grounds that it does not indicate that the people in question are also not Jews, in fact in at least one passage Swedenborg indicates that he considers Jews to be a category of Christian. This occurs in §54 of his 1763 work *Sacred Scripture,* where he speaks of the understanding of Scripture "in the Christian world" and goes on to name specifically the Reformed, the Catholics, and the Jews. A relevant parallel can be found in the Qur'an, which speaks of the أَهْلُ ٱلْكِتَابِ, *'ahlu-lkitābi,* the "people of the book," meaning "those who have the Torah, the Gospel, or the Qur'an." This delineation corresponds nicely to the definition of *gentes* in the present section as "people who are outside the church, where the Word is not found." [GFD]

201. See §§200–212. [GFD]

202. The reference is to Swedenborg's 1758 work *Other Planets.* [GFD]

203. The Latin word here translated "superficial matters" is *externis,* which could also be translated "external things." [GFD]

204. In eighteenth-century Europe, where complex detail was the fashion in everything from music to painting to narrative, high style was virtually synonymous with the ornate. [GFD]

Notes to §§311–317

205. See §§582–588. [GFD]

206. Both theologian Friedrich Christoph Oetinger (1702–1782) and the Idealist philosopher Friedrich von Schelling (1775–1854) lamented this skepticism and welcomed Swedenborg's rebuttal of it. On Oetinger, see especially Benz 1947; on Schelling, see Horn 1954. [GFD]

207. See §§421–535. [GFD]

Notes to §§318–328

208. See note 200 above. [GFD]

209. This principle may be better known today in the form of the dictum of the early Christian theologian Cyprian (about 200 to 258 C.E.) that "outside the church there is no salvation" (Walker 1970, 67 note 22). [RHK]

210. The ideas of this section—how a combination of good motives and good actions lead to heaven—are expanded in the passage headed "It Is Not So Hard to Lead a Heaven-Bound Life as People Think It Is," §§528–535 below. [RHK]

211. Swedenborg's work *Other Planets* was published in 1758 along with *Heaven and Hell*. [GFD]

212. The Latin term translated "early church" is *ecclesia antiqua*, Swedenborg's label for the church that existed after the times signified by the Flood in the Bible (Genesis chapters 6–9); in some translations this is rendered "the ancient church." See §115 above and §327 below for Swedenborg's view of a succession of "churches" from the beginning of the human race. [RHK, GFD]

213. The Latin term translated "Near East" is *orbis Asiatici*, "Asiatic world." For Swedenborg, this does not refer to the continent now known as Asia but to the geographical world of the Hebrew Bible (see the list of place-names in §324 below). [JSR]

214. Micah's mother had spent 1100 shekels (about 28 pounds) of silver for a carved image and a cast idol for him. Micah then persuaded a young Levite sojourner named Jonathan to be his priest in exchange for room and board. But six hundred members of the tribe of Dan in search of a place to live stole Micah's images and persuaded his young Levite to leave Micah and be their priest instead. Micah rallied his neighbors and complained to the Danites, "You took away my carved images that I made, and the priest, and you went away. What do I have left?" But he gave up trying to recover them as he saw that the six hundred were too strong for his group. [JSR]

215. Swedenborg says elsewhere that in the spiritual world thoughts and associations are visibly projected around the people who are having them. *Secrets of Heaven* 6200 explains that whatever someone is thinking about is represented in the spiritual world as a central point, around which can be seen everything one has ever associated with it. For example, when Swedenborg thought about someone, an image of that person was in the middle, and around it, looking like the wings of a bird moving up and down, were visual forms of all the thoughts and experiences Swedenborg had ever had in relation to that person (*Secrets of Heaven* 6200). Here Swedenborg determines a group's nationality from the images he sees around them. [JSR]

216. In several passages—most of them in *Supplements* and *Spiritual Experiences*, but prominently too in *True Christianity*, especially §§837–839—Swedenborg describes the spirits and angels who had lived their earthly lives in continental Africa, particularly the inland regions (see *Supplements* 76 and *Spiritual Experiences* [= Swedenborg 1889] §4777), as excelling in spiritual perception and interior judgment. Also see below, §514, and the parallel to the present passage in *Secrets of Heaven* 2604. [RHK, JSR]

217. The Latin term here translated "the early church" is *ecclesia antiqua*; see notes 2 and 212 above. [RHK]

218. On Swedenborg's method of referring to locations in spiritual space see note 22 above. [JSR]

Notes to §§329–345

219. This way of describing the location of a particular heaven, or rather a specific segment of heaven, derives from the schema set forth in §§59–67 above (the passage under the heading "The Whole Heaven, Grasped as a Single Entity, Reflects a Single Individual"), especially §65. [RHK]

220. Swedenborg's frequent assertions that all people—including even infants—are born into evils of every kind and in themselves are nothing but evil are balanced by assertions that each person is created in the image and according to the likeness of God

(Genesis 1:26, *Secrets of Heaven* 51), with heaven as his or her intended goal, and that means of salvation are provided by the Lord. In fact, he says, human beings "as they are in themselves" are nonexistent hypotheticals, since the Lord's inflowing presence is necessary for moment-to-moment existence—all of us on earth and all angels are recipients of life from the Lord (*Divine Providence* 4) and the realization of this is the beginning of life and regeneration (*Secrets of Heaven* 20 and throughout). See also note 188 above. Furthermore, this passage should not be taken as evidence of a negative attitude toward children. Reports from Swedenborg's contemporaries suggest that in fact he had a spontaneous affection for children and a remarkable rapport with them (see Tafel 1890, 541, 723–724, 725). [RHK]

221. Compare Jeremiah 31:29–30. [RHK]

222. The Latin here translated "before they had learned to talk at all" is *quum adhuc prorsus infantiles essent,* literally, "when they still were completely infantile." The context suggests that *infantiles,* "infantile," is intended in its etymological sense of "not speaking." [GFD]

223. In Swedenborg's theology a plane (Latin *planum*) is a field of activity, a receptive level or area lower down into which a higher level flows or falls, at which it comes to a stop, and through which it operates. For instance, one's conscience is a plane into which angels especially flow (*Secrets of Heaven* 6207). If someone lacks conscience, the inflow from angels has no plane in that individual, that is, it finds no home, no platform, no "base of operations" in him or her. [JSR]

Notes to §§346–356

224. The Latin word translated "those who have justified" is *justificantes,* used here, as frequently, in the theological sense of absolving others from guilt. [GFD]

225. The Latin word here translated "illumination" is *lumen,* "light," often contrasted with a more affirmatively intended *lux,* though the two words have the same basic denotation. [GFD]

Notes to §§357–365

226. This and the following sections take up a common theme of Swedenborg's: that spiritual state and motivation determine the quality of a state or action, and material conditions and activities are neither good nor bad in themselves apart from those motivations. See §222 above. [RHK]

227. See the passages cited in §471 below. [GFD]

228. The term here translated "non-Jews" is a form of the Latin noun *gentes,* elsewhere translated "non-Christians," as discussed in note 200 above. In this instance the translation "non-Jews" is required by the context. [GFD]

229. The first edition here reads Psalm 40, but apparently Psalm 45 is intended. Furthermore, the versification of Psalm 45 differs in Latin and English Bibles. Thus Swedenborg cites as verse 12 what is verse 13 in English Bibles. [JSR]

Notes to §§366–386

230. See §60 above, where the parallel terms "understanding and intention" are used instead of "intellect and volition." [RHK]

231. Swedenborg frequently distinguishes between different kinds of love by specifying their object (for example, "love for oneself" *[amor sui]*, "love for the Lord" *[amor in Dominum]*), but treats "marriage love" *(amor conjugialis)* as a kind of technical term, categorizing it by type. The current passage provides a good definition of the term at one level. However, Swedenborg sees this ideal relationship between a married man and woman as corresponding to spiritual, heavenly, and divine manifestations of marriage love—the union of love-for-what-is-good with love-for-what-is-true, the union of the good itself with the true itself, and the union of love with wisdom in God. This is presented most completely in his 1768 work *Marriage Love*. [RHK]

232. Swedenborg here, like Schmidt 1696 (see note 5 above), translates the Hebrew idiom for "become" (הָיוּ לְ, *hāyû lǝ*) with strict literalism as "be into." [GFD]

233. See §§87–102 and 103–115 above. [JSR]

234. As evidence that they married within their clans Swedenborg elsewhere points to Genesis 24:2–9, in which Abraham has his servant swear that he will find Isaac a wife from his own country and kindred, with the result that Abraham's son marries Abraham's nephew's daughter (see *Secrets of Heaven* 3024, especially the last subsection). In fact, as Swedenborg notes in the section just cited, the Israelites were forbidden to marry outside the extended family (Deuteronomy 7:3). [JSR]

235. In the more extensive treatment of polygamy in *Marriage Love*, Swedenborg states that it is not a sin for people whose religion allows it (§348), and even mentions a "lower Muslim heaven" where polygamy is practiced (§343). He insists, however, that the practice prevents people from becoming truly spiritual (§347). [GFD]

236. In the first edition, this section and the following one are both numbered 382. [GFD]

237. The Latin word rendered "fiery gems" is *pyropis;* in classical Latin it refers to ruddy bronze; in Swedenborg it refers to red gems, sometimes rubies. He would have been aware of its derivation from a Greek word meaning "fiery-looking." Hans Helander identifies the adjectival form of this word as a possible "neologism of sense"; see Swedenborg [1715] 1988, 27. [GFD]

238. Elsewhere Swedenborg suggests that repentance gives one the power to reopen heaven (see *Revelation Explained* [= Swedenborg 1994–1997] §798:6). [JSR]

Notes to §§387–394

239. See notes 94 and 135 above. [RHK]

240. At this point, the first edition omits the superscript letter that indicates Swedenborg's footnote, but it is clear that it is appropriately placed here. [GFD]

241. The lower earth is elsewhere defined as a region below the world of spirits, close to hell but not in it. See §513 and note a there; *Revelation Unveiled* 845:2; *Secrets of Heaven* 4728. [JSR]

Notes to §§395–414

242. For an extensive account of such an experience, see *Marriage Love* 2–25. [JSR]

243. The "two loves of heaven" are love for the Lord and love for our neighbor. See §15 above. [RHK]

244. That is, love for oneself and love of the world. See §18 above. [RHK]

245. Swedenborg opens his 1768 work *Marriage Love* with a sequence of stories about people allowed to experience what they imagine heaven to be, which in each case turns out after just a few days to be nightmarish (§§2–25). One such account shows people being disabused of the notion that heaven is perpetual worship and glorification of God (*Marriage Love* 1–3, 9). [GFD]

246. This variety of heavenly individuals and communities, like the Lord's variations in appearance to different individuals (§55 above), underlies Swedenborg's universalism: there is a heaven for everyone who loves the Lord and loves her or his neighbor. [RHK]

Notes to §§415–420

247. Although in Swedenborg's time there were many theories regarding the date of creation, the most generally received was 4004 B.C.E., determined by James Ussher (1580–1655), Archbishop of Armagh, using time periods given in the Bible. [JSR]

248. This passage is extracted almost verbatim from §§2–4, 6, and 126 of Swedenborg's 1758 work mentioned in the introductory paragraph, *Other Planets,* which sections in turn are lightly edited from *Secrets of Heaven* 6697–6698 and 9441. In the first edition of the present work, the material here indented is set off by flush-left quotation marks on each line of text. [GFD]

249. See §321 above. [GFD]

250. On only the poor being accepted into heaven, see Matthew 19:23–24, Luke 14:21; on only the elect being accepted, see Matthew 24:31, Mark 13:27; on only people in the church and not people from outside being accepted, see perhaps John 3:18; on only people for whom the Lord makes intercession being accepted, see Romans 8:29–34; on heaven being closed when it is full, see perhaps Revelation 14:3; and on the time for this being foreordained, see Revelation 20:2–7. [GFD]

Notes to §§421–431

251. The "world of spirits" *(mundus spirituum),* defined in this chapter, is a technical term in Swedenborg's usage throughout his works. It refers to the region "halfway between heaven and hell" in which people spend their "halfway state after death" before going to either heaven or hell (§422). The world of spirits is not to be confused with the spiritual world *(mundus spiritualis),* although the former is part of the latter. When he refers to the spiritual world Swedenborg means heaven, the world of spirits, and hell. [RHK, JSR]

252. This is a topic Swedenborg explains from many angles, perhaps trying to correct what he considered a serious flaw in contemporary thinking—the belief that deciding between faith and charity (thoughtfulness toward others), the true and the good, and the intellect and the will involved either/or choices. See notes 32, 47, and 50 above. [RHK]

253. This promise is not apparently fulfilled. The only mention of spirits coming out of hell in the remainder of the book is the brief mention of evil spirits "going in and out of various hells" as part of their second state in the world of spirits (§510). [JSR]

Notes to §§432–444

254. Swedenborg uses "spirit" *(spiritus)* most frequently to denote the nonmaterial aspect of human life, as well as to name the whole nonmaterial category of reality in

which the human spirit is included. "Soul" *(anima)* appears less often, sometimes (as here) as a distinct term, other times as a clarifying synonym (for example, the phrase "soul or spirit" in *Secrets of Heaven* 443, 444, 446) and less often as a technical term in his psychological theory (see note 49 above). [RHK]

255. The Latin word here translated "agent" is *subjectum.* "Agent" here is parallel to "tool" *(instrumentum)* in §432 immediately above: it is more illustrative than technical. [GFD, RHK]

256. Here, and frequently throughout his work, Swedenborg rests considerable weight on the Latin distinction between comparative and superlative forms (see, for example, §§33 and 270 above): animals possess a "spiritual nature," which could be called an "inner" or "relatively inward" *(interior)* nature, but they do not have an "inmost" *(intimum)* nature. [GFD, RHK]

257. This section is identical to §39 above except for the substitution of *velim,* "I should like to" for *ultimo licet,* "Lastly, I may"; and the addition of *de quibus n: 38,* "discussed in §38." [GFD]

258. This state is commonly called the *hypnagogic* state. [RHK]

259. Swedenborg elsewhere mentions being permitted to experience a phenomenon (automatic writing) purely to edify him, and not so that he can develop it as a regular practice. See *The Old Testament Explained* (= Swedenborg 1927–1951) §§1150, 1892, 6884, and especially 7006. [RHK]

260. See *The Old Testament Explained* (= Swedenborg 1927–1951) §943. [JSR]

Notes to §§445–452

261. In Swedenborg's day, cardiac and respiratory motion—classically measured by pulse, and by mist on a mirror held near the nose and mouth of an unconscious person—were the commonly accepted indicators of life (their absence defining death). [RHK]

262. The account that follows through §450 is substantially edited from interchapter material in *Secrets of Heaven* 168–189 and 314–318. [GFD]

263. The Latin word here translated "center" is *septum,* which has the same literal meaning as the English word *septum.* [GFD]

Notes to §§453–460

264. "Form" is used here in the sense of an Aristotelian "formal cause." Form is distinct from "shape" in that it refers to the aspect of a thing that adapts a substance to a purpose—as a spoon must have the *form* of a concavity to fulfill its purpose, whatever exact *shape* the concavity might take (shallow, deep, oval, etc.). See note 149 above. [RHK]

265. No second state is defined here, but the three states are described in full detail in §§491–520 below. [RHK]

Notes to §§461–469

266. See just below, §§462b–469. [JSR]

267. This section and the following are numbered 462 in the first edition.[GFD]

268. See especially §§551–575. [GFD]

269. Revelation 3:5; 13:8; 17:8; 20:12, 15; 21:27; 22:19; see also Psalms 69:28. [JSR]

270. The translation "the disappearance of intelligence" here is based on the assumption that an error occurs in the first edition; it reads *intelligentia appareat,* which would translate "the appearance of intelligence," and is directly contrary to the sense of this section. [GFD]

271. The first edition adds *non autem ultra eum,* "but not beyond it," which suggests that we are dealing with an incomplete rewriting of some such sentence as ". . . they are steeped . . . at the level of their affection . . . but not beyond it." [GFD]

Notes to §§470–484

272. The Latin words here translated "machines" and "robots" are *automata* and *simulachra.* [JSR]

273. The translation "I discovered" corresponds to the phrase *illi comperti sunt* in the first edition. This Latin phrase seems here and in the following sentence to be used in a passive rather than in the usual deponent sense, literally, "they were discovered/it was discovered" *(compertum).* [GFD]

274. The Latin word here translated "belief" is *persuasio,* which often in Swedenborg refers to a false or incorrect belief. [GFD]

275. The reference is to Swedenborg's 1758 work *Last Judgment.* [GFD]

276. Where the translation reads "whatever," the first edition has *qui,* a masculine plural form that is nonsensical in this context. [JSR]

Notes to §§485–490

277. Swedenborg encouraged self-examination as an essential first step in spiritual growth toward salvation, and as part of what he called "true repentance." See *Secrets of Heaven* 1608:2, and 7178; and especially *True Christianity* 535, 461, and 563. [RHK]

278. Parallelism would lead one to expect a statement that the cellars, crevices, and darkness correspond to false things. [GFD]

279. A reference to Isaiah 64:4, which is also cited in 1 Corinthians 2:9. [GFD]

Note to §§491–498

280. On the nature and function of a "plane" see note 223 above. [JSR]

Notes to §§499–511

281. On the nature and function of a "plane" see note 223 above. [JSR]

282. See §§461–469. [GFD]

283. Swedenborg often makes negative comments about the Roman Catholic religion. He sees particular problems with the vicarship of the pope, as he believes it takes power away from Jesus Christ. Yet although he mentions evil Catholics here and in §§535:2–3 and 587:2, he observes that Catholics also go to heaven (*True Christianity* 567:7, 821). In an account of a memorable occurrence Swedenborg talks at length with Pope Sixtus V (1520–1590), whom he reports to be leading one community of many in the spiritual world made up of angelic Catholics (*Revelation Unveiled* 752). [JSR]

284. Swedenborg here again cites the 1758 work referred to in this edition as *Last Judgment.* [GFD]

285. See §§548, 550. [GFD]

Notes to §§512–520

286. See note 149 above. [RHK]

287. For a discussion of this biblical passage see §346 and following. [JSR]

Notes to §§521–527

288. This chapter summarizes Swedenborg's response to his contemporaries who believed that a soul could be saved from hell exclusively through "faith alone," through "grace alone," or through preemptive mercy. He felt that they—equally with those who believed in salvation by deeds or "works alone"—had distorted biblical teaching on the unity of faith and works, and on the balance of divine mercy and human freedom. See note 32 above. [RHK]

289. In the phrase translated "owl . . . another," Swedenborg actually uses two different words for "owl," *noctuam* and *bubonem*. [GFD]

Notes to §§528–535

290. This chapter balances the preceding one, summarizing Swedenborg's response to those who believed that souls were saved from hell exclusively by good deeds or "works," including pious behavior in that category. [RHK]

291. Swedenborg's numbering of the Ten Commandments follows Schmidt 1696 (see note 5 above). Under the first three, those that regard spiritual life, it includes having no other gods, not taking God's name in vain, and remembering the sabbath; as the middle four, which concern civic life, it includes honoring one's father and mother, not committing murder, not stealing, and not committing adultery; and as the final three, which concern moral life, it includes not bearing false witness, not coveting one's neighbor's house, and not coveting anything else belonging to one's neighbor. See *Secrets of Heaven* 8860–8912 and *True Christianity* 283–331. [RHK]

292. The passage in Luke quotes Psalms 118:22–23. Passages parallel to Luke are found in Matthew 21:42 and Mark 12:10. The passage in Matthew 21:44 includes the mention of those who fall upon the stone, though this is not found in Mark. [GFD]

Notes to §§536–544

293. The importance of this balance or equilibrium in the divine management of creation is shown in Swedenborg's 1764 work *Divine Providence* 21–23 (where Swedenborg directs readers back to *Heaven and Hell* 589–603). [RHK]

294. See §§589–603, and especially §598. [GFD]

295. See §600. [GFD]

296. This epistemological assertion has over fifty parallels in Swedenborg's theological works. "Perception" *(perceptio)* is defined in *Secrets of Heaven* 104: "Perception is a certain internal sensation from the Lord alone, as to whether a thing is true and good. . . . A person living spiritually [but not in a heavenly way] has no perception, but has conscience. A spiritually dead person does not even have conscience." The issue becomes more complex in *Divine Providence* 24: "An opposite destroys as well as exalts perceptions and sensations: it destroys when it mingles them with itself and exalts them when it does not . . . [so] the Lord most carefully separates what is good and what is evil within us . . . just as he separates heaven and hell." [RHK]

Notes to §§545–550

297. In Swedenborg's view, perception and enlightenment are closely interrelated. See note 296 above. [RHK]

298. This section provides one of Swedenborg's more decisive resolutions to the tension between our being "born into evils" and "born for heaven": he suggests that the

evil is real and present, but the Lord is real and present, too, offering omnipotent help in resisting evils if we will accept it. [RHK]

299. This is one of the rare instances in which Swedenborg refers ahead to a specific section number. We must presume that he inserted the number when he was making his fair copy for the printer, and that his first draft had reached §574 by this time. It may also be noted that §574 begins with a reference back to this passage. In his unpublished work *Revelation Explained* (composed 1757–1759; = Swedenborg 1994–1997) for which we have both first draft and fair copy, it seems that Swedenborg updated his fair copy frequently and wrote it in fairly short sections. [GFD]

Notes to §§551–565

300. The Latin phrase here translated "are . . . their essential selves" is *in se est.* This might also be translated as "are in themselves." [GFD]

301. The Latin word here translated "breath" is *animam,* which means both "breath" and "soul." [GFD]

302. See note 102 above regarding "love for oneself." [RHK]

303. This and the following section are both numbered 558 in the first edition. [GFD]

304. As a young man, Swedenborg had been personally acquainted with and favored by the charismatic Swedish king Charles XII (1682–1718), whose imperial ambitions were shattered at Poltava in 1709. Charles's expansionist ventures were eventually to leave Sweden virtually bankrupt. While Swedenborg publicly celebrated Charles's heroism in his prose poem *Joyous Accolade* (= Swedenborg [1714] 1985), he privately despaired of Sweden's fortunes under his leadership. [GFD]

305. The equation of the Catholic church with the Babylon of the Book of Revelation 14:8; 16:19; 17:5; 18:2, 10, 21 (and other passages) was taken largely for granted in eighteenth-century Lutheran thought. [GFD]

306. The reference is to Swedenborg's 1758 work *Last Judgment.* [GFD]

307. For a parallel account that goes into greater detail see *Revelation Unveiled* 153. [JSR]

Notes to §§566–575

308. For a list of such passages in the Bible, see the end of §575. [JSR]

309. A textual omission between the last sentence and this one is strongly suggested both by the lack of any antecedent for *illa,* "these," and by the fact that *mala,* "evils," is capitalized in the first edition in spite of its being preceded by a colon rather than a period. [GFD]

310. The versification of Joel differs in Latin and English Bibles. Swedenborg's first edition reads 3:3, 4 here, following Latin versification; in English versions this passage is 2:30, 31. [JSR]

311. The versification of the end of Malachi differs in Latin and English Bibles. Swedenborg's first edition reads 3:19 here, following Latin versification; in English versions this passage is 4:1. [JSR]

Notes to §§576–581

312. The tense shift at this point is Swedenborg's. [GFD]

313. Due to the brevity of Swedenborg's descriptions and the unfamiliarity of the phenomena he is describing, the translation of this paragraph is relatively conjectural. On emissaries, see §§601 and 603:9 below.[GFD]

Note to §§582–588

314. The 1758 work Swedenborg refers to here is called *Last Judgment* in the present edition. [JSR]

Notes to §§589–596

315. The Latin word here translated "energy" is *conatus,* a word used in this denotation by Swedenborg and several of his contemporaries, though its literal meaning is "effort" or "endeavor." [GFD, RHK]

316. The Latin word here translated "in what is evil" is *malo,* "evil"; the word *in* is supplied from the parallel with the previous phrase *in bono,* "in what is good," though the preposition is not present in the first edition. [GFD]

Notes to §§597–603

317. Latin has no indefinite article, but one is necessary in English here (implying as it does that the freedom being discussed is one kind or type of freedom and not freedom itself) because the third paragraph of this section speaks of "this freedom" *(hoc liberum).* [RHK]

318. The Latin word translated "reality" is *esse.* See note 110 above. [GFD]

319. Swedenborg may have himself in mind here, since he had been intensely occupied with just such a search when he experienced the call to his career as visionary. His effort yielded the massive *Dynamics of the Soul's Domain* (= Swedenborg [1740–1741] 1955), which he judged to have failed in its primary purpose, and the first stages of the even more ambitious *The Soul's Domain* (= Swedenborg [1744–1745] 1960). [GFD]

Works Cited
in the Notes

Acton, Alfred. 1955. *The Letters and Memorials of Emanuel Swedenborg*. Vol. 2. Bryn Athyn, Pa.: Swedenborg Scientific Association.

Benz, Ernst. 1947. *Swedenborg in Deutschland: F. C. Oetingers und Immanuel Kants Auseinandersetzung mit der Person und Lehre Emanuel Swedenborgs*. Frankfurt am Main: Vittorio Klostermann.

Dole, George F., and Robert H. Kirven. 1992. *A Scientist Explores Spirit*. New York and West Chester, Pa.: Swedenborg Foundation.

Ehman, K.C.E., ed. 1859. *Friedrich Christoph Oetingers Leben und Brief, als urkundlicher Commentar zu desen Schriften (Beyer und Rosen)*. Stuttgart: J. F. Steinkopf.

Ernesti, Johann August. 1760. Review of *Secrets of Heaven,* by Emanuel Swedenborg. *Neue Theologische Bibliothek* 1:515–527.

Frazier, Scott I. 1998. "Echoes from the Past: A Look at Classical Influences within Swedenborg's 'Golden Age.'" *Scripta: Bryn Athyn College Review* 1:27–44.

Hjern, Olle. 1990. *Swedenborg och hans vänner i Göteborg*. Stockholm: Nykyrkliga Bokförlaget.

Horn, Friedemann. 1954. *Schelling und Swedenborg: Ein Beitrag zur Problemgeschichte des deutschen Idealismus und zur Geschichte Swedenborgs in Deutschland, nebst einem Anhang über K.C.F. Krause und Swedenborg sowie Ergänzungen zu R. Schneiders Forschungen*. Zürich: Swedenborg-Verlag. English version: *Schelling and Swedenborg: Mysticism and German Idealism,* translated by George F. Dole, West Chester, Pa.: Swedenborg Foundation, 1997.

King, Kristin. 1999. "The Power and Limitations of Language in Swedenborg, Shakespeare, and Frost." *Studia Swedenborgiana* 11(3):1–63.

Kirven, Robert H. 1965. *Emanuel Swedenborg and the Revolt against Deism*. Ann Arbor: University Microfilms.

———. 1988. "Swedenborg's Contributions to the History of Ideas." In *Emanuel Swedenborg: A Continuing Vision*. Edited by Robin Larsen. New York: Swedenborg Foundation.

Kirven, Robert H., and Robin Larsen. 1988. "Emanuel Swedenborg: A Pictorial Biography." In *Emanuel Swedenborg: A Continuing Vision*. Edited by Robin Larsen. New York: Swedenborg Foundation.

Montanus, Benedict Arias. 1657. *Biblia Universa . . . cum Latina Interpretatione*. Leipzig: Christian Kirchner.

Schmidt, Sebastian. 1696. *Biblia Sacra, sive Testamentum Vetus et Novum ex Linguis Originalibus in Linguam Latinam Translatum*. Strasbourg: J. F. Spoor.

Sigstedt, Cyriel Odhner. 1981. *The Swedenborg Epic: The Life and Works of Emanuel Swedenborg.* New York: Bookman Associates, 1952. Reprint, London: Swedenborg Society.

Swedenborg, Emanuel. 1872. Marginal notations in *Biblia Sacra, sive Testamentum Vetus et Novum.* Translated by Sebastian Schmidt. Stockholm: Societas Photo-Lithographica.

———. 1889. *The Spiritual Diary of Emanuel Swedenborg.* Vol. 4. Translated by George Bush and James F. Buss. New York: Swedenborg Foundation.

———. 1927–1951. *The Word Explained.* 10 vols. Translated and edited by Alfred Acton. Bryn Athyn: Academy of the New Church.

———. [1742] 1950. *Rational Psychology.* Translated by N. Rogers and Alfred Acton, and edited by Alfred Acton. Philadelphia: Swedenborg Scientific Association.

———. [1740–1741] 1955. *The Economy of the Animal Kingdom.* Translated by Augustus Clissold. Two volumes. Bryn Athyn, Pa.: Swedenborg Scientific Association. Reprint of edition of 1845–1846, London: W. Newbery, H. Bailliere; Boston: Otis Clapp. A more accurate translation of the title of this work is *Dynamics of the Soul's Domain.*

———. [1744–1745] 1960. *The Animal Kingdom.* Translated by J.J.G. Wilkinson. Two volumes. Bryn Athyn, Pa.: Swedenborg Scientific Association. Reprint of edition of 1843–1844, London: Wm. Newbery. A more accurate translation of the title of this work is *The Soul's Domain.*

———. 1983–1997. *Experientiae Spirituales.* 6 vols. Edited by J. Durban Odhner. Bryn Athyn, Pa.: Academy of the New Church.

———. 1984. *Emanuel Swedenborg: The Universal Human and Soul-Body Interaction.* Translated by George F. Dole. New York: Paulist Press.

———. [1714] 1985. *Festivus Applausus in Caroli XII . . . in Pomeraniam Suam Adventum* [Joyous Accolade for Charles XII's . . . Arrival in His Own Pomerania]. Edited and translated by Hans Helander. Uppsala: Acta Universitatis Upsaliensis.

———. [1715] 1988. *Camena Borea* [Northern Muse]. Edited and translated by Hans Helander. Uppsala: Acta Universitatis Upsaliensis.

———. 1994–1997. *Apocalypse Explained.* Translated by John C. Ager and revised by John Whitehead. West Chester, Pa.: Swedenborg Foundation.

———. [1758] 1995. *Heaven and Its Wonders and Hell; from Things Heard and Seen.* Translated by John C. Ager. West Chester, Pa.: Swedenborg Foundation.

———. 1998–2000. *Emanuel Swedenborg's Diary, Recounting Spiritual Experiences.* 2 vols. Translated by J. Durban Odhner. Bryn Athyn, Pa.: General Church of the New Jerusalem.

Tafel, Rudolph Leonard. 1875. *Documents concerning the Life and Character of Emanuel Swedenborg.* Vol. 1. London: Swedenborg Society.

———. 1890. *Documents concerning the Life and Character of Emanuel Swedenborg.* Vols. 2–3. London: Swedenborg Society.

Van Dusen, Wilson. 1981. *Uses: A Way of Personal and Spiritual Growth.* New York: Swedenborg Foundation.

Walker, Williston. 1970. *A History of the Christian Church.* 2nd ed. Revised by Cyril Richardson, Wilhelm Pauck, and Robert T. Handy. New York: Charles Scribner's Sons.

Index to Preface, Introduction, and Notes

The following index, referenced by page number, covers material in the translator's preface, the introduction, and the scholars' notes. References to the Bible in this material are listed under the heading "Scripture references." (References to the Bible that appear in the translation proper are treated in a separate index.) For topics in Swedenborg's footnotes, see the index to the translation.

A

Addison, Joseph, 67
Advent of the Lord, 459 note 14
Africans, 44 note 18, 477 note 216
Ager, John, 5
Alexander VI, Pope, 35
Almond, Philip, 43
Angels, 469–470 note 125
   African, 477 note 216
   communication among, 17
   described, 16–17, 43, 47
   establishing communication with, 475
     note 187
   gender of, 473 note 168
   guardian, 18
   as intermediaries, 29–30
   language of, 17, 471 note 147
   powers of, 471 note 139
   receiving instruction from,
     16, 18
Apocalyptic scenarios, 27–28
Appearances, 469 note 122
Arcana Coelestia, 10–11. *See also*
   Secrets of Heaven
Archaic worldviews, 24–28
Aristotle, 471 note 149, 481 note 264
Assheton, William, 67
Astronomy, Swedenborg's interest in, 468
   note 111
Athanasian Creed, 460 note 19
Augustine, 32, 33, 36
"Auras," 462 note 39
Aussichten in die Ewigkeit, 45, 69
Automatic writing, 481 note 259

B

Babylon of Revelation, the Roman Catholic
   church as, 484 note 305
Bacon, Francis, 24

"Balance"
   in the divine management of creation, 483
     note 293
   in Swedenborg's view of regeneration, 475
     note 186
Balzac, Honoré de, 58–59, 64
Baroque views on life after death, 65–69
   in interpreting *Heaven and Hell*, 39–45
Barrett, Benjamin, 5
Baxter, Richard, 42
Being, "single," 462 note 33
"Belief," 482 note 274
Benedict XIV, Pope, 39
Bengel, Johann Albrecht, 457–458 note 7
Bering, Vitus, 40
Berkeley, George, 33
Bible. *See also* Scripture references
   book titles Swedenborg used, 84, 468 note
     106, 469 note 121, 469 note 124
   interpretations of, 457–458 note 7
   spiritual meaning within literal, 1
   Swedenborg's citations from, 457 note 5
   taking literally, 457–458 note 7
   translations of, 457 note 5
Blake, William, 64
Bodin, Jean, 43 note 17
Body. *See* Human body
Boehme, Jacob, 58
Bonde, Count Gustaf, 50–51
Book of life, 471 note 145, 481 note 269
Borgia, Rodrigo, 35
Boswell, James, 41, 42–43, 69
Boyle, Robert, 23
Brain function, Swedenborg's insights into,
   467 note 98
Bread, 467 note 93
"Breath," 484 note 301
Bruno, Giordano, 24
Bultmann, Rudolf, 28
Bunyan, John, 66

Index to Scriptural Passages in *Heaven and Hell*

The following index refers to passages from the Bible cited in the translation of *Heaven and Hell,* including Swedenborg's footnotes. The numbers to the left under each Bible book title are its chapter numbers. They are followed by verse numbers with the following designations: bold figures designate verses fully quoted; italic figures designate verses given in substance; figures in parenthesis indicate verses merely referred or alluded to. The numbers to the right are section numbers in *Heaven and Hell;* subsection numbers are separated from section numbers by a colon. (Passages from the Bible cited in the preface, introduction, and scholars' notes can be found under the heading "Scripture references" in the separate index of those elements.)

Table of Parallel Passages

The following table indicates passages in *Heaven and Hell* that parallel passages in Swedenborg's other theological works. (For a bibliographic list of these works, see pages 80–84.) The table is based on John Faulkner Potts's *Swedenborg Concordance* (London: Swedenborg Society, 1902), 6:859–864; on a table of passages parallel to *Heaven and Hell* composed by Norman Ryder (n.p.: Swedenborg Society, 1982; mimeographed); and on new research by Jonathan S. Rose.

Reference numbers in this table correspond to Swedenborg's section numbers; subsection numbers are separated from section numbers by a colon.

Heaven and Hell	Parallel Passage
39	*Heaven and Hell* 435; *Last Judgment* 25:5
47	*Spiritual Experiences* 2104
86:2–4	*New Jerusalem* 298–300
86:5	*New Jerusalem* 303
86:6	*New Jerusalem* 304
86:7–9	*New Jerusalem* 305
86:10	*New Jerusalem* 306
86:11–12	*New Jerusalem* 307:2
86:13	*New Jerusalem* 309
108:2	*Spiritual Experiences* 2475
159	*Spiritual Experiences* 4639
185	*Spiritual Experiences* 4292
212	*Spiritual Experiences* 5779, 5780, 5782
231	*Spiritual Experiences* 881, 1754
238	*Secrets of Heaven* 2304
241	*Spiritual Experiences* 5112–5114, 5620; *Sacred Scripture* 90:2
260	*Spiritual Experiences* 4671, 5562, 5578–5579, 5581, 5621; *Sacred Scripture* 90:1; *True Christianity* 278
261	*Spiritual Experiences* 5579
263	*Spiritual Experiences* 5571, 5584
270:5	*Spiritual Experiences* 5153
273	*Spiritual Experiences* 5566; *Secrets of Heaven* 4295:3

Heaven and Hell	Parallel Passage
356:15	*New Jerusalem* 34
363	*Heaven and Hell* 480
381	*Secrets of Heaven* 2742
382a	*Spiritual Experiences* 4156; *Secrets of Heaven* 2735
385	*Secrets of Heaven* 2733; *Marriage Love* 481
386	*Secrets of Heaven* 2744
387	*Spiritual Experiences* 5158
403	*Secrets of Heaven* 454
404	*Spiritual Experiences* 3986; *Secrets of Heaven* 456
405	*Spiritual Experiences* 2104; *Secrets of Heaven* 457
406	*Secrets of Heaven* 548
406:2	*Spiritual Experiences* 4104
407	*Spiritual Experiences* 3872
408	*Spiritual Experiences* 1234
410	*Spiritual Experiences* 314; *Secrets of Heaven* 543
411	*Spiritual Experiences* 5101
412	*Spiritual Experiences* 1990; *Secrets of Heaven* 540
413	*Secrets of Heaven* 545
417:2–6	*Secrets of Heaven* 6697–6698, 9441; *Other Planets* 2–4, 6, 126
419	*Secrets of Heaven* 10784; *Other Planets* 168
430	*Secrets of Heaven* 2851:2–3
435	*Heaven and Hell* 39; *Last Judgment* 25:5
438	*Spiritual Experiences* 5645
439	*Secrets of Heaven* 1882
440	*Spiritual Experiences* 56, 651, 653; *Secrets of Heaven* 1883
441	*Secrets of Heaven* 1884
442	*Secrets of Heaven* 1885
448	*Spiritual Experiences* 1092; *Secrets of Heaven* 168
449:1	*Spiritual Experiences* 1092–1094; *Secrets of Heaven* 169, 170, 172, 176
449:2	*Spiritual Experiences* 1096, 1097, 1099, 1100; *Secrets of Heaven* 171, 173, 175, 1518

Heaven and Hell	**Parallel Passage**
449:3	*Spiritual Experiences* 1102; *Secrets of Heaven* 177
450	*Spiritual Experiences* 1106, 1115–1116; *Secrets of Heaven* 314–316
456	*Last Judgment* 17
465	*Spiritual Experiences* 4410; *Secrets of Heaven* 2479
466	*Secrets of Heaven* 2492
467	*Secrets of Heaven* 2494
480	*Heaven and Hell* 363; *Marriage Love* 524:3
534	*Spiritual Experiences* 5798
558a	*New Jerusalem* 70
559	*Secrets of Heaven* 7375; *New Jerusalem* 71
562	*New Jerusalem* 75
564	*New Jerusalem* 72–73
565	*New Jerusalem* 76–77
582	*Supplements* 36–38
597	*New Jerusalem* 149
598	*New Jerusalem* 149
599	*New Jerusalem* 149

Index to *Heaven and Hell*

The following index covers the translation of *Heaven and Hell,* including Swedenborg's footnotes. For references to passages from the Bible and to topics treated in the preface, introduction, and scholars' notes, see the separate indexes to those elements.

Reference numbers in this index correspond to Swedenborg's section numbers in *Heaven and Hell;* subsection numbers are separated from section numbers by a colon.

Biographical Note

EMANUEL SWEDENBORG (1688–1772) was born Emanuel Swedberg (or Svedberg) in Stockholm, Sweden, on January 29, 1688 (Julian calendar). He was the third of the nine children of Jesper Swedberg (1653–1735) and Sara Behm (1666–1696). At the age of eight he lost his mother. After the death of his only older brother ten days later, he became the oldest living son. In 1697 his father married Sara Bergia (1666–1720), who developed great affection for Emanuel and left him a significant inheritance. His father, a Lutheran clergyman, later became a celebrated and controversial bishop, whose diocese included the Swedish churches in Pennsylvania and in London, England.

After studying at the University of Uppsala (1699–1709), Emanuel journeyed to England, Holland, France, and Germany (1710–1715) to study and work with leading scientists in western Europe. Upon his return he apprenticed as an engineer under the brilliant Swedish inventor Christopher Polhem (1661–1751). He gained favor with Sweden's King Charles XII (1682–1718), who gave him a salaried position as an overseer of Sweden's mining industry (1716–1747). Although he was engaged, he never married.

After the death of Charles XII, Emanuel was ennobled by Queen Ulrika Eleonora (1688–1741), and his last name was changed to Swedenborg (or Svedenborg). This change in status gave him a seat in the Swedish House of Nobles, where he remained an active participant in the Swedish government throughout his life.

A member of the Swedish Royal Academy of Sciences, he devoted himself to studies that culminated in a number of publications, most notably a comprehensive three-volume work on natural philosophy and metallurgy (1734) that brought him recognition across Europe as a scientist. After 1734 he redirected his research and publishing to a study of anatomy in search of the interface between the soul and body, making several significant discoveries in physiology.

From 1743 to 1745 he entered a transitional phase that resulted in a shift of his main focus from science to theology. Throughout the rest of his life he maintained that this shift was brought about by Jesus Christ, who appeared to him, called him to a new mission, and opened his perception to a permanent dual consciousness of this life and the life after death.

He devoted the last decades of his life to studying Scripture and publishing eighteen theological titles that draw on the Bible, reasoning, and his own spiritual experiences. These works present a Christian theology with unique perspectives on the nature of God, the spiritual world, the Bible, the human mind, and the path to salvation.

Swedenborg died in London on March 29, 1772, at the age of eighty-four.